POLAND

Executive Editorial Director David Brabis
THE GREEN GUIDE – POLAND
Editor	Béatrice Brillion
Writers	Laure Dabo, Jean-François Breuiller, Arnaud Galy, Laurent Gontier, Arnaud Léonard, Julie Wood
Translators	Elisabeth Morris, Grace Coston
English Edition Editor	Grace Coston
Correction	Jane McDonald
Cartography	Alain Baldet, Thierry Olin, Jean-Michel Perreau
Photo Editors	Cécile Koroleff, Eliane Bailly, Stéphanie Quillon, Marie-Christine Petit
Production Coordinators	Pascal Grougon, Jacqueline Pavageau, Danièle Jazeron
Layout	Didier Hée, Jean-Paul Josset, Frédéric Sardin
Design	Agence Rampazzo
Cover Design	Laurent Muller
Production	Pierre Ballochard, Renaud Leblanc

Contact Us

The Green Guide
Michelin Travel Publications
One Parkway South
Greenville, SC 29615
USA
☏ 1-800-423-0485
www.michelintravel.com
michelin.guides@us.michelin.com
or
Hannay House, 39 Clarendon Road
Watford, Herts WD17 1JA, UK
☏ 01923 205 240 - Fax 01923 205 241
TheGreenGuide-uk@uk.michelin.com

2006 Edition

Special Sales

For information regarding bulk sales, customized editions and premium sales, please contact our Customer Service Departments:

USA	1-800-423-0485
UK	(01923) 205 240
Canada	1-800-361-8236

Note to the reader

The Green Guide,

culture in motion

Do you like to spend your holidays on the move? If you enjoy getting away during your vacation or for a long weekend, if you enjoy seeing new places, take The Green Guide along. You will find ideas for things to do and see, travel tips and up-to-date practical information to minimize the guesswork involved with travel.

The world is a changing place. Travellers need information that keeps up with events and provides the latest on new hotels and restaurants, current prices, opening times, etc. Even monuments and other popular tourist destinations regularly undergo restoration, add attractions or close temporarily while improvements are being made. Museums acquire new works, new amenities are offered; suggested touring itineraries may be enhanced by new discoveries.

The Green Guide takes these changes into account; we constantly reassess the relative interest of each attraction on our scale that identifies places as highly recommended (the famous three-star rating), recommended (two stars) and interesting (one star). We visit the attractions, evaluate them with ratings and describe what you'll discover when you visit them.

The Green Guide was created to facilitate and enrich the experience of travel. Today, we continue to publish guides with you in mind: a traveller who wants to learn more about the unique character of the region he or she has set out to explore. Simple, clear and easy to use, it is a family-friendly guide as well. The 👫 symbol highlights places children will especially enjoy: zoos, theme parks, unusual museums and special tours or workshops for children that are offered at major tourist attractions including monuments and natural heritage sites.

There is just one reason our team is dedicated to producing quality travel publications – you, our reader. After all, we want you to enjoy travelling as much as we do!

The Michelin Green Guide Team
michelin.guides@us.michelin.com
TheGreenGuide-uk@uk.michelin.com

PLANNING YOUR TRIP

GETTING TO KNOW POLAND

CITIES AND SIGHTS

The inside front cover flap of this guide shows a map of Poland with the **Principal Sights** of interest. This map identifies:

    Starred sights and attractions,

    Suggested itineraries.

In the section of the guided devoted to **Sights**:

    The **main tourist attractions** are presented by region,

    Other attractions are listed under the heading "Nearby",

    Practical information is found on the green pages at the end of each chapter.

CONTENTS

SIGHTS

Tram in Kraków

WHEN AND WHERE TO GO

Poland's assets across the seasons

WHEN TO TRAVEL TO POLAND

Poland enjoys a continental climate tempered by an oceanic influence along coastal areas. Each season is attractive for specific reasons.

Summers are hot and sunny, with an average daily temperature of 25°C sometimes rising above 30°C, in particular inland where winds are less prominent and temperatures can therefore become stifling. The tourist season reaches its peak in July and August when tourists and Polish holiday-makers converge towards the same places. Sailing is a major activity in the Masurian lake region from May to the end of August whereas mountainous regions and nature parks attract rambling enthusiasts. It is also during that period that tourist activities are in full swing (festivals, organized activities in the skansens etc). It is essential to make reservations in advance and to bear in mind that the cost of accommodation is higher (high-season prices) than at any other time of the year.

Spring and **autumn** are undeniably the most pleasant seasons to visit Poland: the weather is mild, days are fairly long, tourist crowds are manageable and they are ideal periods for sport and outdoor activities. In spring, the awakening of nature is spectacular throughout the country; it is the ideal time for discovering the many national parks. In May, for instance, the park of Kórnik Castle, south of Poznań, boasts splendid magnolias in full bloom. In autumn, Polish forests are bedecked with an infinite variety of colours ranging from green to bright red, through a whole palette of yellows. And, from the second fortnight in September, one can hear stags belling.

Winters are cold and dry over most of the country but damp near the Baltic; don't forget to take warm clothing. Temperature oscillate around 0°C except in January and February, which are the coldest months of the year, when the average temperature sinks to a few degrees below zero. Snow covers the major part of the country, but is not so abundant in coastal areas. In the mountains, snow cover is generally excellent in winter (January, February and March) and winter sports enthusiasts can practise ski as well as snowshoeing.

In Masuria, this is also the time when ice-yacht competitions take place. Winter can also be the ideal season for cultural tourism (visiting towns and museums).

A town and its surroundings in a few days

Warsaw and above all Kraków are exceptionally fine destinations for a weekend. Their international airports put them within easy reach. By prolonging the weekend by one or two days, you will also be able to enjoy the cities' immediate surroundings.

WARSAW

Allow at least four days in order to make the most of the town.

Poland's capital has been undergoing constant change for the past few years. Skyscrapers now stand next to buildings erected during the Communist period. Everything seems to be going very fast. Traces of the old régime are still noticeable in the social atmosphere, in some people's attitudes and in the architectural heritage, but

Malbork Castle in the winter

Western lifestyle is gradually taking over. The whole situation forms a most "exotic" mixture, to say the least. Tour the Old Town, admire the splendid way in which it was rebuilt after the last war. Stroll through the streets lined with 17C and 18C houses. This highly touristic area looks completely different at night. Visit the Historical Museum and, from the castle, go towards the New Town along the Royal Way which used to lead to the sovereigns' summer residence in the Łazienki Park, south of the town. In the centre, the Palace of Culture is Warsaw's symbol. Walk across Konstytucji Square decorated with huge lampposts and take a detour via the National Museum and the War Museum. The north of the town bears traces of the Jewish district decimated by the Nazis. Visit the Nożyk Synagogue, stand in silent remembrance before the remains of the ghetto wall. A visit to the Historical Institute and to the Jewish cemetery, one of the largest in Europe, will inform you on the history of this community. A short way out of town, at the western exit, the Kampinos nature park is the ideal place to escape the hustle and bustle of the town and the locals love to go and relax there on their days off work. 130km south-east of the capital, on the banks of the Wisła, **Kazimierz Dolny** is a pleasant town, entirely built in Renaissance style, which is well worth a day trip.

KRAKÓW

Spend a minimum of two days in Kraków.

It is a peaceful medieval city, one of the rare towns in Poland to have come out of the war unscathed. If you don't have much time, restrict yourself to the historic centre around the Rynek and the Cloth Hall, to the buildings of the famous Jagiellonian University and to the visit of Wawel Castle and its Cathedral, the Polish kings' pantheon. Spend at least one evening in the Jewish district of Kazimierz.

If you can spend longer in town or if a brief first stay gave you a taste for more, you can devote a week to the discovery of the city's museums and monuments, and enjoy the atmosphere of its streets to the full. Kraków is best toured on foot, in particular the Old Town, surrounded by the Planty, and Kazimierz.

Excursions from Kraków include the sprawling **Wieliczka** salt mine in the south or the all too famous **Auschwitz Camp**. For each of these excursions, allow an hour to an hour and a half for the journey and a whole day for the visit. Nearer town, the suburban site of **Zwierzyniec** offers fine rambles in a rustic setting dotted with ancient mounds, and 10km east of Kraków, you can visit **Nowa Huta**, a communist town built from scratch round a village which still retains it Cistercian monastery as well as a modern church, the Arch. 15km to the north-west, you wil find the impressive **Ojców nature park** where limestone rocks create rugged landscapes with steep-cut dips.

Suggested itineraries

Below are some suggestions to discover Poland's main geographical regions.

GDAŃSK AND THE BALTIC COAST

Allow one week to visit the region in depth.

Discover the Tri-City (Trójmiasto) which includes **Gdańsk, Sopot** and **Gdynia**. Extending over a distance of more than 35km, this conurbation is easily accessible by public transport. Take time to stroll along the streets of the former Danzig, an ancient Hanseatic city razed to the ground during the war and magnificently rebuilt to its former appearance. Two days will enable you to visit the whole town. Fancy a more festive atmosphere? Escape for a day to Sopot, the seaside

C. Hervé-Bazin / MICHELIN

The jetty at Sopot

resort where casinos contribute to create a more frivolous atmosphere than in Gdańsk. Not far from there, Gdynia, a port built to provide Poland with an outlet to the sea when Danzig was a German port, features an architectural heritage dating from the 1920s-1930s. Discover another aspect of the coastal fringe by exploring the **Hel peninsula**, a long strip of land only a few hundred metres wide, where pine trees grow on sandy soil. You can spend the night in one of the many establishments of the old fishing port of the same name situated at the tip end of the peninsula. It will suit bathing enthusiasts, who will also enjoy Sopot and, further south, the beaches stretching along the Vistual delta. Further north, the coast extends west towards the German border. Here, you can cycle or ramble through the **Słowiński nature park**, famous for its shifting dunes gaining year after yeat on the pine forest. In **Łeba**, widely considered as THE fashionable seaside resort, you will find several fine beaches. It could be fun to spend the night there to discover the jet-set feel of the place.

Extending inland from Gdańsk is the **Kashubian Switzerland** or Little Pomeranian Switzerland (Szwajcaria Kaszubska). The Kashubian influence, deeply marked by traditions, can be felt around the town of Kartuzy. Finally, reserve one whole day for a visit to the famous huge **Malbork Castle** (south-east of Gdańsk), the jewel of the Teutonic Knights' architecture.

TORUŃ AND GREATER POLAND: THE ORIGINS OF THE POLISH STATE

Allow four days to a week to discover the region which saw the birth of the Polish State.

Toruń is probably one of the most pleasant towns in Poland. Small, well preserved, it offers visitors a fine stroll among Gothic buildings, mostly brick built. Stroll around the Rynek with its imposing town hall, along the banks of the Wisła. The Hanseatic city is best toured on foot and, after a day going round all the sights, you can have a peaceful night within the ramparts. Devote half a day to the visit of **Chełmno**, a small prosperous town during the golden age of the Hanseatic League, surrounded by well-preserved fortifications, situated some 30km

on the way to Gdańsk. From there you can head for Poznań, located one hundred kilometres south of Toruń. On the way, stop by the archaeological site of **Biskupin**, known as the Polish Pompei, and get an insight into life in Poland during the neolithic period. Slightly further on, **Gniezno** boasts a sanctuary dedicated to St Adalbert whose life is recalled through the low-reliefs of a huge bronze door. Between Gniezno and Poznań, the Ostrów Lednicki archaeological reserve offers the possibility of seeing the remains of the palace of the first Polish sovereign on an island in Lake Lednica.

Poznań is a lively city with a long-standing tradition of fairs. It boasts one of the finest and largest Ryneks in the country. Surrounding the imposing town hall are the Baroque and Classical façades of houses which were restored after the last war. Take time to discover the narrow streets and numerous churches. Two days should be enough to make the most of the town. Devote one day to a tour of the nearby **castles of Kórnik** and **Rogalin**. If you have some time left, go to **Kalisz**, no doubt the oldest town in Poland, and visit **Gołuchów Castle** nestling in a lovely park and **Antonín Hunting Palace** nearby.

A WEEK THROUGH "YESTERDAY'S" EUROPE

From the time it joined the European Union, Poland has been its eastern "rampart"! If it is clear that Ukraine has embarked on a political and economic programme of modernization, the situation in Belarus is much less straightforward. Both countries played a role in the development of Polish culture which still bears their imprint. Indeed, populations of Ukrainian and Belarusian origin live in the eastern regions of Poland, perpetuating their traditions, their folklore and also sometimes their political memory. **Białystok**, **Lublin**, **Zamość** or **Przemyśl** are striking examples of this. The main interest of these towns, In addition to the rich architectural heritage found in and around them, lies in the imprint of their mixed culture: Jewish influence in Lublin, Orthodox in Białystok, Graeco-Catholic in Przemyśl, military in Zamość. Exploring these towns offers the opportunity of stepping back in time and rediscovering Europe as it was before the 20C conflicts.

NEW
Michelin Green Guide: expand your holiday horizons

- *New cover*
- *New layout*
- *New information*
- *New destinations*

MASURIA

Allow three days to discover the region but if you wish to enjoy its nature to the full, you will have to stay longer.
From spring to the beginning of autumn is the best time to discover Masuria. In winter, the thick snow cover and biting cold offer the possibility of enjoying ski touring, fishing through a hole in the ice and ice-yachting.
With the exception of **Reszel**, a small, welcoming Gothic town, towns are devoid of interest. A few kilometres away, the Baroque sanctuary of **Święta Lipka** is one of the most popular places of pilgrimage in Poland. 20km to the east, **Kętrzyn** is the site of one of the castles of the Teutonic Knights and a good base from which to visit the **Wolf's Lair**, Hitler's general headquarters, from where he supervised military operations in the East. The site is now a fortified ghost town on the edge of the **Masurian lakeland** extending eastwards. In summer, the ports of Giżycko, Węgorzewo and Mikołajki attract a crowd of yachting enthusiasts who enjoy sailing on the lakes, some of which are now nature reserves. The surrounding forests are crisscrossed by renowned hiking trails. Continuing eastwards for about 70km leads you to the far reaches of Poland. Still relatively unexplored by tourists, these regions boast lakes and dense forests around the towns of **Suwałki** and **Augustów**. Starting from the latter, there are fascinating canoeing itineraries along the canal of the same name.

WROCŁAW AND THE SUDETEN

Allow one week.
Wrocław is full of surprises. A tour of the capital of Lower Silesia will take at least 2 or 3 days. You will need that much time to walk across the Rynek lined with splendidly restored houses, to stroll along the bustling streets, livened up year-round by the important student population. Take a stroll along the banks of the Oder, explore Ostrów Tumski, this former island which stil retains its cathedral and several churches. Parks and open spaces will give you a chance to take a break and children will love the zoo which became famous all over the country through a television programme.

According to the amount of time at your disposal and what you fancy, you will have the opportunity of heading for the Karkonosze region and of discovering the town of **Jelenia Góra** and the ski resort of **Karpacz**. Rambling and the discovery of nature are activities on offer less than 100km from Wrocław. Stop on the way to visit the wooden churches of **Jawor** and **Świdnica**, listed by UNESCO. 80km south of Wrocław, the **Kłodzko area** offers rambles in the heart of the Table Mountains with their jagged landscapes. The Bear Cave and the network of tunnels of Kłodzko Fortress will take you into the depths of the earth. End your round tour with a visit to **Paczków,** a town sometimes referred to as the Polish Carcassonne. A 350km round tour starting from Wrocław will enable you, over three days, to see all these sites and even to make a detour to the peaceful towns of **Opole** and **Brzeg**; the area surrounding the latter boasts some ten wooden churches containing rediscovered 14C frescoes.

FORMER EASTERN PRUSSIA - ELBLĄG AND OLSZTYN

Three or four days at least are necessary to get an overall view of this region, but you will need one week to explore it thoroughly.
Slightly set back from the Baltic coast, **Elbląg** is a fine Hanseatic town, rebuilt in traditional style without completely excluding modern architecture.

F. Soreau / MICHELIN

The Basilica in Święta Lipka

A visit to the renowned gallery of contemporary art is recommended. The town is the starting point of boat trips on the **Elbląg Canal**, which offers an unusual attraction: along part of the course, boats are pulled up onto the land and hoisted on rails. The trip as far as Ostróda, with its fine Teutonic castle, lasts 11 hours, which can prove terribly boring. This is why it is advisable to concentrate on the section of the journey which negotiates the 5 most spectacular locks. 15km north-east of Elbląg, the town of **Frombork** has based its tourist trade on its association with Copernicus who was a canon of the cathedral and is buried inside. Visit the impressive fortified cathedral towering above the Wiślany laguna: in fine weather, the Russian town of Kaliningrad can be seen from the top of the tower. 60km south-east of Elbląg, **Olsztyn**, a little-known but pleasant town spread across several hills and boasting many parks, makes a good overnight stop. Do not miss the medieval castle. End the round tour in **Lidzbark Warmiński**, a town dominated by one of the most spectacular Gothic castles , once the residence of the bishops of Warmia.

CARPATHIANS AND TATRAS

Allow at least one week.
It is possible to travel through the Polish mountains in a week, from **Zakopane** to **Sanok**, along a 400km long itinerary, taking time for the occasional ramble.
From Zakopane south of Kraków to Sanok at the south-eastern end of the country, Poland looks like a mountainous region: small mountains like the Beskid (East or West), Alpine areas like the Tatras around Zakopane or small, rounded, almost deserted mountains like the Bieszczady. These regions all retain their strong traditions both in architecture and in folk arts and crafts. Rambling paths, which often lead through the heart of nature parks, are well marked and open to all levels of difficulty. When you visit this mountain range, you are also permanently skirting Slovakia. The Tatra Mountains extend much more in Slovak than in Polish territory and if you sail down the Dunajec Gorge in the Pienini, you will have a Polish cliff on one side and a Slovak one on the other!

A Tour of Polish Towns by Train

If you are mainly interested in Polish towns why not tour the country over two weeks comfortably settled in first-class velvet-covered seats or, if your budget objects, in second-class seats covered with imitation leather. Travelling by train is not expensive, it is pleasant and you are always taken to the very heart of cities. From Warsaw to Gdańsk via Malbork, from Gdańsk to Toruń, Poznań and then Wrocław. From Wrocław to Kraków and from the latter back to Warsaw, you will have the opportunity of seeing a great deal of Poland's cultural wealth. And, to help you organize your trip, look up the Polish railways website : www.pkp.pl

LITTLE POLAND AND WOODEN CHURCHES

Allow one week along the small roads of the South.
All over Little Poland, you will see brown panels with the words "Szlak Architektury Drewnianej" signaling some remarkable wooden monument. Most of the time it is a church. The most famous churches, on UNESCO's World Heritage List, are **Lipnica Murowana**, **Binarowa**, **Sękowa** or **Dębno**. However, these gems must not hide the forest! Villages situated south-east of Kraków, towards **Nowy Sącz** and **Gorlice** boast wooden churches built between the 15C and 19C which have withstood the ravages of time. Located beyond the administrative boundaries, the **West Beskid** and the **Bieszczady** also contain treasures waiting to be discovered. Visitors who don't have that much time are advised to go on a tour of regional skansens.

Excursions across the border

Being surrounded by as many as 7 different countries, Poland offers a wide choice of excursions across her borders. Make sure that you hold the necessary documents, and eventually visas. In some countries, you will need the international green card for your vehicle. Make inquiries before leaving as requirements differ considerably. If you rent a car, ask the hiring company to confirm that you are allowed to cross the border with the vehicle.

Sites on UNESCO's World Heritage List

Kraków's historic centre(1978)
The Wieliczka salt mines(1978)
Auschwitz Concentration Camp(1979)
Białowieża Forest(1979)
Warsaw's historic centre(1980)
The Old Town of Zamość (1992)
The castle of the Teutonic Order at Malbork (1997)
The medieval city of Toruń (1997)
Kalwaria Zebrzydowska : mannerist architectural ensemble and landscape pilgrimage park (1999)
The churches of peace in Jawor and Świdnica (2001)
Wooden churches in the South of Little Poland (2003)
The Muskau Park/Park Murzakowski (2004)

IN UKRAINE

EU nationals do not need a visa.
Even though the country may not always be readily accessible on account of its political history and of its culture, a weekend excursion to **L'viv** (300km east of Kraków) is recommended. The town is accessible by a regular bus service or by car. Bear in mind that the border is a real border where problems can still arise from time to time. Situated 80km further on, L'viv is the capital of western Ukraine, therefore of the Carpathians. The majority of the population speaks Ukrainian and most Ukrainians are practising Graeco-Catholics. They were at the origin of the Orange Revolution which swept away the last leaders having risen to power with the help of the ex USSR. L'viv is on UNESCO's World Heritage List. Surprisingly spared by the Nazi occupation forces and by the Soviet power, L'viv is a mixture of Jewish, Armenian and Polish culture. Its architectural heritage, both religious and secular, its many icon and painting museums and its parks located in the town centre make it a great weekend destination. The youth of this university town is enthusiastically open to the world and foreigners from Western Europe are very welcome. Beware, few hotels are adapted to "European" standards and those that are are also very expensive! We advise you to go through a travel agency (or your hotel) from Kraków, Przemyśc, Lublin, Zamość (Zamojski Hotel). Inquire at their Tourist Offices *(see practical pages)*.

IN SLOVAKIA

A simple identity card (or passport) is necessary to cross the border.
From Zakopane situated in the Tatras (border post of Łysa Polana south of Zakopane or Chynze in the north), from the Pienini (border post of Piwniczna), or from Barwinek in the Beskid, south of Krosno, the **Slovak Tatras** are easily accessible. Apart from the exceptional natural environment, it is pleasant to cross the border and encounter a different cultural atmosphere. The great number of Tziganes on the roads and their camps and villages are, of course, not tourist sights, but they confer to the region its undeniable character. The most interesting town for an excursion of a few hours or a couple of days is **Bardejów**. It is a Gothic and Renaissance city on UNESCO's list. The surrounding area boasts many wooden churches similar to those one sees in Poland. The village of Medzilaborce, some one hundred kilometres east of Bardejów. and close to the Polish border post of Barwinek, houses the **Warhol Family Museum of Modern Art**. And indeed, the parents of the founder of pop art, who emigrated to the US in 1913, were natives of a mountain village close to Medzilaborce. Besides documents connected with his family, the museum houses original works by the artist, some of them from the Andy Warhol Foundation for the Visual Arts in New York.

IN RUSSIA

A visa is essential. It will cost you €80 and you will need a letter of invitation or a hotel reservation.
Caution and vigilance should be applied because Kaliningrad is not always safe and one should be aware of it.
From Poland, there are two ways

L'viv

of enter Russia or, more precisely, the **Kaliningrad enclave**. One way is from Gdynia, the port of Gdańsk, from where boats sail towards Kaliningrad. The other consists in crossing the border 90km north of Olsztyn via road 51. Kaliningrad is then 40km away. The most remarkable German monument left in the former Königsberg, destroyed by the raids of the British army and then by the assaults of the Red army, is the red-brick Gothic cathedral. The town houses the grave of Emmanuel Kant who was born and taught in this town.

IN BELARUS

A visa is essential to cross the border. From Białystok, you can reach the town of **Hrodna**, also known as Grodno, 83km away. This well-preserved city, which has a population of 300 000, is famous for its historic architectural heritage and above all for its 12C wooden church and its 16C church. Further south, on the Polish border, the town of **Brest** is renowned for its fortress where the Russians withstood German attacks in 1941. 60km north of the town, you will ba able to explore the Belarusian side of the Białowieski primeval forest, known there under the name of **Belavezhskaya Puscha**.

IN LITHUANIA

Now that the country has joined the EU, a passport is sufficient to enter Lithuania.
Vilnius lies some 70km from the Polish border. Allow at least two days for an excursion starting from Suwałki or Augustów. Situated at the confluence of the Vilnia and the Neris, the town was almost entirely rebuilt after the Second World War. It is nevertheless a splendid Baroque city, on UNESCO's World Heritage List, with the full flavour of the Baltic States.

IN THE CZECH REPUBLIC

An identity card (or a passport) is all EU nationals and Swiss citizens need to enter the Czech Republic.
In winter, snow makes it difficult to cross the check points which are located along the mountain ranges. Indeed, passes are often closed at this time of year.
Prague, accessible via the E65 and E67 highways from Jelenia Góra and Kłodzko, lies only 100km from the Polish border. If the well-known sights of the Czech capital appeal to you, allow at least two days for this excursion. if you are short of time, then you might prefer to stay on the Czech side of the mountains which the Republic shares with Poland.

IN GERMANY

An identity card (or a passport) is sufficient for EU nationals.
If you go through Wrocław or the Sudeten, you will no doubt be surprised to learn that the nearest town is neither Warsaw nor Gdańsk but **Berlin**. 350km separate Wrocław from the German capital. Roads are in good condition. Do not hesitate to take two days from your schedule in order to soak in the Berlin atmosphere and visit the town's main museums.

BEFORE LEAVING

Useful addresses

TOURIST INFORMATION

Where to go when you start planning your trip.

Polish National Tourist Office London – Level 3, Westec House, West Gate, London W5 1YY ✆: 08700 675 010 (brochure line) fax: 08700 675 011
e-mail: info@visitpoland.org
www.poland.dial.pipex.com

Polish National Tourist Office New York – 275 Madison Avenue Suite 1711 New York, NY 10016 ✆: (212) 338-9412 Fax (212) 338-9283
e-mail: pntonyc@polandtour.org
www.polandtour.org

EMBASSIES AND CONSULATES

Embassy of the Republic of Poland, London – 47 Portland Place London W1B 1JH ✆: 0870 774 2700, fax: 0870 774 2755
e-mail: polishembassy@polishembassy.org.uk
www.polishembassy.or.uk

Embassy of the Republic of Poland Canada – 443 Daly Avenue, Ottawa, Ontario K1N 6H3, ✆ 789 0468, fax 789 1218.
ottawa@polishembassy.ca

Embassy of the Republic of Poland United States –2640 16th Street, NW Washington, DC 20009 ✆: (202) 234-3800 Fax (202)328-6271
e-mail: polemb.info@earthlink.net

ASSOCIATIONS

U.K. –The Polish community outside Poland amounts to 40 million and is thus second largest diaspora in the world, next to that of China. There are about 2 million Poles living in the UK. The Polish Cultural Institute is a non-profit organisation associated with the Polish Ministry of Foreign Affairs, dedicated to promoting Polish culture in Britain. The aim of the Institute is to bring contemporary Polish culture to a wider British audience through programmes featuring art, film, theatre, music and literature. As well as holding events in the beautiful English heritage building in the heart of London's West End, they also take their events to venues around the UK.

Polish Cultural Institute –34 Portland Place London W1B 1HQ ✆: 0870 7742 900 fax : 0207 637 2190
Office hours : 10.00am - 4.00 pm Monday to Friday
pci@polishculture.org.uk
There is also a list of about 100 Polish associations in the UK on the web site www.zpwb.org.uk/eg/poles-in-uk.php
U.S. – Polish traditions are alive and well in the U.S., in particular around Chicago, where many immigrants settled. The Polish Cultural Institute in New York is a diplomatic mission of the Ministry of Foreign Affairs of the Republic of Poland.

Polish Cultural Institute – 350 Fifth Avenue Suite 4621 New York, NY 10118 ✆: (212) 239-7300, fax (212) 239-7577
http://polishculture-nyc.org/pci.htm

PolskiInternet.com was created in 1998 in Chicago, to promote all Polish and Poland-related web sites on the internet in different languages. Their goal is to introduce Polish Culture and Heritage to all interested parties and to help Poles around the world reach their countrymen for social and/or business needs. While they do not focus on any specific geographic region, most visitors and featured web sites are from the United States of America. This is one of the largest directories of Polish associations in the world.

Cadd Services of Chicago, PolskiInternet.com –P.O. Box 56099, Chicago, IL 60656-0099, U.S.A. ✆: (773) 544-8809 fax: (773) 594-9449.

CYBERSPACE

Everything about Poland– www.poland.gov.pl – A vast panorama of Polish history, society, economy. Information for tourists and business travellers. You can learn the national anthem or catch up on the latest regional news, listen to Polish radio and download a screensaver for your desktop.

WWW.Poland.com offers information and advertising related to travel and business in Poland. There are special offers for hotels, rental cars and package tours, and a chat forum as well as a brief section on Polish culture.

A few other sites of interest:
European Information Centre – www.cie.gov.pl Information on Poland in Europe.

For the best little places, follow the leader.

Looking for the latest news on today's best hotels and restaurants? Pick up the Michelin Guide and look for the Bib Gourmand and Bib Hotel symbols. With 45,000 addresses in Europe, in every category and price range, the perfect place to dine or stay is never far away.

A better way forward

Ministry of Culture –
www.mk.gov.pl
Polish Literature –
www.polska2000.pl
Cultural news–
www.culture.pl

Formalities

DOCUMENTS

Identity card, passport

Nationals of countries within the EU need only a national identity card. Nationals of other countries must be in possession of a valid national passport.

Visa

No visa is required for nationals of one of the EU countries or of one of the 15 countries having signed an agreement with Poland (including Switzerland). A visa is however required for Canadian nationals.

Driving licence

If you wish to drive in Poland, you need to have a valid national driving licence.

International Student Card

Students and teachers will find the International Student or Faculty Identity Card (ISIC) very useful to obtain discounts and various advantages.
Additional information from: **STA Travel – U.K**. *☏ 0870 1 600 599, Call Centre Opening Hours 9am-8pm (Mon-Fri) 9.30am-5.30pm (Sat)10am-4pm (Sun), over 60 offices around the country. www.statravel.co.uk*
STA Travel – U.S. *5900 Wilshire Blvd, Suite 900, Los Angeles, CA 90036 ☏ 1-800-223-7986. www.isicus.com*

CUSTOMS

It is forbidden to import into Poland raw meat or home-cured meat, dairy products, flowers or pot plants and exotic animals. It is also strictly forbidden to carry weapons as well as drugs or dangerous products.

PETS

If you are travelling with your pet, take with you the animal's health record and make sure that its vaccination against rabies is valid.

Getting there

BY AIR

In view of the development of low-cost airlines, flying is now the most practical and economical means of going to Poland.

LOT Polish Airlines

The national airline (www.lot.com) offers domestic and international service. The airline is a member of the Star Alliance, and they have offices in London, New York and Chicago.

BY COACH

Eurolines - *www.eurolines.com* This is the largest network of international coach companies serving all of Europe. In the U.K., you can call the **National Express** dedicated booking line ☏ 08705 808080, the Disabled Persons Travel Helpline ☏ 0121 423 8479, the textphone line for customers who are deaf or hard of hearing ☏ 0121 455 0086. www.nationalexpress.com The Eurolines web site **www.eurolines.com** has information on their pass offer for low-cost travel between Europe's classic cities: 15 or 30 days unlimited coach travel between 40 cities. You can pre-book your first journey and for all other journeys book as you travel.

BY RAIL

It's easy to travel from the UK to Poland by train. Take Eurostar to Brussels and a high-speed train to Cologne, then the direct air-conditioned sleeper train 'Jan Kiepura' from Cologne to Warsaw. Alternatively, take Eurostar to Brussels, the overight train from Brussels to Berlin, then an air-conditioned express from Berlin to Warsaw, Kraków, Poznań, Wrocław or Katowice. The journey from London to Warsaw or Kraków is safe and comfortable, with couchettes and sleeping-cars for the overnight part and a restaurant car for meals. An experience in itself! Allow 24 hours for travel. You can book the whole trip online at www.seat61.com
Polrail has information about travelling by train in Poland (www.polrail.com).

BY CAR

Do not forget the car registration papers, but the International Insurance

Green Card is no longer required now that Poland is a member of the EU. However, Swiss nationals are still required to have it with them; if they don't, they run the risk of being fined several thousand Zlotys. It is possible to acquire one at the border posts, before entering Poland.

Main highways leading to Poland

Michelin Motoring Atlas Europe shows different itineraries for driving to Poland from anywhere in Europe. Poland has borders with Germany, the Czech Republic, Slovakia, Ukraine, Belarus, Lithuania and Russia. Below are the main highways leading into Poland from each border.

E 28: German border, Kokbaskowo, Szczecin, Koszalin, Słupsk, Gdynia, Gdańsk.

E 30: German border, Świecko, Poznań, Konin, Warsaw, Siedlce, Biała Podlaska, Terspol, Belarusian border.

E 36: German border, Olszyna.

E 40: German border, Zgorzelec, Wrocław, Opole, Kraków, Rzeszów, Przemyśl, Medyka, Ukrainian border.

E 67: Czech border, Słone, Kudowa Zdrój, Wrocław, Piotrków Trybunalski, Warsaw.

E 75: Czech border, Cieszyn, Bielsko-Biała, Katowice, Częstochowa, Łódź, Toruń, Gdańsk.

E 77: Slovak border, Chyżne, Kraków, Kielce, Warsaw, Ostróda, Elblag, Gdańsk.

E 462: Czech border, Cieszyn, Bielsko-Biała, Wadowice.

Border posts open 24h/day

With Germany
Lubieszyn, Kołbaskowo, Rosówek, Krajnik Dolny, Osinów Dolny, Kostrzyn, Słubice, Świecko, Gubinek, Olszyna, Łęknica, Przewóz, Jędrzychowice, Zgorzelec, Sieniawka, Porajów.

With Ukraine
Medyka, Korczowa, Hrebenne, Dorohusk, Zosin.

With Belarus
Terespol, Koroszczyn, Sławatycze, Kuźnica, Białostocka, Połowce, Bobrowniki.

With Russia
Gołdap, Gronowo, Bezledy.

With the Czech Republic
Bogatynia, Zawidów, Czerniawa, Jakuszyce, Przełęcz Okraj, Lubawka, Golińsk, Tłumaczów, Paczków, Kudowa Słone, Głuchołazy, Boboszów,
Konradów, Trzebina, Pietrowice, Pietraszyn, Chałupki, Cieszyn Boguszowice, Cieszyn, Leszna Góra, Jasnowice.

With Slovakia
Zwardoń, Korbielów, Chyżne, Chochołów, Łysa Polana, Piwniczna, Konieczna, Niedzica, Barwinek.

With Lithuania
Ogrodniki, Budzisko.

Internet route-planning

You can obtain personalized itineraries, addresses of hotels and restaurants, as well as practical and sightseeing information about places on the way through Michelin's route-planning service *www.viamichelin.com*

Booking accommodation

Several websites offer the possibility of making reservations for various types of accommodation in Poland. If you do not wish to plan your stay in advance, these services wil enable you to refine your choice of hotels.

Hotels

Discover Poland Online - *www.discover-poland.pl*

Hotels in Poland - *www.hotelsinpoland.com* Good selection of historic residences and palaces in addition to the more classic type of establishment.

All Hotels & Travel in Poland - *www.polhotels.com* Fairly comprehensive but very austere.

Hotels Poland - *www.hotelspoland.com*

Old Town Apartments - *www.warsawshotel.com* Renting an apartment can be an interesting alternative to staying in a hotel.

Warsaw airport, home port for LOT Airlines

E. de Malglaive / GAMMA

Farm holidays

Agrotouristika - *www.agritourism.pl.* Very comprehensive with photos and detailed information about the accommodation on offer.

Time

Winter: GMT + 1; Summer: GMT + 2. There is no time difference between Poland and Western Europe except Britain. Poland like the rest of Western Europe is always one hour ahead of Britain. Official time changes occur on the same date throughout Western Europe.

Money

CURRENCY

The Polish unit of currency is the Złoty (which means "golden"). The local abbreviation is Zł and the internatonal one is PLN.
On 21 February 2006, the exchange rate was 3.77 PLN for one Euro, 5.52 PLN for one British pound and 3.16 PLN for one US dollar.
One Złoty is divided into 100 Groszy. There are notes of 10, 20, 50, 100 and 200 Złotys and coins of 1, 2, 5, 10, 20, 50 groszy and 1, 2, 5 Złotys.

For convenience sake, have some small change handy as well as low-denomination notes. The Euro is sometimes accepted, but this is unpredictable, so be sure to have local currency at hand.

EXCHANGE

Exchanging money on the side is illegal and, in addition, one runs the risk of being swindled.

There are bureaux de change (**Kantor**) everywhere: in Post Offices, large hotels, airports and shopping streets. They only exchange cash, not travellers' cheques. Their opening times are variable and, when they are not open 24h/day, they usually work from 9am-6pm during the week and until noon on Saturday. They do not charge commissions.

The exchange rate is available daily on the Polish National Bank website *www.nbp.pl*

BANKS

They are generally open from Monday to Saturday 8am-6pm.

ATM machine in Warsaw

Travellers' cheques

Travellers' cheques offer a reliable means of insuring against theft. On the other hand, it is not always easy to convert them into cash and commissions can be rather hefty.

ATM machines

They are now available in the main streets of most town centres, in railway stations, airports and shopping centres. Instructions are in English, German and sometimes French.

CREDIT CARDS

Major bank cards are accepted in the greater part of the country. Credit cards are accepted without difficulty in large hotels and restaurant, not so much in more modest establishments. In case of loss or theft, dial: *48 22 515 31 50 or 515 30 00.*

BUDGET

Staying in Poland will not make you go bankrupt. For a comfortable double room, you should allow a minimum of 250 to 300 PLN per night in Warsaw and other large towns, 160 to 205 PLN in a lesser establishment. A room in a B & B costs around 100 PLN.
Meal in a restaurant: this varies, of course, according to the nature and standard of the establishment. Allow between 6 and 25 PLN for a dish and 15 to 50 PLN for a meal.

What to pack

It depends on the time of year when you are travelling and on the kind of activity you intend to practise when you are there. You will be able to find everything you need as far as staple goods are concerned, and brands are often the same as in Western Europe.

If you are planning to take part in sport activities, remember to take walking shoes and warm clothing, particularly in spring and autumn. They are useful in mountainous areas and to visit caves and underground sites.

Also pack a first-aid kit, although everything it may contain can be found in Polish pharmacies.

Photographers will find in specialised boutiques the equipment necessary to transfer digital photos onto a CD for next to nothing.

Useful tip

The **Polish card**, which has been distributed free in Tourist Offices in Poland since 2004, enables visitors to benefit from many reductions conceded by several hotels, restaurants, museums, tourist sites and boutiques all over the country.

WHEN YOU ARE THERE

Useful addresses

TOURIST INFORMATION

Tourist Offices – Every town wanting to promote its cultural heritage has a Tourist Office with, more often than not, English-speaking staff.
Available literature is often abundant and of good quality: brochures about sights, detailed rambling maps...

PTTK (Polskie Towarzystwo Turystyczno Krajoznawcze)– The Polish Association for the promotion of tourism and the discovery of the country has a vast network of offices in Poland's major cities. It has, for decades now, been looking after footpaths and river courses as well as a few regional museums specialised in the discovery of nature.

Polish Association for the Promotion of Tourism

WARNING

Poland is a safe country and, as elsewhere, a few elementary precautions are necessary to avoid trouble: do not carry too much cash on you, avoid being out and about too late at night, particularly outside town centres, around railway stations or in parks. Night trains generally have a bad reputation but if you keep an eye on your luggage, you should have no trouble. Do not leave anything of value inside your vehicle, rented and foreign cars being the favourite target of thieves, and when you are driving from one town to the next, always keep at hand the highway emergency number and the traffic police number. Polish Law applies zero tolerance as far as drugs are concerned. Therefore, do

not give in to temptation. Finally, do not forget that, just like many eastern countries, Poland is invaded with all types of imitations of luxury products (clothes, perfume, handbags...) and it is, of course, strictly forbidden to export such goods to the West.

EMERGENCIES

The numbers indicated below should be kept at hand. Telephone operators do not always speak English and, if you can't make yourself understood, try, as a last resort, to get in touch with your embassy.

Police: 997 (free call), 112 from a mobile (free call)

Fire brigade: 998 (free call)
Medical emergency: 999 (free call)

Number for foreigners staying in Poland: 0 800 200 300 (free call), (22) 601 55 55. Functions from 1 May to 31 October. In English, German and Russian.

EMBASSIES AND CONSULATES

British Embassy Warsaw

Al. Róż 100-556 Warszawa - ✆ 22 311 00 00 fax 22311 03 11, e-mail: info@britishembassy.pl consular@ britishembassy.pl

American Embassy and Consulates

U.S. Embassy Warsaw – *Aleje Ujazdowskie 29/3100-540 Warsaw ✆ 22 504-2000*

U.S. Consulate General in Kraków – *ul. Stolarska 931-043 Kraków ✆ 12 424-5100 fax: +48 12 424-5103*

Consular Agency in Poznań – *ul. Paderewskiego 861-770 Poznant 61 851-8516 Fax +48 61 851-8966*

Canadian Consulate Warsaw

ul. Jana Matejki 1/5, 00-481 Varsovie. ✆ 22 829 80 51

Getting around

BY AIR

Domestic flights are operated by the Polish ariline **Lot**, connecting the airports of Warsaw, Kraków, Poznań, Lublin, Łódź, Katowice, Gdańsk, Bydgoszcz, Rzeszów.

Information from the Warsaw office
- *al. Jerozolimskie 65/79.* ☎ *0801 703 703* and *22 9572* for mobile users. *www. lot.com* (website in English).

BY RAIL

The Polish State Railways **PKP** (Polskie Koleje Państwowe) network includes over 25 000km of lines. Most places are therefore accessible by train.
Express trains, **Intercity** and **Eurocity**, operate long distance routes, directly linking major cities. Their timetables are marked in red with an R next to the time.
"Fast trains" are in fact rather slow since they stop more often than express trains. They are also marked in red.
As for **normal trains**, they are really slow!

pkp.com.pl

The rail company's official site is useful for planning train travel inside Poland, with schedules and routes.

All trains offer the choice between first and second class. First-class seats, which are inexpensive compared to Western European prices, are covered with velvet and very comfortable. One gets the impression of travelling in a bygone age.
All stations have a left-luggage office; allow 8 PLN per day.
Words to know to get around in a station:
głowny : central station (useful information since all major towns have several stations).
tor : track
peron : platform
Don't forget night trains for long journeys, but it is sometimes essential to reserve couchettes a long time in advance

BY COACH

Trains are a better choice over long distances, but buses, although slower, are often the only means of reaching remote places, particularly in mountainous regions or rural areas.
A few private companies operate services between large towns. Bus terminals are often situated near railway stations and sometimes share the same ticket office. Private companies usually have their own terminal.

Information for the State company **PKS**: *www.pks.pl* a very comprehensive website providing timetables and destinations.

BY TAXI

Taxi ranks are indicated by a panel "Taxi". A higher rate applies to journeys undertaken on Saturday, Sunday and at night (between 10pm and 6am) or well as beyond urban areas. The first kilometre costs around 4 PLN, thereafter the charge is 2 PLN per kilometre. In Warsaw and Kraków, taxis waiting outside stations and at the airport are likely to charge more. In all Polish towns, you can ring for a taxi, see the practical information about each town. Always make sure that the meter is working. A journey in town should cost between 5 and 20 PLN.

BY PUBLIC TRANSPORT

In large towns, you will usually have the choice between tramway, bus or metro (in Warsaw only). Tickets can be bought in RUCH kiosks and in hotels. There are travel cards for 1 day, 1 week and 1 month. Information is available from Tourist Offices.

BY CAR

Driving licence
In order to be able to drive in Poland, you must have a valid passport and a driving licence (international if possible). The green card is no longer necessary since Poland is now a member of the EU.

Car hire
Renting a car in Poland will cost you between 100 and 400 PLN per day depending on the model. It is possible to drive a rented vehicle through the neighbouring countries except those situated beyond Poland's eastern border. Most companies will agree, for an additional fee, to your giving the car back in another agency.
Large international companies are all represented in Poland but there are also more modest private companies. Internation reservation services:
Europcar – ☎ *0 825 358 358 ou www.europcar.com*
Hertz – ☎ *0 825 861 861 and www.hertz.com*

In Poland :
Avis – Warsaw : *in the centre - ☎ and fax (022) 630 73 16 - Okecie Airport:*

*(022) 650 48 72 - fax 650 48 71 - informations: *0800 1 200 10
Gdańsk : *(058)301 88 18 - fax 301 88 24
Poznań : *and fax (061) 851 77 78
Wroclaw : *(071) 372 35 67 - fax 343 09 28
Bydgoszcz : *and fax (052) 349 35 87
Kraków: *(012) 421 10 66
Katowice: *and fax (032) 58 44 18

Budget – *Central reservation:* *(022) 630 72 80 - fax 630 69 46 - Okecie Airport: *(022) 650 40 62 - fax 650 40 63

Europcar – *Central reservation:* *(022) 853 66 77 - fax 853 47 86 - Okecie Airport: *(022) 650 25 64 - fax 650 25 63

Hertz – *Central reservation:* *(022) 621 02 39 - fax 629 38 75 - Okecie Airport: *(022) 650 28 96 - fax 650 34 90 - *Recorded information:* *0 800 1 43 789
Gdańsk: *(058) 301 40 45
Katowice: *(032) 59 99 47
Kraków: *(012) 429 62 62
Lublin: *(081) 533 20 61
Łódź: *(042) 633 21 49
Olsztyn: *(089) 527 57 93
Poznań: *(061) 853 17 02

National – *Central reservation:* *(022) 868 75 74 - fax 868 75 25 - Okecie Airport: *and fax : (022)650 47 33

Polish car hire companies:

Auto atelier – *Office in Gliwice:* *and fax (032) 279 59 67
Kalisz: *and fax (062) 768 15 07
Ostrow Wielkopolski : *and fax (062) 768 15 01 - www.autoatelier.pl

Local Rent A Car – *Office in Warsaw:* *(022) 826 71 00

Global Poland – *Warsaw, Okecie Airport:* *and fax (022) 650 14 83
Cracovie : *and fax (012) 259 15 90
WEST - *Office in Kraków:* *(012) 648 75 44

Road conditions

The road network is well developed but road surfaces vary a lot. A few sections of motorway, marked with the letter E followed by a figure, lead out of the urban areas of Warsaw and Wrocław. There are two long sections, one running along a north-south axis and linking Łódż and Bielsko-Biała (via Częstochowa and Katowice) and the other running from west to east and linking the German border and Kraków (via Wrocław and Katowice). The rest of the network, being constantly renovated, consists of narrow roads and two-lane main

roads (their number is preceded by an A in the case of international roads). The oldest of that last category are often dotted with potholes dug in the asphalt by the weight of lorries. On the most recent roads, the hard shoulder is used by vehicles to overtake, even if the highway code and common sense are against this kind of practice. Expect to see cars coming towards you and driving in the middle of the road! In any case, lorries and farm vehicles, difficult to overtake, often slow traffic down. Don't base yourself on the number of kilometres to calculate your journey time. The distance between Warsaw and the Masurian Lakes (around 240km) represents a 4hr drive.
In winter, snow cover blocks the passes linking Poland with the Czech Republic and with Slovakia. In isolated regions such as Podlasie, many roads also become impassable.

Maps and plans

Michelin map 720 Poland, on a scale of 1:700 000, gives and excellent view of the whole country.
The road atlas published by Copernicus is useful, as is the general map published by Demart. There are practical maps available for large towns, making it possible to locate each single street and indicating pedestrian and one-way streets.

Highway code

Traffic drives on the right and the Polish highway code is similar to those currently used in the rest of Europe. Indeed, road signs are international. Right of way is indicated by road signs but bear in mind that, in town, right of way must be given to tramways at any time.

Speed limits:

60km/hr in built-up areas,
110km/hr on dual carriageways
130km/hr on motorways.
Vehicles towing a caravan must reduce their speed to 70km/hr.

Lights:

Dipped lights must be switched on all day from 1 October to 1 March .

Safety precautions:

Wearing a seat belt is compulsory and children under 12 must sit in a safety seat. The use of a mobile phone while driving is allowed so long as it is not hand-held.
All vehicles must be equipped with an extinguisher and a warning triangle.

DISTANCE BETWEEN THE MAIN TOWNS									
	Białistok	Kraków	Gdańsk	Łódź	Lublin	Olsztyn	Poznań	Warsaw	Wrocław
Białistok	–	490	4132	367	260	227	503	193	539
Kraków	490	–	597	242	295	508	450	296	275
Gdańsk	413	597	–	357	506	268	313	345	448
Łódź	367	242	357	–	261	315	221	139	208
Lublin	260	295	506	261	–	373	477	166	433
Olsztyn	227	508	268	315	373	–	330	218	466
Poznań	503	450	313	221	477	330	–	312	168
Warsaw	193	296	345	139	146	218	312	–	352
Wrocław	539	275	448	208	433	466	168	352	–

In built-up areas, you must comply with the injunctions of police officers in uniform or civilian clothes. Outside built-up areas, you must comply with injunctions of police officers in uniform or in civilian clothes if they are standing near a police car.

Road signs

They are similar to those used in Western Europe although there are a few specific panels essentially concerning built-up areas. The road sign marking the entrance to a built-up area features the outline of a town. Crossed by a red line, the same panel indicates the end of the built-up area. A road sign featuring a little girl holding a balloon means that children are often crossing at that spot.

Drinking and driving

A zero tolerance applies to drinking and driving on the road. Any intake of alcohol, even the slightest, by the driver of a vehicle can lead to a hefty fine and an arrest. When it reaches 0.5mg/litre of alcohol in the blood, the simple breach of the law becomes a criminal offence and the offender runs the risk of being sent to prison for up to two years with immediate effect. This procedure can last several months.

Parking

Most towns are now equipped with parking ticket machines. In smaller towns, a municipal employee sells parking tickets (around 2 PLN/hr). His presence guarantees the safety of your vehicle but if you have to park overnight, choose a enclosed guarded car park. These car parks are located on the edge of town centres. Allow 30 PLN per night.

Fines

The penalty for failing to observe any of the highway code rules is a fine ranging from 100 to 500 PLN. Points taken from driving licences is a additional penalty that applies in some cases and, in view of agreements between Poland and countries that also use this system, foreign offenders in theory run the risk of having points taken from their own licence. In reality, a hefty fine is all you risk.

Fuel

Poland has a more than adequate number of petrol stations belonging either to Polish companies such as CPN, Petrochemia Plock, Rafineria Gdańsk, or to distributors of private companies. Most petrol outlets, particularly those located on main roads, are open 24hr/day. Others are open from 6am to 8pm or even 10pm. All types of fuel are available. 94-octane petrol is marked in yellow, whereas 95 and 98-octane unleaded petrol is marked in green.

Pedestrian crossing

B. Brillion / MICHELIN

Also on sale is unleaded U95 petrol intended for cars without a catalytic converter, as well as diesel. Allow about 4.20 PLN for a litre of petrol and about 3.7 PLN for a litre of diesel.

Breakdown

The **Starter** patrol offers roadside assistance. You can call it on ℰ (61) 831 98 00, 600 222 222 and on 609 222 222.

The **Polish Automobile and Motorcycle Federation**, (**PZMot**) provides roadside breakdown service. Within a 50km radius of main towns, a simple phone call will enable you to benefit from the federation's free breakdown service if you have an AIT (Alliance Internationale de Tourisme) card or are a member of a motoring club affiliated to the Fédération Internationale de l'Automobile. For the addresses and phone numbers of roadside assistance services, apply to the Polish Automobile and Motorcycle Federation, *ul. Kazimierzowska 66 à Varsovie* - ℰ *(22) 849 93 61 or (22) 849 93 62 and the emergency number 9637 open 24h/day.* There are also many private companies.

Where to eat

Eating and above all eating well will not cost you a lot in Poland where restaurants are plentiful and varied.

IN MIECZNY BARS

The **Bar Mleczny** (milk bar) is a real Polish institution and a legacy from the Communist era, operating as self-service establishments. They attract a modest clientele and offer simple traditional dishes; one often eats well for about 10 PLN in these snack bars where helpings are copious. You will have no problem understanding the menu in Polish since dishes are visible behind the counter and you'll just need to point to what you want.

IN RESTAURANTS

Restaurants intended for tourists, where the decor is often outrageously exuberant, make a point of offering a wide choice of dishes. But the cuisine often shows a lack of inventiveness; therefore, try and eat in a more discreet establishment, renowned for its specialities and, if your budget allows, don't hesitate to go to a gourmet restaurant.

Some of them offer real Polish specialities while many others offer typical dishes from Poland's neighbours such as Ukraine. Besides classic restaurants, there are pizzerias and chain restaurants halfway between fast-food and world-cuisine restaurants, serving a selection of Greek, Tex-Mex or French-inspired dishes. These establishments are popular with young trendy consumers who live in large cities. However, they offer no real interest from a gastronomic point of view.

Opening times

Restaurants are usually open without a break from 11am or noon to 10pm. Some of them specify that they are open "until the last customer goes". Don't forget that the Poles have dinner early, around 7pm, and that the last customer could be leaving around 9.30pm. Chain restaurants alone stay open later, until around 11pm. Meal times in Poland are different from those in most other countries of Western Europe. **Breakfast** is very copious (eggs, charcuterie, dairy products) and enables one to hold out for a good part of the day. Towards midday, Poles have a very light snack, but the second meal which could be compared to **lunch**, is only taken at the end of the working day, around 4pm. The third, lighter meal, **dinner**, is taken around 7pm. People in large cities do not observe these meal times and dinner is often taken fairly late.

Menu

In more modest establishments, the menu in Polish will no doubt give you a hard time and the opportunity to have unusual but interesting culinary experiences. The menu of restaurants that are more used to tourists is at least in German or English, sometimes in Russian, less often in French. Menus often consist of some ten pages since everything is described in detail. Next to each dish is the quantity served, in grammes…. a good way of choosing according to one's appetite!

The bill

Although one can have a copious meal in a milk bar for some ten złotys, a meal in a more classic establishment costs between 35 and 40 PLN. In a high-class restaurant, the bill can vary from 175 to 1 000 PLN, wine included. Tips, on the other hand, are not included and it is recommended to leave an additional 10%.

Little Red Riding Hood

But Little Red Riding Hood had her regional map with her, and so she did not fall into the trap. She did not take the path through the wood and she did not meet the big bad wolf. Instead, she chose the picturesque touring route straight to Grandmother's house, and arrived safely with her cake and her little pot of butter.

The End

Where to stay

There are many accommodation options in Poland. Prices vary but are considerably lower than in Western Europe.

Practical info

In the practical pages concerning each town described in this guide we offer you a selection of restaurants and hotels suitable for all budgets.

HOTELS

There are hotels of all categories, for all tastes and at all prices. Their number has been increasing over the past few years. Hotels dating from the Communist period have not all disappeared. Some of them were restored and adapted to a more modern and pleasant level of comfort, others, now becoming rare, still boast the atmosphere of bygone days: huge marble halls, brown wallpaper or wall-to-wall carpet, neon lights, outdated furniture and beds (when they are not downright dilapidated). A real journey back in time!

However, over the past few years, modern establishments have sprung up, particularly in some town centres undergoing full renovation programmes. From comfortable hotels displaying one to five stars (with parking and bellboy, even sauna) to charming guesthouses, there is a wide choice which is bound to satisfy your needs.

Reservation system of the Polish tourist and hotel services: *www.dis-cover-poland.pl*

It is also possible to make reservations on the following booking websites:
www.polhotel.pl
www.hotelsinpoland.com
www.polhotels.com
www.hotelspoland.com
And for Warsaw:
www.warsawshotel.com

Orbis is the largest hotel chain in Poland. Its members are usually 4 or 5-star hotels.
To make reservations at hotels of the Orbis Group: ☏ *0-801 606 606 and (+48-502) 805 805 - www.orbis.pl*

Charming hotels

This kind of accommodation is beginning to grow. On offer, for example, are former granaries magnificently restored in Toruń, Reszel Castle or the Antonin hunting lodge in Greater Poland.

BUDGET ACCOMMODATION

Several options of budget accommodation are available through organisations such as youth hostels, pensions, tourism centres, private rooms associations (towns or villages in the most touristic regions).

You can book a place in a youth hostel by applying to the **Polish Youth Hostel Federation (PTSM)** : *ul. Chocimska 28 - 00-791 Warsaw - ☏/fax: (22) 849 83 54 - www.ptsm.com.pl*

In some towns, **student hostels** welcome visitors in summer and during university holidays, in particular in Warsaw, Kraków, Wrocław, Poznań and Gdańsk.

Private rooms

It is probably the most pleasant way of discovering Polish people and rural life. Some Tourist Offices propose farm holidays. A Polish website list region by region all the farms offering a **stay in the country**. Polish and English version: *www.agritourism.pl*
Whether they are in towns or in the country, private rooms are indicated by panels marked **Noclegi** (night) or **Pokoje** (room).

Campsites

The network of campsites (232 in all) covers the whole Polish territory. Campsites are located near large towns and tourist centres; they are generally open from 1 May or 1 June to 15 or 30 September.

Polish Federation of Camping & Caravaning (PFCC) : *ul. Grochowska 331 - ☏ (22) 810 60 50 - www.pfcc.info*

Traditional houses on the main square of Wrocław

Useful tip

In towns, most hotels of a certain standard propose lower tarifs during weekends (often half price).
It is not necessary to pack products like soap or shampoo, most establishments consider that they owe it to their reputation to provide these to their customers.

Health

No vaccine is required.

British Travellers

During a temporary stay in Poland, British Citizens are entitled to emergency medical treatment on the same terms as Polish nationals on production of a **European Health Insurance Card (EHIC)** issued in the UK before leaving the country.

The **EHIC replaced Form E111,** which remained valid until the end of 2005. The EHIC is available free of charge through most United Kingdom Post Offices or through the UK Department of Health via their website or by telephoning 0800 555 7777 and obtaining their leaflet "Health Advice for Travellers".

The EHIC is not a substitute for medical and travel insurance.

You will find further information about health insurance in Poland on the web-site: *www.nfz.gov.pl/ue*

Travellers from outside the European Union should ask their travel agent or insurance agent about medical coverage when travelling abroad.

American Travellers

If an American citizen becomes seriously ill or injured abroad, a U. S. consular officer can assist in locating appropriate medical services and informing family or friends. If necessary, a consular officer can also assist in the transfer of funds from the United States. However, payment of hospital and other expenses is the responsibility of the traveler.

Before going abroad, learn what medical services your health insurance will cover overseas. If your health insurance policy provides coverage outside the United States, carry both your insurance policy identity card as proof of such insurance and a claim form. Although many health insurance companies will pay "customary and reasonable" hospital costs abroad, very few will pay for your medical evacuation back to the United States. Medical evacuation can easily cost

$10,000 and up, depending on your location and medical condition.

The Social Security Medicare program does not provide coverage for hospital or medical costs outside the U.S. Senior citizens may wish to contact the American Association of Retired Persons for information about foreign medical care coverage with Medicare supplement plans.

Any medications being carried overseas should be left in their original containers and be clearly labeled.

The booklet "Health Information for International Travel" may be obtained through the Superintendent of Documents, U.S. Government Printing Office, Washington, DC 20402. For detailed information on physicians abroad, the authoritative reference is The Official ABMS Directory of Board Certified Medical Specialists published for the American Board of Medical Specialists and its certifying member boards. This publication should be available in your local library. U.S. embassies and consulates abroad maintain lists of hospitals and physicians. Major credit card companies also can provide the names of local doctors and hospitals abroad.

EMERGENCIES

Once you are in Poland, if you find yourself in difficulty, you will be able, as a foreign visitor, to obtain help and advice – in English, German or Russian – by dialling the following numbers: *0800 200 300* (free call from a land line) or *+48 608 599 999* (paying call from a mobile). The line operates from June to September, from 8am-8pm.

Polish doctors are competent whatever the establishment. However, public hospitals are run on a much tighter budget than private ones. Their equipment is usually less efficient and there are an insufficient number of beds.

Practical info

You will find addresses of hospitals, and pharmacies in the practical pages of large towns.

PHARMACIES

There is no difference between Polish and Western European pharmacies. The same medicines are available. Their staff often speak English.

Communications

POST OFFICES

Post Offices are located in town centres and generally open weekdays from 8am to 7pm and on Saturday morning. Stamps can be bought in Post Offices or in kiosks (RUCH). To send a letter to an EU country you need a 2.10 PLN stamp, to the US, 2.50 PLN. EMS-Pocztex courier service can be used from any Post Office in town.
Allow roughly a week for mail to reach Britain or the U.S.
Postal codes in Poland have five figures. Large towns may have more than one code. For example, in Warsaw, the codes begin with 00-033 and continue.

Telephone card

Practical info

At the beginning of all practical pages for each town in the guide, you will find the postal code and phone code of the town and region.
Poland's country code is 48.

TELEPHONE

To be able to phone from a public booth, you must buy cards of 25, 50 or 100 units in kiosks or at the reception desk of some hotels.
To phone Poland from abroad: dial the international access code (usually 00) then 48 (country code), followed by the area code (omitting the initial 0) and the number of the person you are calling.

To phone abroad from Poland:
for the UK, dial 00 then 44 followed by the area code (omitting the initial 0) and the number.
Other useful country codes:
Ireland: 00 + 353
Canada : 00 + 1
USA: 00 + 1
Australia: 00 + 61
New Zealand: 00 + 64

Local and national calls:
within one region, dial the subscriber's number omitting the initial 0. From one region to another, dial the area code (including the initial 0).
Some area codes:
Warsaw: 022
Gdańsk : 058
Kraków: 012

Mobile phones
Poland uses the GSM network which also covers the rest of Europe. The GSM cover is efficient over the whole of the country. Before going, ask your phone company to activate your international access. Bear in mind, however, that all calls (including in-coming calls) will be charged at the rate of international calls, even if you are calling someone in Poland. You could be faced with a hefty bill.

INTERNET

There are plenty of Internet cafés in Poland, even in small towns where, however, tarifs are sometimes prohibitive. Allow 4 PLN for one hour's connection.

Shopping

Opening times
Shops are usually open from 10am to 6pm from Monday to Friday, with shorter hours on Saturday. International brands are gaining ground and their prices are not very different from those charged in Western Europe. In major towns, some shops selling food and alcohol remain open late at night and sometimes 24hr/day. In all Polish towns you will find small kiosks where you will be able to buy anything and everything: postcards, sweets, cigarettes and newspapers.
In the North of the country, along the Baltic and in Masuria, **amber** is plentiful. Necklaces, pendents and earrings make lovely gifts. In view

- **a.** 🍄 *Meals served in the garden or on the terrace*
- **b.** 🍇 *A particularly interesting wine list*
- **c.** 🍺 *Cask beers and ales usually served*

Find out all the answers in the Michelin Guide "Eating Out in Pubs"!

A selection of 500 dining pubs and inns throughout Britain and Ireland researched by the same inspectors who make the Michelin Guide.

- for good food and the right atmosphere
- in-depth descriptions bring out the feel of the place and the flavour of the cuisine.

The pleasure of travel with Michelin Maps and Guides.

Souvenir stand

C. Hervé-Bazin / MICHELIN

U.S residents arriving from anywhere other than a U.S. insular possession may bring back $800 worth of items duty free, as accompanied baggage. Keep your receipts with you. One liter (33.8 fl. oz.) of alcoholic beverages may be included in your exemption if you are 21 years old. The exemption includes not more than 200 cigarettes and 100 cigars

Tourists can recover VAT (a 22% tax in Poland) on purchases over 200 PLN. The simplest way is to make any large purchases in a store with a "tax free" offer advertised (have your passport and return ticket handy).

Daily life from A to Z

ADMISSION TIMES

Opening times of museums (usually closed on Monday) and other tourist sites mentioned in this guide were taken down on location. In reality, opening hours are less than reliable, and even unpredictable, particularly off season and in more remote areas. Be patient and do not hesitate to ring the door bell or knock at the door: it can happen that a keeper will eventually let you in and allow you to see a hidden collection.

ELECTRICITY

Polish plugs provide standard continental 220-volt current. There is always a plug in hotel rooms for a laptop or a mobile-phone charger.

PUBLIC HOLIDAYS

1 January: New Year
Easter: Sunday and Monday
1 May: Labour Day
3 May: Constitution Day
Corpus Christi: Thursday, variable feast
15 August: Feast of the Assumption
1 November: All Saints' Day
11 November: Independence Day
25 and 26 December: Christmas

TOILETS

There are public toilets everywhere; they are generally well kept by adequate staff. One is expected to leave a tip. Women's toilets are marked with a circle, men's toilets with a triangle.

of the development of synthetic amber, caution is recommended, and it is best to go to official dealers. You will find the finest items in Gdańsk. In rural regions, particularly mountainous regions, there are interesting **textiles** to be bought, both for clothing and decorating purposes. Keep an eye out for **contemporary designers** whose work is often quite fanciful. Travel souvenirs include fine **art books** which will remind you of the sites and monuments you visited. And last but not least are Polish **posters**, whether political, cultural or defending a cause.
Remember: you need special permission to take any work of art or book dating from before 1945 out of the country.

FOOD AND DRINK

There is a wide choice here. **Vodka** is, of course, at the top of the list. There are varieties for every taste from the bison herb drink to more austere or sweeter varieties. Polish **beer** also has unconditional admirers. **Charcuterie** is also popular, in particular sausages and smoked ham...and there are the different **cheeses**, including the tasty **oscypek** that has a delicate smokey flavour. Toruń, famous for **pierniki**, is the capital of gingerbread.

Allowances
Residents of E.U. Member States are allowed to bring home 10 l of alcohol, 90 l of wine, 110 l of beer and 200 cigarettes.

WHAT TO DO AND SEE

Sport and leisure activities from A to Z

Local and regional Tourist Offices publish brochures and literature and will answer inquiries about activities that can be practised in their region. To find our selection, look up the sections "Where to go" and "Sport and leisure" in the practical pages of towns and sites.

BOAT TRIPS

All lakes and rivers of a reasonable size lend themselves to boat trips. Private companies organise cruises sometimes lasting several hours, from the simple nautical trip to the elaborate themed trip. For instance, Lake Wigry in Podlasie offers ideal conditions for the discovery of its hidden treasures. On the Masurian lakes, boat trips take visitors on a tour of nature reserves and small sanctuary islands where a multitude of protected birds find refuge. In Toruń and Wrocław, excursions on the river offer a new insight into the wealth of history and architecture of these towns.

CANOEING AND KAYAKING

The North-East of the country is the most suitable region for this kind of activity, in particular the River Krutynia, which flows through a vast forest south of the Masurian Lakes, and along the renowned course of the Czarna Hańcza prolonged, via an impressive series of locks, by the Augustów Canal. Elsewhere, the rivers Dewęca and Drawa, in the Brodnica region welcome canoeing enthusiasts.

South of Kraków, it is possible to canoe down the Dunajec and Bobr mountain streams. It's a little more demanding than paddling along peaceful rivers but certainly more stimulating.

Polish canoeing-kayaking Federation (PZK) – Ul. Ciołka 17, 01-445 Warsaw, ✆ (+48-22) 837 14 70 and 837 40 59. www.pzkaj.pl

CYCLING

Cycling and rambling are probably the best ways of discovering Poland. Indeede, cycling will be more suitable for travellers who do not have enough time to explore a region on foot. Many towns suggest discovery trails in surrounding areas, very often in collaboration with bike-hire companies. For instance, the Tourist Office in Poznań publishes a map of the many itineraries starting from the town centre and linking Kórnik and Rogalin castles or running along the footpaths of the Greater Poland National Park.

Polish Cycling Federation (PZKol) – Ul. Afrykańska 7a - 03-966 Warsaw ✆(+48-22) 671 99 10 - www.pzklo.pl

FISHING

Fishing is a year-round activity. In winter, frozen lakes lend themselves to fishing though a hole in the ice, in particular in the Masurian Lakeland where perches are the most common fish, closely followed by eels. Next to Pomerania, this is the most renowned fishing region. Fishing for trout in the tumultuous mountain streams of the Bieszczady is also a sought-after activity. Salmon, on the other hand, is plentiful at the mouth of rivers and the Baltic offers almost 500km of coastline suitable for sea-fishing, the prize catch being cod.

In Poland, one must hold a licence in order to be allowed to practise fishing, whether it be sea-fishing or fresh-water fishing.

The **Polish Fishing Association (PZW)** – ul. Twarda 42, 00-831 Warsaw, ✆ (+48 22) 620 89 66. www.pzw.pl will be able to tell you how to obtain a licence.

GUIDED TOURS

In towns, they are usually scheduled by the **PTTK**. This organisation includes polyglot guides who propose personalised guided tours, based on what you feel you'd like and how much time you have. You will find their details in the practical pages of each town.

In addition, each fairly important town proposes discovery trails; apply to Tourist Offices. In Warsaw for instance, there is a special itinerary for discovering the Old Town, the Royal Way, the Wilanów Palace and the main monuments. Another trail is devoted to the Jewish heritage. In Toruń, boat trips along the river Wisła propose a discovery of the town from the river which brought is wealth during its heyday.

HUNTING

Polish forests are rich in various kinds of game. It is possible to hunt deer (September to February), roe-deer (May to September), wild boar (April to February), hare (October to January) and even partridge (September to October). The best hunting grounds are to be found in the North-East of the country as well as in the Bieszczady region. Roe-deer live mainly in Masuria, Pomerania and Greater Poland where Prince Antoni Radziwiłł, who no doubt knew that, had a sumptuous wooden hunting palace built. As for deer, they can be found in the majority of Poland's forests.

Polish Hunting Federation (PZŁ) – Ul. Nowy Świat 35, 00-029 Warsaw, ✆ (+48-22) 826 20 51. www.pzlow.pl

ICE-YACHTING

in winter, when lakes and rivers are caught under a thick cover of ice, yachting enthusiasts always find a way to practise their favourite sport. Ice-yachting is becoming more and more popular in Poland. It is essentially practised in the North-East, on the lakes and canals of Masuria, Warmia and Pomerania. The small town of Mikołajki gathers a great number of ice-yachting enthusiasts.

Lake near Smolniki de Suwalki

P. Ciesla / Hoa qui/Age

MOUNTAINEERING

The southern border is the only part of Poland where one can practise mountain climbing. In the Tatras, for instance, Zakopane is the ideal base from which to set out on an expedition. Guides and equipment are available on location.

Polish Mountaineering Federation (PZA) – Ul. Ciołka 17, 01-445 Warsaw, ✆ (+48-22) 836 36 90. www.pza.org.pl

MUSEUMS

Museums are closed on Mondays. Admission costs between 5 and 15 PLN (without a guide). Some museums only accept groups by prior appointment. For those which are located outside towns, allow the cost of parking in addition to admission charges. Photos are usually forbidden. Some museums allow them against payment of an additional charge of about 20 PLN. Explanations are often but not always in English. Plan your visits carefully, as museums usually close around 3 to 4pm.

NATURE PARKS

Love to ramble through unspoilt nature? The wealth of Polish nature and the determination to preserve this unique heritage led to the opening of no fewer than 23 nature parks throughout the country. Many environments and ecosystems are represented. There is a genuine effort to develop and enhance these areas and, running through each of them, are marked paths and discovery trails intended to make ramblers aware of the unique natural wealth of each site. In the Gór Stołowych National Park, Nature carved a fantastic landscape which forms the setting of fascinating rambles, as in the Karkonosze where paths running along the mountain slopes offer the opportunity of seeing ibex once imported from Corsica. In the Wigierski Park, in the North-East of Poland, lakes and forests form the basis of the environment. Well-kept marked paths make it possible for ramblers to encounter beavers, the symbol of the region. A few kilometres to the north-west of Kraków, bats living in caves are the mascot of the tiny Ojców nature park. Here, the limestone strata carved by erosion forms spectacular landscapes through which paths wind their way past

S. Sauvignier / Michelin

a. *Coteaux de Chiroubles vineyards (Beaujolais) ?*
b. *The vineyards around Les Riceys (Champagne) ?*
c. *Riquewihr and the surrounding vineyards (Alsace) ?*

Can't decide ?
Then immerse yourself in the Michelin Green Guide !

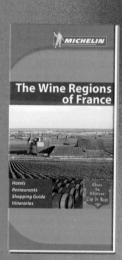

- Everything to do and see
- The best driving tours
- Practical information
- Where to stay and eat

  The Michelin Green Guide:
  the spirit of discovery.

castles perched on high ground and churches nestling on the waterside. The seaside is just as fascinating with the Słowiński Park and its strange shifting dunes. As for the Białowieski Park, it boasts the oldest primeval forest in Europe.

RAMBLING

Forests, mountains and nature parks abound, the choice is yours. The Polish countryside lends itself beautifully to walking.Tracks and footpaths are plentiful and well marked. In each region, you will find a selection of maps detailing the various itineraries. Sometimes, journey times between two trails, whichever way you tackle them, are indicated and the different sights you will meet on the way are described, so that you may make the most of your visit to a given region. The Polish authorities, particularly in the case of nature parks and protected areas, are making tremendous efforts to mark and maintain trails, many of which are the only means of getting to certain places. If you can afford the time, do not hesitate to explore the countryside. It is the best way to discover the rural side of Poland.

RIDING

Riding is a popular activity in Poland which can be practised as part of a package tour or through private riding centres and holiday farms. Riding across the Bieszczadki National Park is a sought-after experience as are riding tours along the Baltic beaches. It is, of course, possible to make longer tours, in particular along the 250km long Transjurassic track linking the Kraków area to Częstochowa. In the Beskid and the Bieszczady, enthusiasts can enjoy riding small mountain horses known as Hutsuls (Hucuły).

PTTK Sub-commission of Mountain Horse-riding Tourism (Podkomisja Górskiej Turystyki Jeździeckiej PTTK) – *Ul. Jagiellońska 6,* ☏ *12 421 21 13. www.pttk.pl*
Polish Horse-riding Federation (PZJ) – *Ul. Cegłowska 68/70, 01-809 Warsaw,* ☏ *(+48-22) 834 73 21. Fax 834 52 28. www.pzj.pl*

SAILING

The ideal region for sailing enthusiasts is no doubt Masuria. Lakes Śniardwy and Mamry, one of the largest in Poland, offer fine sailing opportunities. An important network linking lakes, canals and rivers makes it possible to sail over distances of nearly 200km. The main ports are Giżycko, Węgorzewo and Mikołajki.

Sailing is also a popular activity on the Baltic Sea, in the bay of Gdańsk and around the Hel peninsula. For beginners, the Szczecin laguna is ideal as there are calm waters around the Trzebież marina. From there, it is possible to reach the island of Wolin, a former Viking colony and now a nature park.

Polish Sailing Federation (PZŻ) – *Ul. Chocimska 14, 00-791 Warsaw,* ☏ *(+48-22) 848 04 83. Fax 848 04 82. www.pya.org.pl*

SEA BATHING

With over 600km of coastline along the Baltic Sea, Poland offers a large number of beaches backed by cliffs, lagunas, or extending along estuaries. In West Pomerania, sea bathing takes place around Szczecin. But the Gdańsk region has the greatest number and variety of beaches. Sopot, reminiscent of Deauville, is the great favourite. A little further north, Łeba is somewhat similar. More discreet are the resorts of Kołobrzeg, Międzyzdroje, Darłowo and Ustka, which are not devoid of charm. Finally, the sand strip of the Hel peninsula offers a long stretch of beaches dotted with fishing villages. Bear in mind that water is a little cold here. But it is said to be very invigorating.

ONT Pologne

Sailing is a popular sport in Poland

SKIING

Polish ski resorts have, over the past few years, gained a good reputation throughout Europe. Snow cover is significant and of good quality between November and April, but the best skiing season in fact only extends from January to March; landscapes are charming and prices very affordable. Cross-country skiing, Alpine skiing and snowboarding are, of course, the main activities, not forgetting snowshoeing tours and sleigh rides.

A must for skiing enthusiasts, **Zakopane**, in the heart of the Tatras, is Poland's winter sports capital. Well provided with runs and skilifts, it offers the possibility of skiing at an altitude of over 2 000m. Among other nearby resorts worth visiting is Bukowina Tatrzańska. Skiing is also one of the Beskid's major activities, in the town of Szczyrk for instance, With an altittude of around 1 000m. In the Sudeten, the resort of Szklarska Poręba, on the slopes of Mount Szrenica, boasts a run which is lit at night. The ski runs of nearby Karpacz are on the slopes of Mount Kopa.

Cross-country skiing forms part of the activities on offer in high-altitude resorts but also in the valleys of the Tatras and in the Beskid. Near Szklarska Poręba, in the Sudeten, the annual Piast race takes place in January. In the low-lying areas of the country's north-eastern region, it is possible to practise cross-country skiing in the picturesque wooded area around Suwłaki and the Masurian Lakes.

More information is available on the website *www.skiinginpoland.com*

SLEIGH RACING

This Polish tradition normally takes place around Carnival time in the Tatra and Beskid Mountains. However, soon after the first snowfalls, sleighs pulled by horses can be seen throughout the country.

SPAS

Poland has some forty spa centres open year-round. The various thermal springs provide treatments suitable for a range of complaints. The most widespread means of treatment are mineral baths, mud baths, drinking mineral water, inhaling and hydrotherapy.

For information, apply to the **Economic Association of Polish Spas** – *Ul. Rolna 179/181, 02-729 Warsaw, ℘ (022) 843 34 60. www. sanatoria.com.pl*

Spas are essentially located in or near mountainous regions. Thus the Kłodzko region boasts four spas:Duszniki Zdrój, Kudowa Zdrój, Polanica Zdrój and Lądek Zdrój. All kinds of illnesses are treated there, from respiratory complaints to skin diseases and rheumatism. In the Beskid, Krynica and Ustroń specialise in the treatment of metabolism disorders, including obesity. Other spas, situated at the foot of mountains, include Polańczyk, in the Bieszczady region, Iwonicz Zdrój, near the Carpathians, Rabka, between Kraków and Zakopane, and Cieplice Zdrój, close to Jelenia Góra in Silesia. South of Warsaw is Konstancin and one can take the waters in Ciechocinek near Toruń. The town of Inowrocław has its own treatment centre. However, a special mention should go to the **Sanatorium in Wieliczka**, south of Kraków, for originality, because it uses the facilities of the impressive salt mines which give local water such specific properties.

WILDLIFE WATCHING

This is a much more peaceful way of hunting. Wolves still roam round the forests in the Suwłaki region while beavers colonize the numerous lakes. You can hear stags bell in Augustów Forest or in the Białowieża Mountains. The Masurian Lakes are dotted with islands which are all sanctuaries for protected bird species. In the Białystok region, the Białowieski nature park offers visitors the rare privilege of meeting Europe's last bisons.

Feasts and festivals

Poland has a vast choice of festive events. The main ones are listed below but new ones appear every year. You can see a list of events for the current year on the following website: *www.culture.pl*

RECONSTRUCTIONS AND HISTORICAL PAGEANTS

The Poles love reconstructions of major episodes of their history. At the prehistoric site of Biskupin, an archaeological festival takes place every year during the third week in September. In Gniew, in Pomerania and in Gołub-Dobrzyń, near Toruń, medieval tournaments are reenacted. In Frombork Castle, the siege of 1410 is reenacted at the end of July.

FEBRUARY

Warsaw – Poster Biennial . Every two years in spring.
Toruń – Old Nowa Jazz.

MARCH

Kraków – Rękawka Festivities .
Wrocław – Singing Actors Festival.
Poznań – Jazz Festival.
Toruń – Klamra Theatre Festival.

EASTER MONDAY

Kraków - Easter Fair.

APRIL

Kraków - International jazz Festival.
Wrocław - jazz Festival.

Toruń - Toruńki Nauki Szuki Festiwal.

MAY

Kraków - Film Festival.
Zakopane - Country Fair.
Częstochowa - Queen of Poland's Feast. 3 May.
Toruń - Kontakt Theatre Festival.

JUNE

Kraków - Town Festival. 5 June.
Kraków - Festival of Jewish Culture.
Kraków - International Short Film Festival.
Wrocław - Wrocław Non Stop. End of the month.
Opole - Polish Song Festival. End of the month.
Poznań - Malta International Theatre Festival.
Toruń - Song of Songs Festival.
Gdańsk - international Festival of Organ Music. Until the end of August.

JULY

Kraków - Street Theatre International Festival.
  - Summer Jazz Festival.
Zamość - International Folk Festival.
Toruń - Toruń Muzyka i Architectura: July and August.
Gdańsk - Northern People Folk Festival.
  - Baltic Sail: International Regattas.
  - Street Theatre Festival.

Folk dancers

W. Buss / MICHELIN

B. Kaufmann / Michelin

- **a.** *Hollywood Studios (California)?*
- **b.** *Tabernas Mini Hollywood (Spain)?*
- **c.** *Atlas Film Studio (Morocco)?*

Can't decide ?
Then immerse yourself in the Michelin Green Guide !

- Everything to do and see
- The best driving tours
- Practical information
- Where to stay and eat

The Michelin Green Guide:
the spirit of discovery.

AUGUST

Krynica - Jan Kiepura Music Festival. Two weeks in mid-August.

Zakopane - Mountain Areas Folk Festival. Last week in August.

Częstochowa - Feast of the Częstochowa Virgin. 26 August.

Kudowa Zdrój - international Music Festival.

Duszniki Zdrój - Chopin Festival.

Gdańsk - Shakespeare Festival.

AUTUMN

Kraków - Jewish Culture Month.

SEPTEMBER

Częstochowa - Harvest Festival. 1st Sunday in September.

Zawoja - Folk Song and Dance. End of the month.

Wrocław - Wratislawia Cantans.

Kłodzko - Theatre Festival.

Gdańsk - Feature Film Festival.

OCTOBER

Warsaw -Jamboree Jazz Festival.

NOVEMBER

Kraków - Jazz in Kraków. 1 November.

Poznań - Masks, International Theatre Festival.

DECEMBER

Kraków - Christmas Crib Competition.

Warsaw - International Film Festival (Warszawa Film Fest).

Further reading

HISTORY AND MEMOIRES

A Concise History of Poland by **Jerzy Lukowski and Hubert Zawadzki** (Cambridge University Press, 2001). From medieval times to the present; the authors describe how Polish society developed under foreign rule in the 19C and how it was altered by and responded to 45 years of communism, and developments since its collapse. Jerzy Lukowski is Senior Lecturer in Modern History, School of Historical Studies, at the University of Birmingham, UK. He is also the author of *The Partitions of Poland* (Addison Wesley, 1998), and *Liberty's Folly* (Routledge, 1991). Herbert Zawadzki is Teacher of History at Abingdon School. He spent the first ten years of his life in various Polish resettlement camps across the length and breadth of Britain. He has written for several journals and contributed to the Cambridge Encyclopedia of Russia and the former Soviet Union. This book includes helpful, well-chosen maps and illustrations and a seven-page bibliography of works in English

Napoleon's Campaign in Poland 1806-1807 by **Francis Loraine Petre** (Kessinger Publishing, 2004; paperback Greenhill, 2001). The author (1852-1925) was a member of the group of prominent soldiers, scholars and authors which was virtually responsible for the introduction of the serious analytical study of military history to British academic life. Petre's five volumes on the Napoleonic Wars have remained in print over the years, for their scope, detail and clarity are unequaled. *Napoleon's Campaign in Poland* is a brilliant overview of Napoleon's vaunted army confronting some of its most worthy opponents.

The Spring Will be Ours: Poland and the Poles from Occupation to Freedom by **Andrzej Paczkowski** (Penn State Press, 2003). This is the first English-language book to focus on the turbulent half century in Poland from the outbreak of World War II in 1939 when state socialism collapsed. It offers an analysis of contemporary Polish history.

Remembering a Vanished World: a Jewish Childhood in Interwar Poland by **Theodore S. Hamerow** (Berghahn Books, 2001). The author, a prominent historian, was born in Warsaw in 1920 and spent his childhood in Poland and Germany. His parents were members of the best known Yiddish theater ensemble, the Vilna Company. They were thus part of an important movement in the Jewish community of Eastern Europe which sought, during the half century before World War II, to create a secular Jewish culture, the vehicle of which would be the Yiddish language. Combining the skills of an experienced historian with the talents of a natural writer, the author not only brings this exciting part of Jewish culture to life but also deals with ethnic relations and ethnic tensions in the region and addresses the broad political and cultural issues of a society on the verge of destruction. Thus a vivid portrait emerges that captures the feel and atmosphere of a world that has vanished forever.

The Pianist: The Extraordinary True Story of One Man's Survival in Warsaw, 1939-1945, by **Wladyslaw Szpilman** (Picador, 2002). This is the amazing story of Szpilman's survival amid the rampant inhumanity of the Warsaw ghetto. His memoir describes the hiding, bravery, and incredible good luck that saved him. His prodigious talent also proved indispensable to his survival. First published in Polish in 1946 and long supressed, the autobiography reveals the triumph of the soul, the flourishing of the artistic sensibility, even in the face of the most hellish circumstances. Roman Polanski's recent film based on this book, won the highest honor at the Cannes Film Festival and won three Academy Awards.

The Long Walk: The True Story of a Trek to Freedom by **Slavomir Rawicz** (The Lyons Press, 1997). The extraordinary story of a group of prisoners who escape from a Siberian prison and walk thousands of miles to freedom in British-controlled India. First published in Britain in 1956, once out of print, the book now sells 30,000 copies a year, and has been reissued with a new introduction. A cult classic, it spurs many debates on just how "true" the story is, but it is a great read in any event.

FOR YOUNG READERS

Poland by **Sean McCollum** (Carolrhoda Books, 1999). With the help of an older reader, young children can take a first look at the world using this appealing book. A friendly text and design present the country's landscape and describe in easy-to-understand language its main ethnic and cultural features. Full-color photos, simple sidebars, emergent-reading-level glossary, pronunciation guide, further reading list, and index complete the presentation.

How to Draw Poland's Sights and Symbols by **Melody S. Mis** (The Rosen Publishing Group, 2004). This fun art-instruction book helps children draw simple things (the Polish flag) as well as major monuments (Malbork Castle) to engage the young traveller. There is also a "fact list", time line and glossary.

LITERATURE

Contemporary Writers of Poland by **Bł Aszak Danuta** (Lulu Pres, 2005). The anthology is a wide presentation of contemporary writers of Poland, the generation following the two recent Nobel Prize winners, Milosz and Szymborska. It consists of two parts: poetry and a few short stories

Adam Mickiewicz – To a Pole, the name Adam Mickiewicz is emblematic of Polishness and greatness. It is generally agreed that Mickiewicz's three masterpieces are *Dziady Part III*, *Kśięgi narodu polskiego i pielgrzymstwa* (The Books of the Polish Nation and Pilgrimage) - both published in 1832 - and *Pan Tadeusz* (1834). *Kśięgi narodu polskiego i pielgrzymstwa* is a cycle of moral tales and parables written in a quasi biblical style and preaching the cause of national freedom. Mickiewicz advocated in these tales the application of Christian principles to the relations between nations as well as individuals. Any child in Poland, however, also knows his *Ballady i romanse* (Ballads and Romances), his humorous poem *Pani Twardowska*, his poems about unrequited love. In *Do matki Polki* (To a Polish Mother), he sarcastically suggests to Polish mothers that they put their children in chains, rather than let them play with toys, in preparation for political oppression.

Without Dogma: a Novel of Modern Poland by **Henryk Sienkiewicz** (Kessinger Publising, 2004). By the prolific novelist, storyteller, and winner of the Nobel Prize for Literature in 1905. Among Sienkiewicz's (1846-1916) most famous novels is the widely translated and several times filmed *Quo Vadis* (1896). His strongly Catholic worldview deeply marked his writing. Sienkiewicz's works have been published in 50 languages.

The Street of Crocodiles by **Bruno Schulz** (Penguin Classics, 1992). Interest in Schulz's work has grown recently (Cynithia Ozick made the author a protagonist of a short story), and good translations are now available. Born in Drohobych, western Ukraine, he rarely left his native city which he viewed to be the center of the world and was a penetrating observer of life there. His stories are replete with descriptions of the town's main streets and landmarks, as well as with images of its inhabitants. Schulz was also a painter, though many of his works appear to have been lost. On November 19, 1942, the writer and artist was shot in the streets of Drohobych by the Gestapo.

Cosmos and Pornografia: Two Novels by **Witold Gombrowicz** (Grove Press 1994). "BUT let me tell you about another, even more curious adventure." Thus begins this strange existential voyage that has won fans around the world – despite the lack of a really good translation in English. Another favourite by the same author: *Ferdydurke* (Yale University Press 2000). A masterpiece of European modernism, first published in 1937, this novel was banned first by the Nazis then by the Communists. Humorous and absurdist, although it may no longer strike the modern reader as subversive, this exuberant book has finally been given the excellent English translation it deserves.

Jerzy Kosinki (1933–91), an American writer, was born in Łódź. He taught at the University of Łódź before emigrating to the United States in 1957. Among his novels, widely available, *The Painted Bird* (1965), describes surrealistic scenes, the nightmarish world of a child adrift in remote villages, faced with the hostility and cruelty of Polish peasants. *The Steps* (1968), a sequel, shows the boy becoming an adult. This book won the National Book Award. *Being There* (1971) is a satire of American popular culture: a simple-minded gardener named Chance is elevated to the role of sage elder, thanks to wisdom gleaned from TV. The 1979 film version stars Peter Sellers and Shirley MacLaine. Kosinski's final novel, *The Hermit of 69th Street*, is a portrait of a writer at the end of his rope. It is in part a response to accusations made against him of relying on editorial assistants to do his work. Kosiński committed suicide in 1991.

The Tin Drum by **Günter Grass** (Vintage Paperbacks 1997). A classic book (and film) with Gdańsk as background, by a native of the city. *The Flounder* (Picador, 1989) is another book by the same author.

Czesław Miłosz (1911-2004) received many awards for his poetry, including the Nobel Prize in 1980. His collection of essays, *The Captive Mind* (1953) is well known, and he also published novels and an autobiography. His many books have been translated into English. Shortly before his death, he published the volume *New and*

Collected Poems 1931-2001 (Ecco, 2001), a good overview of his work from beginning to end.

POLISH COOKING

A Treasury of Polish Cuisine: Traditional Recipes in Polish & English by Maria de Gorgey (Hippocrene Books, 1999). A bilingual cookbook with chapters on Soups and Appetizers, Main Courses, Desserts, and two special holiday chapters—one devoted to "Wigilia," the festive Polish Christmas Eve Dinner, and one to "Wielkanoc," the Polish Easter Luncheon

The Art of Polish Cooking by **Alina Zeranska** (Pelican Publishing Co 1989). 500 delicious recipes, as well as menus for authentic Polish meals.

Old Polish Traditions: In the Kitchen and at the Table (Hippocrene International Cookbook Classics S.) by **Maria Lemnis** and Henryk Vitry. Recipes and history of Polish culinary customs, Polish hospitality, holiday traditions, the exalted status of the mushroom. Over 100 recipes for traditional family fare.

A few films

Man of Marble by Andrezj Wajda, 1976.

Double Life of Véronique by Krysztof Kieślowski, 1991.

Schindler's List by Steven Spielberg, 1993.

The Pianist by Roman Polanski, 2001.

© Adagp, Banque d'images, Paris 2006

"Oedipus Rex Strawinski", by Roman Cieslewicz (1961)

Plan
Discover
Explore

Also in the same collection:

Europe
- Amsterdam
- Andalucia
- Austria
- Belgium, Grand Duchy of Luxembourg
- Berlin
- Brussels
- Europe
- Germany
- Great Britain
- Greece
- Hungary, Budapest
- Italy
- Ireland

- London
- Nertherlands
- Poland
- Portugal
- Prague
- Rome
- Scandinavia, Finland
- Scotland
- Sicily
- Spain
- Switzerland
- Tuscany
- Venice
- Vienna

France
- Alsace Lorraine Champagne
- Atlantic Coast
- Auvergne Rhône Valley
- Brittany
- Burgundy Jura
- Châteaux of the Loire
- Dordogne Berry Limousin
- France
- French Alps
- French Riviera

- Languedoc Roussillon Tarn Gorges
- Normandy
- Nothern France and the Paris Region
- Paris
- Provence

- The Wine Regions of France

Other places in the World
- California
- Canada
- Chicago
- Florida
- Mexico
- New England
- New York City
- Pacific Northwest

- Quebec
- San Francisco
- USA East
- USA West
- Washington DC

- Thailand

Kazimierz Dolny on the Wisła

POLAND

In spite of a generally accepted notion, Poland is not just a vast plain where wooded areas planted with pines and birches alternate with strips of cultivated land. On the contrary, the country offers a rich and varied nature: Alpine-type mountains and strange granite rock formations, primeval forests, innumerable lakes, protected marshes sheltering an exceptional flora and fauna, huge shifting sand dunes...These landscapes are not always accessible by public transport but their environmental value, which is unique in Europe, unquestionably make them worth a detour.

W. Bibikow / Hoa qui/Age

Tatras Mountains

Geography

Poland extends 650km from north to south and 690km from east to west, covering an area of 312 700sq km, which makes it the **ninth largest country in Europe**. The imaginary lines linking the northernmost and southernmost points of the continent (North Cape in Norway and Cape Matapan in Greece) and its east and west boundaries (Central Ural in Russia and Cabo da Roca in Portugal) intersect near Warsaw, which places Poland at the **centre of Europe**. The general shape of the country is rather rounded, with a crest-like strip of land, the Hel Peninsula (34km long for an average width of 500m), jutting out into the sea. The country has over **3 000km of borders** to which should be added 694km of coastline along the Baltic. It is bordered to the north by Russia over a distance of 210km (Kaliningrad region), to the east by Lithuania (103km), Belarus (416km) and Ukraine (529km), to the south by Slovakia (540km) and the Czech Republic (790km) and to the west by Germany (467km).

NATURAL AREAS

Poland is essentially a region of **lowlands**, forming part of the great north European plain. Indeed, the word "Pole" means "field" and "plain" in Polish. The average altitude is 173m and 91% of the territory lies below 300m. The southern part of the country alone is mountainous but the highest point does not rise above 2 500m. Poland's topography features five main natural regions: the sandy Baltic coastline and lakeland in the north, the great central plain, the plateaux and the foothills bordering the various mountain ranges in the south. The oldest massifs (the **Sudeten**) date from the Primary era whereas the higher **Carpathian range** consists of younger Alpine-type mountains from the Tertiary era. The largest human concentrations in the country are settled in the areas where the Hercynian bedrock is rich in coal, lignite, copper, sulphur, zinc, lead and rock salt (**Silesia**). During the Quarternary era, the great Scandinavian ice sheet (inlandsis) advanced across the plain and reached the foot of these mountains. The fertile silts (loess) deposited in front of the ice cap ensured the agricultural wealth of the Lublin plateaux, of Little Poland and of Lower Silesia around Wrocław. As the **inlandsis** receded, a process which ended only some ten thousand years ago, it carved the landscapes of Masuria and of Pomerania, forming a chaos of **lakes** and wooded **morainic hills** characterized by infertile podzolic soils. The ice sheet considerably disrupted the draining of the land and the course of the country's two great rivers. The **Wisła** or **Vistula** (1 087km) and the **Oder** or **Odra** (912 km) drain northwards practically across the whole country before flowing into the Baltic. But their course sometimes veers at right angles and follows an east-west direction. The Wisła runs right across the centre of Poland and flows into the Gulf of Gdańsk. Its main tributary is the River Bug (730km) which acts as an eastern border along part of its course. The Oder has its source in the Czech Republic and forms a natural western border with Germany. Its main tributary is the Warta (753km). These rivers already feature the same characteristics as Russian rivers: they are frozen in winter and swell dramatically in spring when the snow melts. However, they are navigable during part of the year and well connected with one another by canals.

THE COASTAL PLAIN ALONG THE BALTIC

The Polish coastal fringe, between 40 and 100km wide, stretches along the Baltic, forming a fairly straight, sandy low-lying zone. Extending over a distance of 694km, it is only indented to the west by the Gulf of Szczecin (Oder Delta and Bay of Pomerania) and to the east by the Gulf of Gdańsk (Wisła Delta). The landscapes feature long **sandy beaches** (very crowded in summer lined by dunes and forests of conifers. During the Tertiary era, the resin from these trees became fossilised in the form of **amber,** sometimes trapping insects or pieces of plants. The amazing brightness of amber led ancient peoples to believe that it resulted from sun rays being solidified in the waves and later thrown back onto the beach. Amber, used for making jewellery and ornaments, was at the origin of a flourishing trade which reached it peak during the 2C AD. **Gdańsk** is still today the world's amber capital and an important shipbuilding centre (including the conurbation). The coastline features several natural treasures, among them the Słowiński National Park (on Unesco's List of World Biosphere Reserves) where one can ramble among huge **shifting dunes** over 30m high and a few shallow coastal lakes. On the other hand, water in the Baltic is **five times less salted** than in the North Sea or the Atlantic. That is why the subaquatic fauna is scarce (few molluscs and jellyfish for instance). Large cetaceans (whales…) are also rare because of the shortage of food, of the relative shallowness of the sea, of the total absence of tidal movements and of the difficulty of going through the Danish straits leading to the high seas.

THE LAKE REGION: POMERANIA AND MASURIA

The north of Poland is an area of low hills (200 to 300m) dotted with lakes. **Pomerania** extends from the German border (Oder) to the Wisła Valley. Lying east of the river, **Masuria** stretches to the country's eastern border. This region of Poland features some 9 300 lakes with an area of over 1ha, in other words more than 1% of the country's total area. It offers a landscape which is **unique** in Europe. Pomerania boasts the greater number of lakes but the two largest lakes are situated in Masuria (Lake Śniardwy has an area of 114sq km, Lake Mamry 109sq km). Connected with one another by canals and rivers, the lakes form vast waterways. Many people practise angling and **sailing**, particularly in Masuria and the longest nautical course totals 91km! The area shelters a great variety of aquatic flora and fauna. Lake Łukajno is on the List of World Biosphere Reserves and one can get a glimpse of wild ducks, swans, herons etc. Landscapes feature sparsely populated wooded hills. Rye, oats, potatoes and flax grow on the meagre soil part of which is devoted to pastures. **Unemployment** is very high in this region which has few large urban centres.

THE GREAT CENTRAL PLAIN

Central Poland consists of several vast plains, cut from east to west by wide valleys. West of the Wisła are the plains of **Greater Poland** (through which flows the Warta) and of Kujavia; to the east are the plains of **Masovia** (drained by the middle Wisła) and of **Podlasie**. Together they form landscapes of lowlands offering little contrast. In fact, this central openland area extends from Berlin to Moscow and, for centuries, men, traders, travellers but also invaders have passed through it. Located here is the cradle of the Polish State, Gniezno, as well as one

Biebrza marshes

C. Hervé-Bazin / MICHELIN

of Poland's economic centres, **Poznań**, and of course the capital, **Warsaw**. It is one of the country's most **dynamic** regions. The landscapes are monotonous as they are in all stone-free sandy lowlands. Birch and pine forests alternate with strips of open cultivated land. The **Kampinos** primeval forest, lying west of Warsaw, attracts visitors interested in World Biosphere Reserves; the meeting of the Wisła and of the Scandinavian inlandsis resulted in a unique landscape of sand dunes covered with vegetation and of marshland. The Polish plain gets little rain but the thick layer of sandy clay often accounts for insufficient drainage of the soil which creates an environment of **marshland** and **peat bogs** (such as the amazing **Biebrza Park**). Soils are on the whole mediocre but they were improved in the west by one hundred years of Prussian occupation, through intensive use of chemical fertilizers.

FOOTHILLS AND LOW PLATEAUX

The Wisła and Oder valleys run through relatively low plateaux: Silesia, Little Poland, Lublin plateau and western Galicia. This southern area features an exceptional combination of agricultural and mining resources. It was therefore natural that it should attract human settlements, with a high rural population density in the Rzeszów and Sandomierz basins, and enormous **urban concentrations** in Silesia and in the ancient trading and cultural cities of **Kraków, Lublin** and **Wrocław**. The industrial basin of **Upper Silesia** is renowned for its important reserves of coal around **Katowice**. However, the region is currently undergoing a complete **redevelopment** programme. The **Little Poland** plateau is dominated by an ancient Hercynian massif, the Holy Cross Mountains (the highest peak, Mount Łysica culminating at 612m), prolonged northwards by the Częstochowa Jurassic plateau. This area is the oldest from a geological point of view. There are important mineral deposits. The undulating landscapes feature karstic ridges dotted with medieval castles (eagles' nests around Kraków). The **Galicia** plateau is marked by fertile valleys and rich pastures alternating with sterile sandy soils and marshland. The **Lublin** alluvial plateau, covered with loess and fertile deposits, is one of Poland's main wheat-producing regions.

THE SUDETEN AND CARPATHIAN MOUNTAINS

The southern mountain ranges are unquestionably the country's natural borders. They include the Sudeten to the west (border with the Czech Republic), and to the east part of the western Carpathians (border with Slovakia). Although this area represents less than 10% of the country's territory, it nevertheless occupies an important place in the Poles' collective imagination, both as the source of the country's two main rivers and as a holiday and recreation area rich in traditions. This is therefore Poland's top **tourist region**. Lying to the south-west of the country, the **Sudeten** stretch over a distance of 250km and their highest peak, Mount Śnieżka, culminates at 1 602m. These mountains offer many spa and ski resorts, as well as impressive nature parks, for instance in the Table Mountains (Góry stołowy) featuring some fascinating rock formations. The highest massif in this area is known as the Giant Mountains (Karkonosze), a granite range where moufflons gambol over stangely shaped rocks (sunflower, horses' heads, pilgrims...).

To the south-east, the Carpathian fringe includes the **High Tatras** (Tatry), the **Beskid** (Beskidy), the Pieniny and the Bieszczady. Mount Rysy, the highest peak of the High Tatras crystalline massif, south of Kraków, culminates at 2 499m. Winter sports resorts such as **Zakopane** are very popular and the Tatras National Park welcomes over 2 million visitors every year. Scattered over the park's territory are some 30 lakes filled with crystal-clear water, known as "stawy", the most famous being Morskie Oko, the "Eye of the Sea" (covering 35ha and 51m deep) and many mountain streams sometimes featuring spectacular waterfalls (Wielka Siklawa, 70 m high). In springtime, fields known as "hale"are covered with thousands of crocuses. Many caves can also be visited. The **Beskid** are the country's second highest mountain range, culminating at 1 725m (Mount Babia Góra). Four stages of vegetation can be observed. In the **Pieniny National Park**'s limestone mountains, mountain rafts go down the Dunajec Gorge, which, in places, looks like a deep grand canyon.

Poland's last Carpathian mountain range, the **Bieszczady**, culminating at 1 343m (Mount Tarnica), is particularly wild and sparsely populated. High pasture areas, called "połoniny", are exceptionally beautiful. This park and those of the Giant Mountains, of the Tatras and of the Beskid, are listed by UNESCO as part of the Cultural and Natural World Heritage.

Population patterns

With an average of 122 inhabitants per sq km, the Polish population is unequally spread throughout the territory. The North of the country is sparsely populated, in contrast with the **Warsaw** conurbation (2.3 million inhabitants) and the industrial region of Upper Silesia (the **Katowice** conurbation has reached 3.5 million inhabitants!). Poland was originally an essentially rural country but today **65%** of its population lives in **urban areas** and there are more than 40 towns with over 100 000 inhabitants. In addition to the two conurbations already mentioned, there are three other large concentrations of slightly

National parks

Poland boasts 23 national parks (covering around 3 150sq km) and 1 368 nature reserves, some of them with a unique fauna and flora. The most famous is the **Białowieża Park**, one of Europe's only two parks to be both on the list of World Biosphere Reserves and on UNESCO's World Heritage List. It represents the last area of the huge primeval forest which used to cover most European plains one thousand years ago. In all, nine national parks are on the list of World Biosphere Reserves: four mountain parks two forest parks, one lakeland park, one coastal park and one marshland park.

over one million inhabitants each: **Kraków**, Poland's former capital on the River Wisła, **Łódź**, the large textile city and **Gdańsk-Gdynia-Sopot**, the twin ports on the Baltic. The Polish population is also concentrated in other large towns such as **Wrocław, on the Oder** (640 000 habitants), an important centre of metallurgy as well as of the chemical and food processing industries, **Poznań**, on the River Warta (570 000), one of the country's oldest towns, **Szczecin**, a major port on the Baltic (413 000), Bydgoszcz (369 000), a large industrial city in the Lower Wisła Valley, **Lublin** (356 000) specialised in consumer goods and **Białystok** (292 000), Poland's second most important textile centre.

Climate

Poland enjoys a **temperate climate**, featuring well-defined seasons and in particular **cold dry winters** and **hot rainy summers**. However, the climate can vary significantly from one year to the next. Apart from the specific mountain climate which applies to the South of the country, the climate over the rest of the country marks a **transition** between the oceanic and continental influences. The great north-European plain is an area where masses of humid air from the Atlantic or the North Sea come into contact with dry air from the inland regions of the Eurasian continent. Consequently, there are temperature variations from west to east and from north to south. The main characteristics of Poland's climate are **unstable weather conditions** and a frequent cloud cover; there are only between 30 and 50 clear days in a year. Dominant influences come from the west during the summer months (rainfall is 2 to 3 times more abundant than in winter and the average temperature is around 18°C) and from the east in winter (average temperature - 3°C), particularly in December and January (the coldest month). The intermediate seasons are hardly noticeable. The hottest month is July, when the average temperature is between 16 and 19°C. Warm days with temperatures of at least 25°C, ideal for tourism, can be expected in Poland from May until September ("golden autumn"). Their number increases as one moves away from the sea and closer to the mountains. In general, the North-west of Poland, close to the Baltic sea, enjoys a predominantly temperate oceanic climate with damp snowy winters and cool summers (sea breeze) with alternating periods of rain and sunshine. In the eastern part of the country, continental influences are more obvious, with harsh winters lasting over four months and drier summers. The main characteristic of mountainous areas is the presence of **snow** for the major part of the year. In the Sudeten, snow falls during 120 days and in the Tatras this can be extended to 145 days. In the Tatras Mountains one can sometimes experience the foehn, a violent wind, fairly warm and dry, called "halny" in Polish.

Flora

Poland may look like a largely agricultural country but 28% of its territory is covered with forests. They are planted with conifers (70%) in particular forest pines, the remainder being mixed (resinous like spruce and fir or deciduous like oak, beech, hornbeam or birch). Although the major part of Poland's forested regions have been cleared to make way for farming activities, one can still see areas untouched by human activities: some thirty "puszcze" or "bory", primeval forests, extend over part of the territory. The gems of Polish flora include first of all the ancient Rogalin **oaks**, hundreds of which grow in the large forest situated near Poznań. Famous for their longevity, the oldest (over 700 years) have all got a name, Bartek, Chrobry, Lech, Czech and Rus, and are the heroes of many legends. Giant trees up to 50m high grow in the **Białowieża primeval forest**. In view of the absence of natural barriers that would limit plant migration, most species are transitory (apart from a few endemic species in the Carpathian Mountains). There are, for instance, some berries belonging to Eurasian species and North-American such as cranberry (borówka), blackcurrant (czarna porzeczka) or bilberry (jagoda), which the Poles

Environmental Issues

In Poland, "ecologically disastrous" zones concern 11% of the country's total area and 36% of the population. Poland has to face a high level of **air pollution** caused by the release of toxic gases by factories powered by coal or lignite. Nearly three quarters of the country's trees are affected by **acid rain**. Forests in the South-west are particularly spoiled because winds carry polluting elements released by Poland but also by Germany and the Czech Republic. Poland must also face **water pollution** problems caused by the release of toxic products by industries, large conurbations and even agriculture. 4/5 of all main rivers and the Baltic coast are severely polluted. However, some progress has been made. **Pollution measurements** now fall into line with EU standards and there are many more sewage treatment plants and antipollution filters (factories and cars) than before. The safeguard of the environment is well on its way but it requires time and heavy investments.

like a lot. Mushrooms too are plentiful and chanterelles and cepes are on all the tables at the beginning and at the end of the summer. If you arrive at the right time, you can even pick them without getting off your bike!

Fauna

Local fauna is almost identical to that found in the rest of Europe. Among domestic animals, dogs and **horses** are particularly dear to the heart of the Poles who raise renowned breeds and enter them into many competitions. Moreover, horse riding is a great national tradition and Polish breeding of Arab horses is famous throughout the world. Animals in parks and gardens peacefully cohabit with the local population. Birds come willingly to an outstretched hand to peck at some seeds or squirrels answer your call ("Basia, Basia..." Polish people say) and get hold of the hazelnut or walnut you are holding out to them. From the point of view of variety and number of species, the animal world is considerably richer than the plant world. There are, in Poland, 93 species of mammals, 406 species of birds, nine species of reptiles, 18 species of batrachians and 55 species of fish. **White storks** hold a special place within the bird population. Poland is called the paradise of storks:

a quarter of the European population of storks nests here because the birds find many places to build their nests and clean areas rich in food. The Poles are particularly fond of this animal and from March on, they look up at the sky and wait for the familiar clatter. Birdwatchers also have their own paradise: the **Biebrza marshes**. 263 bird species can be spotted in these marshes during the brooding season as well as during the migration period. The valley is one of the last places in Europe where aquatic and marshland birds can live, because most marshes on the European continent were drained. This king of environments is also very much appreciated by birds of prey resulting in the highest number of different species (25) in Europe. In these marshy areas, one also meets **elk**, the most powerful members of the Cervidae family, and **beavers**. Another peatbog park on the list of World Biosphere Reserves is the **Polesie** National Park, east of Lublin. The national emblem of Poland is traditionally the **white-tailed eagle**, the country's largest bird of prey. A very small number of them nests in the North of the country, mainly on the Island of Wolin (this national park is also renowned for its cormorants and otters) and along the Baltic coast. Another interesting sight is the Nietoperek **bat reserve** in Greater Poland, which consists of a huge bunker built by the Germans between 1925 and 1941, where a few thousand bats hibernate every year. Poland also offers amateurs of mammals an impressive spectacle: **bisons**, the largest European animals are protected in several national parks including the Białowieża National Park where there are over 250 specimens. All thoroughbred bisons born in Polish nature reserves are given names starting with the syllable "Po", for example "Poranek" or "Pomruk". The high mountains in the South of the country shelter a particularly rich fauna. The most interesting wild species are **chamois**, **moufflons**, **deer**, **marmots** and **royal eagles**. Other large mammals are equally protected in Poland: the huge **brown bears, wolves, lynx, wild cats**. Most rare species live in the Bieszczady, where you will find the vastest wild open spaces in the country.

R. Czerwiński / ONT Polska

Lynx

HISTORY

Poland has, since the Middle Ages, ranked among the great European states. It had its heyday in the 16C when it became a centre of Renaissance art and of religious peace. However, the nobility, powerless to deal with the decline of the major trade routes, handed the country over to her powerful neighbours: Poland ceased to exist as an independent country between 1795 and 1918. Yet it was during this period that the stateless nation took shape. After 1945, the country, by then ethnically homogeneous, stood up to the USSR through the Church and the working class yearning for the end of socialism. These differences led the West to think there was "another Europe", but the entry of Poland into the EU was a reminder that her history fully shares in the major events that shaped Europe.

Biskupin Museum

From the first villages to the arrival of the Slavs

The oldest traces of mining activity on Polish soil go back to 3 500 B.C. Krzemionki Opatowskie, near Kielce, is one of the world's best-preserved flint- quarrying sites. The sandy subsoil covering a major part of the country prevented the first settlers from establishing structures that could have left traces still visible today. The best known sites were preserved in mud and silt which covered them over after they were abandoned. The first town mentioned in written records was situated in **Greater Poland**: Kalisz was quoted in the 2C AD as being a trading port on the **amber route**, between the Baltic and the Mediterranean. The Poznań region seems to have been an important stopover along this trade route. And it was here that the Slavonic tribe of the **Polanie** settled around the 6C; later they gave their name and her first kings to their country.

👁 *The Biskupin lake town (550 BC).*

CHRISTIAN KINGS AND CONQUERORS (10C and 11C)

The 10C and 11C saw periods of intense struggle in the region between Western and Eastern Christians. Whereas the great majority of Slavonic leaders opted for Byzantium, the **Piast** dynasty of the Polanie joined Rome in order to halt the expansionist intentions of the Holy German Empire. Prince Mieszko was christened in Gniezno and his son Bolesław was crowned as the first king of Poland by the Pope in 1025. Strengthened by their Roman support, the two men managed to conquer vast territories (Pomerania, Silesia, Little Poland). In AD 1000, the borders of the kingdom were already those of present-day Poland. Many missionaries Christianised the region. These events created a bond between Poland and the Latin world. The Spaniard Ibrahim ibn Yaqub and the Frenchman Gallus Anonymus left detailed descriptions of their visit to Piast country.

👁 *The Romanesque doorway of Gniezno and Wrocław cathedrals.*

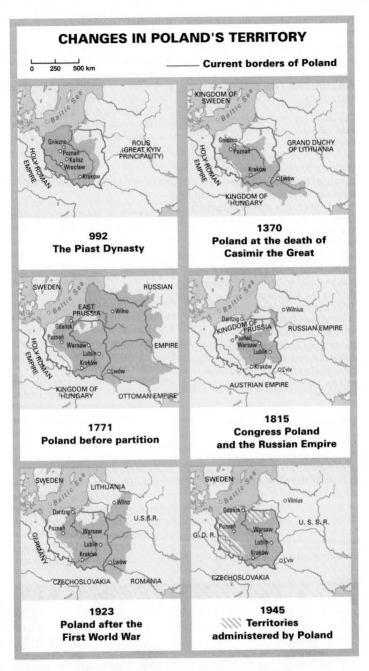

CHANGES IN POLAND'S TERRITORY

——— Current borders of Poland

0 250 500 km

992
The Piast Dynasty

1370
Poland at the death of
Casimir the Great

1771
Poland before partition

1815
Congress Poland
and the Russian Empire

1923
Poland after the
First World War

1945
Territories
administered by Poland

POLITICAL WEAKENING
BUT ECONOMIC EXPANSION
(12C AND 13C)

During the 12C and 13C, rivalry between heirs to the crown and feudal division of land left Poland wide open to invasion. Faced with incursions by the **Teutonic Knights** and the **Mongols** or Tatars, the Piast kings chose to transfer their capital to Kraków. Following the invasions which left whole territories deserted, Polish princes welcomed German and Dutch settlers and allowed them to retain their legal and fiscal structures, well adapted to a trade-based economy. Many Jews, persecuted in Western Europe, also found refuge here. The arrival of these people resulted in urban and commercial expansion. Thousands of villages and scores of towns were created and granted liberties and privileges (Wrocław in 1242, Poznań in 1253, Kraków in 1257). Many monasteries were built, in particular by

53

the Cistercians who brought with them their know-how in farming.

👁 *Malbork Castle, Cistercian abbeys at Trzebnica, Lubiąż and Wąchock.*

KAZIMIERZ THE GREAT
(1333-1370)

The last king of the Piast dynasty, **Kazimierz III**, appropriately known as "the Great", accomplished many things: he unified the kingdom and strengthened the State, he welcomed immigrants, in particular Jews, he built churches and fortresses, he encouraged the development of towns (the towns of Kazimierz Dolny and Kazimierz, now a district of Kraków, are named after him). Kraków, in fact, became an important European centre: its **university** (1364) was one of the first in Europe. One should not therefore be surprised by what Jan Długosz, the first Polish historian, wrote around 1470: "Kazimierz received a country built of wood and left it built of bricks".

👁 *The Collegium Maius in Kraków, the town hall in Wrocław, castles in the Polish Jura, the medieval cities of Paczków and Kwidzyń, Gothic cathedrals in Kraków, Gniezno and Poznań, churches in Chełmno.*

UNION WITH LITHUANIA

Kazimierz having no legal heir, the great Polish lords decided to join in matrimony one of their queens and a still pagan Lithuanian duke. The union between the two states was then sealed for four centuries and the new **Jagiellonian dynasty** took charge of a huge territory able to face the threatening Teutonic Knights. The task was completed in 1410 with the resounding victory at

Grunwald (Tannenberg) and at the end of the Thirteen Years War (1454-1466), when Poland recovered the city of Gdańsk. The country then stretched from the Black Sea to the Baltic and included part of Ukraine and Belarus, being thus the largest European State.

👁 *The Russo-Byzantine frescoes in Lublin, wooden churches in the Pieniny and the Carpathian foothills, Gothic monuments in Toruń and Gdańsk, Pelplin Cathedral.*

The Golden Age (16C)

Poland's Golden Age came in the 16C. The Baltic towns, liberated once and for all from Prussian domination, could form associations with the wealthy merchant cities of the **Hanseatic League**. In 1569, The Lublin Union enabled Poland and Lithuania to have one single Diet (or Parliament) and the same sovereign. The country's economy prospered, thanks to a dynamic middle-class, a large number of peasants and a powerful nobility. The "Nihil Novi" constitution (1505) forbade the monarch to take important decisions without the Diet's agreement. It was these magnates and the urban élite who opened Poland to the influence of humanism (symbolized by the astronomer **Copernicus**), of the Renaissance and of the Reformation. The **Renaissance** first flourished in Kraków, at the Jagiellonian Court, where King Sigismund, a patron of the arts, commissioned the construction of a new chapel for the royal castle from two Italian artists, Francesco Fiorentino and Bartolomeo Berecci. Important Polish towns had sumptuous town halls (ratusz) built: the Poznań town hall, the largest in the country, was built by Giovanni

Łańcut Castle

Battista Quadro. Others were erected in Tarnów (Giovanni Maria Padovano) and Chełmno. In 1581, Bernardo Morando began the construction of Zamość, the pearl of the Polish Renaissance, also known as "the Padua of the North". The magnates' castles and palaces were also commissioned from Italian artists: Santi Gucci for Baranów, Galeazzo Appiani for Krasiczyn, Matteo Trapola for Łańcut and Nowy Wiśnicz, the Parra Brothers and Bernardo Neurone for Brzeg. At the end of the century and at the beginning of the next century, the city of Gdańsk, then the country's largest town, called on the best **Flemish architects and artists**: the Van den Block family, Johan Voigt, Anton van Opberghen. The Reformation met with a certain success as the elite wished to oppose the monarch and to seize the clergy's estates. As early as 1564, the Jesuits, who were Catholic agents of the Counter-Reformation, arrived in Poland with the aim of founding a number of colleges. However, whereas Europe was torn apart by the wars of religion, Poland appeared like an oasis of peace and a refuge for heretics. In 1573, one year after the St Bartholomew massacre, the Warsaw Confederation proclaimed that all religions were equal. The development of Protestantism, based on the reading of holy texts in the national language, was accompanied by the emergence of Polish which gradually replaced Latin. At the end of the 16C, Russian first names were given a Polish flavour and finally disappeared. Prompted by the development of printing, the national literature expanded.

👁 *The Wawel Royal Castle and Sigismund's Chapel, town halls in Poznań, Tarnów and Chełmno, Zamość's ideal city, the castles and palaces of Baranów, Krasiczyn, Łańcut, Nowy Wiśnicz and Brzeg, the town centres of Gdańsk and Kazimierz Dolny.*

A KING UNDER SUPERVISION AND A DIVIDED NOBILITY (17C)

Like the Piasts before them, the Jagiellonians left the scene of history through lack of heirs. Worried about the hostile intentions of their neighbours, Polish aristocrats decided to elect their new king themselves and did not rule out foreigners. However, each election gave rise to intrigues between the magnates and foreign powers. Between 1587 and 1668, Poland was governed by a Catholic branch of the Swedish **Vasa** dynasty who, at the very beginning of the 17C, decided to transfer the Polish capital from Kraków to **Warsaw**. With the help of the Jesuits, the Vasa undertook to convert the country and its neighbours to Catholicism. Polish patriotism then became mixed with religious fanaticism and this was the cause of constant bad relations with the neighbours. There were successive wars against the Swedish Protestants, the Moslem Turks and Tatars and the Orthodox Russians and Ukrainians. After the terrible Swedish invasion of 1655-60, nicknamed "deluge", the country lay waste and the population, depleted by the black death, was reduced by a third. Polish art of that time is heavily marked by the macabre and the need for atonement. There was a sudden abundance of miraculous Virgins, dances of death, hermitages and calvaries. The magnates adapted palaces, churches and monasteries to the **Baroque** style. These edifices are full of portraits of aristocrats sporting long Turkish-style caftans and wearing a long moustache and a feathered bonnet over a partly shaved head. The term "**Sarmatism**" derived from the name of the nobility's mythical ancestors, describes the cultural specificity of this megalomaniac class shutting itself off from the rest of the world. This aristocracy dealt a second fatal blow to the kingdom in 1652 by demanding that decisions taken by the Diet be unanimous ("**liberum veto**"). The fact that **King Jan III Sobieski** was acknowledged as the saviour of Christendom after he liberated Vienna besieged by the Turks, did not empower him to halt the country's political decline. The last scuttling of Poland's independence took place in 1717, when the aristocrats granted Russia a say in their privileges: Poland then became in reality a **Russian protectorate.**

The Constitution of 3 May 1791

From 1775 onwards, a powerful nationalist movement was formed in Poland. Inspired by the French Revolution and the work of the Constituent Assembly; these patriots aimed to abolish the elected monarchy and the "liberum veto", grant more rights to the Third Estate, assert national sovereignty and find a balance between the power of the legislators, of the government and of the judges. On 3 May 1791, the Diet adopted this Constitution in spite of hostile reactions. It followed the American example (17 September 1787) and preceded the French (3 September 1791). The 3rd of May is now Poland's National Day.

👁 *The skulls chapels at Kudowa and Czerma, the hermitages in Wigry Park, Baroque monasteries at Częstochowa, Święta Lipka and Legnickie Pole, Warsaw's royal castle, the palaces of Wilanów, Ujazdów, Nieborów, Kielce, Białystok and Ujazd.*

THE LAST POLISH KING:
(1764-1795)

In 1764, Prussia and Russia imposed their candidate to the crown, the Pole **Stanisław August Poniatowski**. This open-minded aristocrat, influenced by the spirit of the Enlightenment, chose as his second name that of the first Roman Emperor in order to show that he intended to reform the archaic structures of the State. However, his country was the object of negotiations between Prussia, Russia and Austria. During the first Partition in 1772, the three states seized about a third of the territory. In spite of this, Poniatowski invited to his court the greatest painters and sculptors of the time. Thus **Canaletto** could paint views of Warsaw which were very useful when the town had to be rebuilt after 1945. The king succeeded in persuading the Diet to adopt a liberal constituition. But Russia, considering that the "revolutionary spirit" was gaining ground in the country, chose to send her army supported by the Polish nobility who were in favour of the Ancien Régime. In 1793, the second Partition further reduced the size of the country and in 1795, after the national insurrection, led by Tadeusz Kościuszko, failed, the **third Partition** wiped Poland from the European map for the next 123 years.

👁 *The Łazienki Palace, The Arkadia Park.*

THE BRIEF NAPOLEONIAN HOPE

After the disappearance of the Polish State, Paris became the main refuge of political exiles. France being at war with Austria, General **J. H. Dąbrowski** obtained from the Directoire in 1796 the permission to organise the first "**Polish legions**" with Polish soldiers captured by the Austrian army, in the hope of liberating the country. "March, march, Dąbrowski, from Italy to Poland […], Poland is not dead as long as we live" are the words of their song, written by J Wybicki, which later became the national anthem. The legions fought several battles but were finally sent to Saint-Domingue in 1802 to crush the

black population's rebellion; the first consul, Bonaparte, was not yet ready to sacrifice the fragile European balance to further the Polish cause. Subsequently, there was a divide among the Poles between those who advocated cooperation with Russia (Adam Czartoryski) and those who favoured support from western powers. This opposition lasted for decades and influenced the country's destiny on many occasions. And yet, in 1806-07, Napoleon, recently crowned Emperor of the French and at war with Prussia, easily triggered off a Polish uprising in the territories occupied by the Prussians. The land taken from Poland by Prussia then formed the **Grand Duchy of Warsaw**, granted a constitution and the Napoleonic code in 1807-08. In 1809, the Polish army led by **Prince Poniatowski**, took part in the victory against Austria, who had to cede to the Duchy the major part of the territories she occupied (including Kraków). Urged by the Poles to restore a real kingdom, Napoleon led them to expect, in 1811, that their independence would depend on the outcome of his war with Russia. However, in spite of the strong mobilization of Polish soldiers and civilians, the disaster in Russia sealed the political fate of the Duchy, from then on occupied by the Tsar's troops.

CRUSHED REBELLIONS AND INTENSE EMIGRATION

In 1815, the Congress of Vienna which shared out the remains of Napoleon's Empire, became in fact a fourth Partition of Poland. A Polish kingdom or "Congress Kingdom of Poland" was officially created, but the tsar was

Lwów and Wilno

Marshal Piłsudski compared Poland to a bretzel, empty in the centre but full on the edges. In 1918, he did his utmost to see that the northern and eastern territories were returned to Poland, however these were definitively lost in 1939. Among these border regions, the Lithuanian Vilnius (Wilno) and the Ukrainian L'viv (Lwów) are still dear to the heart of the Poles. The two towns which became Polish in the 14C long shared in the country's main historic events, even after the partitions: while Vilnius welcomed the poets Mickiewicz and Słowacki and became the cradle of Polish Romanticism, L'viv experienced political autonomy as the main town of Galicia.

declared king. The Congress then shared the remainder of the territory between Poland's three neighbours. In the annexed provinces, Prussians and Russians rapidly set up a policy of integration and encouraged a sometimes massive influx of settlers. The **autonomous republic of Kraków** alone could carry on with its political and cultural activities: it became a refuge for the Polish nation. Nationalist **insurrections** took place in Poland in 1830 (November insurrection), 1846, 1848 (the Peoples' Spring throughout Europe), 1861, 1863 (January insurrection) and 1905 (following the first Russian revolution), but they did not lead to anything. The result, each time, was an intensified Russification and Germanization. After each of these insurrections, waves of political refugees left their homeland. As early as 1830, over 5 000 Poles went into exile in France; they included the poet **Mickiewicz**, the composer **Chopin** and the politician **Adam Czartoryski** : their fame explains why this exodus was known as the "**Great Emigration**".

THE INDUSTRIAL REVOLUTION

Despite what is generally believed, the Polish population of the late 19C is not exclusively made up of farmers. Although W Reymont was awarded the Nobel Prize for his novel entitled *Peasants*, he also wrote a work called *The Land of Great Promise*, in which the town of **Łódź** appears like a tower of Babel of the textile industry. Łódź is a multicultural town (46% Polish, 34% Jewish, 20% German and 2% Russian) but it claims to be the Polish Manchester.

👁 *Industrial architectural ensembles in Łódź.*

A difficult independence

Between 1905 and 1914, the political troubles which shook Europe rekindled the Poles' hopes for independence. However, when the First World War started, Poles who were recruited by the Russians had to fight their brothers of the Polish legions integrated into the Austro-Hungarian army and led by **Joseph Piłsudski**. It was he who proclaimed the independent republic on **11 November 1918**. Postwar treaties granted Poland several territories including the famous "**Danzig Cor-**

ridor" as well as the richest part of Silesia. But the Entente did not succeed in agreeing on the eastern borders: the project of the English minister Curzon was not unanimously endorsed. Russia and Poland therefore decided to fight it out. During the battle which took place near Warsaw in August 1920, known as the "**miracle of the Wisła**", Poland, with the help of French General Weygand, repelled the enemy and regained its historic territories of Belarus and Ukraine. But the country found it very difficult to manage its newly acquired independence: the numerous minorities demanded rights, political parties tore each other apart and a financial crisis shook the economy. Between 1919 and 1930, 495 000 Poles settled in France, essentially in the coal mines of the Nord-Pas-de-Calais region.

General Piłsudski, portrait by W. Kossut (b 1928)

Rue des Archives

To boost the economy, in 1924 the Diet launched the construction of the port of Gdynia. In May 1926, following a coup d'état, Piłsudski was first elected Minister of War before gradually gaining total control of the government at the end of the 1920s and beginning of the 1930s when the world economic crisis hit the country. His programme was based on the "**sanacja**", the "cleaning up" of the State; but this meant the internment of opponents. Poland also signed pacts of non-agression with the USSR and later with Germany. However, as early as March 1939, Hitler demanded that Poland give up Danzig and grant Germany important rights over the corridor.

The German-Soviet invasion (1939-1941)

On 1 September 1939, at 4.45am, the battleship "Schleswig-Holstein" fired its heavy guns at **Westerplatte**, a Polish enclave in the port of Gdańsk, while German tanks crossed the border. Prior to the invasion, Germany had secretly signed a pact with the USSR anticipating a partition of the country. On 17 September, Soviet troops in turn invaded Poland. The country could not fight back without western help; Germany and the USSR shared the land and thousands of Poles were imprisoned, deported to the Reich (almost one million) and the goulags of the Arctic and of Kazakhstan (over one million) or murdered by the Soviet secret police. Meanwhile, a government in exile, led by **General Sikorski**, was formed, at first in Angers then in London after the French defeat in June 1940. There was a turning point in June 1941 when Hitler threw his army across Polish territory to attack the USSR. Following a meeting in London between Sikorski and a Soviet representative, 75 000 Polish soldiers were liberated from the goulags and General Anders was asked to organise this newly formed army corps.

👁 *The Wolf's Lair, in Kętrzyn*

GHETTOS AND DEATH CAMPS

It is essential to stress the difference between the fate of non-Jewish Poles and that of Jewish Poles. As early as October 1939, the German governor of Poland explained that "Poland would be treated as a colony: the Poles will become the slaves of the Great Reich". All those who refused to submit, in particular the elite, were sent to concentration camps or Labour Camps: Stutthof (near Gdańsk), Auschwitz, Gross-Rosen (near Wrocław), Majdanek (near Lublin) and Płaszów (near Kraków). As for Jewish Poles, they were treated differently. At first, they were parked in **ghettos**; there were 400 in Poland alone, the most important being in Warsaw, Łódź, Kraków, Białystok, Lublin, Częstochowa, Kielce, Tarnów, Radom and Włocławek. Then, from the autumn of 1941, when the Nazis decided to implement the "final solution", it was in Poland that the **death camps** were set up. The reason behind this decision was that the country had a greater number of Jews and it was far enough to avoid arousing the curiosity of the German population. Therefore, between November 1941 and June 1942, the Nazis transformed Auschwitz and Majdanek into death camps and created five more death factories: Chełmno (Kulmhof), Bełżec, Birkenau (Auschwitz II), Sobibór and Treblinka. Around **2 700 000** people perished in those six camps. On 19 April 1943, rather than wait passively to be transferred to the camps and murdered, the Jews of the **Warsaw Ghetto** chose to rebel, although they knew it was hopeless. It took the Germans three weeks of fierce fighting to crush the rebellion.

It is impossible to convey in a few lines the reality of these ghettos and death camps in Poland. Various first-hand accounts of this reality are available: life in the Warsaw Ghetto (A. Czerniakow, M. Edelman, J. Korczak, H. Seidman, E. Ringelblum, M. Halter, W. Szpilman) or in the Łódź Ghetto (D. Sierakowiak, A. Cytryn) and in Auschwitz (Rudolf Hoess, Elie Wiesel, Martin Gray, Primo Levi, Rudolf Vrba, Jo Wajsblat), not forgetting films like *Shoah* by C. Lanzmann, *Night and Fog* by A. Resnais and, more recently *The Pianist* by R. Polański based on W. Szpilman's autobiography.

👁 *The Auschwitz and Majdanek death camps, the Treblinka Memorial, monuments connected with ghettos in Warsaw, Kraków and Łódź, Emanuel Ringelblum' Archives in the Warsaw Institute of Jewish History.*

The Katyń tragedy

Stalin personally hated Poland. For him, that country was the Germans' gateway into Russia. Taming Poland was tantamount to (according to his own words) trying to "saddle a pig". On 5 March 1940, Stalin ordered his secret police, the NKVD, to murder the 25 700 Polish prisoners, including 15 000 officers and non-commisioned officers who represented the cream of the national intelligentsia. These executions are a symbol of Soviet cruelty and love of deceit: 200 people were killed every night by a German bullet in the back of the head. On 13 April 1943, the Germans discovered the mass grave in Katyń, near Smoleńsk (another two are located in Tver and Kharkov); but the Soviets always denied responsibility. It was only on 14 October 1992 that Boris Yeltsin acknowledged the facts in front of Lech Wałęsa, yet many Russians continue to deny them.

Poland and the Jews

Raising the subject of the Jews in Poland can be tricky. The Poles' dominant feeling is one of deep injustice: how can they be considered antisemitic when the country was the main refuge of European Jews and the Polish institutions never took part in the persecution and subsequent extermination of the Jews? In dealing with this sensitive question and differing opinions, clichés and historical over-simplifications usually dominate any debate: the anti-Polish side, including in particular American and European Jews, hold against Poland the waves of antisemitism of the period between 1930 and 1960, when the Jews were used as scapegoats to justify the country's successive humiliations. The Poles, on the other hand, defend themselves, with E. Wiesel's support, by reminding their detractors that, during the war, even if all Jews were victims, all victims were not Jewish and that, in spite of the fact that helping a Jew was immediately punishable by death, a few thousand Jews were saved by Poles, in particular by the Żegota organisation (6 600 Poles have been honoured as "Righteous among the nations" by Israel). In fact, Poland is only beginning to come out of a phase of suppression, of refusing to see the difference and of a kind of "competition between victims". Since the discovery of the Kielce pogrom (4 July 1946) in 1996 and of Jedwabne (10 July 1941) in 2000, Polish historians have been courageously working in depth and they no longer hesitate to shed light on shady areas of their national history. Tourist offices are planning itineraries "in the footsteps of the Jews" and a large Museum of Jewish Poland is due to open soon in Warsaw.

👁 *Jewish districts in Kraków, Warsaw, Łódź, Wrocław, Lublin, Sandomierz, Kielce and Lesko, cemeteries in Tarnów, Szydłowiec, Chęciny and Leżajsk, synagogues in Łańcut, Zamość, Nowy Sącz, Tykocin, Bobowa, Sejny, Szydłów, Włodawa and Pińczów.*

RESISTANCE MOVEMENTS AND WARSAW UPRISING:
(AUGUST-OCTOBER 1944)

Throughout the war, French and Polish officers worked together at deciphering messages sent by enemy troops (Enigma Code device). Polish troops took an active part in the Italy landings (Anders at Monte Cassino) and in Normandy. The Polish Government in London was involved in the creation of a **clandestine State** in Poland, something unique in Europe, with its own army, schools, press and justice. The Poles' great uprising against German occupation began in Warsaw on **1 August 1944**. In order to prevent the advancing Red Army from taking control of the country, the **Inland Forces** (AK) decided to attack. There followed street-by-street fighting throughout the capital actively supported by the majority of the population. But the shortage of weapons and **Stalin**'s decision to refuse to help the insurgents forced them to surrender on **2 October**. The fighting, which lasted 63 days cost the lives of 18 000 AK soldiers and 150 to 200 000 civilians. The Germans razed 70% of the town after evacuating the population.

The number of Polish victims of the Second World War is considerable: to the **2.9 million Polish Jews** (88% of their population) who disappeared are to be added around **2 million people**, including 1.5 million due to the Nazi occupation and 500 000 due to the Soviet occupation, not forgetting the **50 000 Polish Tziganes** (67% of their total population).

In all, 15% of the country's population perished. The ruins of Warsaw fell into the hands of the Red Army in January 1945. It is then that the national liberation committee, formed in Lublin by the communists became the self-proclaimed provisional government of Poland. At the **Yalta Conference** held in the early part of 1945, the British and American governments obtained from the Soviets the assurance that free elections would be organised. However, this conference took place at a time when the Allies needed the help of the Soviets; Stalin could therefore impose his will.

👁 *The museum of the Warsaw Uprising.*

Uprising in the Warsaw ghetto: Arszalkowska street in flames, 1944

B. Ullstein / Akg-images

POPULATION TRANSFERS

Although the Curzon line was officially accepted in the east (it partly followed the course of the River Bug), the western border along the Oder-Neisse was not officially recognised for fear of violent German reactions. Thus Ukraine and Belarus gained territories from Poland who, in turn, recovered territories inhabited by **6 million Germans**. What occurred therefore was an east-west shift of population. In the west, there was a real colonisation of the "**recovered territories**"; the number of private farms went up to 3 million, without a care for the consequences this splitting up would have on crop yields. In the east, millions of Poles had to leave the "lost territories", although 2 millions chose to stay in the USSR. These population transfers meant a real tragedy for these millions of people: not counting the few thousand Poles who left France and Belgium to settle in the recovered territories, the vast majority of those who settled in the West came from the lost territories; they travelled 600km and, on arrival, settled in a farm just abandoned by a German family. The new Poland was built on an ethnically homogeneous territory, all the more so as most of the Jews who survived the war left the country between 1947 and 1950.

Satellization and Stalinization (1947-1956)

During the legislative elections of January 1947, denounced as non-democratic by Western powers, the socialist-communist coalition won 85% of the votes; they decided to merge to form the **PZPR** (Polish United Workers' Party). **W. Gomułka**, who wished Poland to follow her own road to socialism, was brushed aside in favour of B. Bierut. The satellization of the country was underway: the **Kominform**, the consultative body of the different communist parties was created in Szklarska Poręba, in Poland, in September 1947. In 1949, Soviet Marshal K. Rokossovski was nominated Polish Minister of War. The **Palace of Culture and Science**, built in Warsaw between 1952 and 1955, was the symbol of this forced friendship between the Russian and the Polish people. It was in Warsaw that was signed in May 1955 the famous **Warsaw Pact** between the USSR and the popular democracies, intended to be the counterpart of NATO.

On the economic front, forced industrialization was launched together with the nationalization of several thousand businesses; but the collectivization of agriculture was a failure and later had to be abandoned. The PZPR governed the PRL, Poland's Popular Republic, in a totalitarian fashion with considerable help from the secret police and Soviet "advisers". **Repression** did not only concern political opponents such as soldiers of the AK or Catholic priests (**Cardinal Wyszyński** was imprisoned in 1953), but also the Party's rebellious civil servants.

👁 *Warsaw's Historical Museum, the Nowa Huta industrial complex.*

UPRISINGS AND DASHED HOPES

In February 1956, hope was revived in Poland when **Khrushchev** denounced Stalin's crimes. After the **Poznań uprisings**, the Party chose to call **Gomułka** back. However, from 1962, Polish leaders adopted a hard line once more. In order to stifle the student protest of March 1968, the government lauched an **antisemitic campaign**: over half the 25 000 Jews still living in Poland went into exile. On 8 September 1968, a Pole, Ryszard Siwiec, immolated himself in Warsaw during a public event in protest against Warsaw Pact aggression in Czechoslovakia and Polish participation in it. Serious economic problems led the govenment to modify its foreign policy particularly in order to obtain economic and technological aid from the prosperous Federal Republic of Germany,

Nikita Kroutchev and Władysław Gomułka in Warsaw, 1959

Milestones of Poland's history

966 - Conversion of Mieszko to Christianism
1309 - Teutonic State around Marlbork
1385 - Marriage of Jagiello of Lituania and Hedwig of Poland
15 July 1410 - Teutonic Knights defeated at Grunwald
28 January 1573 - Eternal peace between religions proclaimed by the "Warsaw Confederation"
1596 - Capital transferred to Warsaw
1685 - Ottomans stopped in front of Vienna by Jan III Sobieski
3 May 1791 - First liberal Constitution in Europe
1794 - Kościuszko insurrection against the three occupying countries
24 October 1795 - Third Partition and disappearance of Poland
1807 - Grand Duchy of Warsaw formed by Napoleon
1815 - "Congress Kingdom of Poland" in the hands of the tsar
29 November 1830 - November insurrection
22 January 1863 - January insurrection
11 November 1918 - Independence of Poland
15 August 1920 - "Miracle of the Wisła" enabling Poland to push Russia back
12 May 1926 - Piłsudski in power after a coup d'état
1-17 September 1939 - Soviet-German invasion
19 April-20 May 1943 - Warsaw Ghetto Uprising
May 1944 - Monte Cassino victory in Italy
1 August-2 October 1944 - Warsaw Uprising
January 1947 - Large communist victory after rigged elections
June 1956 - Poznań riots
March 1968 - Persecution of intellectuals and antisemitic purge
14-18 December 1970 - Workers riots in Gdańsk, Gdynia, Elbląg and Szczecin
16 October 1978 - Election of Karol Wojtyła as Pope
August 1980 - New workers riots in the Baltic shipyards
31 August 1980 - Gdańsk agreement between Solidarność and the government
12-13 December 1981 - Martial law decreed by General Jaruzelski
5 April 1989 - Round Table agreement between Communists and Solidarność
September 1989 - T. Mazowiecki, first non-communist head of government
12 March 1999 - Poland joins NATO
1 May 2004 - Poland joins the EU

ready to recognise the Oder-Neisse line officially in exchange for emigration being granted to Germans residing in Poland. On 7 December, **Willy Brandt** went to Warsaw to sign this agreement and symbolically stood in silent remembrance on the site of the former Warsaw ghetto. That same month, demonstrations took place in Gdańsk, Gdynia, Szczecin and Elbląg. Gomułka was replaced by **E. Gierek**, a former miner who lived in France and Belgium and wished to modernize the economy by borrowing from the West. The Poles lived in euphoria for assets were flooding into the country. But the injection of huge sums into an economy already weakened by the oil crisis only increased the country's indebtedness. In 1976, inflation was at 60%, strikes paralysed the country and new riots shook Radom and Ursus near Warsaw, where the famous tractors used in communist countries were made. In 1978, the election of **Karol Wojtyła** as pope and his visit to Poland the following year encouraged the Poles to seek intellectual and political freedom.

Solidarność and martial law (1980-1986)

In 1980, the economy collapsed. After the government decided to raise food prices, new demonstrations took place in August in the **Baltic shipyards**. The movement spread to hundreds of thousands of workers. Led by **Lech Wałęsa**, they managed to force the government to accept the **Gdańsk Agreement** (31 August). Among the strikers' 21 demands were the right to strike, the right to information, salary rises and the liberation of political prisoners. Gierek was brushed aside and the authorities finally recognised the independent trade union **Solidarność** (Solidarity). In December 1980, the awarding of the Nobel prize for literature to the exiled poet **C. Miłosz** took on a symbolic meaning. A year later, **General Jaruzelski**, supported by the Soviets (who had definitively abandoned the possibility of a military intervention in December 1980), declared **martial law** during the night of 12 to 13 December 1981. He assumed full powers, dissolved Solidarność and had 6 000 persons interned, including the main leaders of the union. Places of worship then became the only places enjoying a kind of semi-liberty even through priests did not escape repression (murder of **Father Popiełuszko** by the secret police in 1984).

ROUND TABLE AND END OF COMMUNISM

The nomination of **Gorbatchov** at the head of the USSR in 1985 marked a turning point. The Polish government had to face passive resistance from a growing proportion of the population. in April-May 1988, a new wave of industrial strikes prompted the communist reformers to suggest negotiations with the opposition; Solidarność was chosen as sole representative when it had already lost a great deal of its influence. Finally, on 5 April 1989, the so-called "**Round-Table**" agreements were signed: they included the creation of a Senate composed of freely elected members and semifree elections for members of the Diet. During the legislative elections of 4 June 1989, Solidarność won an overwhelming victory. The trade union approved the election of Jaruzelski to the presidency and, in September, T. Mazowiecki, a close colleague of Wałęsa, became the first head of a coalition government. The PZPR was dissolved on 30 January 1990 and, on 9 December, Lech Wałęsa was elected President. The Third Republic was born. The withdrawal of Soviet troops stationed in Poland began in April 1991 and ended in October 1992.

Great figures

NICOLAUS COPERNICUS
(1473-1543)

A true Renaissance mind, Copernicus studied in Poland and in Italy and obtained a doctorate in canon law in 1503. A mathematician, translator, economist, doctor of medicine and cartographer, he is known above all for his work as an astronomer. Thirty six years of research enabled him to show that although it is true that the Moon is a satellite of the Earth, the Earth's axis is not fixed. Shattering the medieval vision of the world which placed man at the centre of the universe, the ideas of Nicolaus Copernicus had a considerable

philosophical impact and sparked off violent reactions lasting for more than two hundred years. His main work, *De revolutionibus orbium coelestium*, was probably written around 1520 (original manuscript kept in Kraków's Jagiellonian Library). It was published for the first time in 1543, a few days before the death of its author, in the Protestant town of Nuremberg.

👁 *Toruń and Frombork.*

FRÉDÉRIC CHOPIN (1810-1849)

Born in Żelazowa Wola of a French father settled in Poland, Chopin composed music before he could even read. At the age of 20, he decided to leave Warsaw and never returned to his native country. It is in Nohant, in the estate of his mistress and muse George Sand, that he composed the major part of his most remarkable works. Although Chopin is acknowledged as one of the fathers of Romanticism, his music is very personal, featuring harmonies well ahead of his time and sounds characteristic of Polish folklore. His repertoire is centred round the piano but he was the first composer to make piano music artistically autonomous by using chords, arpeggios, keys and scales not as a setting but as a real musical colour. Suffering from tuberculosis, he died in Paris and is buried in the Père Lachaise cemetery. His heart is set into a wall of the nave of the Holy Cross Church in Warsaw. The major part of his work is kept in Poland at the Frédéric Chopin Society and at the National Library. The international Chopin Competition takes place in Poland every five years.

👁 *The residences of Żelazowa Wola and Antonin, Ostrogoski Palace and the monument in Łazienki Park in Warsaw.*

MARIE CURIE-SKŁODOWSKA
(1867-1934)

Maria Skłodowska was born in Warsaw and began her studies by following clandestine lectures in occupied Poland. In 1891, she left for France to obtain a doctorate. After discovering an article by physicist H. Becquerel about mysterious rays emitted by uranium, M. Skłodowska began a programme of research about this still-unnamed phenomenon. She was the first woman to defend her thesis at the Sorbonne and later to hold her own chair there. Thus she paved the way for other women in the field of Science. Holding a degree in mathematics and in physics, she was also the first person to

Statue of Copernicus on Toruń's market square

be awarded two Nobel prizes: the Nobel Prize for physics in 1903, jointly with her husband Pierre (who died the following year) and Becquerel, for the discovery of radioactivity, and the Nobel Prize for chemistry in 1911 for the discovery of radium (later used to treat cancer) and polonium (given that name as a tribute to her country). She died of Leukemia caused by that same radium. Her ashes and those of her husband Pierre, were transferred to the Panthéon in Paris in 1995.

👁 *The Curie Museum in Warsaw.*

JOHN PAUL II (1920-2005)

Karol Wojtyła was born in Wadowice, near Kraków. His youth was marred by the death of his mother and his brother. While he was studying humanities at the philosophy faculty in Kraków, he discovered he had a passion for the theatre and for writing. It was during the Second World War that his vocation was revealed to him: in 1942, after the death of his father, he entered the clandestine seminary in Kraków and was ordained priest in 1946.

He became a bishop in 1958 and Paul VI nominated him archbishop of Kraków five years later, then cardinal in 1967. The years 1960-70 turned him into one of the main instigators of the collapse of communism; by tricking the communist regime and sometimes standing up to it, he succeeded for instance in having a church built in the vast workers' complex of Nowa Huta. The choice of Karol Wojtyła, on 16 October 1978, as the first non-Italian pope for over 400 years, was no accident. His first words "Don't be afraid, open your countries' frontiers, and economic and political systems" sounded like a signal to the Poles. His visits to Poland in 1979, 1983 and 1987 were increasingly triumphant. He was venerated not to say adored by almost all the Poles and his death on 2 April 2005 gave rise to huge ceremonies throughout the country.

LECH WAŁĘSA (1943)

Lech Wałęsa was born in 1943 in Popowo, in a province annexed by Germany at the time. After driving agricultural machines, he got a job as a shipyard electrician, taking part from 1970 onwards in strikes and rapidly becoming a charismatic leader capable of gathering around him hundreds of workers. In 1980, he led the strike at the Gdańsk shipyard and founded the trade union Solidarność. He wanted to act the "Gandhi way", on a long term basis, in a non-violent fashion inspired by Christian charity. The Pope, who supported him, received him in January 1981. Invited by the French trade unions and the non-communist left, he made a triumphant visit to Paris in October 1981. Arrested on 13 December 1981, he was released in November 1982 and placed under house arrest. In June 1983, he had another meeting with the Pope and in October he received the Nobel Prize for Peace. In May and August 1988, he resumed his role as leader during a new wave of strikes in Gdańsk but, in view of the government's violent reaction, he called for the fighting to stop. In December 1988, he was allowed to go to France where, together with A. Sakharov, he was received with great honours by F Mitterrand. Later, he took part in negotiations with the communist authorities which led on 5 April 1989 to the "Round-Table" Agreements. The next day, Jaruzelski met Wałęsa, whom he had not seen since 1981. Yet another visit by Wałęsa to Rome showed the many sceptical Poles that the Pope approved this careful march towards a semi-democracy. In 1990, he was elected President of

Lech Wałęsa during a Solidarność Convention

the Republic. However, having fallen out with his former Solidarność allies, confronted with the difficult economic transition and the rise in unemployment, he became painfully aware of his isolation, in particular during the cohabitation with the left between September 1993 and November 1995. Beaten by a former communist at the presidential election of 1995, he was humiliated at the 2000 election (barely 1% of the votes).

Political figures

Stanisław Leszczyński (1677-1766) – Philosopher-king of Poland, known as the Beneficent, exiled and subsequently Duke of Lorraine.

Maria Leszczyńska (1703-1768) - Daughter of the above, wife of Louis XV and a patron of science in Poland.

Tadeusz Kościuszko (1746-1817) – Hero of the War of Independence in the US and of the 1794 Uprising.

Jan Henryk Dąbrowski (1755-1818) – General, founder of the Polish Legions who gave his name to the national anthem.

Józef Poniatowski (1763-1813) – Prince, loyal to Napoleon who made him Marshal of France; died heroically at the battle of Leipzig and his name is inscribed on the Arc de Triomphe in Paris.

Adam Czartoryski (1770-1861) – Prince and politician, who became his country's unofficial ambassador at the Hôtel Lambert in Paris.

Maria Walewska (1789-1817) – Napoleon's mistress, who symbolized Polish women in the eyes of many Frenchmen.

Jarosław Dąbrowski (1836-1871) – One of the leaders of the January insurrection and then of the Paris Commune.

Józef Piłsudski (1867-1935) – Major figure of European history, in particular in 1920 when he halted the Red Army.

Władysław Sikorski (1881-1943) – Head of the Polish Government in exile, he died in a mysterious plane accident.

Ubu (1896) - Imaginary tyrant of Poland, a country situated "nowhere" by Alfred Jarry.

Tadeusz Mazowiecki (1927-) – One of the founding members of Solidarność, very close to the Pope, first non-communist head of government in Eastern Europe.

Zbigniew Brzeziński (1928-) – Jimmy Carter's adviser, who played a major role in East-West relations.

Ryszard Kukliński (1930-2004) – Member of the Polish army's High Command and important CIA spy.

Bronisław Geremek (1932-) – Major intellectual, committed on the side of Solidarność then to the construction of the European Community.

Lech Kaczyński (1949-) – President of Poland since 2005, a conservative and a Catholic.

Aleksander Kwaśniewski (1954-) – First ex-communist President, freely elected.

The Polish plumber (2005-) – Symbol of the difficulty of opening the labour market in Europe and new picture of the "Pole" after those of the lancer and of the miner. the anthem in 1980.

Mazurek Dąbrowskiego

The **Polish National Anthem** is set to a lively Mazurka. The patriotic hymn was written shortly after the country lost its independence and was divided up between Austria, Russia, Prussia. The author of the "Song of the Polish Legions in Italy" – as the anthem was originally called – was Józef Wybick. He composed it in July, 1795 in Reggio di Emilia in Italy, as the Polish legions, led by general Jan Henryk Dąbrowski were marching out to support Napoleon's army.

After the failure of the final effort to save Poand during the Kościuszko Insurrection in 1794, many Poles emigrated to France, in the hopes that one good turn would deserve another and that Napoleon Bonaparte would support the restoration of Poland as an independent state.

The Tsarist and Prussian governments banned the song in 1815 (after the defeat of Napoleon) and again in 1860. Yet it continued to serve rebellious Poles: against the Russians (1830, 1863); during the 1848 Spring of the Nations; as the anthem of the student union (Zwiazek Burszow, 1816-1830). The students sang: "March, march, the youth/ go first as it should be/ following your leadership/ we will become a nation again."

At the end of the 19C, the song was modified to suit the context of the times ("March, March, the Poles, to fight and to work"). Dąbrowski was replaced by other military leaders, as current events required.

Finally, in 1926, "Dąbrowski's Mazurka" was officially recognized as the Polish national anthem. The title of the anthem was listed the first time in the Constitution of the Polish People's Republic in 1976: the Sejm approved the official text and music of the anthem in 1980.

Poland is not yet lost
while we live we will fight
For all that our enemies have taken
from us.

Refrain:
March, march Dąbrowski
from Italy to Poland
Under your command
we will reunite with the nation.

We will cross the Wisła and Warta Rivers,
we will be Poles,
Bonaparte showed us how to win.

Refrain: March, march...

Like Czarniecki to Poznan, after Swedish
annexation,
We will come back across the sea
To save our motherland

Refrain: March, march...

Father, in tears, says to his Basia: "Just
listen,
It seems that our people
Are beating the drums."

Refrain: March, march..

ART AND ARCHITECTURE

Despite its geographic position, Poland, allied with the Roman Catholic Church since 9966, has always had close ties to Western culture. Thus it has been more common to speak of art in Poland rather than Polish art specifically. Then, because the country was twice erased from the map of Europe, Polish nationalism, at a loss for political expression, maintained its unity and strength through art. This cultural movement, while authentic, was also widely influenced by the West. Some have suggested that Polish contemporary art owes its identity to others. But Poland, a nation at the crossroads of East and West, has developed a culture that is unique and truly distinctive.

Doors of the Gniezno Cathedral

G. Sioen / Rapho

Styles

Many civilisations passed through this vast plain, leaving traces found during archaeological excavations. Prominent among them were the Scythians with their animal-style decor and the Sarmatians (4C) with their strongly geometric art from the steppes.

ROMANESQUE ART

After the conversion of Prince Mieszko I to Christianism in 966, Poland entered the sphere of western art. Religious stone architecture was introduced. Pre-Romanesque forms of architecture, drawing their inspiration from Bohemia, can be seen in the Church of SS Felix and Adauctus on Wawel, in Poznań Cathedral and in the Piasts' castles in Ostrów Lednicki, Giecz and Premyśl.

There are few traces left of the first churches which were small rotundas (Cieszyn) and of the first 10C and 11C cathedrals, except for the second crypt (St Leonard) of Wawel Cathedral and St Andrew's Church in Kraków, which looks like a fortress-church with its complex combination of towers and galleries

(*Westwerk*). This tendency to fortification is evident in the churches of Opatów, Płock and Tum.

From the mid-12C, Romanesque architecture flourished in the ornamentation of **doorways** (Tum, St Mary Magdalene of Wrocław), of façades (the Church of the Hospitallers in Zagość) and rare carved pillars in Strzelno.

The remarkable mid-12C **bronze doors** intended for Płock Cathedral (today in Novgorod) as well as those in Gniezno are inspired from Mosan art.

Also dating from this period are a few miniatures and some extraordinary items of sllver- and goldwork.

THE CISTERCIAN TRANSITION

During the years when the Cistercian Order was extending its zone of influence, between 1140 and 1300, 25 monasteries of various origins were created. Mainly established in Little Poland between the Oder and the Wisła (Jędrzejów, Sulejów, Wąchock, abbey of Mogiła near Kraków), and in Silesia (in Trzebnica, the introduction of open-work windows heralds the late-Gothic style), Cistercian architecture is better preserved there than in Greater Poland where, being rarer, it disappeared or was considerably remodelled during the Baroque period. The Cistercians, initiating the transition from the Romanesque to the Gothic styles, introduced elements of Gothic architecture with semi-circular arches and ribbed vaulting at the beginning of the 13C. In Pomernia, Cistercians who were dependent on German and Danish communities (Kołbacz, Oliwa), adapted the Gothic style of Western Europe to a brick-based architecture, followed in this way by the Franciscan and Dominican mendicant orders who also built brick monasteries such as the Dominican church in Sandomierz (1226), considered to be Poland's first brick-built church.

GOTHIC ART

Setting itself apart, Silesia developed its own regional school of Gothic architecture best represented by the basilicas of Strzegom and Wrocław (St Elizabeth's and St Mary Magdalene's churches) before coming under the influence of the Parler, a family of architects from Prague.

Gothic art in the North

The North of the country saw a flourishing of "Backsteingotik", a German expression used to refer to brick-built Gothic edifices, characteristic of Poland and Northern Germany. The Teutonic Order erected vast castles on a square plan, the most important of which, situated in Malbork, was like a fortress-monastery, similar to the strongholds of Syria and Palestine. This northern Gothic featured massive walls and elaborately decorated gables as illustrated by Frombork Cathedral, Orneta Church, Toruń Cathedral and Lidzbark Warmiński Castle as well as by churches boasting naves of equal height such as the Basilica of Our Lady in Gdańsk. Pelplin Cathedral offered the first example of English-style star vaulting.

Gothic art in towns

In the mid-14C, the influence of the monasteries was gradually replaced by that of the Crown, represented by the builder-king, Kazimierz the Great, who is said to "have found Poland built of wood and left it built of stone". New powers granted to towns based on urban charters (*prawo miejskie*) promoted a new kind of layout featuring a vast central market square (*rynek*) dominated by a town hall (*ratusz*) and a parish church (*kościół farny*); the finest example of this town planning is

undeniably Kraków, which symbolizes the power of the local middle class. Throughout the kingdom of Poland, large basilicas such as the cathedrals in Kraków, Gniezno, Poznań and Wrocław were erected on the foundations of existing buildings, some fifty castles (Ojców, Będzin, Olsztyn, Ogrodzieniec) were built and almost as many churches including, in particular, the three-naved collegiate church in Sandomierz, boasting fan and star vaulting, and the twin-naved Wiślica Church. The Church of the Holy Cross in Kraków spreads its star vaulting over a single central pillar with a palm-like capital. In the 14C, at the time of the accession to the throne of the Jagellons, the **Flamboyant Gothic** style, with its ribbed vaulting and elongated pointed arches, its profusion of windows and of decoration and the emphasis on vertical lines met with a growing success which spread throughout the provinces.

Gothic sculpture

The oldest wooden sculptures date from the 12C and 13C and, at the beginning of the 15C, the Virgin and Child became one of the favourite themes of Polish sculpture, under Italian influence. The Krużlowa Madonna, attributed to an artist from Little Poland, is the most famous and characteristic example of the "delicate style". It was also during this period that **Gothic altarpieces** acquired their definitive shape, featuring a vertical triptych with moving panels surrounding a carved centrepiece. With **Veit Stoss**, who worked in Kraków during the last quarter of the 15C, Polish sculpture found a new lease of life. His altarpiece of the Dormition of the Virgin in St Mary's

Dormition of the Virgin in St Mary's Church in Kraków, Veit Stoss

R. Czerwiński / ONT Polska

Church in Kraków and the tomb of King Kazimierz Jagiello in Wawel Cathedral inspired artists until the middle of the 16C even though new trends born of the Italian Renaissance were already spreading.

At the same time, Poland was exposed to the influence of masters from Russia, as attested by the Byzantine-style frescoes decorating the Collegiate Cathedral of Sandormierz and those adorning the Holy Trinity Chapel in Lublin, dating from 1418.

THE RENAISSANCE

Sigismund I (married to an Italian) invited Italian artists to Wawel thus bringing to Poland the more decorative art of the Renaissance. Between 1507 and 1532, while Germany, Bohemia, Masovia and Podlasie remained loyal to the late-Gothic style, the royal castle on Wawel Hill was transformed under the influence of Florentine architecture, as shown by the fine main courtyard surrounded by three superposed arcaded galleries, and the coffered ceiling of the Audience Hall, otherwise still basically Gothic. Supervised in turn by Francesco from Florence, Bartolommeo Berecci and then Benedykt from Sandomierz, these remodellings prompted the kingdom's wealthy magnates to want to compete, which is what they did in Little Poland in the middle of the 16C in the palaces of Krzyżtopór, Krasiczyn or even Baranów, near Sandomierz, known as the little Wawel.

Although it only borrowed a few decorative elements from the Renaissance style, religious architecture owed to Bartolommeo Berecci one of the masterpieces of the Polish golden age (*Złoty Wiek*): the famous Sigismund Chapel added onto the side of Wawel Cathedral, on which many constructions were modelled.

The most flourishing towns at the height of their power built sumptuous town halls (ratusz) often surmounted by a crenellated tower, such as the Poznań town hall erected by Giovanni Battista Quadro. The lower part of the roofs of many buildings were enhanced by decorated attics. Threatened by a Turkish invasion, towns surrounded themselves with brick-and-earth fortifications such as the extremely well-preserved Barbican in Kraków, dating from the 15C. A whole city, Zamość, built from 1579 onwards, was designed by one single Italian architect, Bernardo Morando, along the lines of a Renaissance-style town-planning project, although Eastern influences appeared in the middle of the

17C with a group of Armenian houses. Most prominent in Gdańsk and in the Hanseatic cities, the Dutch Mannerist style was promoted by Anton van Opbergen, the architect of the Old Town Hall, by Abraham and Wilhem van den Blocke, and by the painter Hans Vredemann de Vries.

The sculptors Santi Gucci, Gian Maria Padovano and Jan Michałowicz, who worked on magnificent funerary monuments, intended for the royal family and the nobility, and on the decoration of many other monuments, rank among the most talented artists of their time. Finally, the painter-monk Stanisław Samostrzelnik from Mogiła Monastery produced important mural paintings.

THE BAROQUE STYLE

The Renaissance period undeniably bore the imprint of the Jagiellonian royal dynasty, but from the beginning of the Baroque period, the dominant influence was that of the Vasa royal dynasty, Sigismund III (1597-1632) who transferred the capital from Kraków to Warsaw in 1596 and his son Ladislaw IV (1632-1648). Coinciding with the arrival of the Jesuits in Poland, the Baroque style became the official style of the Counter Reformation which made its first appearance in the Church of SS Peter and Paul in Kraków. Designed as a scaled-down version of the Roman church of Il Gesu de Vignola, without aisles, designed on the Latin Cross plan, with a dome soaring above the crossing, it was the work of the Italian architect Giovanni Trevano, whereas the interior decoration (intended to hide the brickwork) was made by the stucco artist Baltazar Fontana. Having arrived in Poland around 1665, the Dutch architect Tylman Van Gameren, who designed the Krasiński Palace in Warsaw and St Anne's Church in Kraków, softened with a touch of Classicism the exuberance of the initial Italian style. Other fine examples of pure Baroque style are to be found in the Jesuit Church in Poznań and in the Church of the Nuns of the Holy Sacrament in Warsaw, boasting elegant façades; on the other hand, the town of Gdańsk was not particularly marked, apart from the Royal Chapel, by the architectural style of the Counter Reformation. At the time, architects generally tended to remodel old edifices in the Baroque style. Indeed, the Gothic interior of many a church was enhanced by Baroque decorative elements and enriched with marbles and stuccos.

Architecture

Gothic Military Architecture

Malbork: Teutonic castle (14C)

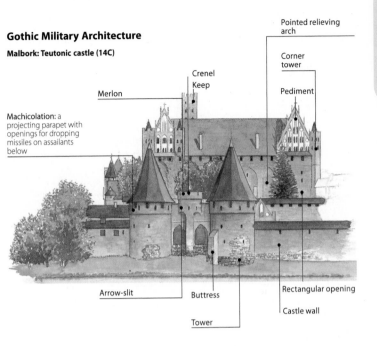

- Pointed relieving arch
- Corner tower
- Crenel
- Keep
- Merlon
- Pediment
- Machicolation: a projecting parapet with openings for dropping missiles on assailants below
- Arrow-slit
- Buttress
- Tower
- Rectangular opening
- Castle wall

Flamboyant Gothic Architecture

Wrocław Town Hall (2nd half of the 13C, remodelled in late Gothic style)

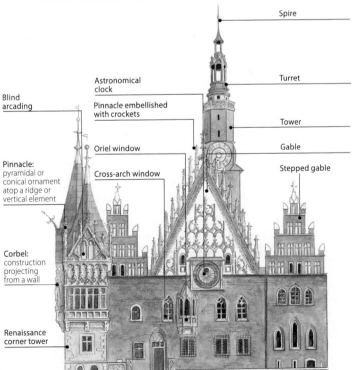

- Spire
- Turret
- Astronomical clock
- Blind arcading
- Pinnacle embellished with crockets
- Tower
- Gable
- Oriel window
- Pinnacle: pyramidal or conical ornament atop a ridge or vertical element
- Cross-arch window
- Stepped gable
- Corbel: construction projecting from a wall
- Renaissance corner tower

H. Choimet/MICHELIN

Renaissance Architecture

Kraków: The Cloth Hall (16C, remodelled in neo-Gothic style in the late 19C)

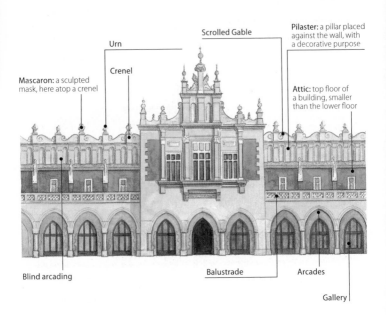

Pilaster: a pillar placed against the wall, with a decorative purpose

Scrolled Gable

Urn

Crenel

Mascaron: a sculpted mask, here atop a crenel

Attic: top floor of a building, smaller than the lower floor

Blind arcading

Balustrade

Arcades

Gallery

Renaissance Architecture remodelled as Baroque in the 18C

Zamość Town Hall

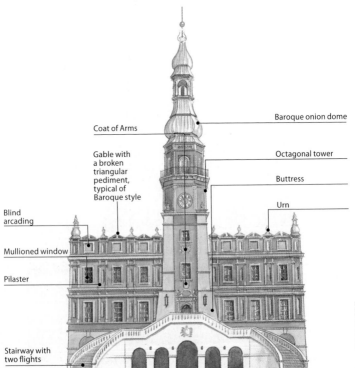

Baroque onion dome

Coat of Arms

Octagonal tower

Gable with a broken triangular pediment, typical of Baroque style

Buttress

Urn

Blind arcading

Mullioned window

Pilaster

Stairway with two flights

H. Choimet/MICHELIN

Baroque Jesuit Architecture

Kraków: Church of SS Peter and Paul

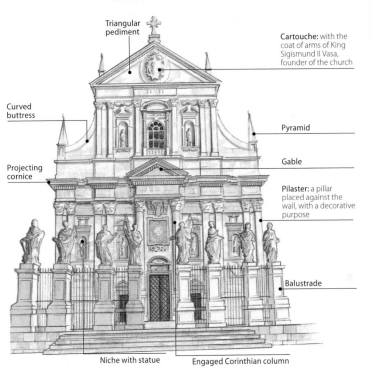

Triangular pediment

Cartouche: with the coat of arms of King Sigismund II Vasa, founder of the church

Curved buttress

Pyramid

Gable

Projecting cornice

Pilaster: a pillar placed against the wall, with a decorative purpose

Balustrade

Niche with statue

Engaged Corinthian column

Dutch Mannerist Architecture

Gdánsk: Golden House

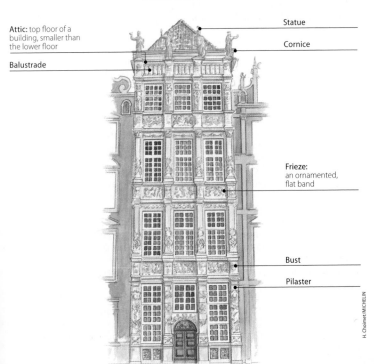

Attic: top floor of a building, smaller than the lower floor

Statue

Cornice

Balustrade

Frieze: an ornamented, flat band

Bust

Pilaster

H. Choimet/MICHELIN

Built at the beginning of the 18C, the Rococo bishop's palace in Kielce, decorated by Antoni Frączkiewicz, showed a French influence which, strengthened by the bonds uniting the Polish and French courts, became more and more prominent. At the same time, following the victory against the Turks in 1683, the Eastern influence could be seen in the minor decorative arts. It was the period when "Sarmatism" (*Sarmatyzm*) was fashionable; this concept of another age, returning to a strange "East/West" blend, was favoured by Polish aristocrats who wished to rediscover, through the splendour of ceremonies and the magnificence of costumes, decor and weapons, the virtues and military glory of their Sarmatian ancestors. Associated with costume, the so-called Sarmatian portrait, introduced at the end of the 16C, remained fashionable until the 18C. Another type of typically Polish production also fashionable at that time were the portraits used to decorate coffins (*portret trumienny*).

This was also the period when important royal art collections were assembled and interest for the arts resulted in the acquisition of works by Rubens in particular (he made portraits of the first two Vasa kings) or by masters of Dutch painting. Daniel Schultz from Gdańsk, trained in Holland, was then the official painter of the royal family, whereas the Venitian Tommaso Dolabella adapted Italian Mannerism to religious and historical subjects.

Painting and graphic arts

A ROYAL PATRON OF THE ARTS

The Age of the Enlightenment brought with it a more international artistic period than Sarmatism had been, with its specifically Polish character in spite of the Oriental influence. King Stanisław August Poniatowski, a dedicated patron of the arts, great connoisseur of French culture and enthusiastic art collector, attracted to his court a number of foreign artists, in particular from Italy and France. In charge of the remodelling and furnishing of the interior of the royal castle in early classicist style were the French architect Victor Louis (1731-1800) and the Italian Dominico Merlini (1731-1797), who became the king's first architect after Jacob Fontana.

The Italian painter, **Marcello Bacciarelli** (1731-1818), the king's main artistic adviser, settled in Warsaw in 1766 to take charge of the artists working at the Royal Castle. His task was, more specifically, to decorate the ceilings of the rooms of the new Łazienki summer royal residence, built jointly by the architect from Dresden Jan Chrystian Kamsetzer and by Merlini, and modelled on the Petit Trianon in Versailles. Another eminent artist staying at the Polish court was Bernardo Bellotto known as **Canaletto the Younger** (1720-80), who painted renowned *vedute* (townscapes with characters), just like his famous uncle. French artist **André Le Brun** (1737-1811), a disciple of Pigalle, was in charge of the royal sculpture studio while the painter **Jean-Pierre Norblin de la Gourdaine** (1745-1830), a protégé of Prince Czartoryski, introduced Poland to genre painting and battle scenes, a theme later developed by his pupil **Aleksander Orłowski** (1777-1832).

With the 1795 Partition and the end of the monarchy, the "styl Stanisławowski" was taken up by the Polish nobility who commissioned many palaces to be built or rebuilt in Palladian, neo-Classical style by master builders such as Stanisław Zawadzki and Szymon Bogumił Zug or in neo-Gothic style by Piotr Aigner. During the 19C, the division of the country between the three great neighbouring powers strengthened Austro-Hungarian, Prussian and Russian architectural influences, for instance in Warsaw where late neo-classicism recalls St Petersburg.

PAINTING AND NATIONALISM

Antoni Brodowski (1784-1832), who studied in Paris, was Poland's most outstanding neo-classicist painter whereas **Piotr Michałowski** (1800-1855) is considered as the country's greatest Romantic painter. Often compared to Géricault, this famous artist, who specialised in painting horses, also admired the Napoleonic period which he illustrated through many paintings. Inspired by Cervantes's Don Quixote, he made many portraits of working-class people in the vein of Daumier.

Sharing his time between Vienna and Paris, **Henryk Rodakowski** (1823-1894) was a great society portrait painter, an exponent of the realist style, admired in particular by Eugène Delacroix and Théophile Gautier.

Since the court no longer governed public and artistic life, the second half of the 19C saw many artists go into exile. While Prussian Poland went through an enforced Germanization process and, following the 1863 insurrection, tsarist repression became fierce (Austro-Hungarian Galicia enjoyed relative freedom after 1861), some Polish artists turned to subjects and symbols of a national nature, art thus becoming a substitute for politics.

A great master of Polish historical painting, **Jan Matejko** (1838-93), founder of the "Kraków School", had many pupils (the most talented later rejected his style), and devoted his entire output to the "awakening of his enslaved nation's conscience". His huge compositions, overcrowded with characters, illustrate the great periods of Polish history. Deeply concerned with the preservation of his native Kraków's artistic heritage, he took part in the interior decoration of St Mary's Church. The lithographs of young **Artur Grottger** (1837-67) are inspired by the same themes.

The main exponent of realism in landscape painting, **Józef Chełmoński** (1846-1914), left contemplative works illustrating peasant or daily-life scenes. On the other hand, his contemporary, **Witold Pruszkowski** (1846-1896), was a precursor of symbolism.

Particularly concerned with light, **Aleksander Gierymski** (1850-1901) produced genre scenes which can be classified as pre-Impressionist painting. Fascinated by Paul Gauguin, **Władysław Ślewiński** (1854-1918), who spent a major part of his life in Britanny, had strong links with the Pont-Aven School and influenced Wyspiański and Mehoffer.

Characterized by a blend of symbolism and realism, the work of **Jacek Malczewski** (1854-1929), a pupil of Matejko, stands apart. Painted in ever brighter colours, his eccentric self-portraits (featuring some surrealist elements) magnify the personality of an artist who is also affected by the thwarted destiny of his country. The National Museum in Poznań houses the major part of his work.

Another pupil of Matejko, **Maurycy Gottlieb** (1856-79), of Jewish origin, tried during his brief life to reconcile the Jewish and Christian traditions in an original way.

At first close to Impressionism which he discovered in Paris, **Władysław Podkowiński** (1866-95) left few works, yet his *Madness*, exhibited in 1894, influenced by the emerging symbolist movement, was the talk of artistic circles. His friend **Józef Pankiewicz** (1866-1940), always open to French influences which he promoted among young Polish artists, was the main exponent of Impressionism in Poland before adhering to symbolism.

The excellent portrait-painter **Olga Boznańska** (1865-1907), known for her subtle range of colours, settled in Paris in 1894 and became one of the main exponents of post-Impressionism. In a more sombre vein, **Witold Wojtkiewicz** (1879-1909), who died prematurely, left a few most original Expressionist works, often featuring morbid and grotesque imaginary elements.

SYNTHESIS OF THE ARTS : YOUNG POLAND

Founded in Kraków in 1898, the Young Poland movement (*Młoda Polska*) was a blend of several pre-existing artistic trends (Impressionism, naturalism, symbolism, Expressionism) which gathered multifaceted talents. Marked by a return to Romanticism, repressed by the positivist period, and tinged with new-found spirituality, it was one of the expressions of decorative Art Nouveau (*Secesja*).

A versatile creator, **Stanisław Wyspiański** (1869-1907), born in a family of artists from Kraków, was considered as the father of modernism. Before he devoted the last ten years of his life to the theatre, he produced graphic works, mainly pastels, including intimist canvases such as portraits or landscapes as well as monumental projects such as the polychromes decorating Kraków's Franciscan Church and above all the magnificent stained-glass windows he made for the same church.

Private Collection/The Bridgeman Art Library

"Portrait of a Child", by Jan Matejko (1883)

"Dancers", by Józef Mehoffer (1869-1946)

The Bridgeman Art Library

Although he was a pupil of Matejko and later worked with him, his works betray the influence of the Viennese Secession, of French Art Nouveau (through a stylised rendering of plants) and even of Japanese art. His friend, the artist **Józef Mehoffer** (1869-1946), excelled in the decorative arts and became famous for the stained-glass windows which he made for the collegiate church in Fribourg (Switzerland) and which bear the mark of Art Nouveau. His painting is imbued with a unique feeling of intense delight and happiness.

Having also studied in Kraków, **Włodzimierz Tetmajer** (1862-1923) devoted his expressive, colourful art to the peasantry. **Wojcieh Weiss** (1875-1950), highly influenced by Przybyszewski's writings, produced amazing Expressionist paintings at the turn of the 20C, before returning to a more traditional style.

Having the same name as his famour son, **Stanisław Witkiewicz** (1851-1915) is essentially known as an art critic and theorist through his anthology *Our Art and Criticism* (1871) which influenced many a young artist. He also invented the so-called Zakopane architectural style inspired by popular art from mountainous areas.

Strongly influenced by Rodin during his stay in Paris between 1914 and 1922, **Xavery Dunikowski** (1875-1964) was THE great Polish sculptor whose style incorporated Cubist fragmentation and considerably evolved subsequently. Also worth mentioning is **Bolesław Biegas** (1877-1954), who settled in Paris in 1902 and whose sculptures (also influenced by Rodin) and paintings are essentially symbolist.

THE PRECURSORS OF MODERN ART

After Poland recovered its independence in 1918, defending the national culture became a secondary issue and there was a blossoming of more radical artistic movements comparable to those of Western Europe. Led by a few exceptional figureheads, the Polish avant-garde showed a desire to experiment in the midst of a riot of artistic expression. The art magazine **Zwrotnica** founded by Tadeusz Peiper (1891-1961) was used as a forum for theoretical debate by the Polish avant-garde in the 1920s.

Exiled in Paris, **Tadeusz Makowski** (1882-1932), who was mainly influenced by Gauguin and Polish popular art, was probably the first to take into consideration the advent of Cubism, but it was above all in the work of **Zbigniew Pronaszko** (1885-1958) that the first Cubist elements were to be found. Combining Futurism and Cubism, **Tytus Czyżewski** (1880-1945) initiated a trend in Kraków in 1915, which was at first described as Polish Expressionism but soon evolved towards a more formal radicalism whose exponents adopted in 1918 the name of Formists (*Formiści*), while a dissident group from Warsaw, founded by painter Eugene Zak, took in 1922 the name of "*Rytm*". Prolonging this trend, the eminent logician **Léon Chwistek** (1884-1944) devised a theory, known as "Zonism" (*Stresfizm*), about unity of form and colour.

More or less connected with this movement are the graphic works of the multidisciplinary artist **Stanisław Ignacy Witkiewicz** (1885-1939) known as **Wit-**

kacy, initiator of naturalism and founder of the "Pure Form" theory. In addition to complex theoretical essays about art, he created in 1924 his "Firma Portretowa" of which he was the only member and for which he portrayed his contemporaries in a twisted and psychologically arbitrary way. He ranks among the best-known 20C Polish painters and his contribution in the field of photography was also substantial. The graphic works produced by **Bruno Schulz** as an illustrator, consisting of strange drawings, can be associated with this Expressionist trend.

More inclined towards internationalism than the Formists who aim to define a national art, are the founders of the Expressionist group Bunt (Revolt), centred round the magazine Zdrój published in Poznań and including **Stanisław Kubicki** (1899-1934) who later drew nearer to German activism. Close to the Bunt group, the group of Jewish artists **Jung Idysz**, including Jankel Adler, was based in Łódź.

Kisling of Montparnasse

Born in a Jewish family from Kraków in 1891, **Moïse Kisling** was the pupil of Pankiewicz before he settled in France in 1910 and became one of the typical exponents of the Paris school.

COLORISTS OF THE "PARIS COMMITTEE"

Art became diversified during the interwar period which gave rise to many schools and different trends sometimes radically opposed. For many Polish artists, Paris represented, during the first decades of the 20C, the hub of modernism in art. In order to quench their "thirst for modernity", which drove them to reject academicism still in force in Poland, a handful of young Polish artists arrived in Paris in 1924 and settled there for six years, founding the "**Paris Committee**" (Komitet Paryski). Subscribing to a post-Impressionist and fauvist line advocating the dominance of colour, these pupils of Pankiewicz called themselves "kapists" or "KP" from the name of their leader **Józef Czapski** (1896-1993), a symbolic figure of contemporary Polish history who settled permanently in France after the war. One of the rare officers to have survived the Katyń massacre, he repeatedly denounced, in several works, the crimes perpetrated by the Soviets. Another two founders

of the Paris Committee were **Zygmunt Waliszewski** (1897-1936) and **Jan Cybis** (1897-1972). A prize named after the latter is now awarded in Poland to a work in the artistic field. The influence of the colorists, who were of no interest to the avant-garde, in Polish art teaching during the postwar period was important and long-lasting.

THE CONSTRUCTIVIST INFLUENCE

From 1924 onwards, a new trend which had already appeared in Moscow and Berlin, Constructivism, entered Warsaw's artistic scene. Castigating the academic colorist trend of the kapists, the exponents of Constructivism advocated a radical break in order to retain pure form only, without any content whatsoever. Inspired by Soviet art and the Suprematism of Malevitch whom they welcomed in Warsaw in 1927, they rejected all nationalist elements.

The father of Polish abstraction, **Henryk Stażewski** (1894-1988) ranks among the pioneers of the avant-garde of the 1920s and 1930s. He was the main exponent of Constructivism and, from the 1960s onwards, he devoted himself to the rigour of geometric abstraction. Co-founder of the communist group Blok in 1924, then a member of Praesens (founded by the architect S. Syrkus) from 1926 on, he later joined the a r (artyści rewolucyjni) and, during the 1930s, he exhibited as part of the Parisian groups Cercle and Carré, and Abstraction-Création. Linked to the latter, **Maria Nicz-Borowiak** (1896-1944) was also a major exponent of Polish Constructivism, as

"Jasienski at the Grand Piano", by Jozef Pankiewicz (1908), Pankiewicz National Museum, Kraków

Did you know?

Born in Kiev, Ukraine, in 1879, the Russian painter and writer, father of the white square on a white background (1917), Kazimir Malevitch, had Polish parents who were deported to Ukraine following an insurrection against Russian occupation. This was also the case of the dancer and choreographer Vaslav Fomitch Nijinski, who was also subjected to the Russian integration process.

was **Mieczysław Szczuka** (1898-1927), theoretician and editor of the magazine Blok, close to the sculptress **Teresa Żarnower** (1895-1950). Founder in 1929 of the avant-garde group "a r" (revolutionary artists), **Władysław Strzemiński** (1893-1952) initiated the first modern-art gallery inaugurated in February 1931 in the industrial city of Łódź which aimed to mount one of the first permanent art exhibitions showing works by the world's avant-garde. He distanced himself from Malevitch and Tatlin by developing his theory of "Unizm" from 1927 onwards and applied to his own painting the principles of "space-and-time rhythms". His wife **Katarzyna Kobro** (1898-1951), a sculptor formed in Moscow as he was, adapted the simple juxtaposition of area to spatial works. Connected with the Praesens Group, **Kazimir Podsadecki** (1904-1970) distinguished himself in the use of the "Functionalist" photomontage technique. Theoretician of "mecanofacture" then initiator of the Blok Group before going to France in 1928, **Henryk Berlewi** (1894-1967) is considered as one of the precursors of Op Art or Optical Art.

Before he perfected his "factorealism", the painter **Marek Włodarski** (1903-60) joined the Artes Group, created in Lvov in 1929, who later moved on to the committed realist trend of Socialist-realism.

POSTWAR CONTEMPORARY ART

With the establishment of communism, artists became employees of the State and closely dependent on the Ministry of Culture's sponsorship, a situation which continued into the 1980s. The painter of the Autodidacte Group **Andrzej Wróblewski** (1927-1957) used his method "neo barbaryczna" to further the edification of Socialism. The same applies to **Maria Jarema** (1908-58), co-founder of the Kraków Group with Henryk Wiciński (1908-43), who later moved on to abstraction before collaborating with Kantor. A member of the communist

group "Phrygian Cap", **Bronisław Wojciech Linke** (1906-62) combined satire and surrealism. The ZPAP, Union of Polish Artists, decided in June 1949 in Katowice to adopt Social Realism which ended in 1955. The end of the Soviet internationalist style gave rise to many new trends such as the **55 Group** exhibiting their "visual metaphors" in the Krzywe Koło (Twisted Circle) Gallery in Warsaw or the **Grupa Krakowska II** of **Tadeusz Brzozowski** (1918-1988), hostile to any form of esthetism. The 1960s inaugurated a period of diversity featuring all the western trends of Modernism. A "total artist" according to his own definition, **Tadeusz Kantor** (1915-90), who belonged to the Grupa Krakowska, began his informal period in 1948 by organising an avant-garde art exhibition around his Metamorphoses. His first medium, painting, gave him a decisive experience which led him to object to human representation and to adhere to the idea of the Fine Arts borrowing forms of action, of "performance art" and happenings, the first of which took place in 1965 in the **Foksal Gallery** in Warsaw, founded by artist **Włodzimierz Borowski** (1930).

Memento Mori

Born in France in 1931, the artist **Roman Opałka** went back to live and study in Poland between 1935 and 1979 (he was deported to Germany in 1940). According to an anecdote, the fact that his wife waited for a long time in a Warsaw hotel in 1965 prompted him to conceive his project of formal painting: the passing of one's own lifetime comprehending "art as life", a subtle petaphysical reflection on time and the infinitely small.

He then began to give concrete expression to the count down of his own existence by painting white numbers lined up on a black background, on canvases with identical measurements based on his own size (196x135cm). Prolonging this long line of numbers from painting to painting, he got to one million in 1972 and then added 1% of white to the black background on each new canvas, which became greyer and greyer until the numbers and the background became one. At the same time, he started recording his voice in 1972 and took a picture of his face at the end of each working day. All these details formed part of a global project which will be finalised with the death and therefore the last canvas of the artist. As he is now nearing the six millions, how many numbers separate him from the end of his human life and of his work completed at last?

A remarkable creator of modern tapestry when she started out, **Magdalena Aba-kanowicz** (1930), became one of the artists best represented in the world's main museums with her outdoor monumental sculptures.

Noteworthy artists also include **Jonasz Stern** (1904-88), who devoted himself to "painting matter" and incorporated in his paintings organic waste, and **Władysław Hasior** (1928-2000), who studied in Zakopane and produced amazingly poetic assemblages. Also worth mentioning are the technical experiments around the human body of **Alina Szapocznikow** (1926-73) or the church polychromes of Orthodox artist **Jerzy Nowosielski** (1923), as well as the "wild expression" canvases of **Leon Tarasewicz** (1957), not forgetting the works of conceptualist artists **Ryszard Winiarski** (1936) or **Roman Opałka** (1931). Zdzisław Beksiński, Józef Szajna, Edward Dwurnik, Kazimierz Mikulski, Jerzy Beres, Jan Lebestein, Zbigniew Makowski, Krzysztof Wodiczko, Jarosław Kozłowski, are also important figures on the 20C Polish artistic scene and there are always many artists ready to take over from their predecessors.

Finally, one should not omit, in the field of popular art, the painters **Eugeniusz Mucha** (1927) and **Nikifor** (1895-1968), a self-taught artist who has been compared to Henri Rousseau, known as "le Douanier" (toll-inspector).

POLISH POSTERS

Being the preferred support of political and cultural life (theatre, cinema, opera, jazz, circus), poster painting, which evolved from graphic art of the Art Nouveau and Constructivist periods, flourished in Poland towards the end of the 1950s. Propaganda posters, marked by Soviet realism, were closely subjected to controls and censorship, but cultural posters, although also commissioned by the state, enjoyed the relative cultural liberation which followed the events of October 1956. Free from advertising constraints, "outside commercialisation", the popular art of poster painting was

"The dove of peace and the reconstruction of Warsaw", by Eryk Lipinski-Trepkowski (1945)

represented by talented graphic artists who managed to maintain a certain level of independence and artistic integrity, rejecting the esthetic dogmas of Socialist realism. The production, which attests a real avant-garde creativity, rapidly led critics and art historians to speak of a Polish school of poster painting whose main exponents, acknowledged abroad, were in the 1960s Jan Lenica (1928-2001), also a cartoon film maker, Roman Cieślewicz (1930-1996), Tadeusz Trepkowski, Henryk Tomaszewski, Waldemar Świerzy, Jan Młodożeniec, Franciszek Starowiejski. The new generation includes Maciej Buszewicz, Jacek Staniszewski and Michał Batory who has lived in France since 1987 and now works on posters for such theatres as the Théâtre de la Colline and the Théâtre de Chaillot.

In 1966, the first Biennial International Poster Festival took place in Warsaw and, in 1968, an annex of the National Museum dedicated to this "street art" was created within the Wilanów Palace, near Warsaw.

Also worth mentioning is the Triennial International Engraving Festival which has, since 1966, been exhibiting the work of "Kraków's famous school of engraving".

CULTURE

"If there were no Poland, there would be no Poles", in the words of Ubu, the hero of French playwright Alfred Jarry's absurdist drama. Self evident? Perhaps, but if authors and artists in exile had not been steadfast in keeping the country alive though their works, Poland, which by the 18C had been absent from the map of the world for 120 years, might have disappeared altogether. Following the 1918 reunification, nationalist cultural movements gave way to the exuberance of the avant-garde. Artistic expression was then plunged deep into one of history's darkest moments, the trauma of the Holocaust and the censure of Soviet rule.

Agence Bernand

"The Dead Class", by Tandeusz Kantor, in performance by the Cricot 2 Theatre of Kraków, at the Théâtre National de Chaillot in Paris (1977)

Literature and Drama

INSPIRED LITERATURE

It appears that the oldest known sentence expressed in Polish came from a chronicle from the Henryków monastery in Silesia some time after AD 1270. Insignificant and spoken by a Polish peasant, it was taken down by a German Cistercian monk. In fact, until the 16C, Polish literature – owing to the importance assumed by the Church – was in Latin and reserved for an elite, as attested by the Annales Poloniae, historical chronicles by the Jesuit **Jan Długosz** (1415-1480). The first book in Polish was printed in 1513 and, although the Protestant **Mikołaj Rej** (1509-69) is usually seen as the father of Polish literature, it is considered that popular language first flourished with the poet **Jan Kochanowsk**i (1532-1586) and that the national language established its pedigree with the Jesuit preacher **Piotr Skarga** (1536-1612).

Associated with the Counter Reformation are the works of Wacław Potocki (1621-96) and Samuel Twardowski (1600-61), an exponent of the elegiac form, who drew his inspiration from Spanish sources. **Jan Chryzostom Pasek** (1636-1701), who wrote famous Memoirs sitll appreciated today, comes through his incredible war adventures as an extraordinary storyteller and swashbuckler, prefiguring the Polish historical novel. **King Jan III Sobieski** (1674-96), another battlefield regular, leaves a first-class account in the form of correspondence addressed to his French-born wife Mariette. 18C Polish literature generally drew its inspiration from 17C French authors as illustrated in the moralizing drama of Franciszek Bohomolec (1720-84). The Age of Enlightenment produced the "prince of poets" and archibishop of Warmia, **Ignacy Krasicki** (1735-1801), a talented moralist and satirist, author of famous fables.

A COUNTRY TORN APART... EXILED POETS

Following the partitions of Poland in 1795 and then again in 1815, the tsarist oppression, imposed by the absolute ruler Nicholas I, supplied Polish Romanticism with an exceptionally fertile compost for its development. The "Great Emigration", which followed the repressed insurrection of November 1830, gave a voice to the conscience of three great poets for whom literature, intended to convey patriotic feelings, became the only means of expression capable of safeguarding the national identity.

Adam Mickiewicz (1798-1855) is the most famous national bard of that period. Born in Lithuania, he was forced into a triumphant exile as early as 1823. and never saw his beloved country again. An idealist both in morals and in politics, he left a vast epic poem *Pan Tadeusz* and one of the sacred plays of the Polish drama repertoire, *Ancestors*.

Juliusz Słowacki (1809-1849), the archetypal Romantic melancholiac, left a varied production marked by the mystical impulses of a man who saw himself as a spiritual guide. In response to *Ancestors*, he also wrote a Romantic drama on the theme of the insurrection, *Kordian*. His patriotic poetry, becoming more and more exuberant, drifted, at the end of his life, towards Messianic symbolism. Buried in Montmorency's Polish cemetery, his remains were transferred in 1927 in Wawel Cathedral, as those of Mickiewicz had been in 1890.

Zygmunt Krasiński (1812-1859) was born in France and wrote in both languages. He is essentially known as the author of a social drama, *The Non-Divine Comedy*, on the theme of the silk-workers' uprising in Lyons, which ranked him as the most universal writer of the Romantic generation. He also left a colossal amount of correspondence.

POSITIVIST LITERATURE

The failure of the January 1863 insurrection resulted in the emergence of the positivist period, marked by realist trends as well as social and political transformations, which led to the ultimate consecration of prose.

Representative of the historical novel, the works of prolific writer **Józef Ignacy Kraszewski** (1812-87), strongly inspired by French authors, find a perfect equivalent in Marejko's paintings. Although **Józef Korzeniowski** (1797-1863) was probably the best exponent of the realist novel, it is the name of **Henryk Sienkiewicz** (1846-1916) that is still remembered today. Famous author of the best-seller *Quo Vadis*, an epic novel about the beginnings of Christianism

in ancient Rome, translated into 100 languages, this workaholic is mainly known in Poland for his historical *Trilogy*, for which he was awarded the Nobel Prize in 1905. Another positivist figure is **Bolesław Prus** (1845-1912) who, under the pen name of Aleksander Głowaski, wrote *The Doll*, one of the most famous Polish social novels. The first great female literary figure, **Eliza Orzeszkowa** (1841-1910) depicted with benevolence, in a populist vein, the world of ordinary people in the Polish provinces. **Adam Asnyk** (1838-1897) and **Maria Konopnicka** (1842-1910) rank among the best poets of this generation.

THE "YOUNG POLAND" RENEWAL

In reaction to the realist trend came the modernist Young Poland (*Młoda Polska*) movement which is today considered as a period of the national history in its own right. The expression, which first came about in 1898, refers to the neo-Romantic movement which maintained that art as a creator of worth was an object of veneration and creators alone were capable of achieving national renewal. The advent of this movement caused a change in sensitivity and style which affected all the arts.

An advocator of bohemian life and of Satanic literature, for ever in search of the "bare soul", **Stanisław Przybyszewski** (1868-1927) is considered as a precursor of that movement. Following a long stay in Berlin where he met Strindberg and Munch, he settled in Kraków and gathered the new trends under the banner of *Moderna*, centred on the magazine *Życie* (*Life*). An independent and original artist, he durably influenced a good deal of writers and artists.

Stanisław Wyspiański (1869-1907) stands as a significant figure of the movement, not only in the field of pictorial art, but also drama, with his famous play *The Wedding*, a tragi-comic parable about the fate of Poland, which renewed drama and revolution.

The main prose writers include **Wacłav Berent** (1873-1940), **Stefan Żeromski** (1864-1925), described as the "conscience of Polish literature", and above all **Władysław Reymont** (1867-1925), whose huge four-volume epic novel entitled *Peasants* is considered as a national saga, for which its author was awarded the Nobel Prize for literature in 1924.

THE "THREE MUSKETEERS": GOMBROWICZ, SCHULZ AND WITKACY

The interwar period saw the emergence of three exceptional literary figures whose talents have now been recognised. In a country henceforth liberated from the patriotic ideal necessary to form a nation, their intellectual quest turned to new paths. Self-appointed by Gombrowicz himself, these "three musketeers" were three marginal artists who, each in his own way, furthered the cause of the Polish literary avant-garde.

"Portrait of a Man", by Stanislas Ignacy Witkiewicz (1924), National Museum, Warsaw

Stanisław Ignacy Witkiewicz known as **Witkacy** (1885-1939), a fascinating figure of modern literature, was first and foremost an artist with many talents.The son of an interesting painter, art critic and theoretician, this indomitable individualist, based in Zakopane, initiated a theory of art reflecting a metaphysical obsession for "pure form". His parodic dramas (difficult to translate and incomprehensible to many), which illustrate the search for pure drama, made him a precursor of the 1950s' theatre of the absurd. His doomwatch theory, his anxiety about the future of our European civilisation and his prophecy of the loss of the individual, led him to commit suicide in September 1939, when Poland was invaded by the Nazis.

Bruno Schulz (1892-1942), whose talent is gradually being recognised, was a Jewish writer (and illustrator) born in Galicia (now Ukraine) whose exuberant style and sensual sensitivity were unequalled. His unusual literary output included two sets of short stories, *Steet of Crocodiles* and *Under the Sign of the Hourglass*, in which he evokes his childhood in a metaphorically enigmatic style. He died tragically, shot down in the street by a bullet in the head fired by an SS officer.

Wishing to distance himself from the vicissitudes of History, **Witold Gombrowicz** (1904-1969) left Poland for good in 1939 and settled first in Argentina, then in France. His corrosive and deeply pessimistic works include his audacious first novel, *Ferdydurke*, which depicts a man shaped from the outside, unauthentic, caught in a vice-like conflict between maturity and immaturity and condemned to "never be himself". His other famous novel *Pornography*, which places eroticism at the centre of his work, expresses the paradoxical immature liking of humanity for imperfection and youth.

LITERATURE IN THE POSTWAR YEARS

The worldwide catastrophy, which had been forecast by many intellectuals, left Poland – with the German occupation and the extermination of the Jews – deplete of her intellectual elite. Yet from this chaos emerged the amazingly mature verse of the young poet **Krzysztof Kamil Baczyński** (1921-44), killed in action during the Warsaw Uprising.

During the immediate postwar period, writers pledged themselves to the new régime and placed their hatred of Nazism at the service of the new government. Under the influence of Stalinism, the country's cultural policy adopted a harder line and some writers (Władysław Broniewski) became fully implicated. Faced with such a dilemma, Tadeusz Borowski committed suicide in 1951 and Czesłau Miłosz fled and went on to analyse in *The Captive Mind* the processus of collective paranoia which threatened intellectuals at that time. Several important texts by exiled writers, gathered round the periodical Kultura, were published at the Paris Literary Institute by Jerzy Giedroyć, an important intellectual figure of the Polish emigration. Yet Polish writers were among the first within the Communist block to stand up against ideological conformism and to reject the dogma of Socialist Realism, starting with two novels by Leon Kruczkowski: *Revenge* and *The Germans*.

Using the theme of war, **Jerzy Andrze-jewski** (1909-1983) was one of the first to free himself from the communist power. Less of a protester, **Jarosław Iwasz-kiewicz** (1894-1980) left a rich and varied production. **Tadeusz Konwicki** (1926), also a film maker, was at first in favour of the communist power but in two of his novels he recalls how he progressively distanced himself. Before settling in Paris in 1972, **Adolf Rudnicki** (1912-1990) witnessed the tragedy that Poland's Jewish population lived through.

A POLISH SCHOOL OF POETRY

A major figure of postwar Polish literature, the poet and essayist **Czesław Miłosz** (1911-2004), awarded the Nobel Prize for Literature in 1980, had a long literary career that began before he went into exile in France and later in the US. His works include in particular a History of Polish Literature. Poland's latest Nobel Prize for Literature was awarded in 1996 to the poet from Kraków **Wisława Szymborska** (1923), who writes in a pithy, pared down style. Other important poets include **Tadeusz Różewicz** (1921) and **Zbigniew Herbert** (1924-1998) with his *Mr Cogito*, the Polish double of Paul Valéry's Monsieur Teste. The playwright and novelist **Sławomir Mrożek** (1930), who emigrated to France in 1963, writes satirical, burlesque stories and mocking plays inspired by the theatre of the absurd. The field of science fiction boasts the most translated of Polish writers, **Stanisław Lem** (1921-2006), whose novel *Solaris* (1961) was successively adapted for the screen by Andreï

Tarkowski then Steven Soderbergh. More recently, international critics have welcomed the work of two reporters, **Hanna Krall** and **Ryszard Kapuściński**, who wrote the remarkable "Ebony" about Africa.

POLISH THEATRE

Traditionally dominated by the experimental National Theatre in Warsaw and the more conservative Old Theatre in Kraków, drama is a living art in Poland. The term theatre may seem too narrow to describe the work of the independent and permanently avant-garde artist that **Tadeusz Kantor** (1915-90) was. In 1955, he founded Kraków's Cricot 2 Theatre, named after the prewar literary café mainly popular with painters, where he imposed his own vision of the world, away from officially approved ideologies, through an informal but brutally radical theatre, aiming to destroy all form. In 1963, he imposed his "zero theatre", which conveyed the absolute discrepancy between text and dramatic art. After his show *The Dead Class* in 1975, he developed his "Theatre of Death". Anecdote, plot and action were reduced to nothing; there was no more performance, no illustration of the play, no expression from the actors who were neutralised, just Kantor, ever present on stage, like a conductor, surrounded by objects, machines, packaging and dummies.

Another important figure of Polish drama was **Jerzy Grotowski** (1933-1999), with his Laboratory Theatre in Wrocław, extended by the Garzienice Centre of Theatrical Research where **Włodzimierz Staniewski** developed his "theatre ecology".

Wojtek Pszoniak, Jerzy Radziwłłowicz, Jerzy Stuhr, Andrzej Seweryn are world-famous Polish actors.

Polish Cinema

POLISH CINEMATOGRAPH PIONEERS

The first Polish cinematographic show took place on 14 November 1895 in Kraków but it was only in 1908 that a French film maker from the Pathé Frères company, Joseph-Louis Mundviller, made – under the pseudonym Jerzy Meyer – the first Polish fiction film: *Anthony, for the First Time in Warsaw*. Yet, as early as 1894, Kazimierz Prózyński tested a camera called "pleograph", and in 1898, Bolesław Matuszewski published the first Polish theory of the

Czesław Miłosz

C. Felver / Corbis

cinema in his brochure entitled *A New Source of History*. Instantly popular, the cinema developed steadily until the country became independent in 1918, with a production of about 30 films a year, During the following decade, which witnessed the début of one of Poland's first great academic film directors, Aleksander Ford, the national output slackened in favour of foreign productions, in particular French films, before being obliterated by the great world conflict which caused many actors and technicians to leave the country.

FROM STATE CINEMA TO EMANCIPATION

After the war, three films contributed to the renewal of Polish cinema now under State control. In 1947, *Forbidden Songs* by Leonard Buczkowski (one of Poland's greatest box-office successes) then in 1948, *Truth has no Frontiers* by A Ford and *The Last Stage* by Wanda Jakubowska, depict war and its consequences without any pretence, just before the brutal Stalinization that took place between 1949 and 1953 and the generalization of a clearly propagandist cinema. In the mid-1950s, as the Socialist Realist trend led to an artistic deadlock, it was severely questioned by a new generation of film makers, mostly trained at the cinema school created in 1948 in Łódź, who more or less succeeded in avoiding ideological demands and making it increasingly difficult for the communist power to appropriate them politically. The double success of Andrzej Wajda's film *Kanał* (they loved life) at the 1957 Cannes Festival, then of *Mother Joan of the Angels* by Jerzy Kawalerowicz (1922) at the 1961 Festival, both films winning

the Jury's Special Prize, confirmed the existence of this original Polish New Wave which some saw as the precursors of other European new waves.

THE POLISH SCHOOL OF CINEMA

A symbolic figure of this *nowa fala*, **Jerzy Skolimowski** (1936) began his career by making very personal films, including *Distinguishing Features, none* (1964), *Walk-over* (1965) and *The Barrier* (1966), before embarking, under pressure from the censorship, on a more chaotic and not always convincing international career, which however includes the noteworthy *Deep End* (1970) and *The Shout* (1978).

Andrzej Munk (1921-1961), undoubtedly one of the most talented film makers, made *Eroïca* in 1957 and *Luck to Spare* in 1960, two films in a short career of just four films, marked by scepticism and above all irony and featuring characters engulfed by the great flood of History.

Walerian Borowczyk (1923), who started out as a master of cartoons, was the first film maker to emigrate to France in 1959 (thus setting an example); he later specialised in erotic films from the ambitious *Immoral Tales* to the more commercial and depressing *Emmanuelle 5*.

Andrzej Wajda (1926), noticed in the 1960s for his stylistic hesitations and questionable themes, convincingly came back in 1977 with the highly political *The Marble Man* and again in 1981 with *The Iron Man*, awarded the Palme d'Or in Cannes. The following year, he made, in France, a memorable *Danton* with G Depardieu and W. Pszoniak in the key roles. With over 30 films to his credit (he is preparing a new film about Katyń), the so-called father of Polish cinema receives award after award, inclu-

W. Krzysztof / Gamma

Andrzej Wajda

ding an Oscar for the whole of his work. He had the honour of becoming a member of the Institut de France and to assume political responsibilities in Poland at the time of Lech Wałęsa's Presidency.

Other noteworthy figures of Polish cinema include **Wojciech Has** (1925-2000) who made *Farewell* in 1958 then *Clepsydre* in 1972 and **Kazimierz Kutz** (1929) author in 1960 of *Nobody Calls*, followed a year later by *Panic in a train*.

An international film maker

Born in Paris in 1933, Roman Polanski graduated in 1959 from the Cinema School in Lódź, then, in 1963, his first feature film, *Knife in the Water*, written in collaboration with Skolimowski, was nominated for the Oscar of the best foreign film. This was the only feature film he made in Poland before chosing to emigrate. Abroad, he made multigenre films, often acclaimed by critics and public alike; he adapted *The Tenant* (1976), a novel by a writer of Polish extraction, Roland Topor, then went on to make several remarkable films, reaching the top of his career with the success of *The Pianist*, filmed in Poland in 2001, winner of many awards.

THE CINEMA OF MORAL ANXIETY

Belonging to a generation of film makers anxious to free themselves from the traumas of the war, or at least decided to deal with them less directly, **Krzysztof Zanussi** (1939) made his mark in 1969 with his very first film, *The Crystal Structure*, as the leader of a new trend in which one can detect the social criticism of a political system relying on corruption. Consistently producing from abroad films in the same stylistic vein known as "moral anxiety", this film maker, often accused of being too intellectuel, questions us about faith in his last film *Life as a Sexually Transmissible Terminal I llness* (2000). Undermined by the emigration of its main protagonists, Polish cinema made in Poland, which hardly existed in the mid-1980s, showed signs of dying until **Krzysztof Kieslowski** (1941-1996) gave it a creative impulse and a new lease of life. He became famous through his cycle entitled *Decalogue* (1988-89), a remarkable series of ten films of about an hour each, produced for television and illustrating a modern application of the Ten Commandments. His last films *The Double*

Life of Veronique (1991) and the trilogy *Three Colours* (1993-94), both French co-productions, met with significant success, no doubt amplified by the participation of French actresses Irène Jacob, Julie Delpy and Juliette Binoche.

Filip Bajon (1947) with *Aria for an Athlete* (1979), Agnieszka Holland (1948) with *Provincial Actors* (1979) and *Europa, Europa* (1990), Wojciech Marczewski with *Escape of the Freedom Cinema* (1990) and more recently Krzysztof Krauze (1953) and Robert Gliński (1952) today share and prolong the same creative vein.

The unclassifiable film maker **Andrzej Żuławski** (1940) only made two films in Poland *Third Part of the Night* in 1970 and, two years later, *The Devil*, banned by the board of censors; he then went on to make films in France and produced tormented, even hysterical films rarely acclaimed by critics and often unintelligible to the public. His last film *Szamanka*, made in Poland in 1996, was no exception to the rule.

THE CINEMA OF NEW-FOUND FREEDOM

After the collapse of Communism and the progression towards a market economy, the very nature of film producing changed and forced most film makers to look for financing outside Poland, even if the State continued to invest in some prestigious projects such as the Polish-American co-production *Schindler's List* (1993) by Steven Spielberg, filmed in Kazimierz, Kraków's former Jewish district. The new generation also called on their illustrious elders for epic films inspired by the classics of Polish literature: Wajda, for instance, adapted in 1999 the famous poem by Adam Mickiewicz, *Pan Tadeusz*, and Kawalerowicz undertook in 2001 to adapt for the screen the no less famous novel *Quo Vadis ?* New directors confirmed during the 1990s include Andrzej Kondratiuk (1936), Janusz Kijowski (1939), the actor Jerzy Stuhr (1947) who turned director and Jan Jakub Kolski (1956), whose adaptation of Gombrowicz's famous novel, Pornography, came out in a few French cinemas in March 2005.

Finally, it is worth mentioning the excellent production, during the period 1957-70, of **Polish cartoons** by film makers like Jan Lenica, Walerian Borowczyk, Witold Giersz who enjoyed a worldwide reputation, as well as the still strong Polish tradition of documentary film-making, illustrated by Marcel Łoziński, following in the steps of Kazimierz Karabasz, author of the famous *Musicians* (1960).

Music

A highly musical nation, Poland can be proud to be the native country of a genius: Chopin, an eminently national yet at the same time universal composer. A"tree" to be reckoned with, that hides a precious "wood" of contemporary music.

FROM THE ORIGINS TO ROMANTICISM

The first music pieces, kept in the national archives, date from the 11C, but the Polish school of Gregorian then polyphonic chant developed under the Piasts and later under the Jagiellonians with, in particular, Nicolaus of Radom in the 15C and, in the 16C, Nicolaus Gomólka who marked the climax of Renaissance music. They were not followed by any original first-class composer and one can safely say that Polish classical music was born during the Romantic period.

An endearing figure of Romantic music, **Frédéric Chopin** (1810-1849), born to a Polish mother and a French father, both of them musicians, arrived in Paris in 1831. Apart from a few orchestral and chamber-music compositions, he wrote essentially for solo piano, having since childhood been a virtuoso of that instrument. He composed in an inexhaustible variety of styles (preludes, nocturnes, waltzes, polonaises, mazurkas). Drawing his inspiration from the depth of human feelings and from Polish folklore, he produced, from his close collaboration with his piano, some of the finest pages of Western music. As an ultimate symbol for this composer whose soul was both exalted and tormented and whom Georges Sand called "this dear corpse", his body is buried in the Père Lachaise cemetery while his heart lies in the Church of the Holy Cross in Warsaw.

Eclipsed by Chopin's creative shadow, his near contemporary **Stanisław Moniuszko** (1819-1872), who composed cantatas and lieder (based on texts from the great national poets), is considered, on account of his *Halka* and *The Enchanted Manor* as the true father of Poland's modern national opera, even though the first Polish operas (Italian opera was introduced in Warsaw in 1628) were written by Maciej Kamieński (1734-1821) and Jan Stefani (1746-1826). A childhood friend of Chopin, **Oskar Kolberg** (1814-1890), who studied Poland's musical folklore, is considered as a pioneer in the field of Polish ethnomusicology. The virtuoso violinist **Henryk Wieniawski** (1835-1880) gave his name (as Chopin did for the piano in Warsaw) to a famous Polish festival which takes place every five years in Poznań.

Frédéric Chopin (1810-49) Polish pianist and composer

THE NEGLECTED 20C "CHOPIN"

Comparable to Bartok in Hungary or Janaček in Czechoslovakia, **Karol Szymanowski** (1882-1937) was the main architect of the renewal of 20C Polish music. Co-founder with Karłowicz, Fitelberg, Różycki and Szeluto of the neo-Romantic group "Young Poland" which tried to imitate the progressive trends of Western Europe, he initiated in 1927 the creation of the Association of young Polish musicians, who flocked to be trained in France, in particular by Nadia Boulanger. His whole work, deeply rooted in various fields of culture and nourished by a rich travel experience, can be divided into three periods: romantic, impressionist (with a touch of orientalism for instance in *Myths* op.30) and Polish. For the last one, he searched for the national musical roots which were secondary in his previous works but now formed the base of his musical structure. His ballet *Harnasie* (The Bandits), influenced by folk music from the Tatras, was created in Paris in 1936. His last compositions, which were essentially vocal, include masterpieces like his opera King Roger (1926), based on a libretto by Iwaszkiewicz and his Stabat Mater (1929). Although his works are still rarely recorded and need to be discovered, there is no doubt that he opened the way for a whole generation of musicians and established the trends of contemporary Polish music.

THE WAYS OF THE CONTEMPORARY AVANT-GARDE

From the 1960s, Poland was undoubtedly held as an avant-garde country in the field of contemporary music. Yet one could not speak of a Polish national school, because composers came from very varied backgrounds and worked from different angles.

After strictly academic beginnings, **Witold Lutosławski** (1913-1994) drew his inspiration from folk music before approaching dodecaphonism and experimenting with random devices as in his *Venitian Games* and his 2nd Symphony, probably his best composition. in 1970, his cello concerto was created in London by Mstislav Rostropowitch. Less well known, **Tadeusz Baird** (1928-1981), Kazimierz Serocki (1922) and Jan Krenz (1926) formed the 49 Group with the intention of composing serial music of a high artistic standard but more accessible to the listener. The first two co-founded the Warsaw Autumn Festival of contemporary music still acclaimed today. The name of **Andrej Panufnik** (1914) is rather more associated with sound experiments.

Krzysztof Penderecki (1933) is the most famous contemporary Polish composer. His complex musical language is mainly based on musical colour. A master of choral music, he excels in religious compositions. His *Dies Irae* and his *Passion According to St Luke* rank among his most famous works. He also composed a mystical opera, *The Devils of Loudun* (1967), but came back in the 1980s to more traditional, neo-classical forms. His exact contemporary, also inclined towards spiritual quests, **Henrik Mikołaj Gorecki** (1933) composes deeply mystical music such as the famous and peaceful 3rd symphony known as the "symphony of plaintive songs". His two quartets, composed for the Kronos Quartet, are equally remarkable.

OTHER MUSICS

An exponent of minimalist music, **Wojciech Kilar** (1932) is also a great composer of film music, in particular for Polanski for whom he wrote the sound track of *The Pianist*. Other noteworthy composers include **Jan A. P. Kaczmarek** and **Zbigniew Preisner**, official and much appreciated composer of the sound tracks of Kieślowski's last films. Poland also boasts great virtuosi in the field of classical music, such as the tenor Jan Kiepura (1902-1966), the pianist Arthur Rubinstein (1886-1982), a great friend of Szymanowski, the harpsichord player Wanda Landowska (1879-1959) and Witold Malcuzynski. Ignacy Jan Paderewski (1860-1941) should be added to the list: the virtuoso pianist and politician became Prime Minister of the first independent government of the new Poland in 1919.

Internationally known Polish **jazz musicians** include the trumpet player Tomasz Stańko, the saxophonist Zbigniew Namysłowski, the singer Urszula Dudziak and the now legendary pianist Krzystof Komeda (1931-69), who wrote the sound tracks of Polanski's first films.

Gamma/Camera Press/PR/IN/PA

Conductor Krzysztof Penderecki

FOLK ARTS
AND TRADITIONS

Pictures circulated by the media between the postwar period and the 1980s gave a grey and dull account of Polish society. Although the political context was bound to lead to this kind of conclusion, greyness and dullness are not among the original values of Polish culture. Popular arts and folklore, which have come back into the limelight since the opening-up of the country to the world, are full of colour and life. A yearning for bygone days, imagined as better than the present, which often shows through festivals and costumes, is not a Polish specificity. It is common to many countries deeply attached to their cultural and religious roots!

Folk dancers

TRADITIONS PERPETUATED IN SPITE OF HISTORY

Anybody visiting Poland will be surprised by the diversity and endurance of traditions. Whether pagan, religious or, by some mystery, a blend of both, regional cultural features are countless. The Poles' attachment to their roots is all the more intense since the 20C tried its best to destroy them. Marxism never approved what could involve spirituality and recall the memory of Poland before the Communist era. And yet, as soon as the régime collapsed, stables and barns released the memories and rituals of former times. The Polish diaspora, spread throughout the world, contributes to maintain the country's cultural identity by financing all kinds of associations. Those who emigrated always made a point of organising nostalgic reunions, thus keeping alive regional customs and rites. Aware of the attraction this wealth of traditional folklore has on foreigners, each region tries to regulate the succession of events.

Handicraft, traditional music festivals, folk dancing and religious celebrations actively contribute to perfect the colourful festive image that the country wishes to promote. The Festival of Baltic Fishemen, the Festival of Silesian miners, the Beskid Transhumance Festival, the great Easter pilgrimages and the historic reconstructions are excellent tools at the disposal of the public for the discovery of the country.

Traditional architecture

SKANSENS

like many central European countries, Poland boasts numerous skansens. Skansen, a word of Scandinavian origin, refers to an outdoor ethnographic museum gathering together buildings illustrating a region's architectural traditions. Skansens are often laid out in vast parks and include churches, farms, mills, manor houses or simple apiaries. Most of the buildings date from the 17C to the 19C. They are not replicas but authentic dwellings or places of worship carefully taken apart and moved from their original site then reassembled by master craftsmen. Visitors can walk into the dark rooms of farmhouses and look at farming implements or objects of daily life. They can see how the most modest rural homes were suitably equipped to be self-sufficient. Churches, often consecrated, where religious services are still held, are often richer than in towns, for they are looked after by the curators and watched, mostly by elderly people who earn an additional income by working for a few hours in the skansen. One can easily get the impression of walking through a village of the past. Farm animals roam around, adding to the convivial atmosphere. Organisers of festivals or traditional feasts regularly stage these events in skansens.

TRADITIONAL HOUSING, BETWEEN WOOD AND BRICK

It is no accident that skansens first appeared in the cold regions of Sweden and now flourish in central European countries such as Poland. They no doubt offer the best solution (apart from books) for preserving a nation's rural heritage. It is a fact that traditional materials used by people living along the Baltic coast, in the plains of Masovia or in the Tatras mountains did not withstand the test of time. Wood, which always formed the basis of constructions, could, unfortunately, stand up neither to snow and variations in temperature between winter and summer, nor to invaders of all sorts who overran the country torch in hand. It is in the southern and eastern parts of Poland that the tradition of wooden architecture remains the strongest. From the Opole region to Podlasie via the Podhale and Little Poland, there are many wooden farms, villas and churches. In the Zakopane area, wooden constructions are still being built according to aesthetic criteria dating from the end of the 19C. In the heart of Little Poland, wooden houses are often whitewashed then painted in bright colours, in particular blue. In all these regions, roofs are covered with shingles or sometimes thatched. Further north, in Greater Poland or in Pomerania, and east, in Silesia and in the Łódź area, brick replaced wood with the advent of Gothic architecture. Castles, churches and large monuments in towns were often only built during the brick period. As for stone-building which reached its peak all over Europe during the Roman-esque period, there are practically no trace of it left since Poland did not really exist then and therefore few architectural ensembles were built at the end of the Middle Ages. Stone only came back in fashion during the Renaissance. It was thanks to the Italian, French or Northern European architects, who were invited by Polish sovereigns to design their castles or their cities, that it became again a sought-after building material.

There are a few regional specificities such as granite houses in the villages of the Biebrza Valley or half-timbered buildings, dating from the 16C to the 20C, in the vicinity of Swołowo or Kluli on the Baltic coast.

Traditional crafts

In Poland, as in many other countries, it is often difficult to tell the difference between regional handicraft, illustrating a tradition, and a simple souvenir. Anachronic "Russian dolls" are on offer next to jewellery made with amber from the Baltic or Podhale glass icons. There is an impressive amount of handicraft on offer in markets, galleries and on the parking areas of major tourist sites. And yet, during the long Communist period, popular artistic expression, often connected with religious beliefs, was not encouraged. One must conclude that handicraft, like folk dancing and regional costumes was so dear to the heart of the Poles that they could not do without them. The growing tourist industry will certainly not stop the expansion of these crafts. Raw materials such as wood, wool or leather form the basis of traditional crafts. In all the markets one finds legions of **wooden boxes**

Orthodox church in Podlachia

C. Hervé-Bazin / MICHELIN

Easter eggs decorated in the traditional Polish way

carved with geometric or floral motifs. Clothes made from **wool** dyed with natural colouring agents are a reminder that Polish climate can be harsh. Even though **tobacco pouches** and **pottery** are closely linked with Kashubia, **lace** with Little Poland, straw mats and furniture with Podlasie, it is obvious that regional specificities are more or less erased by the expanding tourist trade. Fortunately, a few crafts have retained their authentic creativity.

WYCINANKI OR PAPER CUT-OUTS

In the 19C, peasant women made decorative paper cut-outs using knives and scissors intended for shearing sheep. The technique later improved until the Wycinanki became real paper lace decorations adorning walls and windows; they illustrate symbolic shapes such as moons, stars, arabesques or flowers. Offered to friends, the Wycinanw are also essential elements of religious festivals. The Kurpie region, between Masovia and Podlasie, the Łowicz area and Masovia as a whole are traditionally strongly attached to the Wycinanki tradition.

PISANKA OR DECORATED EGG

Another tradition requiring know-how and precision is that of the **Pisanka** or decorated egg. Once a pagan tradition, it became an Easter symbol celebrating the Resurrection of Christ just like the awakening of nature. These eggs can be found in many shops all over the country, but the tradition originates from the Carpathian regions. The Łemko populations

from Ukraine or Slovakia, the Hutsul from the Romanian Carpathians and the Poles close to Belarusian culture are the initiators of this technique. Eggs are decorated with drawings made with beeswax, and dipped in several coloured liquids. Strong heat then eliminates the coats of wax, revealing 3 or 4 colour motifs which draw their inspiration from various sources, including religious symbols, geometric shapes and only rarely human figures. The eggs are sometimes made of wood and decorated with rough floral motifs.

GLASS PAINTING

Extremely popular since the 18C, paintings on glass were, owing to their low cost, intended for a rural or mountain clientele. Many can still be found today in Little Poland. Themes used are sacred or profane. Glass icons can be seen in many houses, churches and even cemeteries, as in Zakopane's old cemetery. Representations of Mary and Jesus are probably the most frequent. The technique has hardly changed. The

Amber

support is a piece of window glass on which the artist paints a mirror image of his subject. He first draws the outline in gouache then fills in the motifs with colours.

AMBER
FROM THE BALTIQUE

Although amber is sold all over the country, it remains the symbol of the Baltic. This resin, fossilized some 40 million years ago, offered by the sea like a precious gift, is the raw material that contemporary designers continue to cut. Workshops in Gdańsk, Warsaw and large towns turn this "gold of the North" into jewellery, lamps, medals or clocks.

Festivals and feasts

DANCING, COSTUMES
AND FESTIVALS

Polish folk-dancing troupes go all over the world to present shows organized like military parades. The warm colours and the dynamism of the young artists charm their audiences. If they have so much success on the international stage, it is because Polish folklore is so rich and varied. In the 19C, Oskar Kolberg, a learned man, drew up a repertoire of the country's music, songs and dances, taking care to note regional differences. His study is still used as reference.

The **Mazurka**, a dance in triple time, of which Chopin was the main exponent with a contribution of some fifty piano pieces, is one of the most popular dances in Poland and one of the best known throughout the world. It has emigrated to Russia, the US, Sweden and France. Composers as different as Ravel, Debussy or Tchaikowski have drawn their inspiration from it.

A few other dances, either in their classical or flolk version, belong to the country's cultural heritage, including the **Polonaise,** the Kujawiak or the Krakowiak. As its name implies, the latter is one of the leading folk dances of Little Poland. All of them liven up summer festivals and family banquets in traditional inns.

Most Poles find it quite natural to belong to a folk group or to attend the numerous festivals dedicated to regional songs and dances. Caring deeply for one's roots and showing it openly is common in all age groups. The impressive quantity of summer

events, during which all the generations celebrate their cultural background together, therefore comes as no surprise. Women wearing headscarfs, yellow, blue or green silk blouses and full skirts walk onto the stage, eager to dance. They are accompanied by men looking virile and impetuous, wearing sleeveless jackets and peacock feathers on their hats. If you do not have the opportunity of attending one of these festivals, just switch the television on and zap through the regional channels. Some of them are keen on broadcasting events of this kind.

ONT Pologne

Christmas crib in Kraków

Religious festivals

The conviction and faith of Polish Catholics, although shaken by the postwar Communist régimes, continue to influence the life of the country. The consumer society which has been pouring in since the 1990s and the spiritual disengagement which affects many European countries do not seem to make an impression on John-Paul II's compatriots. In addition to Sunday Mass, religious feasts are fervently celebrated.

CHRISTMAS CELEBRATIONS

As in many countries, Christmas in Poland brings families together, whatever their religious convictions. A visit from Father Christmas or St Nicholas is perfectly compatible with the celebration of the birth of Christ. The most fervent observe a short period of fasting before giving in to the temptation from the twelve ritual dishes on the evening of 24 December. Strict observance of the tradition requires abstaining from meat, but carp and pike are on the menu in many homes in addition to mushroom soup, pierogis or stuffed cabbage. For dessert, there are pastries made with white cheese and dried fruit (sernik), and cakes with poppy seeds (makowiec). Then at last it is time for presents! Later on the guests go to church to hear the midnight Mass (Pasterka). The congregation sing Christmas carols and assert their faith while marvelling in front of the crib bathed in light and colour and full of characters.

THE KRAKÓW CRIBS

Even though all churches in Poland have cribs, in Kraków, a real event is organised around the "manger in Bethleem". Every year at the beginning of December, artists exhibit their cribs at the foot of Adam Mickiewicz's statue. For over 60 years now, this competition has gathered together between 130 and 150 cribs, sometimes as tall as a man. They must all draw their inspiration from Kraków's architecture and include some of the town's legendary figures. Jesus can therefore be next to the dragon or the trumpet player playing the Hejnał. After celebrating the winner, the Historical Museum takes charge of the works.

PUPPETS AND WINTER DISGUISE

At Christmas time in the regions of the Beskid, Kraków, Lublin and Rzeszów, some villages uphold the tradition of the collection. Children carrying a star and a crib go from house to house, wishing people happiness in exchange for sweets; they are accompanied by a puppet depicting a Tzigane, a devil, death or an aurochs. If handled well, the latter can have....chattering teeth! The Museum of Lublin Castle exhibits puppets of that kind. The origin of this parade is the story of King Herod ordering the "Massacre of the Innocents".

NEW YEAR AND CARNIVAL

The New-Year and **Carnival** celebrations also offer the opportunity of parading in the company of puppets and masks. Tziganes, Jews, bears, devils or beggars are the characters most often represented. Today these popular events have almost disappeared.

EASTER

This is the second most important celebration. On Palm Sunday, homes are decorated with willow branches covered with white catkins while most Poles paint very elaborate decorative motifs on eggs which are then blessed in church on Holy Saturday with other food stuff (including a small lamb made of cake or sugar) which will be eaten the next day after Mass. Easter Monday is marked by massive spraying of water in the streets for good luck.

ALL SAINTS' DAY

On this occasion, Polish cemeteries are lit with thousands of candles. Public transports are full of people carrying yellow chrysanthemums and flower stalls do a brisk business.

Military legends

THE LAJKONIK

The richly clothed Tatar chief (the khan) parading on his horse is known by all visitors to Kraków's Market Square. The legend goes back to 1287, when the Tatars invaded the town. One night, the inhabitants of the village of Zwierzyniec summoned up their courage and attacked the Tatar camp, killing the khan. This brave deed continues to be celebrated in Kraków. An actor, disguised as the Khan, walks around the Cloth Hall, thus perpetuating the tradition. In addition, every year in June, on the last day of the Corpus Christi week, a grand costumed procession makes its way from Zwierzyniec to the Market Square. The Lajkonik walks along the streets in search of a few złotys, gently beating those who contribute; according to the modern legend, fortune will smile on them later. As for the mayor of the town, it costs him a few glasses of wine!

THE BROTHERHOOD OF THE ROOSTER

The Brotherhood of the Rooster is 700 years old. Archers, crossbowmen and arquebusiers used their skills to protect their villages and strongholds. These occasional warriors were not soldiers but tradesmen, bourgeois or craftsmen and they belonged to a Brotherhood which adopted the rooster, symbolizing night watching, as its emblem. Kraków continues to celebrate the

Brotherhood of the Rooster, Kraków

descendants of these brave marksmen. On the first Monday after the eight days of the Corpus Christi Feast, the members of the present-day Brother-hood of the Rooster parade in medieval costume and challenge each other in friendly fashion during great competitions...by aiming at wooden roosters.

KULIG, A WINTER GAME

The kulig in its original form has gone for ever. Even though some people are trying to make it fashionable again, it is impossible to imagine that it could regain its former craze! The kulig was a game reserved for wealthy aristocrats wishing to relax and amuse themselves during the Christmas festivities or around Ash Wednesday. It consisted in a cavalcade of horse-drawn carts filled with jolly fellows who went across the countryside from manor to manor. They danced, ate and drank a lot until they didn't feel the cold anymore. Some were disguised as priests, others as Tziganes or Jews. The 20C put a stop to this somewhat excessive amusement, but the principle seems to be coming back with the help of tourists and the advent of a well-off young generation.

Polish cooking

Copious and rich in calories, Polish cuisine has skillfully appropriated the various influences of the populations who occupied the country over the centuries. The Baltic, the numerous lakes and rivers, the mountain ranges and the great plains provide each region with its specific products.

ALL OVER POLAND

Soups

Any good meal starts with soup and Poland having as wide a choice of soups as France has of cheeses, you will be offered mushroom soup, sorel soup, sauerkraut soup or crayfish soup served with a varied selection of ravioli or meat balls. The most common soups on the menus of restaurants or private homes are:

Barchtche which belongs to the History of cuisine. In the old days, country people prepared this soup from sour fruit picked in forests. Later beetroot replaced these berries. The sour taste was preserved by adding fermented beetroot juice (**kwas**), lemon or vinegar.

Żurek, or white barchtche, which is just as popular, is a soup made from fermented rye flour juice served with salami.

And finally **flaki po warszawsku** or **Warsaw-style tripe** which is a mixture of shin of beef and tripe seasoned with paprika, ginger and nutmeg.

Meat

Whether grilled, coated with breadcrumbs, or covered with onions or prunes, **pork** is the Poles' favourite meat.

Poultry follows closely. Polish-style chicken, stuffed with breadcrumbs, egg and parsley, and duck stuffed with pieces of apple and soaked in red wine while cooking are the two most famous recipes.

The many nature areas and dense forests offer a choice of **game**. Hare, wild boar and roe-deer are particularly appreciated by hunters' families or by those who know where to find this kind of meat. As for **partridge**, once it is stuffed with bread soaked in milk, currants and juniper, it reminds young generations that, in the old days, royal and feudal hunts always ended with gargantuan feasts.

Beef is not so well liked, except for **steak tartare** the origin of which goes back to the times when Mongol horsemen invaded central Europe, stocking their supply of raw meat under their saddle.

Fish

On the fish side, Polish cuisine is privileged in being able to use only choice fish or very tasty ones: **sturgeon** from the Baltic, **pike** from pure fresh-water streams, or **pikeperch** from the lakes. **Carp**, which is probably the most commonly found fish on restaurant menus year-round, becomes a traditional festive dish on Christmas eve in homes all over Poland. As for **herring**, it is a popular cheap dish: laid out in small rolls stuffed with cucumber and hard-boiled egg or marinated in a mixture of oil and onions. Herring and vodka go very well together, it seems.

Polish trilogy

Pierogi are small crescent-shaped ravioli made from a simple dough consisting of flour, water, eggs and salt. This forms the base of a large number or creative variations. Among the most common are the Russian-style pierogi filled with white cheese, onions and potatoes, others being stuffed with mushrooms and cabbage. As a dessert, pierogi are filled with fruit: cherries, strawberries or bilberries.

Marinated cucumbers (ogórki kiszone) are eaten throughout the meal. As an appetizer with beer, as a first course or as a main course with other vegetables. These cucumbers are picked before they are ripe and look more like gherkins. They are pickled in brine made with cherry, vine and oak leaves, dill, coriander and a spoonful of white vinegar and brandy. They are reckoned to reduce the effect of vodka, which remains to be verified!

Cabbage is used in many ways, raw and cooked, but it is also the essential ingredient of a dish unanimously appreciated by Polish gourmets, bigos. Served as a first course or as a meal in itself, this kind of Polish-style sauerkraut is a mixture of several types of cabbage, pork, mutton or veal, game, mushrooms and even prunes, seasoned with many spices such as hot pepper from Jamaica, cardamom or nutmeg, not forgetting Madeira.

REGIONAL CUISINE

In Masuria and Warmia, forests and lakes are an inexhaustible source of high-quality products such as **fish dumplings** or pikeperch served with **crayfish tails**. More unusual are goose or duck's-blood soup (czernina z golcami), and **Masurian gingerbread** (piernik) flavoured with chicory.

Anyone interested in drawing up a list of all the recipes based on **potatoes** should definitely go to Poland. Potato croquettes, mashed potato, potato noodles, potato soup, potato salad... potatoes are everywhere. More original are **onions stuffed with mushrooms** (gały cebulowe).

Smoked cheese from Oscypek

The high number of miners in need of sustaining food and the proximity of Germany, Austria and the Czech Republic had a significant influence on Silesian cuisine. Specialities include the following: **Silesian noodles** made from potatoes; **krupniok**, made from offal, buckwheat flour and blood; **Silesian stuffed roll**, consisting of a slice of beef seasoned with mustard and stuffed with bacon, sausages and cucumbers pickled in salt.

The Polish court, for a long time based in Kraków, made it a point of honour to have a variety of European dishes on her menu. **Hungarian goulash**, **Vienna schnitzel** or **Russian-style pierogi** are quite at home in Little Poland.

Oscypek, a smoked cheese made from ewe's milk in shepherds' huts and **bryndza**, another cheese made from ewe's milk but unsmoked, are the tasty ambassadors of the Podhale region. Oscypek is on sale on the pavements of Zakopane. Cut into slices, covered with dill and heated in an oven for a few minutes, it goes very well with brandy.

Charcuterie from Kurpie, a small region situated between Masovia and Podlasie, is renowned for its smoking technique using **juniper wood**. Juniper also flavours a local beer that is reputed to give credence to the toast, «To your health»! Except in the region along the border with Germany, around Zielona Góra, Polish wine-growing is nonexistent.

POLAND TODAY

Since 1989, Poland has been faced with a gigantic task: that of moving from a state-controlled economic system and an authoritarian goverment to a market economy and potitical democracy. This "metamorphosis" could not be achieved without radically changing society, mentalities and traditions. What stage has Poland reached today?

Celebrating the entry of Poland into the European Union, Warsaw, April 30 2004

Democracy in Poland

A LARGE, HOMOGENEOUS AND RATHER YOUNG POPULATION

With **38.1 million inhabitants**, Poland represents 8.4% of the EU population. However, since 1999, the Polish population has been going down slowly. This is due to a lower birth rate, to a death rate which is still fairly high (over 8%) and to a definitely negative migration balance (many Poles leave to find work in other EU countries).

Poles form around **97 %** of the country's population, the remainder consisting eessentially of Germans, Ukrainians and Belarusians. The Polish population is one of the youngest in Europe, even though it is gradually getting older. People over 65 represent only 13% of the population and over one third of the total number of inhabitants is under 25. Life expectancy is still lower by three years than the EU average, the main cause being neither the excessive intake of alcohol and tobacco nor the rich food and the deterioration of the health service, but pollution.

RAPID ECONOMIC TRANSITION

In 1989, the country's economic situation was alarming: hyper-inflation (700%), enormous debts, an obsolete, inefficient industry and backward agriculture. The **state-controlled system** which had been the rule for over forty years, had prevented the Poles, at least partially, from realising that the world was changing. As early as 1990, the Minister of Finance, L. Balcerowicz, imposed "**radical remedies**" on the country in order to launch it into the market economy. These reforms continued to be implemented even though, between 1993 and 1997, the left being in power slowed down the process of privatisation. The return of Balcerowicz as Minister of Finance in 1997 attest the people's will to continue his policy of reforms: **massive privatisations**, development of the free market rules, radical decrease of public debts and inflation, convertibility and reinforcement of the złoty, creation of the Warsaw stock exchange, income tax levied on individuals and a value-added tax (VAT). The aim was simple: maintain a **6-7 % growth** in order to reduce the gap between Poland and EU countries. This vigorous policy paid off: the GNP increased by 42% between 1990 and

2002 and inflation is now stabilised around 2-3%. Although it reached 5.4% in 2005, the growth rate has been slowing down, in particular because of the unfavourable economic climate in the EU. It could very well go down to 3.5% in the years to come. It was mainly the 2 million small and medium-sized businesses created in the trade and services sector (food and computing stores, clothes shops, car dealers...) which helped boost the Polish economy and employment. They employ 55% of the working population and produce 1/3 of the GNP. However, they have to compete with foreign hypermarkets (Leclerc, Auchan, Carrefour, Casino-Géant, Ikea Decathlon, Leroy Merlin...). In fact foreign buyouts mainly concerned the most lucrative sectors: alcohol (Polmos bought by Bacardi and Pernod-Ricard), telecommunications (TPSA bought by France Télécom)...

Today, it is considered that privatisations are finished. Three examples illustrate the creation of factories by large companies, **Michelin** in the field of tyres, Dell in computing and the much earlier case of Fiat established before 1939. The private sector now generates 80% of the economic activity even though the public sector still employs 1/3 of the working population. In spite of this, tricky problems are plentiful. **Agriculture** employs almost a quarter of the working population (on small plots averaging 6ha) and only produces 4% of the GNP. At least half of the two million farms will disappear during the coming years and the others will have to be radically modernized. Other difficulties arise from the coal **mines**, which are showing a loss and are in debt, and from the steel industry which requires heavy investments as well as massive lay-offs.

INSTITUTIONAL AND ADMINISTRATIVE REFORMS

In 1997, Poland acquired a new **Constitution**, the previous one dating from 1952. Today, Poland's institutions are similar to those of France. Executive power is in the hands of a **President, elected by universal suffrage** for a five-year term renewable once, who has a right of veto in Parliament. Legislative power belongs to **two houses**, elected by direct universal suffrage for four years, the Diet (460 members elected by revised proportional representation, which gives a bonus to the largest parties) and the Senate (100 members elected by majority vote). In 1998 a reform of administrative autonomy introduced a third degree of decentralisation (districts or powiaty) and the number of regions (województwo) was reduced from 49 to 16.

THE DIFFICULT LEGACY OF THE OPPOSITION

Democratization saw the emergence of a **great number of short-lived parties.** There is a proverb that says: "where 4 Poles are gathered, there are already 5 political parties". Among the main parties, the oldest are those on the left, in particular the **SLD** (Democratic Left Alliance), formed from the ruins of the former Communist party. Samoobrona (Self-Defence), the populist agrarian party led by A. Lepper, which caught the public's attention, claims to be situated on the extreme left. The anti-communist movement extended, after 1989, from the centre to the extreme right. The **intellectual, democratic trend** was represented by different parties in succession, including the Freedom Union (UW) whose main representatives are T. Mazowiecki, B. Geremek, L. Balcerowicz. **The liberal trend** is led by the PO, Civic Platform, founded in 2001 by men such as D. Tusk and J. Rokita. The conservative and Christian-Democrat trend is represented by the **PiS** (Right and Justice, also founded in 2001) with the twins Jarosław and Lech Kaczyński (the country's current President) and Kazimierz Marcinkiewicz (current Prime Minister). Finally, the League of Polish Families (LPR) is an ultra-Catholic, nationalist and anti-European party.

To purge or not to purge?

The compromise reached during the "Round Table" talks in 1989 provided for a peaceful transition from the Communist system to democracy and excluded a purge of the civil service. The second left/right cohabitation even implemented a processus of general redemption which culminated in 2004-05 when L. Wałęsa agreed to meet W. Jaruzelski on a television set and when the leader of Solidarność and President A. Kwaśniewski invited each other to official and even private functions. And yet, for a few years now, the question of the purge or "lustration" has become fashionable again. Poland has not, until now, made the Communist archives public, unlike other East European countries. However, in February 2005, after the release on the Internet of a list of 240 000 names, the debate was reopened within Polish society and the nationalist right made lustration one of its war horses.

CHANGES IN POWER AND "COHABITATION"

In 1989-1990, the right wing held the Presidency (L. Wałęsa) and Parliament. In September 1993, the legislative elections brought the victory of the left wing taking advantage of the population's discontent linked with the rapid social and economic reforms. This first change in power, shared at the time by other east-European countries, was marked by a short cohabitation; in November 1995, L. Wałęsa was beaten at the presidential election by A. Kwaśniewski, a former Communist of the SLD, reelected on the first ballot in October 2000. The period 1997-2001 was in turn marked by a left/right power-sharing, known as "cohabitation", ending in September 2001 when the legislative elections were won by a left-wing coalition. But the political climate turned sour: split of the governmental coalition in March 2003, scandals linked with corruption and increasing unpopularity of the Prime Minister, replaced in May 2004. In September and October 2005, the legislative and presidential elections led to the second change in power: the right wing came back and the left wing was crushed. However, the high level of abstention (between 50 and 60%) confirmed the politicians' representation crisis.

A RADICALLY TRANSFORMED SOCIETY

Poland's **GNP** per inhabitant is twice as low as the EU average and the IDH which measures the level achieved in terms of life expectancy, education and income per inhabitant, ranks the country 36th in the world. The average salary is around €500 net per month (€200 for the guaranteed minimum wage), but this average is distorted by very high salaries, in particular in Warsaw where they are twice as high as anywhere else. **Unemployment**, a real national calamity, concerns around 3 million people (18% of the working population) including 85% who do not get unemployment benefits (benefits are only paid for six months and are in the region of €150 per month). Young people under 25 and the over 45 who have no diplomas are worst off. About 30% of the total income of households comes from State assistance. However, budget restrictions and price increases make life difficult for the most under-privileged who think that their country has moved from the era of full wallets and empty shops to that of full shops and empty wallets. In spite of the evident emergence of the middle classes in large towns, Poland still functions on **two levels**: there are those who were able to follow the modern economic movement and the others. Health and education are also on two different planes: private establishments , which have very high fees and public establishments, forced by budget restrictions to be less well equipped and understaffed. The pensions' reform (the country has 9.5 million pensioners) is underway, combining some capitalisation with the present share-out system but many elderly people are obliged to have financial help from their children. One of the consequences of these difficulties is the existence of a black market economy which is believed to represent over a quarter of the GNP and to involve over one million people who do not declare their work and their income although they sometimes receive social benefits.

An education system undergoing sweeping reforms

Poland has, since the 1990s, become aware of the necessity of reforming its education system: the adult population included only 7% graduates and differences between regions were important, in particular between town and country. Responsibility for the school network was transferred to local authorities, teacher training was developed, school-leaving age was raised to 18, levels were modified to match European and American systems (development of nursery schools, creation of colleges or gimnazjums, and of vocational schools). In 2005, the school-leaving certificate (matura) became a national exam, less dependent on the appreciation of individual establishments, which should, in the future, enable pupils to enter a higher-education establishment without having to take an entrance exam. In 1989, only 10% of the 19-24 age group undertook higher-education studies, today their number has risen to 40%, even though half of them only attend weekend or evening classes (paying) because they have another activity during the week or the day. But the 5% of the GNP that the State spends on education (the OECD's average) are still insufficient in view of the country's demographic pattern. One of the consequences of this situation is the flourishing of private establishments. The majority of nursery schools and 2/3 of higher-education providers are now private. In towns, advertisements for fee-paying language tuition abound.

FRANCO-POLISH FRIENDSHIP

In 1991, the presidents of both republics, L. Wałęsa and F. Mitterrand signed a treaty of friendship and solidarity between the two countries, the term solidarity having in fact never been used before in diplomatic language. In 2004, the Polish Season in France, Nowa Polska, enabled French and Polish people to celebrate and rediscover the history of a close and unusual relationship between the two peoples, who never fought each other, a very rare example in European history. This closeness is symbolized by the love stories of Marie-Louise de Gonzague and Ladisław IV, Marie d'Arquien (Marysieńka) and Jan III Sobieski, Maria Leszczyńska and Louis XV, Maria Walewska and Napoleon Bonaparte, George Sand and Chopin, Mme Hanska and Honoré de Balzac, Maria Skłodowska and Pierre Curie or, more recently, Sophie Marceau and Andrzej Żuławski. It may be a known fact that Polish borrowed many words from French ("à propos, vis-à-vis, cul-de-sac, dossier, en face, enfant terrible, passe-partout, calembour, fondue, pruderie, fiole, abat-jour, paysage, gendarmerie, garde-robe…") but the reverse is also true: riding ("calèche, cravache"), pastries ("baba, meringue"), clothes ("chapskas") not forgetting dances such as mazurkas, polkas and polonaises.

Poland in the EU

BETWEEN THE EU AND THE US?

As early as 1994, Poland clearly showed its economic inclination towards the EU and its military inclination towards the US: the country applied for EU membership and, at the same time, joined NATO's "Partnership for Peace Agreement". In May 1997, Poland was invited into the **Atlantic Alliance** (in fact, full membership became official on 12 March 1999) and, in December, the country's application for EU membership was accepted. In Copenhagen in 2002, Poland was one of the ten countries designated to join the EU (membership came into effect on 1 May 2004). In 2003, there was a hardening of West-European opinion following Poland's decision to support the US intervention in Irak and to buy F-16 planes rather than French Mirages or Swedish Gripen. However, the referendum on EU membership in June 2003 was

Symbol of Poland in the European Union

a success in Poland: 77.4% of the population voted "yes", but the Poles rejected the project of European constitution in favour of the Nice Treaty (2000), which gave them more bargaining power. The European Parliament election in June 2004 was marked by a record abstention rate (almost 80%) and nearly half the new Polish members of the European Parliament can be said to be Euro-sceptics. However, the success of Poland's entry into the EU is gradually gaining the approval of the most reticent: farmers, who were very pessimistic two years ago, had to admit that direct European subsidies were flooding in at the rate of 55 euros per ha (nearly 1.5 billion euros paid to 1.4 million farmers representing 85% of all farmers) and that exports of farm produce (milk, sugar beet, meat, cheese, butter) had increased by over 40% since membership came into force. Today, the EU is Poland's main trading partner (70% of exports and 60% of imports) and it brings into the country 3/5 of foreign capitals. Poland could, within a few years, join the euro zone but no date has yet been fixed since the country's budget deficit (nearly 4% of the GNP) is higher than the European limits. As for the opening of the labour market, it depends on bilateral agreements: the United Kingdom, Ireland, Sweden and Switzerland are, for the moment, the only countries to have signed agreements with Poland. Over half a million Poles have tried their luck in Europe since Poland's entry in the EU. Many of them are seasonal workers, who are already back, but members of the medical and computing profession opt for longer stays.

DIFFICULT RELATIONS WITH THE NEIGHBOURS

In November 1990, Poland signed with Germany an "Agreement of friendship and neighbourly relations", guaranteeing the inviolability of the borders and the rights of the German minority in Poland. In August 1991, the meeting of the Polish, German and French foreign-affairs ministers marked the timid beginning of a trilateral cooperation known as the **Weimar Triangle**. In addition, four **Euro-regions** are developing on the western border. However, the memory of the atrocities perpetrated by the Nazis is still very present in the mind of the Poles and when Berlin speaks of the dramatic situation endured by six million Germans "displaced" in 1945 or the possible compensations their descendants could claim, feelings run high. The recent gas pipeline project between Russia and Germany, which by-passes Poland, was also the source of heated arguments. Since Poland partly depends on Russia for its oil, she must humour V Poutine in spite of serious disagreements. The recent diplomatic crisis between Poland and Belarus, close to Moscow, shows that relations between these countries are not yet normalized. It is no longer the case with **Ukraine**: the Poles were the staunchest supporters of the "orange revolution" which led the pro-western side to power to the great displeasure of Moscow. There are still many Poles living around L'viv and economic relations between the two countries are important. Warsaw has stepped up security checks along this border to be ready to join the Schengen area but her visa policy is very supple. Three Euro-regions were set up on the eastern border. To the

Polonia

Poland has, for the past century, had a strong emigration tradition, the most important waves of emigrants taking place between 1900 and 1918 and after 1945. Nearly fifteen million Poles or persons of Polish origin live abroad. They form "Polonia", so dear to the heart of the Poles in the "old country" since almost every family has relatives abroad.

Nearly ten million of them live in the US (particularly in Chicago), almost 2 million live in Russia and in the former Soviet republics, one and a half million in Germany and one million in France. There are also Polish minorities in Canada, Brazil, Australia and the United Kingdom.

south, Poland founded in February 1991, together with Hungary and Czechoslovakia, a group known as **Visegrad** to reinforce the positions of the three partners in the processus of European integration. Seven Euro-regions were created on the southern border. To the north, Poland is a member of the Council of Baltic States and a Euro-region was created.

THE IMPORTANCE OF THE CHURCH

With around **95 % of Catholics,** including over 60% who practise their religion, Poland is one of the few countries of Europe where religion is so important. Attendance at the 15 000 churches and chapels is still high and Sunday Mass gathers church-goers of all ages. Every year on 15 August, 4 to 5 million pilgrims go to Częstochowa to pray in front of the icon of the Black Virgin, the protector and patron saint of Poland. The number

Welcoming the Pope in Gdańsk

of marriages remains high (marriage in church is recognized by the law) and the average age for a first marriage is around 27 (against 30 in the EU). The two cohabitations nevertheless revealed some differences of opinion about the place of religion in the State (in particular on the question of abortion, the concordat and sexual education in public schools). Some people today object to what they consider as an excessive involvement of the church in political affairs or to the verbal faux pas of certain Catholic fundamentalists who can be heard on Radio Maryja, on the Trwam television channel or who express their ideas in the Nasz Dziennik daily newspaper.

SOLIDARITY AND FAMILY TRADITIONS

The Poles can at first appear slightly cold or obsequious to a European from the West; this is mainly due to variations in social behaviour. In Poland, you would rarely greet someone you meet but don't know yet you would use several polite phrases when introduced. This is when you can really discover the extent of the Poles' hospitality: a Pole will do everything he can to help you if you are in difficulty. From the dark hours of their history, the Poles have retained an acute sense of duty, towards themselves and their family but also towards others and towards their nation. Family ties are particularly strong, especially since the shortage and high cost of housing often compel several generations to live under the same roof, even though the divorce rate is rising. Houses and apartments are often still blessed on 6 January and the first letters of the name of the Three Kings are then written with chalk on the doors. Respect between generations is very high, although misunderstandings sometimes arise between those who spent most of their life under the Communist régime (the over-45s), those who lived during both periods (the 30-or-so-year-olds) and the young who were born after the mid-80s.

Religious feasts offer the opportunity of gathering the whole family and often friends as well. **Christmas** is the most important feast in the year. It is celebrated three days running by the whole Polish population. Christmas Eve (Wigilia) officially starts when the first star appears in the sky. Before the beginning of the traditional meal, families share the consecrated bread and exchange good wishes. The meal consists of twelve dishes (without meat but with the famous carp) then children, accompanied by carol singing, discover the presents left by St Nicholas at the foot of the Christmas tree. Later on, the midnight Mass gathers round the crib all the residents of the district.

Easter is the second most important celebration. On Palm Sunday, homes are decorated with branches of willow tree covered with white catkins and most Poles paint elaborate decorative motifs on eggs which are then blessed in church on Good Friday, together with other foodstuff (including small lambs made of pastry or sugar) which will be eaten the next day after Mass. Easter Monday is marked by massive spraying of water in the streets for good luck.

Finally, on All Saints' Day, Polish cemeteries are lit with thousands of candles.

Weekends are also privileged moments for the Poles who recharge their batteries in the country (barbecues on lake shores during the fine season, mountain activities in winter). Contrary to what happens on working days, when meal times are disturbed, weekends make it possible to enjoy the five traditional meals, breakfast at 9am, a second "breakfast" at midday, then lunch at 3pm, "tea" at 5pm and dinner at 8pm. The main meal takes place in the middle of the afternoon (oblad) and usually includes soup, a main course with meat and crudités and sometimes a cake for dessert, served with tea or a fruit tea (kompot), even vodka or wine on special occasions.

Warsaw by night

A. Galy / MICHELIN

Warsaw★★★

Warszawa

POPULATION 1 688 944 – MAP OF POLAND A2 – WOJEWÓDZTWO OF MASOVIA

Lying on the border of East and West and described by writer Witold Gombrowicz as "the place where eastern and western cultures are abolished", Warsaw looks like no other European town. A martyr of the Second World War which literally reduced it to ashes, it gives the impression of being a vast building site with an odd mixture of reconstructed picturesque prewar districts and Baroque edifices, of concrete Stalinist blocks and ultramodern buildings. Yet even if this urban anarchism tends to baffle visitors and locals alike, it nevertheless reflects the unique moving personality of this unusual capital, the showcase of Poland's past sufferings and ambitions for the future.

- ▶ **Getting your bearings** – 294km from Kraków and 343km from Gdánsk.
- 👁 **Not to be missed** – The Old Town, the Palace of Culture and Science, the Łazienki Park, the Jewish memorials.
- 🕐 **Planning your visit** – Allow 2 days to see the main sights, 3 days to add a themed tour (see box).
- 👫 **With your children** – The Fotoplastikon, the zoo and numerous parks.

Visiting Warsaw

Warsaw is a vast conurbation through which flows the **Wisła**. Lying on the west bank, to the north, are the reconstructed old districts: the **Old Town** and the **New Town**. Farther south is the **Centre**, a business area centred round the Palace of Culture and Science, and the old residential districts of **Żoliborz** and **Mokotów** and finally, further south still are two large **parks, Ujazdowski** and **Łazienki** as well as **Wilanów Palace.** The city's main thoroughfare known as the Royal Way forms a north-south axis from the Old Town down to Wilanów. Located on the east bank, the working-class **Praga**, the only district that escaped destruction during the war, seems to have found a new lease of life thanks to the many artists who are settling there.

Warsaw in three days

1st day – Start from the Castle Square, then walk through the streets of the Old Town and of the New Town . After having lunch in this area, you can go back to the Castle Square and from there walk down the Royal Way) (Krakowskie Przedmieście and Nowy Świat).

2nd day – After exploring the Palace of Culture and the surrounding district, take a stroll through Ujazdowski and Łazienki parks and visit Wilanów Palace.

3rd day – If you are interested in sights connected with Jewish culture, follow our itinerary through the former Ghetto and visit the Museum of the Warsaw Uprising. You can also explore the National Museum.

Background

Prior to being Poland's capital – Warsaw entered history relatively late: although evidence of a first settlement dates from the 10C, it was only at the end of the 13C that the new city was built on the hill where the royal castle now stands. After it became the capital of the duchy of Masovia in 1413, the town expanded rapidly both economically and culturally. When the duchy was incorporated into the Kingdom of Poland in 1526, on the death of the last Masovian prince, Warsaw became the obvious choice as the seat of political power of the new kingdom established in 1569 by the Treaty of Lublin joining Lithuania and Poland. The Diet (legislative assembly) immediately decided to have its headquarters here and in 1573, Warsaw was, for the first time the chosen venue for the coronation of King Sigismund III who, after his Wawel castle was destroyed by fire, finally agreed to the centralisation of royal power and officially transferred the capital from Kraków to Warsaw in 1596.

A capital symbolizing a painful national history – Its new status placed the town at the heart of the long and painful chapter of Polish history which soon began. Indeed, from the mid-17C to the Second World War, Poland and Warsaw entered into

Warsaw by Canaletto (1778), National Museum, Warsaw

a period of incessant conflicts and wars. Between 1655 and 1658, the Swedes and the Transylvanians invaded the kingdom on three occasions and plundered the Polish capital. Ruined and robbed of its cultural assets, Warsaw continued to decline slowly until Saxon princes, under pressure from Russia and Austria, undertook to rebuild, extend and embellish the town between 1697 and 1763. By creating the "Saxon Axis", perpendicular to the Royal Way, and establishing their residence in its centre, they opened the way for a new era of urban planning characterised in particular by the construction of large vistas. Stanisław II Poniatowski, Catherine of Russia's candidate elected in 1764, a young, forward-looking monarch and a great art lover, completed Warsaw's transformation into a modern urban centre and encouraged the construction of Baroque and later Classical edifices. The second half of the 18C thus marked the "**Golden Age**" of Warsaw by then the undisputed centre of the country's political, economic, commercial and industrial life as well as the centre of Polish Enlightenment. However, in 1795, following the third Partition of Poland, Warsaw was annexeeed by Prussia and lost it status as political and artistic capital. It regained some of its influence during the interlude of the Grand Duchy of Warsaw (1806-15) which gave back to the Poles their own government and central administration, but the Congress of Vienna soon put the town under Russian control. The Russians' liberal attitude did not, however, hinder the economic and intellectual development of Warsaw and the first university was inaugurated in 1818. In 1831, the failure of the anti-Russian uprising led to severe reprisals: Warsaw was relegated to the rank of mere provincial town and its cultural and educational establishments were purely and simply closed. It was only at the onset of the First World War that Russian domination began to falter, giving way to the German army who occupied the town. Polish independence was only regained in 1918 and Warsaw became once more the capital of a free country.

Recovery plans for the ruined economy, the restoration of an independent national administration, programmes of urban planning, of land and social reforms, the reopening of places of worship and of educational establishments: as the seat of power, Warsaw was the focus of attention of the population whose expectations were high. Unfortunately, once again, the people's hopes for a new lease of life and all the energy they poured into rebuilding their city were shattered at the outbreak of the Second World War.

The Warsaw Mermaid

Once upon a time, two sister mermaids lived on the shores of the Baltic. One day, they got lost while swimming; the first one, who was stranded in the Danish straits, now sits at the entrance to Copenhagen's harbour. The second swam up the Wisła and, on her way, met two lovers, Wars and Sawa; she asked them to found the town and to give it their combined firstnames. Promising to stay and come to the rescue of Warsaw's inhabitants whenever they were in danger, the little mermaid, armed with a sword and a shield, became the emblem of the town.

The Second World War – In September 1939, Hitler invaded Poland and, within a few weeks, Warsaw was occupied by the German army. This marked the beginning of the darkest years of the town's history: its leaders were deported or imprisoned, educational establishments were closed once more and, as early as 1940, the entire Jewish population was transferred to a **ghetto** area and subjected to repressive measures and starvation. When, at the beginning of the summer of 1944, Hitler's army began to pull back as Soviet troops moved forward, the Polish resistance movement organised an **uprising** in order to hasten the liberation of Warsaw. However, this heroic initiative proved to be a disaster: armed clashes, unsupported by the Russian allies, left 200 000 dead on the Polish side. Wild with rage and a desire for vengeance, Hitler ordered the systematic destruction of the Polish capital. At the end of the war, 850 000 Warsaw residents, i.e. two thirds of the population, were either dead or missing. Warsaw, reduced to ashes, was no more than a name on the map of Europe.

A capital city in the process of radical transformation – For a while, one of the courses of action contemplated was to leave Warsaw in ruins, as a kind of open-air museum of the horrors of the Second World War. The idea was eventually abandoned and Warsaw was patiently rebuilt. Since the collapse of the communist regime, the town has, for the first time in its history, fully recovered the status of political, economic and cultural capital of Poland. The resurrection of Warsaw, a city in perpetual change, is a history lesson for the whole of humanity.

1 The City's Old Districts PLAN II

It is no doubt paradoxical to use the term "old districts" for a town practically razed to the ground and rebuilt... and yet you will have the definite impression of discovering urban areas constructed over the past centuries and now called: the Old Town (Stare Miasto) which used to include some medieval monuments, the New Town (Nowe Miasto) built in the 17C and 18C, the Theatre-Opera district (19C) and the Royal Way.

THE OLD TOWN (STARE MIASTO)★★

The Old Town is entirely pedestrianised; it is possible to find parking space in the adjacent streets. Allow 2hr for the tour of the area, half a day if you include a visit to the museums. It is advisable to try and avoid the weekend crowds of tourists.

WARSAW Plan I

0   250   500 m

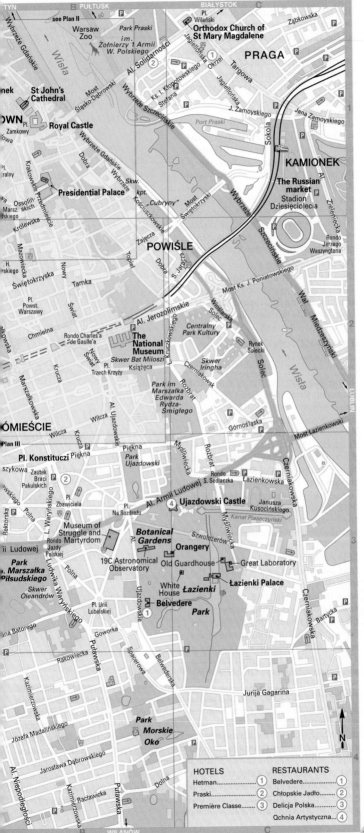

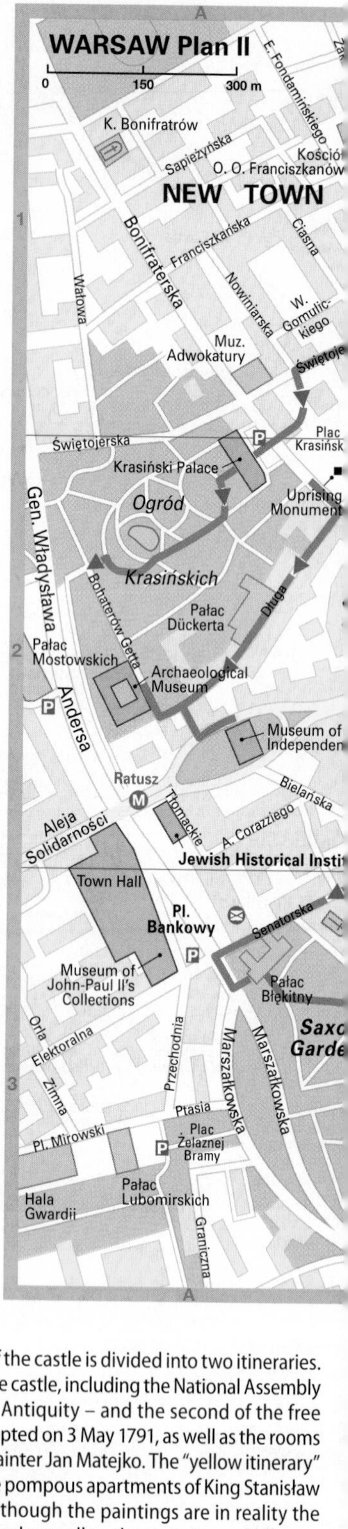

The Old Town forms one of Warsaw's finest architectural ensembles, but above all the most poignant evidence of the Polish nation's will to recover her honour scorned by the ravages of the Second World War. Entirely destroyed, it was meticulously rebuilt after reproductions dating from the 18C, essentially with funds donated by the Polish diaspora and thanks to the tenacity of the voluntary work force. In 1982, this unprecedented undertaking earned the town a place on Unesco's World Heritage List. Bordered on the east by the River Wisła above which it towers (the best viewpoint over the city is located in Praga on the opposite bank) and in the west by its ramparts, the Old Town features a picturesque central market square (Rynek) surrounded by a grid-plan network of streets.

The obvious starting point of a tour of the Old Town is **Castle Square**(Plac Zamkowy) with, in its centre, the **bronze column of King Sigismund III** (1644). From there, the tour continues along the colourful paved streets.

The Royal Castle

(Zamek Królewski)★ B2

Plac Zamkowy 4. ☎657 21 70. Sun-Mon 11am-6pm, Tue-Sat 10am-6pm, last admission 1hr before closing. 18/12 PLN, free admission on Sunday. Guided tours by appointment, daily except Sun, 85 PLN. Allow 2hr for the visit.

Erected in the 14C then remodelled in Baroque style, the Royal Castle was the home of the dukes of Masovia and of the kings of Poland before becoming the seat of Parliament and then, from 1918 onwards the official residence of the President of the Republic. After the war, the communist authorities were not in favour of its reconstruction which was finally undertaken in 1971 under pressure from the country's intellectual elite. The main structure and interiors of the castle were completed in 1988, whereas the Kubicki arcades in the inner courtyard and the adjoining Tin-roofed Palace (Pałac pod Blachą) were still undergoing restoration work in 2005. Although the building is a replica, most of the castle's paintings and furniture, taken to a safe place at the beginning of the war, are originals. The visit of the castle is divided into two itineraries. The "blue itinerary" covers the main parts of the castle, including the National Assembly where the first European Constitution since Antiquity – and the second of the free world after that of the United States – was adopted on 3 May 1791, as well as the rooms containing frescoes by the famous romantic painter Jan Matejko. The "yellow itinerary" leads through the most prestigious rooms: the pompous apartments of King Stanisław August Poniatowski, the Canaletto Room (although the paintings are in reality the work of his nephew Bellotto), the Royal Chapel as well as the sumptuous Ballroom where Polish high society used to waltz away under the captivating allegorical fresco by Bacciarelli, *The Dissolution of Chaos*. On Sundays, there is only one itinerary offering a selection of rooms from the above itineraries.

WARSAW Plan II

0   150   300 m

NEW TOWN

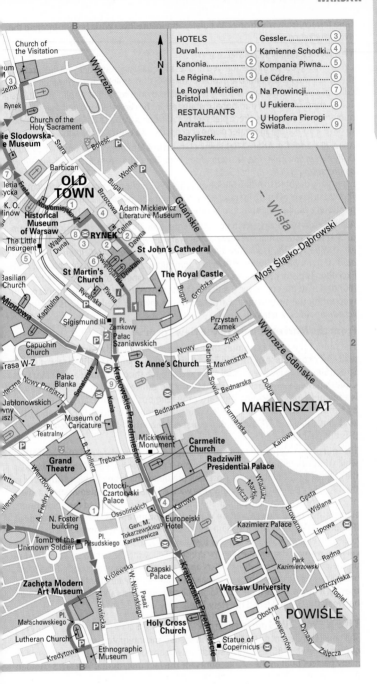

HOTELS
Duval.................... ①
Kanonia................. ②
Le Régina.............. ③
Le Royal Méridien
Bristol.................. ④

Gessler.................. ③
Kamienne Schodki.. ④
Kompania Piwna..... ⑤
Le Cédre............... ⑥
Na Prowincji.......... ⑦
U Fukiera.............. ⑧
U Hopfera Pierogi
Swiata................. ⑨

RESTAURANTS
Antrakt................. ①
Bazyliszek............. ②

St John's Cathedral (Archikatedra Św. Jana)★ B2

Ul. Świętojańska 8

This is the town's oldest and main place of worship. Built in Gothic style at the beginning of the 14C, the cathedral contains the Renaissance tombs of the last Masovian princes and a 16C Crucifix with real hair on Christ's head. In addition, the crypt houses the ashes of famous Poles, such as Henryk Sienkewicz, awarded the Nobel Prize for literature in 1905, and pianist Ignacy Paderewski.

Dziekania Street, on the right of the cathedral, leads to the pretty triangular Kanonia Place, lined with **houses** which once belonged to the **canons** of the Warsaw Chapter. Note, in the centre, a bronze **bell** dating from 1646, damaged during its construction. The amazing little passageway situated before Jezuicka Street, leads to the Gnojna

Góra terrace, from which one can quietly admire the River Wisła before entering the lively market square.

The Rynek (Rynek Starego Miasta)★★ B1

Lined with colourful multi-storeyed houses of Renaissance and Baroque inspiration, the Rynek was in fact, until the middle of the 19C, the administrative, commercial and cultural centre of Warsaw, staging fairs and festivities as well as public executions. Today, some of the best traditional restaurants in the capital are located here and the numerous outdoor cafés offer a pleasant break in fine weather; it is also quite enjoyable to have a drink from the water pumps occupying the centre of the square.

At no 20 stands the **Adam Mickiewicz Literature Museum** (Muzeum Mickiewicza) *Daily except Sat: Mon, Tue, Fri 10am-3pm, Wed-Thu 11am-6pm, last admission 30min before closing. 5 PLN.*

Essentially devoted to Adam Mickiewicz, the 19C cult Romantic writer, author of *Pan Tadeusz*, a jewel of Polish literature, this museum also stages usually very interesting temporary exhibitions about Polish literature from the 18C to the 20C.

All the façades lining the north side of the square are those of the **Historical Museum of Warsaw** (Muzeum historyczne starej Warszawy)★ *Rynek n°28. ☎635 16 25. Daily except Mon. Tue, Thu 11am-6pm, Wed, Fri 10am-3.30pm, Sat-Sun 10.30am-4.30pm, last admission 1hr before closing. 5 PLN, free admission on Sun. Allow 2hr for the visit.*

Excellent as history museums go, it covers all the aspects of Warsaw's life from its foundation to the end of the 1980s. Not to be missed is the short documentary film recounting the systematic destruction of the town by the Nazis in 1944 *(English version on Sat-Sun at noon).*

From the Market Square to the New Town A-B1

The tour of the town continues through Nowomiejska and Szeroki Dunaj Streets which offer a glimpse of the Old Town's backyards, then on to the pleasant Piwna Street. Lined with jeweller's, bookstalls and antique shops, it also boasts **St Martin's Church** (Kościól Św.Marcina)★. This 14C Gothic edifice featuring a Baroque interior is a favourite of newlyweds who, after the religious ceremony, are congratulated by family and friends in the arcaded courtyard. Note also that Adam Jarzębski, the king's musician and 17C author of the first guidebook of Warsaw, written... in verse (!) is buried inside.

The tour of the Old Town would not be complete without a detour via Podwale along which the brick **ramparts** were rebuilt in order to restore its original charm – whereas the original fortifications, having lost their usefulness, had already been dismantled in the 19C. The open path surrounding the walls is lined with commemorative plaques placed there as a tribute to foreigners who at some time supported the Polish cause, such as the French poet Alfred de Vigny. The **Monument of the Little Insurgent** (Pomnik Małego Powstańca) is undoubtedly the most poignant memorial along Podwale: enormous helmet on his head and rifle in hand, he pays tribute to the children who died during the Warsaw uprising. Following the ramparts, which feature on their north side the statue of Wars and Sawa, the lovers who founded the town, one comes across the **Barbican** (Barbakan): originally a point of entry and defence of the city, it now attracts traditional local painters and artists and marks the transition between the Old Town and the New Town.

THE NEW TOWN (NOWE MIASTO)★ A-B1

This small but elegant district, created in the 15C and integrated into the municipality of Warsaw in the 18C, features a specifically peaceful atmosphere. The presence of many palaces built in the 17C accounts for the fact that, during Warsaw's "Golden Age", a number of Polish aristocrats settled here.

Freta Street B1

Freta Street is lined with galleries, cafés and places of worship and one should go through the porches of the houses to get a glimpse of the courtyards and parks hidden behind the façades.

No 16 is the birthplace of Marie Skłodowska-Curie, twice awarded the Nobel Prize for her discovery of radium and of polonium in 1903 and 1911. The house is now the **Marie Skłodowska-Curie Museum ★** *(Tue-Sat 10am-4pm, Sun 10am-2pm. 8 PLN)* dedicated to the life and work of the great physicist.

New Town Square B1

Freta Street leads to the New Town Square, as peaceful as the Old Town Square is buzzing. On the east side, the **Baroque Church of the Holy Sacrament** (Kościól

Royal Castle and column of King Sigismund III

Sakramentek), commissioned by Queen Maria Sobieska in memory of her husband's victory over Turkish troops in Vienna in 1683, contains the funerary chapel of the Sobieski dynasty.

The **Church of the Visitation** (Kościół Wizytek), built in Gothic style at the beginning of the 15C, is famous for its bell tower used as a landmark from the opposite bank of the Wisła.

Krasiński Square (Plac Krasińskich) A1

At the foot of the glass building housing the Supreme Court stands the very controversial **Uprising Monument** (Pomnik Powstania Warszawskiego). Erected on the spot where AK (National Army) troops launched their assault against the Nazis on 1 Aug 1944, this imposing metal sculpture represents armed insurgents coming out of their underground hiding places to attack the Germans but also their desperate retreat into the city's sewers.

The **Krasiński Palace** (Pałac Krasińskich), which houses the special collections of the National Library, closes off the square. Designed by Tylman von Gameren at the end of the 18C, it is one of the finest Baroque edifices in Warsaw. It is unfortunately not open to visitors who can, however, stroll through the gardens at the back of the palace. In the 19C, these gardens were the meeting place of Warsaw's high society.

Długa Street A2-B1

The Długa Street exit gives direct access to the **Archaeological Museum** (muzeum archeologiczne), housed in a 17C arsenal, which displays archaeological collections of Polish prehistory *(ul. Długa 52. Daily except Sat, Mon-Fri 9am-4pm, Sun 10am-4pm, 6 PLN)*. Opposite is the **Museum of Independence** (muzeum Niepodległości, *Al. Solidarności 62. Daily except Mon, Tue-Fri 10am-5pm, Sat-Sun 10am-4pm, 5 PLN)* offering an interesting analysis of the national history by recounting Poland's incessant struggle against her hostile and powerful neighbours led by Russia and Germany.

Miodowa Street B2

Walking up Długa Street, you will enter what used to be the very centre of the aristocratic town: Miodowa Street, exclusively lined with 18C Baroque and neo-Classical palaces, the most prestigious being the **Borch Palace** (no 13), now the residence of the Primate of the Catholic Church, the **Radziwiłł Palace** by Tylman von Gameren, and the **Pac Palace** (no 15), with its distinctive mouldings over the main entrance (original row of Empire-style curved arcades), which houses the Ministry of Health. Along this road, you will also find the **Basilian Church** (Kościół Bazylianów, at no 16), Warsaw's only Uniate church, as well as the **Capuchin Church** (Kościół Kapucynów), repository of the heart of Jan III Sobieski.

THE NORTHERN DISTRICTS OF THE TOWN CENTRE

These elegant districts are accessible via Senatorska Street.

Museum of Caricature (muzeum Karykatury) B2

Ul. Kozia 11. Daily except Mon, Tue-Sun 11am-5pm, Thu until 6pm. 5 PLN, free admission on Sat.

This tiny yet amusing museum stages temporary exhibitions devoted to Polish caricaturists – a highly appreciated genre in Poland – the most famous of them being Eryk Lipiński.

Theatre Square (Plac Teatralny) B2

Before the war, Theatre Square was the elegant part of the city centre. Long neglected, it regained some of its former character following the restoration of the Old Town Hall buildings (now the head office of a bank). Erected during the 1820s by Corazzi, the **Grand Theatre** (Teatr Wielki)★ features a fine classicist façade decorated with Greek sculptures, and its interior rotunda is well worth a look. Rebuilt and extended after the war, the Grand Theatre combines the Opera and the National Theatre as well as a small museum occasionally hosting temporary exhibitions about the history of Polish drama. The interior is however only accessible during performances.

Senatorska Street continues towards the bustling Bankowy Square.

Bank Square (Plac Bankowy)★ B2

The west side is entirely taken up by **Warsaw's Town Hall**, an imposing complex of buildings designed by Corazzi at the beginning of the 19C, in front of which stands the statue of the famous poet Juliusz Słowacki. Next door, the **Museum of John-Paul II's Collections** (Muzeum Kolekcji im.Jana Pawła II) *(daily except Mon, Tue-Sun 10am-5pm, 7 PLN)* houses a collection of around 400 paintings on religious themes. Donated by the Caroll-Porczyński family to the Polish Church, the collection is however controversial because the authenticity of some of the works is doubtful.

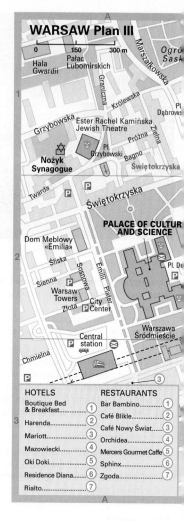

HOTELS

Boutique Bed & Breakfast	(1)
Harenda	(2)
Mariott	(3)
Mazowiecki	(4)
Oki Doki	(5)
Residence Diana	(6)
Rialto	(7)

RESTAURANTS

Bar Bambino	(1)
Café Blikle	(2)
Café Nowy Świat	(3)
Orchidea	(4)
Mercers Gourmet Caffe	(5)
Sphinx	(6)
Zgoda	(7)

Saxon Gardens (Ogród Saski)★ A-B3

On the way south to the town centre, one crosses the magnificent Saxon Gardens. Laid out by Tylman von Gameren for August II at the beginning of the 17C, these gardens miraculously escaped destruction during the Second World War. With over a hundred species of very old trees, they are the finest green lungs of the city. The main alleyway, featuring a 19C fountain, the town's first water tower and a sundial, ends with a group of elegant Baroque statues symbolizing the Virtues, Science and the Elements.

Exit on Piłsudskiego Square.

Piłsudskiego Square B3

Situated just behind the park's statues, the **Tomb of the Unknown Soldier** (Grób Nieznanego Żołnierza) was erected in 1925 to commemorate the anonymous heroes who died while fighting for Poland's independence; it contains the ashes of an unknown soldier who defended Lwów (now L'viv in Ukraine), mixed with earth from the battlefields of the First World War. It is located under the arcades of the old Saski Palace, which is all that remains of the Saxon kings' former residence destroyed during the war.

Its strong symbolic meaning makes it the obvious rallying point for important gatherings, and indeed it is here that the demonstrations organised by Solidarity in the 1980s were launched and that, more recently, thousands of Warsaw residents watched the broadcast of John-Paul II's funeral. This vast, most of the time deserted square is an

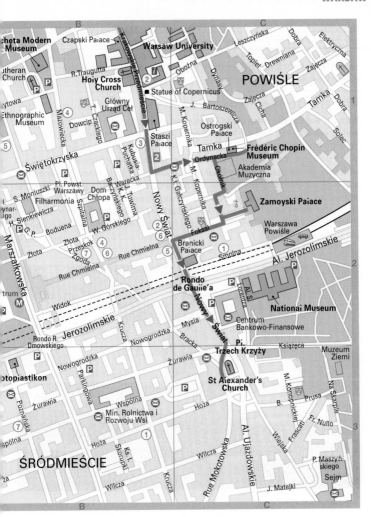

unusual mix of various architectural styles. Adjoining the former **Europejski Hotel** (currently closed), a former 19C palace converted into a luxury hotel during the communist era and today returned to its original owners, and opposite the Stalinist bunker of the **Victoria Hotel**, is the **glass edifice built by Norman Foster.** Inaugurated at the beginning of 2004 and highly controversial because of its proximity to the Grand Theatre, it houses restaurants, galleries and luxury boutiques grouped around the splendid fountain adorning the inner courtyard, as well as offices in the upper floors.

Zachęta Modern Art Museum (Galeria Zachęta)★ B3
Plac Małachowskiego 3, on the corner of Piłsudskiego Square and Mazowiecka Street ℘ 827 58 54. Daily except Mon, Tue-Sun 10am-6pm, Thu until 8pm. Around 10 PLN.
The edifice, built at the beginning of the 20C as the permanent headquarters of the Warsaw Applied Arts Society, houses Poland's most important museum of contemporary art. Its collections, originally more substantial than today, included such works as Matejko's *Battle of Grunwald* but they were hidden in the National Museum at the outbreak of the war and remained there afterwards.

Heading for the Town Centre
From Małachowskiego Square, follow Mazowiecka Street.
A short detour via Kredytowa Street will enable you to see the 18C **Lutheran church** (Ewangelicko-Augsburgski) and admire its huge dome, Warsaw's largest. Chopin gave his first concert here at the age of 14 and the church, renowned for its excellent acoustics, still holds regular choral and chamber-music concerts.

Facing the church across the street, the **Ethnographic Museum** (Muzeum Etnograficzne. *Tue, Thu, Fri, 10am-4pm, Wed 11am-6pm, Sat-Sun 10am-5pm. 5 PLN, free admission on Wed)* will be of particular interest to lovers of popular art with its impressive collection of traditional folk costumes from all over Poland; some of the temporary exhibitions are also worth looking at.

The modern centre PLAN III

With the **Palace of Culture and Science** as its focal point, Warsaw's commercial and business centre looks different from the usual town centre, rather like a vast building site where it is at first difficult to get one's bearings. The area is a strange mix of skyscrapers and futuristic buildings erected along wide Stalinist avenues lined with a medley of hotels, luxury boutiques, residential blocks from the communist era, fragile-looking stalls and displays of miscellaneous products (flowers, fruit and vegetables, clothes, jewellery and perfume) sometimes laid directly on the ground. This hodgepodge, which offers a pleasant visual surprise, reflects the contrasts which characterize a society still relatively poor yet engaged in a fast process of economic transformation.

Palace of Culture and Science

The Centre is laid out on a grid plan with two main thoroughfares travelled by a fleet of colourful and often crammed tramways. **Jerozolimskie Avenue** runs through Warsaw from east to west over several kilometres. Towering above it is the LOT skyscraper whose shimmering glass structure reflects the Palace of Culture and the **Central Station** (Warszawa Centralna). Despite repeated announcements about its forthcoming restoration, the station is in a totally neglected state, in striking contrast to the adjoining ultra-modern commercial centre. **Marszałkowska Avenue** is the main north-south axis. Several underground passageways, swarming with people and buzzing with activity, run perpendicular to it, as is often the case in large Central European towns. Starting behind the shopping precinct (Galeria Centrum) extending along the east side of the avenue, **Chmielna Street**, a pedestrian shopping street of smaller proportions, leads straight to the Royal Way.

Palace of Culture and Science (Pałac Kultury i Nauki)★★★ A2

Palace of Culture and Science (PKIN) – 1 Plac Defilad (main entrance and parking in Marszałkowska Avenue) – Panoramic terrace, daily 9am-8pm, 15 PLN. For additional information consult the excellent website www.pkin.pl (in Polish and in English).
A "Present from the Soviet nation to the Polish nation", the Palace of Culture and Science has become, such is the irony of history, the landmark and symbol of Warsaw. Commissioned by Stalin and designed by Lew Rudnyew, this impressive 231m-high edifice, visible within a 30km radius and boasting 3 288 rooms, was built in just 3 years (1952-55) by 3 500 Russian workers cooped up in an isolated area. The Palace of Culture houses the Technical Museum, a congress hall, two theatres, a cinema, a club, a café and administrative offices. The history

of the palace has, over the past fifty years been enriched with anecdotes, from the series of suicides which followed its inauguration to the disappearance in the early 1990s of Stalin's statue set into the west façade, not to mention the Rolling Stones' memorable concert in 1967. After the collapse of the communist regime, the Palace of Culture's future became a major urban issue for Warsaw and razing it to the ground was even considered for a while. Long hated by the Varsovians (who jokingly say that the best view of Warsaw is from the top of the palace because it is the only spot from which it cannot be seen!), the Palace of Culture has become less and less controversial, mainly on account of the nearby skyscrapers which seem to soar even higher. A lift takes visitors up to the top of the PKIN (30th floor), from which one can, in summer and in fine weather, study the map of Warsaw and look out towards the Masovian plains surrounding the city; the view is probably even more stunning under snow in winter.

Fotoplastikon★ B3
al.Jerozolimskie 51. Daily except Sun, Mon-Fri noon-5pm, Sat 11am-2pm. Time: 20min. 8 PLN.
The last display of its kind in Europe. Fotoplastikon allows people to glimpse life throughout 20C century Warsaw via a selection of 3D images. During both wars it was fully operational, acting as contact point for the Polish underground during Nazi occupation.

From Rondo R. Dmowskiego, head south along Marszałkowska Avenue which leads to **Constitution Square** (Plac Konstytucji)★ – referring to the constitution of 3 May 1791– a fine example of Socialist-realist architecture imbued with a certain symmetrical harmony, featuring cold, grandiose constructions decorated with low-relief sculptures celebrating the Polish people at work. The adjoining streets are becoming part of the new and increasingly sought-after residential district of the town centre. **Mokotowska Street,** lined with boutiques and antique shops, among the most remarkable in Warsaw, is particularly recommended for shopping addicts.

2 The Royal Way PLAN II-PLAN III
The Royal Way, Warsaw's most famous tourist trail, owes its name to the fact that it links the various Varsovian residences of Polish kings. Stretching 4km from the Old Town's Castle Square, where the kings had their main residence, to the Wilanów Palace where they retired in summer, via the Ujazdów hunting palace and the imposing Łazienki Park. All the sights lining the Royal Way cannot be visited in the space of one day, it seems natural, therefore, to begin with the first section from Castle Square south along Krakowskie Przedmieście to Trzech Krzyży Square.

KRAKOWSKIE PRZEDMIEŚCIE (The Kraków Road)
As early as 1596, many Varsovian aristocrats wanted to establish their residence along this street to be near the king who had recently settled in the Old Town. Today, Krakowskie Przedmieście is one of Warsaw's main thoroughfares, lined with the President of the Republic's residence and the University buildings as well as several historic churches and houses from the 17C and 18C.

St Anne's Church (Kościół Św. Anny)★ PLAN II B2
Located at the beginning of the street is the church where royal princes used to swear homage and loyalty to the king. Built in 1454 by Princess Anne of Masovia for the Bernardine Order, it was destroyed by the Swedes in 1656 then rebuilt in Baroque style during the course of the next century. The only remaining parts of the initial edifice are the brick-built Gothic presbytery adjoining the nave and the dome of the chapel. The church also features a sumptuous "crystal vault" and an original organ. From the northern side of the courtyard, you can climb to the top of the belfry *(May-Sep 10am-5pm, 2 PLN)* for a fabulous view of the river banks.
Before continuing, make a detour down to the small **Mariensztat District,** whose paved streets, lined with old houses and small cafés, are a haven of peace unjustly ignored by strollers *(there and back via Bednarska Street).*
Immediately past the **Mickiewicz Monument** (one of the many of its kind dedicated to the poet throughout the country), you will see a church, slightly recessed from the street.

Carmelite Church (Kościół Karmelitów)★ PLAN II B3
This is one of the rare edifices in Warsaw to have escaped unscathed when the town was destroyed at the end of the Second World War. Built by Schroeger in the 17C, it is one of the first examples of true Classical style in Poland, featuring a delicately carved façade crowned by an unusual globe, while the interior contains a monumental high altar by Tylman von Gameren.

The Royal Way

Potocki-Czartoryski Palace PLAN II B3

This palace where Napoleon is said to have met Maria Walewska now houses the Ministry of Culture (as well as a modern art gallery hosting generally interesting temporary exhibitions).

Radziwiłł Presidential Palace (Pałac Radziwiłłów)★ PLAN II C3

℘ 695 13 23, for all information about visits.

It is here that the Warsaw Pact was signed in 1955 and that **round-table talks** were held in 1989 between the communist authorities and the leaders of Solidarity.

Walk past the art deco building of the **Bristol Hotel** and the adjoining gardens.

Warsaw University (Uniwersytet Warszawski)★ PLAN II C3

The extended university buildings occupy the whole second half of Krakowskie Przedmieście. Founded in 1818, the Warsaw University was closed by the tsar in 1832 in reprisal for the 1830 insurrection and it was only reopened in 1915. During the Nazi occupation, studies were forbidden and thousands of clandestine teachers and students were murdered.

As in most large cities throughout Poland, particularly in Kraków, a clandestine university was introduced; this tradition of a "moving university" continued during the communist era, when eminent opposition personalities gave regular lectures in public, each time in a different venue. The university campus still boasts magnificent monuments.

The **Kazimierz Palace** (Pałac Kazimierzowski), located on the main campus courtyard, was a royal summer residence before being Frédéric Chopin's home until 1827; it is now the home of the rector of the university.

The **Czapski Palace** (opposite, across the street), was also inhabited by Chopin from 1827 to 1830; this fine Baroque edifice now houses the Academy of Fine Arts.

Holy Cross Church (Kościół Św. Krzyża)★ PLAN II C3

The church, facing the university's main entrance, was destroyed during the 1944 uprising, at the end of a two-week battle between the insurgents and the Nazis, which took place inside the building. This fine Baroque church, flanked by two towers, later witnessed regular confrontations between students and the communist authorities. The statue of Christ at the entrance, carrying the Cross on his back, remains a symbol of the martyred city. Varsovians also love this church because it contains Chopin's heart (in the pillar on the north side of the nave).

Staszic Palace (Pałac Staszica) PLAN III B1

This palace, which is the headquarters of the Polish Academy of Science, closes off Krakowskie Przedmieście, whereas, facing it, the statue of Copernicus (Pomnik Mikołaja Kopernika) symbolically opens New World Street (Nowy Świat).

NOWY ŚWIAT

This extension of the Royal Way, dating from the middle of the 17C, is somewhat unduly known as Warsaw's Champs-Élysées. Razed to the ground during the Second World War, this long avenue lined with boutiques, cafés and restaurants is mainly interesting for having had a number of personalities from the Polish art and literary world as residents, among them Joseph Conrad (at no 45).

Frédéric Chopin Museum (muzeum Fryderyka Chopina)★ PLAN III C1
Ul. Ordynacka/Okolnik, daily except Tue 10am-2pm, 5 PLN.
Housed in the solemn late-17C **Ostrogski Palace**, the museum displays various objects that belonged to Chopin, including the last piano on which he played – still used for occasional concerts *(every Monday evening from May to September)* organised by the Frédéric Chopin Foundation, which has its headquarters in the palace.
Return to Nowy Świat via Foksal Street.

Zamoyski Palace★ PLAN III C2
This neo-Renaissance palace was, in 1863, the scene of an attempt to assassinate the tsarist governor. In reprisal, the building was confiscated after being ransacked by Cossacks who went as far as to throw one of Chopin's pianos out the window; the instrument belonged to the composer's sister who lived in the palace at the time. Today, it is one of the rare palaces in Warsaw to be open to the public. It houses the **Polish Architects' Association** and an **architectural centre (SARP)**, a pleasant café-restaurant with a terrace and the famous **Foksal Gallery**, one of the finest galleries of contemporary art in town *(Mon-Fri noon-5pm, free admission)*. The gallery has been a cult place for contemporary and avant-garde artists since the beginning of the 1960s. It was at that time the first place in Warsaw to host performances directed by the already famous Kraków artist and theatre director, Tadeusz Kantor.

Finally, beyond the neo-Gothic **Branicki Palace** (on the corner of Smolna Street), which houses the finest pharmacy in Poland, Nowy Świat leads to the Charles de Gaulle Roundabout.

Charles de Gaulle Roundabout (Rondo de Gaulle'a)★ PLAN III C2
At the junction of the Royal Way and Jerozolimskie Avenue, this roundabout is one of the busiest in town. Of all the buildings surrounding it, the most striking is the imposing edifice which once housed the headquarters of the **Polish Communist Party** (Budynek KC) and became the city's Stock Exchange after the collapse of the communist regime. Since then, the Stock Exchange has been moved to adjoining premises and today the building only houses private businesses. However, the originality of the roundabout is mainly due to the **palm tree** standing in its centre, since the presence of this kind of tree in the middle of Warsaw is somewhat surprising. The tree was planted here on the initiative of artist Joanna Rajkowska who, after a trip to Israel, thought of planting a palm tree in the capital's Jerusalem Avenue. This also has a symbolic meaning: in Polish, palm tree *(palma)* is a figurative expression qualifying something absurd, a description which, according to the artist, applies rather well to Warsaw. Far from being unanimously approved, the palm tree on the Charles de Gaulle Roundabout is on its way to becoming as much of a symbol as the Palace of Culture...

Three Crosses Square (Plac Trzech Krzyży Square) ★ PLAN III C3
The Royal Way itinerary continues to Trzech Krzyży Square, in the middle of which stands **St Alexander's Church** (Kościół Św. Aleksandra)★. Built in 1818 in honour of Tsar Alexander I of Russia, who was also king of Poland, the church was modelled on the Pantheon in Rome before being transformed into a cathedral. Following its destruction during the war, the original church alone was rebuilt and its charm makes it a sought-after venue for weddings. Wiejska Street, heading south from the square, leads to the buildings of the **Polish Parliament** (Sejm), erected in the 1920s after Poland had regained her independence in 1918.

Ujazdowski and Łazienki Parks PLAN I

Its vast peaceful parks feature undoubtedly among Warsaw's main attractions and they are obviously the reason why Varsovians prefer the second part of the Royal Way which stretches along some 2.5km of uninterrupted green open spaces from Ujazdowskie Avenue (south of Trzech Krzyży Square) to Łazienki Park, by far the most beautiful and famous park in Poland.

Ujazdowskie Avenue and Park B3

Ujazdowskie Avenue is one of the capital's most elegant avenues. Lined with 19C villas boasting beautifully carved façades (most of them now occupied by embassies), it leads to the park of the same name entered by crossing the express way which unfortunately cuts across the Royal Way. Before penetrating deep into the park, take a look at the **Museum of Struggle and Martyrdom** (Muzeum Walki i Meczeństwa, *al. Szucha 25, on the corner of al. Ujazdowskie and Armii Ludowej. Wed-Sun. 9am-4pm. Donation required*), the former headquarters of the Gestapo, which recalls once more the tragic fate of the Polish capital by commemorating the thousands of persons who were tortured and murdered in this place during the Second World War.

The Ujazdów Esplanade goes back in time further than Warsaw's history. This hamlet, whose origins go back to the 12C, was in fact the favourite resting place of Masovian princes, until they decided to settle on the hill where the Old Town stands. However, the site remained a princely hunting ground until Anna Jagiellonka, the wife of King Stefan Barory, decided at the end of the 16C to have a royal residence built; this formed the initial structure of **Ujazdowski Castle★** (Zamek Ujazdowski, *Tue-Sun 11am-5pm, Fri until 9pm – 5 PLN*). After the Polish capital was transferred from Kraków to Warsaw, King Sigismund III extended and modernised the castle. Although the basic structure features the Renaissance style, the enlarged entrance, the curved roofline and the decorative turrets are in typical Polish Baroque style, otherwise known as Vasa style. The two large curved staircases linking the castle to the canal, built along the axis of the entrance, date from the first half of the 18C. The Zamek, as Varsovians call it, is now an active **contemporary art centre**, Warsaw's second modern art centre after Zachęta. Regularly hosting great international exhibitions of painting and photography, performances, jazz and experimental-music concerts, the centre displays the works of Poland's young artists on a permanent basis. This temple of contemporary art also houses a trendy restaurant (Quchnia Artystyczna, see Practical Warsaw), a café, a cinema showing art films, as well as a boutique and an art bookshop.

Łazienki Park (Park Łazienkowski)★★ B-C3

Łazienki park is accessible either from Ujazdowski Park by crossing Agrykola Street, or through the main entrance, al. Ujazdowskie no 106 (Open daily from 8am to dusk, 4pm in winter).

A former hunting ground adjoining Ujazdowski Castle, Łazienki was bought in 1760 by King Stanisław August, who transformed it into an English-style park. Standing by the main entrance, the Chopin monument welcomes strollers who, when the weather is fine, flock to listen to the concerts of classical music taking place beneath it *(May to Sep, every Sat at 3pm and Sun at 11am)*; carrying the sound to the audience scattered around on the grass, the circular pond adds to the charm of these events in which the greatest international artists take part. It is also the venue for "studies" and "mazurkas", readings from works by Mickiewicz and other Romantic poets. Across the main path stands the elegant **Belvedere** (Belweder)★, initially owned by King Stanisław August who set up a manufacture of ceramics inside. This Royal residence, built around 1660 then redesigned in the 1820s for the benefit of Warsaw's governor, became the official residence of the leaders of the Polish State at the end of the First World War; after the Second World War interlude during which it was taken over by the Nazi governor Hans Frank, it was inhabited for ten years by General Jaruzelski, then by President Łech Wałęsa (before the presidential palace was transferred to Krakowskie Przedmieście); today, the Belvedere is still used for official receptions. Walking down the main path, you will pass in front of the **White House** (Biały Dom, *Tue-Sun 9am-3.30pm, 5PLN)*, where the Count of Provence, the future Louis XVIII stayed during his exile from 1801 to 1804, then the **Old Guardhouse** (Stara Kordegarda, *Tue-Sun 9am-4pm, free admission*), before reaching the Park's main monument, the **Łazienki Palace★★** (Pałac Łazienkowski, *Tue-Sun 9am-4pm, 12 PLN. Arrive early to avoid long queues)*. Commonly known as the "palace on the water", this neo-Classical edifice, designed by Merlini for Józef Poniatowski between 1772 and 1793, is held as the best memorial to Poland's last and most cultured king. Partially damaged during the war, the palace was rebuilt but the furnishings and the collections, which had been taken to a safe place, are originals. On the ground floor, the decorations at the base of the walls are a reminder that the palace was initially

Pałac Łazienkowski, the "palace on the water"

only a "bathhouse" (*łazienki* meaning "baths" in Polish), whereas the ballroom and the painting gallery testify to the classical taste of King Stanisław and to his ability as an art collector. Despite the fact that the German army siezed the best items, including three Rembrandts, there remains an interesting collection of Dutch and Flemish paintings. Upstairs, the king's private apartments boast, among others, a painting by Bellotto depicting the original bathhouse. Facing the palace, the amphitheatre, featuring a decor of antique ruins set on an island and inhabited by peacocks, regularly hosts performances in summer. A little further on, the **Great Laboratory** (Wielka Oficyna), the former officers' training school where the 1830 anti-tsarist conspiracy was instigated, houses the **Jan Paderewski and Polish Expatriates in the United States Museum** *(Tue-Sun 10am-3pm, 6 PLN)*, inaugurated in 1992 on the occasion of the return to Poland of the remains of the famous composer exiled in America. Opposite stands the **Myśliwski Palace**, a present from the king to his nephew Józef Poniatowski, which imitates the decorum of the main Łazienki Palace *(daily except Tue, 9.30am-4pm, 4 PLN)*. As you walk back towards the north side of the park, you will come across the **Orangery**★ (Pomarańczarnia, *Tue-Sun 9am-3pm, 6 PLN)*, one of the few remaining wooden theatres in Europe to feature its original 18C decor (1788); it now houses a sculpture gallery. A little higher up, opposite the **19C Astronomical Observatory** (Obserwatorium astronomiczne, *Tue-Sun 9.30am-3.30pm. Free admission)*, the **Botanical Gardens**★ (Ogród Botaniczny, *Mon-Sat 9am-7pm, Sun 10am-7pm. 4 PLN)* provide a pleasant ending to the stroll through the parks. Laid out in 1818, the gardens boast a collection of some 7 000 species of plants; note in particular the rose garden and the medicinal-herb garden.

The Royal Way continues south towards Wilanów via the residential district of Mokotów.

Wilanów

Access: ul Stanisława Kostki-Potockiego 10/16 (free parking). By bus, from the town centre, nos 116, 117, 130, 139, 164, 180, 519, 522, 700, 710, E-2.
Situated south of Warsaw, Wilanów is a very pleasant district surrounding the palace, its park and outbuildings, which include a charming church.

Wilanów Palace (Pałac Wilanowski)★★

Open daily except Tue 9am-4pm. Summer opening times (mid-May to mid-Sep): Wed until 6pm and Sun until 7pm. Last admission 1hr before closing. 20 PLN. Allow 135 PLN for a group of 5 persons with a guide.
Wilanów Palace shows Jan III Sobieski (1677-96), crowned king of Poland in 1674, as a dedicated art lover, connoisseur and patron of the arts.

A troubled history – Erected during the late 17C and extended by its successive owners, the palace is a typical example of Baroque country residence, "between courtyard and garden". Jan III Sobieski originally named his summer residence Vila Nova which over the years became Wilanów.

Wilanów Palace

After the king's death in 1696, the palace passed to his sons then was purchased in 1720 by Elżbieta Sieniawska and later by other Polish families. In 1799, it was acquired by Stanisław Potocki. This man of letters, author of many treatises on art and aesthetics and enlightened collector, created in Wilanów one of the first public museums in the world. During the Second World War, the German army occupied the palace and set up barracks inside. After the war, it became state property and subsequently underwent extensive restoration work. It was reopened to the public in 1962 after the Polish government had retrieved most of the works of art stolen by the Germans.

Tour of the palace – The exterior ornamentation and interior paintings and sculptures are remarkable. The sculptures and low-reliefs decorating the façade, inspired from Antiquity, are a tribute to the Sobieski dynasty and the king's military successes. The interior of the palace is a blend of three main architectural styles: original Baroque rooms of King Jan III Sobieski in the central part, 18C interiors in the south wing and in the pavilion adjoining the palace, and finally 19C interiors in the north wing, the palace's most recent part, decorated and remodelled by the Potocki family.

The tour starts on the first floor with the portrait gallery, whose main interest lies in the numerous posthumous portraits placed on coffins, a specifically Polish custom. Beyond the Great Crimson Room and the Etruscan Study, you enter the oldest part of the palace. It was here that the Potocki Museum was set up; the marble slab bearing the inscription "cunctis patet ingressus" (accessible to all) recalls the precursor spirit which led to these works of art being shown to the public. The tour continues on the ground floor with Jan III Sobieski's apartments, the chapel designed by Henri Marconi and the royal library.

The Gardens★
Daily 9am to dusk – 4.5 PLN (free admission on Thu).
The gardens are at the back of the palace. They were laid out in the French style on a dual-level terrace decorated with sculptures symbolising the four stages of love (reserve, the first kiss, indifference and the first quarrel). The original sundial is the work of the great Polish astronomer Jan Heweliusz, who invented the telescope.
Beyond the Orangery (temporary exhibitions, same opening times as the palace), is the English-style park, adorned with sarcophagi, columns and obelisks. A Roman bridge, a Chinese kiosk and the pumps room evoke Antiquity, Oriental Art and the Middle Ages.

Poster Museum (Muzeum plakatu)★
Tue-Thu 10am-4pm, Sat-Sun 10am-5pm. 4 PLN.
This museum, housed in a modern building next to the palace, is dedicated to an art form in which the Poles have always excelled: poster painting.
Whether they were made for advertising, the cinema, the theatre, politics or tourism, there are so many posters in this collection that they have to be displayed in rotation through thematic temporary exhibitions.

Muranów and Mirów – The former Jewish Ghetto

PLAN II

Like other Polish towns such as Łódź, Białystok or Kraków, Warsaw had, for centuries, one of Europe's most important Jewish communities, estimated in 1939 at 370 000 persons, which represented a third of the population; in May 1945, that number was reduced to 300. Although Warsaw's prewar Jewish community was scattered throughout the whole town, not residing exclusively in any particular district, today the only traces of this community to be found are located in and around the former ghetto, in the districts of Mirów and Muranów, and, to a lesser extent, in Praga, across the River Wisła. The extermination of the Jews is still generally a taboo subject in Poland; however, in Warsaw as in other Polish towns, above all in Kraków, the nucleus of a Jewish community is reappearing and, with the support of the diaspora, these people are actively endeavouring to keep alive the memory of the Shoah and to revive their ancestral culture.

Useful tips for the visit: *Places connected with Jewish culture being on the whole badly signposted or even not at all, it is advisable to use a detailed map and to follow the practical information inserted in the text.*

Jewish Historical Institute (Muzeum Żydowskiego Instytutu Historycznego)★ A2
Ul. Tłomackie 6, behind the Peugeot Tower in Bankowy Square. ☎827 92 21. Mon-Wed, Fri 9am-4pm, Thu 11am-6pm. 10/5 PLN.

The visit of the Institute is an excellent introduction to the discovery of the tragic history of Warsaw's Jewish community. Founded immediately after the war on the site of the former Jewish Library, it hosts two permanent exhibitions: one of them is devoted to Jewish art (sacred and secular works of art) and the other to the Warsaw ghetto *(see the 35min film – in English, German, Hebrew and Polish)*. The Institute also houses a research centre and a substantial stock of information about the history of Polish Jews since the 17C; these are not directly accessible to the general public. Finally the essential **Guide to Jewish Warsaw** *(10 PLN)* is on sale here. On the site now occupied by the Blekitny Wiezowiec (Blue Skyscraper) once stood the **Great Synagogue** (Synagoga na Tlomackiem – the greatest synagogue in Poland). The synagogue was blown up by the Nazis in 1943. According to a story told by Warsaw Jews, a rabbi placed a curse that no other building would ever be built on the site of the synagogue. Which may be the reason why the construction of the Blue Skyscraper took more than 30 years. It was finished in early 1990s.

The Path of Remembrance of Jewish Martyrdom and Struggle★★ A2

This "Path of Remembrance" starts from Bohaterów Getta Square featuring the **Ghetto Heroes Monument** (Pomnik Bohaterów Getta), unveiled among the ruins of the ghetto on 19 avril 1948 for the 5th anniversary of the Ghetto Uprising. The sculpture "Struggle", carved on the west façade of the monument, represents the

> ### The Warsaw Ghetto
>
> The Warsaw Ghetto was the largest "Jewish residential district" (according to the official terminology) in Nazi Europe: a 3m high and 18km long brick wall isolated 30% of the population (around 50 000 people) on only 2.4% of the town's area (400ha). The "Great Action" which, on 22 July 1942, saw the transfer of 265 000 Jews to the death camp at Treblinka, marked the beginning of a policy of massive extermination. Resistance within the ghetto began to get organised under the command of the ŻOB (Jewish Fighting Organisation), using arms smuggled into the ghetto. The Ghetto Uprising started on 19 April 1943; taken by surprise, the German army took a month to retaliate. A few thousand Jews only managed to escape, the others were shot on the spot or deported. The story of the Warsaw Ghetto, faithfully told in HW Szpilman's book *The Pianist*, which inspired Roman Polanski' film, remains one of the darkest episodes of the Shoah.

ghetto insurgents whereas the sculpture carved on the east façade symbolises the "March towards Extermination". The monument is covered with labrador slabs, originally ordered from Sweden by Hitler who, anticipating an early victory, intended to have a monument built in Warsaw to the glory of the Third Reich. The plaque located next to the monument and bearing the inscription "Zegota 1942-45" commemorates the organisation intended to help the Jews, created by the clandestine Jewish State at the time of the Holocaust. Of all the organisations that were active in Europe during the Second World War, this was the only one to be financed by a government, that of the exiled Polish Republic.

The Path of Remembrance continues along Zamenhofa Street, where there are **19 granite plaques** commemorating, in Polish and Hebrew, significant events and personalities of the ghetto: historian Emmanuel Ringenblum (no 5), ŻOB (Jewish Fighting Organisation) Commander in chief and leader of the Ghetto Uprising, Mordechai Anielewicz (no 10), Janusz Korczak (no 15).

Further up, on the **site of the former ŻOB Bunker** *(ul. Miła 18)* stands an amazing and poignant monument: a heap of rubble, its height representing that of the rubble left after the destruction of the ghetto. Note, in the adjacent streets, a number of houses built on the same level: pressed by the urgency of the situation and unable to cope with the extent of the damage and of the reconstruction work needed, the postwar communist authorities decided to erect new blocks of flats directly on the ruins of the ghetto.

The Path of Remembrance ends on the **Umschlagplatz** *(ul. Stawki 10)* where, from July 1942, Warsaw Jews were systematically gathered and loaded into cattle wagons bound for Treblinka. The simple white-marble **monument** erected at the end of the 1980s and representing those very cattle trucks used to transport the Jews, is covered inside with 400 Jewish first names, poignantly symbolizing the 300 000 Jews deported from Warsaw to the death camps. On the side wall, inscribed in Polish, Hebrew and Yiddish, one can read this verse from the Book of Job: "O earth do not conceal my blood, let it cry out on my behalf". In 1988, a **stone** was also placed on the very spot where the trains started. It bears the following inscription: "Through this path of suffering and death, during the years 1940-1943, over 300 000 Jews went from the Warsaw ghetto to the death camps".

On the other side of the street stands one of the rare houses to have survived the destruction of the ghetto: it is, ironically, the house occupied during the war by the SS officer supervising the Jews' departure from the Umschlugplatz.

The Jewish Cemetery (Cmentarz Żydowski) PLAN I A1
Follow Stawki Street then turn left onto Okopowa and continue until you reach the main entrance to the cemetery, at no 49/51 (daily except Sat 10am-4pm).
Established in 1806, it is one of the rare Jewish cemeteries still in use in Poland. Having miraculously escaped severe damage during the war, the cemetery contains some 250 000 graves, including those of some illustrious Polish Jews: the ophtalmologist and inventor of Esperanto, Ludwig Zamenhof, the writer DH Nomber, or even Janusz Korczak. (A guide of the graves is available from the caretaker at the entrance to the cemetery, but it is wiser to ask the Jewish Historical Institute for a copy prior to your visit).

South of the Jewish cemetery, the **Janusz Korczak Orphanage** *(ul. Jaktorowska 6 – walk along Okopowska then turn right halfway down Towarowa. Ask the caretaker to let you into the building),* which survived the war, is still used as an orphanage. The imposing statue and the commemorative plaque at the entrance pay tribute to the doctor who died in Treblinka with the deported Jewish orphans whom he joined of his own free will. Andrzej Wajda chose this event as the subject of one of his films, *Korczak*.

Around Grzybowski Square
The remaining memorial sites and places of Jewish worship and culture are grouped around Grzybowski Square, on the south-eastern border of the Mirów district, near the Palace of Culture. The most striking of these is undoubtedly the **fragment of the ghetto wall**★★ *(ul. Sienna 55. Ring the entry-phone at no 100 or wait for one of the building's residents to open the gate. The wall is in the courtyard on the left, beyond the porch).* This tiny brick wall is all that remains of the 3m-high rampart which, from November 1940 to July 1942, sealed off Jewish Varsovians from the rest of the capital's Polish population. The commemorative plaque recalling the ghetto dates was placed here in 1992 by the Israeli president during the "inauguration" of the fragment of the wall; a second plaque mentions that two stones from the wall were transferred to the Holocaust Museum in Washington. Further up, on the corner of Grzybowski Square and Prozna Street, the only buildings that survived the destruction of the ghetto attest to Warsaw's prewar red-brick architecture. On the other side of the square, the **Nożyk Synagogue**★, the only synagogue in Warsaw to have escaped total destruction, was reopened in 1983 following complete restoration. It features a fine interior architecture *(ul. Twarda 6, Thu 10am-3pm).* Adjoining the synagogue, the **Ester Rachel Kamińska Jewish Theatre** *(Plac Grzybowski 2)* recreates popular shows given by the prewar Jewish community. The building is also the headquarters of several Jewish associations.

Ghetto Heroes Monument

Praga, popular and arty Warsaw PLAN I

(Tramways nos 23 and 32 from Bankowy Square, or no 25 from Jerozolimskie Avenue – stop at Wileńska).

The popular, working-class Praga district is still not appreciated by residents of the west bank of the Wisła. Yet, as the only district to have survived the war, it offers an authentic atmosphere and an interesting stroll away from the traditional tourist trail. Moreover, it contains Warsaw's oldest buildings, boasting façades scarred by gunfire during the Second World War.

Orthodox Church of St Mary Magdalene (Cerkiew Św. Marii Magdaleny)★ C1

ul. Solidarności 52.

This fine ochre and gold edifice (1869), built for the benefit of the railway workers of Wileńska Station, is one of the best examples of Russian influence in Warsaw: a large neo-Byzantine structure, surmounted by several onion domes and an interior in perfect condition *(access is only possible during daily services, at 5pm)*.

The artists' quarter (C1)extends over the north-east perimeter (between *Targowa, 11 Listopada and Konopacka streets*). Drawn to abandoned factories and buildings in which they set up their studios, painters, sculptors and comedians are slowly bringing Praga back to life; the pioneers set themselves up in the now cult building standing at no 3 Inżynierska Street. As for Ząbkowska Street, rightfully considered until recently as the capital's notorious crime centre, it has now been renovated and is becoming an area highly sought after by artists. Past no 50 Targowa Street, the district's oldest building (1819), you will see the **Różyckiego Bazaar**, the longest-surviving bazaar in Warsaw. Established in 1902, it is now only a pale reflection of what it once was; however, it retains a little of its magic appeal in winter, when people come to buy salmon laid out on the snow-covered stalls.

The Russian market (stadium Dziesęciolecia)★ C1-2

Reached by tramway no 25, stop at Plac Washingtona, only in the morning, daily 6.30am-1pm.

Built on the rubble in the 1950s, the stadium became, after the collapse of the communist regime, the centre of the illegal imitations trade. Although deemed dangerous and cleaned up since Poland joined the European Union, it remains one of Warsaw's great attractions (beware of pickpockets) with its sellers from all parts of the world: many Vietnamese and residents of the nearby ex-Soviet republics, Belarus, Ukraine etc. From the top of the stadium, there is a fine view of Warsaw on the other side of the Wisła.

Praga also had an important concentration of Jews before the war as attested by the **Brodno Jewish Cemetery** *(on the corner of ul. Odrowąża and Św. Wincentego, tram way no 3 from ul. Targowa)*, the oldest in town. Founded in the 1780s, it was intended for the poorest Jews.

Finally, Praga is famous for the **bears in Praski Park** *(tramway nos 23 and 32, stop at Praski)*. Since 1949, over 400 bears have been raised here before being transferred to zoos in the four corners of the world. The three current residents seem to have a friendly contact with passers-by in Solidarności Avenue.

"Battle of Grunwald" by Jan Matejko (1878), National Museum, Warsaw

The Warsaw Zoo (Miejski Ogród Zoologiczny) B1

ul. Ratuszowa 1/3. Daily 9am-7pm, last admission 1hr before closing. 12/6 PLN). Opened in 1928, the zoo houses elephants, lions, dolphins as well as a large colony of reptiles and birds. It was used as a hiding place by many Jews during the war, thanks to the collaboration of its former famous director, Jan Żabiński.

Museums PLAN I

The National Museum (Muzeum Narodowe)★★ B2

Al. Jerozolimskie 3. Tue-Sun 10am-4pm, Thu noon-6pm. 12 PLN, free admission on Sat. Housed in a large building inaugurated in 1938, Warsaw's National Museum contains valuable collections of medieval and ancient art, of Polish art from the 16C to the 20C and of decorative arts.

The **Faras Gallery** *(on the ground floor)* is in itself worth a visit. It presents frescoes and architectural elements from a Christian cathedral in the Sudan. The site of Faras, one of those which were flooded by Lake Nasser when the Assouan dam was built, was excavated by Professor Kazimierz Michałowski and his team from 1960 to 1964. Among other treasures, they saved the 120 remarkable murals decorating the cathedral. The proceeds of the excavations was shared between Poland and the Sudan. Today it is possible to admire, displayed in specially adapted rooms, the sixty or so frescoes dating from the 8C to the 14C, including the charming portrait of St Anne (8C) and Christ in Majesty (11C) with the symbols of the evangelists. Note also some red-sand-stone architectural elements and the fine collection of Coptic Crosses.

Kazimierz Michałowski (1901-1981)

Founder of the Polish school of mediterranean archaeology, this eminent archaeologist launched many excavation programmes in Egypt including those at Edfou (1936), Deir el Bahari (1961) and Faras.

The **gallery of medieval art** *(on the ground floor)* consists of seven rooms displaying splendid sculptures, altar-pieces and paintings from all over Poland. Admire in particular the series of Gothic works, featuring a wealth of delicate details, from the region of Wrocław and from Silesia, including St Luke and the Virgin Mary (1506) or the sculpted group comprising the Virgin Mary and St John (1500) whose faces are very expressive.

The **painting galleries** *(1st and 2nd floors)* are rich in works from the various European schools of painting: the Italian School (Boticelli, Tintoretto), the French School (Nattier, Watteau), the Dutch School (Jordaens) and the German School. However, the **gallery of Polish painting** *(1st floor)* deserves special attention. The huge canvas by Jan Matejko **"The Battle of Grunwald"** is a must; painted in 1878, it depicts the defeat inflicted on the Teutonic Knights by the Polish army. In a totally different class, Józef Mehoffer's works, inspired by Art Nouveau, convey an impression of happiness, for instance his *Strange Garden* (1903) or his paintings on glass.

The Museum of the Warsaw Uprising (Muzeum Powstania Warszawskiego)★★ A2

ul. Przykopowa 28. Daily 10am-6pm, Thu until 8pm. 4 PLN, free admission on Mon. Exhibitions in English and detailed information freely available to the public at every stage of the visit.

Opened in 2005, this museum was designed by architect Wojciech Obłutowicz to be housed inside the brick building of a former tramway power station. Using modern scenographic means (film screening, photos, reconstruction of sound effects etc), it offers a day-by-day account of the bloody episode of the Warsaw uprising against Nazi troops between 1 August and October 1944. This symbolic and desperate attempt by the Polish resistance caused over 200 000 deaths and is still painfully present in the collective memory.

The Warsaw Uprising

After the uprising of the ghetto followed by its total destruction in 1943, it was the turn of the Warsaw population, worn out by the Nazi occupation, to rebel against it in 1944. The insurrection was launched on 1 August at 5pm by the National Army, a resistance organisation. Many Varsovians became impromptu fighters. During 63 days, until 2 October, there was incessant street fighting. 18 000 insurgents were killed and there were many more deaths (180 000) among the civil population. Russian troops stationed in Praga, on the other side of the Wisła, just watched without intervening and waited for the end of the fighting before entering the devastated city.

The visit of the museum is extremely moving particularly when one is confronted with the photos of all those talented boys and girls cut down in the prime of youth for having fought the Nazi troops in a city in ruins, while the Russians were waiting in Praga, on the other side of the Wisła.

Nearby

Kampinos National Park (Kampinoski Park Narodowy)★★ A1

20km from Warsaw Town Centre. By car: to reach the northern edge of the park, follow E 77 towards Gdańsk then exit at Dziekanów-Leśny or Palmiry; to enter the park through the south, follow road 580 towards Sochaczew, then exit at Leszno or Kampinos. Frequent bus services from Warszawa Zachodnia bus station (towards Kamion and Gostynin. Last bus for returning to Warsaw at 6pm). Finally, a more picturesque way to get to the park is by narrow-gauge railway from Sochaczew (Apr-Oct. Departure every 30min. 4 PLN).

Kampinos, a rare example of a nature reserve on the edge of a large town, is Poland's largest nature park (38 000ha). Situated along the Wisła Valley, it offers splendidly varied landscapes of marshland, forests and dunes sheltering a remarkable fauna and flora. Since the 1950s, the park has successfully carried out a policy of protection and reintroduction of endangered species: beavers, lynx, wild boars and elks, the latter having multiplied so much that they now migrate to other forested areas. Many birds (white storks, lapwings, kingfishers etc) have made their home among the 1 100 species of plants, the most famous of which is the black birch; the best spot to admire them is in the vicinity of the village of Dziekanów-Leśny, on the northern edge of the park.

Excursions to Kampinos are made easier by the complex network of footpaths, cycle tracks and, in winter, cross-country skiing tracks. The classic itinerary from Truskaw to Palmiry (5km), lined with small wooden houses whose inhabitants sell their honey, enables visitors to admire the beauty of the park while discovering its tragic history. A vast wooded region close to Warsaw, Kampinos was an obvious resitance centre during the numerous wars that shook Poland. The small **Truskaw Museum** *(Tue-Sun 9am-3.30pm. 3 PLN)* recounts the episodes of insurrection against Russian troops in 1863, as well as those of the Second World War when the Nazis chose Kampinos as the place of execution of the first Polish Jews in 1940; over 2 000 of them are buried in the "war cemetery" in Palmiry.

Another particularly pleasant itinerary, which leads deeper into the forest, stretches over 12km from Leszno to Kampinos, where there is a charming 18C **wooden church**. The ramble can be extended as far as the fascinating **Granica Museum**, devoted to the park's fauna and flora *(Tue-Sun 9am-3.30pm. 4 PLN)*.

Pułtusk★ (population 4 637)

70km north of Warsaw. Follow road 61 towards Suwałki. Bus service from Warszawa Zachodnia bus station every 15min.

M. Rawluk / ONT Pologne

Pułtusk

This charming market town through which flows the River Narew (a tributary of the Wisła) offers a relaxing setting very much sought after by the Varsovians. The town had its heyday in the 15C and 16C, when it became the official residence of the bishops of Płock. Its Jesuit College, founded at the beginning of the 16C, trained numerous Polish politicians and contributed to spreading education throughout the eastern part of the country, traditionally at a disadvantage. In 1806, Napoleon fought a battle against the Russians which led to the Tilsit agreement founding the duchy of Warsaw. Pułtusk hit the headlines again in 1868, when a mighty meteorite crashed to earth in the vicinity. Finally, during the Second World War, 85% of the town was destroyed and half the population exterminated.

Pułtusk was rebuilt after the war with the help of late-18C illustrations. Today, one can admire the market square (**rynek**), reckoned to be the longest in Europe (400m), featuring in its centre the Gothic tower of the town hall which houses the **Regional Museum**. The rynek is closed off to the north by the Gothic collegiate church, remodelled in Renaissance style in the 16C by Venitian architect Giovanni Battista. Renaissance frescoes were discovered inside.

The south side of the square is occupied by the huge horseshoe-shaped **castle**, once the residence of the bishops of Płock.

The castle was remodelled many times before being rebuilt in 1974 and given by the government to the association of the Polish diaspora; it then became the **Polish House** (Dom Polonii), a centre where Poles from all over the world meet. It was turned into a comfortable hotel for Poles from foreign countries but also open to all.

Żelazowa Wola (Dom Urodzenia Fryderyka Chopina w Żelazowej Woli)★

54km west of Warsaw, on the edge of Kampinos National Park, near Sochaczew. The best way to get there is by bus (3 direct buses a day) from the Warszawa Zachodnia PKS bus terminal. Trains also run from Warszawa Centralna PKP Central Station or from Warszawa Śródmieście Station to Sochaczew but one must then take a local bus (no 6). ℘ (046) 863 33 00. Open May-Sep 9.30am-5.30pm, Oct-Apr 10am-4pm; closed Mon, 1 Jan, Easter Sun, 1 Nov, 24 Dec and public hols.

The manor of Żelazowa Wola, the birthplace of **Frédéric Chopin** (1810-1849), is now a museum. This fine residence originally formed part of the estate of Count Skarbek for whom the composer's father, Nicolas Chopin, a Frenchman, worked as a private tutor. The restored house, furnished in period style, and its surroundings are imbued with a very pleasant atmosphere but, unfortunately there are very few mementoes of Frédéric Chopin to be seen.

The charming adjoining park is the setting of open-air concerts given by music-school students *(Sat in Jul and Aug)*. On

---

Where to stay in Pułtusk

Dom Polonii – *Zamek. ℘ (48) 23 692 9000 – www.dompolonii.pultusk.pl. 52 rooms from 250 to 390 PLN.*

A three-star hotel with restaurant and gymnasium in the historic setting of the castle.

Sundays, on the other hand *(from the 1st Sun in May to the last Sun in Sep, at 11am and 3pm)*, admirers from all over the world flock to listen to the concerts given by renowned soloists.

Treblinka

100km north-east of Warsaw. The simplest way to get there without a car, is to join a guided tour. Alternatively, you can take a train to Małkinia and, from there, a bus to cover the last 8km (6 buses a day). From the bus stop, it is a 5min-walk to the parking area of the site. Open daily 9am-7pm, Nov-Mar until 5pm.

Laden with tragic memories, the site of the Treblinka concentration camp is a memorial to the 800 000 Jews who died there. Built next to the Treblinka I work camp, the Treblinka II death camp, which functioned from July 1942 to November 1943, was entirely dedicated to the "final solution". Covering 17ha, it was divided into two zones: one area was set aside to accommodate the SS, the other contained the three gas chambers to which ten more were soon added. From the train, deportees were taken to the gas chambers and their bodies were subsequently cremated. 12 to 17 000 people could thus be eliminated every day. In November 1943, the camp was dismantled, all trace of its macabre activity was erased and the site was reforested. On 10 May 1964, the Treblinka Memorial was inaugurated. There is no reconstruction but a vast central monument bearing the inscription "Never again", surrounded by a symbolic cemetery with 17 000 stones recalling the camp's sinister daily quota. In 1978, a stela was erected to the memory of Janusz Korczak.

Chopin's house

Practical Warsaw

Phone code – 022
Postal code -begins with 00-033

Useful addresses

TOURIST OFFICE (IT – Informacja Turystyczna) – ℰ94 31 (tourist informations in English – daily, May-Sep 8am-8pm, Oct-Apr 8am-6pm) – www.warsawtour.pl – The 4 branches of the Tourist Office handle accommodation and guided tours but only provide very basic literature about Warsaw.

- Plac Zamkowy 1/3 (Castle Square in the Old Town) – ℰ635 18 81 – Mon-Fri 9am-6pm, Sat 10am-6pm, Sun 11am-6pm.

- Okęcie Airport (Arrivals hall, next to the news-stand) – daily, May-Sep 8am-8pm; Oct-Apr 8am-6pm.

- Central Railway Station (Dworzec PKP Warszawa Centralna – main hall) – daily, May-Sep 8am-8pm; Oct-Apr 8am-6pm.

- Bus Station (Dworzec PKS Zachodnia – next to the ticket office) – daily 9am-5pm.

Canadian Embassy and Consulate – al. Matejki 1/5 – ℰ584 31 00 – Mon-Fri 10am-noon, 1-3pm – www.canada.pl.

Police – ℰ997 (112 from a mobile phone). Central Station – Ul. Wilcza 21.

Medical emergency – ℰ999.

Hospital and clinics

Szpital Dzieciątka Jezus (general public hospital) – Ul. Lindleya 4 – ℰ628 41 75.

Capricorn (private clinic) – Ul. Podwale 11 – ℰ831 86 69 – Mon, Wed, Fri. 8am-10pm; Tue, Thu, Sat-Sun and public hols 8am-9pm. Consultations in English.

Duodent (dental surgery) – Ul. Nowolipki 21 – ℰ838 82 68 – Mon-Fri 8am-8pm, Sat 8am-2pm. Consultations in English.

24hr/day pharmacy (Apteka) – Central Station (Dworzec Warszawa Centralna) – al. Jerozolimskie 54 – ℰ825 69 86.

Post office (Poczta) – There are many post offices, in particular at the airport, in the Central Station and in the rynek of the Old Town (Mon-Fri 8am-8pm, Sat 8am-1pm). Central post office : ul. Świętokrzyska 31/33 (daily 24hr/day). Sale of stamps for mailing abroad, phone cards, urban transport tickets and fax service. Long queues (about 20min).

Telephone – Public phone booths in stations, at the airport, in shopping precincts and subways crossing the main thoroughfares. Magnetic cards for sale in post offices and RUCH kiosks.

ATM machines (Bankomat) – There are many cash dispensers throughout the town as well as at the airport, in railway stations and in hotels. It is quite easy to withdraw cash 24hr/day.

Banks – Pekao-SA – Plac Bankowy 2 (on the first floor of the Blue Tower) – Mon-Fri 8am-7pm, Sat 9am-4pm – It is possible to draw cash on presentation of a bank card and a passport (counter no 9). The bank also exchanges American Express traveller's cheques.

Bureaux de change (Kantor) – There are many bureaux de change for changing money throughout the town; their rates are similar. Those at the airport and in the Central Station remain open 24hr/day.

Western Union (international money orders) – Ul. Długa 27 -- Mon-Fri 8am-6pm.

Internet cafés

Casablanca – Ul. Krakowskie Przedmieście 4/6- Mon-Fri 9am-1pm, Sat 10am-2pm, Sun 10am-midnight – 9 PLN/hr. Student-style café.

Simple – Ul. Marszałkowska 99/101 – daily 24hr/day – 4 PLN/ hr.

Grocery stores

Albert – Ul. Marszałkowska 112 (inside Galeria Centrum) – Mon-Sat 6am-11pm, Sun 10am-8pm.

Sklep nocny – Ul. Nowy Świat 53 – daily 7am-5pm.

International press – EMPIK (Galeria Centrum: Mon-Fri 7am-10pm, Sat 9am-10pm, Sun 11am-8pm; ul. Nowy Świat 15: Mon-Sat 9am-10pm, Sun 11am-7pm) – TRAFFIC (ul. Bracka 15 – Mon-Sat 10am-10pm, Sun 10am-7pm).

Where to go

The **Warsaw Tourist Office** organises guided tours of the town in collaboration with **tour operators**. The classic tour includes the Old Town, the Royal Way, the Wilanów Palace and the main monuments (Tomb of the Unknown Soldier, Ghetto Heroes Memorial, etc). Prices vary according to the season, the language, the duration of the tour and the number of people (allow for instance 120 PLN/pers for a 3hr tour in English). It is recommended to appy directly to the Tourist Office (ℰ94 31 – www.warsawtour.pl) or to the following tour operators : Trakt (ul. Kredytowa 6 – ℰ827 80 68 – daily 8am-6pm) or Mazurkas Travel (ul. Długa 8/14 – ℰ635 66 33 – www.mazurkas.pol.pl – daily 8am-6pm), who also organise thematic guided tours (Jewish Heritage and Frédéric Chopin Trail).

Oki Doki Hotel (Plac Dąbrowskiego 3 – ℰ826 51 12) organises good-quality guided tours (open to everybody) at unbeatable prices: a 5hr tour of the Old Town, the New Town, the former Jewish Ghetto and 20 historic sites (in English only. Dai ly except Wed and Sun, noon-5pm. 20 PLN/pers. Reservation advisable) and a tour exclusively dedicated to the Jewish Heritage (in English. Daily 11am-4pm. 30 PLN /pers, Students 20 PLN. Reservation required). Recommended.

No 180 bus – This line linking most of the capital's tourist sites offers visitors an overall view of Warsaw for the price of a single ticket (daily 7am-11pm). Stops at Rondo de Gaulle'a and all along the Royal Way.

Useful magazines and brochures – The following monthly magazines (in English) provide all the necessary information about Warsaw (including practical information, hotels, cafés, clubs and restaurants, exhibitions, as well as a map of the town and a description of the main tourist sites): *Warsaw in your pocket (5 PLN)*, *Warsaw Insider (8 PLN)*, *Poland WhatWhereWhen (free)*. They are available in hotels and foreign-newspaper retailers mentioned above.

Getting around

Frédéric Chopin Airport (Port Lotniczy im. Frederyka Chopina) – *Ul. Żwigry i Wigury 1* – ☎*650 42 20 (information in English about international flights)* – Warsaw Airport, situated 10km from the town centre, handles all domestic and international flights (including "low-cost" companies: departures and arrivals in Etiuda Terminal, 300m from the main terminals). There are two options to reach the town centre: 175 bus which goes to Warsaw Centre, stops at the railway station, along the Royal Way and in the Old Town (Departures every 15min from 5am-11pm, opposite the arrivals hall. Tickets -*bilet normalny* 2,40 PLN- available at the Ruch kiosk in the arrivals hall – Extra ticket compulsory for each large piece of luggage); or one of the taxis queueing up at the terminal exits (journey to the centre 30/40 PLN. Beware : it is imperative to turn away taxis offering their services verbally within the airport compound, they are either illegal or much dearer and not insured).

Central Railway Station (Dworzec PKP Warszawa Centralna) – *al. Jerozolimskie 54 (access from the avenue via the subways)* – ☎*94 36* – Regular train services to every Polish town as well as to the capitals of neighbouring countries. Ticket-office staff usually do not speak English, it is therefore advisble to go to the central hall information point first or to browse the excellent website *www. pkp.pl* (in English). Only problem: destinations must be mentioned in Polish). Platforms *(peron)* are located below ground.

Bus stations -

The Central Station **(Dworzec Centralny PKS Warszawa Zachodnia** – *al. Jerozolimskie 144)* handles the main part of the international traffic as well as the domestic traffic from the south and the west of Poland. Take the 508 bus at the exit to go to the town centre.

The Praga Station **(Dworzec PKS Stadion)** handles traffic to and from the north, east and south-east of the country. Take Tramway no 25 to get to the town centre.

Public transport – Warsaw boasts an excellent public-transport network – Information: ☎*94 84* or *www.ztm.waw.pl (website in English)* – **Tramways** are recommended for journeys in the town centre *(daily 5am-11pm)*. **Buses** are best

for the Royal Way *(daily 5am-11pm)*.The **underground** has only one north-south line *(daily 5am-0.15am)*. One **ticket** system common to all these means of transport: single ticket *(bilet jednorazowy* 2.40 PLN, valid for one journey on one means of transport only), daily ticket *(bilet dobowy* 7.20 PLN – valid 24hr from the time it is stamped, on all means of transport), 3-day ticket *(bilet trzydniowy* 12 PLN – valid 72hr from the time it is stamped, on all means of transport), weekly ticket *(bilet tygodniowy* 24 PLN). Children under 4 and people over 70 travel free. 50% concession for students with an ISIC card. Tickets can be bought from Ruch kiosks or post offices. Bear in mind that 3-day and weekly tickets are not on sale in the Ruch kiosks located in the Central Station and in the airport, nor at the city's ZTM public transport headquarters (*ul. Senatorska 37*). Frequent controls (86 PLN fines payable on the spot in cash for non-residents). There is no pocket map of the transport network, but the journey description and the timetable are posted at the stops.

Taxis – Taxis must be reserved by phone (from a mobile, dial 22 before the number) – MPT (☎*919* – CB accepted. Service for disabled travellers) and WA-WA (☎*96 44*) have English-speaking operators. Be sure to avoid illegal taxis, many of whom hang out in the vicinity of the Old Town (only accept or wave down taxis with the name and telephone number of their company on the roof, and fares clearly marked on the back passenger window).

Vehicle hire – There are many hire companies at the airport, including: AVIS – ☎*572 65 65* – *www.avis.pl* – (there is a very useful branch in the town centre, in the Marrott Hotel).
HERTZ – ☎*500 16 20* – *www.hertz.com.pl*.
24hr/day breakdown service – ☎*981 and 96 33*.
24h/24 supervised car parks- In the Old Town: *ul.Senatorska 3*; in the centre: *Marc Pol (in front of the Palace of Culture)*.
Bike hire – The Oki Doki Hotel offers by far the best prices, see address below *(8 PLN/hour, 37 PLN/day)*.

Warsaw underground entrance

ONT Pologne

Where to stay

As capitals go, Warsaw offers a relatively limited choice of hotels; however, it is not generally difficult to find accommodation, even without prior reservation, because the volume of tourists is still low. Since prices vary quite a lot between weekdays and weekends and also according to the season, it is advisable to apply directly to the hotels or to take a look at their website.

IN AND AROUND THE OLD TOWN

Kanonia – *Ul. Jezuicka 2* – ☎635 06 76 – www.kanonia.pl – *42 rooms 28 PLN/pers.* – ▭ *9 PLN* – This quiet, well-kept youth hostel offers a roof in the most picturesque narrow street of the Old Town for a very modest price. No curfew and Internet access. Open year-round.

Hotel Praski – *al. Solidarności 61* – ☎818 49 89 – www.praski.pl – *33 rooms 160/270 PLN* ▭ – **P** – **&** – Situated on the other side of the Wisła yet only one tramway stop from the Old Town, this standard hotel, clean and recently renovated, undeniably offers good value for money.

Hotel Hetman – *Ul. Kłopotoskiego 36* – ☎511 98 00 – www.hotelhetman.pl – *68 rooms 330/380 PLN* ▭ – **P** – **&** – This hotel, boasting spacious rooms, simply painted in light sand colours, offers all the facilities of a three-star establishment for a slightly lower price. Located in a peaceful tree-lined street in the Praga district, near the zoo and one tramway stop from the Old Town. Internet.

Duval – *Ul. Nowomiejska 10* – ☎831 91 04 – www.duval.net.pl – *4 apart. 390 PLN* ▭ – This residence situated in the heart of the Old Town comprises 4 studio apartments, meticulously furnished in different styles (retro, Polish, Japanese and "classy"), all equipped with an Internet connection. Breakfast is served in a pleasant kitchen-cum-living room where the suspended fireplace blends perfectly well with the wooden furniture and the old piano. Reservation advisable.

Le Régina – *Ul. Kościelna 12* – ☎531 60 00 – www.leregina.com – *61 rooms 580/1180 PLN* ▭ – **P** – **&** – Housed in an 18C restored palace in the heart of the New Town, this luxury hotel is impressive on account of the monastic silence which reigns inside. The walls of all the rooms are decorated with hand-painted frescoes. Excellent French restaurant. Swimming pool and gymnasium. WIFI Internet connection.

Le Royal Méridien Bristol – *Ul. Krakowskie Przedmieście 42/44* – ☎551 10 00 – www.lemeridienbristol.com – *205 rooms 540/1560 PLN* ▭ – **&** – Ideally situated along the Royal Way, between the centre and the Old Town, the Royal Méridien Bristol is Warsaw's only 5-star hotel. Art Nouveau entrance hall, carefully decorated rooms, high-class restaurant,

swimming pool and irreproachable staff. Undeniably the best place to stay at in Warsaw, budget permitting.

CENTRE

Oki Doki – *Plac Dąbrowskiego 3* – ☎826 51 12 – www.okidoki.pl – *30 rooms 145/185 PLN, 10 rooms for 4-8 pers. 45/55 PLN/pers.* – ▭ *9 PLN* – **P** – This youth hostel is undoubtedly one of the best moderately priced establishments in the town centre. Single or double rooms decorated by local artists, very convivial staff and numerous tourist services including: organisation of guided tours, bike rental, information about outings, etc. No curfew. Free Internet access. Reservation required.

Mazowiecki – *Ul. Mazowiecka 10* – ☎827 23 65 – www.mazowiecki.com.pl – *56 rooms 150/248 PLN* ▭ – The ideal situation of this hotel, halfway between the centre and the Old Town, its low prices and the most romantic adjoining restaurant where breakfast is served largely make up for the plain outmoded yet neat rooms (bathrooms are either individual or on the landing). Bear in mind that the street is very busy (ask for a room overlooking the courtyard).

Boutique Bed & Breakfast – *Ul. Smolna 14/7* – ☎829 48 01 – www.bedandbreakfast.pl – *4 apart. 200/360 PLN* – **P** – 4 apartments of a high standard, decorated with flowers and equipped with wooden furniture, situated in a pleasant and peaceful street adjacent to the Royal Way; one really feels at home here. The Queen apartment, with its spacious living room and jacuzzi, is obviously highly recommended… It is also recommended to ask the convivial owner for a reservation.

Harenda – *Ul. Krakowskie Przedmieście 4/6* – ☎826 26 25 – www.hotelharenda.com.pl – *43 rooms 250/315 PLN (at weekends, the 2nd night is free)* ▭ – **P** – This hotel offers outdated rooms which are not, unfortunately, up to the same standard as the elegant reception area; it is nevertheless a place one can justifiably recommend on account of its situation at the junction of the Old Town, the Centre and the Royal Way and also of the attractive discounts applied at weekends. Bear in mind that there is a noisy nightclub in the basement at weekends.

Première Classe – *Ul. Towarowa 2* – ☎824 08 00 – www.premiereclasse.com.pl – *126 rooms 169 PLN* – ▭ *18 PLN* – **P** – Standard yet bright and modern rooms, all fitted with individual bathrooms. Located along a dull avenue, but at the crossroads of the main bus and tramway lines.

Residence Diana – *Ul. Chmielna 13a* – ☎505 91 00 – www.residencediana.com – *46 apart. 360/890 PLN* – ▭ *42 PLN* – **P** – **&** – THE high-standard place to stay in the centre: this recent welcoming residence, boasting a contemporary design apt to satisfy every taste, is located in a fine inner courtyard, in the pedestrian shopping area of the town centre. Apartments (for 2 persons) come in all sizes and prices. The residence offers all the services of a 4-star hotel (Internet access, plasma-screen TV, dry-cleaner's, jacuzzi, etc) and continental restaurant. A pleasant discovery.

Hotel Rialto – Ul. Wilcza 73 – ☎ 584 87 00 – info@hotelrialto.com.pl – 33 rooms 1161 PLN – ☒ 72 PLN – 🄿 – ♿ – Situated in a quiet spot and housed in a fine Art Déco building dating from 1906. The rooms boast a personalised decor with the latest comfort. High-quality restaurant with 1930s-style decor and furniture.

Hotel Mariott – Al. Jerozolimskie 65-79 – ☎ 630 63 06 – mariott@it.com.pl – 491 rooms 817 PLN – ☒ 86 PLN – 🄿 – ♿ – Housed in a recent building with beautiful views of the town and the latest comfort. High-class Italian restaurant and another restaurant serving traditional Polish cuisine.

Eating out

Warsaw offer a wide range of quality restaurants, usually serving from noon to 10pm without a break.

OLD TOWN

Kamienne Schodki – Rynek 26 – ☎ 831 08 22 – daily noon-last customer – 55 PLN – Excellent value for money for this traditional restaurant situated in the rynek.

Na Prowincji – Ul. Nowomiejska 10 – ☎ 831 98 75 – daily noon-11pm – 30 PLN – This small Italian restaurant featuring stone walls and diffused lighting, makes a welcome change from the traditional Polish restaurants in the Old Town.

Kompania Piwna – Podwale 25 – ☎ 635 63 14 – Mon-Fri 11am-1am, Sat-Sun noon-1am – 40 PLN – This vast popular tavern offers by far the best value for money in the Old Town. Traditional family-style dishes and generous helpings. In the evening, avoid the room at the back, which is extremely noisy.

Bazyliszek – Rynek 1/3 – ☎ 831 18 41 – daily noon-midnight – 80 PLN – This restaurant with a long-standing family tradition offers a wide choice of Polish specialities in a carefully preserved historic decor: the hunter's room (sala myśliwska) and the knight's room (sala rycerska) are recommended.

Gessler – Rynek 21 – ☎ 831 16 61 – daily noon-last customer – 70 PLN – Warsaw's oldest restaurant comprises a high-class room upstairs and a tavern in the basement. The latter, a labyrinth of vaulted rooms splendidly decorated as late-19C farmhouse interiors, is well worth a visit. Prices are unfortunately rather prohibitive.

U Fukiera – Rynek 27 – ☎ 831 10 13 – daily noon-last customer – 100 PLN – This very famous Polish restaurant consists of three imposing dining rooms lit by candlelight and a superb inner courtyard. Elaborate menu and impeccable service.

NEW TOWN

Antrakt – Plac Piłsudskiego 12 – ☎ 827 64 11 – daily noon-last customer – 30 PLN – This small café-cum-restaurant housed inside the Grand Theatre offers simple good-quality food in a warm friendly decor characteristic of literary cafés of the interwar period.

CENTRE

Sphinx – Ul. Szpitalna 1 – ☎ 827 58 19 – daily 11am-1am – 30 PLN – Snacks and traditional dishes in a setting featuring overabundant decorations: the place is not interesting in itself, apart from the fact that it is Warsaw's most popular restaurant. Students, business men and whole families come for a meal or a snack at any time of the day.

Zgoda – Ul. Zgoda 4 – ☎ 827 99 34 – Mon-Sat 9am-11pm, Sun noon-11pm – 35 PLN – A bright, well-kept restaurant offering traditional cuisine at very competitive prices for this area. The large tables are ideal for a family meal and there is no deafening background music. Non-smoking dining room.

Orchidea – Ul. Szpitalna 3 – ☎ 827 34 36 – Mon-Sat 10am-midnight, Sun noon-last customer – 40 PLN – An excellent establishment offering a delicious fusion-style cuisine at reasonable prices; the staff is really charming.

Bar Bambino – Ul. Krucza 21 – Mon-Fri 7am-8pm, Sat 9am-5pm – 15 PLN – 🚭- This milk bar is an example of its kind: simple cooking, generous helpings; mixed clientele. The place is highly recommended as it provides an insight into the former canteens of the communist period.

Chłopskie Jadło – Plac Konstytuji 1 – ☎ 339 17 17 – daily noon-midnight – 50 PLN – This "farmhouse kitchen" is without a doubt THE restaurant not to be missed in Warsaw. The food is unbelievably excellent and the enormous helpings are accompanied by large loaves of fresh bread placed directly onto the large wooden tables. All the dishes are delicious, starting with the placki (potato pancakes) and the smalec (streaky bacon, a speciality of the house). Service is quick and the atmosphere extremely convivial. It is essential to reserve the day before.

Delicja Polska – Ul. Koszykowa 54 – ☎ 630 88 50 – daily noon-last customer – 40 PLN – Delicious dishes, a fairy-tale decor, efficient, discreet service and moderate prices: this restaurant is one of Warsaw's small gems. Do try the house liquor (nalewki kresowe), made from walnuts and bilberries.

ROYAL WAY

Café Nowy Świat – Ul. Nowy Świat 63 – Mon-Fri 9am-10pm, Sat-Sun 10am-9pm –

This hundred-year-old café,(see Taking a break) also offers a choice of dishes.

U Hopfera Pierogi Świata – *Ul. Krakowskie Przedmieście 53 – ☏828 73 52 – daily 11am-last customer – 30 PLN* – A charming little restaurant exclusively and competently dedicated to the national speciality, i.e. *pierogi* (stuffed ravioli).

Mercers Gourmet Caffe– *Ul. Nowy Świat 21 (go through the porch and walk to the end of the alley. Basement of the building on the right) – ☏826 38 77 – daily 11am-last customer – 100 PLN* – This high-class restaurant is the perfect place to try the best Polish specialities served in a warmly and richly decorated setting. Ideal for tête-à-tête dinners by candlelight. Reservation advisable.

Qchnia Artystyczna – *Zamek Ujazdowski– ☏625 76 27 – dialy 11am-last customer – 70 PLN* – Housed in the contemporary art centre, this restaurant is by far one of Warsaw's least typical eateries. It proposes Polish and continental dishes, elegantly served in a pared down decor renewed with each new exhibition hosted by the art centre. The potato-and-salmon pancakes *(placki z łososiem)* are a must. The town's finest terrace in summer.

Belvédère – *Parc Łazienki, ul Agrykola 1 (entrance via Parkowa Street) – ☏841 22 50 – daily noon-last customer – 120 PLN* – The capital's most elegant restaurant obviously offers a faultless menu and an exceptional setting which alone would justify the high prices: in the heart of Łazienki Park, inside the historic Orangery, where the luxuriant vegetation, the suspended aviary and the winter garden create a unique atmosphere.

PRAGA

Le Cèdre – *al Solidarności 61 (level with the Praski tramway stop, just after crossing the Wisła) – ☏670 11 66 – daily 11am-11pm – 40 PLN* – The only real restaurant in Praga serves excellent lebanese food. Take away service.

Taking a break

Most bars and cafés also serve meals throughout the day.

OLD TOWN AND NEW TOWN

Stacja Rynek – *Rynek 15 (in the basement, on the corner of Świętojańska and Zapiecek streets) – daily noon-midnight* – A haven of peace in the midst of the Rynek's bustle, cleverly blending old furniture and elements of modern decoration.

Metal Bar – *Rynek 10 (at the end of the corridor) – daily 11am-midnight* – A tiny modern, peaceful bar offering Internet access until midnight for a minimal sum.

Chimera – *Ul. Podwale 29 (in the courtyard beyond the porch) – Mon-Fri 3pm-1am, Sat-Sun 1pm-1am* – This informal café, invisible from the street, has a large shaded terrace; fantastic in summer.

To Lubię – *Ul. Freta 10 – daily 10am-10pm* – This bright, cosy café offers a large choice of teas and coffees as well as mouth-watering homemade cakes. A small drawing area is set aside upstairs for children. No smoking.

Jazz Café Helicon – *Ul. Freta 45/47 – Mon-Fri 11am-midnight, Sat-Sun 11am-1am* – This café/record shop hosts jazz concerts by renowned Polish and international musicians (every Tue, Thu and Sun at 7pm).

CENTRE

Café Kulturalna – *Palace of Culture and Science (on the side of Marszałkowska Avenue. Entrance on the left of the Palace's main entrance) – Mon-Sat noon-last customer, Sun 3pm-last customer* – This peaceful café, imbued with a literary and artistic atmosphere, offers the possibility of getting an insight into the Palace of Culture. Concerts and previews regularly take place in the evening.

Wedel – *Ul. Szpitalna 8 – Mon-Sat 8am-10pm, Sun noon-8pm* – The temple of the famous Warsaw chocolate-maker serves the best hot chocolate in town as well as copious and succulent breakfasts at reasonable prices. Non-smoking room.

Między Nami – *Ul. Bracka 20 – Mon-Wed, Sun 11am-11pm, Thu-Sat 11am-1am* – This favourite haunt of Warsaw's trendy youth offers, in summer time, the best terrace in the town centre and good-quality snacks at moderate prices.

Fukiera restaurant in the Old Town

Antykwariat – *Ul. Żurawia 45 – Mon-Fri 11am-11pm, Sat-Sun 1-11pm* – Walls covered with old books, an indoor garden and an oriental room: this café is a must whatever the season and the time of day.

Café Karma – *Plac Zbawiciela 3/5 – Mon-Fri 7.30am-10pm, Sat 9am-10pm, Sun 10.30am-10pm* – The ideal place to relax after a tour of the town or a shopping afternoon. Spacious and equipped with comfortable teak chairs spread around an ancient central fireplace, the café attracts a local clientele as well as the actors of the nearby theatre.

ROYAL WAY

Tea Art – *Ul. Bednarska 28/30 – daily 10am-10pm* – A charming tearoom furnished with bric-à-brac in the romantic district of Mariensztat.

Café Nowy Świat – *Ul. Nowy Świat 63 – Mon-Fri 9am-10pm, Sat-Sun 10am-9pm* – This hundred-year-old café, the legendary haunt of the Polish intelligentsia, is imbued with a unique atmosphere... crowded as it is with students and teachers from the nearby university buildings. Fine cuisine and excellent pastries. You can look at newspapers and magazines from all European countries and from the US as well. In summer, pleasant terrace located in the inner courtyard. Non-smoking room.

Café Blikle – *Ul. Nowy Świat 33 – Mon-Fri 9am-10pm, Sat-Sun 10am-10pm* – The ancestor of Warsaw's cafés (1869) offers delicious dishes and pastries (rose-jam doughnuts, *rogalik z różą*, are a speciality). Terrace in summer and non-smoking room.

PRAGA

Łysy Pingwin – *Ul. Ząbkowska 11 – Mon-Thu 10am-10pm, Fri-Sat noon-last-customer, Sun 1-6pm* – Amusing café crowded with local artists; the walls are covered with old film posters and vinyl LPs from the 1970s/80s on sale for 10 PLN each. Excellent sandwiches made to order.

Pracownia Krawiecka – *Ul. Inżynierska 1 – Tue-Sat 9.30am-last customer, Sun 7.30pm-last customer* – This unassuming bar, looking quite Bohemian inside, also serves toasts for a moderate price.

On the town

Information brochures – Magazines mentioned in the Where to go section offer a rich and varied selection of night-time events (concerts, cinemas, theatre, previews, etc) and the monthly *Aktivist* provides the comprehensive programme of clubs and current music concerts (freely available from bars and some restaurants).

WHERE TO HAVE A DRINK

Concentration of clubs and cafés in ul. Foksal, Mazowiecka and Żurawia/Trzech Krzyży.

Melodia – *Ul. Nowy Świat 3/5 – ℰ583 01 81 – Mon-Sat 4pm-last customer* – This elegant piano-bar, decorated with warm refined colours, hosts jazz and world music concerts every evening.

SHOWS AND ENTERTAINMENT

Casino – Casinos Polands – *al Jerozolimskie 65/79 – ℰ630 63 64 – daily 11am-7am – Admission 4 PLN* – Housed on the top floor of the Marriott Hotel, this casino offers a breathtaking view of Warsaw by night.

Cinemas – Kinoteka (multiplex housed in the Palace of Culture, always impressive!) – Kino Iluzjon (*ul. Narbutta 50a)*: a marvellous cinema with creeking wooden foldaway seats, dedicated to the classics of Polish and international cinema, boasting a retro café, ideal after the show – Kino Lab (*Zamek, al. Ujazdowskie 6 – Cross the main hall, entance in the inner courtyard on the right):* the small auditorium of the contemporary art centre shows art films from various countries.

Grand Theatre and National Opera (Teatr Wielki / Opera Narodowa) – *Plac Teatralny 1 – ℰ826 50 19 – www. teatrwielki.pl.* **National Philharmonia (Filharmonia Narodowa)** – *Ul. Sienkiewicza 10 – ℰ551 71 49 – www. filharmonia.pl.*

Friends of Frédéric Chopin Society (Towarzystwo mienia Fryderyka Chopina) – *Ul. Okólnik 1 – ℰ827 54 71.*

Fabryka Trzciny – *Ul. Otwocka 14 (in the Praga district) – ℰ619 05 13 – www. fabrykatrzciny.p*l. A former factory, converted into an elegant centre of art and culture, regularly hosting good-quality jazz, as well as current and world music concerts.

Shopping

Warning : shops are usually closed on Saturday afternoon and on the afternoon preceding a public holiday, except in shopping centres.

POLISH TRADITIONAL HANDICRAFTS

The following shops offer a wide choice of wooden objects, ceramics, household linen, folk costumes, as well as the famous colourful eggs and small boxes in painted wood.

PolArt – *Rynek Starego miasta 10 – Mon-Fri 10am-6pm, Sat 10am-2pm.*

Cepelia – *Ul. Chmielna 8 – Mon-Fri 10am-7pm, Sat 10am-2pm.*

Arex Folk Art Gallery – *Ul. Chopina 5 – Mon-Fri 10am-7pm, Sat 10am-2pm.*

POSTERS AND CONTEMPORARY ART

Galeria Polskiego Plakatu – *Rynek Starego miasta 23 – daily 10am-7pm – www.poster.com.pl –* This boutique, devoted to Polish poster painting and graphic art offers an impressive choice of film, theatre, opera and circus posters, mostly collector's items, some of them very rare.

Galeria Plakatu Włodka Orła – *Plac Na Rozdrożu (in the subway) – daily 2-6pm – www.polskiplakat.link2.pl –* This famous and unusual stall belongs to a poster lover... low prices.

Galeria Raster – *Ul. Hoża 42 m 8 (ring the entryphone at no 8. Top floor) – Tue-Sat 3-8pm –* This independent gallery, laid out like a private apartment, exhibits the works of many artists among the most forceful of the Polish avant-garde. Wide range of prices.l

Galeria De Sign – *Zamek Ujazdowski – Tue-Sun 11am-5pm, Fri 11am-7pm –* Furniture and highly original contemporary china.

CLOTHES AND JEWELLERY

Metal Galeria – *Rynek Starego Miasta 8 ; Ul. Chmielna 32 – Mon-Fri 11am-7pm, Sat 11am-3pm* – The finest jewellery shop in Warsaw, selling limited editions of original items exclusively made by Polish artists.

DW Art Gallery – *Ul. Nowy Świat 52 – Mon-Sat 11am-7pm* – This boutique sells Polish designer jewellery, original decorative objects as well as unusual tea and vodka sets.

Polscy Projektanci – *Ul. Chmielna 30 – Mon-Fri 11am-7pm, Sat 10am-4pm* – A small boutique exclusively devoted to Polish designers. Clothes and handbags from the most classic to the most extravagant, in a wide range of prices.

Fur shops – *Ul. Chmielna and Nowy Świat.*

BOOKS

Bookshop of the contemporary art centre – *Zamek Ujazdowski – Tue-Sun 11am-5pm, Fri 11am-9pm* – A fine selection of art books at interesting prices, some of them dedicated to Polish artists, as well as beautiful books about Warsaw and Poland with lovely photographs.

GROCERY SHOPS

Blikle – *Ul. Nowy Świat 35 – Mon-Sat 10am-8pm* – The famous temple of traditional biscuits and cakes.

Skarby Smaku – *Ul. Hoża 43/49* – Traditional homemade organic products (cheese, ginger bread from Toruń, cakes from Podlasie, etc), presented in the convivial decor of an old kitchen. Gift-baskets.

BAZAARS AND MARKETS

Two popular and picturesque flower, fruit and vegetable markets: **Hala Mirowska** *(Plac Mirowski – Mon-Sat 7am-4pm)* and **Hala Banacha** *(ul. Grójecka 95 – Mon-Sat 7am-2pm).*

"Russian Market" – *Stadion Dziesięciolecia (tramway no 25 starting from the central station or Rondo De Gaulle'a, stop at Rondo Waszyngtona) – daily 6.30am-1pm* – The biggest open market in Europe. Ordinary bric-à-brac

items are on sale, but the place deserves a visit for its atmosphere and the unique feel of this huge stadium, especially under snow in winter (go up to the very top in order to look inside the stadium; the market is held on the outside)

Stodoła photo market – *Stodoła Hall, ul. Batorego 10 (Underground stop Pole Mokotowskie) – Sun 10am-2pm – 4 PLN* – Professional and amateur photographers alike will find this market particularly attractive. Interesting prices.

SHOPPING CENTRES

Galeria Centrum – *Ul. Marszałkowska 104/122 (opposite the Palace of Culture and Science – Mon-Fri 9.30am-9pm, Sat 9.30am-8.30pm, Sun 10.30am-5pm.* All brands.

Arkadia – *Al. Jana Pawła 82 – Mon-Sat 9am-9pm, Sun 10am-8pm* – Europe's largest shopping centre, inaugurated in 2004.

Sport and leisure

Ski-jumping and bobsleigh – Ski Slope – *Park Szczęśliwicki, ul. Drawska 22 – ☎823 86 75 – Open 1 Nov to 31 Mar: Mon-Fri 2-10pm, Sat-Sun 10am-10pm.* To get acquainted with ski-jumping, THE national sport.

Ice rinks – Torwar – *Ul. Łazienkowska 6a – ☎621 44 71 – Sat-Sun, entrance at 11am and 5pm* – Ice rink of the Palace of Culture and Science (on the side of ul. Świętokrzyska): a must if you visit Warsaw in winter.

Festive events

Biennial Poster Festival – Poster Museum (Muzeum Plakatu) – Every two years, the next one will take place in spring 2006.

Jazz Festival Jamboree – *Every year in October* – The biggest international jazz Festival in Central Europe.

International Film Festival (Warszawa Film Fest) – Every year at the beginning of October- *www.wff.pl*

Łódź ★

POPULATION 785 134 – MAP OF POLAND A2 – WOJEWÓDZTWO OF ŁÓDŹ

Łódź (pronounced "woodge"), the country's second largest town, occupies a place apart from other towns in Poland. Entirely built in the 19C at the time of the industrial revolution, it instantly became the "Promised Land" described in the novel by Władysław Reymont, laureate of the Nobel Prize of Literature, and adapted for the screen by Andrzej Wajda. Smoke from the slender brick chimneys still rises over the horizon, while the famous Cinema School and the original villas and manufactures in the town centre, house many museums and host numerous festivals, thus attesting to the capital role played by Łódź on the Polish cultural scene.

- ▶ **Getting your bearings** – 120km south-west of Warsaw, 230km north-west of Kraków.
- 👁 **Not to be missed** – Piotrkowska Street, the White Factory, the Modern Art Museum.
- 🕐 **Planning your visit** – Allow a minimum of one day; allow two days to enjoy your visit to the full.

Background

The Polish Manchester – In 1820, tsarist Poland chose the small town of Łódź as the centre of its newly created textile industry. As early as 1823, the first working-class district was built at the instigation of Jewish manufacturers. Łódź rapidly became a "Promised Land" for thousands of farmers from the surrounding region and for Polish and foreign investors who flocked to the town. The suppression of trade barriers between Poland and Russia in 1850 led to a considerable increase in textile exports and, during the second half of the 19C, Łódź became the world's top textile centre and a cosmopolitan metropolis. It was administered by Othodox Russians while the factories were run by Protestant German industrialists who, together with the Jews, founded the main manufactures employing Catholic Polish workers.

The Second World War broke out during the first half of the 20C, just when the textile industry was beginning to decline. The town was occupied by the German army as early as September 1939. The Nazis set up Poland's first ghetto in the centre of Łódź, where 260 000 Jews were confined and starved before being sent to the death camps. The Radogoszcz district was partly turned into a transit camp, while other camps, exclusively intended for children and Tziganes were created.

Łódź is still an industrial centre today, but it is above all proud of the place it holds on Poland's cultural scene: it boasts many museums including a prestigious Modern Art Museum, a famous Cinema School, hosts several art festivals and is considered as the Polish capital of techno music.

Exploring

Because it was built in the 19C, Łódź has no old rynek, no historic castle but centres round the famous **Piotrkowska Street**, the town's main thoroughfare, 4km long and entirely pedestrianised. The 19C architecture draws its inspiration from the neo-Gothic, neo-Renaissance, neo-Baroque and Art Nouveau styles equally applied to the factories and to the industrialists' bourgeois residences. The old market square (Plac Kościelny) to the north, dominated by the two brick towers of the neo-Gothic Church of the Assumption, has lost its role as the main square.

Piotrkowska Street ★

It starts from **Plac Wolności** featuring the former town hall in neo-Classical style (1827) and, behind Kościuszko's statue, a charming Uniate church. Piotrkowska and the streets perpendicular to it are lined with a series of magnificent bourgeois houses. The former residence of the printer Jan Perersilgy at no 86 is quite impressive with its wealth of architectural details (including Poland's only statue of Gutenberg). Take a detour via **Moniuszki Street**, lined with an uninterrupted rown of fine neo-Renaissance houses, before returning to Piotrkowska Street and the splendid **Palace of Wilhem Schweikert** (no 282), headquarters of the Centre of European Studies. Further down, the **Olympia Manufacture**, followed by several villas owned by industrialists, successfully blends different architectural styles. Opposite and close to each other are the town's two most important churches. The neo-Gothic **St Stanisłas Cathedral** (Archikatedra im Św. Stanisława Kostki)★ features a rather dull brick façade, but the stained-glass windows and the interior, which has a particularly spacious feel to it, come as a surprise. The Lutheran **St Matthew' Church** (kościół Św. Macieja) is the parish church of the descendants of the old German oligarchy; recitals are frequently given on the romantic-style organ, one of the finest of its kind in Poland. The **Kinderman Villa** (ul. Wólczańska 31/33) is undoubtedly the most brilliant example of Art Nouveau style introduced in Poland. Finally, the renowned **Herbst Palace** (ul. Przędzalniana 72. Daily except Mon And Fri 10am-3pm, 3 PLN) looks from the outside like one of those Renaissance villas built by Palladio in the north of Italy. The Catholic-inspired interior decorations are exceptionally fine and attest to the wealth of this family of German industrial magnates.

Łódź

Jewish Cemetery (Cmentarz Żydowski)
Ul. Bracka. Daily except Sat 9am-3pm. 4 PLN. The Jewish community of Łódź (30% of the local population) was practically wiped out during the Second World War. The synagogues and the old cemetery were razed to the ground, but the "New" Jewish cemetery founded in 1892 survived; with over 180 000 graves, it is the largest in Europe. Its overgrown alleyways are conducive to meditation.

Things to see

The Town's Historical Museum (Muzeum Historii Miasta.)★
Ul. Ogrodowa 15. Tue, Thu-Sun 10am-2pm, Wed 2-6pm. 7 PLN, free admission on Sun. The museum offers the added interest of being housed in Europe's most elaborate manufacturing complex of the Industrial Revolution period; this includes first of all the Poznański Palace, standing as a brilliant example of the way the emerging industrial middle class adopted the aristocratic taste for the Baroque style, then the "Poltex" factory (still in operation), the warehouses and, across the street, the workers' homes. Several rooms inside the museum are devoted to the famous musician Arthur Rubinstein.

Textile Museum (Muzeum Włókiennictwa)★
l.Piotrkowska 282. Tue-Fri 9am-4pm, Sat-Sun 11am-4pm. 5 PLN, free admission on Fri. Located inside the neo-Classical building of the White Factory (Biały Młyn), the first mill to be equipped with a steam engine (1838), the museum illustrates the saga of the textile industry in Łódź in an entertaining way by underlining its social implications. Impressive display of machinery and fabrics from the 16C to the 19C.

Modern Art Museum (Muzeum Sztuki)★★
Ul. Więckowskiego 36. Tue 10am-5pm, Wed, Fri 11am-5pm, Thu noon-7pm, Sat-Sun 10am-4pm. 7 PLN, free admission on Thu. Founded in 1925 and housed in another Renaissance Palace once owned by the Poznański family, this was one of the first avant-garde museums in the world. Created on the initiative of Władysław Strzemiński, an exponent of Polish Constructivism and a founder of the a.r. ("avant-garde du réel") group, the museum added its valuable contribution to the history of contemporary art in Poland. The collection includes abstract, constructivist, surrealist and figurative works by Polish avant-garde artists of the first half of the 20C: Kobro, Stażewski, Strzemiński (a revelation for anyone who is not familiar with his work), etc.
The collection of the a.r. group was the second museum collection of avant-garde art in Europe (after the Hanover Abstract Cabinet, opened in 1927). The museum also houses one of the great international collections of 20C painting (works by Chagall,

Mondrian, Kisling, Nolde, Ernst, Klee, Arp, Léger, Picasso, etc) as well as an excellent collection of socialist-realist works from the Stalinist period.

Cinema Museum (Muzeum Kinematografii)★

Plac Zwycięstwa 1. Tue noon-5pm, Wed-Sun 10am-3pm, 6 PLN, free admission on Tue. Housed in the fortress-style palace of the Scheibler family, this museum acknowledges the fact that Łódź ranks among the top producers of filmmakers in Europe. Temporary exhibitions illustrating the history of Polish cinema, as well as the life and works of its most famous representatives.

Practical Łódź

Postal code – 90- 000
Phone code – 046

Useful addresses

Tourist Office – Al. Kościuszw 88 –
✆ 638 59 56 – *cit@uml.lodz.pl* –The helpful staff speaks English. Many useful brochures. The town's website – *www. uml.lodz.pl* – in English offers a wealth of information.

Central post office – *ul. Tuwima 38.*

24hr/day Internet café- *ul. Piotrkowska 81.*

Getting around

Łódź Fabryczna PKP Railway Station – *Pl Salinskiego 1.* Warsaw (departure every hour) and all destinations to the north and east.

Łódź Kaliska PKP Railway Station – *al. Unii Lubelskiej 3/5* Destinations to the south and west.

PKS Bus Station – *Pl. Saliński ego 3.* Regular bus service to all the main towns and the surrounding areas. Bus to Warsaw every hour (from 6.45am to 8.45pm).

Where to stay

Grand Hotel – *ul. Piotrkowska 72 –* ✆ 633 99 20 – *www.orbis.pl* – *161 rooms: 145/380 PLN.* Fine Belle Époque establishment where Roman Polanski stays during his frequent visits.

Déjà-Vu – *ul. Wigury 4/6 –* ✆ 636 20 60 – *45 ch – 19 rooms: 145/380 PLN.* Amazing B &B establishment recreating the atmosphere of the industrial districts in the 1920s. Prices are set accordingly but the illusion is guaranteed.

Polonia Hotel – *ul. Narutowicza 38 –* ✆ 632 87 73- *www.hotelstp.com.pl* – *55 rooms, 80/120 PLN.* Basic comfort but excellent value for money and the hotel is clean. Halfway between the bus and railway stations and the town centre.

Youth Hostel – *ul. Legionów 27 –* ✆ 633 03 65 – *www.youthhostellodz.w.pl* – *630 66 80 – 72 rooms – 35/45 PLN -.* Neat, central and open year-round.

Eating out

Piotrkowska street boasts a great many restaurants and cafés, most of them offering classic Polish dishes. Do not hesitate to step into the inner courtyards where there are very pleasant terrace-cafés in summer.

Restauracja Polska – *ul. Piotrkowska 12 – 55 PLN.* High-class traditional Polish setting and cuisine. The place is ideal for a dinner by candlelight.

Ziemia Obiecana – *ul. Wigury 4/6 – 636 70 81 – 40 PLN.* Adjoining the Déjà-Vu guesthouse, this restaurant is really worth a detour, for its excellent homemade cuisine served in a fascinating turn-of-the-20C decor. Reservation advisable.

Figaro – *Ul. Piotrkowska 92 – 20 PLN.* Amusing café-cum-restaurant boasting a futuristic design and attracting an interesting clientele of artists and actors from the nearby theatres. Traditional snacks served in an original fashion.

On the town

The town's rich nightlife is concentrated along Piotrkowska Street. Many cafés, pubs and music bars.

Fabryka – *ul. Piotrkowska 80.* Incredible pub housed in a former textile factory. Noisy but undoubtedly worth a visit if only for its decor.

Łódź Kaliska – – *ul. Piotrkowska 102 –* Splendid café covered with mirrors, hidden at the end of an alleyway signalled by a reproduction of theStatue of Liberty.

Film School

Kazimierz Dolny★

POPULATION 3 658 – MAP OF POLAND A2 – WOJEWÓDZTWO OF LUBLIN

Having long thrived on trading and on its favourable situation on the banks of the Wisła, Kazimierz Dolny is now a sleepy little town attracting colonies of artists who keep on immortalizing its image. The history of Polish painting and that of Kazimierz Dolny have been closely linked since the 19C.

- ▶ **Getting your bearings** – 45km west of Lublin, near Puławy, on the banks of the Wisła.
- 👁 **Not to be missed** – A stroll along the Wisła, between the ferry in the west and the Natural History Museum in the east.
- 🕑 **Planning your visit** – Allow one day to stroll through the hilly countryside around the castle and the Rynek, to visit the museums and to cross the river to go and see Janowiec Castle.

Background

On the banks of the Wisła – According to legend, the founder of Kazimierz Dolny, King Kazimierz the Great, loved a beautiful Jewish maiden named Esther, who lived in the village of Bochotnica. In order to live their love in secret, the king had a 4km-long tunnel dug between the castle he had just had built and the village of his beloved. The reality is less romantic. The castle was erected to fight the Tatar invasions and it proved very useful later to defend the prosperous trading town. In the 17C, although it had barely over 2 000 inhabitants, Kazimierz Dolny ranked among the richest towns in Poland. Wheat granaries were dotted along the Wisła, cattle breeding and the timber and wine trades were thriving. This flourishing period was halted by various calamities: Swedish invasions between 1655 and 1660, followed by epidemics of cholera and plague.

The Good-Luck Dog

Sitting on the Rynek, near the parish church, is a small bronze dog, who has been quietly watching passers-by since 2001. If you touch his nose and make a wish, it should be granted. Children, who are too small to reach his nose, touch his paws...apparently the result is the same. Originally, a dog from the village of Janowiec, on the other side of the Wisła, used to swim across to get little treats from tourists. He was replaced by this good-luck dog. Judging by the patina of his nose and his paws, there must be a great number of wishes!

A village of artists – At the end of the 19C, at the instigation of a few painters, including **Władysław Słewiński**, the village became the favourite haunt of generations of artists and their students armed with canvases and brushes. During a long stay in France, Słewiński became the student and friend of Gauguin, at a time when the latter was turning the Breton village of Pont-Aven into a temple of artistic and pictorial expression.

Having returned to Poland, Słewiński applied the idea of his French friend to Kazimierz Dolny and attracted many artists to the village. The upheavals and dramas of the 20C upset the harmony and creative emulation of this favoured environment, all the more because many of the local painters were Jewish. However, the setting and the light inherent in Kazimierz Dolny continue to fascinate new generations of artists and the town boasts many studios and art galleries.

Exploring

The Rynek★

This vast paved square has a lone well in its centre. In the 14C, it was surrounded by wooden houses followed, in the 17C, by fine residences built with the local limestone, such as the **twin houses of the Przybyła Family** (Kamienice Przybyłów)★★ in the purest Renaissance style, featuring low-relief sculptures depicting characters and animals. Situated on another side of the square is the Baroque **Gdańsk House**. These buildings attest the wealth of the village merchants in the past.

The Rynek rises to the north up a hill, at the foot of which stands the **parish church** (Kościół Farny) famous for its organ built in 1620 by Szymon Liliusz and for its baptismal font dating from 1587.

Gold- and Silverwork Museum (Muzeum Sztuki Złotniczej)

Ul Zamkowa 2. May-Sep 10am-5pm; Oct-Apr 10am-3pm. Closed hols and day following 1 Jan, Easter Sunday, 1 May, 11 Nov, 24 Dec. 6 PLN. The museum displays collections of classic gold- and silverwork made between 1650 and 1880 – ciboria, crosses, candelabra, tea sets, lights from all over Poland, on the ground floor, and from Paris Toulon, St-Petersburg, Copenhagen or Dublin upstairs. In addition to these collections, the museum shows jewellery by contemporary Polish designers. Sometimes decorated with amber, these pieces of jewellery were created between 1960 and 2000 by artists from Warsaw and Wieliczka.

Towards the Castle ruins

Zamkowa Street leads up to the **Castle ruins**. You can make a detour by following the path on the right beyond the museum and climbing **Three Crosses Hill** (these crosses were erected during the plague and cholera epidemics). The magnificent **views** of the village and the Wisła are the main purpose of this ramble.

Walk back down the same way; as you reach the parish church, turn left onto Krzywe Koło Street which leads to the former Jewish district.

Old synagogue

Modelled on the synagogue built in 1677 and destroyed by the Nazis in 1939, this edifice shows precisely where the former Jewish district was located.

Small Market Square (Mały Rynek)

This is still one of the liveliest spots in the village, boasting numerous boutiques and art galleries as well as stalls on market days.

Reformed Franciscan Monastery (Kościół Reformatów)

It is possible to enter the courtyard and ask to see the well with its huge wheel located in an inner courtyard. During the Second World War, this place was the headquarters of the Gestapo; the Nazis took the stelae in the Jewish cemetery (situated where the Jewish memorial now stands) and used them as partitions between the prison cells located in the basement of the monastery.

Walk down towards Nadrzeczna Street and turn left.

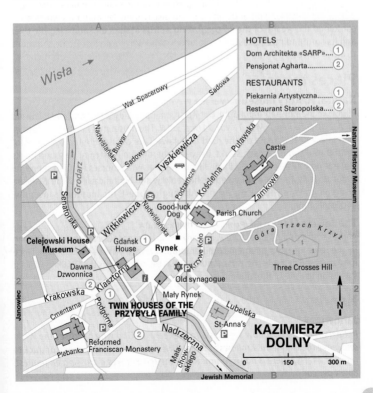

Twin houses of the Przybyła Family

Celejowski House Museum (Kamienica Celejowska)★
Ul Senatorska 11. May-Sep 10am-5pm, Sun noon-7pm; Oct-Apr 10am-3pm. Closed hols and day following 1 Jan, Easter Sunday, 1 May, 11 Nov, 24 Dec. 5 PLN.
This remarkable **Renaissance residence** built in 1630 by a wealthy merchant, Bartolomeo Celejowski, houses a museum devoted to the **history of Kazimierz's artist colony** (Kolonia artystyczna w kazimierzu). The village and its surroundings were used as models by generations of artists and the result is a collection of water colours, paintings on wood or cardboard, black-and-white sketches…The museum also contains works made by members of the colony during their travels through Europe. A few glass display cases and ethnographic compositions evoke the local Jewish community.

Continue along Senatorska Street, lined with painting galleries, towards the end of the village and the River Wisła. A long **path**★ running along the banks offers the possibility of walking up or down river and discovering the granaries which once contained the wealth of the village. Taking a stroll at dusk and admiring the river and its surroundings makes it easy to understand why Kazimierz Dolny continues to attract artists.

Places to see

Natural History Museum (Muzeum Przyrodnicze)★
Puławska 54. May-Sep 10am-5pm; Oct-Apr 10am-3pm. Closed hols and day following 1 Jan, Easter Sunday, 1 May, 11 Nov, 24 Dec. 5 PLN. The museum is housed in a former riverside wheat granary on the road to Puławy. One can admire the collection of stuffed and mounted foxes, storks, beavers or herons while listening to sound tracks illustrating forest sounds or village life at the time when horses reigned supreme. Unfortunately, the shows devoted to the geology and biological life of the Wisła are reserved for Polish-speaking visitors. Although modest, the museum is inventive and interesting.

The Jewish Memorial (Pomnik Ofiar Holokaustu)★
About 1km from the centre of Kazimierz Dolny, along the road to Opole Lubelskie. Standing by the roadside is a monument commemorating Jewish victims of the Shoah. Since it was erected in the 1970s, this monument has been known as the "Wailing Wall". It stands on the site of the former Jewish cemetery.

Nearby

Janowiec★
In Kazimierz Dolny, follow signposts to the ferry (PROM) which crosses the Wisła and leave the village via Krakowska Street. Drive some 2km along a road or track to reach the ferry. There is no fixed timetable, the ferry makes a crossing on request. 8 PLN per car.

Janowiec Castle (Muzeum Zamek w Janowcu)
May-Sep Mon 10am-2pm, Tue-Fri 10am-5pm, Sat-Sun 10am-7pm; Oct-Apr Tue-Fri 10am-3pm, Sat-Sun 10am-4pm. 8 PLN. Free admission to the park.
This castle, built in pure Renaissance style at the beginning of the 16C and now unfortunately in ruins, was one of the most splendid of its kind in Poland. It once comprised some 100 rooms and as many as 10 ballrooms. All that remains today are a few exhibition halls, an 18C manor and a horse-drawn carriage museum in the park. Most fascinating of all are the **panoramic views** of the Wisła and of the village of Janowiec with its pink Renaissance church.

Practical Kazimierz Dolny

Postal code – 24-120
Phone code – 081

Useful addresses

PTTK Tourist Office – *Rynek 27 -*
℘ *881 00 46 – www.kazimierzdolny.pl – pttk_kazimierz_dolny@poczta.onet.pl – year-round Mon-Fri 8am-5.30pm, Sat-Sun 10am-5.30pm.*
Police – ℘ *997*
Emergency/ambulance – ℘ *998*
Taxi – *The taxi rank is in front of Rynek 2.* ℘ *881 03 38.*
ATM machine – *In the Rynek, on the corner of Naswiślańka Street and the path leading up to the parish church.*

Getting around

Parking – It is forbidden to park the car along the streets of the town centre and in the Rynek, but there are car parks at the entrance to the town, on the road to Puławy and along the River Wisła. Some private courtyards in the centre are at the disposal of motorists for the sum of 3 to 5 PLN/hr.
Bus Station – *Situated at the entrance to the town, on the road to Puławy, at the foot of Castle Hill.* Buses no 12 and 14 operate a regular service to Puławy; journey time: 15min. From there it is easy to go to Warsaw and Lublin by bus or train.

Where to stay

Dom Architekta « SARP » – *Rynek 20 –* ℘ *883 55 44 – sarp@dom-architekta.pl – 30 rooms: 160 PLN.* In exchange for having the pleasure of sleeping in some of the Rynek's historic houses, one must make a few concessions about modern facilities. Large vaulted rooms and furniture from another time account for the old-world charm.
Pensjonat Agharta – *Ul Krakowska 2 –* ℘ *882 04 21 – www.agharta.com.pl – 5 rooms: 200 PLN, 1 apart.* This splendid place, in a peaceful location at the foot of the monastery, is both an extremely comfortable guesthouse and an art gallery. The atmosphere suggests Indonesia or Birma and there is no doubt that the owners have taste. Breakfast but no meals.

Eating out

Piekarnia Artystyczna – *Ul Nadrzeczna 6 –* ℘ *881 06 43 – www.sarzynski.com.pl.* This establishment is a real institution with many facets: pâtisserie, tearoom, bar, high-class restaurant and vaulted cellar reserved for wine and cigar lovers. The large house is divided into many rooms where everyone finds a suitable product or price.
Restauracja Staropolska – Ul Nadrzeczna 14 – ℘ *881 02 36 – 60 PLN.* This restaurant is dedicated to Polish cuisine and it is delicious. Dark murals, black-wood furniture and clocks ticking away convey the impression of a Sunday family meal. Excellent and entertaining for those who like their food and enjoy watching what goes on around them.

Taking a break

Café Antałek – *Mały Rynek 4/5 –* ℘ *mobile 0 695 910 499 – Sat-Sun 10am-midnight, Mon-Fri 10am-10pm.* This art gallery also sells antiques and bric-à-brac. Objects for sale are displayed on the terrace and in front of the door. One can have a beer or a cup of tea next to a statue of the Virgin or a postwar radio set.

Shopping

There are many art galleries of varying quality. The main ones are located around the Rynek and along Senatorska Street.
Lamus Gallery – *Ul Plebanka – Daily noon-5pm.* This gallery run by the artist Maja Fidea Parfianowicz is located in a tiny wooden house built 150 years ago. The young woman sells her own paintings, but she also has a flair for digging out antiques, icons painted on glass or trinkets and to turn the little space she has into a delight for the eyes.

Festive Events

Folklore Festival – During the last week in June.Songs and dances from all over Poland.
Festival of Popular Orchestras – At various times during the summer. It offers musicians the opportunity of mingling with artists.

Lublin★★

POPULATION 358 354 – MAP OF POLAND A2 – WOJEWÓDZTWO OF LUBLIN

Lublin is one of those towns bearing the indelible marks of the historic events linking Poland and the Jewish people. Every stone in the historic centre carries the memory of peaceful times or of periods of horror. Problems of ownership are delaying the restoration of the streets surrounding the Rynek and the dilapidated look of some districts increases the ambient feeling of sadness. And yet, Lublin has many assets, a thriving cultural life, a lively student population and a rich architectural heritage.

- ▶ **Getting your bearings** – 165km south-east of Warsaw, this is the last town before reaching the border with Belarus and Ukraine.

- 👁 **Not to be missed** – Between the Rynek and the Grodzka Gate, the numerous cafés, tearooms or restaurants offering a journey to the heart of Jewish culture through music and a range of flavours.

- 🕓 **Planning your visit** – Allow one day to visit the historic centre and the castle; half a day to go to the Majdanek concentration camp and to the Skansen on the outskirts of town.

Background

Culture as a peaceful weapon – The first signs of life on the hills of Lubin appeared around the 6C but it was only at the end of the Middle Ages that a city was formed. Traders and travellers between Western Europe and Central Asia built a town which was granted a municipal charter in 1317 by Prince Władysław Łokietek. In 1569 the Union between Poland and Lithuania, known as the Lublin Union, was signed here, heralding the beginning of the town's prosperity. During the 16C, the town surrounded itself with defensive ramparts pierced by gates equipped with drawbridges. From the top of its loess hills, the town overlooked a vast marshy area which made it easier to defend. Taking advantage of its trading power and of its geopolitical role between Kraków and Vilnius, Lublin encouraged the various communities residing within its walls to express their differences. Ruthenians, Jews, Hungarians, Italians or French formed a creative cultural mosaic: for example, it was in Lublin that the first book in Polish was published: *The Paradise of the Soul* by Biernat of Lublin, who is considered as the "father of written Polish"; the Renaissance poet Jan Kochanowski, a friend of Pierre de Ronsard and translator of his works, lived and died in Lublin. Famous names of Polish music, such as Jan of Lublin who invented the organ tablature or Henryk Wieniawski after whom a famous violin competition was named, are celebrated in Lublin. Later political upheavals did not really interfere with the city's cultural life. Neither the invasion of the Union by Cossack or Swedish troops in the 17C, nor the repeated usurpation of power by the Habsburg Empire at the end of the 18C and then by the Russian at the beginning of the 19C, could destroy the town's cultural diversity. However, the first world conflict and above all the second succeeded in turning Lublin into a martyred town. The extermination of the Jews by the Nazis, symbolized by the Majdanek death camp, is a dark shadow hovering over the town that many residents of the historic centre are trying to dispel by promoting Jewish culture. Culture and art are once more Lublin's peaceful weapons.

Exploring

FROM THE CASTLE TO THE "DEPTAK"★★

This itinerary goes through the Old Town (Stare Miasto) towards the main shopping street on the west side of the city, known as the Deptak to shorten its rather long name: Krakowskie Przedmieście Avenue.

Castle★

Situated on the loess hill, the castle was rebuilt in 1824 in neo-Gothic style to be used as a prison. It covers the remains of the castles erected in the Middle Ages and of the royal fortress built between the 14C and 16C. All that remains from the latter period are the chapel and the tower. Most of the castle is occupied by a museum.

Lublin Museum (Muzeum Lubelskie)★ and **Chapel of the Holy Trinity** (Kaplica Św. Trójcy)★★ *Wed-Sat 9am-4pm, Sun 9am-5pm. The chapel is in the courtyard of the castle, which can be reached via the museum. Same opening times. 6.5 PLN.*

The museum is famous for Jan Matejko's painting, the "**Union of Lublin**". This painting, its imposing dimensions matching its political impact, symbolizes the first attempt at unifying the great kingdoms of Europe. Matejko's other artistic and political work is a painting entitled *The admission of the Jews to Poland in 1096*. in addition, you will be able to see collections of archaeological and prehistoric items, medals and coins from the 14C to the 19C, weapons or even ethnographic objects such as splendid fabrics.

The interior of **the Gothic Chapel** is entirely covered with **Russo-byzantine frescoes★★** in perfect condition, which are real masterpieces. Commissioned from the Russian Master Andrew in 1418 by King Władisław V Jagiello, they attest to the harmonious relations between the different Christian cultures which cohabited in Poland in the 15C.

Castle Square (Plac Zamkowy)
Situated at the foot of the steps leading to the castle gate. The curved houses surrounding it are facing the hill and the monument.

Grodzka Gate (Brama Grodzka)
From Castle Square, a paved path leads to this gate opening onto the Old Town. Built in the 14C and remodelled in 1785, the gate will always remain the symbol of the separation between Catholic and Jewish districts.

Walking along Grodzka Street, which shows how much behind schedule the town's restoration planning is, you will pass in front of no 5 housing a small **Museum of Pharmacy**, then you will come to a square on the left where St Michael's parish church was built in the 13C and subsequently entirely destroyed by the Russians in the middle of the 19C. From the square, where the ruins are now the locals' favourite meeting place, you will enjoy a magnificent view of the castle. A little farther up, you will arrive at the Rynek.

Rynek★★
Its centre is occupied or rather dominated by the **Royal Tribunal**, a building of excessive dimensions in comparison with those of the square. It is the former Town Hall built in 1578 and remodelled in neo-Classical style in 1781.

Surrounding the Rynek are a **few richly decorated houses**, sometimes featuring strange colours, which were enhanced by tasteful restoration work.

Klonowicz House at no 2, was occupied in the 16C by the poet and mayor of Lublin who gave it his name. The house was remodelled in neo-Classical style in the 18C. The medallions depicting poets or musicians only date from 1939.

No 8 is the **House of the Lubomelski family**, built in Renaissance style in 1540. The interior *(not open to the public)* is decorated with polychrome paintings on the theme of Epicurian pleasures and Love!

The **House of the Konopnic family,** at no12, erected in 1512, and later rebuilt, boasts splendid sculptures round the windows and on the façade. Masculine and feminine bodies, dragon heads and masks, as well as medallions featuring the owners are visible from the Rynek.

Lublin Old Town

Kraków Gate (Brama Krakowska)★

This Gothic architectural emblem of Lublin provides valuable information about the ramparts surrounding the town in the 14C. The gate was altered several times over the centuries: it was given a clock in the 16C and a Baroque roof in the 18C.

The tower houses the **Lublin Historical Museum** (Muzeum Historii Miasta Lublina)

Wed-Sat 8am-4pm, the 2nd and 4th Sun of the month 9am-5pm. 3.5 PLN.

The collections of maps of the city or the portraits of local 20C leaders cannot possibly interest foreigners. However, the most inquisitive will learn that the president of the Lublin region between 1837 and 1939 was called Jerzy Albin de Tramecourt. His parents were French and he was killed in the war in 1939. In any case, the museum is worth a visit for the **panoramic view** of Lublin one gets from the top floor.

Nearby is the Gothic tower rebuilt in the 1980s.

Follow Jesuit Street (Jezuicka), which starts from the Kraków Gate.

Baroque Cathedral and Trinity Tower★

This 40m-tall tower dominating the Old Town houses the Diocesan Museum.

Dominican Church and Monastery

The construction of this ensemble began in 1342 and was completed in several stages. Originally built in Gothic style, it was remodelled during the Renaissance period.

Head back towards the Kraków Gate and cross Lubartowska Avenue towards the new Town Hall. It marks the beginning of the pedestrian shopping avenue, Krakowskie Przedmieście, known as "deptak".

IN THE FOOTSPEPS OF LUBLIN'S JEWS★

An itinerary signposted by panels bearing a blue star of David links the different sights connected with the history of the town's Jewish community. If you wish to follow it in detail, we advise you to apply to the Tourist Office for a brochure in English.

This itinerary starts from Castle Square, a vast esplanade which was once a lively built-up area reserved for the Jewish community. Having turned it into a ghetto in 1941, the Nazis destroyed it in 1943 and sent the Jewish community to the Majdanek concentration camp.

Walk up towards the castle before following a panel pointing to the site of a **synagogue** destroyed in 1943, on Tysiąclecia Avenue.

At the junction of Kalinowszczyna and Sienna streets, there is an entrance to the **old Jewish cemetery★** with graves going back to 1541. Buried here are many rabbis and other influential members of the community.

The **new Jewish cemetery,** laid out in Walecznych Street in 1829, is still used by the Jewish community. It contains a monument commemorating the Holocaust and the graves of Jewish soldiers who served in the Polish army between 1944 and 1945.

The marked itinerary follows Lubartowska Avenue back to the historic district. Along this avenue, you will see the old University of Talmudic Studies, the former Jewish Hospital and the Cultural Centre. At no 10 Lubartowska avenue stands the town's only **synagogue** to have survived the war. A few paces further on is the **Monument to the Ghetto Victims.**

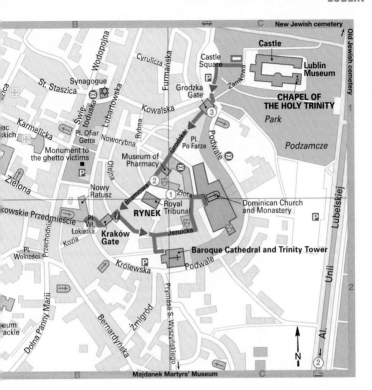

Nearby

Majdanek Death Camp and Martyrs' Museum
(Muzeum Martyrologii na Majdanku)

4km south-east of Lublin. Ul Męczenników Majdanka 67. Apr-Oct 9am-4pm, Nov-Mar 8am-3pm. Parking: 3 PLN.

Majdanek camp was first established in October 1941 as a work camp under SS control. Polish or Russian prisoners of war and many Jews worked in weapons factories set up near the camp's electrified barbed wire fences and watchtowers. Majdanek became a death camp in April 1942. It then held different kinds of victims of the Nazis' concentration and extermination policy: Jews, 130 000 of whom, transferred from France, Belgium, the Netherlands, Slovakia, Greece and of course from other parts of Poland, were gassed or machine-gunned. On 3 November 1943 alone, 17 000 Jews were machine-gunned during an operation named "Harvest Feast". To the 230 000 Polish soldiers or civilians were added Russians, Belarusians, Ukrainians and Tziganes from central Europe, which brings the total number of victims to 360 000. Part of the camp was reserved for children. The camp included as many as 144 barracks and several gas chambers over an area of around 3sq km. The fact that the camp is close to the town adds a feeling of unease to this emotional experience. Indeed, from the path linking the commemorative monument to the mausoleum containing the ashes of the victims, one can see that the first houses are almost against the barbed wire. History will never stop weighing down the collective conscience.

Lublin's Regional Ethnographic Museum (Muzeum Wsi Lubelskiej)★
About 3km from the town centre, On the road to Warsaw. Warszawska 96. Apr-Oct 9am-4pm, Sun until 5pm; Nov-23 Dec Fri-Sun 9am-3pm. 6 PLN.

Lublin's skansen, extending over 25ha of wooded undulating countryside, features rural buildings such as farms or mills as well as sacred monuments. On Sunday morning, Mass is celebrated in the church, on the roadside. In spring and summer, the skansen becomes a real live theatre setting used for folk festivals or reconstructions of rural life in the past. Many domestic animals roam around freely, which adds to one's impression that the place is lived in.

Practical Lublin

Postal code – 20-
Phone code – 081

Useful addresses

Tourist Office – *Ul Jezuika 1/3 -* 🕿 *532 44 12 – www.lublin.pl – itlubln@onet.pl – Mon-Fri 9am-5pm, Sat 10am-3pm.* The Office, situated at the foot of the Kraków Gate, is well stocked with useful literature. It is a very pleasant place to draw up one's programme for visiting the town.

Getting around

Railway Station – *Plac Dworcowy – About 2km from the town centre heading for Przemyśl.* The extremely busy central station serves all the major cities: Warsaw, Kraków, Wrocław, Poznań or Gdynia.

Bus Station – *Al. Tysiąclecia – Located opposite Castle Square, across the avenue, the bus station is right in the town centre.* There are frequent buses to Kazimierz Dolny, Sandomierz or Zamość. Departures for Warsaw every 2hr and for Kraków once or twice a day.

Where to stay

Europa Hotel – *Ul. Krakowskie Przedmieście 29 -* 🕿 *535 03 03 – www.hoteleuropa.pl – 60 rooms 380 PLN, 280 at weekends.* The hotel belongs to the Prestigious-Hotels chain. Luxury and comfort are obvious in the rooms as well as in the nightclub and in the restaurant.

Lwów Hotel – *Ul. Bronowicka 2 -* 🕿 *745 57 09 – www.btm-lwow.pl – btm@neostrad.pl – 19 rooms 240 PLN.* Lwów is the Russian name of the town of L'viv in Ukraine. The rooms are tastefully furnished and are equipped to a three-star level of comfort. The staff's uniforms , the paintings of Lwów on the walls and the background music attest to the closeness of Ukraine. *(See also "Eating Out").*

Waksman Hotel – *Ul. Grodzka 21 -* 🕿 *532 54 54 – www.waksman.pl – 4 rooms 200 PLN.* The rooms, furnished in Louis XVI or Victorian style, overlook the royal castle. This ideally situated hotel underlines both its retro feel and comfort.

Eating out

Restaurant of the Lwów Hotel – *(See "Where to Stay")* 80 PLN. Delicious cuisine featuring Ukrainian, Polish, Mediterranean and South American dishes. Try the soup prepared with wild mushrooms, served inside a loaf of bread and the veal with chanterelles.

Mandragora – *Rynek 9 –* 🕿 *536 20 20 – www.mandragora.lublin/pl – 1pm-midnight. 60 PLN.* Located in a historic house, the three dining rooms are imbued with Jewish nostalgia and souvenirs. The establishment, which is both an art gallery and a high-class restaurant, offers a harmonious blend of culture and flavours. Sale of traditional Jewish music. Double bass recital at weekends.

Złoty Osioł – *Ul. Grodzka –* 🕿 *532 90 42 – noon-midnight – 60 PLN.* This inn in the heart of the city serves typically Polish cuisine.

Taking a break

Magia – *Rynek 8 –* 🕿 *534 51 41 – www.magia-lublin.pl – 10h- 21h.* Charming tearoom and wine bar, where one can also buy various teas and herbal teas, jams and confectionery. A tiny, chic, cosy and convivial place.

On the town

Szeroka 28 – *Ul. Grodzka 21.* 🕿 *534 61 09 – www.szeroka28.com – Sun-Thu noon-11pm, Fri-Sat noon-midnight.* Located beneath Grodzka Gate, this convivial café-cum-restaurant is the favourite haunt of lovers of Klezmer music. For years now, every saturday at 8.30pm, the Lubliner Klezmorin have been inviting their audience to sing and dance to the sound of a clarinet and a violin. (Concert: 15 PLN).

Shopping

Galeria Autorska Michałowski – *Ul. Grodzka 19 – 10am-6pm.* Whether he is depicting Jewish life in the interwar period or painting landscapes along the Wisła, Bartłomiej Michałowki puts all his sensitivity and technique into his work.

Zamość★★★

POPULATION 66 820 – MAP OF POLAND A2– WOJEWÓDZTWO OF LUBLIN

With the expansion of the European Union to 25 members, Zamość became one of the most eastern cities in the European political space, very close to Ukraine. Can anyone dream of a finer gateway? This town known as the "Padua of the North" is a pearl inspired by the Renaissance. It remains relatively unknown to travellers today, in spite of being recognised by UNESCO in 1992 as a World Heritage Site.

- **Getting your bearings** – 250km south-east of Warsaw, 130km from L'viv, the regional capital of the Ukrainian Carpathians.
- **Not to be missed** –The Rynek Wielki, the tour of the ramparts and the Rotunda.
- **Planning your visit** – Allow one day to explore the town and almost another day to visit the museums.

Background

One man's ideal town – The name of **Jan Zamoyski** (1542 -1605) hovers over the town. Zamość is the fruit of the erudition and ambition of this man who wanted to make his mark in his country's history. Having studied at the Padua university in Italy, where he discovered the spirit of the Renaissance, he founded an entirely new town which reflected his taste and personality. The city's date of birth was 3 April 1580. Zamość was designed on a pentagonal plan, prolonged to the west by a rectangle enclosing the Zamoyski Palace, and surrounded by fortifications. Jan Zamoyski commissioned the Venitian architect **Bernardo Morando** to carry out this idealistic project. The two men had a deep understanding of each other and Zamość was built within a few years. All the edifices were built with the same enthusiasm, fully complying with the architectural criteria of the Renaissance: the Rynek Wielki and its bourgeois houses, the Town Hall, the fortifications, the academies and the residence of the Zamoyski family. Jan Zamoyski's wish, shared by his architect, was to separate the spiritual and religious part of the town from the districts occupied by craftsmen and merchants. On the whole, the religious and academic edifices stand outside the town centre, whereas the traders' houses together with the salt and water markets are gathered in the Rynek Wielki and along the adjacent streets. In spite of the Tatar, Swedish, Russian or Nazi invasions which sometimes spoilt the harmony of certain elements, the ensemble is still breathtaking. The genius, the ambition and the creative obsession of Jan Zamoyski and Bernardo Morando have withstood the ravages of time and of men for 425 years.

A. Galy / MICHELIN

Zamość Town Hall

Exploring

One's first encounter with Zamość inevitably takes place on the Rynek's cobblestones and it is a good idea to start with a visit to the Tourist Office inside the town hall.

THE RYNEK WIELKI★★★

This perfect square with 100m sides, dominated by the 52m high **Town Hall Tower**, attracts visitors like a magnet. Unlike what can be seen in other towns dating from the same period, the **Town Hall ★★** does not stand in the centre of the square. It would seem that Jan Zamoyski did not want it to outshine his own palace and preferred to have the communal house integrated with the rest of the architecture. From the top of the strangely pink town-hall staircase, built a century later, one can encompass the whole structure of the square. The geometric uniformity of the arcades and of the straight streets reaching out to the remains of the red-brick ramparts, is impressive. Jan Zymoyski dreamed of a corner of Italy, his wishes were granted. The Rynek Wielki boasts the pale yellow or blue of a Venitian or Florentine piazza. Pigeons, pizzerias and groups of tourists reinforce this impression of the "Padua of the North". In the morning, secondary school children and students walk across the square to their respective Academy or music schools. In the evening, the square becomes a vast football ground or a cabaret stage for buskers. Football and Comedia del Arte… Italy still! Fortunately, the Rynek Wielki is by no means a museum district.

The **Armenian houses★★**, situated on the right of the town hall as you face it, differ from the Rynek's other bourgeois houses in their exuberant ornamentation added in the 17C to comply with the Oriental tastes of their owners, wealthy merchants from Armenia. **No 30** in Ormiańska Street is the **Wilczkowska House** housing the **Zamojskie Regional Museum** (Muzeum Zamojskie) *(see "Things to see")*. Next comes the **Bartoszewiczowska House** at n° 26, also known as the house "under the lion" or "under the angel", then the house "under the couple" at **no 24** and finally a yellow house known as "under the Virgin" at **no 22**. They are all surmounted by attics and painted in striking colours, often either ochre or purple. Walking round the square beneath the arcades, one discovers the characteristic unity of the decorations on the doors. These doors are often originals, sculpted and featuring a wealth of decorations. By going through the corridors or down the staircases beneath the arcades with their painted ceilings, one reaches a series of cellars converted into bars or restaurants.

TOUR OF THE TOWN

Improve on your overall impression of the town by following Grodzka Street running through the Rynek Wielki from west to east. Heading east along the street leads to one of the town gates: the **former L'viv Gate**. Go through the gate to find yourself outisde the ramparts. It is possible to walk along the still intact bastions for a few hundred metres, then to re-enter the Old Town at the level of St Catherine's Church (Kościół Świętej Katarzyny). Carry on along Akademicka Avenue as far as the ensemble formed by the **former Zamoyski Palace** and the **Cathedral.** The latter retains all its characteristic features, in particular the campanile, but the palace suffered a lot of damage under Soviet influence, being drowned in concrete! Its renovation is apparently programmed…

Cathedral of the Resurrection of Christ and of St Thomas the Apostle (Katedra Wniebowstąpienia i Świętego Tomasza)★

Ul. Kolegiacka – Daily 10am-4pm.

Built between 1587 and 1598, under the supervision of Bernardo Morando, the collegiate church, now a cathedral, is one of the finest religious monuments from the Renaissance period in Poland, with its typical vaulting in Polish mannerist style. The artistic treasures it contains include the "Annunciation" painted by Carlo Dolci and the monumental Rococo-style silver tabernacle. The chancel houses four superb paintings representing the life of St Thomas, the patron saint of Zamość. In the Zamoyski chapel, several crypts are accessible to visitors. They house the funerary monuments of the town's founder, of his family, of the main dignitaries and of artists or scholars. Note a white-marble naturalist sculpture, made in Italy, depicting Tomasz Zamoyski, who died in 1638. From the **campanile** *(May-Sep 10am-4pm. Free admission)* there is a **panoramic view★★** of the Old Town.

Museum of Sacred Art (Muzeum Sakralne Kolegiaty Zamojskiej)

Ul. Kolegiacka. May-Sep 10am-4pm. Oct-Apr sun only 10am-4pm. 6 PLN.

Set up near the cathedral in the historic house, known as the "Infułatka", of the mitred abbot (name given to an abbot who had the same rank as a bishop), the Museum of

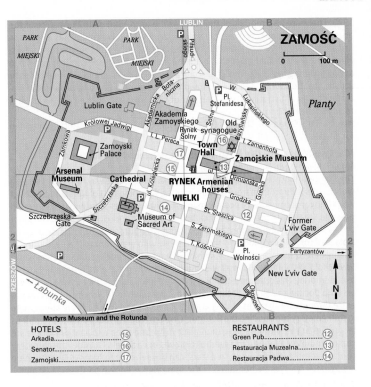

ZAMOŚĆ

0   100 m

Sacred Art is interesting for its collection of liturgical garments, for its few items of gold- and silverwork and for its bronze fonts.

From the cathedral, one can return to the Rynek Wielki along the western part of Grodzka Street.

Things to see

Zamojskie Museum – Regional Museum (Muzeum Zamojskie)★★

Ul. Ormiańska 30. Tue-Sun 9am-4pm. Closed hols and the day after. Visit: 45min. 8 PLN.

The museum is housed inside the Armenian houses. On entering this place full of history, one feels the omnipresence of Jan Zamoyski and of those close to him. Paintings, statues or prints attest the influence of the Hetman (commander in chief) in shaping the history of his town. The museum contains several different collections of paintings, prints, military equipment and wooden religious sculptures. The many themes illustrated underline the eclectic impression. The displays and the lighting are carefully arranged, but the museum lacks explanations in foreign languages. No captions are needed of course to appreciate old photographs of the Rynek Wielki, showing a garden laid out on the square, once divided into plots. The same applies to the 16C Italian furniture inlaid with ivory, to the traditional 19C and 20C clothes, boots and scarves, to the pottery decorated with brown and green motifs from the Carpathian mountains and to the collections of cut stones dating from the Mesolithic or Palaeolithic periods. A room is devoted to a style of naive painting, featuring bright colours and a clumsy sense of perspective, and depicting peasant scenes, weddings... This museum should suit those who like to flit about in a museum, not troubling themselves with any particular theme.

Arsenal Museum (Muzeum Barwy i Oręża "Arsenał")★

Ul Zamkowa 2. Tue-Sat 9am-4pm.

The Arsenal is a long white building, standing in the district of the cathedral and of the former Zamoyski Palace. This weapon store was built around 1582 to stock the war trophies taken by the Hetman's armies as well as the presents he received. The collections were for the most part damaged or plundered during foreign invasions. It was remodelled in neo-Classical style in 1820 and a storey was added. Today it houses, quite appropriately, a Military Museum containing many 16C armours, 17C and 18C swords and sabres as well as crossbows and French or Austrian rifles from

1820. There are also models of the town as it was in 1580 or 1825. In spite of the absence of scenic effects, the most moving and impressive collections are on the first floor. They consist of paintings or drawings made by the soldiers themselves, illustrating their life in the trenches or on the front line during the conflicts of 1915-16 and later during the 1930s. The idyllic comradeship, soldiers armed with mandolins or accordions, troops marching under the protective gaze of Christ who blesses them, almost all the illustrations make a point of shrugging off or masking the painful reality of the fighting.

Nearby is the **Open-air Military Museum** *(Jun-Oct 9am-4pm)* specifically intended for amateurs of Second-World-War weapons.

Martyrs Museum, the Rotunda (Droga Męczenników Rotundy)★★
May-Oct 9am-6pm. Free admission.
The Rotunda is located beyond the Szczebrzeska Gate (on the way to Kraków) inside a wooded park. Built 500m from the Old Town and forming part of the fortifications, it was an advanced post and a powder magazine linked to the town by an underground passage. It is a vast circular red-brick building with doors opening onto the inner courtyard. In 1939, Nazi troops used it for a sinister purpose. The Rotunda became a place of torture, execution or transit for those who were sent to the death camps, mainly Bełżec. Members of the Jewish community, local intellectuals, partisans and Soviet soldiers, some 8 000 in all were murdered within these walls now considered as a memorial. This gruesome toll does not take into account the convoys of prisoners who flocked to Zamość at the end of the war when the Nazi army was trying to erase through fire all traces of their crimes. Plainness and simplicity are appropriate in the cemetery surrounding the Rotunda. One can read a few explanations in various languages at the entrance gate. Thereafter visitors need no explanations. There are commemorative plaques and symbolic graves in each cell. Outside, the cemetery contains tombstones on which "red stars" can be seen next to "stars of David", where anonymous martyrs are honoured in the same way as known partisans.

The Town-Hall Photo Gallery (Galeria Fotografii « Ratusz »)
Rynek Wielki 13. Free admission.
The premises of the Tourist Office host temporary exhibitions of photography.

Practical Zamość

Postal code – 22-400
Phone code – 084

Useful addresses

Tourist Office - *Rynek Wielki 13 – ☏ 639 22 9 – zoit@zamosc.um.gov.pl -www.zamosc. pl*. The office is located under the town-hall tower.

Municipal police – *Rynek Wielki 13 - ☏ 986*

Post office – The Tourist Office sells stamps and a post box is at the disposal of visitors.

ATM machine – *Ul. Grodzka 2* – Pekao office and cash dispenser, near the Senator Hotel.

There is a 24hr cash dispenser in the reception area of the Zamojski Hotel.

Internet Café – Kawiarenka internetowa – *Ul Żeromskiego 26.* 11am-6pm (Sat noon-4pm).

Getting around

PKP Railway Station – *Ul. Szczebrzeska 11 – ☏ 639 34 01* . Very little traffic. Trains to Warsaw and Kraków.

PKS Bus Station – *Ul. Hrubieszowska - ☏ 639 49 86*. Private minibuses leave for Lublin every 20min.

Regular service to Warsaw, Lublín, Kraków, Łódz, Rzeszów and Przemyśl .

To go to L'viv, in Ukraine, one must first go to Tomaszów south of Zamość. Buses bound for Ukraine leave at 6.35am and 2.10pm.

Taxi – Lux Taxi ☏ 96 24, Damel Taxi ☏ 96 26, Hetman Taxi ☏ 96 21.

Bike hire – Atlanta – *Ul Partyzantów 37.*

Supervised car park– *Ul Sadowa.* 24hr/day

Where to stay

Arkada Hotel – *Rynek Wielki 9 – ☏ 638 65 07 – makben@wp.pl – 25 rooms: 120 PLN* ⌷ 🅿. The hotel is ideally situated inside one of the houses in the Rynek. The rooms are simple but neat. The dining room overlooks the town hall. Enclosed car park.

Senator Hotel – *Ul Rynek Solny 4 – ☏ 638 99 90 – 44 rooms, 2 suites – 268 PLN* ⌷ *weekdays – 190 PLN* ⌷ *weekends.* The hotel is located on a square behind the town hall where the old salt market stands. It occupies an old house, entirely restored and modernised, the rooms are tastefully furnished and the general atmosphere is convivial.

Zamojski Hotel – *Ul Kołłątaja 2/4/6 – ☏ 639 25 16 – zamojski@orbis.pl – 45 rooms, 5 studios, 4 suites – Room: 285 PLN weekdays – 190 PLN weekends* ☐. 10m from the Rynek Wielki. The town's top luxury hotel offers very high-quality facilities and services. The architect worked on the lighting to create the impression of being in a winter garden.

Eating out

Most eateries are located around the Rynek. A few Polish restaurants are listed below, but if you wish to enhance your impression of the town's Italian atmosphere, you can also try one of the many **pizzerias** located under the arcades of the Rynek Wielki. They are called: Verona, Il Tempo, Italiana, la Cantina … You will be spoiled for choice!

Muzealna – *Ul. Ormiańska 30, ☏ 638 73 00 – daily 9am-midnight, winter 11am-midnight – 25 PLN*. This restaurant is housed in a cellar near the town hall. It specializes in traditional Polish cuisine. The delicious soups are a meal in themselves. Ask for a table in the rooms at the back.

Padwa – *Ul. Staszica 23 – ☏ 638 62 56 – daily 11am-11pm – 30 PLN*. Located in an old tastefully restored house with a very bright ground floor, this restaurant offers a wide choice of red wines from all over the world. The Gulash soup (5 PLN) is remarkable. Salads with a variety of fresh vegetables.

Green Pub – *Ul. Staszica 2 – ☏ 627 03 36 – Daily 1-10pm – 30 PLN*. Situated near the L'viv Gate, this convivial restaurant boasts an original decor. Everything is either green or orange. Helpings are generous and the menu does not lie: when it says "diablo", it really means that it's hellishly spicy.

On the town

Jazz Café -Kawairnia Kosz – Jazz Club – *Ul. Zamenhofa 3, ☏ 638 60 41.*Jazz is very much appreciated in Poland. where many internationally famous artists perform. Zamość has its jazz temple. The Kosz Club is located in the former Jewish district, near the synagogue. The concert hall is housed in the former baths. For the past 35 years, Jerzy Zdybel and his friends have

A façade in Zamość

brought jazz, blues and occasionally other kinds of music to life in this place, which is also the soul of the "International Meeting of Jazz Vocalists" taking place every year on the first weekend in October. A charming place run by enthusiasts. Regular concerts on Thursday, Friday and Saturday nights.

Shopping

Hala Targowa – *At the bottom of ul. Grodzka, next to the L'viv Gate Sat 9am-5pm, Sun 9am-3pm*. This shopping centre, occupying part of the bastion, is an amazing place which smells both of sausages and cologne. Behind the building is a small typical market: kantors, toilets, newsagent, grocery shop, cafés etc.

Stefanidesa Square – *Ul. Przyrynek, near St Catherine's Church, behind the Senator Hotel weekdays 11am-6pm, Sat noon-4pm*. Taxi rank, kantors and small bazaar-style boutiques.

Festive events

Hetman fair – A historical costumed reconstruction in the heart of the Old Town. Takes place during the first two weekends in June.

International Folklore Festival – In July.

Jazz Festivals – Several jazz festivals take place every year, including one in June and another one in September. The "International Meeting of Jazz Vocalists" takes place every year during the first weekend in October.

In the Białowieża Forest

Białowieża Forest★★

Puszcza Białowieska

MAP OF POLAND D2– WOJEWÓDZTWO OF PODLASIE

Studied by scientists the world over, the Białowieża Forest half-opens its doors to visitors. Its first-class ecological interest cannot allow trampling by bipeds. Bisons, wolves and beavers are the kings of the forest. For a long time, they were hunted by kings and tsars alike, until the animals and their environment became protected and watched over like gems.

▶ **Getting your bearings** – 100km south-east of Białystok; the forest extends across Poland and Belarus.

👁 **Not to be missed** – The road which the tsar followed to reach Białowieża.

🕐 **Planning your visit** – Allow one day to explore the areas of the Park open to visitors. Outside the Park, the Forest is freely accessible. Allow half a day to discover the Tzars' Trail.

👪 **With your children** – A tour of the Bison Reserve and a visit to the Park's Natural History Museum offer the best opportunity for observing bisons!

Background

The European bison, an omnipresent but discreet emblem – This powerful omnivorous animal whose adult male weighs between 500 and 900kg and reaches a height of 1.80m, is the most imposing quadruped living in Europe at the moment. Kings of Poland and later tsars of Russia hunted it, yet it was always a protected species. In the 16C, bison hunters who had no permission from the king were condemned to death and, until the beginning of the 20C, a balance was maintained between hunting and the animal's reproduction cycle. During the First World War, poachers and soldiers upset this balance and, as early as 1919, there was not a single bison left in the Białowieża Forest.

In the 1920s, scientists who studying the reintroduction of bisons drew up a list of the natural resources of the forest and concluded that protective action was needed for the forest environment as a whole, including streams, soil, flora and fauna. Today, the Białowieża Forest and its Belarusian equivalent are on UNESCO's World Heritage List. The Park which covers part of the forest is only accessible under very strict conditions. Scientists manage the herd of bisons and oversee their reproduction. There are, at present, some 700 bisons in the Polish-Belarusian controlled area.

Exploring

Białowieża Forest Park★★

All the tours start from the village of Białowieża, where information is available (see Practical Białowieża).

The strictly protected Orłówka area – The Orłówka protected area is described as a primeval forest because it has never been exploited by man. Bordered by the River Hwoźna in the north, the River Narewka in the west and Belarus in the east, this is the most strictly protected area of the Park. Unfortunately, visitors are barred from the major part of the 4 750ha.

Tour – *Entry into this zone is through the Palace Park situated in the centre of Białowieża. The way into the park is via a road on the left of the red-brick Orthodox church.*

🐾 One must be accompanied by an official guide. The 7km itinerary, representing an easy walk of three hours across flat but often marshy terrain, offers an insight into the natural resources of the forest: 450-year-old oak trees soaring up to 40m, marshy areas covered with sturdy or uprooted spruce, pines once used as beehives by bee-keepers disregarding the ban on entering the area imposed by the tsar.

The Hwoźna protected area – This area, located west of the River Narewka and north of the Hwoźna, covers over 50 000 ha. Past and present interference by man deprives it of its primeval character. It does not have the exceptional characteristics of the Orłówka zone but is, nevertheless, a magnificent rambling area.

Entry is via the village of **Narewka**. It is crisscrossed by many marked tracks for hiking or cycling and for cross-country skiing in winter. This is a privilege granted to the public who is bound to abide by the rules for the protection of nature.

Things to see

Wildlife Park and Bison Reserve (Rez Pokazowy Zwierząt)

If you are arriving from Hajnówka, the Reserve is on the left of the road, 2km from the entrance to Białowieża. 9am-5pm. 8 PLN. Lovers of unspoilt nature and wild spaces might be disappointed, but one must admit that this reserve undoubtedly offers the best solution for getting a glimpse of a bison, a wolf or a deer. Small Polish horses known as "tarpans" also live in this area.

Białowieża Park Natural History Museum
(Muzeum Przyrodniczo Lesńym Białowieskiego Parku Narodowego)★★

Park Pałacowy - Apr-Oct 9am-4.30pm; Nov-Mar, Tue-Sun 9am-4pm. 10 PLN.
The museum is located inside a 50ha park where Tsar Alexander II's residence once stood. It was destroyed in 1944 except for rather picturesque wooden pavilions and farm buildings now used by the Park's employees. The museum is a vast edifice surmounted by a tower from the top of which there is a panoramic view of the forest. Taxidermy and film showings provide different kinds of encounters with animals. It is also a means of reviving ancient hunting traditions and helps visitors to appreciate the work of scientists for the protection of nature.

Nearby

Hajnówka

This small town came into being recently thanks to the timber industry. It is an entry point into the Białowieża Forest. Its strong Orthodox and Belarusian identity is illustrated by the vast contemporary-style **church** built in 1982 (*ul. Ks. A. Dziewiatowskiego*). Not to be missed is the small **museum** devoted to Belarusian culture (*ul. 3-go Maja 42, Open Mon-Fri 9am-2pm*).
An imposing statue of Lenin stands on the roof of the **"U Wołodzi" Café★** which, with its timeless decor, is something of a real "Skansen" (ethnographic museum).

Small tourist train

(Ticket: 20 PLN)
A railway line links Hajnówka and the forest village of Topiło. The station is situated on the way out of Hajnówka, along the road to Białowieża, opposite the cemetery. Follow the signposts: "Kolejki Leśne w Puszczy Białowieskiej". This tourist train offers

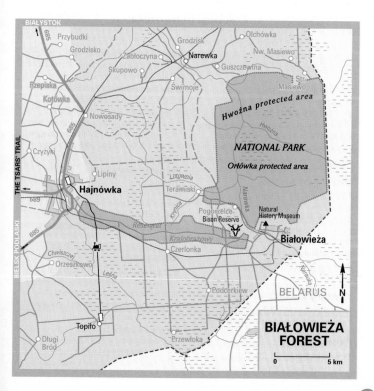

Bison roam in Białowieża National Park

a different way of approaching the forest. There are scheduled stops along the way (11km) to enable you to discover the forest and its characteristic flora.

The Tsars' Trail★

(about 30km)

The trail links Hajnówka and Bielsk Podlaski, going through the villages of Nowe Berezowo, Czyże, Łoknika, Pasynki ou Widowo. This is the road that the tsars and their guests followed when they went bison hunting. The villages, whose inhabitants had to light the way with torches as the convoy went by, all boast **Orthodox churches** with amazing shapes and colours. The road ends in Bielsk Podlaski where churches are renowned for their decorations and the quality of their icons. The icon tradition is flourishing thanks to an Icon Technical School, which is unique in Poland.

Practical Białowieża

Postal code – *17-230*
Phone code – *085*

Useful addresses

PTTK Tourist Office – *Kolejowa 17 - ☎ 681 22 95 - www.pttk.bialowieza.pl - pttkbialowieza@wp.pl - Tue-Sat 8am-4pm, Sun-Mon 8am-3pm.* Located in a small yellow house hidden on a square next to the Zubrówka Hotel. It is possible to book a guide, hire a horse-drawn cart or a bike.

Białowieża Forest Park – *Park Pałacowy 11 – ☎ 681 23 06 – www. bpn.com.pl*

Guides' Office – Lucyna Szymura - *Park Pałacowy 5 - ☎ 681 28 98 - bup@o2.pl -* Guides organize 3hr rambles through the Orłówka Protected Area (165 PLN) and guided tours of the Natural History Museum (20 PLN).

Getting around

Frequent buses link Białystok, Bielsk Podlaski or Hajnówka to Białowieża.

Where to stay

Żubrówka Hotel – *Ul. Olgi Gabiec 6 - 681 23 03 - www.hotel-zubrowka.pl -60 rooms 320 PLN.* A luxury hotel for those who look for comfort and service even if it means losing some of the forest atmosphere.

Dwór Soplicowo – *Ul. Krzyże 2a - ☎ 681 28 40 - www.dwor-soplicowo.pl - 32 rooms, apart. 220 PLN, 450 PLN.* A modern building with thatched roofs and 19C furniture. It's exactly how we imagine a bison-hunting lodge, with 21C comfort on top.

Pensjonat « Sioło Budy » *–"Budy" in Białowieża – ☎ 681 29 78 – www.kampio. com.pl -10 rooms 90 PLN.* Ideal to play at being a wild man in relative comfort. The hamlet of "Budy" is something between a Skansen, a scouts' camp and a country house.

Eating out

Restauracja Carska – *Ul Stacja Towarowa - ☎ 602 243 228 - 100 PLN.* The decoration and the cuisine are refined.Try the sturgeon or the game. French red wines are well represented.

Karczma u Jankiela – *In the courtyard of Dwór Soplicowo - 50 PLN.* The place upholds the genuine tradition of Polish inns; empty stomachs will be delighted.

Białystok★

POPULATION 291 660 – MAP OF POLAND D2– WOJEWÓDZTWO OF PODLASIE

Białystok is the capital of Podlasie. Following the industrial revolution, it became one of the jewels of Polish industry, in particular textiles. Although built around a Baroque architectural ensemble and a red-brick Catholic cathedral, the town is far from having a homogeneous cultural background. Situated at the crossroads of Catholicism and Orthodoxy, it also boasts descendants of Tatar horsemen who have remained faithful to the Moslem religion.

▶ **Getting your bearings** – 195km north-west of Warsaw, on the doorstep of Belarus

👁 **Not to be missed** – The houses or palaces which formerly belonged to textile factory owners who brought prosperity to the town in the 19C.

🕐 **Planning your visit** – Allow half a day to visit Białystok, and half a day to follow the Tatar Trail in the vicinity of the town.

Background

Motherland of Esperanto – For centuries, daily life in Białystok has taken into account an amazing mosaic of cultures, religions and languages. In the 19C, the town had a population of 30 000 including 3 000 Poles, 18 000 Jews, 5 000 Germans and 4 000 Russians. This fragmentation was also present in the social and professional structures: although Russian was the official language, "intellectuals" spoke Polish, workers German, shopkeepers Hebrew and farmers White Russian, spoken today throughout Belarus. Communities and districts lived side by side without any real unity. Faced with this situation, a precocious and sharp-witted adolescent from the ghetto undertook to create a common language. **Ludwik Zamenhof**, born in Białystok in 1859, with a degree in ophtalmology from the University of Moscou, invented Esperanto. This man who spoke a dozen languages, completed his invention at the age of 28 and went on to translate Shakespeare, Gogol and the Bible. He died in Warsaw in 1917. Today, some 150 universities throughout the world teach Esperanto.

Exploring

Lipowa Street runs through the centre of Białystok.

Cathedral of the Assumption★

The cathedral's 72.5m-high flamboyant towers stand at the western end of Lipowa Street. The neo-Gothic red-brick edifice, erected between 1900 and 1905 was designed as an annexee of the Baroque church, known as the white church, dating from 1627.

Branicki Palace★

On the other side of Lipowa Street. The original palace, like many districts, was destroyed during the Second World War and the building we see today was entirely rebuilt. It is named after the family who gave this "Podlasie Versailles" its definitive appearance over several generations. Completed during the 18C, the palace was a thriving centre of art and science which brought fame to Białystok. The kings of Poland and later the Austrian Emperor Josef II frequently stayed in the palace. Today, it houses the Academy of Medicine. However, it is possible to enter the place and discover a few rooms and the chapel. A vast park, alternating between the French and the English styles, leads to the **Planty**. From this park laid out on the site of the former ramparts, one can reach another protected open space known as "Las Zwierzyniecki".

A. Galy / MICHELIN

Moslem cemetery

Follow Lipowa Street eastwards to the former Town Hall.

Former Town Hall

Built in the 17C, it now houses the **Podlasie Regional Museum** (Muzeum Podlaskie) (*Ul. Rynek Kościuszki 10. Tue-Sun 10am-5pm. 4.5 PLN*). The basement, devoted to wine growing and to enjoying wine, is particularly interesting.

Orthodox Church of "St Nicholas the Miracle Worker"
(Kościół Sw Mikołaja)★

Erected in 1843, it is a reminder that Białystok includes more followers of the Orthodox religion (80 000) than any other Polish municipality.

The street leads to Independence Square, dominated by the monumental modern **St Roch's Church**. The foundation stone was laid in 1927 but the building was only completed in 1946. Shaped like a star, it is surmounted by an 8m-high bell tower.

Near the cathedral and the Branicki Palace, in Warszawska Street, there are a few examples of **palaces built for company directors** from Warsaw or Łódź, who contributed to the region's economic prosperity.

Nearby

In the footsteps of Moslem Tatars★★

The first Tatars settled in Lithuanian and Polish territories at the beginning of the 15C. Having fought against Christian armies, some of them sought refuge in Lithuania. They sided with the Poles against the Teutonic Knights, in particular at the Battle of Grunwald. In 1679, King Jan III Sobieski, who could no longer pay them, offered them land in Podlasie. Their descendants still live in Kruszyniany and Bohoniki, two tiny villages nestling round mosques and cemeteries. Religious festivals witness the return of relatives living in Warsaw, Gdańsk or Białystok. Before 1939, there were around ten such villages. The mosques were burned down by the Nazis or the communists and the population was exiled.

Sokółka – *40km north-east of Białystok along road 19.*
The **Sokółka Regional Museum** (Muzeum Ziemi Sokólskiej) (*Ul. Grodzieńska - Tue-Fri 8am-5pm, Sat-Sun 9am-5pm. 4 PLN*), although modest, offers additional background information about the origin of Tatar presence in Podlasie.

Bohoniki – *From Sokółka, follow road 674 towards Krynki for about 3km.* The mosque built in 1900 was entirely restored in 2005. The cemetery is located on the way out of the village, on the left at the end of a tree-lined alleyway.

Kruszyniany – *Drive to Krynki and continue south for about 10km.* The mosque erected at the end of the 19C is Poland's oldest. The cemetery, situated in the grove behind the mosque, features late-17C graves.

Practical Białystok

Postal code – *15-000*
Phone code – *085*

Useful addresses

Tourist Office – *Ul. Malmeda 6 – ☎ 732 68 31 – www.podlaskieit.pl - 8am-4pm.*

Getting around

Railway station – *Ul Kolejowa 26.* 9 trains a day to Warsaw (journey time: 2hr 30min). Also regular services to Kraków, Gdynia, Gliwice or Poznań .

Bus station – *Ul Bohaterów Monte Cassino 8.* Many buses leave Białystok bound for various destinations including Warsaw, Wrocław, Gdańsk and Rzeszów. There are also buses bound for Belarus, Lithuania and Western Europe.

Where to stay

Branicki Hotel – *Ul. Zamenhofa 25 – ☎ 665 25 00 - www.hotelbranicki.com - 32 rooms. 305 PLN, weekends 250 PLN.* Charming high-class hotel (sauna, cigar club, night-club and private car park). It is located in a quiet street close to the centre.

Eating out

Sabatino – *Ul Sienkiewicza 3 - ☎ 743 58 23 - noon-midnight - 50 PLN.* A large, rather bare room, jazz or blues-style music and diffused lighting form the decor. On the menu: Polish dishes as well as an amazing Provençal soup and Italian specialities.

Tatarska Jurta – *Kruszyniany. ☎ 710 84 60 - 30 PLN* - Dżenneta Bogdanowicz welcomes you into her own home, opposite the mosque. Tatar meals based on meat pies and soups are simple and copious.

Biebrza National Park ★★
Biebrzański Park Narodowy
MAP OF POLAND C2 – WOJEWÓDZTWO OF PODLASIE

The short River Biebrza which has its source between Białystok and Augustów, overflows and spreads across marshland. Elk and beavers have adopted this aquatic environment as their domain and birds descend in all seasons on this territory which seems to have been created for them. Birdwatching enthusiasts and all those who love rambling with rubber boots on will not be disappointed.

▶ **Getting your bearings** – 60km north-west of Białystok, between Łomża and Augustów.

👁 **Not to be missed** – Storks' nests, vacant or not according to the season.

🕐 **Planning your visit** – Allow two days to explore the whole park and half a day to visit Tykocin.

👥 **With your children** – A peaceful canoe trip down the River Biebrza.

Background

The largest marshland area in Central Europe – "The Polish Amazon", as some people call it, is one of the last living marshes in Europe. The Biebrza National Park, looking like two pyramids joined at the top, is similar in shape to an hourglass. Inaugurated in 1994, it covers an area of 592sq km, which makes it the largest in Poland. It extends across the whole river basin after which it is named and can be divided into three zones. The first, in the north, is the least visited. The second, covering the middle course of the river, consists essentially of humid forests of alders and several marshes including the Red Marsh (Czerwone Bagno). It is in this zone that the bulk of the elk population lives. Reintroduced during the 1950s, elk have since then proliferated and now number around 500. The southern part of the basin mainly consists of marshes and quagmires. It is, of course, the paradise of birdwatchers who can observe as many as 270 different species including great snipes, now rare, and numerous sedge warblers.

Exploring

In order to gain access to the Park, one must first go to the central information office, situated in the heart of the reserve, on the river bank facing the village of Goniądz, starting point of our itineraries. *Open Mon-Fri 7.30am-3.30pm, Sat-Sun (summer only) 7.30am-7.30pm. Brochures and maps are available here and you will be able to reserve the services of a guide or hire a canoe (5 PLN/hr, 30 PLN/day) or a kayak (4 PLN/hr, 20 PLN/day). Inside the Park, there are 500km of footpaths, 3 cycle tracks and 135 km of waterways. Admission charge to the Park: adults 4 PLN/day, children over 7 2 PLN/day. There is a separate admission charge to itineraries within the Red Marsh (same as the Park). Bear in mind that going through marshland in springtime can be tricky.*

The southern part of the Park by car

No road runs through the Park; however, it is possible to follow a road which skirts the park over a distance of 100km. Starting from Goniądz, drive south-west to Radziłów, then to Wizna via Brzostowo and Burzyn. 10km from Wisna, on the Kurpiki road, head north towards Laskowiec, and drive to Goniądz via Gugny. Villages are sometimes situated a few hundred metres from the road. It is recommended to visit the villages, most of which are built on floodland. There are many paths heading in all directions, always well signposted and the Park administration has built observation towers, often located along the road. In addition to birdwatching, these towers offer magnificent panoramic views of the flat landscape, which would otherwise be difficult to see.

🐦 The northern part of the Park on foot

Starting from Grzędy. As the crow flies, Grzędy lies 10km north of Goniądz. By road, it is best to skirt around the west side of the Park and to follow the road between Grajewo and Rajgród.
The 18km hike takes about 8hr on foot. Follow the red markings. The track runs deep into forests of conifers and several hundred-year-old oaks. Rare, hot-climate plants grow on the Grzędy sand dunes. Elsewhere there are vast expanses of reeds. Halfway there, there is an amazing view from the Wilcza Góra viewing tower which overlooks the marshes.

The southern part of the Park on foot

Starting from Gugny. See "the southern part of the Park by car".
This 10km ramble *(follow the red markings)* takes four hours including a pause at each of the two viewing towers. The first tower is said to be ideal for watching elk and deer at sunset... However, you'll still need luck!

Canoeing through the Park from north to south

There are many options for canoeing down the Biebrza and its marshes at leisure. From north to south, villages with accommodation hiring facilities are Lipsk, Sztabin, Dolistowo, Goniądz, Osowiec and Brzostowo. Itineraries vary from 8 to 25km. Everyone can find an option to suit him or her, taking physical condition into account as well as the size and composition of the family. Wisna is the village situated furthest south. Hiring a canoe in these villages is only possible after having acquired a sailing permit from the Park authorities in Lipsk, Sztabin or Osowiec-Twierdza.

Nearby

Tykocin

30km south-east of the Biebrza Park, slightly north of the road linking Łomża and Białystok.
Tykocin is a sleepy Baroque village lying along the River Narew. The **Church of the Holy Trinity**, built between 1741 and 1750 by Jan Klemens Branicki, is renowned for its organ and high altar, both original. Evidence of the Catholic past can be seen on the left as you enter, in a disused seminary built in 1633, and farther on in the village beyond the gates of a Benedictine monastery still occupied by the monks.

Tykocin Regional Museum (Muzeum w Tykocinie) – *Ul. Kozia 2. 10am-5pm except Mon. 5 PLN.* The most moving building in Tykocin is undoubtedly the former synagogue. Turned into a museum, this place which withstood all the barbaric acts of the 20C now houses liturgical objects such as the Torah, crowns for Torah, Talithim, Hanukka lights... displayed in glass cabinets; in the middle of the edifice stands the Bimah where the scriptures were read. Close to the synagogue is another part of the museum housing paintings, archaeological finds and a reconstructed pharmacy.

Pentowo, the Stork Village

1km from Tykocin, along the road to Kiermusy. 2 PLN, guided tour 10 to 30 PLN depending on the option chosen.
From inside a farmyard, one can observe some twenty storks' nests.

Practical Biebrza

Useful addresses

BIEBRZA - GONIĄDZ
Postal code – 19-110
Phone code – 086
Biebrza National Park – *Osowiec-Twierdza 8 -* ℘ *272 06 20 - www.biebrza.org.pl - biebrza@biebrza.org.pl*

TYKOCIN
Postal code – 16-080
Phone code – 085
Tourist Office – *Ul. Złota 2 -* ℘ *718 16 27 - www.tykocin.doc.pl - Mon-Fri 7.30am-3.30pm.*

Where to stay and eat

BIEBRZA - GONIĄDZ
Bartłowizna – *Ul. Nadbiebrzańska 32 -* ℘ *272 06 30 - www.biebrza.org.pl - bartek@biebrza.com.pl - 36 rooms 140 PLN.*

Meal 50 PLN. This recent hotel complex offers a great variety of accommodation as well as the facilities of a traditional inn. All necessary information about hikes, canoe and guide hire are also accurately provided.

TYKOCIN
Dworek nad Kąkami – *Kiermusy 12 -* ℘ *718 70 79 - www.dworek.com.pl - 10 rooms, apart., chalets : 250 PLN- 800 PLN. Meal 60 PLN.*
Located in a delightful setting in the heart of the forest, this establishment is a blend of elegant hunting lodge, antiques gallery and 17C farmhouse. The retro look of the rooms is underlined by the absence of a telephone and a TV set. Here everything is done to inspire nostalgia and to offer peace and quiet as well as top-quality service.

Suwałki

POPULATION 42 927 – MAP OF POLAND D1– WOJEWÓDZTWO OF PODLASIE

Tucked away in the north-east corner of the country, in the northern part of the Podlasie region, the Suwałki lakeland is undoubtedly one of the least known areas of Poland. Its wild unspoilt wooded landscapes dotted with lakes submitted to harsh weather conditions in winter, are reminiscent of Arctic regions. Indeed, this northern area is close to Russia, Lithuania and Belarus, whose influence can sometimes be detected in the customs, the atmosphere of the villages and the cuisine.

- ▶ **Getting your bearings** – Suwałki is 280km north-east of Warsaw.
- 👁 **Not to be missed** – Rambles through nature parks, between lakes and forests.
- 🕐 **Planning your visit** – Because the region is so remote, it seems sensible to devote at least two days to it. Bearing in mind that towns have very little of interest to offer, do not hesitate to seek accommodation in the countryside.

Background

The glacial period which, at these latitudes, ended later, left a landscape marked by deep valleys and depressions today filled in by some 100 lakes among the deepest in Poland. Populated by Prussian and Lithuanian tribes in the past, the Suwałki region was often contested, occupied and subdued. In 1795, the third partition of Poland ceded it to Prussia. In 1807, Napoleon made it part of the duchy of Warsaw and it was returned to the kingdom of Poland 8 years later. Created in the 17C by Camaldolese monks from Wigry Monastery, Suwałki reached its heyday in the 19C. The native town of film director Andrzej Wajda has only one asset from a touristic point of view: its ideal location at the centre of a vast region of lakes which lends itself to rambling and discovering magnificent landscapes.

Exploring

Nestling inside a meander of the River Czarna Hańcza, which flows down from the Suwałki Landscape Park, the city gathers round the long main avenue running in a north-south direction.

The **small regional museum** (Muzeum Okręgowe w Suwałkach, *ul. T. Kościuszki 81 – Tue-Fri 8am-4pm, Sat-Sun 9am-5pm, 5 PLN*) is interesting for its brief presentation, with the help of archaeological finds, of the Yotvingians (also known as Suduvians), an extinct Baltic people who left several necropoles in the area. Explanations are in Polish. The first floor houses paintings by 19C local artist Alfred Wierusz Kowalski.

At the town's eastern exit, along Bakałarzewska Street, several **cemeteries** testify to the various influences which converged here over the centuries, each religion having its own. The tiny Moslem area has no gravestones. As for those which were

Wigry Monastery

spared when the Jewish cemetery was destroyed by the Germans in 1942, they stand together, forming a commemorative monument, in the centre of an austere grass-covered enclosure. The Orthodox area is dominated by the wooden structure of a church built at the end of the 19C.

Nearby

Wigry National Park (Wigierski Park Narodowy)★
5km east of Suwałki. 2 PLN/day/pers.
The hilly terrain of this vast 15 000ha park was formed during the glacial period. Around forty lakes, some of them no larger than a simple waterhole are scattered among hills, peatbogs and forests. The nature reserve is named after the largest and most sinuous of these lakes, Lake Wigry. The River Czarna Hańcza flows into it from the west as a mountain stream and comes out on the east side as a wide waterway. It flows through the park then meanders southwards over a distance of 95km through the Augustów Forest, on its way to the Belarusian border; this is one of the finest courses for canoeing enthusiasts. Pines and firs grow on the shores of the lakes together with oaks, alders and birches. It is the habitat of a rich fauna, including beavers, the real mascots of the Park. 130km of marked tracks offer the possibility of exploring the reserve on foot or by bike.
The information centre located In the village of Krzywe, at the entrance to the Park, has a lot of literature in stock, some of it in English. The **Ethnographic Museum** housed in a former barn contains farming tools and machinery as well as objects of daily life. Next door, a small **Natural History Museum** introduces visitors to the diversity of the local flora and fauna. Beavers are, needless to say, ever present.

Camaldolese Monastery (Klasztor Kamedułów)★★
It stands on a promontory which was once an island in Lake Wigry. The land was ceded in 1667 to the Camaldolese monks, an order close to the Benedictines, by the Polish king Jan Kazimierz. The monks soon built a Baroque church, a monastery and several small hermitages, not to mention the outbuildings, from the smithy to the indispensable brewery. The influence of the monastery extended over a radius of 50km and the town of Suwałki was founded in the 17C. In 1800, the Camaldolese monks were expelled by the Prussians. The buildings suffered greatly during the two world wars but were superbly restored and the place is now imbued with serenity. It is possible to stroll among the 15 houses once occupied by the monks. The isolated bell tower is a fine observatory which provides a panoramic view of the region. Today the complex is a **hotel** charging very reasonable prices. A small exhibition recalls John-Paul II's visit in 1999.

Boat trips on the lake *(www.wigry.war.pl). Departure point at the foot of the monastery. Daily cruises from May to October 10am-4pm. Trips last 1hr 30min.*

Yotvingian Cemetery (Cmentarzysko Jaćwingów)
5km north of Suwałki, alongside road no 8, signposted to the left by a white panel marked "Szwajcaria". A very special atmosphere pervades this promontory covered with pines, where one can vaguely see some 100 funerary mounds.

Suwałki Landscape Park (Suwalski Park Krajobrazowy)★
15km north-west of Suwałki. Founded in 1976, the park covers 6 200 ha. It is probably one of the coldest spots in Poland. Formed by a glacier which retreated rather late, the deeply carved landscape looks most picturesque in winter under the white snow cover. Over 100 lakes are scattered across the undulating area where the flora and fauna show Nordic characteristics. Lake Hańcza, the deepest lake (108m) in the Central European plain, is filled with water as clear as that of a mountain lake. The Cisowa Góra hill, the region's 256m-high symbolic summit, sometimes referred to as "Suwałki's Fujiyama", towers above the eastern shore of the lake.

Ramble around Lake Jaczno – *Starting from Smolniki. 7km, allow 2hr 30min.* The park lends itself to discovery-rambles such as this one.
In the village of Wodziłki *(from Jeleniewo, follow the road skirting the southern border of the park then turn right after 5km, by a white-brick bus shelter)*, founded around 1788 by a Russian Orthodox community, you will see a wooden late-19C church.
The Park's Tourist Information Centre: *7km west of Jeleniewo, in a place called Turtul -* ℘ *569 18 01, www.spk.org.pl, open Jul-Aug 8am-5pm, Sat 9am-5pm, winter Mon-Fri 8am-3pm, bike hire 4 PLN/hr)*

Augustów (population 29 713)
33km south of Suwałki along road no 8.
Built on the edge of the forest by lakes Necko, Białe and Sajno, the town was founded

in the 16C by King Sigismund August and named after him. The road linking Warsaw and St-Petersburg and above all the canal dug between 1824 and 1839 brought prosperity to the town in the 19C. During the 1920s and 1930s, it was a holiday resort sought after by the elite. Today it is an unattractive spa town and a water sports centre. The small **Augustów Regional Museum** (Muzeum Ziemi Augustowskiej, *ul. Hoża 7 – 3 PLN. Open Tue-Sun 9am-4pm*) houses an ethnographic collection of ancient objects of daily life. A Museum annexe (Dział Historii Kanału Augustowskiego), housed in a wooden building located at the extremity of the peninsula (5 Ristopada Street), features an exhibition of archives and documents relating to the Augustów Canal.

The Augustów Canal

What was Poland's largest investment in the 19C links the Wisła and Niemen basins to enable trading with the Baltic to take place. Spread along 110km (80 in Poland) are 18 locks (14 in Poland) negotiating a 50m difference in level. The canal crosses many lakes (Necko, Rospuda, Biale, Studziennicze...). Cruises organised by the **Żegluga Augustowska Company** (✆ *643 28 81/643 21 52, www.it.mazury.pl/eglugaaugustowska*) between May and September link Augustów with the Przewięż lock and Lake Studzienicze, both situated 7km east of the town *(tours last from 1 to 3hr).*

Augustów Forest
(Puszcza Augustowska)

It starts on the eastern outskirts of town and extends 40km eastwards to the Belarusian border. A network of cycle tracks and footpaths runs across this wooded plain covering 115 000ha, mainly planted with pines and firs. Marshes and peatbogs cover the southern part where alders also grow. Trees well over a hundred years old can be seen in places.

Practical Suwałki

Postal code – 16 400
Phone code – 087

Useful addresses

Augustów Tourist Office - *Rynek Zygmunta Augusta 44* - ✆ *643 28 83* - open May-Aug Mon-Fri 8am-8pm, Sat-Sun 10am-6pm, Sep-Apr Mon-Fri 8am-5pm. This office has the widest choice of information in the region. Free Internet access.

Wigry National Park Information Centre - *À Krzywe* - ✆ *563 25 62* - www.wigry.win.pl - open Jul-Aug daily 7am-6pm, Mon-Fri 7am-3pm off season. Wide choice of information, some in English, about themed rambles, various activities, bike and boat hire points.

Railway station - Suwałki : ✆ *94 36, 566 22 35* - Augustów : ul. *Kolejowa 8,* ✆ *644 36 36*

Bus station - Suwałki : *ul. Utrata 1b,* ✆ *566 27 63* - Augustów : *ul. Rynek Zygmunta 4,* ✆ *643 36 49*

Where to stay

Jaczno – *In Smolniki, inside the Suwałki Landscape Park* – ✆ *568 35 90* - www.jaczno.pl – 10 rooms - 300 PLN. The rooms are located in small log cabins gathered on a peninsula on the western shore of Lake Jaczno. A delightful place, all the more charming when surrounded by snow in winter.

Hôtel du couvent des Camaldules (Dom Pracy Tworczej w Wigrach) – *16-412 Stary Folwark* - ✆/fax *563 70 00* - www.wigry.org -160 PLN. Make a point of spending a night in this unusual decor.

Eating out

Albatros – *Ul. Mostowa 3 à Augustów* – ✆ *087) 643 21 23* – 15 PLN. Classic Polish cuisine, copious helpings served in a rather outmoded setting.

Polski – *Ul. Kościuszki 59 à Suwłki*– ✆ *565 01 93* – 10 PLN. Tiny tavern offering popular specialities. Regular customers are a reassuring guarantee of quality.

Pod Jelonkiem – *Ul. Sportowa 7* – ✆ *568 30 21* – 15 PLN. Small restaurant in the village of Jeleniewo, 12km north of Suwałki, where one can enjoy delicious regional dishes based on potatoes (Kartacz: potato and minced-pork pie).

Festive events

Polish Championship of Unusual Boats: in July in Augustów.

Musical Summer: classical music in July and August in Suwałki.

The Masurian Lakes ★

MAP OF POLAND C1– WOJEWÓDZTWO OF WARMIA-MASURIA

Situated in north-east Poland and bordered by the Russian Kaliningrad enclave, Masuria spreads its numerous lakes, rivers and canals between forests and voluptuous hills. In summer, it is the paradise of sailing and water sports enthusiasts but also of nature lovers keen on lakes and isolated islets colonized by swans, cormorants and cranes who, inevitably, turn lake cruising into a fascinating birdwatching adventure. Winter here is one of the harshest in Poland. Snow covers the landscape which can be explored on skis or by sleighing and the frozen lakes are ideal for fishing through a hole in the ice or ice-yachting. Here nature reigns supreme and the rare towns offer little of interest.

▶ **Getting your bearings** – 240km north of Warsaw and 65km east of Olsztyn.

👁 **Not to be missed** – Canoe trips down the rivers.

🕐 **Planning your visit** – Allow three days to explore the region.

👫 **With your children** – The organised lake cruises will delight them.

Background

The land of a thousand lakes – From the largest to the smallest, there are, in fact, 3 000 of them! The weight and slow to-and-fro motion of the glaciers, which covered the region over 10 000 years ago, gave shape to the hilly landscape with its peatbogs and basins. The string of lakes extends along a north-south axis. Lakes Śniardwy (110sq km) and Mamry (102sq km), Poland's largest, are in the centre of a vast waterway system formed by rivers and canals, which can reach a total of 200km. Stretching to the south is a plain through which flows the River Krutynia; it is covered with the dense pine Forest of Pisz (86 000ha) where one can encounter wolves, bisons and lynx. The fauna is extremely varied. Some islets, such as those in Lakes Mamry and Dobsko, and remote lakes, such as Lake Łukajno near Mikołajki, are real nature reserves. Swans, cormorants, herons, ducks, black-headed gulls live in total freedom, far from the threats of civilisation. Pine, oak and birch forests such as the Forests of Pisz, Skalisko and Borecka shelter deer, wild boars and beavers.

A border area – Masuria's history was the logical consequence of its strategic position. The region was a melting pot of cultures, German, Russian, Lithuanian and of religions, Catholic, Protestant and Orthodox. Prussian tribes from the Baltic were Christianised here, sometimes brutally, by the Teutonic Knights at the end of the 13C. Poles and Germans occupied the first towns then, after the Second World War, the region became entirely Polish. The inhabitants of German descent were replaced by Polish farmers from Ukraine which, by then, had been joined to the Soviet Union.

The green lung of Poland – Protected from intensive industrialisation and urbanisation, the Masurian Lakes region fully deserves its nickname of "green lung of Poland". The first tourists who came at the end of the 19C made no mistake. It is today more than ever the favourite destination of Warsaw's residents who rush in as soon as they have a day's holiday. It is difficult to find accommodation in summer. Less popular and between two seasons, autumn and spring offer more subtle aspects of nature: its awakening from April to June and its fireworks of colours from September to November. The climate is also more changing and capricious then and the sailing season is limited to the period from June to September. However, the beauty of nature will delight ramblers, anglers and hunters.

Giżycko

(Population 30 000)

Situated on the isthmus separating Lakes Kisajno and Niegocin, Giżycko is one of Masuria's largest towns and the capital of water leisure activities in Poland. Thanks to its central location, it is the ideal starting point of a tour of the region either to the north or to the south. It gets very crowded in summer and visitors looking for peace and quiet will no doubt prefer to escape to the surrounding area. The resort is of limited architectural interest.

Before being returned to Poland in 1946, the town was called Lötzen under the Prussian and German occupation. The **Gothic castle** (Zamek Pokrzyżacki) built by the Teutonic Knights in the 14C has all but disappeared; all that remains is a wing remodelled in the 16C and 17C and now allowed to fall into decay. It stands on the banks of the Łuczański canal dug between 1756 and 1772 in order to link lakes Niegocin and Kisajno. It is spanned by a wooden **swing bridge** (Most Obrotowy), built between 1856 and 1860. It is one of only two specimens remaining in Europe.

One monument alone (but what a monument!) is of interest in Giżycko.

Boyen Fortress (Twierdza Boyen)

Ul. Turystyczna 1. Open daily 9am-dusk. 5 PLN

Situated on the western edge of town, this huge star-shaped fortress was, for a whole century, the key to the lake region's defence. Intended to protect one of the rare isthmuses preceding the border with Russia, it was built between 1844 and 1848 at the instigation of the Prussian war minister, General Hermann von Boyen. Modernised at the end of the 19C, it played an essential role in the resistance put up against the Russian breakthrough in 1914 and became a military hospital between 1941 and 1944. The Polish army later occupied it. It is now abandoned and overgrown apart from the moat which has been turned into an open-air theatre and stages concerts and various performances.

A small **museum** *(May-Sep)* is housed on the ground floor of one of the casemates. It illustrates the history of the fortress (fine scale model which gives a good idea of the enormity of the structure) and contains souvenirs of the Second World War in Masuria as well as photographs of Giżycko in the past. One room is devoted to an exhibition of documents and objects connected with the Solidarity trade union. Take a quick look at the collection of works by local artists, rather dwarfed by being too close to reproductions of famous masterpieces.

1 North of Giżycko

Several lakes lie north of Giżycko: Lakes Kisajno, Dargin and Dobskie, the latter being classified as a nature reserve. Next comes Lake Mamry. The surrounding area can be explored taking as a starting point the town of Węgorzewo reached via road 63.

Pozezdrze

First stop on the way to Węgorzewo, 12km from Giżycko. This village dating from the 16C was chosen by Heinrich Himmler, head of the SS, as his headquarters between 1940 and 1941. Half a dozen bunkers with over 2m thick concrete walls still remain. The best preserved is Himmler's private bunker, featuring double walls.

Węgorzewo (population 11 756)

20km south of the Russian border and 25km north of Giżycko.

This small town on the shores of Lake Mamry had a troubled history. The Galindian tribe was supplanted in the 13C by the Teutonic Knights who left a massive and austere castle restored in 1980 (private property). The Swedish wars, the 18C plague and the Second World War caused serious damage. Holiday resort during the 1920s, it was returned to Poland in 1946 when it was given its current name. The town has no monument of interest apart from a small museum combined with an **ethnographic park** (Muzeum Kultury Ludowej, *ul. Portowa 1, Mon-Fri 8am-6pm, Sat-Sun 10am-3pm, 5 PLN*). It displays the usual objects of daily life and comes to

Giżycko Marina

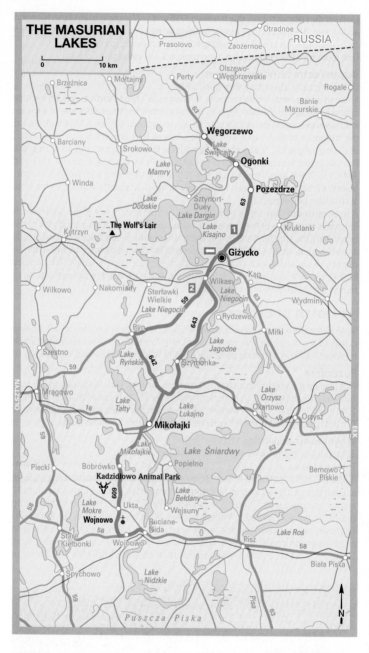

THE MASURIAN LAKES

0 — 10 km

life during the workshops (pottery, weaving, lace-making and basket-making) organised by local craftsmen.

Węgorzewo is the ideal base for an excursion to the north-eastern part of the lake region. 7km to the south-east, the large beach of the village of Ogonki overlooks Lake Święcajty from which it is possible to reach the River Sapina by canoe.

2 South of Giżycko

Two routes lead to Mikołajki. The first and undoubtedly the most pleasant skirts Lakes Niegocin and Jagodne (32 km). Leave Giżycko along road 59 and, as you exit the village of Wilkasy, turn left onto road 643. The second route (40km) follows road 59 then road 642 which makes a detour via **Ryn** where you can see the **Gothic-style castle**, built in the 14C by the Teutonic Knights then remodelled in the 19C, and the Dutch-style **windmill** standing on the edge of town.

Mikołajki (population 3 901)

Built on an isthmus separating Lakes Mikołajki and Tałty, this small resort with a population of 4 000 is one of the most pleasant in the whole lake region. It came into being in 1726 following the union of several villages on the site. Round the square which boasts a fountain adorned with a crowned fish, a symbol of what the area owes to fishing, historic houses from the 18C and 19C recall this past. Invaded by pleasure-boat owners who bring life to bars and restaurants in the marina, the town sets its pace to the rhythm of its activities and concerts. One hour's walk leads to **Lake Łukajno**, east of the town, a nature reserve sheltering a colony of a thousand mute swans.

From Mikołajki, road 609 runs south through the forest towards Ruciane-Nida.

Kadzidłowo Wildlife Park (Park Dzikich Zwierząt w Kadzidłowie)

13km south of Mikołajki, a road turns right towards this 60ha park, home to deer, fallow deer, tarpans (small Polish horses) as well as donkeys and goats... and even a bison. A kind of mini-zoo shelters specimens of all the animals living in the forest: beavers and lynx, as well as numerous birds, from storks to owls and waders. Nearby stands a **traditional house★**, splendidly restored in 2004 (Muzeum Chata Podcieniowa XIX w) (*5 PLN*). Inside are the kitchen, living quarters with all the furniture and utensils, and a classroom which only lacks pupils and a teacher.

Rejoin road 609, continue south to the village of Ukta as far as a panel signalling the Orthodox monastery of Wojnowo on the right.

Wojnowo Orthodox Monastery and Church (Klasztor Staroobrzędowców w Wojnowie)

It is here that, in the 19C, Russian Orthodox monks known as the Old Believers, who rejected the 17C reform of Patriarch Nikon, sought refuge in order to practice their faith, opposing all changes and banning tobacco, vodka and tea. Settling on the shores of a lake, the members of the community organised their life around a house of prayers and a church decorated with magnificent icons. A small wooded promontory shelters a tiny cemetery with many Orthodox crosses.

Continue south until you reach road 58 then turn left towards Ruciane-Nida.

Ruciane-Nida (population 4 994)

This is the most southern town in the lake region. Formed by the union of two villages, it extends along the forested shores of lakes Bełdany and Nidzkie. All tourist activities as well as the restaurants are concentrated in the modest Rucian district. The harbour is the departure point of northbound boat trips along the lakes.

Practical Masurian Lakes

Postal code – 11500
Phone code – 087

Useful addresses

Giżycko Tourist Office - Ul. Warszawska 7 - ☏ 428 52 65 - www.gizycko.turystyka.pl - Open May-Aug Mon-Sat 8am-7pm, Sun 10am-6pm, Sep-Apr Mon-Sat 8am-4pm, Sun in Sep 10am-6pm. Efficient office, well informed about the region. English and German-speaking staff.

Mikołajki Tourist Office - www.mikolajki.ot.pl - Open Jul-Aug 9am-8pm. On the square, opposite the fountain with the fish.

Węgorzewo Tourist Office - Pl. Wolności 11 - ☏ 427 40 09 - www.wegorzewo.pl -

Open Jun-Aug Mon-Fri 9am-5pm, Sat 10am-3pm, Sun 10am-2pm, off season Mon-Fri 9am-4pm. Useful brochures, English spoken.

Ruciane-Nida Tourist Office - Ul. Dworcowa 14 - ☏ 423 19 89 - Open 9am-5pm. Best information about the lake region available here.

Giżycko Port Authority - Ul. Kolejowa 9 - ☏ 428 25 78.

Navigation office - In Giżycko. ☏ 428 56 51. To be contacted in the event of a sailing accident.

Emergency Unit - ☏ 601 1001 00. Medical help to persons involved in a sailing accident.

Emergency Regional Centre - ☏ 112 (from a mobile phone). Medical help and rescue.

INTERNET

Very little difference from one establishment to another. Allow about 4 PLN/hr and reckon on opening hours from about 9am to 8pm.

Giżycko
Cyber Klub Romix - Ul. Olsztyńska 15b.

Mikołajki
Kawiarenka Internetowa - Ul. Kolejowa 6.
Usługi Informatyczne - Ul. Szkolna 4d.

Where to go

Lake cruises

Off season, any boat trip with fewer than 10 passengers is cancelled.

Masurian Sailing Company (Żegluga Mazurska) -

In Giżycko -Al. Wojska Polskiego 8 -
☏ 428 25 78 ,

Mikołajki Office - ☏ 421 61 02,

Ruciane Office- ☏ 423 10 43,

Węgorzewo Office - ☏ 562 22 0 .
Departure from the ports of Mikołajki, Giżycko, Węgorzewo, Ruciane-Nida. Tickets are sold on board or at the counters. The company proposes round trips as well as excursions from one port to another. **Average price for the journey Giżycko - Mikołajki** (4hr 30min) 50 PLN,

Giżycko - Węgorzewo (2hr 30min) 35 PLN, **Mikołajki - Ruciane-Nida** (2hr 30min) 40 PLN, 2hr cruises on Lake Śniardwy 25 PLN. Trips aimed at discovering a lake or a nature reserve (1 to several hours) are also organised from every port. A few trips only take place in spring and autumn.

Some small companies propose thematic itineraries based on birdwatching or fishing. Inquire at tourist offices.

Getting around

On land –Train timetables are available on the following website: www.rozklad.pkp.pl (in English). For bus timetables, look up www.pks.mragowo.pl.

On water – The regular services provided by the **Masurian Sailing Company (Żegluga Mazurska)** (see **Where to go**) are a pleasant if slower alternative to land transport.

GIŻYCKO

Railway station - Pl. Dworcowy -
☏ 94 36. Giżycko is situated on the line linking Olsztyn and Kętrzyn to Białystock. It is the region's busiest station.

Bus station - Next door to the previous one ☏ 428 50 87

WĘGORZEWO

Bus station - Ul. Armii Krajowei -
☏ 427 25 51.

MIKOŁAJKI

Railway station - Ul. Kolejowa.

Bus station - Not a real bus station, just a simple bus stop pl. Kościelny 1.

RUCIANE-NIDA

Railway station - Ul. Dworcowa - ☏ (089) 533 66 87.

Bus station - Ul. Dworcowa - ☏ 423 31 48.

Where to stay

There are many hotels and B & Bs; tourist offices provide exhaustive lists. The closer to the lakes the accommodation is the more expensive it is. Not surprisingly summer is the most expensive season, up to 50% more, and many establishments are closed from November to April.

IN GIŻYCKO

The 3 hotels below are located in the same peaceful area, at the town's north-western exit, 100m from a small creek in Lake Kisajno.

Europa Hotel - Al. Wojska Polskiego 37 - ☏ 429 30 01 - fax 429 25 54 - www.hoteleuropa-gizycko.pl - 215 PLN, 180 PLN from Nov to Apr, 🛏,🅿. Perfect comfort awaits you in this simple, restful hotel; note that the rooms have a warm atmosphere. Give preference to those overlooking Lake Kisajno.

Mazury Hotel - Al. Wojska Polskiego 56 - ☏ 4298 59 56 - www.hotelmazury.prv.pl - 46 rooms - 240 PLN in Jul-Aug, 200 PLN in May-Jun and Sep, 🛏,🅿. Located 100m from Lake Kisajno, this establishment is already old and somewhat outmoded yet it has the advantage of making you feel at home.

Helena Hotel - Al. Wojska Polskiego 58 - ☏ 429 22 09 - www.mazury.com.pl - 48 rooms - 200 PLN in Jul-Aug, 150 PLN in May-Jun, Sep-Oct., 🛏. Large family hotel named after its owner. The rooms are small but attractive and the place is welcoming. Large banquet hall where special evenings are organised.

Zamek Hotel - Ul. Moniuszki 1 - ☏ 428 24 19 - www.cmazur.elknet.pl - 12 rooms - 180 PLN in Jul-Aug, 140 PLN in May-Jun and Sep, 🛏,🅿.On the edge of a park, close to the canal and the ruins of the castle, this strange motel boasts a private garage under each of the rooms. The decor is slightly timeless but the place is pleasant and there are a few pitches for tents.

Tajty Hotel - Ul. Przemysłowa 17 - ☏ 428 01 94 - fax 428 00 87 - www.hoteltajty.com.pl - 46 rooms - 214 PLN, 160 PLN from Nov to Apr, 🛏,🅿. On the shores of Lake Tajty, slightly away from the village of Wilkasy south of Giżycko. The rooms are adequate if rather ordinary, but the remoteness of the place guarantees peaceful undisturbed nights.

IN MIKOŁAJKI

Amax Hotel - Al. Spacerowa 7 - ☏ 421 90 00 - www.hotel-amax.pl - 16 rooms - 250 to

390 PLN depending on the season, ⌦ closed Dec-Apr. On the other side of the lake, facing the lights of Mikołajki, this hotel probably offers more peace and quiet than any other. It may lack character but it fulfils its role of luxury establishment to perfection. Sauna and jacuzzi, swimming pool, beauty and fitness centre.

Mazur Hotel - *Plac. Wolności 6 - ☏ 421 69 41 - www.hotelmazur.com.pl - 28 rooms - 200 PLN ⌦ closed Nov-Apr.* A must in Mikołajki. A maze of corridors leads to vast bedrooms, generally quiet except when the street livens up on summer nights. Choose a room overlooking the courtyard!

Caligula Hotel - *Pl. Handlowy 7 - ☏ 421 98 45 - www.caligula.pl - 17 rooms - 200 PLN from Jun to Aug, 160 PLN the rest of the year, ⌦.* Small hotel with tiny but comfortable and well-appointed rooms. Some of them have a mini-balcony. This place which seems to attract ice-yachting enthusiasts offers a convivial welcome.

IN WĘGORZEWO

Vena Romantik Hotel - *20km west of Węgorzewo, at a place called Karłowo, north of the municipality of Srokowo - ☏ 427 62 44 - www.venaromantik.com - 25 rooms - 160 à 230 PLN depending on the season and the room, ⌦.* Located on the heights overlooking Lake Rydzówka which stretches eastwards, this hotel is a real paradise in the heart of nature, surrounded by pastureland for horses. Wooden cottages with refined pastoral decors (animal skins, flowers). A must see!

Nautic Hotel - *Ul. Słowackiego 14 - ☏ 427 20 80 - www.nautic.pl - 12 rooms - 210 PLN ⌦.* Nice little hotel in the town centre, on the banks of the canal flowing into Lake Mamry. The rooms are small but neat and the hospitality warm. Fine terrace overlooking the canal, where one can have a meal or enjoy an ice-cream.

IN RUCIANE-NIDA

Nidzki Hotel - *Ul. Nadbrzeżna - ☏ 423 64 01 - www.hotel.nidzki.ta.pl - 33 rooms - 225 PLN from May to Sep, 170 PLN from Oct to Apr, ⌦.* This superb luxury hotel is proud to offer personalised service. The magic appeal of this isolated place, built on the wooded shores of Lake Nidzkie, and the charm of the large rooms are reminiscent of Canada.

Barbara and Mirosław Gworek's B & B - *Głodowo 10 - ☏ 423 18 02.* A little corner of paradise at the extremity of a peninsula, 9km north of Ruciane-Nida. The 3 double rooms at 60 PLN per night are rather basic, but, for 150 PLN, one can rent one of the two superb apartments on two levels situated next to the fish smoke-house. Family welcome and tiny grocery store, two reasons for staying several days.

Oberża pod Psem - *Kadzidłowo 1, 8km north of Ruciane-Nida on the way to Mikołajki - ☏ 425 74 74.* Danuta and

Krzysztof Worobiec's B & B consists of 5 rooms in two traditional houses. The coal-burning stove adds it contribution to the background heating, but you will not be sorry to have spent a night in an authentic Polish family home. Allow 120 PLN for a double room.

Eating out

IN GIŻYCKO

Karczma Pod Złotą Rybką - *Ul. Olsztyńska 15 - ☏ 428 55 10 - www.mazury.info.pl/zlota - 35 PLN.* This small unassuming restaurant specializes in fish from the lakes. Indulge in anything fishy you fancy on the menu: fish soup, fish by the weight, fried or served with a sauce, large dish of 5 different fish from the lakes including pikeperch and eel.

IN MIKOŁAJKI

Kuchnie Świata - *Pl. Wolności 13 - ☏ (088) 769 91 38 - 35 PLN.* Located along the promenade running by the lakeside, near the footbridge. Festive atmosphere, huge dishes and grilled-meat specialities. Useful to know: the place closes late.

Tawerna Pod Złamanym Pagajem - *Ul. Kowalska 3 - ☏ 421 51 65 - 20 PLN.* In the marina. Even if the place is more of a snack bar than a restaurant, it has the atmosphere of a sailors' tavern. Specialities include kotlet schabdwy, pierogis and bigos.

IN WĘGORZEWO

Karczma - *Ul. Zamkowa 10 - ☏ 427 32 23 - 15 PLN.* A small inn along the main road. Wooded surroundings and small terrace unfortunately overlooking the road and the traffic. However, the cuisine is good and the service attentive. This is the most commendable restaurant in town. Halina, the owner, offers sound advice for choosing a dish.

IN RUCIANE-NIDA

Kolorada - *Ul. Dworcowa 6e - ☏ 423 65 31 - www.kolorada.mazury.info. 40 PLN.* This restaurant insists more on the variety of the dishes on offer than on their originality. World cuisine is on the menu: greek, tex-mex and even French. Helpings are copious if not refined.

Oberża pod Psem - *Kadzidłowo 1, 8km north of Ruciane-Nida on the way to Mikołajki - ☏ 425 74 74 - 30 PLN.* A real inn housed in a log cabin with rustic-style furniture. On the menu, the inevitable bigós, but also wild boar with potato pasta and other Polish delights.

Shopping

Panels (marked "Miód") on the roadside signal the possibility of buying honey directly from the bee-keeper. Between Mikołajki and Ruciane-Nida, go up to Kadzidłowo (see text). At the **"Dog's Inn" (Oberża pod Psem)** it is possible to buy homemade bread and plum jam (powidła śliwkowe), pies (pasztet) or even smalec, a kind of lard with bacon cubes for frying or using as a spread with a little salt.

Sport and Leisure

SAILING

This is the best way to discover the lakes. In Giżycko, Węgorzewo, Sztynort, Mikołajki and Ruciane-Nida there are boat-hire companies and marinas able to provide supplies and services. There are many hiring companies; bear in mind that the most important ones offer the best guarantees. The highest prices *(between 300 and 500 PLN per day)* are applied in July and during the first fortnight in August as well as during long weekends such as 1 to 3 May. The lowest prices *(around 200 PLN per day)* are applied in May and September. *Allow around 500 PLN for the deposit and at least 100 PLN per day for the skipper.* Beware: the insurance does not cover the theft of the engine.

Allow 5-12 PLN for a night in a port and, in addition, 2 to 4 PLN per crew member. One can, however, moor on the lakes for a night but it is forbidden to tie the boat to a tree. A map showing the varying depths is a must to avoid being stranded.

SAILING IN GIŻYCKO

Mazur Wind - *Ul. Klonowa 19 - in Wilkasy - ℘ 428 01 72 - www.mazurwind.pl.* In a village south of Giżycko, on Lake Niegocin. With ten years' practice, the owner certainly knows his business and his boats are well looked after. Trips with or without skipper.

Marina Bełbot - *Ul. Przemysłowa 17 - in Wilkasy - ℘ 428 03 85 - www.marina.com.pl.* Boat hire from late Apr to late Sep. On the shores of Lake Tajty. Appreciated within the profession, the company offers a wide choice of boats.

Almatur - *Ul. Moniuszki 24 - ℘ 428 59 71 - fax 428 58 98 - www.sail-almatur.pl.* Boat hire from late Apr to the first fortnight in Oct. On the shores of Lake Kisajno. At the western exit of Giżycko, turn right opposite the stadium.

SAILING IN WĘGORZEWO

Port Keja - *Ul. Braci Ejsmontów 2 - ℘ 427 18 43 - www.keja.com.pl.* In Węgorzewo harbour. Several sizes of boats accommodating 4 to 8 persons. *Allow 140 to 450 PLN per day in high season, depending on the model chosen.*

CANOEING

Canoeing is ideal for exploring rivers and small lakes, but it is not recommended to venture out to the middle of the lakes whose waters can be turbulent. There are many itineraries to choose from; inquire from the hiring company and tourist offices. Like pleasure-boats, canoes must carefully avoid the numerous bird sanctuaries. It is important to obtain all the necessary information.

Hiring a canoe costs between 25 and 50 PLN/ day.

A few canoeing courses – The most famous follows the **River Krutynia** over a distance of 103km, from Ruciane-Nida to Sorkwity. It goes through Piska Forest in a north-west direction.

Starting from Gyżycko, another two-day course links **Lakes Niegocin and Śniardwy** via Lakes Tyrklo and Buwelno. It goes through a narrow valley, gouged out by glaciers and now flanked by wooded hills; one must organise the transport of the canoes over the 9km wide land strip separating the last two lakes.

Starting from Węgorzewo, it takes 10hr to canoe down the **River Sapina** which leads to the village of Kruklanki, north-west of Giżycko.

PEDALO

Numerous possibilities in the leisure centres located on the lake shores. *Allow 6 PLN/hour.*

RIDING IN GIŻYCKO

At Gajewo Hotel *in Giżycko - ul. Suwalska 5 - ℘ 429 27 67 - www.gajewo.pl. Allow 40 PLN for one hour's riding.*

BIKING

8 marked itineraries, from 36 to 67km, crisscross the region of Giżycko. The tourist office in Giżycko provides a brochure with detailed information about each one and signals bike-hire centres (including some hotels). *Allow 15 to 20 PLN/day.*

A 50km **loop circles Lake Mamry**, starting from Węgorzewo, and an 80km itinerary runs round Lake Śniardwy, starting from Mikołajki, via Lake Łukajno.

RAMBLING

All tourist offices provide a detailed map of the itineraries available.

In the Ruciane-Nida region, do not miss **Pisz Forest** (Puszcza Piska) covering an area of at least 86 000ha. Pines are the dominant species but there are also oaks and birches. It is possible to get a glimpse of some deer, roe deer, wild boars and tarpans, the small Polish breed of horses.

FISHING

In the clear water of the lakes in summer, through a hole in the ice in winter. Perch, tench and eel. *Permit: 15 PLN per day to 50 PLN per week.*

Festive events

Ice-yachting week : in Węgorzewo in March. Ice-yachting races.

International Folk Festival: Węgorzewo mid-August.

In summer, there are **Festivals of sea songs**. The most famous is the Giżycko Festival which takes place in mid-July. The Węgorzewo Festival, WegoSzanty, which takes place in August, is gaining in importance.

Kętrzyn

POPULATION 28 619 – MAP OF POLAND C1–WOJEWÓDZTWO OF WARMIA-PODLASIE

For visitors arriving from Olsztyn, Kętrzyn is the last town they come across before reaching the Masurian Lakes region. Though less spectacular than other popular tourist areas, the undulating surrounding area with its fields and scanty forests boasts historic sites well worth a detour.

- ▶ **Getting your bearings** – 250km north of Warsaw and 92km north-east of Olsztyn.
- 👁 **Not to be missed** – A stroll along the narrow streets of Reszel or along the river.
- 🕐 **Planning your visit** – The four sites can be visited in the space of two days. Do not hesitate to allow slightly more time for Reszel and the peaceful atmosphere of its streets.

Background

A base for Christianisation

In 1329, the Teutonic Knights erected a fortress on the banks of the River Guber, on the site of a Prussian village, Rast. Christianisation of the region and of the Lithuanian peoples did not altogether go smoothly. The town, which became Rastenburg, was taken several times and fell again under the control of the order who founded St George's Church (Kościół św. Jerzego), a massive, fortified edifice. Walls soon surrounded the town, but that did not stop it being siezed by the Prussians in 1454 and by the Russians in 1758. In 1807, Napoleon's armies stopped here on their way to Moscow. The closeness of Hitler's General Headquarters made it a choice target during the Second World War at the end of which the town was handed back to Poland and given its current name.

Things to see

Stretching along Sikorskiego Avenue, the town has a certain historic feel about it. This can be due, as you turn a corner, to a ruined fortification, the massive tower of a church, the outline of a castle but above all to the line of edifices rebuilt after the war in 19C style.

Castle and museum

Pl. Zamkowy 1. Open Mon 10am-3pm, Tue-Fri 10am-5pm, Sat-Sun 10am-4pm. 5 PLN.
This fine building dating from the late 14C is the town's only attraction. Built on a square plan around a bailey, it was once surrounded by a curtain wall. Taken again and again, it was remodelled in the 18C and almost totally destroyed in 1945. The restoration work did not spoil its Gothic appearance, partly conveyed by its brick walls, but do not expect to find inside any monumental fireplace or vaulted ceiling, you are

The Wolf's Lair

169

more likely to think you've entered an administrative building from the communist period. A **museum** displays a few Gothic sculptures, 17C furniture, a few masonic objects as well as a funerary flag made for a 3-year-old child around 1667. On the upper floor, the history of the town is illustrated by a collection of postcards and municipal archives, whereas small Chinese statues in marble and ivory are displayed in another room.

Nearby

Reszel★ (population 5 224)
18km south-west of Kętrzyn.
This charming little town lying in the heart of hilly countryside, occupies a strategic site on the edge of a steep plateau overlooking the River Izera. Built in the 13C by the Teutonic Knights on the site of a Prussian settlement, it has retained its characteristic grid plan centred on a tiny Rynek. In 1808, the last witch in Europe was burned at the stake here.

In the centre of the **Rynek** stands the Classical-style **town hall** rebuilt in 1815. The town offers a pleasant stroll along its narrow paved streets, now and then revealing the remains of the medieval ramparts or an 18C timber-framed barn (Spichrzowa Street).

The monumental **Church of SS Peter and Paul** (Kościół śś. Piotra i Pawła) stands in the southern part of town. Built in the 14C, it is dominated by a 65m high massive square tower. The interior is a blend of Empire and Rococo styles. Nearby, in a field overgrown with wild grass, stands the former elegant presbytery, now unfortunately left to fall into decay.

The **two old 14C bridges**, the Fishermen's Bridge (Most Rybacki) and the Low Bridge (Most Niski), span the ravine dug by the river which offers fine walks along its banks.

The **Gothic castle**, at 3 Podzamcze Street, in the eastern part of town, is the emblem of Reszel with its towers soaring up to the sky from a height overlooking the river. Built from 1350 onwards, it was one of the key elements of Prussia's defence system. In the 16C, it lost some of its military importance and became for a few years the hunting lodge of the bishops of Warmia based in Lidzbark Warmiński. In 1795, the Prussian authorities turned it into a prison. In 1822, the refectory and the bishops' living quarters were transformed into an evangelical church to which was added a strange tower looking as if it were built of concrete. Today it is a **Museum of Modern Art** *(open Tue-Sun 9am-5pm, 3 PLN)* which stages temporary exhibitions. The castle surrounds a central courtyard, the south and east wings now housing a hotel. From the top of the tall keep, cylindrical over a square base, the **panoramic view** of the region is splendid. The whole edifice is surrounded by a curtain wall, the latrines tower alone being linked to the castle.

Święta Lipka Baroque Monastery★
10km south-east of Kętrzyn, 5km south-east of Reszel.
Ul. Podzamcze 3. Open Tue-Sun. 3 PLN. Located in a dale framed by two lakes, the "Baroque Pearl of Northern Poland" owes its name of Holy Lime Tree to a fine legend. A chapel was built on the site of the famous lime tree then razed by the Protestants. The **Baroque monastery** was built between 1687 and 1693 at the instigation of the Jesuits. Many craftsmen from Reszel took part in its construction. The holy tree has, for centuries, been attracting a crowd of pilgrims and the sanctuary, which used to stand on the border of Catholic Polish Warmia and Protestant Prussia, long assumed an important political significance. Today it is famous for the concerts given on its monumental organ, dating from 1721 and featuring mechanical statues.

On its **west front**, a Virgin in Majesty in the hollow of a tree recalls the legend. The interior, decorated with gold, contains a reproduction of the sacred lime

The Legend of the Holy Lime Tree

At the beginning of the 14C, a man condemned to death was rotting in the dungeons of Kętrzyn Castle. The Virgin Mary answered his prayers and his repentance by sending him a piece of wood and a knife and asking him to carve a statuette of her, which he did in the space of a few hours and with such talent that the judges, convinced this was a miracle, released the prisoner. On his way to Reszel, the man placed his work in the branches of the first lime tree he saw, in order to comply with his saviour's wishes. Miracles and cures promptly followed.

tree adorned with ex-votos. The bright blue pillars framing the dark walnut-and-lime altar rise up to the vaulting covered with frescoes and kings' portraits.
The **cloister**, featuring the Stations of the Cross, forms a square enclosure round the church. The four corners are adorned with the domes of Baroque chapels decorated with trompe-l'oeil Biblical scenes.

The Wolf's Lair
(Wilczy Szaniec Wolfschanze)★

In Gierłoż, 9km north-west of Kętrzyn. Open from dawn to dusk. Parking and admission charge (7 and 8 PLN).
Invisible from the road running through the woods, this real fortress once housed the Eastern Front High Command. Built between 1940 and 1942 by the Todt Organisation, the Wolfschanz covers 18ha dotted with 80 buildings including 50 bunkers. The walls of several of them, in particular Hitler's personal bunker and that of the highest Nazi dignitaries, are 8m thick. This small town produced its own electricity and had its own airfield, railway line and even cinema. The ensemble, surrounded by barbed wire and minefields, was camouflaged under a huge net of artificial vegetation which was changed according to the season. Elite troops and an anti-aircraft system defended it. Today it is a vast area covered with ruins over which nature is regaining control. Held by the iron bars reinforcing the concrete, the remains of the bunkers blown up by the fleeing Germans in January 1945 seem to have been frozen on the spot by the explosion. At the beginning of the path running through the ruins, a plaque marks the site of the building where the assassination attempt against Hitler took place on 20 July 1944.

Attempt on Hitler's Life

It was undertaken by a handful of plotters gathered round Count Claus von Stauffenberg, an officer who had served in France, Poland, Russia and North Africa. The plot aimed at killing Hitler in order to end a war that many believed lost and thus to preserve what remained of Germany. On 20 July 1944, von Stauffenberg took part in a meeting of the High Command. Well known, trusted by Hitler, he easily avoided being checked and succeeded in placing his bomb in the room where the officers were. Nevertheless, the operation failed, Hitler, miraculously protected by part of the strong wooden table, was only wounded. Unmasked, the conspirators were pitilessly hunted down and punished.Marshall Rommel, who took part in the plot was forced to commit suicide.

Practical Kętrzyn

Postal code – 11 400
Phone code – 089

Useful addresses

Kętrzyn Tourist Office - *Pl. Piłsudskiego 1 - ☏ 751 47 65 - Open May to August daily 9am-9pm, the rest of the year Mon-Fri 9am-5pm, Sat 10am-2pm. Located in a room of the town hall. Some literature in English.*
Reszel Tourist Office - *Open Mon-Fri 10am-6pm, Sat 10am-1pm. Housed in the town hall.*

Getting around

Railway station - *Ul. Dworcowa 10 - ☏ 752 30 45 et 94 36.*
Bus station - *Ul. Dworcowa 1 - ☏ 752 32 10.*

Where to stay

KĘTRZYN
Zajazd Pod Zamkiem u Szwagrów - *ul. Struga 2 - ☏ 752 31 17 - www.zajazd. ketrzyn.pl - 4 rooms - 140 PLN. Situated at* the foot of the castle, this pleasant inn which also has a restaurant, offers rooms with four beds, located under the eaves, perfect for families.

RESZEL
Zamek w Reszlu - *Ul. Podzamcze 3 - ☏ (089) 755 02 16 - www.reszel.iap.pl - 21 rooms - 230 à 250 PLN. The best address in the whole region. For a reasonable price, you can spend the night in the magnificent Reszel castle in the highly romantic setting of one of the vast rooms with stone walls. In addition, the Polish restaurant is excellent.*

Eating out

RESZEL
Rycerska - *Ul. Rynek 7 - t (089) 755 00 16 - Open daily 11am-9pm - 25 PLN. This small brand new restaurant features a rather discreet and pleasant medieval-style decor. The menu includes fine traditional dishes prepared with care and served with a smile.*

Lidzbark Warmiński★

MAP OF POLAND C1 – WOJEWÓDZTWO OF WARMIA-MASURIA

Famous for being the site of the battle between Napoleon and the allied forces of Prussia and Russia, Lidzbark Warmiński boasts one of the best preserved medieval castles in Poland which came through all the wars unscathed.

- ▶ **Getting your bearings** – 50km north of Olsztyn.
- 👁 **Not to be missed** –The collection of Russian icons.
- 🕐 **Planning your visit** –Allow around one hour to visit the castle.

Background

Mentioned as early as the 10C at the confluence of the Rivers Łyna and Symsarna, this is one of Warmia's oldest cities and a former regional capital. Still visible are sections of the fortifications, including the **Main Gate** (Brama Wysoka), erected in the 13C by the Teutonic Knights to defend their military base. The bishops who ruled this powerful diocese between 1350 and 1795 were mainly Polish. Nicolaus Copernicus, the nephew of one of these bishops, Łukasz Watzenrode, lived in the town from 1503 to 1510. It is in the vicinity of the city, called Heilsberg at the time, that in June 1807 Napoleon won a decisive victory against the Prussian and Russian armies.

Lidzbark Warmiński Castle

W. Buss / MICHELIN

Castle (Zamek)★

Pl. Zamkowy 1. Open Jun-Aug Tue-Sun 9am-4pm, off season 10am-4pm. 5 PLN. Explanations in Poiish, sometimes in English.

The impressive Gothic edifice, brick built on a square plan with square corner towers, was the residence of the bishops of Warmia. A footbridge spanning the wide moat leads to the mound where it was erected in the 14C. The large Gothic doorway gives access to an inner courtyard from which one can see, on the first floor, a delicate arcaded gallery often compared to that of the royal castle in Kraków. On the walls protected by the gallery, are traces of vast frescoes, now severely damaged. A flight of steps leads to the basement where an impressive room supported by pillars houses reproductions of paintings illustrating Napoleon's victory. Another staircase leads farther down still to a succession of vaulted rooms with stone floors where ancient guns are displayed. The different floors of the fortress which now house the **Warmia Museum** (Muzeum Warmińskie), feature a succession of rooms covered with Gothic vaulting containing pictures of famous guests (such as Copernicus), period furniture and objects. A few murals are sometimes visible under the whitewash covering the walls. They are particularly well preserved in the great hall of Ignacy Krasicki, known at the time as the poet-bishop. Although remodelled in Rococo style in the 18C, the chapel, adorned with stucco and gilded decorations, retained its medieval vaulting from which gilded angels are hanging. Close by, the brick-paved Great Refectory, the finest hall in the fortress, contains a collection of 15C and 16C polychromes. A series of coats of arms is painted above the checked polychrome frescoes running right round the walls. Via the audience hall and the library, which now displays 17C and 18C paintings, one gets to the 2nd and 3rd floors whose modern architectural style contrasts with the Gothic style. The collections of modern and contemporary Polish paintings are less interesting than the magnificent exhibition of **Russian icons** from the 17C to the 20C.

Olsztyn ★

POPULATION 172 467 – MAP OF POLAND C1 – WOJEWÓDZTWO OF WARMIA-MASURIA

Lying halfway between Warsaw and Gdańsk, Olsztyn is surrounded by 10 post-glacial lakes (to the west) and by vast forests, which make a visit to the capital of Warmia-Masuria particularly pleasant. The picturesque gorge of the River Łyna over which towers the medieval fortress runs through the town. Olsztyn was for a long time torn between the Prussian and Polish influences but it now looks like a young, dynamic and verdant city, where Michelin has set up a large factory. The small historic centre, meticulously restored, offers a pleasant surprise, even if there are few major monuments.

- **Getting your bearings** – 200km north of Warsaw, 180km from Gdańsk.
- **Not to be missed** – The castle, student bars in the old town.
- **Planning your visit** – Allow half a day to visit the town.

Background

Mentioned for the first time in chronicles dating from 1348, the foundation of this town in the Warmia diocese, decreed by papal bull, seems to have coincided with the construction of the castle in the 14C.

At first it came under the rule of the Teutonic Knights who had conquered it but it was integrated into Polish territory following the Treaty of Toruń in 1466. Unlike Elbląg who became Protestant after the Reformation in 1525, Olsztyn remained Catholic and formed a kind of ecclesiastical, relatively autonomous state administered by the princely bishops of Warmia who had christianised it. Having fallen under Prussian control and been renamed Allenstein after the first Partition of Poland in 1772, it continued to remain the heart of the Polish national and cultural movement in Warmia, in spite of the growing number of German immigrants who settled in the town during the second half of the 19C. Subjected to enforced Germanization

Floods of Tears at the Origin of the Town

Alina, the faithful wife of a Prussian tribal chief, made the mistake of rejecting the advances of a local witch's son. When the dangerous lover obtained from his mother the death in battle of the troublesome husband, Alina and her lady's maids cried so much that their floods of tears turned into a river which was named **Łyna** after the unfortunate wife. The Prussian name of the town, **Allenstein**, is said to derive from that of the river… but some say that it is more likely connected with the famous stone known as *Alue Status*, located inside the Lutheran church.

during the Second World War, it became Polish again at the end of the conflict which left it partially in ruins (40% of the town was destroyed) and practically drained of

High Gate

B. Brillion / MICHELIN

its inhabitants. The whole German population was then expelled and replaced by Poles arriving essentially from the eastern territories annexeed by the Soviet Union, but also from Lithuania.

Exploring

The medium-size **Historic Centre** (Stare Miasto) is bound by the meanders of the River Łyna in the south and by the fortifications erected at the end of the 14C, formerly pierced by three gates, of which only the **High Gate** (Brama Wysoka) remains.

Rynek★
Small and steep, partially surrounded by arcaded Gothic houses, it is centred round the former town hall now the municipal library.

St James's Cathedral (Katedra Św. Jakuba)
Built from 1380 onwards against the former town walls, it is surmounted by a massive 63m-high tower, featuring fake arcades, erected between 1562 and 1596. The interior covered with fine crystalline and netlike **vaulting★★** resting on 10 pillars, is bathed in a light conducive to meditation, diffused by modern multicolour stained-glass windows. Note the **Gothic tabernacle** (on the right of the high altar) and the beautifully carved, painted and gilded 16C **triptych★** of the Holy Cross, situated at the end of the north aisle, transferred from the church of the same name in 1802.

Castle★★
This attractive brick-built edifice, dating from the 14C, is surrounded by a large moat (laid out on the right as an amphitheatre), spanned by a stone bridge guarded by a statue of Copernicus. This castle was the head office of the Warmia Chapter's administration, whose treasure was kept here. Today it houses the Regional Museum.

Museum of Warmia and Masuria (Muzeum Warmii i Mazur)★★
Ul. Zamkowa 2. Jun-Sep Tue-Sun 9am-5pm; Oct-May Tue-Sun 10am-4pm. 6 PLN.
The colourful ground-floor rooms house a fine portrait gallery. The first floor of the east wing features the *komnaty Kopernikowskie*, a series of rooms with splendid crystalline vaulting linked to the memory of Copernicus who resided in the castle and was appointed administrator of the Chapter's Treasury between 1516-19 and 1520-21. In 1521, he took an active part in the city's defence against the attacks of the Teutonic Knights. The first room *(Sala Kromera),* a former chapel, is prolonged by the old refectory which contains a collection of silverware; the room at the end is devoted to Copernicus and his work. The tour continues on the upper floor with an ethnographic exhibition about Warmia and Masuria and with the visit of the castle tower. In the courtyard, next to the well, you will see a statue known as the Prussian Woman (*pruska baba*) found in Barciany, probably carved by Prussian pagan tribes from the Baltic who once lived in the area. As you come out of the castle, note, immediately after the bridge, the **evangelist church,** rebuilt in neo-Gothic style in 1899, which features under the high altar a sacrificial stone called *Alue Status*, probably a relic of an ancient pagan cult.

Copernicus' statue stands guard over the castle bridge

By the backway, you can reach the **Fish Market Square** (Targ Rybny), laid out on the site of the former medieval Mill Gate. On the square stands the building formerly occupied by the *Gazeta Olstyńska* newspaper, now an annexee of the museum.

Dom "Gazety Olsztyńskiej" (Muzeum Warmii i Mazur)
Ul. Targ Rybny 1. Jun-Oct Tue-Sun 9am-5pm, Nov-May Tue-Sun 9am-3.30pm. 5 PLN. Explanations in Polish only.

This annexe of the Museum of Warmia and Masuria is housed on three levels inside the first premises used by the *Gazeta Olsztyńsk*a, the main newspaper of the Polish community in Eastern Prussia, which was published between 1886 and 1939. Essentially devoted to the history of the Polish National Movement in Masuria and Warmia, the museum is concerned with local heroes and other important regional figures of the 20C, mostly unknown outside Poland, apart from Pope John-Paul II who visited Olsztyn in 1991. In the staircase, an interesting series of photographs shows Olsztyn after it was destroyed and then rebuilt. An ethnographic section housed in the basement illustrates aspects of daily life in rural areas in the past.

Beyond the High Gate lies the Upper District (Górne Przedmieście) centred round the **new neo-Baroque Town Hall**.

On the heights overlooking the town stand the **Planetarium** and, housed in a former 19C water tower, the **Astronomical Observatory**.

Nearby

Morąg (population 14 657)
Situated halfway between Elbląg and Olsztyn (50km from each of these towns).

This small town of Prussian origin was the birthplace of philosopher and poet of the Age of Enlightenment **Johann Gottfried Herder** (1744-1803). Standing in the middle of the peaceful **Rynek** and preceded by two French guns from the 1st Empire, the elegant, Gothic-style, former **Town Hall** (Ratusz) now houses the Tourist Office (*Mon-Fri 8am-4pm, Sat 10am-2pm - www.morag.pl*). Between the square and the church is the monument erected to commemorate the local celebrity, opposite the house where he was born. Behind the Gothic church one can see the ruins of the old Teutonic castle dating from the 13C; the courtyard features the gloomy sight of four gallows complete with ropes ready for use... an "artistic installation" conceived by the current owner of the castle.

J.G. Herder Museum (Muzeum im. J. G. Herdera)★★
Ul. Dąbrowskiego 54 . Tue-Sun 9am-5pm - 6 PLN. Explanations in Polish and German.
Do not miss this small but attractive museum housed inside the Pałac Dohnów, built between 1562 and 1571 then remodelled in the Baroque period. The right wing, devoted to Helder and his contemporaries, will be of great interest to amateurs of German culture. Born in Mohrungen (Morąg) in 1744, Herder died in Weimar in 1803, having spent the years between 1762 and 1769 in Königsberg and Riga. The left wing houses a collection of 18C portraits and 17C Dutch prints, a long gallery displaying 17C paintings from the Dutch School as well as several reconstructed rooms containing period furniture in Baroque, Second Empire, Art Nouveau and Biedermeier styles. The

> **Practical Morąg**
>
> The owner of Dohnów Castle lets the first-floor Renaissance apartment. *For 250 PLN, it accommodates up to five persons. Contact Anita Borlnicka on ℰ 089 757 42 98 and book two weeks in advance.*

visit is enhanced by an exhibition of works by painter Hugo Landheer (1896-1963) and by temporary exhibitions of contemporary art on the ground floor.

Olsztynek (population 7 673)
25km south of Olsztyn.
Founded in the 14C by the Teutonic Knights, this modest town was the birthplace in 1764 of lexicographer **Mrongowiusz** to whom a small museum is dedicated. It was also one of Poland's bastions of Protestantism and the disused Protestant church in the Rynek now houses the **Salon Wystawowy** *(May-Sep daily except Mon 9am-5pm, Oct-Apr daily except Mon 9am-4pm. 3 PLN),* devoted to temporary exhibitions of graphic arts.
It was also here, at the exit of the town in the direction of Gdańsk, that stood the Hindenburg Mausoleum commemorating German victory over the Russians in 1914. It was entirely destroyed by Soviet forces in 1945. 500m away stood the Stalag IB Hohenstein POW camp, where French prisoners were detained during the Second World War. Today, one comes to Olsztynek to visit its skansen.

Olsztynek Ethnographic Park (Skansen) (Muzeum Budownictwa Ludowego (Park Etnograficzny)★
Ul. Sportowa 21, 11-015 Olsztynek ℰ   089 519 21 64. 15-30 Apr Tue-Sun 9am-3pm, May daily 9am-5.30pm, Jun-Aug Mon-Fri 9am-5.30pm, Sat-Sun 9am-6pm, Sep Tue-Sun 9am-4.30pm, Oct Tue-Sun 9am-3.30pm. May-Aug: 7.50 PLN, Sep: 6.50 PLN, Oct: 5.50 PLN. On presentation of your ticket, keepers will open locked buildings. Note also that there is a cheaper ticket allowing visitors to look at the buildings from the outside only. Allow 2hr for the visit. Literature in English (5 PLN), with a useful map of the site.
This skansen, originally set up in Królewiec (the former Königsberg and the present Kaliningrad in Russia), is Poland's oldest and largest open-air museum. Moved to Olsztynek between 1938 and 1942 to form with the Hindenburg Mausoleum a monumental ensemble named Tannenberg, devoted to east Prussian architecture in the past, it comprises some fifty reconstructed or original buildings from Warmia, Masuria, Podlasie (eastern bank of the Lower Wisła) and Lithuania, scattered in green surroundings. Some houses illustrate special themes: weaving, traditional costumes, painted furniture, domestic life. At no 29, ask for the music box to be activated. After having admired the windmills, end your visit with a look at the fine painted-wood Protestant church and note the temptation scene depicting a particularly suggestive Eve.

Grunwald
Museum of the Battle of Grunwald (Muzeum Bitwy Grunwaldzkiej)
18km south-west of Olsztynek, on the territory of the municipality of Stębark. May-15 Oct: 8am-6pm. 6PLN - charge for supervised parking. ℰ   089 647 22 27.
Just like the English have come to associate 1805 with the Battle of Trafalgar, all Polish schoolchildren have learned to think of 1410 as the year of the Battle of Grunwald. The site where it happened seems to have remained unchanged. In these peaceful meadows took place on 15 July 1410 the most important European battle of medieval times, which sealed the fate of Poland for the first time. During the course of the bloody fighting that involved some 60 000 men, the Polish king Władysław Jagiełło, commanding a Polish-Lithuanian coalition, defeated the Teutonic Knights' army. Every year, this event, which has become a symbol of Polish national resistance, is commemorated during a grand historical pageant spread over several days, which draws brotherhoods of "Knights" from the four corners of Europe.

Behind the double commemorative monument erected in 1960, consisting of 11 high metal pillars and a stone monument, there is a small **museum** concealed in the hillside, which displays a few objects connected with the battle and presents a 23min film recalling the great moments of the massacre. 400m further *(follow the footpath)*, you will see the ruins of a chapel erected a year after the defeat, on the spot where the Grand Master of the Teutonic Order, Ulrich von Jungingen, is believed to have died.

Practical Olsztyn

Postal code – 10-000 à 11-041
Phone code – 089

Useful addresses

Tourist Office (IT)– *Ul. Staromiejska 1 - On the left of the High Gate leading to the Rynek - ✆/fax 535 35 65 -wcit@warmia. mazury.pl - www.warmia-mazury-rot.pl - Oct-May Mon-Fri 8am-4pm, Jun-Sep Mon-Sat 8am-5pm (until 6pm in Jul-Aug).*

Internet access – *On the 1st floor of the municipal library located in the centre of the Rynek. 2 PLN/hr.*

Where to stay

Szkolne Schronisko Młodzieżowe w Olsztynie. *Ul. Kościuszki 72/74 – ✆527 66 50 - fax 527 67 70 - ssmolsztyn@ptsm.com.pl - www.ptsm.com.pl/olsztyn -🍴 - P.* This large yellowy building is none other than the local HI-registered youth hostel, offering 70 beds in rooms with 1, 2, 3, 4 and 6 beds. Fully equipped kitchen.

Hotel Wysoka Brama– *Ul. Staromiejska 1 - Between the TO and the gate of the same name - ✆/fax 527 36 75 - www. hotelwysokabrama.olsztyn.pl -🍴 - 25 rooms - 100 PLN - 🛏10 PLN.* Visitors with tight budgets will appreciate the basic but neat rooms of this hotel; also on offer are several rooms without bathroom for 58 PLN and a dormitory.

Hotel Pod Zamkiem–*Ul. Nowowiejskiego 10 - ✆535 12 87 ✆/fax 534 09 40 - hotel@olsztyn.com.pl - www.hotel.olsztyn. com.pl - P - 15 rooms - 190 PLN, 🛏.* Isolated within the castle park, this Secession-style villa – the town's former music school – features an entrance hall and a staircase worthy of a hunting lodge.

Polsko-Niemieckie Centrum Młodzieży. *Ul. Okopowa 25 – ✆534 07 80 - ✆/fax 527 69 33 -centrum@maxi.pl - www.pncm. olsztyn.pl - P - 22 rooms - 200PLN - 🛏19PLN.* This Polish-German youth centre, ideally situated below the castle (to the left of the amphitheatre), is no longer what its name implies. The initial customers have been replaced by business people and the hotel-cum-restaurant has adapted its standard accordingly.

Hotel Warmiński – *Ul. Głowackiego 8 - ✆ 522 14 00 - fax 533067063 - www. hotelwarminski.com.pl - hotel@hotel-warminski.com.pl - 127 rooms - 74 PLN.* Don't judge this hotel by its unattractive concrete-block appearance; inside, the rooms are very pleasant and comfortable.

Hotel «Villa Pallas»– *Ul. Żołnierska 4 - ✆/ fax 535 01 15 -www.villapallas.pl - P - 32 rooms - 250 PLN 🛏.* Comfortable rooms housed in a huge villa full of staircases and corridors and situated on the heights overlooking the town. Elegant dining room with appetizing à la carte menu.

Eating out

Świeże Zupy –. *Ul. Św. Barbary 1 - Sun-Thu 11am-10pm (Fri-Sat until midnight).* An establishment sought after by the locals who flock inside at any time of the day to enjoy a mouth-watering bowl of homemade soup, *5 PLN for a small bowl, 7 PLN for a large bowl.*

Różana café – *Ul. Targ Rybny 14 - On the right before the bridge leading to the castle - ✆/fax 523 50 39 - daily 11am-10pm.* The best restaurant in the old town dedicated to the most fragrant of flowers, as can be guessed from the colour of the walls, the mural frieze and their presence on every table. The cost is not excessive for all that.

Staromiejska – *Ul. Stare Miasto 4/6 At the top of the Rynek - ✆ 527 58 83 - daily 10am-10pm.* The locals' favourite place in the late afternoon for a chat and a beer or tea and biscuits. In the evening, it is an elegant old-world restaurant. Outside terrace. Retro-style waitress wearing a lace blouse and high white booties. 3 dining rooms.

Restaurant Przystań – *Ul. Żeglarska 3 - ✆ 523 77 73 - daily noon-10pm.* This restaurant on the edge of a lake, is sought after for its setting and traditional cuisine Drinks are served in the middle of the lake in summer.

Taking a break

Filmowy Bar Kawowy – A bar dedicated to the cinema where one can take a tea or coffee break. In the south-west corner of the Rynek. *Open daily 4-9pm.*

On the town

The town centre may have few attractive restaurants, but it has a great many pleasant, convivial bars.

Ostróda-Elbląg Canal★★
Kanał Ostródzko Elbląski

MAP OF POLAND C1 – WOJEWÓDZTWO OF WARMIA-MASURIA

Dug between 1848 and 1876 on the basis of a project by Dutch engineer J.G. Steenke, the Ostróda-Elbląg canal linking the Baltic and the south of Prussia is, on account of the original solutions adopted to solve technical difficulties, a unique masterpiece of hydrographic art. 80.4km long (including 40km of canal dug to link the six lakes), it forms the main section of a several-pronged system. Unfortunately, no sooner was the project completed that the advent of the railway made this ingenious system obsolete and it never had any real commercial value. It is now only operating for tourists.

▶ **Getting your bearings** – Ostróda is 36km west of Olsztyn and Elbląg is 61km east of Gdańsk.

Discovering

The 9.6km situated between the villages of Całuny Nowe and Buczyniec, where the water level difference reaches 99.5m, form the most interesting stretch. In order to negotiate this level difference between Lakes Drweckie and Drużno, five successive slipways are used like ladders to link the various waterway levels. Once in front of a slipway, boats are hauled along rails by a system operated by hydraulic power. While one of the structures goes up on one side, the other goes down and the boats cross over land.

Cruises – *The company's main office is in Ostróda (Ul. Mickiewicza 9A ℰ/fax 089 646 38 71 / 0 801 350 900 . Daily 7am-3pm, Jun-Aug 7am-6pm) on the edge of Lake Drweckie. In Elbląg, the office is situated in a basement, 50m beyond the Vivaldi Hotel (Ul. Wieżowa 14 ℰ/fax 055 232 43 07), but one can also call in the morning at the landing stage situated opposite St Nicholas's Church. A complete cruise costs 85 PLN (concessions 65 PLN, luggage 16 PLN, bike 32 PLN), a cruise as far as Buczyniec costs 70 PLN. www.inf@zegluga.com.pl / www.zegluga.com.pl. Snacks available on board.*

A fleet of five boats provides daily service in July and August, and a less regular one in low season (May-Sep). Cruises go in both directions from Elbląg or Ostróda; departure at 8am, arrival in the other town around 7pm. The complete journey between the two towns lasting 11hr might seem fastidious. A good way to compromise is to do half the journey (5hr) from Elbląg to Buczyniec, the village where there is the last and most spectacular slipway. In Buczyniec, a small **museum** *(May-Sep daily 10am-6pm, 2 PLN)* illustrates the story of the project and you can also visit the powerful hydraulic machinery *(4 PLN)*.

By road – *To watch boats going up the slipways, go to Buczyniec (diversion along the road beyond Pasłęk from Elbląg or at Morzewo from Ostróda) between 12.30 and 2pm.*

Nearby

Elbląg (population 128 016)
Seeing a few old photographs of Elbląg's former quays would convince you that the town would have continued to compete with Gdańsk, had it been spared by the war. The old Protestant city of Elbing, daughter of the mythical old Prussian sea port of Truso and of the Hanseatic trading town founded by the Teutonic Order, is slowly rising from its ashes. It is possible to visit the **Galeria El w Elblągu** *(Ul. Kuśniersko 6 - Mon-Sat 10am-6pm, Sun 10am-5pm - 4PL)*, a symbolic Polish gallery of contemporary art housed since 1961 in the former Gothic St Mary's Church (Kościół Mariacki).

Ostróda (population 33 698)
Napoleon's admirers will be delighted to learn from a commemorative plaque in the courtyard of the small much-restored Teutonic **castle** occupied by the municipal library and the tourist office *(on the 1st floor on the ledt as you enter, Mon-Fri 8am-4pm)* that the great man "stayed in this castle from which he governed the Empire" from 21 February to 1 April 1807.

Frombork★★

POPULATION 2 598 – MAP OF POLAND C1 – WOJEWÓDZTWO OF WARMIA-MASURIA

This small sleepy town, facing the laguna north of the Wisła estuary, is no doubt the most qualified for the coveted title of "Copernicus's city". Indeed, it is here that the illustrious astronomer spent the greatest part of his life and carried out most of his research, from 1509 to his death in 1543. The former Frauenburg (Our Lady's town), which was for a long time the capital of the Warmia diocese, is still dominated by its charming fortified cathedral picturesquely situated at the top of a cliff overlooking the town and the sea and offering, in fine weather, a good view of the shores... of Mother Russia. Copernicus was, for over 30 years one of the cathedral's canons, which earned him the privilege of being buried inside the cathedral.

- ▶ **Getting your bearings** – 94km east of Gdańsk and 32km north-east of Elbląg.
- 👁 **Not to be missed** – The panorama from the cathedral's former bell tower.
- 🕐 **Planning your visit** – Allow 2 to 3hr to see all the sights. Bear in mind, however, that some museums are closed on Sundays and Mondays.

Background

Initially established in Braniewo, the cathedral of the Warmia diocese, too exposed to the Prussian threat, was moved to Frombork at the end of the 13C while the bishops chose to reside in Lidzbark Warmiński. Frombork remained for a long time under the influence of Braniewo and attempts at creating a maritime trading port were repeatedly crushed by Braniewo and Elbląg. Having no fortifications, the town was often plundered, in particular by the Swedes in 1626, and, following the Prussian annexeation in 1772, it only resumed its official role as residence of Warmia's bishops in 1837 and retained it until 1945.

Exploring

The only part of the town (80% of which was destroyed) to have been spared by the disasters of the Second World War is **Cathedral Hill** where most of the sights are located. It can be reached on foot from the lower town via a stepped path which skirts the walls (to the left) and enters the courtyard on the south side through the **Main Gate** (Brama Główna). *Admission to the courtyard is free, but there is an admission charge to the buildings (including the cathedral).*

Dominating the **Lower Town** and looking somewhat like a keep, the tower (14C-16C) adjoining the tourist office deserves it name of Water Tower (wieża wodna). In 1571, it was fitted with a system enabling it to supply water to Cathedral Hill through a network of oak pipes. Today it houses a pleasant café where one can take a break and sit at a table on one of the levels leading to the summit which offers a fine **panoramic view** of the town (May-Sep 8.30am-8.30pm; Oct-Apr 9am-4pm. 3 PLN). Note the burned-out roof of the massive St Nicholas's Church (kościół św. Mikołaja), now disused, one of the rare relics that were retained in the Lower Town.

Cathedral Hill (Wzgórze Katedralne)★★★

Information available from the Cathedral Museum. 9am-4.20pm - Ul. Katedralna 8 - 𝒫 243 72 18 - www.frombork.art.pl

Cathedral (Katedra)★★
Mon-Sat 9.30am-5pm. 4 PLN
Erected between 1329 and 1388 at the top of a cliff, on the site of a previous wooden cathedral built in 1280, it boasts a specific feature: it is surrounded by ramparts. Start by walking round the building and note that some elements were added to the Gothic structure, for instance St George's Chapel (15C) and St Saviour's Chapel (1732-35). Take time to admire the unusual **west front**, flanked by two octagonal turrets. The porch shelters a remarkable stone doorway decorated with a string of characters which runs on along the ribs of the vaulting. The interior, surmounted by fine star vaulting, contains some twenty Baroque altars, as many as 101 funerary plaques (essentially Warmian bishops and canons) and 19 epitaphs. One of these, located on the first pillar in the nave, immediately to the right of the chancel, was made in the 18C to commemorate Copernicus, since the great man's body is buried somewhere under a slab without anyone knowing exactly where. Note the seven orange hats

hanging from the chancel vaulting: they belonged to the seven Warmian bishops who became cardinals, whereas the papal tiara is that of Enea Silvio Piccolomini who, with the support of the Polish king, became pope under the name of Pius II. The late-Baroque black-marble **high altar**, replaced in 1752 the magnificent late-Gothic **polyptych** (1504) now in the north aisle. Note the **Baroque pulpit** (1785) and the fine **organ** (1684) renowned for its rich tone which, combined with the excellent accoustics of the place, offers the possibility of splendid concerts in summer *(on Sundays from June to August)*. Also noteworthy is the Baroque Chapel of the Saviour, at the end of the south aisle, closed off by an imposing **wrought-iron railing** framed by a trompe-l'oeil painting. Finally, two paintings located on each side of the side entrance are worth looking at: St Anthony and the Procession of the Holy Body of Christ.

Frombork Cathedral

Copernicus Museum (Muzeum Kopernika)★
Tue-Sun 9am-4pm. 4 PLN. Explanations in Polish and German.
Housed in the former Gothic Bishops' Palace remodelled during the Baroque period, the museum is essentially devoted to Nicolaus Copernicus (Mikołaj Kopernik) (1473-1543). Having visited the ground-floor exhibition of archaeological finds and fragments of stained glass from the late 19C and early 20C, originally in the cathedral, go to the first floor where a room is entirely devoted to the great astronomer. Drawing their inspiration from a famous three-quarter portrait, artists represented him in many different styles, using various techniques, including a masculine version of the Mona Lisa. Acting as canon of the Warmia Chapter during 30 years, Copernicus completed numerous missions in the course of his duties, as the exhibition shows. Having initiated a monetary reform, the author of the famous *De revolutionibus orbium coelstium*, published in Nuremberg and, as the story goes, seen by him for the first time on his death bed, was also asked in 1510 to draw up a map of the region; several copies of this map are exhibited and will enable you to understand better the complicated history of Warmia for many years caught in a pincer movement by Prussia. On the 2nd floor, international contemporary artists expose their ideas about heliocentricism. The last room presents a few telescopes.

Radziejowski Tower (Wieża Radziejowskiego)
Open daily 9.30am-5pm. 4PLN
Situated in the south-west corner of the curtain wall, this former Gothic steeple, which rises 70m above the nearby sea, offers an exceptional panoramic view. Halfway up the tower, a **Foucault pendulum** confirms the earth's rotation. A spiral staircase then leads up to an outside gallery, level with the Baroque spire, from which the **panoramic view★★★** of the Wisła's laguna is breathtaking. In fine weather, one can even get a glimpse of the Russian town of Kaliningrad at the extremity of the bay. In the basement, a **planetarium** puts on six shows a day *(6 PLN)*.

Copernicus Tower (Wieża Kopernika)

Mon-Sat 9am-5pm. 3 PLN

Built before 1400, destroyed and rebuilt several times (the last time in 1965), this square tower is the oldest part of the fortifications. It is thought to have been the scientist's study (those who say that it was his home are wrong) and celestial observatory. The reconstruction of this Renaissance scientist's study is not exceptional and by no means a must see.

Hospital of the Holy Ghost and St Anne's Chapel (Szpital św. Ducha i Kaplica św. Anny)★

Ul. Stara (on the left as you leave by the main door, then straight on). Tue-Sat 9am-5pm. 3 PLN

Situated outside the cathedral enclosure, this former medieval hospital from the late 14C, which was recently restored, houses a modest **Museum of Medicine** (Dzial Historii Medycyny). Past the entrance and the lovely paved floor, you will see the remains of a heating and waste-water disposal system. However, the main interest lies in the traces of **frescoes** painted on the walls of the chancel rotunda in the chapel. These naive paintings, illustrating the Last Judgement in the form of sketches, feature a wealth of small devils fighting over the souls of the damned.

Practical Frombork

Postal code – 14-530
Phone code – 055

Useful addresses

Tourist Office (IT Globus)– *Ul. Elbląska 2 - At the foot of the Water Tower, in the Lower Town.* ✆ *243 75 00, fax 243 73 54 - globus. frombork@poczta.fm - May-Sep 8.30am-8.30pm, Oct-Apr 9am-4pm.* More of a private boutique - particularly well stocked with books - than a real tourist office. Bike hire available.

Internet–Two computers offer Internet access inside the **Akcent** Restaurant (*Ul. Rybacka 4*).

Getting around

Frombork can be reached by bus or train from Elbląg. There is also a less regular bus service between the town and Lidzbark Warmiński.

Where to stay

Note that a new youth hostel is scheduled to open in one of the orphanage buildings (Dom Dziecka) opposite the cemetery, along the road to Braniewo. You can also find a few private rooms (*Kwatery Prywatne*).

Dom Familijny Rheticus–*Ul. Kopernika 10 -* ✆*/fax 243 78 00 domfamilijny@gabo.pl -*
www.frombork.iq.pl/reklama/rheticus - 🅿 *- 9 apart. (1,2,3 rooms) 192 PLN - room 120 PLN -* ☕ *7PLN (in the rooms).* The place has the feel of a provincial railway station, with its somewhat austere exterior and much more convivial interior (the ground floor is shared with a florist). This welcoming guesthouse, named after Copernicus's only disciple, offers spacious, rooms with high ceilings, each with its own kitchen.

Hotel Kopernik–*Ul. Kościelna 2* ✆ *243 72 86* ✆*/fax 243 73 00 - hotel.kopernik@wp.pl - www.frombork.iq.pl - 32 rooms - 130 PLN -* ☕ *30 PLN -* 🅿. This long one-storey building, painted in yellow and red, contains standardized rooms with balconies, offering a pleasant view of the cathedral. Combined with a restaurant. Off-season discounts.

Eating out

Not much choice really! Several *Fish & Chips* located behind the Water Tower offer a quick-snack option. In one of these, an annexe of the **Akcent Restaurant** (*Ul. Rybacka 4*✆*243 72 75*), situated on the side of the square, you will be able to have a snack in a more conventional setting - prefer the terrace to the dull dining room. The only real alternative is the restaurant of Hotel Kopernik mentioned above.

Kraków in the snow

Kraków★★★

POPULATION 757 547 – MAP OF POLAND C4– WOJEWÓDZTWO OF LITTLE POLAND

Lying at the foot of first uplands of the Carpathian Beskid, on the north bank of the Upper Wisła (Vistula) River, Kraków is Poland's real gem of a city, equal in splendour to the finest European towns and included by UNESCO, as early as 1978, on its very first World Heritage List. This elegant cultural and university metropolis is an ancient royal capital, dear to the hearts of the Poles for whom it represents the birthplace of their nation and of their culture. The remarkable Gothic and Renaissance complex in the town centre may indeed have come through the Second World War virtually unscathed but, on the other hand, the Jewish community of the Kazimierz district suffered a great deal as illustrated in Stephen Spielberg's film, *Schindler's List*. A symbol of "Old Poland" during the communist era, this provincial capital is now a young and dynamic town with nearly 130 000 students, and centres its activities on tourism.

▶ **Getting your bearings** – 294km south of Warsaw, 114km south-east of Częstochowa, 536km south-east of Gdańsk, 220km south-east of Łódż, 100km north of Zakopane.

👁 **Not to be missed** – The Rynek, the altarpiece by Veit Stoss in St Mary's Church, Leonardo da Vinci's *Lady with an Ermine* in the Czartoryski Museum, stained-glass windows by S. Wyspiański in the Franciscan Church, Wawel Castle and Cathedral, the old Jewish district of Kazimierz, the Wieliczka salt mines, the atmosphere of the vaulted cellars of the Old Town's restaurants and cafés.

🕐 **Planning your visit** – Like all beautiful towns, Kraków invites its visitors to extend their stay if they wish to get to know the city thoroughly. However, a minimum stay of three days will enable you to see the essential, thanks to the relatively small size of the town, which makes it the ideal destination for a long weekend.

Background

Foundation of the city – According to legend, Kraków was founded in the 7C by King Krak or Krakus, who rid Wawel Hill of its dragon and whose daughter Wanda chose to drown herself in the Wisła rather than be forced to marry a German prince. Being the main settlement of the Vistulans (Wiślanie, from the Polish name of the River Wisła), Kraków, mentioned for the first time in 965, was incorporated into the kingdom of Poland by Prince Mieszko I. It was the first Christian centre in Poland and, around AD 1000, it became a bishopric then the capital of the Piast duchy and of the Polish kingdom during the reign of **Kazimierz The Restorer** (1038-58) who preferred the city to Gniezno. The 13C was marked by a series of Tatar invasions (1241, 1259-60 and 1287); the 1241 raid was particularly destructive as the timber-built city was reduced to ashes.

R. Mattes / MICHELIN

Rynek seen from a terrace under the arcades

The Tatars

Although the Tatar raids against the city took place in the 13C, Kraków never ceased to commemorate them. In addition to the **hejnał** tradition *(see box p 187)*, there is the **Lajkonik procession** which takes place every year in early June, eight days after Corpus Christi. The origin of this tradition, connected with the last Tatar raid in 1287, remains vague. Some say that members of the rafters' guild from Zwierzyniec prevented a horde of mongols from entering Kraków then put on the khan's clothes and proudly entered the city among popular rejoicing. Nowadays, the procession still follows the ancient tradition, starting from the Premonstratensian Convent and heading for the Rynek. It is led by a richly clothed khan (the costume was redesigned in 1904 by Wyspiański) parading well in front on his wooden horse (lajkonik) and followed by a band of musicians; donations collected from the crowd of onlookers and shopkeepers gathered along the route are said to bring them good luck during the whole year.

Brick and stone replaced wood when it was rebuilt in 1257 during the reign of Bolesław V the Shy, according to the Magdeburg Law, and the grid pattern used at the time remains to this day; fortified during the following century, the town expanded considerably at the foot of the castle. In 1320, Władysław the Short was the first king to be crowned in Wawel Cathedral but it was during the reign of **Kazimierz the Great** (1333-70), the last sovereign of the Piast dynasty, that Kraków really flourished. He built the district which was named after him and, in 1364, he founded the first Polish university, modelled on Prague's: the Kraków Academy, later known as the Jagiellonian University.

The Jagiellon Golden Age – Kraków's Golden Age is situated during the Renaissance period, under the Jagiellon dynasty, founded by Prince Jagiello, Grand Duke of Lithuania, who was converted to Catholicism and baptized in the Polish city before becoming king of Poland under the name of Władysław, through his marriage with Hedwig (Jadwiga) in 1396. The latter bequeathed her possessions to the new university and thus contributed to its growing influence. However, it was essentially in the 16C, during the reigns of Sigismund I the Elder and of his son Sigismund II August, that Kraków had its heyday and became one of Europe's most renowned artistic and scientific centres. The city's combined economic prosperity and artistic expansion were suddenly halted by King Sigismund III Vasa's brutal decision in 1609 to transfer the capital to Warsaw. From then on, the town started declining inexorably.

A city tossed-around between its neighbours – Ransacked by the Swedes in 1655, the town was annexed by the Austrians in 1794 before becoming the free autonomous city of the Kraków Republic in 1815, a status it retained until 1846, when it formed part of the Austro-Hungarian Empire once more. However, from 1861 onwards, it enjoyed relative cultural and political freedom, attracting many artists who gave birth to the Młoda Polska movement, a Polish version of Art Nouveau. But in fact it was only in 1918, at the end of the First World War that Kraków became entirely Polish again. Proclaimed capital of Poland's General Government under Nazi occupation, it was shamelessly looted but was completely spared the disaster of destruction. Proud of its rich heritage, Kraków now enjoys an enviable economic dynamism based on tourism, which means that it will soon be able to replace Łódź as Poland's second city, based on the number of inhabitants.

Kraków today – Seen from the sky, the Old Town looks like a huge pear narrowing round Wawel Castle. Behind the castle lies the medieval town whose ramparts were demolished in the 19C and replaced by the green belt of the Planty. In the north, Rynek Główny, the famous medieval market square, extends over 4 hectares. In the south-east, outside the mdieval walls, the Jewish district of Kazimierz was a separate town until 1820, just like Podgórze situated on the opposite bank of the Wisła. During the socialist era, Kraków became the symbol of the middle-class "Old Poland" but this situation was redressed by the creation in 1949 of a modern satellite city, **Nowa-Huta** (the New Foundry). This industrial workers' area situated some 10km from Wawel generated a considerable amount of pollution which proved detrimental to the old stones of the priceless historic centre.

The Rynek★★★ (Rynek Główny)

TOWN PLAN II A-B2

A tour of the town invariably starts from the Main Market Square, the very heart of the city to which you will always be drawn as if by a magnet. The Rynek was, in medieval times, the centre of Kraków's religious, economic and political life and it remains today the heart of the tourist town. This vast square with sides measuring 200m (i.e. total area: 4ha) is a rare example of well-preserved medieval urban planning. Its layout dates from 1257 when the town was granted its charter by King Bolesław the Shy. The only exceptions to the grid pattern of the square are the small St Adalbert's Church and St Mary's Basilica, built before the square was laid out, as well as Grodzka Street, probably the town's oldest street, which starts from the south-east corner of the square and heads diagonally towards Wawel Castle, thus disrupting the regular layout. A good deal of the town's history lies behind the façades of the 47 houses surrounding the square. Most of them, originally built in the 14C and 15C, were considerably remodelled, particularly in the neo-Classical style, but the majority still boast original architectural features (ceilings with exposed beams, doorways, stucco and polychrome decorative elements).

St Mary's Church★★★ (Kosciół Mariacki) B2

The western half of the nave (entered through the porch) is freely accessible to worshippers. There is an admission charge to the chancel entered via Mariacki Square (south side) - Mon-Sat 11.30am - 6pm, Sun and hols 2-6pm - 4 PLN.

The lofty west front of Kraków's main parish church towers diagonally above the north-east corner of the Rynek. It is the third church dedicated to the Assumption of the Virgin to stand on this site. Rebuilt in Gothic style between 1355 and 1408, it represents the power of Kraków's middle class who financed its construction.

Exterior – The austere **façade** features a late-Baroque **polygonal porch** (1750-52) designed by the Italian architect Francesco Placidi. The side doors are decorated with bronze sculptures of the apostles' heads, the central door with sculptures of

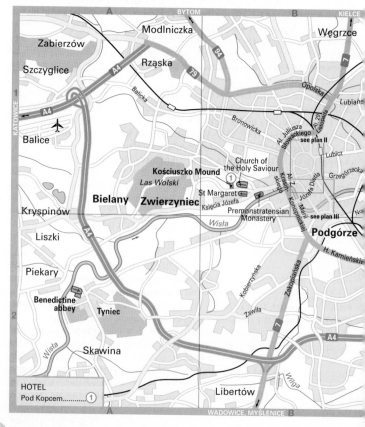

The Hejnał

Have you noticed the crowd that gathers every hour in front of St Mary's Church and looks up to the top of the higher tower? Have you heard a few anxious-sounding notes? Look up towards the last storey of the tower and you will get a glimpse of a trumpet playing a melody based on only five notes. In medieval times, a watchman used to sound the opening and closing of the town's gates and raised the alarm in case of fire or enemy attack. According to legend, during one of the Tatar raids, the watchman's warning of their approach was abruptly interrupted by an arrow which pierced his throat and the melody was cut short. In order to commemorate this event, the melody is still abruptly interrupted today. This custom, established in the 16C, follows a strict ritual: on every hour, the signal is first sounded to the west and then in turn to the other three cardinal points. The ideal place from which to watch the **hejnał** is in front of St Barbara's Church, where the trumpeter in charge acknowledges the applause of the crowd with a friendly greeting.

Should you ever forget the melody, bear in mind that the call (**Hejnał Mariacki**) is broadcast live every day at noon on the Polish national radio station.

Polish saints, carved by Karol Hukan in 1929. The ground floor of the tower known as hejnalica (tower of the bugle call) houses **St Anthony's Chapel** also called "The Criminals' Chapel" (capella captivorum); it was here that criminals spent the night preceding their execution in the company of their confessor. Opposite is the 17C **Częstochowa Virgin's Chapel**, which contains a copy of the famous icon from the Jasna Góra sanctuary (although, according to a local legend, it is the original icon). There are several anecdotes associated with the asymmetrical **towers**, the left tower (81m) soaring above the right one (69m). According to one of these anecdotes, two brothers, both architects, competed in building the towers until one killed the other, thus halting the construction. Locked up inside St Anthony's Chapel (hence the tradition mentioned above), the fratricide was executed the next day but no architect

ever agreed to complete the other tower stained by crime and the municipality was forced to top it with a dome. You might be more enclined to believe this story when you know that the murder weapon, an old rusty knife, is still hanging today under the arcades of Cloth Hall as a reminder that crime never pays. The tower on the right or bell tower was used as the town's belfry, whereas the tower on the left, which served as a watchtower, was surmounted in 1478 by a Gothic cupola comprising 16 pinnacles set round a high central spire girdled by a 350kg gilded crown (sponsored by a burgher in 1666) and topped with a gilded ball. The tower is at the centre of one of Kraków's main legends and attractions: the hejnał.

Interior – Its present appearance is the result of improvements made during the Baroque period (1753-54) by Placidi and followed by renovation work undertaken between 1889 and 1891 by the architect Tadeusz Stryjeński to restore the early-Gothic appearance of the church. The painter Jan Matejko, assisted by his students Wyspiański, Mehoffer and Dmochowski, was commissioned to cover the walls of the central nave with **paintings** (1889-92) and to create some stained-glass windows, including that which decorates the west front based on a design by Wyspiański.

Map caption within image:

KRAKÓW Plan I

0   1,5   3 km

79

Church of the Ark

Nowa Huta

Wanda Mound
▲ 239

skoju

St Bartholomew

Cistercian Monastery of Mogiła

Wisła

Czarnochowice

Zabawa

ielicka

WIELICZKA

▲ WIELICZKA SALT MINE

RZESZÓW

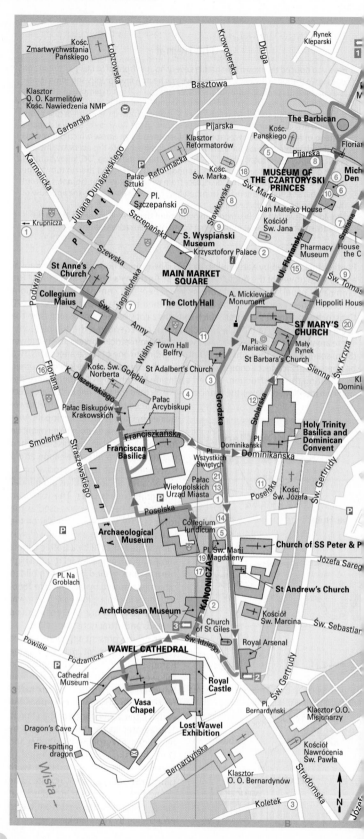

KRAKÓW Plan II

0   100   200 m

St. Worcella
Pawia
Pl. Kolejowy
Kraków Główny
PKP
Dworzec Autobusowy PKS
Lubicz
Westerplatte
Radziwiłłowska
L. Zamenhofa
Théâtre Słowacki
-Croix
Mikołaja Kopernika
Mikołaja Zyblikiewicza
Blich
Wielopole
Józefa Dietla
Teatr. Kameralny

Chancel – From the dark nave, one's eyes are drawn towards the depth of the chancel and the focus of attention becomes the high altar framed by Matejko's paintings against a background of sumptuous 14C **Gothic windows★★**.

The High Altar or Veit Stoss's Altarpiece★★★ – *The opening of the polyptych's panels takes place daily at 11.50am.* The high altar is adorned with a huge five-panelled polyptych elaborately carved in limewood, painted and gilded. This dazzling jewel, which is the prize possession of the church, is the masterpiece of Veit Stoss (1438-1533), a sculptor from Nuremberg, whose name in Polish is Wit Stwosz. Made between 1477 and 1489, this vast 13m-high and 11m-wide altarpiece forms one of the largest Gothic high altars. Decorated with some 200 figures, it illustrates a cycle essentially dedicated to the life of the Virgin Mary. The base features the Tree of Jesse, symbolizing the line of descent of Mary and of Christ. The **main scene** of the central panel of the open polyptych depicts the **Dormition of the Virgin** (according to the scriptures, her last sleep during which her Assumption took place). She is supported by St James and surrounded by the apostles. Above them is a miniature representation of the **Assumption** in which eight angels take Mary, accompanied by Christ, up to heaven. The frame, in the shape of an arc, features the prophets, while the Fathers of the Church are represented in the corners. The central panel is surmounted by an openwork **baldaquin** depicting the **Coronation of the Virgin** surrounded by angels and the two patron saints of Poland, Adalbert on the right and Stanisław on the left. The **side panels** illustrate six happy scenes from the Virgin's life and reveal, when the central panels are folded, twelve low-relief carvings, enhanced by bright colours, depicting the main episodes of the Virgin's life. Caught up in the vicissitudes of the Second World War, this precious altarpiece was dismantled in August 1939 and hidden in Sandomierz. The Germans found it and sent this invaluable booty to Nuremberg Castle where it was discovered at the end of the war, concealed in the cellars. Sent back to Kraków in 1946, it was stored in the stockrooms of Wawel Castle where it remained until it was returned to its original place in the chancel of the church in 1957.

The eastern end of the south aisle houses a very realistic late-Gothic (1496) **stone Crucifix★★**, charged with pathos, another masterpiece by Veit Stoss. Placed in a late-Baroque setting, the Crucifix represents the deeply moving agony of Christ against a background of repoussé silver depicting Jerusalem. Note, in the right angle formed by the chancel and the transept, the imposing **Renaissance ciborium★** (1554) made by Giovanni Maria Padovano, in front of which stands a small panel firmly inviting you to kneel. On the other side of the wall, the lower south corner of the chancel houses the **funerary monument of the Montelupi family** (inspired by the work of Santi Gucci) with stalls surmounted by the busts of the deceased inside recesses. Opposite is the funerary monument of the **Cellari family**. Also noteworthy are the Baroque pulpit and the side chapels, several of which contain fine Renaissance tombs.

St Barbara's Church (Kościół Św. Barbary) B2

This single-nave church overlooking St Mary's Square on the south side of the basilica, built in the 14C and redecorated in the Baroque period, was once a chapel adjoining the parish cemetery used until 1796 and replaced by the small square. Among its contents, note the Baroque ceiling (undergoing restoration work) by Piotr Molitor and, under the porch, a late-15C-early-16C chapel housing a sculpture of Jesus with three of the apostles praying in the Garden of Olives, a work attributed to a pupil of Veit Stoss. The Jesuit convent is adjacent to the church on one side and its other side looks onto the quiet **Little Market Square** (Mały Rynek), the former meat market.

The small **Mariacki Square** boasts a **fountain** surmounted by the statue of a handsome character known as the Student (Pomnik Żaczka): a copy, erected in 1958 by an association of craftsmen, of one of the figures featured on the famous altarpiece by Veit Stoss, which adorns the high altar of the adjacent basilica.

Monument to Adam Mickiewicz (Pomnik Adama Mickiewicza) B2

Opposite the entrance situated on the east side of the Cloth Hall, there is a monument commemorating the romantic poet Adam Mickiewicz (1798-1855). Born in what is now Lithuania in 1798, he never set foot in Kraków during his lifetime. Having died near Constantinople in 1855, he had to wait another 35 years for his remains to be brought to Kraków with great pomp and laid to rest in the crypt of Wawel Cathedral on 4 July 1890. A favourite meeting point of Kraków's residents who gather at its foot in large numbers to wait for their dates, the statue is commonly referred to by the locals as "Pod Adaslem", an expression based on the nickname given to the poet and literally meaning "under Adaś". Carved by Teodor Rygier and inaugurated for the hundredth anniversary of Mickiewicz's birth in 1898, the bronze statue stands on top of a high pedestal surrounded by four allegorical figures symbolizing patriotism, poetry, education and heroism. Precisely because it represented a true national symbol, this monument was one of the first in Kraków to be taken down by the Nazi occupants in 1939 and it was only in 1955, for the hundredth anniversary of the poet's death, that it was replaced by a replica.

The Cloth Hall★ (Sukiennice) A-B2

Lying in the middle of the market square, the imposing shape of the former Cloth Hall, famous for its crenellations decorated with lovely stone grotesques, undoubtedly contributes a great deal to the beautiful appearance of the square. Built at the end of the 14C and dedicated to the cloth trade, it was destroyed by fire in 1555 and immediately rebuilt in Renaissance style by Italian builder Giovanni il Mosca, known as Padovano, who raised it by adding a splendid attic carved by Florentine artist Santi Gucci, designed to hide the steep gables. Spoilt later by the adjunction of many annexees, it was redesigned between 1875 and 1879 by Tomasz Pryliński who added the neo-Gothic side arcades. Devoted, like the arcades, to the tourist trade, the central gallery on the ground floor is today occupied by stalls selling Polish handicraft, whereas the first floor has, since 1883, housed the Gallery of 19C Polish Painting **(Galeria Malarstwa Polskiego)★** *Tue, Fri-Sat 10am-7pm, Wed-Thu 10am-4pm*

Christmas Creches
(szopki)

Every year on the first Thursday in December, a competition is organised at the foot of the Monument dedicated to Adam Mickiewicz. Shaped like castles and churches, the designs of the nativity scenes are inspired by Kraków's architecture. Prize-winning works are then honoured until February by being exhibited in the town's History Museum and the most remarkable of them are included in the museum's permanent collection.

and Sun 10am-3pm - 8 PLN - Free admission on Thu. Access via the stairs located under the arcades, on the east side of the Sukiennice. A tour of the first floor of the Cloth Hall offers an introduction to the masters of 19C Polish painting, whose works have been exhibited here since 1883. Note, in the long gallery on the left, the rustic work of Józef CheCmoński, whose famous panoramic *Foursome* (1881) depicts a team of four galloping horses who seem to be coming straight at the onlooker. The more hypnotic and very symbolic *Ecstasy* (a naked woman lying asleep over a horse's neck) by Władysław Podkowiński made the headlines in 1894. On the belfry side, a whole room is devoted to the Polish Géricault, Piotr Michałowski (1800-1855), who painted numerous horses and riders as well as a number of portraits which are on display. The gallery on the right, devoted to historicist painters, offers the opportunity of admiring Henryk Siemiradzki's great historical panoramas (*Nero's Torch*) and Jan Matejko's monumental works, including the overwhelming *Homage of Prussia in 1525* (1882), a kind of group photo of the high society of that period, which occupies a whole wall of the gallery.

St Adalbert's Church
(Kościół Św. Wojciecha) A-B2
Standing alone in the south-east corner of the Rynek, just where Grodzka Street starts, and facing exactly the same way as St Mary's Basilica, this tiny edifice was the town's first church, built of wood in the 10C on the site where, according to tradition, St Adalbert delivered his evangelical sermons around the year 995. The original building was replaced in the 12C by a Romanesque stone structure, considerably remodelled between 1611 and 1618 until it acquired a Baroque appearance.

The Knife

At the end of the passageway facing the Mickiewicz Monument, you will see a strange metal knife hanging on the left. Two different versions are offered to explain this incongruous presence: the first maintains that it was meant to remind thieves that they would be punished by having their ears cut, the second is linked to a drama which occurred during the construction of the towers of St Mary's Church.

Town Hall Belfry (Wieża Ratuszowa) A-B2
May-Oct daily 10.30am-2pm and 2.30-6pm - 5 PLN.
This imposing 70m-high tower, standing in the south-west corner of the square, is all that remains of the former medieval town hall erected in the 14C and demolished in 1820. The very high steps of the narrow staircase lead up to the clock mechanism and, from there, one enjoys a fine view of the town through the openings in the Baroque cupola which replaced the Gothic spire in 1686. The vast cellars, where the former oubliettes and torture chambers were situated, today house the Ludowy Theatre and a café. From the bottom of the outside staircase guarded by two stone lions, walk left towards Szewska Street and note, on the ground, a commemorative plaque marking the place where, in 1794, Tadeusz Kósciuszko took the oath of allegiance to the nation.

The Cloth HallI

B. Brillion / MICHELIN

Krzysztofory Palace (Pałac Krzysztofory) A1

Rynek 35 - Wed-Sun 10am-5.30pm (closed on the second Sun of every month) - Temporary exhibitions (6 PLN).

Boasting a fine arcaded courtyard with a well in its centre, this opulent 17C palace houses the Historical Museum of Kraków. It owes its name to the 14C statue of St Christopher which used to decorate the façade (others maintain that the famous alchemist Krysztof lived in the house). The first-floor apartments, featuring splendid ceilings decorated by the stucco specialist Baldassare Fontana, contain a wealth of documents and souvenirs related to the town's history (unfortunately captions are in Polish only). The cellars house a famous art gallery connected with the avant-garde art movement, Grupa Krakowska (Kraków Group).

Hippoliti House (Kamienica Hippolitów), an annexe of the Historical Museum (*Pl. Mariacki 3 - Wed-Sun 10am-5.30pm. Closed on the second Sun of every month - 5,20 PLN)* is located on the left of St Mary's Church. The building is named after the family of merchants who came to live in this 14C house in 1599. More recently owned by the Zaleski family, it is sometimes referred to as the "Bourgeois House" because it presents the reconstruction of a middle-class Kraków interior. The two floors are cluttered up with furniture and objects. The edifice is renowned for its 16C wooden balconies overlooking the courtyard.

1 Royal Way: from Matejko Square to Wawel★★★

TOWN PLAN II B1 to A3

The Royal Way (Droga Królewska) was the route followed by the royal family and high dignitaries on their way to Wawel Castle.

Matejki Square B1

Lying outside the Planty, it occupies the site of the market square of the former medieval city of Kleparz, joined to Kraków in 1791. In the centre stands the imposing **Commemorative Monument of the Battle of Grunwald** (Pomnik Grunwaldzki). The original monument, erected at the instigation of the pianist and politician Ignacy Jan Paderewski in 1910, for the 500th anniversary of the battle, was destroyed by the Nazis in 1939 and only replaced in 1976 with a replica made by sculptor Marian Konieczny. Combined with the **Tomb of the Unknown Soldier** (Grób Nieznanego Żołnierza), this ensemble, symbolizing the sovereign Polish State, was, during the 1980s, the epicentre of the political protest initiated by the Solidarity trade union and remains to this day the place where major national events are celebrated.

On the southwestern corner of the square, no 13 is the **Fine Arts Academy**, built in 1879-80. Above the entrance is a bust of Jan Matejko, founder of the first independent art academy in Poland. The building's size echoes the monumental nature of the artist's paintings. He had a studio on the second floor.

Opposite, the Neo-classical headquarters of the **National Bank of Poland** has two allegorical groups on the upper part of the façade. They represent Industry and Agriculture.

The northeastern corner is marked by **Saint Florian's Church** (Kościół sw. Floriana). The first church on this site was Romanesque, but the style is now Baroque. It was built in 1184 as a mausoleum for the relics of St. Florian, the 3rd-century Roman soldier and martyr. The church was a starting point for royal funeral processions to the Wawel Cathedral. John Paul II, then Father Wojtylla, was curate from 1949-51.

The Barbican (Barbakan)★ B1

May-Oct. daily 10.30am-6pm - 5 PLN.

Built in 1499 in response to the Ottoman threat, as an outwork preceding the ramparts and the moats along the axis of the main towngate, this circular bastion, now standing isolated in the middle of the Planty, was originally linked by a passageway, known as "the neck", to the Florian Gate. This is one of Europe's rare example of perfectly well-preserved barbican, its high walls concealing an impressive system of machicolations and loopholes, yet the tour of the inside is somehow disappointing.

The Ramparts and the Planty ★

A 4km-long system of fortifications was erected between 1285 – when the town was granted the privilege to surround itself with ramparts – and the middle of the 16C when the municipal Arsenal was built. The ramparts, having become obsolete with the development of artillery, were demolished by the Austrians at the beginning of the 19C and the double moat was filled in. The area they once covered was gradually replaced by the Planty (plantations) modelled on the Viennese Ring. Kraków residents on their way from the city to the suburbs inevitably go through this green oasis, which was relaid in 1988 and today features many statues, fountains and commemorative monuments as well as plaques marking the site of the former town gates. When the weather is fine, the Planty are the peaceful refuge of lovers, of students revising for their exams and of retired people looking for someone to talk to.

Florian Gate (Brama Floriańska) B1

This is the only remaining town gate out of the eight original ones pierced through the medieval walls; it used to be the main entry point of the Royal Way into town. The 34.5m-high tower, stone-built in the 13C, was completed with red bricks at the end of the next century and its crenellated top was covered in 1694 with a small Baroque cupola. Out of the 39 towers which once rose above the ramparts on both sides of the gate, only three bastions remain and Kraków's street artists now hang their paintings on the stones of the fortified wall.

Florian Street (Ul. Floriańska)★ B1

This main shopping street used to be the start of the Royal Way from the Florian Gate to the Rynek. It was lined with some of the finest houses in town, often featuring Renaissance or late-Gothic doorways.

Michalik's Den (Jama Michalikowa)★★, at no 45, Kraków's finest café, boasts an interior decor worthy of a museum; during the Belle Epoque, it was the headquarters of the local bohemian population, gathered around the literary and artistic movement of Młoda Polska (Young Poland). In 1905, its members set up the Zielony Balonik (Green Balloon) cabaret, famous for its puppet shows. Until 1921, it was under the management of Tadeusz Boy-Zelenski, an author who provided satiric texts for many of the performances. He is also known in Poland for his translation of Marcel Proust's "Remembrance of Things Past".

Jan Matejko House (Dom Jana Matejki)
Ul. Floriańska 41 - Tue-Thu, Sat-Sun 10am-3.30pm, Fri 10am-6pm - 6 PLN - Free admission on Thu. Jan Matejko (1839-1893), one of the most famous Polish painters was born here and spent his whole life in this house; some of his works are on display. Having set himself the task of illustrating Poland's history, he strove to create great historical panoramas, in particular reconstructed scenes of major battles. Highly interested in the town's history, he got involved in the preservation and restoration of many works and buildings, as can be seen from his preliminary sketches of the polychromes painted on the walls of St Mary's Church. Displayed on three levels are paintings, family memorabilia and fine antiques collected by the artist, including eastern and western weapons as well as costumes that he used as models. Note, on the 2nd floor, six carved-wood heads which obviously formed part of a group of 164 such sculptures now missing from the ceiling of the Audience Hall in Wawel Castle.

Pharmacy Museum (Muzeum Farmacji)
Ul. Floriańska 25 - Tue 3-7pm, Wed-Sun 11am-2pm - Closed 1st and 5th Sat of the month. Founded in 1946, this museum, devoted to the history of pharmacy from the Middle Ages to the present, is considered by amateurs as one of the most interesting of its kind.

In order to continue along the Royal Way towards Wawel Castle, walk across the Rynek until you reach Grodzka Street.

Grodzka Street★ B2-3

This elegant street, forming the second section of the Royal Way leading to Wawel, runs south to **Św. Marii Magdaleny Square**, named after St Magdalene's Gothic church that used to stand here until 1811. The square – linking Grodzka and Kanonicza streets – is believed to be the site of the market square of the former Okół district, the first settlement which grew at the foot of Wawel Hill. Today, the square is adorned with a statue of Father Piotr Skarga perched on top of a slender column and with a strikingly contemporary fountain, but it is above all the favourite practice ground of young skateboarders. To the north, the former **Collegium Iuridicum** (no 118), featuring a small courtyard with tiered arcades reminiscent (on a reduced scale) of those of Wawel Castle, today houses the Institute of Art History (Instytut Historii Sztuki), as well as two small university museums with very specific interests: the first (Muszle Egzotyczne) is devoted to shells *(Sun 11am-2pm)*, the second (Motyle Swiata) to butterflies *(Tue-Thu 10am-1pm)*. The former **Jesuit College** (Collegium Broscianum) situated north of the church (no 52) is now occupied by its own former rival, the Jagiellonian University.

Church of SS Peter & Paul★ (Kościół Św. Piotra i Pawła) B2

Access to the crypt and transept: 2,50 PLN - Mon-Sat 9am-5pm and Sun 1-5pm (Jun-Sep until 5.45pm).

Built on the site of a Gothic sanctuary destroyed by fire in 1455, this church was the first Baroque building in Kraków. Its construction, begun in 1596, was based on the model of Roman Jesuit churches such as Il Gesù de Vignola and St Andrea della Valle; a series of mishaps delayed its completion until 1619. Designed on the Latin cross layout, the church has no aisles but several chapels instead and is surmounted by an elliptical dome at the intersection of the nave and the transept. One's attention is first drawn to the elegant, well-proportioned **façade★★**, sheltering (from left to right) the statues of Stanisław Kostka, Ignatius Loyola, Francis Xavier and Aloysius Gonzaga, surmounted on the upper level by those of SS Sigismund and Ladisław. The church being set back from Grodzka Street along an axis at right angles with the street, the façade is preceded by a balustrade designed by Kacper Bazanka to correct the perspective of the church visually. The original monumental statues of the 12 apostles (1723) by Dawid Heel surmounting it were being eaten away by pollution and were therefore replaced by replicas.

Interior – Particularly noteworthy is the **chancel★**, including the black-marble **high altar★** completed in 1735 by Bazanka (who also built the curved balustrade around the organ) and surmounted by a cupola with a semi-circular **stucco decoration★** (1633) by Giovanni Battista Falconi (who sculpted the statues of the four evangelists located in the cupola). The **crypt**, which is less interesting from an artistic point of view, houses the tombs of the fearsome Jesuit preacher and main architect of the counter reform, Piotr Skarga (1536-1612), of W. S. H. Bieliński and of archbishop Andrzej Trzebicki, the latter boasting a sumptuous Baroque decoration. Besides the concerts of classical music which take place regularly, the other interesting feature of the church is its Foucault pendulum demonstrating the earth's rotation by oscillating from the top of the 46.5m-high dome *(Thu at 10am, 11am and noon)*.

St Andrew's Church (Kościół Św. Andrzeja)★ B3

One would never think – judging by the interior, completely remodelled in Baroque style at the beginning of the 18C – that this church of the Poor Clares, dedicated to St Andrew and built between 1079 and 1098, is in fact one of Poland's best-preserved Romanesque edifices. The exterior, bearing numerous scars (sealed-up windows and blocked-up main porch), features several narrow twin windows with a single central column which testify to the defensive purpose of the fortress-church. It was the only church in Kraków that was able to withstand the Tatar attack in 1241 and the population took refuge inside once again during a major fire in 1259. This defensive role is underlined by the beautiful yet austere stone-and-brick **façade★★** surmounted by two octagonal towers with square bases topped in 1639 with Baroque domes.

In striking contrast with the exterior Romanesque austerity, the opulent Baroque interior boasts a rich **stucco decor** (undergoing restoration work) by Baldassare Fontana, a rococo boat-shaped **pulpit**, an ebony **tabernacle** with silver decorations and a lovely patterned **marble floor**. The adjoining convent is known for its rich treasury which is rarely exhibited.

Continuing along Grodzka Street, you will walk past **St Martin's** Lutheran Church (Św. Marcina), dating from the 17C and rarely open to visitors, before reaching the former **Royal Arsenal** (Arsenał Królewski), located at the end of the street, opposite Wawel. Built in the 16C and remodelled in the mid-17C (fine doorway), it has been occupied since 1927 by the sprawling Jagiellonian University. This is the perfect place from which to look up towards the east wing of the castle and to observe the **Kurza Stopka**, an unusual Gothic pavilion, one of the rare parts of the medieval castle erected during the reign of Władysław II Jagiełło. Overlooking a small square, the unassuming single-naved Gothic **Church of St Giles** (Kościół Św. Idziego) has been run by Dominicans since 1595. In this former official place of worship of the Armenian community, Mass has been celebrated in English every Sunday at 10.30 since 1994 and concerts are often organised. Right in front of the building, a wooden cross commemorates the 50th anniversary of the Katyń massacre perpetrated in 1940 by the Soviet NKVD on some 4 500 Polish officers (long blamed on the Germans, it was only acknowledged by the Soviet authorities in 1990).

Wawel Hill★★★
Wzgórze wawelskie
TOWN PLAN II A 3

The hill is freely accessible - daily May-Sep 6am-8pm, Oct-Apr 6am-5pm (the castle's arcaded courtyard closes 1hr before). Closed 1 Jan, Easter, 1 and 11 Nov, 24, 25 and 31 Dec.

Wawel refers to the architectural ensemble standing at the top of a small limestone hill rising 25m above the River Wisła. Standing as a symbol of the glorious episodes of the nation's history, it has been the guardian of Polish national identity since the 11C, with the presence side by side of the Christian sanctuary and of the royal castle representing the close association of religious and secular powers. A place rendered even more symbolic by the fact that Polish kings were not only crowned in the cathedral but also buried there together with many of the nation's illustrious families and famous sons. Having reached its heyday in the 16C, Wawel was abruptly abandoned in 1596 in favour of Warsaw by King Sigismund III Vasa, the king of alchemists, who, according to one legend, left Wawel following an unsuccessful alchemist experiment.

At the foot of the ramp leading to the castle, you will catch a glimpse of the imposing **equestrian statue of Tadeusz Kościuszko** standing at the top of one of the bastions built by the Austrians in 1852. Sculpted by Leonardo Marconi and inaugurated in 1921, it was destroyed by the Nazis in 1940 and was only replaced by a copy in 1960. Along the ramp you will see plaques set into the brick wall inscribed with the names of the generous donors who took part in the castle's restoration during the interwar period. Go through the **Coat of Arms Gate** (Brama Herbowa), beyond which you will find one of the castle's two ticket offices, then through the **Vasa Gate** (Brama Wazów).

To the left of the Vasa Gate stands the cathedral and, slightly offset to the right, the Vicars' house, where you can buy tickets for the visit – inside the cathedral – of the Royal Crypt and of the Sigismund Tower.

Wawel Cathedral (Katedra Wawelska)★★★ A1
Daily 6.30am-5.30pm - Free admission - admission to the tower and the crypt : 10 PLN.
The present sanctuary is the third cathedral to be erected on this site; built in Gothic style at the beginning of the 14C, it replaced a Romanesque edifice of which all that remains today are St Leonard's Crypt and the Silver Bells Tower (Srebrne Dzwony). The cathedral, of surprisingly modest proportions, was built during the reigns of King Władysław the Short and Kazimierz the Great and has not been altered since it was dedicated to SS Stanisław and Wencesław in 1364. From 1320 to 1734, coronations took place in the cathedral, which was also the venue of royal funerals. At first buried in the nave (the oldest royal tomb is that of Władysław the Short, dating from the 14C), Polish monarchs and their families were laid to rest, from the 16C onwards, in the crypt (although a funerary monument in their honour continued to be erected in the nave) which became a national pantheon in the 19C.

Exterior – Once through the **Baroque porch** (1619), your attention will no doubt be drawn to a collection of large **prehistoric bones** hanging on heavy iron chains, located to the left of the entrance. Their presence, said to keep evil forces at bay, is linked to a legend announcing the end of the world and of humanity. Framed with black marble, the magnificent wooden door (1636) is covered with an iron sheet stamped many times with King Kazimierz the Great's monogram, a K surmounted by a crown.

Interior – Standing in the middle of the central nave is the **Altar of St Stanisław★★**, Poland's main patron saint, whose relics are kept in a sarcophagus covered with sheets of chased silver, located under a Baroque black-and-pink marble baldaquin. Made in Gdańsk between 1669 and 1671 by Peter van der Rennen, the reliquary is decorated with

Wawel Cathedral

B. Brillion / MICHELIN

195

scenes illustrating the life of the bishop who became a martyr when he was killed by King Bolesław the Bold on 11 April 1079. Worshipped with particular fervour since its transfer to Wawel in 1254, the saint's tomb was considered as the altar of the nation (Ara Patriae), on which kings laid their war trophies. Surrounded by the four monuments of Kraków's bishops, the altar is preceded along the nave by the sarcophagi of King **Władysław Jagiełło II**★ (on the right) and **Władysław Warnenczyk** (on the left).

The Gothic **Holy Cross Chapel** (Kaplica Świętokrzyska)★ is the only medieval chapel in the cathedral to have retained its original decoration featuring fine **frescoes** inspired by Byzantine art, painted in 1470 by artists from the Russian School of Pskov. In the north-west corner, under a high baldaquin supported by eight columns, lies the sarcophagus of King Kazimierz Jagiello made by Veit Stoss in 1492, the year of his death. Opposite the entrance, the imposing monument erected in 1790 depicting Bishop Cajétan Sołtyk standing on top of his own sarcophagus, from which a black eagle (the family's emblem) is escaping together with an arm holding a sabre, is noteworthy for its fantasy. The fine stained-glass windows in Secession style are the work of Józef Mehoffer.

The first chapel along the aisle, the **Potocki Chapel**, restored in neo-Classical style between 1832 and 1840, is followed by the **Chapel of the Szafraniec Family**, beneath Wikaryjska Tower, an imposing belfry visible from outside. The adjoining **Vasa Chapel**★, named after one of the greatest 17C royal dynasties, is the perfect replica of the Sigismund Chapel; its Baroque ornamentation features a cupola decorated with stucco motifs. The doorway and the bronze decoration of the doors are particularly interesting.

The **Sigismund Chapel** (Kaplica Zygmuntowska)★★★, the mausoleum of the Jagiellon dynasty, is a real masterpiece of Renaissance architecture in Poland. Commissioned by King Sigismund I the Elder, it was built between 1519 and 1533; designed by Bartolomeo Berecci on the square layout and surmounted by a dome, it was given a sumptuous decoration by Italian artists. The cupola was covered on the outside with gilded scales in 1591-92, at the request of Queen Anna Jagiellon. Facing the entrance, the **royal stall** in Hungarian red marble rests against the sarcophagus of Queen **Anna Jagiellon** († 1596). On the right side, set within a two-tiered arcade, the funerary monument (remodelled by sculptor Santi Gucci in 1574-75) of **King Sigismund I the Elder** († 1548) stands on top while that of his son **Sigismund August** († 1572) lies below. Located opposite along the east side and framed by an arcade, the **altar** features a **polyptych** made in Nuremberg between 1531 and 1538. The twelve partly gilded silver panels depict episodes of the life of the Virgin framed by representations of St Adalbert and St Stanisław. The closed panels show 14 scenes by Georg Pencz illustrating the Passion, the Resurrection and the Ascension of Christ. The coffered cupola is decorated with rosettes and surmounted by a lantern bearing the signature of the artist who designed the chapel. Facing the doorway of the chapel is the neo-Gothic (1902) **sarcophagus of Queen Hedwig** († 1399). Made of white Carrara marble, it was inspired by the tomb designed by Jacopo della Quercia for Ilaria del Carretto in the Duomo de Lucca in Tuscany.

Moving along the ambulatory, you will come across the **Olbracht Chapel**★★ which houses, under a fine Gothic vault, the red-marble sarcophagus of King John Olbracht († 1501), lying under a splendidly decorated triumphal arch. It was one of the first examples of a kind of Renaissance funerary monument which later became popular in Poland. Opposite this chapel stands the **Gothic tomb**★★ **of King Kazimierz the Great** († 1370). Behind the **high altar** (1649) are the two exuberant late-Baroque **funerary monuments** (1760) of kings Michael Korybut Wiśniowiecki († 1673) and John III Sobieski († 1696). The chapel opposite houses the **mannerist funerary monument**★★ of **King Stephen Batory**, delicately carved in 1595 by Santi Gucci. At the end of the east part of the ambulatory stands the **altar of the Crucified Lord Jesus**, where Queen Hedwig is said to have had a vision. St Hedwig's Crucifix resting on a silver plaque, consists of an unusual dark-wood Gothic Crucifix, draped with black tulle, which forms part of a Baroque black-marble altar. In the north part of the ambulatory, the recumbent figure of King **Władysław the Short** († 1333) was the first royal tomb built inside the cathedral.

In the left aisle, steps lead down to the **Crypt of the great national poets** (admission charge) which contains, among others, the sarcophagi of Adam Mickiewicz († 1855) and Juliusz Słowacki († 1849), whose remains were brought back from France where they lived in exile. The **Royal Crypt** (Groby Królewskie), linked to the previous one, has, since the 17C, housed the tombs of Polish kings and queens and also of some national heroes such as Tadeusz Kościuszko (1746-1817), Prince Józef Poniatowski

(1763-1813), Marshall Józef Piłsudski (1867-1935) and General Władysław Sikorski. **St Leonard's Crypt★**, the only remnant of the Romanesque cathedral erected in the 11C and 12C, contains the most important series of tombs. It was here that in 1946, a young priest called Wojtyła celebrated his first mass.

Accessible via a staircase located in the sacristy (at the end on the left), the **Sigismund Tower** (Zygmuntowska)★★ offers a close-up view of the five bells of the cathedral reached through an impressive 16C timber roof structure. One of the bells, known as **Sigismund** (1520), is 2.60m in diameter and weighs 11 tonnes; it is the largest bell in Poland and the second largest in the world. Its powerful D major only rings across the city on the most important religious and national holidays and eight to ten men are needed to swing its 350kg clapper.

Cathedral Museum (Muzeum Katedralne) A3
Tue-Sun 10am-3pm
The museum has been housed since 1978 in the chapter house of the cathedral. Its collection of sacred art includes liturgical vessels and clothes as well as historic items; for instance St Maurice's spear, a present from Prussian Emperor Otto III to Bolesław the Brave in AD 1000, Stanisław August Poniatowski's coronation robe, diadems worn by Bolesław the Shy and his wife Kinga and the reliquary containing St Stanisław's skull.

When leaving the cathedral, turn left to admire the south side. In front of you lies the magnificent Arcaded Courtyard (Dziedziniec) of the royal castle.

The Royal Castle (Zamek Królewski)★★ B3
Seat and symbol of royal authority for six centuries, Wawel Castle is a blend of several architectural styles. Preceded by a palatium and later by a princely Romanesque residence, the first castle worthy of the name was erected at the beginning of the 11C by the duke and future king Bolesław the Brave. During the 14C, Kazimierz III the Great, the last sovereign of the Piast dynasty, turned it into an imposing Gothic fortress destroyed by fire in 1499. The 3rd castle was erected at the request of King Sigismund I the Elder who, during the first half of the 16C, commisioned the Italian architects Francesco Florentino and Bartolomeo Berecci to build the Renaissance palace, part of which we can admire today. In 1595, following a fire, the restoration of the north wing was entrusted to Italian architect Giovanni Trevano by Sigismund III Vasa, the same monarch who, a year later, transferred the capital to Warsaw thus starting Wawel's decline. Abandoned from 1655 onwards to successive raids by the Swedes, the Russians and the Prussians, it was turned into barracks after being annexed by the Austrians in 1796 and the hill, which became a military training area, was surrounded by new brick-built fortifications. Ceded to the Poles in 1905, Wawel gave up its role of military garrison but its restoration only began when Poland regained her independence in 1918; Hans Frank, Kraków's Nazi Governor General, was the first to enjoy it when he moved in with his henchmen in 1939. Completed after the war, the full restoration of the edifice enabled it to regain part of its former glory.

Wawel Castle

B. Brillon / MICHELIN

Exterior – The vast inner courtyard, formed on three sides by three magnificent superposed galleries featuring a combination of columns and arcades, is a truly splendid sight, worthy of the most famous Italian Renaissance *palazzi*. Most remarkable is the upper gallery supported by very slender columns and yet covered with a steep, squat roof. The original decoration by Hans Dürer, which adorned the top part of the outside walls of the galleries, has recently been restored. In its heyday during the 16C, the castle was organised in the following way: the ground floor of the north wing contained the Crown Treasury and the administrative offices were housed in the east wing. The king's private apartments were situated on the first floor whereas the state apartments were located on the second floor, known as *piano nobile*. Today the galleries contain five main exhibitions displayed in over 70 rooms. The Lost Wawel exhibition *(see p 199)* cannot be accessed from this courtyard.

The Private Royal Apartments (Prywatne Apartamenty Królewskie)★★ testify to the artistic taste of the Jagiellon dynasty. The main interest of these elaborately decorated rooms lies in the precious collection of Flemish tapestries hanging on the walls of King Sigismund I the Elder's private apartments and of the State apartments located on the second floor. Only 136 out of the 360 16C tapestries (called *arrasy* after the manufacture situated in Arras, France) commissioned by the last monarch of the Jagiellon dynasty, have survived. Designed by painters Willem Tons and Michiel van Coxcle, known as the Flemish Raphaël, most of them illustrate scenes from the Old Testament, such as "Adam and Eve in the Garden of Eden", "Noah's Story" or 'The Erection of the Tower of Babel'. Sent to Russia after the 3rd Partition of Poland in 1795, the precious tapestries only returned to Kraków during the 1920s. Removed to Canada just before the Second World War, the tapestries and other treasures from the castle were only returned to communist Poland in 1962.

Wawel cloisters

The State Apartments (Komnaty Królewskie)★★★ are the castle's major attraction. Several rooms are named after the friezes running underneath the painted ceilings. Starting from the Audience Staircase in the middle of the east wing, you will see to your left a succession of rooms including the **Tournament Room** (from the frieze by Hans Dürer, Albrecht's brother, dating from 1535), the **Military Parade Room** (frieze by Anton Breslau dating from 1535), all decorated with paintings and furniture of Italian origin. At the end of this wing, you will find the **Audience Hall** (Sala Poselska)★★★, undoubtedly the most spectacular room in the castle, once used for royal audience sessions and for debates by the Sejm, the Polish Parliament. Its specificity lies in its splendid decor of carved wooden heads literally springing from the coffered ceiling. This remarkable work was created between 1531 and 1535 by two artists from Breslau, Sebastian Tauerbach and Master Hans Snycerz. Unfortunately, only 30 of the original 194 heads remain. The frieze on the theme of "The Life of Man", which decorates the hall is by Hans Dürer. The rooms located north of the staircase, such as the **Zodiac Room**, the **Planets Room** and the **Battle of Orsza Room**, also owe their name to the friezes made in the early 1930s by Leonard Pękalski. Another noteworthy room is the **Bird Room** (Sala pod Ptakami) featuring fine marble portals, situated at the beginning of the north wing, damaged by fire in 1595, remodelled in Baroque style by the Italian architect Trevano and decorated to suit the taste of the Vasa dynasty. Representative of this trend is the **Eagle Room** (Sala pod Orłem), the old royal court of justice, which houses a series of Dutch and Flemish pictures, including an **equestrian painting** of Prince Ladislas IV Vasa (1624) by Peter Paul Rubens. Finally, the Muses Room leads to the **Senators' Hall** (Sala Senatorska) with its fine Renaissance coffered ceiling. This hall, the largest in the castle, contains a most impressive group of five huge tapestries illustrating scenes from Genesis. The exit is via the Senators' staircase which leads down to the north-east corner of the courtyard.

Housed in some fine Gothic rooms situated on the ground floor of the north-east corner of the castle, the **Crown Treasury** (Skarbiec Koronny) contains a profusion of precious objects connected with the Polish Crown and the kings' coronation (in spite of the fact that the original stock was looted several times, in particular by the Prussians). The prize exhibit is the kings' famous sword, called **Szczerbiec** (the jagged blade), a symbol of bravery used during coronations. The **Armoury** (Zbrojownia) exhibits a rich collection of Polish and European weapons and armours as well as war trophies. Also on display are copies of standards taken from the Teutonic enemy during the battle of Grunwald in 1410. Located in the north-west corner of the castle, the exhibition of **Oriental Art** (Sztuka Wschodu) consists of the spoils of war taken by King John III Sobieski after his victory over the Ottomans in Vienna in 1683, the showpiece being a precious ceremonial tent (undergoing restoration work).

Lost Wawel Exhibition
(Wawel Zaginiony)★ B3

*Open Wed-Mon 9.30am-3pm – Entrance from the Wawel esplanade, near the cafeteria.*Housed on the ground floor and in the cellars of the building which closes the west side of the arcaded courtyard, this exhibition was designed to show what Wawel Hill looked like 1 000 years ago, the main attraction being the reconstructed foundations of the **Rotunda of the Virgin Mary** (or of SS Felix and Adauctus), the oldest stone church on the hill, built in the 10C or at the beginning of the 11C, and possibly Poland's first Christian church. Demolished by the Austrians at the beginning of the 19C, it was rediscovered during excavation work carried out in 1917.

> ### A Sharp Wooden Tongue
> Did you notice a **gagged head** among the carved heads of the Audience Hall ceiling? One day when Sigismund August presided the court hearing, a poor widow unjustly accused of shoplifting was brought before the king. He was about to condemn her when a powerful human voice, which appeared to come down from the ceiling, called out to him: *"August king, pronounce a just sentence"*. This unexpected intervention by one of the heads was enough to convince the king that the woman was innocent but, for fear that this wooden head with a conscience should meddle in the affairs of the kingdom and contest his authority, the monarch ordered the sculptor to cover with a patch the lips of the head which had spoken to prevent it from intervening again.

End your tour of Wawel by walking towards the south-west part of the citadel. Behind the Thieves' keep (Baszta Złodziejska) which houses the castle's second ticket office, one can admire a fine panorama of the meander formed lower down by the Wisła. Slightly to the left is the entrance to the Dragon's Cave (remember to visit the cave last, otherwise, having reached the exit of the cave, you would have to walk right round the citadel in order to go back up.

The Dragon's Cave (Smocza Jama) A3

The cave is accessible from the summit of the citadel via a turret backing onto the fortified wall (an automatic machine dispenses tickets); a spiral staircase (135 steps) leads down into the bowels of the hill, to the deepest part of the cave.

Inside the cave shrouded in mystery, you will only explore 81m out of a total of 270m (so as not to disturb the dragon!). The tour is of no outstanding interest but offers a refreshing interlude in hot weather. The photogenic fire-spitting *(every 2min)* metal dragon (Smok Wawelski), waiting for you as you come out of the cave, was made in 1972 by sculptor Bronisław Chromy.

Leave Wawel via the Bernardine Gate, along the second ramp leading to the castle; this will enable you to get a glimpse of several towers which are all that remain of the 15C fortifications. Having reached the Bernardine Church at the foot of Wawel, you could eventually tour the Kazimierz district by heading east.

The Story of the Greedy Dragon

Once upon a time, according to legend, the peaceful life of Good King Krak's kingdom was threatened by the repeated disappearance of some of its inhabitants who ventured near the Wisła. A young man who narrowly escaped a similar fate revealed the nature of the danger: a horrible dragon had settled on Wawel. The king then offered half his kingdom and the hand of his daughter in marriage to whomever would deliver the town from this curse. Princes and knights tried in vain until a young cobbler claimed he knew how to kill the dragon – on condition that the king gave him his largest sheep. Having filled the animal's stomach with sulphur and tar, he placed it near the cave. At dawn, the town was woken up by a huge explosion. The dragon had swallowed his prey but, feeling extremely thirsty, he had drunk so much water that his stomach had finally exploded. Good King Krak then fulfilled all his promises.

2 From Wawel to the Church of the Holy Cross

A3 to C1

Kanonicza Street★★★ B3

Running parallel to Grodzka Street, this street has undoubtedly the most clerical and aristocratic atmosphere in all Kraków and it is also one of the most beautiful and picturesque streets in town. The medieval character of this slightly winding road has been remarkably well preserved, probably because it was spared by the terrible fire which spread though a large section of the town in 1850. Façades adorned with coats of arms, roofs surmounted by attics, splendid doorways, impressive carriage entrances (do not hesitate to walk through) which conceal magnificent courtyards and sometimes beautiful gardens. It was traditionally the street of Wawel Cathedral's Canons, who had lived there since the 14C and after whom it was named (Kanonicza is derived from *canonicorum*). The twenty or so buildings lining it date from the 14C and 15C but many were remodelled later and show a great diversity of architectural styles.

The first edifice to be erected at the foot of the castle was the 14C **House of Jan Długosz** (at no 25), featuring a fine Renaissance doorway surmounted by an inscription in Latin meaning "No part of Man is better than his mind". This canon, who was the private tutor of King Kazimierz's children and above all Poland's first great historian, lived from 1450 to his death in 1480 in this house now the headquarters of the Papal Academy of Theology. To the left of this corner house, past a plaque indicating that the sculptor's studio of Stanisław Wyspiański's father was located here in the 19C you will see, set in the wall, a low-relief sculpture from 1480 depicting the Virgin with Child.

The **Dean's House** (Dom Dziekański) at no 21, rebuilt between 1582 and 1588 by Santi Gucci, the Italian architect of the Cloth Hall, is one of the most interesting buildings along the street. Behind its splendid **doorway★** and its **façade decorated with sgraffiti** lies a magnificent **Renaissance arcaded courtyard★★** featuring an 18C statue of St Stanisław, bishop and patron saint of Poland, who is said to have lived here. The sides are adorned with the bishops' emblems. The future Pope John Paul II lived in this traditional residence of Kraków's bishops from 1963 to 1967. The floors of the building are now linked to the adjoining Archdiocesan Museum.

Facing the museum at no 16 is the **Copernicus Mansion**, with its courtyard surrounded by a gallery, is a fine example of a successful restoration. No 18 is the **Palace of Bishop Florian of Mokrsko**, rebuilt by architect Jan Michałowicz of Urzedów and featuring a Renaissance doorway and a fine arcaded courtyard.

Bishop **Erazm Ciołek's House** (no 17), combining two Gothic houses, boasts a Renaissance doorway surmounted by a cartouche bearing the royal eagle and the letter "S" referring to King Sigismund and by a fine Gothic window.

Note, at no 15, the composite doorway of the Szreniawa House which is the headquarters of the St Vladimir Foundation (Fundacja Św. Włodzimierza). Adjoining the old Wyspiański Museum at no 9, the Three Crowns House (Pod Trzema Koronami) at no 7 boasts a pleasant summer garden. The Cricoteka Muzeum at no 5 is an information centre open to all those who wish to know more about the life and works of the incomparable Polish artist, Tadeusz Kantor (1915-90). Finally, the building at no 3 offers a façade covered with sgraffiti, fine Renaissance window frames and an elegant rococo doorway.

Archdiocesan Museum (Muzeum Archdiecezjalne)★ A3

Ul. Kanonicza 19-21 - Tue-Fri 10am-4pm, Sat-Sun 10am-3pm - 5 PLN - Free admission on Tue.

Karol Wojtyła lived in this house between 1952 et 1963 when he was only a priest, before being appointed bishop and moving into the apartments adjoining the Dean's House, where he remained until 1967. Many people turn up here out of curiosity to see the reconstruction of his bedroom-cum-study where his furniture, his liturgical clothes and other personal memorabilia, such as a typewriter and even two pairs of skis are respectfully exhibited. However, the main interest of the museum lies in its collection of sacred art, the most interesting part being displayed on the ground floor. Following the first room devoted to the finest painted works is the sculpture department, which houses a remarkable series of the Virgin with Child from the 14C and 15C. Further on are the goldwork, silverware and liturgical garments sections.

Having reached the top of Kanonicza Street, turn left onto the small Senacka Street forming an angle; it is lined with an imposing building. Successively palace of the Tęczyński family, residence of the Benedictine abbots of Tyniec, municipal baths, Carmelite convent and finally Austrian prison in the 19C, this edifice now houses two museums: a small museum devoted to local geology (Muzeum Geologiczne - Thu-Fri 10am-3pm and Sat 10am-2pm), and above all a large archaeological museum (public entrance is at no 3 Poselska Street.

Archaeological Museum (Muzeum Archeologiszne)★ A2

Ul. Poselska 3 - Jul-Aug Mon, Wed, Fri 9am-4pm, Tue, Thu 2-6pm, Sun 10am-4pm, Sep-Jun Mon-Wed 9am-2pm, Thu 2-6pm, Fri, Sun 10am-2pm - 7 PLN - Free admission on Sun.

This educational museum, ideal for arousing children's curiosity, features remarkable displays, such as the collection of Egyptian archaeology housed on the 1st floor, splendidly enhanced by subtle lighting. On the upper floor one learns, through thematic and chronological displays, how the Małopolska (Little Poland) region became populated. Here too, the deliberately educational approach is illustrated by glass cases showing the connection between the evolution of the environment (fauna and flora) and contemporary archaeological objects, and also by a room displaying costumes and accessories and establishing their relation with the evolution of dwellings from 70 000 years BC to AD 1300. The section devoted to funerary rites, including a typological reconstruction of graves, boasts the museum's prize exhibit: an impressive stone **obelisk** from the 10C AD, known

Kanonicza Street

as Światowid Zbruczański and carved on four sides, which was discovered in the River Zbrucz in Podol (Ukraine) in 1848. Before leaving the museum, take a stroll round the adjacent garden with its magnificent display of roses.

Franciscan Basilica (Bazylika Franciszkanów)★★ A2

The construction of the Franciscan Church began in 1255, soon after members of the Order arrived in Kraków in 1237; the project was supported by Duke Bołesław the Chaste and his sister the Blessed Salome who chose to give up her princely status in order to become a Poor Clare and was buried in the chancel in 1269, the year the church was consecrated. It was also here that the pagan Grand Duke Jogaila of Lithuania was baptized in 1386, before he became the Christian King Władysław Jagiełło (1351-1434) of Poland through his marriage with Hedwig. Vandalized during the Swedish invasion then damaged by the great fire of 1850, the church lost its original Gothic appearance during its reconstruction when it became a blend of neo-Romanesque and neo-Gothic styles, but acquired, at the turn of the 20C, some stained-glass windows and mural paintings by Stanisław Wyspiański, which are today its most famous and valuable assets. The splendid **frescoes**★★ covering the walls of the chancel and of the transept combine floral, geometric and heraldic motifs with some figurative scenes. The sumptuous Art-Nouveau **stained-glass windows★★★**, bathing the interior of the church with subtle light, are the artist's unquestionable masterpieces. Best admired in the morning light are St Francis, the Blessed Salome and the Four Elements, located behind the high altar, while the monumental God the Father ordering the world "become" (1904), worthy of Michelangelo, reigns supreme in the middle of the west front (glorious in the late-afternoon light!).

Other must-sees include, on the north side of the nave, the **Chapel of the Passion,** which has been, on every Good Friday since 1595, the starting point of an impressive procession by members of the Brotherhood of the Passion (or of the Beautiful Death). The **Stations of the Cross** (1933) by Józef Mehoffer are painted on the walls. On the opposite side, the south chapel contains a 16C image of the **Madonna of Mercy** by Master Jerzy, a highly venerated figure. Finally, the adjoining **cloister** houses damaged 15C **frescoes** as well as a **painting collection** started in the 16C, containing portraits of Kraków's bishops, including that of Piotr Tomicki by the famous artist-monk of Mogiła's Cistercian Abbey, Stanisław Samostrzelnik.

From the square in front of the church, it is easy to make a detour towards the university district. Originally laid out round the Collegium Maius, the area gradually spread to the old town's first Jewish quarter which was rapidly moved to the present Szczepański before being finally established in Kazimierz. Progressively spreading its annexees in the south-west corner of the Rynek, around three streets, Św. Anny, Jagiellońska and Gołębia, the Jagiellonian "octopus" later reached out with its university tentacles to other parts of the town.

Collegium Maius★★

Ul. Jagiellonska 15 - ✆ 422 05 49 - Mon-Fri 10am-2.20pm (last guided tour) - Apr-Oct until 5.20pm on Thu - free admission on Sat 10am-1.20pm (last guided tour) - Guided tours for groups (20 persons), duration: 20min - main museum 12 PLN - main museum + scientific exhibition and Fine Arts collection (Mon-Fri 1pm, duration 1hr) 16 PLN - Tour in English.

The name Great College means that this is the oldest and most prestigious building of the Kraków University, itself one of the oldest universities of central Europe, founded in 1364 by King Kazimierz the Great. Restored in 1400 by King Władysław Jagiello with the personal gifts made by his deceased wife Hedwig, the Kraków Academy (Academia Croviensis), renamed Jagiellonian University in 1818, extended gradually by acquiring the neighbouring Gothic houses. Remodelled many times over the centuries, in particular in neo-Gothic style during the 19C, it was only restored to its original appearance between 1949 and 1964.

The **inner courtyard** is freely accessible, which enables visitors to witness the brief musical show perfomed everyday at 11am and 1pm by the characters brought to life by the clock mechanism situated above the Golden Door. There are distinct guided tours to the historical section on the first floor and the scientific section on the second floor. The tour starts on the first floor, in front of the **Aurea Door** opening onto the **Libraria** (the reading rooms used to be on the ground floor) prolonged by a vast room devoted to the memory of the best students who attended the university, such as Nicolaus Copernicus (from 1491 to 1495), King Jan III Sobieski (one of the rare sovereigns to have mingled with other students at a university!), Bronisław Malinowski and also Karol Wojtyła. You will see a globe mentioning the American continent as "America noviter reperta", which means "Newly discovered America". The **Stuba Communis**, boasting a Moorish-style stove and a magnificent staircase which led to the bedrooms on the upper floor, was used as a refectory by the teachers. The room contains a fine 14C statuette of King Kazimierz the Great in painted wood, a tribute to the university's founder. Several rooms in succession

Collegium Maius

R. Soberka / MICHELIN

house the **Treasury** displaying the royal sceptres (the crossed sceptres form the emblem of the university) as well as the famous Jagiellonian armillary sphere designed in 1510 by Jan of Stobnica. The next room (a former teacher's bedroom) is entirely devoted to Copernicus and his astronomical instruments. The tour ends with the **Great Hall** (Aula), where the university's major ceremonial events took place, beneath the noble motto inscribed in Latin on one of the walls: "Reason wins over force". Wooden stalls used by teachers are lined along the sides of the room decorated with a collection of portraits and closed at the other end by a fine wooden doorway saved when the former town hall was demolished.

Five rooms on the second floor house the largest collection of scientific instruments in Poland as well as a painting gallery and a collection of medieval art.

St Anne's Church (Kościół Św. Anny)★ A1

Founded in 1689 by the teachers of the Jagiellonian University, this vast church, designed by Dutch architect Tylman van Gameren, is considered as one of the finest Baroque buildings in Poland. Note the clever effect created on the **façade** by the overlapping of the three doorways, in order to counteract the absence of perspective. Particularly noteworthy is the **stucco decoration★★** adorning the nave by Italian artist Baldassare Fontana and the flamboyant high altar (1698) framing a picture of the Virgin with Child in the company of St Anne, painted by Jerzy Eleuter Siemiginowski. The south transept houses a **sarcophagus★** containing the relics of St Jan Kanty (1390-1473) supported by four allegorical figures symbolizing the university's main faculties at the time: Philosophy, Theology, Medicine and Law. The ensemble was made by Baldassare Fontana in 1767, for the canonization of this distinguished professor. The north transept contains the **monument** dedicated to Nicolaus Copernicus bearing the Latin inscription *sapere auso* (know and dare), a likely allusion to the fact that Copernicus only revealed his shattering scientific theories at the end of his life, thus avoiding Giordano Bruno's dreadful fate. Also interesting are the pulpit, the painted stalls and the frescoes of the dome. Renowned organ concerts take place regularly.

Facing St Anne's university church is the **Collegium Nowodworski**, the oldest grammar school in the country where youngsters were supposed to prepare themselves to enter the prestigious university. With its twin-bannister staircase backing onto an arcaded courtyard, this building, erected between 1636 and 1643, forms one of the finest examples of Baroque secular architecture in Kraków. It has, since 1993, been housing the Collegium Medicum of the Jagiellonian University. Standing opposite the Collegium Maius is the **Collegium Kołłątaja** and, farther south, the **Collegium Minus** (1462). At the end of Gołębia Street stands the main building of the modern Jagiellonian University with its façade overlooking the Planty. Built in neo-Gothic style, the **Collegium Novum** (1887) houses the University Headquarters and the local education authority. Opposite is the **Collegium Witkowskiego** (or Collegium Physicum) and, in front of it, a statue of Copernicus holding an astrolabe.

Walk back towards the Franciscan Church.

On the left, the Bishop's Palace was the residence of Karol Wojtiła, the future John-Paul II, from 1967 to 1978 when he moved to the Vatican. Thousands of Kraków's residents gathered here, holding a candle, on the day of his death (2 April 2005) then went on to the Dominican Church.

Behind the east end of St Francis and the bronze statue (1936) of Józef Dietl (1804-78), professor of medicine and president of the Jagiellonian University but above all first elected mayor of Kraków in 1866, stands the Wielopolski Palace, seat of the municipal authorities who acquired it in 1864. Erected between 1535 and 1560 in Renaissance style, it was devastated by the great fire of 1850 but nevertheless retained its original crenellated attic.

Continue straight on towards the Dominican Church.

Holy Trinity Basilica and Dominican Convent
(Bazylika Św. Trójcy i Klasztor Dominikanów)★★ B2

The mother church of Poland's Dominican Order, founded by monks who arrived from Bologna in 1223 at the request of Bishop Iwo Odrowąż, is one of the largest and most important basilicas in Kraków. Erected on the site of a Romanesque church destroyed during the Tatar invasion in 1241, it was consecrated in 1249 then rebuilt several times, in particular in 1872, following the 1850 fire. The relatively well-preserved side chapels, added in the 17C by wealthy aristocratic families, are most interesting.

Interior – The Lubomirski Chapel which features a 17C painted decor, is located in the lower south corner of the nave. Further along, past the late-16C tomb of Prospero Provano surmounted by a fine incubent figure, one comes to the **Myszkowski Chapel★,** erected in mannerist style between 1603 and 1614. It is topped with a dome featuring busts of family members (made by Santi Gucci's workshop) facing each other. Further on still, the Baroque **Rosary Chapel**, built to celebrate the victory of King Jan Sobieski over the Turks in Vienna (1683), houses a representation of the Virgin copied at the end of the 16C from a Romanesque icon originally in Santa Maria Maggiore Basilica in Rome. It has been particularly venerated since it escaped the fire of 1850. Located on the other side, the **Zbaraski Chapel** (1628-33) is noteworthy for its plain yet contrasted black-marble decoration. Further on, a staircase leads to **St Hyacinth's Chapel★**, named after the first Polish Dominican (Jacek in Polish), whose relics are kept in a marble coffin. Built in 1581, it was decorated with stucco around 1700 by Baldassare Fontana and adorned with paintings by the Italian artist Tommaso Dolabella, illustrating the life of the saint. At the end of the nave, a bronze plaque (circa 1500, from a project by Veit Stoss) set in the wall pays tribute to Filippo Buonaccorsi, known as Callimachus, the Florentine humanist who was the tutor of King Kazimierz's children.

The buildings of the adjoining **convent** are grouped around two courtyards, including a beautiful cloister with funerary stelae. Do not miss the mid-13C chapter house and the refectory (2nd quarter of the 13C), decorated with a fine 15C Crucifixion.

Church of the Holy Cross (Kościół Św. Krzyża)★

This Gothic church, its slender red-brick structure offset against the green background of the Planty, is one of the most charming churches in Kraków. It served as the parish church of the Hospitallers of the Holy Spirit of Saxia, an order founded in Montpellier, France, which settled in Kraków in 1244. The present appearance of the edifice dates mainly from the 14C and 15C. The adjoining hospital, closed in the 19C, was demolished in 1891 to make room for the Słowacki Theatre. The almost square nave is surmounted by Gothic palm vaulting supported by a single central pillar featuring a tree-shaped capital; this symbol of the new tree of life represented by the Crucifix is chartacteristic of the Order and omnipresent inside the church. The side walls are adorned with numerous mural paintings (the oldest, decorating the south wall, on your right as you enter, date from the second half of the 16C) which are mainly 19C restorations of Renaissance paintings. Discovered during restoration work carried out in the last ten years of the 19C, they could not be saved in situ and were therefore copied by Wyspiański to be used as models for a later restoration. The most striking painting is that of the "fisherman's mirror" *(Speculum Peccatoris)*. A dignified old man sitting in an armchair emerging from a well, sees his naked body threatened by five swords representing the grave perils of Death, the Devil, Sin and the Word. The fifth and most threatening sword is hanging over his head without any mention of the kind of peril it represents.

Not far from the Church stands the imposing structure of the **Juliusz Słowacki Theatre**, erected between 1891 and 1893, remisniscent of the Opéra Garnier in Paris. Nearby is the **House under the Cross** (Dom Pod Krzyżem), home since 1969 to a delightfully quaint museum devoted to the history of drama in Kraków (*Ul. Szpitalna 21 - Nov-Apr Tue, Thu-Sat and 2nd Sun of every month 9am-4pm, Wed 11am-6pm; May-Sep Tue-Sat and 2nd Sun of every month 10am-5.30pm - 5 PLN).*

Kazimierz★★

TOWN PLAN III

Founded in 1335 as an independent town by King Kazimierz III the Elder and named after him, Kazimierz was surrounded by fortifications at the end of the 14C. The king offered hospitality and granted important privileges to the Jewish community who settled south-west of the Rynek before being resettled north in the area of the present Szczepanski Square. However, following the pogrom of 1494, King John Olbracht moved the Jews to the north-eastern part of Kazimierz where they were told to remain in the vicinity of the present Szeroka Street. At the beginning of the 16C, Jews who were being persecuted in other countries poured into Kazimierz. In 1791, the area officially became a district of Kraków before being turned during the 19C into a true and unique district of Jewish culture. Nowadays, it includes a Catholic part (even if many Jews settled there in the 19C) in the south-west and a Jewish part to the north-east of an area which is slowly emerging from the dilapidated state it had been reduced to at the end of the Second World War. Interest for the Jewish Kazimierz was suddenly aroused in 1989, following the making of Steven Spielberg's film, *Schindler's List*.

The **Podgórze** district, situated on the south bank of the Wisła, includes several memorial places linked with the holocaust of Kraków's Jews, which can be visited.

Pauline Church and Monastery in Skałka (Kościół Paulinów)★ A2

Built on the "rock" (*Na Skałka*) in the middle of a lovely park, the most pastoral of Kraków' churches is, like the Cathedral, a place of worship dedicated to the memory of Stanisław, the martyred bishop. The **idyllic setting★** is enhanced by the presence of a strange four-sided pool (*Sadzawka Św. Stanisława*) with a statue of the patron saint of Poland emerging in its centre, dating from 1731. The present Baroque church (1733-42) is the 3rd maybe even the 4th sanctuary built on this site. The main attraction, placed on the altar dedicated to it in the north aisle, is the tree trunk on which the martyred bishop is said to have been cut to pieces by Bolesław the Bold's henchmen on 11 April 1079, after the king cut off his head on this very spot. Every year on the 1st Sunday after 8 May, St Stanisław's feast day, a large procession winds its way from the cathedral to this church (which contained the saint's grave before its transfer to Wawel). Between 1877 and 1880, the **crypt** cut into the rock in 1792 (accessible from the outside in the middle of the twin-bannister staircase) was turned into a national Pantheon in addition to that already existing in the Wawel crypt.

Posters in the Kazimierz District

The great craftsmen of Polish culture, including the historian Długosz, the writers Siemieński and Kraszewski, the artists Siemiradzki, Wyspiański and Malczewski and the composer Szymanowski were laid to rest in sarcophagi. The latest to be admitted is the poet Czesław Miłosz, buried in great pomp on 27 August 2004.

St Catherine's Church (Kościół Św. Katarzyny)★ B2

This is one of the town's finest Gothic churches; founded in 1363 by King Kazimierz the Great, it was modelled on St Mary's Church on the Rynek, to make amends, as the story goes, for the murder of a man of the church which he ordered. Its history is marked by a succession of disasters: two earthquakes in 1443 and 1786, flooding around 1370 and three huge fires in 1556, 1604 and 1638; to top it all, it was turned into an arsenal by the Austrians during the first half of the 19C. This tragic succession of unfortunate events explains its extremely bare and austere interior in striking contrast with the monumental **high altar** (1634) miraculously spared, which frames a picture illustrating the mystical marriage of St Catherine of Alexandria by Andrzej Wenesta. Also noteworthy is **St Monica's Chapel** (St Augustine's mother), at the end of the south aisle. Outside stands the former 15C brick-and-timber belfry. Adjoining the north side of the church is the cloister of the Augustine Convent which contains early-15C frescoes illustrating in particular the saint's martyrdom.

Walk up Skałeczna Street to Krakowska then turn right towards Wolnica Square.

Wolnica Square B2

Kazimierz's 15C **Town Hall** (Ratusz Kazimierski) stands on the former market place (smaller now than it used to be). Topped on its west side by a fine crenellated attic and dominated by a 16C octagonal tower, it now houses the rich collections of the **Ethnographic Museum** (Muzeum Etnograficzne) including a large number of artefacts illustrating Polish traditional art and culture, in particular through reconstructions of rustic domestic interiors, mainly from the south of Poland. The museum also presents a section displaying objects illustrating the cultures of other continents. The annexee situated nearby (*Ul. Krakowska 46*) is devoted to temporary exhibitions (*Pl. Wolnica Oct-Apr Mon 10am-6pm, Wed-Fri 10am-3pm, Sat-Sun 10am-2pm; May-Sep Mon, Wed-Fri 10am-5pm, Sat-Sun 10am-2pm - 6.50 PLN - free admission on Sun*).

Church of Corpus Christi (Kościół Bożego Ciała) B2

This was the first church in Kazimierz; built in 1340 by the king of the same name, it was completed in the middle of the 15C and remodelled several times. During the siege of Kraków by Swedish troops in the middle of the 17C, the church and its cloister were used as their headquarters by King Carl Gustav and his troops. The interior offers a striking contrast between the austere stone-and-brick architecture and the wealth of ornamentation of the carved Baroque altars. The mannerist high altar frames two paintings attributed to Tomasso Dolabella: a Nativity and a Deposition. Do not miss the stained-glass windows in the chancel, the fine stalls (1632) and the extravagant boat-shaped Baroque pulpit. The Wawel architect, Bartolomeo Berecci, who was murdered in 1537, is buried in St Anne's Chapel.

Continue towards the Jewish part of Kazimierz, via Józefa Street (the tourist office is at no 7).

The **High Synagogue** (Bożnica Wysoka), at no 38, was the third synagogue to be built in the town between 1556 and 1663. It owes its name to the situation of the prayer hall, "high" above street level. You will have to content yourself with admiring the austere façade, pierced by three large windows framed by four massive buttresses, since the building is not open to visitors. No 42 along the same street is a **prayer house** devoted to the study of the Torah (Kowea Itim I'Tora), built in 1810 and restored in 1912. At the end of Józefa Street, you will come to the Old Synagogue entered from the south side which bars Szeroka Street.

Turn right onto Bartosza Street and join the parallel street.

Galicja Jewish Muzeum★ C1

Ul. Dajwór 18 - Apr-Oct daily 9am-8pm, Nov-Mar daily 10am-8pm - 7 PLN.

This museum, inaugurated in June 2004, is based on an interesting approach which consists in taking a fresh look at the Jewish past of Polish Galicia. The objective of the exhibition "Traces of Memory" is to bear witness, through a series of large photographs, to a civilisation which developed during almost a thousand years and suddenly disappeared, practically obliterated from one day to the next. It is reinforced by a temporary exhibition. Good captions in English. Bookshop and cafeteria.

Szeroka Street★★ C1

In spite of its name, it looks very much like a square. Its present name meaning "Large Street" is just as appropriate as its former name of "Main Street". It was the centre of commercial and religious life in the Jewish town from the 15C to the 19C and also assumed the role of market square. Its past bustling atmosphere having long disappeared, it is now the centre of tourist Kazimierz, full of visitors and cars, lined with hotels, galleries, bars and restaurants serving a traditional Jewish cuisine.

Tucked inside the courtyard of the Alef Restaurant is the former **Popper Synagogue** (Synagoga Poppera), founded in 1620 by a wealthy merchant and banker, Wolf Popper, known as The Stork. Vandalized during the war, it was turned in 1965 into a cultural centre open to visitors. The short southern side of the square is closed off by the Old Synagogue. On the opposite side stands the **Jordan Palace** (Pałac Jordanów), otherwise known as the Landau Palace, after the wealthy family who occupied it.

Old Synagogue (Synagoga Stara or Bożnica Stara)★ C1

Ul. Szeroka 24 - Mon 10am-2pm, Tue-Sun 10am-5pm - 7 PLN

This is the oldest surviving Jewish building in Poland. The synagogue was built in Gothic style at the very beginning of the 15C then remodelled in Renaissance style, following the fire that devastated Kazimierz in 1557, by the Italian architect Mateo Gucci. During restoration work undertaken in the early 20C, the 16C level of the building was rediscovered, which explains why it is now below the present street level. Surrounded by a fine wrought-iron railing decorated with the star of David, the synagogue today houses the Jewish section of the town's historical museum, devoted to the history of Kraków's Jewish community.

Remu'h Synagogue and Cemetery
(Bożnica Remuh i Cmentarz Remuh)★★ C1
Ul. Szeroka 40 - Mon-Fri 9am-4pm - 2 PLN. It is compulsory to wear a kippa.
Sometimes called "The New Synagogue" as opposed to the Old Synagogue, it was founded by Israël Isserles Auerbach for his son Moses Isserles (1520-72) also known as Rabbi Remu'h, a scientist, philosopher and eminent Talmud specialist, and built between 1556 and 1558 by Stanisław Baranek. It regained its religious role in 1945 and is now an active place of worship.

The visit of the synagogue is combined with a tour of the **cemetery**★★ (here too, it is compulsory to wear a kippa) which is the oldest cemetery of Kraków's Jewish community and one of Europe's oldest Jewish cemeteries. Situated behind the synagogue, it was created in the year 5331 (1551 on the Christian calendar) and remained the main necropolis in Kazimierz. The most eminent members of the Jewish community were buried here until 1800, when it was closed by the Austrian authorities. Neglected from then on, it was vandalized by the Nazis during the Second World War and became more and more dilapidated until archaeological excavations carried out in 1959-60 revealed the presence of several layers of graves (part of the cemetery which was not excavated still rises 5m above the rest). More than 700 tombs, including very valuable ones from an artistic point of view, were brought to light, restored and carefully replaced. Note that some eminent personalities had a second grave built after the war, when the original one was believed to have definitively disappeared. The **grave** of Rabbi Remu'h, adjoining the western wall of the synagogue, was among the few tombstones spared by the Nazis, a kind of miracle interpreted by Orthodox Jews who flock to the grave as one more sign of the rabbi's holiness and supernatural powers. Fragments of old matzevas were used to build a **memorial wall** against the enclosing wall overlooking Szeroka Street (on the right of the entrance).

Isaac's Synagogue (Synagoga Izaaka)★ B1
Ul. Kupa 18 - Sun-Fri 9am-7pm (Jul-Aug 9am-8pm) - 7 PLN.
The Italian architect Giovanni Battista Trevano and the stucco specialist Giovanni Battista Falconi worked on this imposing Baroque synagogue built between 1638 and 1644 for the wealthy merchant Izaak Jakubowicz. The outside staircase enabled women to reach the gallery reserved for them. The visit is rendered all the more interesting by the viewing of several archive films about the daily life of Kraków's Jewish community before the war and during the German occupation, including in particular films of Nazi progaganda about the Podgórze Ghetto in 1941.

Head towards the **New Square** (Nowy Plac), known in the past as the Jewish Square; in its middle stands a circular covered market hall built in 1900. Between 1927 and the beginning of the war, it was used as a ritual poultry slaughterhouse. Today, the square is surrounded by a great number of trendy cafés which come to life at nightfall; a popular flea market takes place every Sunday morning.

In the corner of the square, along Meiselsa Street, the **Jewish Cultural Centre** (Centrum Kultury Żydowskiej) is the headquarters of the Fundacja Judaica (*Ul. Rabina Meiselsa 17 - Mon-Fri 10am-6pm, Sat-Sun 10am-2pm*). Inaugurated in 1993, it is an exhibition centre and a concert venue. It is worthwhile going in to ask about the programme of events, or to enjoy the tearoom and take a break in the pleasant roof-garden.

Head for Miodowa Street

Tempel Synagogue
(Synagoga Tempel) B1
Ul. Miodowa 24 - variable opening times (more often in the afternoon from 1 to 3pm) - 5 PLN.
Built in 1862 in neo-Romanesque style and given a Moorish-inspired decoration, it is the most recent synagogue in Kazimierz. Reputed to be a progressive (postępowa) synagogue, it was attended by a large number of Jewish intellectuals who

Jewish cemetery

A. Galy / MICHELIN

supported the doctrine of the *Haskala* (light). It was the rendezvous of Kraków's *maskilims* (the enlightened) who called for equal rights, non-denominational education and objected to speaking Yiddish and wearing traditional clothes, thus opposing the precepts of strictly orthodox Jews, supporters of Hasidism. It is today, together with Remu'h Synagogue, one of the two places of worship still active in Kraków. Before the war, a ritual-bath (mikva) establishment stood behind the synagogue.

Follow Miodowa Street towards the new cemetery situated on the other side of the railway line. A short detour via Estery Street will lead you to the Kupa Synagogue (Ul. Warszauera 8), very recently restored.

New Jewish Cemetery (Nowy Cmentarz Zydowski)★ C1

Ul. Miodowa 55 - Sun-Mon 8am-6pm - closes Sat and Jewish hols - Free admission.

Make a point of taking a stroll along the alleyways of this derelict, overgrown cemetery pervaded by a meditative atmosphere. Created in 1800, outside the Kazimierz district of that time, as a replacement of the Remu'h cemetery, it was vandalized by the Nazis who used the matzevas as building material. Bearing witness to the secularization and cultural integration of a growing number of Kraków's Jews, some of the epitaphs inscribed on tombstones are in German or Polish. The most famous graves include those of painter Maurycy Gottlieb (1856-1879) and photographer Ignacy Krieger (1817-1889), whose photos have captured Kraków as it was in the past.

Museums to see

Czartoryski Museum (Muzeum Książąt Czartoryskich)★★★
TOWN PLAN II B1

Ul. Św. Jana 19 - May-Oct Tue, Thu 10am-4pm, Wed, Fri-Sat 10am-7pm, Sun 10am-3pm - 9 PLN - free admission on Thu.

The Museum of the Czartoryski Princes, the direct descendants of the Jagiellon dynasty, is the pride of the city of Kraków; it is housed in three buildings linked by suspended covered galleries: the private Mansion, the Cloister and the Arsenal. The initial stock collected by Izabela Czartoryska in her Puławy palace at the beginning of the 19C was sent to Paris to escape confiscation and was returned to Poland in 1876. Shamelessly plundered by the Nazis during the war, it was partially recovered then nationalized, thus forming part of the National Museum in 1949. The final episode saw the family's heir regain his rights by a court decision in 1991 and bequeath his collection to the Polish nation.

The prize exhibit is undoubtedly the delicate **Lady with an Ermine**, which was only authenticated and officially attributed to Leonardo da Vinci in 1992 when a set of his fingerprints were discovered under the first layer of paint. The princess, who was famous for wrongly attributing works of art, had had the description LA BELE FERONIERE LEONARD D'AWINCI inscribed in the upper left-hand corner, because of the resemblance between this lady and the other lady in the painting by Leonardo displayed in the Louvre Museum. This marvellous work shares a room with another "painting" acquired in Venice in 1807, of which all that remains is the empty frame, symbolically hung on the wall; the painting itself, probably a self-portrait by Raphaël, was "borrowed" by the Nazis in 1939 and never recovered. Another major exhibit is Rembrandt's "**Landscape with the Good Samaritan**", which looks out of place among the other Dutch paintings. Captions are in French, a likely consequence of the collection's long stay in Paris.

KRAKÓW Plan III
KAZIMIERZ

Stanisław Wyspiański Museum (Muzeum Stanisława Wyspiańskiego)★★
TOWN PLAN II A3
Ul. Szczepańska 11 - ℘ 422 70 21 - May-Oct Tue-Wed, Sat 10am-7pm, Thu-Fri 10am-4pm and Sun 10am-3pm - 7 PLN - free admission on Sun.

Recently housed in the 17C Szołayski House, this very pleasant museum contains works and souvenirs connected with the famous Art-Nouveau artist, Stanisław Wyspiański (1869-1907). A leading member of the "Young Poland" movement, the Polish equivalent of Art Nouveau, this native of Kraków, who was very attached to his home town and to Polish national history, was a pupil of Matejko at the Fine Arts Academy. He was essentially a painter but, having more than one string to his bow, he was also a writer, a playwright, a photographer and an architect. The sumptuous stained-glass windows of the Franciscan Church were probably his masterpiece. The museum boasts excellent captions in English and stages interesting temporary exhibitions on the ground floor of the building. Note also the fine series of old photographs of Kraków made by Ignacy Krieger (1820-89).

Kraków National Museum (Muzeum Narodowe)
Al. 3 Maja 1 - May-Oct Tue-Thu 10am-4pm, Wed, Fri-Sat 10am-7pm, Sun 10am-3pm.

Situated in the heart of the new university district, this imposing modern edifice, begun in 1934, was only completed in 1989. The main building (Gmach Główny) of the museum contains the "Weapons and Colours of Poland" gallery, the "Gallery of Decorative Art", the "Gallery of 20C Polish Art" and often stages excellent temporary exhibitions. An imposing commemorative monument, carved by sculptor Marian Konieczny, was erected in 1982 in front of the museum on the occasion of the 75th anniversary of the death of Stanisław Wyspiański.

Józef Mehoffer House (Dom Józefa Mehoffera)★
Ul. Krupnicza 26 - May-Oct Tue-Wed, Sat 10am-7pm, Thu-Fri 10am-4pm, Sun 10am-3pm; Nov-Apr Wed-Thu 9am-3pm, Fri 9am-5.30pm, Sat-Sun 10am-3pm - 6 PLN - Free admission on Sun in winter, on Thu in summer.

Those who appreciate artists' houses should love the peaceful home (and its pleasant adjoining garden) of painter Józef Mehoffer (1869-1946), perfectly preserved in

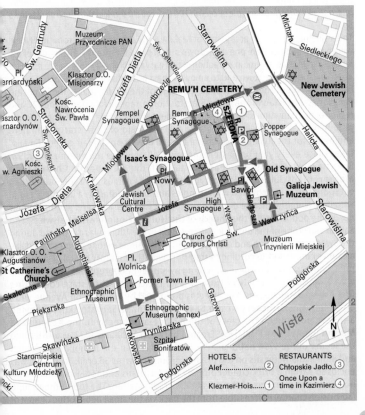

209

its original state. Without being outstanding - the finest room is undoubtedly the Japanese room with its red walls covered with prints - it reflects the personality of this artist-designer with interesting ideas, who was the friend and rival of Wyspiański, born as it happened in 1869 in this house, which Mehoffer bought in 1930.

Manggha Japanese Art Centre (Centrum Sztuki i Techniki Japońskiej "Manggha") A1

Ul. Konopnickiej 26 - Tue-Sun 10am-6pm - 5PLN - Restaurant-bar 10am-7pm (Sat-Sun 8pm).

This futuristic building with outside mirrors reflecting the view of the castle and the Wisła, is placed under the aegis of the Kyoto-Kraków Foundation, created on the initiative of film-maker and director Andrzej Wajda and his wife Krystyna Zachwatowicz. The construction of the building by Japanese architect Arata Isozaki was financed by the prize awarded in 1987 to the film-maker by the Inamori Foundation in Kyoto. The aim of this museum, inaugurated in 1994, is to familiarize the public with Japanese culture through beautiful exhibitions presenting, in rotation, the private collection of writer Feliks "Manggha" Jasieński, bequeathed to the Kraków National Museum in 1920.

"Lady with and Ermine" by Leonardo da Vinci (1485), Kraków National Museum

Nearby

Zwierzyniec ★★ TOWN PLAN I B2

Head for the Salwator (The Saviour) district, at the end of tramway lines no 1,2 et 6. From there you will have to climb another 1.6km to the summit of the Kościuszko Mound, alternatively directly accessible by bus no 100 (infrequent service) starting from Matejko Square.

This walk through green areas west of Kraków, only a few minutes from the Rynek, will enable you to explore one of the town's most pleasant suburbs. The ascent of the Kościuszko Mound, the main attraction of this easy ramble, will allow you to discover another aspect of the town and to enjoy the best possible view of Kraków.

Facing the end of the tram line, on the edge of the Wisła, stands the imposing **Premonstratensian Monastery** (Klasztor Norbertanek), founded in the 12C and remodelled many times. Every year, eight days after Corpus Christi, the Lajkonik parade, whose tradition goes back to the Tatar raid of 1287, starts from here and heads for the Rynek; it is also here that a great popular fair called "Emaus" takes place every year on Easter Monday. Walk towards the mound along Św. Bronisławy Street until you reach, on the left, the 17C **wooden Church of St Margaret** (Kościół Św. Małgorzaty), otherwise known as Gontyna. Built on an octagonal plan, it is covered with shingles and surmounted by a lantern. People who died from the plague during an epidemic were buried here. Slightly higher up, on the opposite side, the **Church of the Holy Saviour** (Kościół Najświętszego Salwatora) is one of the oldest in the city. Built in the 10C, it was destroyed during the Swedish occupation and rebuilt in the 17C. It houses a stone pulpit shaped like a chalice connected, according to tradition, with the memory of St Adalbert who preached here, and an unusual painting by Kasper Kurcz, representing a Crucifix with a musician (1605). Note, just beyond the church, the estate comprising fine Art-Nouveau houses. The street is prolonged by Washington Avenue with, on its left, the **Cemetery of the Saviour** (Cmentarz Salwatorski), occupying a superb position on the crest of the hill; it leads directly to the **Kościuszko Mound** (Kopiec Kościuszki)★★. Erected between 1820 and 1823 as a tribute to the leader of the 1794 national insurrection, this man-made mound, 34m high and 80m in diameter sits on top of a hill (333m) known as Sikornik. In 1853, it was enclosed within a brick citadel built by the Austrians and today occupied by a hotel and the premises of the private RMF radio station. The top of the mound (admission charge) is accessible from the back via the small neo-Gothic Chapel of

St Bronisławy which houses an exhibition devoted to the patriot and national hero. Beneath the hill, you will see a vast meadow commonly called Błonia which is the venue of great popular gatherings such as the grand papal masses celebrated by John-Paul II on his trips to Kraków. Those for whom time is no issue will be able to prolong the excursion on foot towards the vast forestry estate covering over 400ha, dominated by Marshall Józef Piłsudski's Mound and by the Camaldolese Church of the Bielany monastery.

Tyniec★★ TOWN PLAN I A2

Accessible by bus no 112 from the Rynek Dębnicki (on the opposite bank of the Wisła, across the bridge of the same name), by taxi, or in summer by one of the river shuttles moored in front of Wawel.

Perched on a rocky promontory overlooking the south bank of the Wisła, 12km south-west of Kraków, **Tyniec's Benedictine abbey** (Opactwo Benedyktynów Tyńcu) is essentially a fortified church. Benedictine monks arrived from France in 1044 and founded the abbey at the beginning of the 11C. Originally Romanesque (as the right side of the doorway shows) but remodelled several times, the edifice looks today like a Baroque sanctuary with Gothic elements. The church, famous for its summer organ concerts, is the only part of the abbey open to visitors. Inside, note the fine Baroque **pulpit** shaped like the prow of a ship, and the lovely black-marble high **altar** which contrasts with the gilded statues filling the recesses. However, the main asset of the place is its pastoral setting consisting of the **terrace-viewpoint ★★** offering a fine view of the meandering Wisła stretched out below against a background of greenery. In the courtyard, a wooden structure shelters a large well (1620) which has given rise to many legends. Finally, you can stroll along the river and admire the church from the opposite bank which affords a truly delightful view of the abbey perched on its rock.

The Wieliczka Salt Mine★★★ TOWN PLAN I C2

10 km south-east of Krakó - minibus (preferable to trains) stationed in Pawia Street, not far from the railway station, leave visitors near the entrance to the mine (this is not the end of the line) - Ul. Daniłowicza 10 - Ticket office Apr-Oct daily 7.30am-1.30pm and 2-7.30pm; 2 Nov-Mar daily 8am-4pm - closed 1 Jan, Easter Sun, 1 Nov and 24, 25 and 31 Dec - 42 PLN - guided tours (3hr) in English (55 PLN) Jul-Aug at 10 and 11.30am, 12.30, 1.45, 3 and 5pm; in winter at 10am and 12.30pm.

Some foreign tourists plan a trip to Poland with the sole aim of visiting Wieliczka (pronounced Vielichka), a town situated on the outskirts of Kraków, renowned for its **rock-salt mine** (Kopalnia Soli), worked since the 10C and on UNESCO's World Heritage List since 1978. An incredible underground labyrinth dug from the 13C onwards in search of this "white gold" which for centuries represented a real godsend for the Polish kingdom's finances.

After a monotonous descent via a 53-flight staircase you will reach a depth of 64m. There is a permanent temperature of 14°C (take appropriate clothing). You will only tour the first three levels situated at depths of between 64m and 135m, but this vast pit spreads its network of galleries over nine levels. An underground sanatorium, intended for people suffering from allergies, is buried some 211m underground, while the deepest gallery lies at a depth of around 327m. Out of the 300km of existing tunnels, a 3km long section enables visitors to walk along the galleries linking the different chambers. Along the way you will see many attractions including sculptures, salted lakes and deep wells but the climax of the tour is a vast chamber over 54m long, known as the **Chapel of the Blessed Kinga**, the patron saint of miners. It is a real underground sanctuary lit by salt-crystal chandeliers and famous for its numerous low reliefs and carved altars. It is a pity that tours are sometimes conducted at a frantic pace in summer, groups forcing one another out of the successive chambers. At the end of the tour, you can either go back to the surface by lift or prolong your underground excursion by visiting the interesting **museum** (extra charge) situated on level 3 (fairly long walk). In addition to the collection of objects connected with the history of the mine and with mining techniques, the museum contains amazing lifting machines as well as a very beautiful model of the town in 1645.

To complete your visit of the town of Wieliczka (called Magnum Sal in the Middle Ages), take a look at the **castle** (13C-19C) which houses the Museum of the Former Salt Mine, as well as at the 16C wooden Church of St Sebastian, situated on the heights overlooking the town and decorated with fine polychrome paintings in "New Poland" style.

R. Soberka / MICHELIN

Wieliezka Salt Mines

Nowa Huta TOWN PLAN I C1
10 km east of Kraków. Nowa Huta's main square (Plac Centralny) is accessible by tramway no 4, 15 or 22 and bus no 502 or 511.

A prolonged stay in Kraków would be incomplete without a short but instructive excursion to Nowa Huta. A two-to-three-hour stroll through its wide streets will give you an overview of Socialist Realist architecture and an insight into the "Socialist reality" which was the Poles' daily diet during the 1960s. You will also be able to discover, drowned in this ocean of concrete, a few stone patches such as the famous Cistercian church of the old village of Mogiła.

Centralny Square
This central square, which lost its statue of Lenin in 1989, was ironically given "Ronald Reagan" as a second name. From this semi-octagonal, sadly empty central space (some Poles would like Warsaw's Palace of Culture to be moved here), several avenues stretch out in various directions, Solidarity Avenue, General Anders Avenue and John Paul II Avenue (all of them notorious anti-communists!), lined with endless identical residential blocks, mostly grey and drab.

A panel in Roses Alley (Aleja Róż) suggests an itinerary for discovering on foot the various sights of the district and strolling along the most characteristic avenues. Compared to Kraków's charming old streets, these wide thoroughfares look somewhat sinister, even though the foliage of the now mature trees tends to soften the austere appearance of the façades. A good way to see the essential is to tour the town in a taxi and ask to be taken to all or some of the sights.

Situated on the eastern outskirts of the city, at the end of Solidarity Avenue, the **industrial complex** is entered through the very Socialist Realist gate of the Sędzimir Steelworks (Huta im. Sędzimira), owned today by the Indian firm Tycoon Lakshmi Mithal. At the height of its production in 1977, the steelworks employed 38 000 workers with an annual production of 6.7 million tonnes of steel (today's production has stabilized around one million tonnes). Just as important was the pollution generated by the works, which not only endangered the health of the inhabitants but proved very damaging to the old stones of Kraków's historic monuments. The building standing on the left, known as "The Doges' Palace" on account of its crenellated attic but also as "The Vatican", used to house the central administration of the former Lenin steeworks.

Church of Our Lady Queen of Poland, "the Ark"
(Kościół N.M.P. Królowej Polski «Arka») TOWN PLAN I C1
Ul. Obrońców Krzyża 1
A symbol of resistance to communist power, this futuristic church, fervently wanted by Nowa Huta's residents, was only erected in the 1970s. Its long awaited construction even sparked off famous riots after some communists tried to bring down a cross erected by worshippers. Built in the very heart of enemy territory, ideologically speaking, on a foundation stone from St Peter's in Rome, sent in 1969 by Pope Paul VI, this church owes its construction to the inflexible will of

the then archbishop of Kraków, Karol Wojtyła. Nicknamed "The Ark of the Lord", the church is meant to be reminiscent of the boat built by Noah and beached at the top of Mount Ararat; a hardly disguised metaphor illustrating the conviction that Christianism would outlive communism. The interior, bathed in strong light, is impressive on account of the huge Bronze Christ (crucified but without a cross) bending over his worshippers like a sail spread to catch the wind; a very expressive work by sculptor Bronisław Chromy, a native of Kraków. Consecrated in 1977, it was the first church officially erected in postwar Poland and as such this building by architect Wojciech Pietrzyk spurred the construction of many other Polish churches, sometimes built on audacious plans in post-modernist style (less well-known, Nowa Huta's Mistrzejowice Church is another example of this).

The Wanda Mound
(Kopiec Wandy) TOWN PLAN I C1

Ul. Ujastek. Situated south of the Steel-works complex on the way to Mogiła, the Wanda Mound owes its name to one of the daughters of King Krak who chose to throw herself into the Wisła rather than marry the German Prince Rytgier and thus became a symbol of national independence. Probably erected in the 8C, on the site of her grave, this mound is one of Kraków's oldest monuments. Rising to a height of 14m, it was surmounted in the 19C by a marble monument topped with a white eagle designed by painter Jan Matejko, who owned a nearby manor house where he came to find relief from the vicissitudes of urban life; the artist's home is now a **museum** *(Ul.Wańkowicza 25 - lun.-ven. 10h-14h).*

The Cistercian Monastery of Mogiła **(Opactwo Cystersów)★★**

Ul. Klasztorna 11. Looking like an island

The New Steelworks

Such is the evocative name of the new town whose establishment in Kraków's eastern suburbs was decreed by Stalin in 1949 to serve as a model of communist urban planning. A strictly political decision clearly aiming at symbolically punishing a city considered to be too intellectual, too conservative and a hotbed of anticommunism. Presented as a gift from the Soviet nation to the Polish people, this modern town, dedicated to the working class and entirely centred on the huge steelworks complex, was also intended to change Kraków's social structure, dominated at the time by the middle class who, for the most part, had said "No" to the recent referendum seeking popular approval. This naive ambition to create ex nihilo a perfect town that could rival Kraków enabled the historic centre of the latter to escape the whims of Socialist Realist architects.

miraculously emerging from an ocean of concrete, this monastery is one of the rare relics of the old village of Mogiła. Founded by Kraków's Bishop Iwo Odrowążwho presented it to the Cistercians when they arrived from Silesia in 1222, the monastery was named Jasna Mogiła (literally "shining grave") on account of the assumed presence in the vicinity of Princess Wanda's grave. Behind a Baroque west front stands one of the oldest Gothic churches in Poland. Consecrated in 1266 and later destroyed by fire, it was rebuilt in Gothic style in 1447. The most interesting features of the basilica dedicated to the Holy Virgin and to St Wencesław can be seen in and around the transept. Protected by a fine 17C ornamental railing and covered with ex-votos, the Chapel of the Holy Cross (Kaplica Krzyża Świętego), located at the extremity of the north transept, houses the highly venerated Mogiła Cross, miraculously saved from the 1447 fire: tradition requires that worshippers should proceed on their knees round the altar on which it stands. The transept and the chancel of the church (as well as the library of the monastery) have retained frescoes by Stanisław Samostrzelnik, an eminent artist monk from the first half of the 16C. The lovely Gothic cloister adjoining the south side of the church is also adorned with several fine frescoes (including a famous Crucifixion by Samostrzelnik).

Almost opposite the monastery, past the porch of an elegant belfry-tower (1752), stands a **wooden church** dedicated to **St Bartholomew** (Kościół Świętego Bartłomieja). Built at the same time as the monastery and intended for the secular clergy, the church was remodelled and its present appearance dates from 1466. In fact, it is one of the country's oldest wooden churches and a rare example of three-naved sanctuary. In addition to the 16C or 17C baptismal fonts, it contains 18C rococo paintings, which can only be seen during the Sunday services.

Excursions

Kalwaria Zebrzydowska

32km south-west of Kraków, along the road to Wadowice.

Kalwaria (the Calvary) is known throughout Poland as a place of **pilgrimage**. Some forty Baroque chapels suggesting the Golgotha were erected in the hills near the Bernardine monastery dating from 1600. Every Maundy Thursday and Good Friday, the **mystery of the Passion** is re-enacted by local people.

Wadowice

46km south-west of Kraków.

This small industrial town nestling among rolling hills is renowned for being the birthplace of **Karol Wojtyła** (18 May 1920). The future Pope John Paul II spent his childhood and his adolescence here, enjoying rambling (several footpaths which he particularly liked are dedicated to him) and winter sports. Standing on the main square is the Basilica of the Presentation of the Virgin where he was baptized. His birthplace is located In a street behind the square.

John Paul II's Birthplace (Dom Rodzinny Świętego Jana Pawła II) *(ul. Kościelna 7, Oct-Apr Tue-Sun 9am-noon, 2-5pm; May-Sep daily 9am-1pm, 2-6pm, free admission)*. Pilgrims flock to this place year-round and one may have to queue between 30min and 1hr 30min. They all come to pay homage to the Pope's memory and to discover his photos, documents and personal objects as well as many of the garments he wore during his pontificate.

Practical Kraków

Postal code – from 31-000
Phone code – 0(12)

Useful addresses

Kraków Tourist Card (Krakowska Karta Turystyczna). Includes free admission to 32 museums and free travel on the whole MPK public transport network as well as discounts from a selection of shops. Information available at tourist offices, some hotels and travel agencies. *45 PLN for a 2-day pass, 65 PLN for a 3-day pass. www.krakowcard.com*

TOURIST OFFICES AND TRAVEL AGENCIES

Municipal Information Centre (Punkt Informacji Miejskiej). *Ul. Szpitalna 25 - ℘ 432 01 10 - fax 432 00 62 - Oct-May daily 9am-5pm, Jun-Sep 8am-8pm - www. krakow.pl* . This municipal IT Tourist Information Centre is not actually located in the street but in a kiosk standing in the middle of the Planty, halfway between the station (straight on after the subway) and the beginning of the old town (behind the J Słowacki Theatre.)

Ul. Józefa 7 - ℘ 432 08 40 - fax 430 65 03 - Mon-Fri 9am-5pm. This is the second municipal Tourist Information Centre situated in the Kazimierz district, near the crossroads of Józefa and Bozego Ciala Streets.

Małopolskie Tourist Information Centre (Małopolskie Centrum Informacji Turystycznej) – *Rynek Główny 1/3 (Sukiennice) - ℘ 421 77 06 fax 421 30 36 - info@mcit.pl - www.mcit.pl - Oct-Mar Mon-Fri 8am-5pm, Sat 8am-2pm, Sun 10am-2pm; Apr 8am-6pm, Sat 8am-4pm,* *Sun 9.30am-4pm, May-Aug Mon-Fri 8am-8pm, Sat 8am-6pm, Sun 8.30am-4pm; Sep Mon-Fri 8am-6pm, Sat 8.30am-4pm, Sun 8.30am-2pm*. On the ground floor of the Cloth Hall, opposite St Mary's Church: this is the private information centre of the Małopolska region, combined with a shop. Bureau de change.

Cultural Information Centre (Centrum Informacji Kulturalnej) – *Ul. Św. Jana 2 - ℘ 421 77 87 - www.karnet.krakow2000.pl - Oct-Jun Mon-Sat 10am-6pm; Jul-Sep Mon-Sat 10am-6pm, Sun 10am-4pm*.

Comprehensive information about the town's cultural activities. Located at the beginning of St John Street starting from the middle of the north side of the Rynek.

PRIVATE AGENCIES

Jordan Biuro Podróży (Jordan Travel Agency). *Ul. Długa 9 - ℘ 421 21 25 fax 422 82 26 - it@jordan.pl - www.jordan.pl - daily 9am-6pm*. This private travel agency, which owns several branches in town, provides all kind of tourist information. It also runs, on the same spot, a hotel offering good value for money (210 PLN for a double room) despite the fact that some of the rooms are very noisy.

There is another Jordan annexee opposite the station (Centrum Informacji Turystycznej i Zakwaterowania). *Ul. Pawia 8 - ℘ 422 60 91 - fax 429 17 69*

Jarden Travel Agency. *Ul. Szeroka 2 - ℘ 421 71 66 - Mon-Sat 9am-6pm, Sun 10am-6pm*. This agency specialises in tours of the Jewish part of Kazimierz. Fine bookshop on the same theme (Jarden Bookshop).

Promotion and sale office of the Wieliczka salt mine (Biuro Promocji i Sprzedaży Kopalni Soli Wieliczka) : *Ul. Wiślna 12a -* ☎ *426 20 50 - fax 426 20 51 - biuro.promocji@kopalnia.pl - www. kopalnia.pl - Mon-Fri 9am-5pm, Sat-Sun 9am-2pm.*

Kraków's Tourist Guides Association - *Ul. Floriańska 19/6a -* ☎*/fax 422 28 51.*

Kraków's Royal Castle Educational Association (Guides' Office). *Wawel 5 -* ☎ *422 09 04*

Useful tip – Several free small monthly magazines, published in English, are easy to find; *Welcome to Cracow* and *Kraków: What, Where, When* provide up-to-date information about the town. However, the best choice is the fortnightly English-language *Kraków in your pocket* (5PLN), which includes a good selection of addresses.

OTHER ADDRESSES

Emergency service – ☎ 999 (from a mobile, dial 112)

Fire brigade – ☎ 998

Police – ☎ 997.

Police station : *Rynek Główny 29 -* ☎ *24 615 73 17 (24hr a day).*

Main police station in the old town : *Ul. Szeroka 35 -* ☎ *615 77 11.*

Post office – Urząd Pocztowy (Poczta Główna) *Ul. Westerplatte 20 31-045 Kraków 1 -* ☎ *422 24 97 - Mon-Fri 7.30am-8.30pm, Sat 8am-2pm, Sun 9am-2pm.* The main post office is located on the eastern outer edge of the Planty, on the corner of Westerplatte and Wielopole Streets. Poste-restante mail can be sent here and retrieved at counter no 1.

The other post office open on Sat until 8pm is located at *Ul. Lubicz 4* (in front of the railway station); mail posted there is dealt with 24hr/day.

The post office located in Wawel Castle is also open Sat and Sun, Apr-Oct, 10am-5pm (Oct-Mar 9am-4pm).

Most other post offices are open Mon-Fri 8am-7pm and Sat morning until noon, 1pm or 2pm.

Banks and foreign exchange – There are many ATM machines evenly spread around the old town. In most cases it is possible to select an interface in English. There are also numerous kantors (bureaux de change) in the heart of the old town; their exchange rates are similar. The best place to change traveller's cheques is Pekao Bank (*Rynek Główny 31 - Mon-Fri 8am-6pm, Sat 10am-2.30pm*) which takes a reasonable commission.

General Hospital – *Emergencies: Ul. Łazarza 14 -* ☎ *999 ou 424 42 00*

Pharmacy open 24hr/day – Euro Apteka. *Ul. Krowoderska 31 -* ☎ *430 00 05. Apteka: Ul. Galla 26 -* ☎ *636 73 65.*

Internet – Klub U Louisa. *Rynek Główny 13 - daily 11am-10pm - 15min: 1.50 PLN, 1hr: 4 PLN.*

On the south-east corner of the Rynek, inside vaulted cellars, this is the finest place in town for browsing the web.

Internet Cafe. *Rynek Główny 23 - daily 24hr/day. 15min: 1 PLN and 1hr: 3 PLN.*

Foreign newspapers – Empik (Rynek Główny 5) - RKP Central Station - Cracovia Hotel - Francuski Hotel - Saski Hotel - Kiosk in Ul. Sienna - Tabaka Lulka kiosk (Al. Sławkowska 22) - Dukator (Ul. Św. Jana 15).

Almatur. *Rynek Główny 27 - Mon-Fri 9am-6pm, Sat 10am-2pm - www.almatur.pl* Travel agency for students.

Getting around

Airport – The Kraków-Balice John-Paul II international airport (Międzynarodowy Port Lotniczy im. Jana Pawła II Kraków - Balice) is located 11km west of Kraków (*32-083 Balice, Ul. Kpt. M. Medweckiego 1 - www.lotnisko-balice.pl -* ☎ *285 51 20 information 24hr/day).*

Small tourist information kiosk *Kraków in your pocket* (*daily 11am-9pm*).

From the airport to the town centre -

By bus: bus no 192 (towards Plac Bohaterów Getta). Bus stop near the railway station, in Lubicz Street. Around 3 buses every hour from 4.30am to 10.30pm (journey time: 35min). Normal urban ticket. Otherwise: bus no 208 (less frequent) starting from Nowy Kleparz.

By taxi: the journey by taxi costs between 50 and 70 PLN.

Railway station – The main railway station (Dworzec PKP Kraków Główny) is situated north-east of the old town, 5min from the Rynek. *Pl. Kolejowy - international journeys.* (☎ *422 22 48) local journeys (*☎ *422 41 82) - www.pkp.com.pl -* Frequent intercity trains to Warsaw (2hr 50min).

Bus station – The bus station (Dworzec Autobusowy PKS) is adjacent to the railway station (*Pl. Dworcowy - www.pks. krakow.pl*); however, some buses (bound for Zakopane, Oświęcim) start from Kolejowy Square in front of the station.

MPK Public Transport (☎ *9150 - www. mpk.krakow.pl*). Bus or tramway. Single tickets (2.50 PLN) available in kiosks, in offices marked Sprzedaż biletów MPK or from bus and tramway drivers.

Car – The town centre is closed to motor cars except for driving into car parks in the Old Town: *Plac Szczepański, Plac Biskupi (Ul. Powiśle), Ul. Karmelicka.* Parking costs between 3 and 5 PLN per hour.

Taxis – Mega Radio Taxi ☎ *0800 200 200*
Barbakan Taxi ☎ *96-61*
Express Taxi : ☎ *96-29*
Radio Taxi : ☎ *919-*

Wawel Taxi : ✆ 96-66.

Car hire – Europcar, National, Budget, Avis and Hertz have a counter at the airport.

Joka. Ul. Starowiślna 13 (Pałac Pugetów) ✆/fax 429 66 30 krakow@joka.com.pl

Avis. Ul. Lubicz 23 - ✆ 629 61 08 - www. avis.pl

Europcar. Ul. Szlak 2 - ✆ 633 77 73 - www. europcar.com.pl

Hertz. Al. Focha 1 (Hotel Cracovia) - ✆ 429 62 62 - fax 422 29 39 - www.hertz.com.pl

Bike hire – Dwa Koła : Ul. Józefa 5 - ✆ 421 57 85 - daily 9am-6.30pm.

Ul. Dietla 77 - ✆ 422 04 25 - Mon-Fri 9am-6pm, Sat 10am-6pm.

Where to stay

With over four million visitors a year, Kraków is one of the first tourist destinations in Central Europe and finding accommodation is not always an easy task. One positive factor is that most addresses are located within the Old Town or in the immediate vicinity, but the value-for-money ratio (in relation to the local cost of living) is far from being always satisfactory. In the upper categories, even if rooms are comfortable and offer good facilities, they are often far from having the same charm as those in the Old Town.

In summer, there are several possibilities of finding seasonal accommodation, either in youth hostels, or in student hostels. Tourist offices will provide all the necessary information. A 2004 brochure entitled *Sleep cheap in Cracow* lists all types of budget accommodation in detail.

IN THE CENTRE

Waweltur – Ul. Pawia 8 - ✆ 422 19 21 - waweltur@wp.pl - www.waweltur.com.pl - Mon-Fri 8am-8pm (Nov-Jan 7pm), Sat 8am-2pm.

The town's tourist information and accommodation centre is a private agency situated opposite the station; it will find you a room in a private home (86 to 117 PLN) or an independent apartment with a kitchen (200 to 250 PLN depending on the location), that would never be more than a 15min-walk from the Rynek.

Youth hostel – Ul. Oleandry 4 - ✆ 633 88 22 fax 633 89 20 - schronisko@smkrakow.pl - www.smkrakow.pl - 20 PLN /pers. - ⌻ 6 PLN. This is the largest (360 beds) of the town's two permanent youth hostels (2km from the station, near the Cracovia Hotel). The other youth hostel is at Ul. Kościuski 88 in the Zwierzyniec district and there are also some ten private youth hostels.

Hotel Pokoje Gościnne SHERP – Ul. Floriańska 39 - ✆ 429 17 78 - info@hotel-sherp.com.pl - www.hotel-sherp.com.pl - 6 rooms - 210 PLN. This is not strictly speaking a hotel but a boarding-house (some services are not automatic: making the bed and supplying towels!) well situated and managed by an association of Polish architects. It occupies the upper floors of a fine historic building: the former apartments comprise units of two rooms with shared bathroom and kitchen. 240 PLN, breakfast included and served in Michalika's Den next door.

Pokoje Gościnne Wielopole – Ul. Wielopole 3 - ✆/fax422 14 75 - office@ wielopole.pl - www.wielopole.pl - 𝐏 - 12 rooms - 255 PLN - ⌻20 PLN. This very recent hotel situated on the outer edge of the Planty, not far from the Kazimierz district, has both the advantages and disadvantages of new accommodation. Plain, comfortable rooms, boasting standard contemporary furniture with very little charm.

Dom Polonii – Rynek Główny 14 - ✆ 428 04 60 - fax 422 43 55 - www. krakow.zaprasza.net/firma/pokoje/ dompolonii - 3 rooms - 235 PLN - ⌻17 PLN. It is difficult to find a more central place to stay: this apartment, located on the 3rd and top floor (no lift) of a fine building comprises three rooms, two of them overlooking the Rynek. A very sought-after apartment with a kitchen, two double rooms and a total of four beds; reserve well in advance.

Dom Gościnny Uniwersytetu Jagiellońskiego – Ul. Floriańska 49 - ✆/fax 421 12 25 - dguj@if.uj.edu.pl.pl - www.adm. uj.edu.pl - 23 rooms - 320 à 350 PLN ⌻. It is by no means surprising that the sprawling Jagiellonian University should be interested in providing accommodation! Situated in one of the major streets of the Old Town, the university's spacious rooms, most of them single, are not only intended to house teachers. Fine staircase but no lift. There is also an annexe (Bursa Pigonia) of 33 rooms, situated close to the Planty, at no 7a Garbarska Street (✆/fax 422 30 08).

Hotel Pollera – Ul. Szpitalna 30 - ✆422 10 44 - ✆/fax422 13 89 - rezerwacja@pollera. com.pl - www.pollera.com.pl - 𝐏 - 42 rooms - 345 PLN ⌻. Located near the Słowacki Theatre, opposite the House of the Cross, this hotel founded in 1834 by K Poller likes to remind its customers that it is one of Kraków's oldest hotels. Obviously resigned to being deprived of its past splendour, it does not however seem determined to erase completely the wear and tear caused by time and continues to maintain a fairly outdated style. The stained-glass windows in the staircase are the work of Wyspiański. The restaurant is as spacious as a ballroom.

Hotel Europejski – Ul. Lubicz 5 - ✆ 423 25 10 - fax 423 25 29 - he@he.pl - www.he.pl - 𝐏 - 49 rooms - 345 PLN ⌻. In high season, discounted price of 310 PLN for a minimum *stay of two nights*. This huge fin-de-siècle hotel, standing on the left as you come out of the railway station, tries as best it can to conceal its 120 years of existence. Endless corridors lead to standardized rooms (quieter at the back) and to rooms without bathroom at more reasonable prices. Inner courtyard turned into a summer garden.

Hotel Saski. *Ul. Sławkowska 3 – ☎421 42 22 - fax 421 48 30 - info@hotelsaski.com.pl - www.hotelsaski.com.pl - 62 rooms - 360 PLN* 🍽. Rather than dwell on the rooms themselves, one might prefer to enjoy everything that recalls the Belle-Époque, the presence of a liveried doorman, a fine hall with an antique lift still in operation, and a profusion of long corridors. Even though it may not be such good value for money as it was some years ago (one can always book a room without bathroom at 250 PLN), the outdated style still prevails.

Hotel Wawel-Tourist. *Ul. Poselska 22 – ☎ 424 13 00 - fax 424 13 33 - hotel@wawel-tourist.pl - www.wawel-tourist.pl - ▣ - 48 rooms - 380 PLN* 🍽. Located in a quiet street south-east of the Rynek. Partially restored in 1995 in contemporary neo-Art-Nouveau style, this hotel has retained very few original Secession-style features from the National Hotel which succeeded the Black-Eye Inn and occupied the premises from the mid-19C to the early 20C. Customers can choose between retro-style rooms and more modern but also more expensive ones, situated in the new part built onto the back of the hotel.

Hotel Wit Stwosz – *Ul. Mikołajska 28 - ☎ 429 60 26 - fax 429 61 39 - hotel@wit-stwosz.com.pl - www.wit-stwosz.com.pl - ▣ - rooms - 380 PLN - 🍽27 PLN*. This 16C house belonging to St Mary's Church (hence the name of the hotel) is situated in a peaceful street east of the Mały Rynek; it provides a refined setting to the hotel's comfortable and elegant rooms. The 4th-floor rooms are slightly smaller and less expensive.

Hotel Polski – *Ul. Pijarska 17 - ☎/fax 422 11 44 - hotel.polski@podorlem.com.pl - www.podorlem.com.pl - ▣ - 49 rooms - 399 PLN* 🍽. Established near the Florian Gate, inside three old houses recently returned to their former owners, the Czartoryski ducal family, who acquired them in 1913, the White Eagle Hotel is adjacent to the Museum-Palace of the same name. The communal parts are more attractive than the rooms, a little expensive and yet rather ordinary.

Hotel Francuski – *Ul. Pijarska 13 – ☎422 51 22 - fax 422 52 70 - francuski@orbis.pl - www.orbis.pl - ▣ - 42 rooms - 580 PLN - 🍽38 PLN*. This hotel, jewel of the Orbis chain, was, when it was founded in 1912, one of the top luxury hotels in Europe. Completely brought up to modern standards of comfort in 1991, the French Hotel still retains its Belle-Époque palace atmosphere.

Hotel Copernicus – *Ul. Kanonicza 16 - ☎424 34 00 - fax 424 34 05 - copernicus@hotel.com.pl - www. hotel.com.pl - 29 rooms - 850 PLN* 🍽. This luxury establishment concealed behind an austere Gothic façade along Kraków's oldest street, is undoubtedly one of the finest hotels in town. The lovely atrium-style courtyard features wooden galleries leading to the rooms. The swimming pool inside the old Gothic vaulted cellars is a must. Bar on the roof terrace offering a fine view of the castle.

Les Couleurs café

R. Mattes / MICHELIN

IN ZWIERZYNIEC

Pod Kopcem Hotel FM – *Al. Waszyngtona - ☎427 03 55 - fax 427 01 01 - hotel@hotel.fm.pl - www.hotel.fm.pl - ▣ I - 390 PLN* 🍽. An unusual location inside the former military bastions surrounding the Kościuszko Mound, in the Zwierzyniec district (3km/bus 100). The premises are shared by the hotel and the headquarters of the RMF commercial radio, which owns the hotel. It is not more expensive to book a room with a view of Kraków. Discounts at weekends.

IN KAZIMIERZ

Klezmer-Hois – *Ul. Szeroka 6 - ☎/fax 411 12 45 - klezmer@klezmer.pl - www.klezmer.pl - 11 rooms - 320PLN* 🍽. At once hotel, restaurant, art gallery and concert venue, the Klezmer is housed in former Jewish ritual baths located in a fine building on the corner of the wide Szeroka Street. Lovely spacious rooms with a pleasant 30s' atmosphere. The restaurant is recommended and the terrace is very peaceful.

Hotel Alef – *Ul. Szeroka 17 - ☎/fax 421 38 70 - alef@alef.pl - www.alef.pl - 5 rooms - 355 PLN* 🍽. Situated in the middle of the "Wide Street", opposite the old Jewish cemetery, Hotel Alef, housed on three floors, offers five very spacious rooms filled with furniture showing the patina of age, which conveys a pleasant nostalgia for the pre-war period. The undeniably bohemian atmosphere is recreated by a profusion of antiques, as it is in the ground-floor restaurant where the service is casual, sometimes almost offhand. The hotel annexe, located at Ul. Św. Agnieszki 5, has more ordinary rooms (285 PLN).

Eating out

The streets of the old town and of the suburbs boast many eateries of all kinds, each more appealing than the other. Most of them apply similar, generally affordable prices. One way of keeping one's budget under control is to have lunch in one of the popular canteens that still exist. These milk bars would bankrupt traditional restaurants if they didn't close so early (before 8pm). For a modest price of between 10 and 20 PLN, you can have a simple meal – among Polish people – consisting of soup or a starter, a copious main dish and a traditional fruit syrup.

IN THE CENTRE

Bar Mleczny Restauracja Pod Temidą – *Ul. Grodzka 43 - ⌐ - daily 9am-8pm - 10 PLN.*

Undoubtedly the most sought-after self-service milk bar in town, the favourite haunt of students of the Art History Institute and of the Jagiellonian University's nearby Law faculty. A meal consisting of a salad, a main dish and a fruit syrup will hardly ever cost more than 10 PLN.

Bar Kuchcik – *Ul. Jagiellońska 12 - ⌐ - Mon-Fri 10am-6pm, Sat 10am-4pm - 12 PLN.* Close to the Collegium Maius of the Jagiellonian University, this establishment features a plain, unassuming white room which boasts the significant advantage for a milk bar of having a menu in English. And the food is excellent as the house logo suggests. It is also possible to have breakfast here.

Jadłodajnia U Pani Stasi – *Ul. Mikołajska 18 - Mon-Fri 12.30-5pm. Closed July - ⌐ -20 PLN.* Located on the north side of the Mały Rynek, inside the courtyard (accessible via the passageway adjoining the Cyclope Pizzeria) of the "Pod Trzema Lipami" House. This very authentic Kraków eatery is housed in a small vaulted room crowded with regular customers at lunchtime. Sit down before ordering and pay on your way out. Menu in English with a wide choice of "special dishes of the day". *Pierogi* are popular; they go well with a glass of traditional fruit syrup. Prompt service (past the queuing stage) and extremely fresh food.

Bar Grodzki – *Ul. Grodzka 47 - ⌐ 422 68 07 - Mon-Sat 9am-7pm, Sun 10am-7pm - ⌐ - 20 PLN.* Slightly more exclusive than its rival in the same street, this milk bar –

locally called *jadłodajnia* ("dish-of-the-day" restaurant) - is one of the reliable addresses in the district. Menu in English on the wall. Good traditional Polish cuisine including *placki* (potato pancakes covered with goulash or mushrooms) which are particularly appreciated.

Kuchnia Staropolska U Babci Maliny – *Ul. Sławkowska 17 - ⌐ 422 76 01 - Mon-Fri 11am-7pm, Sat-Sun noon-6pm - 10 PLN.* This milk bar gets the top prize for decoration. Fake windows with shutters turned on the inside and the illusion is complete: you get the impression that you are on the terrace whereas you are really in the cellars of the Polish Academy of Arts and Science. Trust your instinct or let yourself be persuaded to try one of the day's specials which are popular with workers, employees, students and retired people alike. Go in then follow the corridor to the glass door and walk down the C staircase.

Różowy Słoń – *Ul. Straszewskiego 23 - ⌐ - Mon-Sat 9am-8pm, Sun 11am-8pm - 20PLN.* Facing the Collegium Novum of the Jagiellonian University, across the green expanse of the Planty, the Pink Elephant is the exact opposite of other traditional milk bars. A kind of original "salad bar/bistro" with walls entirely covered with drawings from American comic strips.

Restauracja Orient Ekspress – *Ul. Stolarska 13 - ⌐ 422 66 72 - daily noon-11pm - 60 PLN.* Climb on board the mythical train for a meal in this restaurant named in 2004 by the Newsweek Polska magazine as the best eatery in town, all categories taken together. You will no doubt prefer to sit in one of the five compartments of the carriage (reservations advisable) rather than in the waiting room located on the right. You will then embark on a gastronomic trip through the European cuisine of the Paris-Istambul journey: excellent and not so expensive as one might fear. Terrace in the inner courtyard.

Wiśniowy Sad – *Ul. Grodzka 33 - ⌐ 430 21 11 - Mon-Thu 10am-10pm, Fri-Sun 10am-midnight - 50 PLN.* The most "melancholic" of Kraków's cafés, in fact a Russian café-cum-restaurant, pervaded by an undeniable nostalgia. A single room where trivial details such as place mats, a samovar, a piano, a mirror, an old column set in the wall and appropriate music are all it takes to recreate a Chekhovian atmosphere. This will hardly surprise you when you know that the translation of the name of the place suggests *The Cherry Orchard*. No smoking.

Restauracja Morskie Oko – *Pl. Szczepański 8 - ⌐ 431 24 23 - daily noon-midnight.*

From the street, one gets the impression that the "Eye of the Sea" (A lake of the

Tatras region) is totally empty. The action takes place in the basement, in a dozen successive vaulted cellars, where the numerous customers sit at long rustic tables to enjoy the colours and flavours of the Tatras mountains. Good to know: on Sundays and Mondays there is no live traditional music.

Restauracja Balaton – *Ul. Grodzka 37 - ℘ 422 04 69 - daily 9am-10pm - 40 PLN.* A restaurant specialising in Polish-style Magyar gastronomy. Opened in 1969, this gastronomic establishment (which refers to the large Hungarian lake of the same name) is, as always, a reliable address. The menu features copious helpings, the service is unrefined but very efficient. Inexpensive and nourishing. In addition, the restaurant offers its guests the possibility of enjoying Hungarian wine instead of Polish beer for a change.

Restauracja Smak Ukraiński – *Ul. Kanonicza 15 - ℘ 421 92 94 - daily 11am-9pm.*

Placed under the aegis of the adjoining Włodzimierza (Vladimir) Foundation, this restaurant housed in two lovely small cellars, plainly decorated, is mainly devoted to promoting Ukrainian cuisine. Don't forget to have a glass of *bras* (3 PLN), an unusual beverage made from soaked bread, which will remind you of a most famous American drink. In summer one can enjoy the coolness of the indoor terrace. It is a shame that the service is so inefficient and that dinner is served so early.

Music Club & Restaurant Kryjówka – *Ul. Sławkowska 11 - ℘ 431 27 19 - daily noon-2am - 40 PLN.* Gastronomy is out of the question in this fine vaulted cellar furnished with large wooden tables placed one against the other, where perfect strangers eat at the same table; people come here to listen to music (not before 9.30 or 10pm) while they have a meal, rather than the opposite.

Gospoda C. K. Dezerter – *Ul. Bracka 6 - ℘ 422 79 31 - daily 11am-11pm - 50 PLN.* For once you won't have to go down into a cellar; this establishment located at street level consists of a succession of three long rooms: the yellow walls are decorated with discoloured photographs illustrating military themes of Austro-Hungarian inspiration. In the kitchen, modern utensils are used to prepare traditional rather cheap dishes from Galicia.

Restauracja Pod Aniołami – *Ul. Grodzka 35 - ℘ 421 39 99 - daily1-11pm - 100PLN.* This restaurant called "Under the Angels" is situated along the Royal Way in a 13C building which, for 300 years housed goldsmiths and their workshops. The small cellars boasting an attractive blend of stone, brick and nice rustic furniture in light-coloured wood have more charm than the garden-courtyard despite the fact that it is decorated with a mosaic mural fountain. A large staff is employed to serve traditional Polish dishes, rather refined but also more expensive than elsewhere.

IN KAZIMIERZ

Chłopskie Jadło – *Ul. Agnieszki 1 - ℘ 421 85 20 - daily noon-midnight - 60 PLN.* The wood-and-earth interior design creates the atmosphere of a mountain inn of the Tatras region. More than a restaurant, this is a real chain paradoxically advocating the authenticity of rural cuisine in mountain areas. This gastronomic institution, always filled with large tourist parties, now owns nine establishments in the country, including two more in Kraków's town centre, along Grodzka and Św. Jana Streets. Huge helpings, omnipresent background music, overwhelmed and not always attentive service.

Once Upon a Time in Kazimierz – *Ul. Szeroka 1 - ℘ 421 12 17 - daily noon-11pm.*

One might reasonably hesitate before going into what looks like four old Jewish workshops from pre-war Kraków, each one with a sign bearing the name of its owner. Inside, the former shops, a general store, a joiner's, a tailor's and a grocer's, have been joined to form the dining area of a restaurant recreating the presumably typical atmosphere of Kazimierz in the past. In fact, the place is obviously intended for tourists yet not at all unpleasant. The menu offers traditional Jewish dishes such as the excellent *Czulent* and the famous stuffed carp.

Restaurant Once Upon a time in Kazimierz

B. Brillon / MICHELIN

Ariel – *Ul. Szeroka 18 - ℘ 421 79 20 - daily 10am-midnight.*

This place is on the way up. It occupies two buildings, one wing being devoted to a private art gallery, the other, symmetrical, housing a café and a restaurant where concerts of Yiddish music are given every evening from 8pm onwards. Good Jewish cooking.

Taking a break

Restauracja U Literatów – *Ul. Kanonicza 7 - ℘ - daily 10am-10pm*. Concealed behind two magnificent old doors, in the street which has the most aristocratic and clerical atmosphere in town, is one of Kraków's most pastoral cafés. You will love, in particular, its charming courtyard, partly paved and partly laid out as a garden (don't pay any attention to the Jardiland-style plastic furniture which is fortunately green), totally cut off from the city. The establishment also owns a restaurant.

Kawiarna Noworolski – *Rynek Główny 1 ℘/fax 422 47 71 - Mar-Nov 9am-11pm, Dec-Feb 9am-9pm*. One of the town's elegant historic cafés, inaugurated in 1910 on the ground floor of the Cloth Hall, close to St Adalbert's Church. Go into one of the restored Art Nouveau drawing rooms – regularly visited by local ladies – or on the terrace, the ideal place from which to gaze at the hustle and bustle of the Rynek.

Kawiarna Jama Michalika – *Ul. Floriańska 45 - ℘ - 422 15 61 - daily 10am-11pm*. Undoubtedly the most famous café in town, if not in all Poland. An awe-inspiring café to be considered like a real museum on account of the numerous works of art decorating its walls. Vaulted rooms plunged in semi darkness, which conceal the interior atmosphere from the street. Cloakroom compulsory. No smoking.

Loch Camelot – *Ul. Św. Tomasza 17 - ℘ 421 01 23 - daily 9am-midnight*. This lovely, somewhat Bohemian café, which attempts to perpetuate the cabaret spirit (Loch Camelot) in its own cellars, is mostly interesting for its large and pleasant terrace recessed on the side of the small St John's Church, whose position out of alignment with the axis of the road creates a fine perspective. Tea (*7 PLN*) or coffee (*6 PLN*), but it is also possible to have a snack, in particular salads and delicious crumbles (*szarlotka*). Some foreign newspapers are at the customers' disposal.

Sklep z kawą «Pożegnanie z Afryką» – *Ul. Św. Tomasza 21 - daily 10am-10pm*. This fine café has, since 1996, been exclusively devoted to... coffee! One can watch the making (with spring water!) of the divine beverage in front of an alignment of small burners. A decor of old postcards and, of course, of old coffee pots and coffee grinders. A boutique devoted to the black nectar occupies the recesses of the place.

Café Larousse – *Ul. Św. Tomasza 22 - Mon-Sat 9am-9pm, Sun 10am-9pm*. A tiny café with only four tables and walls decorated with yellowing plates from the famous illustrated dictionary (yet the kind owner does not know French). Good coffee served with small home-made meringues (5 PLN).

Bunkier Cafe. *Pl. Szczepański 3a - ℘ 431 05 85*. When the weather is fine, the concrete Arts Bunker (*Bunkier Sztuki*) opens its greenhouse to the public; it is a pleasant urban observation post offering a front-seat view of the comings and goings along the green belt of the Planty. Amazing entirely blue café inside the art gallery (admission charge).

On the town

IN THE CENTRE

Bastylia – *Ul. Stolarska 3 - ℘ 431 02 21 - Sun-Tue 1pm-1am, Wed-Sat 1pm-3am*. The illusion is perfect yet this prison never housed any prisoner and is a pure product of a designer's imagination. Since customers have to play the role of prison guards, look inside the cells through the peephole. Charming barbecue-restaurant on the ground floor.

CK Browar – *Ul. Podwale 6-7 - ℘ 429 25 05 - daily 9am- last customers*. Beer lovers should not miss the large cellars of this "royal and imperial" (CK) brewer's where four kinds of home-made piwo are available, either light or brown, from 11.5° to 14.5°. The establishment, which is sought after by young Kraków residents who have been meeting there in large numbers since 1996, is also a restaurant until 10pm.

Café Pauza – *Ul. Floriańska 18 - Mon-Sat 10am-midnight, Sun noon-midnight*. For once, you are not expected to bury yourself in a cellar but to climb the steps to Paradise (take a look, it's written) in order to get to the trendiest bar of the moment, where all the expatriates in town like to meet.

Pub Pod Strzechą – *Ul. Pędzichów 3 - daily 2pm-4am* This slightly out-of-the-way establishment with no exterior sign is housed in a cellar featuring cob walls and reminiscent of African huts; devoted to black music, in particular reggae, it is guaranteed to be almost free of tourists.

IN KAZIMIERZ

Les Couleurs café – *Ul. Estery 10 ℘ 429 42 70 - Mon-Fri 7-2am, Sat 8-2am, Sun 9-2am*. Blue, white and red, these are the dominant colours in this bar where everything is done to evoke France.

Alchemia – *Plac Nowy - ℘ 428 47 80 - daily 10-4am*. Strange atmosphere in this succession of four rooms, each more mysterious and obscure than the other (the last one should be mentioned for it suggests a disused kitchen of former times). This extremely mysterious place, where electricity has been banned and modern facilities disregarded, is only lit by candlelight.

Café Singer – *Ul. Estery 20 - daily 9-3am*. Neither karaoke bar, nor tribute to the famous Yiddish writer, this café celebrates the famous American sewing machines fitted with a shelf on which fabric was originally supposed to rest and now convenient for holding glasses.

Shopping

Galeria Plakatu Kraków – *Ul. Stolarska 8/10 - ☎ 421 26 40 - www.postergallery. art.pl - Mon-Fri 11am-6pm, Sat 11am-2pm.* Polish posters do not have a museum of their own (only a gallery), worthy of this art form in which the Poles excel.

If you are fond of **handicrafts** you will enjoy walking among the stalls located in the central aisle of the Cloth Hall.

Do not leave town without having tasted an **obwarzanki**, a ring-shaped bretzel dotted with various kinds of seeds, sold in the street by hawkers.

Festive events

Easter Fair on the Rynek and Emmaus Fair in Zwierzyniec on Easter Monday.

March: Rękawka Festivities, near Krakus Mound.

Avril: International "Jazz in Kraków" Festival.

May: Kraków Film Festival - Wawel's Dragon Festival.

June: Town Festival (5 june) - Lajkonik Parade - Festival of Jewish Culture - Short Film International Festival.

July : Street Theatre International Festival - Rozstaje Traditional Music Festival - Summer Jazz Festival.

September-mid-October: Jewish Culture Month.

October: International Festival of Ancient Music.

November: Jazz in Kraków for All Saints Day

December: Christmas Crib (szopki) Competition.

Auschwitz Concentration Camp★★★

Oświęcim

MAP OF POLAND C4 – WOJEWÓDZTWO OF LITTLE POLAND

Nothing predestined the small provincial town of Oświęcim to become – after being incorporated by the Nazis into their Third Reich under the German name it assumed for six years – synonymous with Nazi barbarism and a symbol of the Holocaust. Auschwitz, two syllables which evoke the site of the most extensive mass murder ever perpetrated in the history of humanity. Today, Auschwitz is more of a memorial than a museum and, with over 500 000 visitors a year and over 30 million in all since its creation on 14 June 1947, it is one of the most visited sites in Poland.

▶ **Getting your bearings** – 60km west of Kraków (one hour by car).
To get there by public transport from Kraków, it is better to take a regional bus (line no 6 - 9 PLN) in front of the central station rather than take the train which stops a few kms from the site. Journey time: 1hr 30min.

🕓 **Planning you visit** – The two camps of Auschwitz and Birkenau are 3km apart and form one single museum. In order to appreciate all it entails, it is necessary to visit both sites, one after the other. Allow (depending on opening times) a morning or an afternoon starting with the much longer tour of Auschwitz I. The visit of Birkenau, which does not include an exhibition, is shorter.

Because Auschwitz is a memorial and a fortiori because it is a huge cemetery and not just a tourist sight, the emotion aroused by a visit to these concentration camps is strong and often trying. Bear that in mind if you intend to take your children with you. Officially, the visit is not recommended for children under 13, and it is essential to prepare all youngsters for the visit with special care and attention.

Background

A vast cemetery without graves – During the tour of what was the largest Nazi concentration camp and also the largest cemetery in the history of humanity, one question comes to mind but remains unanswered: how was the greatest human extermination ever planned in the history of humanity able to take place? That question is followed by another which today requires a more urgent answer: sixty years after the events, how can we continue to bear witness? Concurrently with the work of the historians, the accounts given by the survivors, inevitably decreasing in number, must be relayed by new generations bound by the duty to keep alive the memory of these events and to go on repeating certain facts and figures linked with this place of evil memory.

Most historians now agree that, between 1940 and 1945, the Nazis deported to Auschwitz at least 1 100 000 Jews, 150 000 Poles, 23 000 Tziganes, 15 000 Russian prisoners of war and 25 000 members of other nations ; in all, 28 different nationalities were concerned. There were Jews from many countries, but Hungarian Jews, believed to number 438 000, formed the largest group, followed by Polish Jews and French Jews. Around 900 000 Jews , i.e. 70 to 75% of all deported Jews were never recorded but led straight to the gas chambers as soon as they got off the death trains. Only 400 000 prisoners were recorded (including 200 000 Jews) and 60 000 of them were still alive at the end of the war. As the Soviet Army approached, the prisoners who were able to walk were taken on "death marches" deep inside the Reich. When the camp was liberated on 27 January 1945, the soldiers of the Red Army only found 7 000 survivors including 300 children in a state of extreme weakness.

Sixty years later, on 27 January 2005, many heads of State and of government met in Auschwitz, together with the last survivors, for a solemn commemoration. Every year since 1988 a "March of the Living" has taken place with the participation of young Jews from every country as a tribute to the victims of the Holocaust.

Things to see

State Museum Auschwitz-Birkenau (Państowe Muzeum Auschwitz-Birkenau w Oświęcimiu)

Ul. Więźniów Oświęcimia 20, 32-603 Oświęcim - ℰ 48 (0)33 843 20 22 - www.auschwitz. org.pl - daily Dec-Feb 8am-3pm, Mar, Nov 8am-4pm, Apr, Oct 8am-5pm, May, Sep 8am-4pm, Jun-Aug 8am-7pm - closed 1 Jan, 25 Dec and Easter Sun - supervised parking area (7 PLN).

Admission to both sites is entirely free. However, there is a charge for the guide service, recommended for a better understanding of the functionning of the camp. You can book a guide by phone +548 (0)33 843 20 22, by fax +548 (0)33 843 22 27, by email dyspozytor-niia@pro.one.pl or on location at the information desk of Auschwitz I Museum.

Before the visit, it is advisable to see the horrifying 15min documentary (charge) about the liberation of the camp by Soviet troops (depending on the days, the showing is at 2 and 3.30pm in Polish, at 3pm in English - 3.50 PLN). In addition, for a better appreciation of the visit, it is recommended to buy a little booklet in English, which offers a map of the site and provides a great deal of interesting explanation.

The *Konzentrationslager Auschwitz* was at once a prison camp, a concentration camp, a work camp and a death camp where the Nazis locked up Jews, Tziganes, homosexuals, communists, members of the resistance, political prisoners, Russian prisoners of war, members of the Polish intellectual elite, priests, Jehovah witnesses, prostitutes and common criminals. At one time, Auschwitz comprised three main camps: Auschwitz I, Auschwitz II-Birkenau, Auschwitz III-Monowitz, as well as over 40 secondary camps scattered throughout the region. Today, the first two camps form the memorial-museum, set up as a State Museum in 1947 following a decision of the Polish parliament, and have been listed as one of UNESCO's Cultural and Natural World Heritage sites since 1979.

Auschwitz I

Established in former disused barracks of the Polish army, the camp was built in April-May 1940 and received its first inmates, 728 Polish political prisoners transferred from Tarnów, in June 1940. It was here that in September 1941, the Nazis for the first time tested a pesticide gas on 850 Poles and Russians, which soon brought considerable wealth to its German manufacturer, Zyklon B. The number of prisoners, many incarcerated for political reasons, oscillated between 12 000 and 16 000 with a peak of 20 000 in 1942 (the year that saw the arrival of women) and a total of 70 000 prisoners died here, some in the gas chamber and the crematorium which functioned in 1941 and 1942. Practically preserved in the state the Nazis left it in 1945, it now houses the main part of the exhibition.

The tour of the camp as such starts when you go through the famous **gate** surmounted by a pernicious inscription stating *"Arbeit macht frei"* (Work makes you free). Standing among lines of poplars, inside the enclosure surrounded by watchtowers and barbed wire, are the red-brick walls of **28 identical blocks** lined on both sides of two central alleys. It would take you several hours to make a careful and exhaustive visit of all the

Entrance to the Auschwitz Concentration Camp

J.-F. Breuiller / MICHELIN

accessible blocks. Start with those at the back, situated along the second alley and devoted to the **so-called general exhibitions** (**Block 4**: Shoah, **Block 5**: Material proof of the crime, **Block 6**: The prisoners' daily life, **Block 7**: Accommodation and sanitary conditions).

On the right at the end of the alley stands the medical experiments and sterilisation block followed by the **Death Block** (no 11), no doubt the most sinister of them all, a section of the camp where obstinate elements were submitted to the most cruel treatment. Between the two, the courtyard was closed in by the Death Wall where thousands of innocents were executed.

From there, go back to the first alley lined with **blocks devoted to national exhibitions.** On the other side of the wall, in line with the central blocks, stood the warehouse containing the stocks of Zyklon B and the prisoners' personal effects confiscated on arrival.

Apart from the France/Belgium Block, most but not all exhibitions have captions in English (next to the national language). Some of the blocks have been equipped with effective, high-quality scenography and provide well-written descriptive texts, although in any event the horrors related in all of the blocks are beyond comparison.

Bloc no 21 attributed to France and Belgium présents a particularly interesting exhibition dedicated to the memory of French deportees. Centred round a few specific cases, it deals with precise examples of deported men and women, assimilated Jews, recent immigrants or political opponents, such as Pierre Masse, Charlotte Delbo, Jean Lemberger, Georgy Halpern, Sarah Beznos. Note that out of some 76 000 Jews who were deported from France (including 69 000 to Auschwitz and over 10 000 children), only 2 500 (i.e. 3%) came back, out of 3 000 members of the Resistance only 969 survived and out of the 20 943 Tziganes sent to Auschwitz 145 had French nationality. Particularly moving is the room displaying photographs of children and teenagers, with short biographical captions stating where they were born, where they lived and when they were deported.

Equally remarkable, the **Hungarian Block (no 20)** takes you, during your visit, along particularly suggestive rail tracks. The **Dutch Block (no 21)**, on the other hand, presents a surprising exhibition with a minimalist scenography against a luminous , clinically white background, which creates an almost serene, reverential atmosphere. When we visited Auschwitz, the Russian block was awaiting a new exhibition. Located in the south-west corner, **Block no 27** is devoted to Jewish martyrology and struggle. Finally, the itinerary leads to the end of the alley on the left, where the gas chamber and the crematorium, converted in 1943 into an anti-aircraft bunker, are located. The gallows nearby was used in 1947 for the public hanging of Rudolf Höss, the first commander of Auschwitz Concentration Camp.

Auschwitz II - Birkenau

A free shuttle links the two camps every hour from 10.30am between 15 April and 31 November. The same shuttle goes at 3.30pm to the Jewish Centre Museum situated in the old synagogue of Oświęcim town centre.

Although Birkenau does not, for most people, have the same sinister ring to it as Auschwitz, it is nevertheless in this camp that the extermination first and foremost of the Jews but also of the Tziganes was systematically planned; it is also from the visit of this camp that one derives the strongest and most harrowing impression. Created ex nihilo in October 1941, 3km from the main camp, near the small Polish village of Brzezinka (Birkenau) meaning "small meadow with birch trees", it looks less like a concentration camp than a camp intended to implement the final solution. Tragically famous is the Death gate beyond which the rail tracks, which were linked in 1944 to the railway network just like those of an ordinary industrial site, enter this terminus of horrors.

Start by climbing to the top of the watchtower above the entrance gate to get an insight into the unbelievable extent of the camp (2x2.5km). Out of the 300 barracks which, in August 1944, housed over 90 000 prisoners, only 45 brick ones and 22 wooden ones were preserved but the outline of the area on which the others stood is marked on the ground. There is no museum here, just a deeply moving site for visitors to wander round.

Walk beside the very long unloading ramp to the **International Monument to Victims of Fascism** inaugurated in 1967. Inscribed in 21 languages, the same commemorative plaque pleads against such odious barbarism ever being repeated. All around are the ruined remains of the crematoria and gas chambers, as well as the ponds into which human ashes were spilled. The creation of the four complexes including gas chambers and crematoria began in 1942 and they were fully operational until the SS blew them up with dynamite in 1944 as the allied armies were approaching, in order to erase all traces of their crimes. Beforehand, on 7 October, a Sonderkommando group, consisting of prisoners whose task was to evacuate the bodies from the gas chambers, had rebelled and blown up crematorium no IV.

Nearby

Auschwitz Jewish Center (Centrum Żydowskie w Oświęcimiu)

Plac Ks. Jana Skarbka 3 32-600 Oświęcim. Located north of the Rynek of the old town of Oświęcim, 3km from the camp - ℘(33) 844 70 02 - www.ajcf.org - daily except Sat and Jewish holidays Apr-Sep 8.30am-8pm, Oct-Mar 8.30am-6pm - 5 PLN.

This museum, which counterbalances the emotional impact caused by the harshness of the camps, aims at providing an insight into the life of the former Jewish community of the town of Oświęcim, in particular during the first half of the 20C. En 1939, before the tragic episode of the Shoah took place and the long-standing Jewish presence in Poland was practically annihilated from one day to the next, the Jews accounted for some 7 000 of the 12 300 inhabitants of the town, i.e. 59% of the total population. It is in this town, considered before the war as a "Jewish town", that were produced famous spirits such as Pesachówa (Pesah Vodka), a product of the renowned Habelfeld Company (the ruins of the former factory can still be seen on the way to the Jewish cemetery along Dąbrowskiego Street).

The museum is housed in the only Jewish building remaining in the town, the synagogue of the Society for the Study of the Mishnah (Chevra Lomdei Mishnayot), a centre of Talmudic studies and its adjoining synagogue completed in 1930 and used as a place of worship until 1939. Devastated by the Nazis who burned it down in March 1941, it was later converted into an arsenal while the Jews were "invited" to leave town and settle in the nearby ghettos of Będzin, Chrzanów and Sosnowiec, from where most of them were subsequently sent to suffer the tragic end that we know. Only about 70 Jews survived the war and most of them emigrated as soon as the war ended in 1945. Recovered by the Jewish community of Bielsko-Biała in 1997, as part of the restitution of the Jewish heritage voted by the neo-communist government, the synagogue was ceded to this foundation based in New York which took care of the restoration and now looks after it. Following the disappearance in May 2000 of the town's last practising Jewish resident, the municipality now makes a point of asserting the continuity of Jewish presence in Oświęcim.

Do not miss the short 14 min documentary (in English), which presents the moving accounts given by Jewish emigrants evoking the Oshpitzin (Auschwitz in Yiddish) of their childhood.

Photographs of prisoners, Auschwitz

The Polish Jura★★
From Kraków to Częstochowa
MAP OF POLAND C3– WOJEWÓDZTWO OF LITTLE POLAND

Short grass and fir trees grow here among twisted limestone rocks scattered around the hiils sometimes crowned with the ruins of former castles. At the extremity of this Polish Jura with its fairy-tale landscape, not far from Kraków, the smallest of Polish national parks nestles inside a deep, remote vale.

▶ **Getting your bearings** – The Ojców Park is located less than 30km north-west of Kraków and the Polish Jura extends 80km further north to Częstochowa.

👁 **Not to be missed** – Rambles through the enchanting Ojców landscape.

🕐 **Planning your visit** – Count half a day to cross the Jura, stopping to visit a few castles along the way. Don't hesitate to spend the night in the Ojców Park. There are delightful rambles to be made early in the morning.

👫 **With your children** – The tour of the caves situated inside Ojców Park is bound to impress them.

Background

The rugged limestone landscapes of the Polish Jura lend themselves to legends which thrive in the thousands of caves and feed on the extravagant shapes of the rocks conveniently transformed into petrified armies and magic dens. It is also an area where History clings to the craggy summits. When Poland was again partitioned in the 14C, the region became a border area which Kazimierz the Great promptly protected by building a series of castles and eagles' nests now in ruins.

Ojców National Park★★ (Ojcowski Park Narodowy)

Some 20km north-west of Kraków. From Kraków, the park is easily accessible via road 778 as far as the village of Skała then along road 773 which runs through the park.

The Prądnik and Sąspówka rivers meet deep inside a valley offering a unique dream-like landscape which lends itself to the most enjoyable rambles. Walking and biking are the best means of getting around to explore this 21sq km park, the smallest in Poland, crisscrossed by five footpaths and four cycle tracks. As you venture along small paths, through the undergrowth and along the riverbanks, you will discover a limestone landscape with no fewer than 400 caves and rock formations with mythical names such as Hercules' Club, the Kraków Gate or the Panieńskie. All around, the forest reigns supreme. The topography accounts for the microclimate which favours a rich variety of plants, including mountain species, and of wildlife, in particular deer and bats, the emblem of the park.

The southern part of the park

It is possible to park the car in Ojców 's vast parking area and from there to visit the main sights on foot via marked footpaths (map available).

Ojców Castle (Zamek w Ojcowie)★

Apr-May and Sep daily 10am-4.45pm, until 5.45pm in Jun-Jul, 3.45pm in Oct and 2.45pm in Nov. 1.65 PLN.

Built in the 14C by King Kazimierz the Great, this castle was the last defence structure before Kraków. The ruins stand on a rocky spur which seems inacces-sible. The fortified main gate, the first floor of which houses a model of the castle in its heyday, leads into the outer bailey where traces of the walls are vis-ible. Note the ruins of the keep and the partially filled-in well, once 40m deep.

Go through Ojców where there are hotels, restaurants and shops.

L. Gontier / MICHELIN

Pieskowa Skała Castle

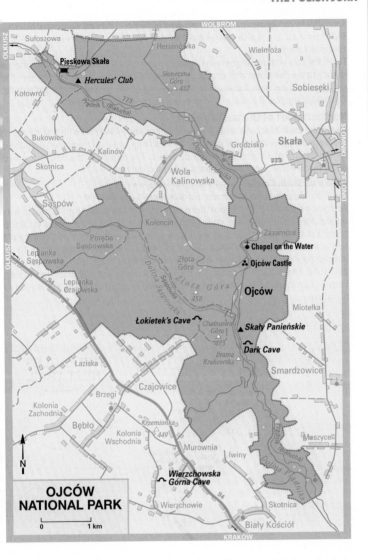

Chapel on the Water (Kaplica na Wodzie) – *Accessible via a footpath starting from the Ojców parking area; allow 10min on foot. The chapel is open for Sunday mass at 8 and 10.30am and at 6pm.*

It was built in 1901 across the River Prądnik following a law which forbade the construction of places of worship on Ojców land... but not on the water.

Footpaths with blue and green markings lead to the caves past the **Skały Panieńskie** boulders which are said to be nuns petrified by God to save them from the Tatars.

Łokietek's Cave (Jaskinia Łokietka) – *Via the footpath with blue markings (45min one way)*. The path runs along the road then through the Kraków Gate (Brama Krakowska) and across the wooded hills.

The cave *(open daily Apr and Nov 9am-3.30pm, May-Aug until 6.30pm, Sep until 5.30pm and Oct until 4.30pm. 6.50/4.30 PLN . Tours start every 20min)* is closed by a railing decorated with a motif recalling a story connected with the place. According to this legend, the web of a spider hid the future king Władisław Łokietek fleeing from the Czech King Wacław II. The 320m long cave consists of several chambers, each named after a room of the cold (7°C) and damp residence of the exiled sovereign.

Dark Cave (Jaskinia Ciemna) – *Via the footpath with green markings (45min one way). Open daily May-Oct 11am-5.15pm. 5.50/3.20 PLN. Tours start every 20min.*

Evidence of human occupation in prehistoric times was found in this cave.

Wierzchowska Górna Cave (Jaskinia Wierzchowska Górna)

Accessible by car; located a few km south-west of the park and well-signposted from the E40. Open daily Apr, Sep-Oct 9am-4pm, May-Aug 9am-5pm, Nov 9am-3pm. 12/10 PLN. Tours start every 20min.

This is the most interesting cave in the area. Over a distance of 370m, the visit offers a chance to see chambers with evocative names: the ballroom, the ossuary (where the remains of a bear were found). Fine concretions such as that of the Wizard's castle. The man is supposed to have lived here during the Neolithic period.

Northern part of the park (by car)

Hercules' Club (Maczuga Herkulesa)★owes its name to a wizard who is said to have challenged the devil to topple the rock. The challenge obviously remained unfulfilled for the delight of amateurs of freaks of nature. The outline of the best-preserved castle in the Polish Jura can be glimpsed behind the rock.

Pieskowa Skała Castle (Zamek Pieskowa Skała)★★
Mon-Thu 10am-3pm, Fri 9am-noon, Sat-Sun 10am-5pm. 10/7 PLN.
Perched on a hillside at the northern extremity of the park, the 14C castle was remodelled in Renaissance style in the 16C. From that period, it has retained a system of fortifications as well as a magnificent high inner courtyard surrounded on each level by arcaded galleries. It is now a museum with an impressive collection of works from the Middle Ages to the 20C, illustrating, in particular, the Italian and Spanish Baroque style; note also Aubusson tapestries, Empire furniture of Egyptian inspiration and a set of German Art Nouveau furniture.

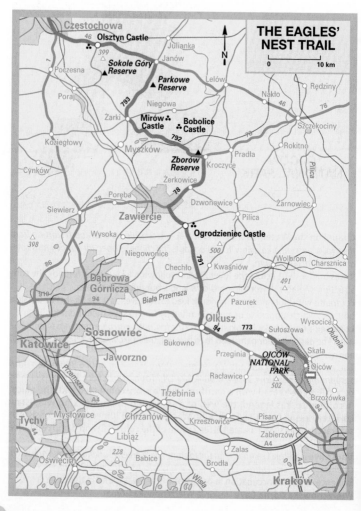

The Eagles' Nest Trail (Szlak Orlich Gniazd)

The Eagles' Nest Trail runs through the Polish Jura from Kraków to Częstochowa over a distance of some 100km. It owes its name to the fortresses erected in the 14C by King Kazimierz the Great to strengthen the kingdom of Kraków and to guard the trade route linking the capital (Kraków) and the rich region of Greater Poland. Over the centuries, the castles came under the control of powerful families who, once the threat of attack had disappeared, adapted the castles to a more comfortable lifestyle and later abandoned them. Built with local stone, the castles or rather their ruins now blend well with the rest of the landscape.

A hiking footpath links some fifteen castles over a distance of almost 160km. *Detailed information is available from tourist offices in Częstochowa or Kraków.* The tour can also be done by car during the course of an afternoon.

From Ojców Park to Częstochowa

Beyond Ojców National Park, the Eagles' Nest Trail runs through hilly countryside where very short grass grows on the chalky soil. A few trees, mainly conifers, gather round outcrops and sometimes spectacular outliers. Between two castles, you can stop in one of the many reserves such as that of **Parkowe** (Rezerwat Parkowe), located south of the town of Janów, or those of **Sokole Góry** and **Zborów,** and stretch your legs through their rugged landscape.

Ogrodzieniec Castle★★ *(Daily Apr-Aug 9am-8pm, Sep-Nov 9am-6pm. 5.5/4.5 PLN),* erected in the 14C on top of the highest hill in the area, was completely remodelled in Renaissance style in the middle of the 16C by one of King Sigismund I's bankers. Destroyed by the Swedes in the 17C, it was partly rebuilt before being finally abandoned around 1810. Its spectacular ruins form a mass of tangled crenellated towers and curtain walls against the rugged landscape.

Slightly further north, the 14C **Mirów** Castle and the **Bobolice** tower are also worth a visit. These twin fortresses were abandoned in the 17C and 18C respectively.

5km south-east of Częstochowa, the relics and the characteristic round keep of **Olsztyn Castle★** stand out above the short grass covering an isolated hill. This residential palace was also destroyed by Swedish troops.

The Practical Polish Jura

Phone code – 012

Useful addresses

Information Centre - *Ojców 15 - ✆ 389 20 02.* Above the grocer's shop "bazar Warszawski".

Park's website - *www.ojcow.pl*

Getting around

Bus– 8 buses a day link the village of Ojców and Kraków's PKS station. *Informations : www.pks.krakow.pl.*

Car – Please note that parking areas at the foot of Ojców and Pieskowa Skała castles fill up very quickly at weekends and on public holidays.

Where to stay

No hotel inside the park but a wide choice of accommodation in private rooms.

Camping Zazamcze - *Ojców 3 - ✆ 389 20 91. 20 PLN for 2 with a car and a tent.* A few pitches are near the road but most of them are by the river. The owner prepares excellent mixed grills.

Bazar Ojcowski - *Ojców 20 - ✆ 389 20 51 - 30 PLN in winter, 25 PLN in summer.* Do not look for a shop, this place is a pleasant house painted in dark colours, located by the riverside, near Ojców's post office. 4 rooms (3 double), in a private house with shared bathroom. One of the rooms has a large terrace. Charming welcome.

Zajazd Zazamcze - *Ojców 1 - ✆ 389 20 83 - 140 PLN for 2 ▭.* In a large house between the river and the edge of the woods. 5 panelled attic rooms above this restaurant serving Polish cuisine.

Eating out

Restaurants are rare inside the Ojców Park. In fine weather, improvised appetizing eating places spring up along the roads, offering bigos, grilled sausages and country bread with poppy seeds.

Gospoda pod Kazimierzem - *Ojców 12 - ✆ 389 20 71 - 30 PLN.* One of the few restaurants in the valley, which doubles up as a bar. The plain but copious cuisine features a few fish dishes.

On the town

Piwnica pod Nietoperzem - *Ojców.* The Bat, a small pub located in the basement of the Ojców post office, mainly serves beer with a few snacks. And, as its name suggests, the place is a den suitable for night owls.

Częstochowa★

POPULATION 250 862 – MAP OF POLAND C3 – WOJEWÓDZTWO OF SILESIA

The spire of the Black Madonna Monastery rising above Jasna Góra Hill warns travellers that they are approaching the Polish Lourdes. Nearly 5 million pilgrims flock to this place every year, 200 000 of them travelling on foot. The town itself may not be very attractive, but the visit of the sanctuary will immerse you in a unique atmosphere of piety and sincere religious fervour.

▶ **Finding your bearings** – 114km north-west of Kraków, 222km south-west of Warsaw.

👁 **Not to be missed** – The view from the top of the bell tower.

🕐 **Planning your visit** – Allow two hours for the visit of the sanctuary.

Faith and Industry

In the 13C, the village of Częstochowa, lying on the banks of the River Warta, excelled in the extraction and processing of iron ore. One and a half centuries later, the construction of the Jasna Góra monastery on the nearby limestone hill brought the town into the pilgrimage era. Pilgrims flocked to the place and so did looters. For several centuries, the city fought back invaders and grew in power and in size. In the 19C, the emblematic avenue of the Very Holy Virgin Mary (Najświętszej Marii Panny abbreviated to al.NMP) linked the sanctuary and the town. During the following century, the town became an important industrial centre.

Things to see

Jasna Góra Monastery

Open daily 5.30am-9.30pm. Free admission.

Icon of the Virgin

In 1382, Ladisław, Duke of Opole, founded the monastery for the Paulite monks who, two years later, were given the icon of the Virgin which brought fame to Częstochowa. According to legend, the credit should go to St Luke, but in fact the icon was probably painted in Byzantium around the 6C. The monastery buildings, spread over 5ha on top of a limestone hill, were surrounded by fortifications to protect them from plunderers. In 1655, the ramparts and, as the rumour goes, the miraculous intervention of the Virgin, halted the Swedish invasion. Thus a myth was born. It is on Częstochowa Hill that the Polish national feeling manifested itself under the protection of the icon of the Black Madonna soon proclaimed Queen of Poland. In the 18C, several sieges failed against the ramparts of fervour and faith. In the 19C, Tzar Alexander I ordered part of the walls to be demolished. However, there remains a wall forming a square reinforced in the corners by bastions. To get past these fortifications, one must go through 4 successive gates. Inside, one can get an overall view from the top of the 106m high **bell tower** *(Apr-Nov 8am-4pm).*

Chapel of the Miraculous Icon★ – A dense reverent crowd continually flocks to this small Gothic chapel with walls covered with ex-votos. The icon of the Virgin looks tiny, set within a Baroque ebony altar. Note the two gashes on the face, a souvenir from the Hussites dating back to 1430, and the jewel-encrusted fabrics offered by pilgrims. The door at the bottom on the right leads to the **sacristy**.

Basilica – This vast three-naved edifice was built between the 15C and the 17C. Note the high altar in Italian Baroque style and the stucco-decorated vaulting.

Knights' Hall★ – This is a quiet place to admire a a reproduction of the icon . A set of 9 paintings, hanging high up on the walls, illustrates the great episodes of the history of the sanctuary, including its foundation and the 1655 siege.

600th Anniversary Museum – The museum's collections illustrate the history of the Paulite Order and of the cult of the icon. Fine collection of musical instruments.

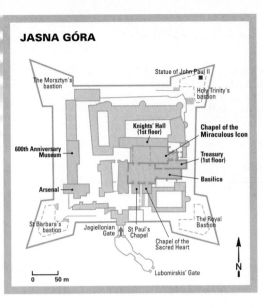

Arsenal – Weapons, armours and oriental trophies recall the military history of the sanctuary and the sieges which it successfully withstood over the centuries.

Treasury - The most precious ex-votos deposited in the sanctuary are displayed. Fine amber items and liturgical dishes are decorated with coral.

Library - Reserved for researchers, the library houses over 8 000 volumes including a large number of precious manuscripts.

Ramparts - Fine view of the monumental Stations of the Cross laid out around the gardens. A monument to John Paul II was inaugurated in 1999.

Leave the sanctuary via Barbary Street lined with souvenir shops: an amazing mixture of plastic Virgins, portraits of the Pope and non-religious items.

Archdiocesan Museum
Ul. Św. Barbary 41 - Tue-Sat 9am-1pm. 2 PLN
Fine collection of sacred art from Częstochowa and the surrounding area: sculptures, paintings, medals. The oldest items date from the 15C.

Practical Częstochowa

Postal code – 42 200
Phone code – 034

Useful addresses

Tourist office – Al. NMP 65 – ✆ 368 22 60 – www.czestochowa.um.gov.pl - open Mon-Sat 9am-5pm.

Jasna Góra Sanctuary Information Centre – ✆ 365 38 88 – May-15 Oct. 7am-8pm, 16 Oct-Apr 8am-5pm, closed during main religious festivals.

Getting around

Parking – Free near the sanctuary; the most difficult task is to find a place.

Railway station – Al. Wolności 21 - ✆ 366 47 89 - www.pkp.pl.

Bus station – Al. Wolności - ✆ 324 66 16 - www.pks.p

Where to stay

Camping Oleńka – Ul. Oleńki 22/30 - ✆ 360 60 66 - 30 PLN for 2 persons with tent and car. 90 PLN for a bungalow for 3. Comfortable accomodation just a street away from the sanctuary. Reservation recommended.

Hôtel Wenecki – Ul. Berka Joselewicza 12 - ✆ 324 33 03 - 30 rooms - 120 PLN, ⌂. A little far from the sanctuary, but very clean with a slight Italian touch. Bright rooms, new and very well-kept.

Eating out

Karczma na Wieluńskiej – Ul. Wieluńska 16 - ✆ 372 62 64 - daily 11am-11pm - 60 LN. Excellent traditional cuisine (pork and cheese roll from the Tatras) served in a refined rustic medieval setting.

Festive events

3 May: Feast day of the Queen of Poland.

26 Aug: Feast of the Częstochowa Virgin.

1st Sun in Sep: Harvest Festival.

In the Zakopane region

R. Mattès / MICHELIN

Bochnia★

POPULATION 29 376 – MAP OF POLAND C4 – WOJEWÓDZTWO OF LITTLE POLAND

The town itself has very little to offer tourists but is worth a visit for its salt mine and a few nearby sights including the historic castle of Nowy Wiśnicz and several wooden churches listed by UNESCO.

- ▶ **Getting your bearings** – 55km east of Kraków along the E40, between Kraków and Tarnów.
- 🕐 **Planning your visit** – Allow about 3hr for the visit of the salt mine, 1hr for the castle and around half a day for the tour of the wooden churches.
- 👪 **With your children** – The unusual and recreational visit of the salt mine.

Things to see

Salt Mine★
Close to the Rynek – Ul Solna 2. Mon-Fri 9.30 and 11.30am, 3.30pm. Sat-Sun 10am-4pm. 26 PLN. www.kopalniasoli.pl
The Bochnia mine was first put into operation in 1248. The lift takes visitors right down into the rock salt seams, at a depth of between 170 and 290m. A small train then takes them to several chapels carved out of the salt and to educational reconstructions. These show bogies and wheels used to get rid of the water as well as dummies clinging to the salt seam, illustrating the difficulties of working the mine. Adults who are enthusiastic about industrial heritage are likely to find all this fascinating. As for children, they will love going down the 140m-long wooden slide sitting on a cushion and steering it like a toboggan. The slide leads directly to a working hall which has been turned into a sports complex where one can play basket ball or volleyball. Other rooms are furnished with bunk beds. This is explained by the fact that the mine is also used as a sanatorium because the air inside is beneficial to the bronchial tubes and the lungs. It is therefore possible to book a night here, as one would in a youth hostel.

Nearby

Nowy Wiśnicz Castle★
From Bochnia, drive 6km south towards Nowy Wiśnicz then follow signs marked "zamek", castle.
Tue-Thu 9am-4pm, Fri 9am-5pm, Sat-Sun 10am-6pm. Last admission 4pm. Guided tours in Polish only, information in English at the ticket office. 5PLN.
From the road, there is a fine view of the castle towering above the village and the wooded hills. The white mass of the Renaissance-style building looks like a trompe-l'oeil stage setting. This impression becomes stronger during the tour of the interior, for many rooms are completely empty and devoid of atmosphere. However, Nowy

Nowy Wiśnicz Castle

Wiśnicz Castle offers a precious account of the country's political and artistic history. The first building to stand on this site was erected during the Middle Ages, when the region lived on salt mining and trade between the East and the Baltic sea, via Hungary.

Nowy Wiśnicz Castle had its cultural heyday during the lifetime of the grand marshall of the Crown, Piotr Kmita, who died in 1553. He was responsible for the Renaissance influence which marked the place. The castle became the favourite haunt of members of the royal family and of the most famous Polish writers. When Kmita died, Nowy Wiśnicz was bought by the extremely wealthy Lubomirski family. Sebastian Lubomirski fortified the castle and gave the exterior the look it has today. Unfortunately, several Swedish invasions during the 17C and, above all, the 1831 fire deprived us of the sumptuous art collection recorded in the inventories, which included paintings by Raphaël, Titian, Veronese and Dürer as well as a collection of manuscripts.

The timbered houses of the village surrounding the castle were destroyed by fire in 1850 and the last precious historical evidence disappeared with them. Bringing the glorious past back to life is not easy. Postwar restoration work spread over thirty years stabilised the building which contains mythological frescoes, models of the castle at different periods and an amazing collection of photographs illustrating the restoration of the castle. Also on display are models of other historic sights in the area, such as the castles of Wawel in Kraków, Baranów Sandomierski or Łańcut. The well-fitted kitchen contains silverware, copper and samovars. The terraces offer a panoramic view of the Carpathian foothills.

It is worth noting that the main square – Rynek – in Nowy Wiśnicz is the ideal place to take a break and relax. Outdoor cafés and benches shaded by tall trees are most inviting.

Wooden churches near Lipnica Murowana★

Starting from Bochnia, drive 12km along the Limanova road to the village of Muchówka, then turn left towards Lipnica Murowana 5km further on.

In 2003, UNESCO included **St Leonard's Church in Lipnica Murowana** on its World Heritage list. The building stands next to an imposing lime tree, on the site of an older pagan temple dating from 1141. The church, built of larch and oak wood, is famous for its 15C paintings and frescoes. It is the ideal starting point of a discovery tour of wooden churches built between the 15C and the 18C. Ten of these are located near Lipnica Murowana. The churches of **Rajbrot** and **Iwkowa** to the south and those of **Pogwizdów** and **Sobolów** to the north as you drive back towards Bochnia are the best examples of 15C and 16C wooden architecture.

Practical Bochnia

Postal code – 32-700
Phone code – 014

Useful addresses

Tourist office – Ul Bernardyńska 10 – ☎ 612 27 62 – poczta@bochnia.pttk.pl

Information on wooden churches and possibility of guided tours – Ul Wiślna 12, 31-007 Kraków – ☎ (+48 12) 430 20 96 - dci@diecezja.krakow.pl

Where to stay

Atlas Hotel – Kopaliny - Stary Wiśnicz - 32-720 Nowy Wiśnicz - ☎ 612 91 25 – 10 rooms - 130 PLN. From the E40 linking Kraków and Tarnów, in Bochnia, turn south to Limanowa and drive for 3km. Family hotel kept by a convivial polyglot. Spacious comfortable rooms, garden and terrace for long summer evenings.

Eating out

Pub 19 Pizzeria – Rynek 19, Nowy Wiśnicz. On the vast village green. Good-quality pizzeria boasting a Wild-West atmosphere.

Tarnów★

POPULATION 119 564 – MAP OF POLAND C4 – WOJEWÓDZTWO OF LITTLE POLAND

Tarnów lies at the foot of the Carpathian mountains, on the edge of the plain. Today a busy hub for the chemical industry, the city looks back with nostalgia on its glorious past, when the town belonged to the powerful Tarnowski family.

▶ **Getting your bearings :** 84km east of Kraków along the road to Rzeszów.

👁 **Not to be missed :** A tour of the ethnographic museum for an insight into the travelling world of gypsies.

🕐 **Planning your visit :** Allow 2hr for visiting Tarnów and its museums.

Background

Renaissance cultural centre – Having stood since 1330 at the junction of trade routes between Russia and Western Europe and between Hungary and the Baltic States, Tarnów became an important cultural and artistic centre in the 16C thanks to Jan Tarnowski. In his capacity as governor of the Kraków region, this wealthy scholar called on Italian artists and established his authority by being tolerant towards the Jews and the many Ukrainian, Austrian, Czech and Scottish immigrants who settled in the town and became prosperous. However, by the end of the century, wars, fires and the cupidity of the local dignitaries had brought Tarnów and its 2 000 inhabitants to a standstill. At the end of the 18C, Kraków restored Tarnów's influence by choosing it as the region's political centre, military headquarters and diocese. A century later, with over 20 000 inhabitants, Tarnów became the third town in Galicia behind Kraków and L'viv (now in Ukraine). In 1939, almost half the town's 56 000-strong population was Jewish and Tarnów was one of the main centres of Jewish thought and culture. Many scientists, jurists, artists and business men contributed to the town's renown. The first 728 Jews deported to Auschwitz (Oświęcim) on 14 June 1940 came from Tarnów.

Exploring

The main way into town is from the road to Kraków. Krakowska, one of the main shopping streets, leads gently up from the station to the historic district surrounding the Rynek.

The Rynek

In the centre rises the imposing **town hall★** – Ratusz – with the regional museum occupying the ground floor. This Gothic building, remodelled many times, today mainly features the Renaissance style. The tower is adorned with the coat of arms of the Sanguszko princes, who were Tarnów's last sovereigns. The square is lined all round with arcaded houses in the Renaissance style. No 20, built in 1565, was always a prominent place: in turn the residence of wealthy Scottish merchants, the seat of

Tarnów Town Hall and Rynek

B. Brillon / MICHELIN

the Masonic Lodge, even a chapel, it is today an annexe of the regional museum. No 21, dating from 1568, is also noteworthy.

Cathedral

Built in the 14C and remodelled in the 19C in the neo-Gothic style, the cathedral contains the magnificent Renaissance mural **graves** of the Tarnówski family and a set of Gothic stalls. Along the narrow street running behind the cathedral stands the Mikolajowski House, built in 1524 in the Gothic and Renaissance styles, now home to the **Diocesan Museum**.

Żydowska Street, which runs off the Rynek beyond nos 20 and 21, leads to one of the former Jewish districts. All that remains of the synagogue, built in 1661 and burned down by the Nazis in 1939, is the **Bimah** where the Scriptures used to be read, now reduced to four stone columns. The Jewish cemetery, which contains numerous more or less well-maintained graves, lies outside the old town. Follow L'viv Street – Lwowska – then head north along the main thoroughfare known as Starodąbrowska. You will find the cemetery 200m further on, on your left.

The Catholic cemetery is situated south of the old town. There you will see a **wooden church** dating from 1440, typical of the Carpathian regional style. To reach it from the Rynek, you need to go down towards the ring road encircling the old town – Targowa Bernardyńska – and then follow Panny Marii Street as far a the church and the cemetery.

Things to see

Regional Ethnographic Museum★ (Muzeum Etnograficzne)

Ul Krakowska 10. Wed, Fri 9am-3.30pm, Tue, Thu 9am-5pm, Sat-Sun 10am-2pm. 4 PLN.
Housed in a fine rustic house, Tarnów's Regional Ethnographic Museum is essentially devoted to the history and traditions of the Gypsy people. Displays of costumes, photographs, paintings and musical instruments enable visitors to feel the atmosphere which characterizes this nomadic people. In a modest educational way, each room throws light on a specific aspect. One is able to follow their migration from India to Europe or the Middle East. Panels introduce the Roma language and its variations over the centuries and successive migrations. Discrimination is not brushed aside. In addition to the repressive laws imposed in the 18C by the monarchs of all countries, there is an uncompromising account of the Holocaust which the Gypsy population suffered. Plain exhibits recall the 35 000 Polish Gypsies exterminated in Treblinka and Auschwitz together with 15 000 French Gypsies, 36 000 Romanian Gypsies and 28 000 Hungarian Gypsies. The cultural tour continues in the garden where there are wooden caravans decorated with traditional Roma motifs. In summer, the garden is turned into a traditional Roma camp brought to life by the sound of the violins, cymbalums and singing of groups which sometimes perform there. Whether they have settled down or are still nomads, whether they are called Gypsies, Bohemians or Romanies, Roma throughout Europe can find here a useful means of communication.

Town Hall Museum (Muzeum Okręgowe)

In the centre of the Rynek. Tue, Thu 10am-5pm, Wed, Fri 9am-3pm, Sat-Sun 10am-2pm. 6.5 PLN.
The museum recounts the history of the town. Interesting collections of armour, coats of mail, firearms and bladed weapons are displayed on the ground floor. Upstairs, the great hall contains many portraits of the various "Hetmans" – commanders-in-chief – who reigned over the town from the 16C to the 18C. Note the engraving depicting Tarnów guarded by its ramparts in 1655 and a splendid etching of Dresden by Bernardo Belloto with a caption in French: "View of the Royal Gallery and part of Notre-Dame Church". France and the French language are being honoured by the museum intent on recalling the diplomatic, political and military relations between Poland and France through engravings, books and paintings.

Nearby

Zalipie

From Tarnów, drive along the Kielce road for 19km to Dąbrowa Tarnowska. Turn left in the town centre and follow the signpost marked "Dom Malarek Zalipie". 12km.
The village of Zalipie is famous for its painted adobe houses and farms which give its full meaning to the expression "popular art". The inhabitants paint colourful frescoes with geometric or floral motifs on their houses, barns, wells and sometimes their furniture and tools.

Zalipie Museum: the House of Women Painters (Dom Malarek)

Coming from Tarnów, on the left side of the road as you enter the village. Open daily. Should the museum be closed, the keys are available from the farm across the road. 5 PLN. Sale of local craftwork.

The museum looks like a small doll's house. The walls are painted blue and yellow and decorated with floral arabesques. The house belonged to the village's first artist, Felicja Curylowa. In 1978 it was turned into the House of Women Painters, Dom Malarek in Polish. The tradition goes back to the turn of the 20C and it has been celebrated every year since 1948 by the inhabitants who organise the painted houses competition in June; however, the tradition is disappearing slowly and it is becoming difficult to spot them in the village. Start with a tour of the museum; then, leaving it on your left, take the first right turn. Drive along slowly and you will be able to see some paintings.

Dębno Castle

22km west of Tarnów, on the road to Kraków, turn left onto a minor road signposted "zamek" (castle). Tue, Thu 10am-5pm, Wed, Fri 9am-3pm, Sat-Sun 11am-3pm. Last admission one hour before closing. Closed Jan-Feb. Guided tours in Polish, unaccompanied visits are not allowed.

Dębno Castle is worth a detour for its surroundings and its successful restoration, a model of its kind. Surrounded by trees and a dry moat, the castle overlooks an undulating landscape through which flows the River Niedźwiedzia. From the time it was built for the Debiński family during the second half of the 15C, this fortified red-brick residence suffered wars, invasions and fires before being restored after the Second World War. A tour of the castle enables visitors to grasp the simplicity of its plan. Four two-storey buildings forming a rectangle are linked by four defensive towers. The tour starts in the inner courtyard which, although relatively bare, successfully conveys the military yet elegant atmosphere. Inside, the wealth of furniture and paintings from the 16C to the 19C comes as a surprise. Note the kitchen and its collection of copper, the concert hall housing a piano used for occasional recitals and the pharmacy with its amazing inlaid furniture. Every year in September, the castle becomes the setting for a tournament in which contestants, dressed as knights, fight their opponents with swords. The half-timbered **chapel** stands 100 metres above the castle.

Practical Tarnów

Postal code – 33-100

Phone code – 014

Useful addresses

Tourist office – Rynek 7 - 𝒫 627 87 35 - www.turystyka.tarnow.pl - centrum@turystika.tarnov.pl - May-Sep: 9am-4pm.

Police – 𝒫 997.

Fire brigade – 𝒫 998.

Taxi – Express 𝒫 9669 - Euro 𝒫 9625, Viva 𝒫 9626.

Internet café – Forum - Ul. Wekslarska 9 - Close to the Rynek - 11am-11pm, Sun: 1-10pm. In the basement of a pizzeria and a café.

Getting around

Bus and railway stations – At the bottom of ul. Krakowska - 10min on foot from the old town. Trains link Tarnów to Kraków throughout the day and the journey lasts about 1hr.

Where to stay

Bristol Hotel – Ul. Krakowska 9 - 𝒫 621 22 79 - www.bristol.tarnow.com.pl - Bristol.tn@poczta.fm. - closed Dec and Jan. - 🅿 - 🖃 - 15 rooms: 280 PLN - 🖾 20 PLN. Located 5 min on foot from the Rynek, this hotel boasting a fine façade overlooking the main shopping street, offers pleasant rooms in various shades of pink.

Eating out

Restauracja Tatrzańska – Ul Krakowska 22 - 𝒫 627 87 35 - 10am-10pm - 50 PLN. The Polish cuisine of this chic and convivial restaurant is refined on account of its taste and its presentation. Most famous icecream in town. Fine background music.

Restauracja Impresja – Rynek 12 - 𝒫 627 89 33 - 11am-10pm - 50 PLN. On the first floor of a building overlooking the Rynek; large attractive room where one can enjoy a refined cuisine including unusual recipes: chicken with gambas, filet mignon with mushrooms.

Kielce

POPULATION 211 810 – MAP OF POLAND C3 – WOJEWÓDZTWO OF LITTLE POLAND

In the 12C, the bishops of Kraków chose Kielce as the seat of one of their residences. The contrast between the lively atmosphere of this student town and commercial centre and its rich architectural past is Kielce's main attraction. Built on a hill, the city is close to the Świętokrzyski National Park with its undulating landscapes offering a wide choice of rambles.

- ▶ **Getting your bearings** – Kielce is on the northern border of the Little Poland region - Małopolska. 120km north of Kraków, on the road to Warsaw.
- ◉ **Not to be missed** – A stroll along the Planty.
- ◷ **Planning your visit** – Allow half a day for the town and its museums, half a day for the skansen in Tokarnia followed by the Sundial Museum in Jędrzejów, and half a day for rambling through the Świętokrzyski National Park.

Background

Cultural university town – Over time, Kielce succeeded in gaining a reputation as a cultural city and an enjoyable one. Being far removed from the finest gems of Polish architecture, the town could easily have become a dull insignificant centre. Instead, it thrives on the dynamism of its students and teachers who account for 20% of the population. Owing to this vitality, Kielce has become a highly artistic city with a cultural centre and houses devoted to music, the stage, photography and dance. The emblem of this success is no doubt Miles Davis whose statue proudly stands in front of the cultural centre and attracts young skaters and bikers who use him as a runway.

Bishops' Palace, Kielce

J. Malburet / MICHELIN

Exploring

On the hilltop, the historic district

The best way to explore Kielce is to aim for the top of the town. From the Rynek, walk up Mala Street, then cross Sienkiewicza Street to reach the **Cathedral** and the **Bishops' Palace**, now housing the **National Museum** *(see Things to see below)*.

Cathedral of the Assumption-of-the-Holy-Virgin

Founded in 1171 by Gideon, a Kraków bishop, it was remodelled and partly rebuilt in the 13C and 19C. Today, it looks like a Baroque church which has retained the simple plan of the original Romanesque edifice.

Walk across the garden laid out over the ruins of the former walls of the **fortress** and make your way over the hill. The area, known as **the Planty**, features a grass-covered stretch, children's games, statues and trees. This steep open space reaches down to several expanses of water where students and young parents like to spend their leisure time in a relaxed family atmosphere. From the bottom of the garden, the extensive view of the architectural ensemble comes as a surprise.

Sienkiewicza Street

Among the numerous shops, banks and exchange offices lining Kielce's pedestrian shopping street are a few historic houses. Starting from the station, look out for no 47, the **Bank of Food Production**, then no 31, the **Wersal Hotel** with its balconies and its tower. No 32 houses the **Żeromskiego Theatre**, inaugurated in 1879, and no 21 opposite is occupied by the **Bristol Hotel**, the oldest establishment in Kielce.

Things to see

Palace and National Museum★★ (Pałac Biskupów Krakowskich)
Plac Zamkowy 1. 9am-4pm. Closed Mon. 6 PLN.
The Kraków Bishops' Palace, built between 1637 and 1641 by one of them, Jakub Zadzik, is a fine example of the architectural style of residences dating from the Vasa period. The façade and most of the rooms were not altered by the passing of time or by rebuilding programmes. Since the 1970s, the building has housed the collections of the National Museum; the gallery of 19C and 20C Polish painting contains the most interesting and one of the richest collections in the country. Upstairs, numerous Gobelins tapestries hang on the walls and most of the ceilings are decorated with frescoes illustrating historic events. Those depicting the 1612 Moscow fire and the arrival of the Swedish delegations in 1635, painted by Tomasso Dolabelli, are particularly striking.

The museum also organises temporary exhibitions often devoted to photography. An annexe of the museum, situated on the Rynek, displays the ethnographic and geological collections *(daily 9am-3pm, closed Mon)*.

Toy Museum★ (Muzeum Zabawkarstwa w Kielcach)
Ul Kościuszki 11. www.MuzeumZabawkarstwa.art.pl. 10am-4pm. Closed Mon. 5 PLN.
The tour of the museum reveals a whole world of china dolls, some of them dating from the 18C, of scale models of planes, cars or trains offered to the museum by private collectors. In addition, there are models of prestigious sailing ships such as the Mayflower, the Cutty Sark or the trio formed by the Nina, the Pinta and the Santa Maria. The most famous Polish sailing ship, the Młodzieży, is also on display. Another room exhibits the work of naive artist Tadeusz Żak, whose speciality was wooden horses and birds. Last but not least are the traditional representations of the witch Babay Jaga, known to all Polish children.

Karczówka Forest Reserve
Leave town heading west towards Kraków. Follow signs marked "Hôtel Karczówka".
A small hill crowned by a church and a monastery, Karczówska is worth a detour for its unspoilt environment and the **panoramic view** it affords of the town and of the surrounding area.

Kadzielnia Nature Reserve
One-hour-long stroll in the southern part of Kielce. The quarry has now been turned into an amphitheatre. Numerous concerts and festivals take place in this mineral environment.

Geological Rambles
The town is famous for its karst topography. Paths running on the outskirts of town offer the opportunity of discovering unusual landscapes and a few renowned karstic caves, including the Kadzielna nature reserve and the "Raj" cave.

"Raj" Cave
On the road to Kraków, about 5km from the outskirts of Kielce. Apr-Nov: 10am-5pm. 8 PLN. With its profusion of stalagmites and stalactites, this is a perfect example of a karstic cave used by Neanderthal man.

Nearby

Obłęgorek
10km from Kielce on the road to Łódź. As you leave Kielce, turn left to Obłęgorek. 10am-5pm. Closed Mon. 6 PLN.
One of the houses in this village belonged to **Henryk Sienkiewicz** (1846-1916). The author of such novels as *The Deluge, Quo Vadis* and *The Teutonic Knights*, was awarded the Nobel Prize for literature in 1905. His home, now a museum, a magnificent over-ornate house, was carefully adapted to offer the best account of the writer's life and work while recreating the atmosphere of aristocratic homes at the turn of the 20C.

Tokarnia's Ethnographic Museum★★ (Park Etnograficzny w Tokarni)
From Kielce, drive 20km along the road to Kraków. The museum is located on the right side of the road as you leave the village of Tokarnia.
Apr-Sep 10am-5pm, Sep 10am-4pm; Oct-Mar Tue-Fri 10am-4pm. Closed Mon. 8 PLN. Full visit: 2hr.
Tokarnia's skansen offers a comprehensive display of traditional rural architecture, farms, houses and other edifices from the Kielce region, which once belonged to farmers, villagers or the local nobility. The 30 wooden buildings scattered around

parkland covering some 80ha were moved from their original site during the 1970s. The group includes farm buildings, a windmill, a church, a school and an herbalist's shed. All of them date either from the 18C or the 19C. There is no call for nostalgia as the vast reconstructed village gives the impression of being lived in. Men are working in the fields and in the gardens. Horses and fowls can be seen in the meadows and each plot of land is under the responsibility of a woman who looks after the garden and makes sure that the houses are clean. Additional information in English is available for visitors with a keen interest. Three buildings are well worth looking at with particular attention:

The Pharmacy, situated at the entrance to the skansen. In the 19C, it served the village of Bieliny. Visitors can admire the usual copper instruments, china jars, microscope and test-tubes on display and, in addition, read amusing details on the information sheet provided, such as the fact that the pharmacy sold powders, plants and...refreshing vodka.

The house of Jan Bernasiewicz, the naive artist who died in 1984 leaving some charming works. His religious and pagan wooden statues are a powerful reminder that Polish naive art always played an active role. Numerous photos of the artist are exhibited in one of the rooms. These portraits, on which he appears mischievous, gruff and modest, present him as the ideal grandfather. And if the photos give a false impression, his works reveal his true nature.

Suchedniów Manor, one of the last places to be visited, stands in striking contrast to the farming world mainly represented in Tokarnia. It was built in 1812 by a local nobleman. Note the solid larch beams carefully assembled, the heating provided by splendid ceramic stoves and the furniture signed by the best crafstmen.

Nowa Słupia Benedictine Abbey

Świętokrzyski National Park★ (Świętokrzyski Park Narodowy)

About 35km from Kielce. Drive along the road to Lublin; in Radlin, turn left towards Ciekoty.

The two main villages of the Park are Święta Katarzyna and Nowa Słupia.

Nowa Słupia Benedictine Abbey

From Nowa Stupia, the abbey can be reached in two ways:

By car – Follow the road skirting the south side of the church towards Święty Krzyż. Drive 500m to the supervised car park (there is a charge for parking). Souvenir shops and bars – snacks – are at your disposal near the car park and the summit.

– Allow 2hr on foot there and back; allow additional time for the visit. The climb is sometimes steep but accessible to all. Town shoes are not recommended.

The path carved out of the rock climbs through the forest. It is sometimes steep but always manageable. The fact that an abbey and a calvary stand at the top motivates elderly Poles to climb up and follow the Way of the Cross while praying.

Once you are on the plateau, you need to walk across a vast grass-covered area to reach the Abbey. The buildings are still occupied by Benedictine monks and Mass is celebrated in the church. The Abbey is accessible by road, but it would be a shame to choose the easy way! The smell of the larches and the birdsongs are unique. Once at the top, you can climb onto the telecommunications relay. From the level accessible to the public, the view extends over the whole area of the Świętokrzyski National Park.

Jędrzejów – Sundial Museum★★ (Muzeum Przypkowskich w Jędrzejowie)

38km from Kielce, on the road to Kraków. Pl Tadeusza Kościuszki 7-8.
Daily except Mon and day following public hols. Oct-Mar: 9am-3pm; Apr-Sep: 9am-4pm. 7 PLN.

This place is fascinating even for those who are not fans of gnomonics – the art of using and constructing dials. The museum occupies the house of the Przypkowski family. Sundials, clocks, watches, globes have pride of place here. All the family members spent their life observing the stars, in particular the sun, and spoilt their eyesight through continually consulting ancient manuscripts as well as modern publications. This marvellous museum is the result of their determined and meticulous pursuit. Many rooms still retain the family furniture and one room alone contains nothing but glass cases entirely filled with miniature sundials. Most of them date from the 16C or the 17C and come from Prague, Madrid, Paris, Augsburg or London. Hundreds of sundials, made from the most precious materials, such as ivory, and elaborately decorated, form the third most important collection in the world. Less serious is the advertisement displayed in a glass case: presumably cut out of an old newspaper (no date is visible), it praises the sundials produced by the Maison du Cadran Solaire in Carcassonne. Before leaving, take the covered passageway to the small garden and stand as far back as possible from the building. You will then notice the astronomical observatory which the Przypkowski family had built on the roof of their house in 1906.

Practical Kielce

Postal code – 25-000
Phone code – 041

Useful addresses

Tourist office – *Plac Niepodległości 1 - ℘ 367 64 36 - informacja@turystyczna. um.kielce.pl - Mon-Fri 9am-4pm, Sat 10am-3pm.*

Getting around

It is difficult to drive into Kielce because the town is surrounded by a network of major roads and panels indicating "Centrum" are not always easy to spot.

Once you have found the Rynek, park your car and continue on foot. Every sight of interest is easily accessible from this square. Tickets allowing you to park are on sale at the small booths located on the Rynek.

Bus and railway station – *Plac Niepodległości.* Buses and trains regularly link Kielce with Warsaw, Kraków, Wrocław, Lublin, Gdańsk and Zakopane. Buses also run to Sandomierz and the Świętokrzyski National Park.

Where to stay

Karczówka Hotel – *Ul Karczówkowska 64 - ℘ 366 26 26 - 28 rooms - 180 PLN .* The

rooms are small but comfortable and neat. Varnished wood and lace give them a cosy look. Away from the town, guaranteed peace and quiet.

Eating out

Pałacyk Zielińskiego – *Ul Zamkowa - ℘ 368 20 55 - Daily 10am-12am - 30 PLN.* Zamkowa Street starts from the garden of the National Museum. At the Pałacyk Zielińskiego, traditional Polish dishes are served in a romantic setting. Piano recitals sometimes take place.

Restauracja Bernasiówska – *Pl Żwirki, Święta Katarzyna. Full meal 25 PLN.* Located north of the Świętokrzyski National Park, this convivial family restaurant extends the warmest welcome to its customers.

Taking a break

Entrakt – *Plac Moniuszki 2 - ℘ 343 20 46. Daily 11am-12am* Situated inside the Cultural Centre, this tearoom which boasts bay windows with engraved words such as "Bordeaux - Armagnac - Cognac", serves excellent cakes. Inside, La Goulue and Toulouse-Lautrec are very prominent.

Sandomierz★★

POPULTION 25 457 – MAP OF POLAND C3– WOJEWÓDZTWO OF LITTLE POLAND

Sandomierz is one of the Gothic gems of Little Poland, with a history going back 800 years. Once a lively trading port on the Wisła, the town found its way to prosperity and became gentrified. For our greatest enjoyment.

▶ **Getting your bearings :** In the most northern part of Little Poland, off road 74 linking Kielce and Lublin.

👁 **Not to be missed** : A walk along the banks of the Wisła.

🕐 **Planning your visit** : Allow a whole day to visit the town and its museums. Spending an evening strolling around the Rynek is also highly recommended.

Background

Exceptionally well-preserved heritage – The history of Sandomierz is marked by the town's tolerant attitude. In 1367, the Jewish community was one of the first to be protected from discrimination by law. Two centuries later, in 1570, The "Sandomierz Agreement" sealed the desire for mutual respect expressed by Calvinists, Lutherans and Moravian Brothers. The city can be said to be the fruit of this harmony, since, as a result, it was only invaded by the Tatars and the Swedes. Still, one may wonder at the exceptional state of conservation of its picturesque heritage, which was neither damaged during the Second World War nor spoilt by the appetite for concrete of Soviet architects. More recently, Sandomierz managed to avoid the usual visual pollution provided by commercial centres on the outskirts of towns. Since these could not be set up on the 7 hills, they were relegated further afield. The only real problem Sandomierz has stems from its unstable subsoil, prone to landslides. During the 1960s, a tragedy was narrowly avoided and enormous quantities of concrete had to be injected into the foundations of buildings to consolidate the whole.

Things to see

Whether you arrive via the **Opatów Gate★,** which is all that remains of the fortress built by Kazimierz the Great in the 14C, or through the narrow cobbled streets climbing up from the castle, you will end up at the Rynek.

Rynek★★

The **Town Hall★** dating from the 14C stands in the centre of this vast sloping square with sides exceeding 100m. Built in the Gothic style, the edifice was simply raised by the adjunction of a Renaissance attic. The most characteristic bourgeois or historic houses are the present post office, known as **Oleśnicki House,** at no 10, the former neo-Classical guardhouse, now occupied by the PTTK tourist information office, and the houses at nos 23, 31 or 27, today the Pod Ciżemką Hotel.

A. Galy / MICHELIN

Town Hall

Underground Gallery (Podziemna Trasa Turystyczna)

Ul Oleśnickich. 10am-4pm. 6.5 PLN. Entrance at the back of Oleśnicki House.

This underground maze was intended to link the houses and shops of the Rynek, in order to protect the goods from pillage during the Tatar and Swedish invasions. The 500m long network of galleries, lined with red bricks, which extends beneath the square required a colossol amount of work. However, the poor settings and the fact that visits are exclusively carried out in Polish are disappointing.

In Zamkowa Street, near the Basztowy Hotel, You will find the "**eye of the needle**", a tiny passageway linking the old town and the street leading to the castle.

Cathedral of Our Lady of the Nativity★ (Kościół katedralny)

Apr-Sep: Tue-Sat 10am-2pm, 3-5pm, Sun 3-5pm. Oct-Mar: Tue-Sat 10am-2pm, Sun 3-5pm. The Tatars and the Lithuanians made a thorough job of destroying the original Romanesque collegiate church, the former in the 13C, the latter in 1349; this prompted Kazimierz the Great to have the present edifice erected in 1360. Since then, this massive example of Gothic architecture has become more impressive. It became a cathedral in 1818 and a basilica in 1960. The interior is decorated with Rococo altars, made of black or white marble in various workshops in Kraków and L'viv (now in Ukraine). The walls of the nave are decorated with very realistic paintings depicting the capture and destruction of the town by the Tatars and the Swedes. Others, known as "**Kalendarium**"★, illustrate, in 12 scenes, the various possibilities of violent death, such as being impaled, cut to pieces or beheaded.

House of Jan Długosz (Diocesan Museum)★★
(Dom Długosza - Muzeum Diecezjalne)

Ul Długosza 9. Apr-Sep: Tue-Sat 9am-4pm, Sun and public hols 1-4pm. Oct-Mar: Tue-Sat 9am-4pm, Sun and public hols 1.30-3pm. The visit lasts 30min.

This red-brick Gothic house, standing behind the cathedral, was built by Jan Długosz in 1476. On the north side, its windows offer a magnificent view of the Wisła. Since 1937 it has been occupied by the Diocesan Museum. Entrance is through a small garden where trees are inhabited by carved-wood characters. The tortuous interior is noteworthy, even if you don't care for sacred art. Room V: the music you hear was recorded on a small 17C organ, kept in a glass case. Room VI: it contains a crib with characters in 18C dress. Room VII: an unusual library presents wooden books, their pages replaced by beetles, acorns or dried moss. The museum also displays splendid ceramics – 16C to 19C – used to line stoves, richly decorated religious garments as well as numerous sculptures and religious paintings of the 15C and 16C, in particular the Three Saints, "Martha, Agnes and Clara", painted in 1518 by an unknown artist, or "Mary with the Child and St Catherine" by Łukasz Cranach.

Castle - Regional Museum★
(Zamek - Sandomierskiego Muzeum Okręgowego)

Mon-Fri: Apr-Sep 9am-5pm; Oct-Mar 9am-3pm. Sat: 9am-3pm, Sun: 10am-3pm. 5 PLN.

The West wing is all that remains of this Renaissance-style castle. The other three wings surrounding the arcaded courtyard were destroyed by the Swedish army in 1656. The castle houses a small regional museum presenting two interesting exhibitions. The first is devoted to contemporary artists who use as their raw material 150-million-year-old sedimentary rocks, mainly from the Świętokrzyski region, and turn them into pieces of jewellery or miniature objects. The second focuses on Polish garments, fabrics and traditions at the turn of the 20C. Photographs dating from the beginning of the 20C take us on a journey back in time.

St James's Church (Kościoł Św. Jakuba)

Standing some one hundred metres above the castle, this church built from 1226 onwards is one of the oldest red-brick churches in Poland. Mainly Romanesque in style, it nevertheless features a high altar dating from 1559 and modern stained-glass windows.

Tour of the castles

Round tour starting from Sandomierz – About 100km - Allow half a day.

One of them is a Baroque-style ruin, the other a Renaissance building turned into a luxury hotel. Striking contrast!

Follow the Kielce road. In Lipnik, before Opatów, turn left towards Klimontów, then take the direction of Iwaniska. The ruined Krzyżtopór Castle is in the Ujazd municipality.

Ujazd - Krzyżtopór Castle (Zamek Krzyżtopór)

This 16C fortified palace, which once symbolized the greatness of the extremely wealthy Krzyżtopór famlily, is now open to all weathers. The only sounds to be heard are the cry of the crows and the rattling of the corrugated-iron sheeting on the roof. Of the star-shaped fortress with five branches equipped with guns, only the skeleton remains. Of the palace which the owners called "the palazzo" in the Italian fashion, all that is left is the memory of magnificent festivities and collapsed windows.

Leave Ujazd and go back to Klimontów where you can pick up the Rzeszów road. Turn right beyond the village of Łoniów. A signpost points to a ferry crossing the Wisła. About 1km further on, turn left at a t junction without any signpost. Drive 4km along a road full of potholes. The 2min ferry crossing is free (two cars at a time). The village of Baranów lies on the opposite bank, a few hundred metres away. Turn right at the first junction, near the police station. The castle stands at the end of the village.

Baranów Sandomierski Castle

Situated away from the village, Baranów Castle shows how fashionable the Renaissance style was with Polish aristocrats in the late 16C. The Leszczińskis asked the Italian architect Santi Gucci to design this elegant residence. Nestling in a 14ha wooded park with areas laid out in the French-style, the edifice lost its defensive character in favour of a more residential look. Four towers surmounted by a cupola – Falconi Tower – and four buildings surround an inner courtyard enhanced by a remarkable staircase leading to the Tylmanowska gallery with frescoes painted on the ceiling. Lived-in until 1939 and hardly damaged during the war, this richly furnished architectural gem has been turned into a luxury hotel.

Practical Sandomierz

Postal code – 27-600
Phone code – 015

Useful addresses

Tourist office – *PTTK - Rynek 12 -* ☎ *832 26 82 - www.pttk-sandomierz.pl 8am-3pm (6pm in summer).*

Getting around

Parking – The historic centre being a car-free zone, it is advisable to park on bd Mickiewicza or in a car park. You can then walk along the park facing the new town. At the end of the park (5min on foot), continue past St Joseph's Church to the Opatów Gate.

Railway station – *Ul Lwowska 35 -* ☎ *832 94 36.*

Bus station – *Ul Listopadowa 22 -* ☎ *832 23 02*

There are regular bus and train services between Sandomierz and Lublin, Kielce, Rzeszów and Kraków.

Where to stay

Basztowy Hotel - *Place Ks.J. Poniatowskiego 2,* ☎ *833 34 50 - www. opiwpr.org.pl - 25 rooms – 270 PLN.* Most modern luxury hotel in the heart of the old town with a rather austere façade. Lively atmosphere.

Ciżemka Hotel - *Rynek 27,* ☎ *832 05 50 - www.sandomierz-hotel.com.pl - 9 rooms - 300 PLN -* 🅿 *20 PLN.* Hotel housed in a listed building with windows overlooking the Rynek. it's impossible to be more immersed in the town's history. The atmosphere, the furniture and the decoration take into account the history of the place.

Królowej Jadwigi Motel – *Ul Krakowska 24,* ☎ *832 29 88 - www.motel.go3.pl - 10 rooms – 170 PLN. Enclosed car park.* This unique motel is furnished like an antique shop. Clocks, water colours and family photographs decorate the restaurant. The owners and staff make guests welcome. Inexpensive yet excellent family cooking. The rooms are plain but neat.

Eating out

30-tka – *Rynek 30 -* ☎ *644 53 12 - 30 PLN.* The terrace overlooks the square and the view is pleasant. Plums and prunes are used in the preparation of most dishes. Original.

Oriana – *Mariacka 5 -* ☎ *832 27 24 - 40 PLN.* Situated away from the hustle and bustle of the Rynek. Ask for a table in the inner courtyard. Traditional Polish cuisine in this excellent restaurant.

Short break

Mała Café – *Ul Sokolnickiego 3.* Everything is young in this tea room: the colour, the music, the staff. It's a tiny place (Mala in Polish) but it's great!

Shopping

Antiques – *Rynek 11 et 18, ul Opatowska 4, 17 and ul Sokolnickiego 10.*

Goldwork – Two jewellery workshops: *Ryszarda and Tomasz Krzesimowscy, ul Opatowska 3. Cezary Łutowicz, Plac Poniatowskiego.*

Łańcut Castle★★★

Łańcut is famous for its vodka and even more for its castle which belonged in turn to the illustrious and extremely wealthy Lubomirski, Czartoryski and Potocki families responsible for its successive alterations over the centuries.

▶ **Getting your bearings** – 20km west of Rzeszów, along the road to Przemyśl.

🕐 **Planning your visit** – It is worth spending a whole day on a thorough tour of the castle, the park and the museums.

Background

In the 17C, Stanisław Lubomorski commissioned a Baroque residential palace from the Italian architect Matteo Trapola. This palace was surrounded by a five-pronged system of fortifications. During the 18C, Princess Izabella Lubimorska, a cultured woman and keen traveller who embodied the spirit of the Enlightenment, undertook the complete remodelling of the interior in the Rococo style. Then, at the end of the 19C, Roman Potocki called on the French architect Armand Beauqué and some of his Viennese and Italian colleagues to add a romantic touch to the castle and the park: the result was the orangery and the stables designed as wings of the palace. The last owner, the wealthy Alfred Potocki, sent furniture and objects abroad in 1944. The castle, now a national monument, contains furniture belonging to the State.

Things to see

Tickets include admission to the castle, the park and the museums. Apr-Sep 9am-5pm (last admission 4pm); Feb-Mar and Oct-Nov 9am-4pm (last admission 3pm). Closed Mon, Dec-Jan, Easter Sat-Sun, 3 May, 1 Nov, 11 Nov. 20 PLN.

Castle and orangery

The castle is a kind of museum of Polish interiors with numerous rooms: bright ones decorated with sculptures, music boxes, Chinese porcelain or elegant furniture, and dark ones containing massive furniture and glass cases full of weapons and armour. The tour of the first floor begins with the portrait gallery of the Potocki family. Because of the many bay windows and openings, the park forms part of the decor as much as the furniture and numerous chinoiseries lying on the furniture or displayed in glass cases. Following the yellow or pink bathroom, the music rooms, the dance hall and the pink-marble dining room comes the long antique gallery decorated with trompe-l'oeil amphorae and low-relief sculptures. The ground floor houses a dark gallery devoted to bladed weapons, including sabres, and pistols.
From the orangery, walk out of the park and cross 3-Go Maja Street.

Former stables

Designed by the French architect Armand Beauqué, they now house the museums.
The Carriage Museum★ presents the superb collection of 19C and 20C horse-drawn vehicles used for attending ceremonies or travelling, bequeathed by the Potocki family; they come from Paris, Vienna or London and also Warsaw and Kielce.
The Icon Museum contains a wealth of 16C and 17C Uniate art from the Przemyśl and Sanok regions and from Slovakia.

The park

A stroll along the alleyways lined with ancient beeches or chestnut trees leads visitors to the orchid house, the riding ring or the music school.

Practical Łańcut

Zamkowa Restaurant – *Established inside the castle.* Very elegant setting and refined Polish cuisine which somehow falls short of one's expectations of such a place. 35 PLN.

Pensjonat Pałacyk Hotel and restaurant –*Ul Paderewskiego 18 -* 📞 *(017) 225 20 43 - www.palacyk.lancut.pl - 10 rooms – 150 PLN Meal 25 PLN.* This is one of our favourites. A miniature palace with a bijou interior. Everything is convivial, elegant and modern.

The restaurant menu, decorated with humoristic drawings, offers the entire range of Polish, Baltic and Ukrainian cuisines. The cinnamon-flavoured cakes and the "zupa gulaszowa" are particularly delicious!

Przemyśl★★

POPULATION 67 955 – MAP OF POLAND D4– WOJEWÓDZTWO OF SUB-CARPATHIA

Considered for a thousand years as a key town by military strategists, Przemyśl can at last enjoy relative peace. Once the largest fortress in the Austro-Hungarian Empire, it became a den of spies during the cold war, but now prefers to promote the skill of its craftsmen specialising in pipes and bells and known throughout the country.

- **Getting your bearings**: On the border with Ukraine, 265km east of Kraków, along the E40.
- **Not to be missed**: A tour of the workshops where bells and pipes are manufactured.
- **Planning your visit**: Allow one day for strolling through the town and visiting the museums. Allow another day for exploring the fortress and the surrounding area.

Background

1000 years of military history – From its very beginnings, Przemyśl was always a source of envy. Its geographical position caused it to be along the path of invasions and at the centre of world conflicts and international tensions. Tatars, Cossaks, Transylvanians and, more recently, Austro-Hungarians, Russians, Nazi or Soviet occupying forces all tried to get control over this route linking Europe and the East. It was only during the 16C and 17C that the city was able to develop its architectural heritage and make its economy prosperous. The major part of the historic buildings we see today date from that period. Yet most of them were destroyed during the disastrous 18C, when Poland was divided. The town's military past had its heyday in the reign of Emperor Franz-Joseph who intended to make Przemyśl the "gateway to Hungary". The army high command decided to make it the most important fortress in the Empire. This involved creating a double network of small forts and of underground galleries as well as arms depots all round the town, sometimes nearly 10km away. This planned action started in 1853 with the fortification work followed in 1855 by the construction of a railway line linking Galicia and Hungary. These two simultaneous projects triggered the town's economic development and a major increase of its population. There were 9 500 inhabitants in Przemyśl in 1850 and nearly 55 000 in 1910. At the beginning of the 20C, the Catholic, Orthodox, Graeco-Catholic and Jewish communities lived in harmony before the two world wars revived interest in the town's strategic position, which resulted once more in decline and misery. 100 000 soldiers died inside the fortress during the First World War.

Thing to see

The foaming River San flowing down from the Polish and Ukrainian Bieszczady separates the modern town from the historic city. Most of the sights of interest are located on the heights overlooking the south bank of the river.

Start from the **Rynek** with its arcaded houses and walk up Kazimierza Wielklego, a pedestrian shopping street, as far as the Clock Tower.

The Bell and Pipe Museum
(Muzeum Dzwonów i Fajek)
Ul. Władycze 3. Tue-Sat 10.30am-5.30pm, Sun 11am-7pm. Closed Mon. 5 PLN.
Housed inside the Baroque-style **Clock Tower**, this museum presents displays on 7 levels, exclusively devoted to two crafts which are still very much alive in Przemyśl: the manufacture of bells and pipes.
Bells: the collection covers the production of bells from the 17C to the 20C. Note in particular the former town hall bell dating from 1740, as well as items produced in the Gdańsk workshops and numerous ships' bells.

Pipe

Pipes: pipes manufactured in various workshops in town are either carved out of wood or made of porcelain. The oldest date from the 17C and 18C. Note in particular the pipe shaped like a horse's head, the property of a Ukrainian Cossack chief, and another one having belonged to a Moravian which humorously depicts his hunting exploits. From the terrace at the top of the tower, there is a panoramic view of the old town and the river.

Return to the Rynek via Franciszkańska Street.

Franciscan Church

The present church was built in the neo-Baroque style on the ruins of the town's first church erected in 1379 and destroyed in the 18C. Artists from the L'viv School made the wood carvings and the frescoes.

Walk a few metres along Asnyka Street to the ensemble formed by the Graeco-Catholic cathedral, the national museum and, further up, the former Carmelite church of St Theresa.

Bells and Pipes Today

It is possible to see some crafstmen at work. The visit of their workshops by tourists is not officially organised but their door is open to those who respect the work of their employees. If you are interested, go to Ostrów, a village situated 5km from the centre of Przemyśl, on the way to Sanok. The workshops are on the side of the road.

Zbigniew Bednarczyk, known as "Bróg", is one of the important master pipers in Przemyśl. His warm personality will fascinate enthusiasts. *Ostrów 324. ℘ 671 08 40.*

For 7 generations **the Felczyński family** has been selling bells cast in its works to churches and ships across five continents. *Odlewnia Dzwonów – Janusz Felczyński, Ostrów. ℘ 670 73 52.*

Ukrainian Byzantine Cathedral

This former catholic cathedral was ceded to the Graeco-Catholics by Pope John-Paul II in 1991, which explains the presence of an iconostasis.

National Museum (Muzeum Narodowe Ziemi Przemyskiej)

Plac t Czackiego 3. Tue-Wed 10.30am-5.30pm, Thu-Sun 10am-2pm. 6 PLN.

Photos, drawings and objects illustrate the daily life and religious observance of the Jewish community in the 19C and early 20C. However, the prize exhibit is the collection of **16C and 17C icons**, due to the historic presence of Orthodox Christians and Graeco-Catholics. Most remarkable is the Passion (1703), one of the gems of the collection. On the second floor, documents and photos illustrate the military and economic role of the fortress, responsible for Przemyśl's prosperity before the world wars.

Catholic Cathedral

This Gothic-style edifice boasts a 71m high Baroque tower.

Katedralna and Zamkowa streets lead to the **castle**. Still visible are traces of the first building which archaeologists date from 992. The base of the castle goes back to 1340; the rest of the edifice was extensively remodelled. Largely destroyed, it serves as the

Krasiczyn Castle

W. Buss / MICHELIN

setting of an outdoor café and the stage of a theatre. The ensemble, surrounded by a vast wooded park, dominates the valley. To walk down to the Rynek, follow Kmity Street then Grodzka Street where the former Dominican monastery is situated.

Fortress (Forty Twierdzy Przemyśl)

Przemyśl fortress was often compared to Verdun. Some thirty fortified sites form a 45km long belt surrounding the town. Sometimes the structures closely follow the contours of the terrain, sometimes they are built underground, forming a line or, less frequently an arc. The small forts were designed to hinder the advance of the tanks, to shelter heavy guns or infantry troops and to protect command posts or telegraph stations. From a military point of view, the fortress seemed impregnable. However, on several occasions during the great 20C conflicts, attacking forces took advantage of an irremediable weakness, hunger! The tour can be made on foot or by bike; simply follow the indications. One should give priority to three main sites and their surroundings:

Siedliska and Jaksmanice: *drive east along the E40 towards Medyka (Ukrainian border). After 10km, turn right towards Siedliska.*

Duńkowiczki and Orzechowce: *drive north along the E40 towards Rzeszów. After 8km, turn left towards Duńkowiczki and Orzechowce.*

Łętownia: *drive west along road 884 over a distance of 8km.*

It is advisable to take a torch.

Nearby

Krasiczyn Castle★★

Drive 8km towards Sanok. The castle is on the side of the road. Guided tours. May-Nov 9am-5pm, every hour; Jan-Apr: at 9 and 11am, 1 and 3pm. 6 PLN.

This Renaissance castle was named after Stanisław Krasicki for whom it was built in 1580. The courtyard, decorated with frescoes depicting noble families, is enclosed by four towers. The Pope's Tower, God's Tower housing a chapel and a crypt, The King's Tower with exhibitions of contemporary art on several levels, and the Nobleman's Tower offering from the terrace a panoramic view of the park planted with some remarkable trees. Ancient oak trees, a Ginkgo biloba, several magnolias and hedges of limetrees make a stroll in the park as pleasant as a tour of the castle.

Practical Przemyśl

Postal code – 33-700
Phone code – 016

Useful addresses

Tourist office – Rynek 1 - ☎ 675 16 64 – www.przemysl.pl - mail@um.przemysl.pl - Mon-Fri 10am-6pm, Sat 10am-4pm. Closed Sun.

Banks – The main banks are situated around the Rynek.

Internet café – Ul Ratuszowa 8 – Very close to the town hall.

Getting around

Bus and railway stations – Ul Czarnieckiego. On the south bank, west of the old town. Regular services to Warsaw, Kraków, Radom, Lublin and Zakopane.

Where to stay

Zamkowy w Krasiczynie Hotel – Inside Krasiczyn Castle - ☎ 671 83 21 – www.hotele.zamkowe.pl - 40 rooms: 210 PLN in the hotel, 230 in the castle. The Renaissance setting of the castle makes this an exceptional place to stay. Luxury rooms and service. Waking up inside the castle surrounded by its park is an unforgettable experience.

Farm holidays - Elżbieta Skrzyszowska – Leszczawa dolna 16, 37 740 Bircza – leszczawa@noclegi-pl.com – about 20km from Przemyśl on the way to Sanok. Charming country house with all modern conveniences. Peace and quiet, natural products. Open year-round.

Eating out

Restauracja « Jutrzenka » - M. Tomaszewska – Pl. Konstucji 3 Maja 6 - ☎ 670 72 40 - www.mtomaszewska.com.pl - 7am-10pm - 40 PLN. Elegant setting reminiscent of the Austrian period. Excellent cuisine, photographs of old times and waltz-like atmosphere. Delicatessen and tearoom.

Restauracja Wyrwigrosz – Ul Rynek 20 - t 678 58 58 - 10am-11pm - 30 PLN. Housed in a large vaulted room, this restaurant offers Polish dishes with a slight Asian flavour. Curry and bamboo shoots served with cabbage!

The Bieszczady★★★

MAP OF POLAND D4 – WOJEWÓDZTWO OF SUB-CARPATHIA

This small mountain area of moderate height extends over Poland, Slovakia and Ukraine, at the southern tip of the Podkarpackie region. Sparsely populated owing to their topography and recent political history, the Bieszczady are today one of the regions most sought after by those who are keen on nature and religious heritage. Here, nature is wild and the landscape alternates between low rounded mountains, covered with green pastures, and wooded valleys with mountain streams rushing through. Sanok is the gateway to the region.

- ▶ **Getting your bearings** – 80km south of Rzeszów, on the border with Ukraine and Slovakia.
- 👁 **Not to be missed** – The works of contemporary artist Zdzisław Beksiński, exhibited on the top floor of Sanok's Historical Museum.
- 🕐 **Planning your visit** – Allow at least two days to ramble through the Bieszczady, enjoy the boat trip on the Solina lake or the small mountain train. In Sanok, allow one day for the visit of the skansen and of the museum.

Background

Systematic depopulation – Inhabited in the Middle Ages by Slavs from the region of Kraków, as well as Ruthenians (people we would today call "Eastern Slavs"), this small territory on the confines of the kingdom of Poland came under Austrian domination in the 18C. During the First World War, the front line separating the Russian and Polish armies crossed the mountains as far as Przemyśl and, in the course of extremely violent fighting, 100 000 Austrians were killed. The Second World War spared the region but the immediate postwar period was tragic. The Polish and Soviet authorities came into conflict with the Ukrainian population. In 1947, the Stalinist regime decided to "solve the problem" by brutally expelling the entire Ruthenian community, causing a blood bath which remained for a long time in the collective memory. Many villages were completely emptied of their inhabitants and abandoned.

Today, many Poles, particularly those from Warsaw or Kraków who are under stress and love vast open spaces, consider the Bieszczady as a kind of "Wild West". The hospitable local population promotes human values specific to their mountain culture. Since 1973, the **Bieszczady National Park** has been entrusted with the task of maintaining a balance between the development of tourism, virtually the region's only source of income, and the safeguard of the environment. Botanists, geologists and zoologists share this ecological playground with ramblers.

Wildlife

Extending over 292sq km, the **Bieszczady National Park** only encompasses the highest part of the mountain range mostly covered with forests (80%). The fauna is particularly varied and plentiful. It is easy to see the numerous **storks** nesting on roofs or electricity poles. Most of the other species – bison, bears, wolves – are difficult to observe. Around 200 European **bison** were reintroduced in the area during the 1960s. In the 1970s and 80s, the males were hunted by the "communist elite", keen on taking trophies, and this greatly compromised their survival. There are also an estimated 90 **bears** who can reach a height of 2.5m and weigh 450kg. They roam around, especially in the forests surrounding Lake Solina and in the Słonne mountains south-east of Sanok. Should you accidentally come face to face with one of them, keep calm and make your retreat without hurrying. Another legendary animal whose name alone scares people is the **wolf**! It is believed that about 210 of them live in small packs of between 5 and 8 animals. Again, you will only meet them by accident and they will disappear without any fuss. There are also 230 **beavers**, 120 **lynx** and numerous birds of prey including **golden eagles**. Because of their wingspan, which can extend to 2m, and the exceptional quality of their vision, they are formidable predators. Last but not least are the pacific **Huculs**, small, very sturdy horses, ideal for rambling. As natives of the Carpathian mountains, they are at home here. The Bieszczady Park and a private owner breed them and treat them like a species to be protected because they are so much a part of the region.

Typical Bieszczady landscape

Round tour through the Bieszczady starting from Lesko★★★

About 150km. In Lesko, take road 893 towards Baligród, along the River Hoczewka.

Baligród

This small town, created at the beginning of the 17C, is known for the quality of its spring water. In the village centre, the rusting shell of a tank recalls the sombre hours of the Second World War. The Jewish cemetery, nestling in a wooded area on top of a hill (follow signposts marked "Cmentarz Żydowski"), and a ruined Graeco-Catholic church are all that remains of the times when the different religious communities lived in harmony.

Cisna

The Majdan - Cisna - Dołżyca - Przysłup railway line (11km)★★

Biuro Fundacji Bieszczadzkiej Kolejki Leśnej Majdan 17 - 38 607 Cisna - ℘ 468 63 35 -Jul-Aug daily; May-Jun, Sep Sat-Sun,hols - departure 10am. - about 2hr 30min. 17 PLN there and back.

Cisna's main attraction is the renovated railway line. At the end of the 19C, the south of the Podkarpacki region was so isolated that the Austrians decided to link Cisna to the L'viv-Budapest railway line. The line was used during the 20C by the Austrian army, then by the Nazi occupation forces and the Russians. Each considered it to be the most efficient means of transporting goods. After the war, the destroyed villages were rebuilt with materials carried by train. Later on, cars and road transport replaced steam locomotives and today tourists can enjoy a section of this very line.

At Cisna-Majdan station, a small unassuming yet moving museum presents a collection of various equipment used by railway workers, uniforms and numerous photos illustrating the construction and renovation of the line.

The company operating the line proposes several options, according to the seasons. During the high tourist season, it is preferable to get on at Majdan rather than at a later stop, as there are a limited number of seats.

Here, nobody indulges in excessive nostalgia! The railway workers and the locomotive are definitely modern, there are no costumes of by-gone days, no faces blackened by coal. The carriages alone, made entirely of wood, take you back to another age. The first section of the line runs through forests. The locomotive stops for a few minutes in Dołżyca, a village razed to the ground in 1947, which came back to life in the 1960s thanks to the wood industry. As soon as the train leaves Dołżyca station, it starts climbing, affording marvellous views. It stops again for a few minutes in Przysłup, which suffered the same fate as Dołżyca. When the train reaches the top of the mountain and the end of the line, the driver and his collegues detach the locomotive and turn it around... Time enough to have a drink and visit a handicraft gallery before returning to Majdan.

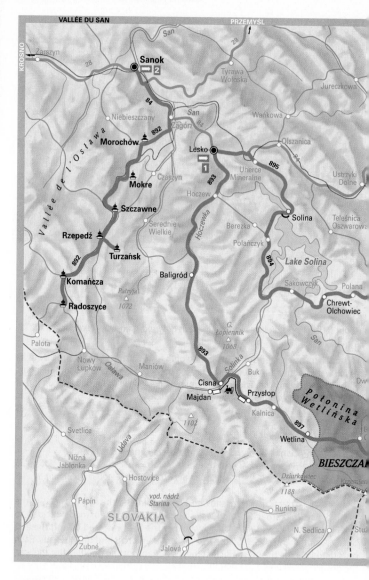

Wetlina

🚶 Ramble through the Połonina Wetlińska massif ★★★

The village, lying at the foot of the Połonina Wetlińska mountains, is the rendezvous of ramblers.

On leaving the village, the road climbs up to a vast plateau where a rambling tour starts. 2hr 15min there and back. Parking fee and admission to the Park: 9 PLN.

The tour presents no special difficulty; however, it is recommended to take a windcheater against the 0 wind blowing at the summit. The stony, fairly steep path runs through a wood then across a vast meadow for the last few hundred metres. The summit boasts a refuge but, above all, an amazing view. No obstacle blocks the 360° panorama unfolding before your eyes. The Polish and Ukrainian Bieszczady, and the Slovak mountains extend as far as the eye can see. No village, no trace of human presence is visible.

Ustrzyki Górne

This village of around 100 inhabitants is a meeting point appreciated by ramblers. The village of Wołosate, signposted on the right of the road, is the starting point of a 2hr ascent of the highest summit (1346) of the Polish Bieszczady, the Tarnica (blue mark). The Bieszczady Park breeds Hucuł horses in Wołosate.

THE BIESZCZADY

One of the finest oriental churches in the Bieszczady is located a few kilometres from Ustrzyki Górne. It stands just before the village of **Smolnik★★**. Originally a Graeco-Catholic church, it is now used by the Roman Catholic community. Built in 1791 in typical Bojko style, it escaped the 1947 massive destruction.

Lutowiska

Lutowiska is a village full of contrasts and excesses. It is known as the "Polish Alaska", not on account of its climate but because of its sparse population. The district of Lutowiska is said to be Poland's least populated, with around 5 inhabitants per sq km. And yet, before the war, the village was an important centre inhabited by Catholics, Graeco-Catholics, Orthodox Christians and Jews. In 1939, there were 3 500 inhabitants, in 1951 only 28 families were left. In the meantime, 650 Jews had been executed by the Nazis in 1942 and the majority of the population had been expelled or killed by Soviet troops in 1947. Cemeteries and a Roman Catholic church are all that remains of these communities. On the other hand, the district can provide accommodation for 1 000 tourists. *On leaving Lutowiska, drive on to Czarna Górna, then turn left to Polana.*

Chrewt – Olchowiec

Just outside Chrewt, there is a hamlet called Olchowiec. Thick smoke can be seen rising on the left side of the road and there is a strong smell of wood. This comes from a traditional charcoal factory built on a mound. This place where men control fire is far from being a tourist centre, yet it certainly deserves a visit. The workers, blackened by working conditions of another age, will kindly let you have a look. A smile, a wave of the hand and respect for their work are enough to open doors.
A steep road running all the way to Solina offers magnificent views of what is sometimes called "the Bieszczady sea".

Solina and its lake

The "Bieszczady sea" is Poland's largest artificial lake, fed by the San and Solinka rivers. It extends over an area of 22sq km and has 150km of indented coastline sometimes forming tiny fjords. This reservoir, which, in parts, reaches a depth of 60m, was created in the 1960s, following the construction of a dam over 650m long. Since then, the Solina lake has been a vast water sports area surrounded by forests where one can go mushroom or berry picking. With their wide choice of sport and leisure activities for the young, its numerous bars, restaurants and discotheques, Solina and its lake are a unique recreation area in the Bieszczady region.

Mini-cruise on the lake★

Leave the car in the parking area by the roadside *(3 PLN)* and walk across the dam to gain access to the beaches, the water sports centre and the restaurants. There is a magnificent view of the San Valley downriver and of the lake upriver. A boat company organises a mini-cruise lasting about 50min *(10 PLN)*. The trip is not exactly unforgettable, but it will enable you to make the most of the exceptional plant and mineral environment.
Beware: the boat only leaves when it is full!
Drive back towards Lesko.

Sanok★★

Population 40 000

Sanok is the gateway to the Bieszczady. The first written mention of its foundation goes back to 1150, but it was not until 1366 that Kazimierz the Great granted the status of township upon Sanok. In 1417, the wedding of King Władysław Jagiełło and Elżbieta Granowska, celebrated in the castle, definitely established Sanok as a royal city, which led noble families to settle in the region. Sanok's political and economic role remained important until the end of the 19C, when the Beksiński and Lipiński families set up the coach and carriage industry which was to become the region's economic driving force. Following the development of technology, coaches were replaced by motorised vehicles. Sanok's expansion in the 20C was due to heavy industries in rubber and mechanical engineering. Dinginess and pollution formed part of the daily life of a population torn between its mountain culture and its industrial activities. The decline of the industrial sector at the end of the 20C forced Sanok to look for new economic prospects. Today, Sanok, which has a fine cultural and religious heritage and is close to the Bieszczady, one of the Poles, Slovaks and Ukrainians' favourite tourist destinations, can look forward to a bright future.

Museum of Folk Architecture★★
(Muzeum Budownictwa Ludowego w Sanoku)

Ul Rybickiego 3 - ℘ 463 16 72 - skansen.sanok@pro.onet.pl - www.bieszczady.pl/skansen - May-Sep daily 8am-6pm, Oct 8am-4pm, Nov-Mar 8am-2pm, Apr 9am-4pm. 9 PLN.

Located on the east bank of the River San, at the foot of the low Słonne mountains, Sanok's skansen enjoys an international renown. The open-air museum was opened to the public in 1958. Spread over 38ha, it provides a valuable insight into the architectural and artistic wealth of the four ethnic groups who lived in the area until 1947.

Most of the buildings erected by the Łemks (Łemkowie) and the Boyks (Bojkowie) stand on the wooded upper part of the museum. The houses and farms of the Pogórzanie and of the Dolinianie were reassembled in the lower part. The sites were selected according to the original settlements, some groups being essentially uplanders and others having mostly lived on the plains.

The museum presents some one hundred buildings, initially erected between the 17C and the 20C, which were thus saved from the inevitable dilapidation threatening wooden structures. Some of the houses, farms and churches are especially interesting. Note in particular the wooden Roman Catholic church dating from 1667, a Łemk Graeco-Catholic church built in 1801 and two Boyk Graeco-Catholic churches dating respectively from 1731 and 1750.

Several craftsmen's workshops were also reconstructed, including wicker-work, pottery, weaving and wood-carving workshops, as well as several windmills.

Historical Museum★★
(Muzeum Historyczne)

Ul Zamkowa 2 - ℘ 463 06 09 – www.muzeum.sanok.pl - muzeum@muzeum.sanok.pl - Tue-Sun 9am-5pm. 6 PLN.

The museum is housed in Sanok's Renaissance manor house, built on the site of a former Ruthenian fortress. The charm of the place and the interest it arouses are no doubt due to the contrasting atmosphere which characterizes the two main exhibitions. Displayed on several floors is a collection of icons, by far the best of its kind in Poland. Some 300 items enable visitors to get a clear insight into the production of icons from the 15C to the 18C and to appreciate the true artistic and liturgical importance of icons in the Eastern Catholic religion. The top floor of the museum is devoted to an exhibition of the works of Zdzisław Beksiński, the world-renowned artist, a native of Sanok.

The Four Ethnic Groups

Four ethnic groups once occupied the region: the **Pogórzanie** around Gorlice, Jasło and Krosno; the **Dolinianie** around Sanok; the **Łemkowie** near the border with Slovakia; the **Bojkowie** in what is now the south of the Bieszczady on the confines of Ukraine and Slovakia.

Bojkowie and Łemkowie were the main victims of the massive deportations which began in 1947. There is little evidence left of Boyk culture apart from Sanok's skansen and the villages of Berehy Górne, Dwernik and Hulskie. The survivors of the cleanup operation now live in the Ukrainian part of the Carpathian region. As for the Łemk people who suffered the same fate, they lived along the River Osława, maintaining strong cultural exchanges with their Slovak brothers. The Łemkowie came back in greater numbers to live in the Bieszczady, thus facilitating the perpetuation of their traditions.

Museum of Folk Architecture, Sanok's skansen

This contemporary painter always arouses interest. His realism, his sinister outlook and his style have been seen in galleries throughout the world. The Osaka Museum in Japan even devotes a permanent exhibition to Beksiński. Sanok is privileged and honoured to have in trust part of his life's work.

Zdzisław Beksiński was assassinated in Warsaw in 2005.

On the trail of wooden churches

The Osława Valley, the Łemk churches trail★★

About 100km there and back, starting from Sanok. Drive south towards Lesko as far as Zagórz, then turn right towards Komańcza.

The River Osława flows into the San at Zagórz. Along the road, which meanders over some forty kilometres through a wooded undulating landscape, there is a string of wooden churches built by the Łemks in the 19C. If visitors are surprised to see so many architectural gems and icons, they should not forget that most of these churches were destroyed during the wars or during the communist era. One more reason to enjoy this itinerary.

On leaving Zagórz, turn right towards Poraż and Morochów.

Morochów Church – *Thanks to the priest living in the presbytery, one can gain access to the church.* A path starting from the road leads to the building perched on a mound. Erected by the Graeco-Catholic community in 1837, it became an Orthodox church in 1961. The interior contains a remarkable 19C iconostasis.

Continue along the road to the village of Mokre.

Mokre Church – *The inhabitants of the house at no 42 along the road will be your guides during the visit.* This brick-built Graeco-Catholic church is recent (1992) and has very little of interest to offer in comparison with its neighbours. However, the iconostasis dating from 1900, on loan from the Icon Museum in Łańcut, is worth looking at.

On leaving Mokre, note the installations of a disused oil well. Continue towards Szczawne. Drive through the village until you reach a railway crossing. The church is on the hill to the right beyond the railway line.

Szczawne Church – *The keys are available from the house at no 20, along the road to Bukowsko. (Note: it is advisable to follow the path from the road to the church and not to walk across the fields...the soil is marshy!).* The church of the Virgin Mary's Dormition, built in 1888 by Graeco-Catholics, is now used by Graeco-Catholics. It is surmounted by an amazing onion-shaped roof. The wooden bell tower, separate from the church, was built a year later. The iconostasis is a contemporary work but the polychrome murals date from 1925.

Continue towards the village of Rzepedź. On entering, turn right onto the road running alongside the stream to the church.

Rzepedź Church – *Sławomir Jurowski, who lives in the first house on the right past the church, has a set of keys.* Built in 1824 and restored in 1896, St Nicholas's Church belonged to the Graeco-Catholic community before passing into the hands of the Roman Catholics after the Second World War. It was recently returned to the Graeco-Catholics. The iconostasis and the three-storey bell tower date from the construction of the church. The polychrome interior decoration dates from 1896.

In the village, turn left towards Turzańsk. Drive through part of the village, the church stands on the left side of the road.

Turzańsk Church – *Teodor Tchoryk, who lives in the house at no 63, shows visitors round.* The church of St Michael the Archangel was erected by Graeco-Catholics in 1803 but is now an Orthodox church. In addition to its late-19C iconostasis and its two early-19C side altars, it boasts a bell tower said to be the highest in Poland for this type of church.

Return to Rzepedź, pick up the road to Komańcza. Go through the village towards Dukla.

Komańcza Churches – The first one is on the roadside. The lower part of the church is brick built whereas the upper part is wooden. A vast cupola covers the building. The history of its construction explains the strangeness of the place. Between 1985 and 1988, in order to find a way round the administrative difficulties and harassment caused by the rigid authorities, the Graeco-Catholic community applied the directives by exploiting their absurdity and they ended up by building a brick church and crowning it with an abandoned wooden church from the nearby village of Dudyńce, which they moved for the occasion. The second church – Church of the Virgin's protection – is a lot more classical. It is a magnificent wooden monument erected in 1802, containing an iconostasis from 1832. It is now used by the Orthodox community, although it was built for the Graeco-Catholics. It is surrounded by a wooden belfry-gate and a churchyard.

From Komańcza, follow the road to Radoszyce. The church is on top of a hill, to the left of the road. It is accessible on foot along a surfaced path.

Radoszyce Church – *Zofia Gusztak, who lives in the house at no 12, near the church, has a set of keys.* St Dimitri Church is Graeco-Catholic. The path leading to it runs under a brick belfry-gate then reaches the plateau where the cemetery is located. Inside, look out for the chancel paintings depicting scenes from the daily life and spiritual life of the Łemki (plural of Łemko).

The San Valley, the icons and eastern churches trail ★★
About 80km there and back starting from Sanok.

Another itinerary, north of Sanok, leads to the discovery of other wooden Graeco-Catholic churches. The route follows the River San towards Mrzygłód. The most typical churches are situated north of this small town, in the villages of **Hłomcza, Łodzina** *(off the road to the left)*, **Dobra Szlachecka** and **Ulucz**. It is without a doubt in **Ulucz** that lies the gem of the whole region. The **Church of the Ascension** *(the keys are available from Genowefa Filip, at no 16 as you enter the village)* is the oldest of Poland's wooden eastern churches. Built in 1510, it is run and looked after by the Museum of Folk Architecture in Sanok.

Practical Bieszczady

Useful addresses

SANOK
Postal code – 38-500
Tourist office – Gregorza z Sanoka 2 - ☏ 464 45 33 - turystyka.sanok@pbp.com.pl - 9am-5pm, Sat 9am-2pm, closed Sun.
Police – ☏ 997
Fire brigade – ☏ 998
Mountain emergency – ☏ 985 (free)
Bieszczady National Park – www.bdpn.pl - bdpn@wp.pl
Headquarters and information : 38-714 Ustrzyki Górne 19 - ☏ 461 06 50
Information centre : 38-713 Lutowiska 2 - ☏ 461 03 50

Cisna tourist office – ☏ 468 64 65 - www.cisna.pl - informacja@cisna.pl - Tue-Sat 8am-4pm.

Getting around

The Bieszczady owe their success to their relative isolation. Fortunately, thanks to public transports, this is not too much of an obstacle to the growth of the region.

Bus and railway stations – They face each other, 10min's walk south of the town centre , on the road to Lesko. There are regular train services to Krosno, itself linked with the major towns in the south of Poland.

Frequent bus services to Kraków and Rzeszów.

Buses of all sizes link the Bieszczady villages at varying intervals.

Where to stay

SANOK

Sanvit Hotel – *Ul. Łazienna 1 – ℘ 465 50 88 - www.sanvit.sanok.pl - biuro@sanvit. sanok.pl - 31 rooms: 134 PLN.* Situated In the very centre of Sanok, this hotel overlooking a wooded park is no doubt the most modern and comfortable in town, even if it is a little cold. Sauna, fitness room and baths await you.

IN THE MOUNTAINS

Pensjonat Leśny Dwór – *38-608 Wetlina - ℘ 468 46 54 - www.bieszczady.pl/dwor - 13 rooms: 260 PLN ½ B ; wooden cottage 4 to 6 pers. : 24 PLN per pers.* Lost in the hills, this large family house is very attractive. The piano, the library and refined decor go well with the weights room, the sauna, the mountain bikes and the delicious cuisine. Warm welcome.

PTTK Hotel Górski – *38-714 Ustrzyki Górne - ℘ 461 06 04 - www.hotelgorski.webpark. pl - hotelgorski@wp.pl - 63 rooms: 180 PLN.* There is a genuine rambling atmosphere in this place. Although it is quite comfortable, this establishment should preferably be reserved for people who enjoy long discussions at night between nature lovers and for those who take advantage of their holidays to get up at dawn. It is a quality hotel with the atmosphere of a youth hostel !

Farm holidays

Daria and Stefan Boiwka – *38-543 Komańcza 147 - ℘ 467 71 34 - 2 rooms: 50 PLN; 100 PLN ½ B.* In Komańcza, at the Dukla road junction, take the road opposite then the first on the left. Follow the path climbing to the left, past the sawmill, to a wooden house. The accommodation is comfortable and, as a bonus, you will meet a charming woman. Daria Boiwka makes folk costumes and manages her own small museum.

Ryszard Krzeszewski – *Chmiel 28 – 38-713 Lutowiska – ℘ : 461 08 34 - koniebieszczady@net.pl - 3 rooms: 60 PLN ½ B.* Ryszard Krzeszewski is an important man in the riding world. Riders can hire Hucuł horses and go rambling in his company. His knowledge of the mountain and of horses together with his interesting personality make him one of the strong characters of the Bieszczady region. Here, although the accommodation is modern and comfortable, its quality is not the customers' priority.

Eating out

SANOK

Bieszczadzka Karczma – *Rynek 12 - ℘ 464 67 00 - www.bieszczady.pl/ karczma - karczmasanok@wp.pl - 11am-* *10pm - 35 PLN.* Ideal to stock up on calories and discover mountain cooking. The interior is a mini-skansen and the terrace is most welcoming for a drink at sunset. The inn situated at the entrance to Sanok's skansen belongs to the same owner. These two addresses are the most likely to satisfy both the palate and the eyes.

Restaurant Jagiellonski Hotel– *Ul. Jagiellonska 49 – ℘ 463 12 08 – 11am-10pm– 60 PLN.* The cuisine is delicious, in striking contrast with the general look of the establishment, which is surprising. It is possible to enjoy original dishes not ususally served in ordinary inns. The place is worth a visit for its appearance and its food!

IN THE MOUNTAINS

Karczma Chata Wędrowca – *38-608 Wetlina – 11am-11pm – 40 PLN.* Located by the roadside, this inn is housed in a large wooden building halfway between the Bieszczady and the "Wild West". Ramblers and locals liven up the place with their incessant chatter about how pure the air is in the area and what a pleasure it is to breathe it, while they drink huge bowls of soup and enjoy mushroom fricassee.

Shopping

Confident in the value of their traditions and of folk art, the Bieszczady craftsmen formed an Association for the Promotion of Local Products. Wooden objects, icons, honey, furniture, fabrics, cheese...the range of products "made in Bieszczady" is amazing. The catalogue published by the Association is available in Tourist offices and offices of the Bieszczady Park.

Bieszczady Centrum Promocji i Certyfikacji Produktu Lokalnego – *Lutowiska 74a - 38-713 Lutowiska – ℘ 461 01 63 - www.bieszczady.pl/produkt - lutgok@poczta.bieszczady.pl*

Sport and leisure

Riding a Hucuł – Many riding farms organise riding tours using this small Carpathian horse. There is a breeding farm and accommodation facilities in the Bieszczady Park. The Park's Information centre can also provide you with suitable addresses according to your riding ability. The Hucuł breeding centre run by the Park is in Wołosate, a few kilometres from Ustrzyki Górne.

Hucuł breeding centre: *Wołosate, 38-714 Ustrzyki Górne - ℘ 461 06 50 - konie@oie. bdpn.pl*

The Bieszczady Riding-tour Club : *Rynek 16 - 38-700 Ustrzyki Górne - ℘ 461 14 15 -*

Biking across the Bieszczady – The Bieszczady Cycle Association : *Ul. 29 Listopada 51/1 - 38-700 Ustrzyki Dolne - ℘ 461 18 78 - www.rowery.bieszczady. info.pl*

Krynica and the East Beskid ★★
Beskides Sądecki – Beskides Niski

MAP OF POLAND C4 – WOJEWÓDZTWO OF LITTLE POLAND AND SUB-CARPATHIA

The East Beskid are split into two mountain ranges of medium altitude. The first, known as the Beskid Sądecki, follows a vertical line between Nowy Sącz and Krynica on the Slovak border. It is appreciated for the beneficial effect of its spas as well as for its colourful architecture and its green undulating scenery. The second, situated further east and known as the Beskid Niski, covers an area extending from Nowy Sącz to Krosno in the north and reaching south as far as the Slovak border via the Dukla pass. Wooden religious architecture is the main attraction. Krynica is the most interesting starting point of a tour of the region.

- ▶ **Getting your bearings** – South-east of Kraków.
- 👁 **Not to be missed** – The oil museum in Bóbrka, near Krosno.
- 🕐 **Planning your visit** – Allow half a day to visit Nowy Sącz and Stary Sącz, two days to make the most of Krynica, a charming spa town, and its surroundings, and spend half a day around Krosno.

Krynica

Krynica owes its charm to the bright colours of its wooden houses painted in light green, blue or yellow and to the luxuriant vegetation of its parks and hillsides, all of this creating a cheerful atmosphere.

Water and Wood

The town has existed since 1547, but the beneficial effects of its mineral springs were only acknowledged at the end of the 18C. The fame of the resort and of its neighbours, Muszyna and Piwniczna, spread rapidly and many doctors set up treatment and fitness centres. In 1856, Józef Dietl, a famous doctor from Kraków University, launched a project for the creation of a spa. The number of baths, pump rooms and places to stay increased and there was an influx of well-off people and artists such as the writer Sienkeiwicz, the painters Matejko and Nikifor, or the musician Jan Kiepura, won over by the peaceful atmosphere and the wooden architecture. The building of a cable car, the creation of ski runs and the arrival of the railway only emphasized the fashion trend. In 1919, around 10 000 people came every year, aspiring to well-being... A fluctuating population rising to 40 000 before the Second World War. After the war, the resort pursued it modernisation and lost its aristocratic character. The Polish communist working class was invited to recharge its batteries in the numerous sanatoriums and guesthouses occupying large grey buildings which spoilt part of the small town's charm. Fortunately, the current authorities understand how important the environment is for visitors and Krynica has now regained the assets which ensured its success.

Promenade Nowotarskiego ★★
You can reach this promenade from anywhere in Krynica. Also known as "**deptak**", it prolongs bd J Piłsudskiego, lined with the town's main shops, and runs parallel to the road leading to Muszyna. Note, at the beginning of the promenade, the **statue of the poet Adam Mickiewicz**, near a bandstand. Most of the spa activity takes place on this large esplanade skirted by the River Kryniczańska. Buildings in 19C style offer a striking contrast with those erected in the 20C.

Springs
The main springs are located in sites known as Nowy Dom Zdrojowy, Pijalnia Główna and Stare Łazienki Mineralne. Another spring, Pijalnia Jana, is hidden inside a park near the Góra Parkowa cable-car station. People can be seen walking about holding a plastic cup or an oddly shaped tumbler filled with foul-smelling water said to have healing powers!

Nikifor Museum (Muzeum Nikifora)
Bulwary Dietla 19. Tue-Sun 10am-1pm, 2-5pm. Closed Mon. 4 PLN.
Nikifor (1893-1968) is considered to be Poland's greatest naive painter. At the height of his career in the 1920s and 1930s, Nikifor distinguished himself by painting self-

Advertisement for a local mineral water

portraits and landscapes. The museum, located in his studio, displays about 100 works by the artist and devotes temporary exhibitions to other Polish painters.

Around Nowy Sącz

Nowy Sącz (Population 85 000)
35km north of Krynica.

This is the largest town in the region. Created in 1292, Nowy Sącz was damaged by many fires throughout its history. At the beginning of the 17C, almost the whole town, the churches and the fortress were destroyed. Later, at the end of the 19C, the northern part of the city was devastated by fire. Lastly, when the town was liberated in January 1945, the partisans blew up the royal castle used by the Germans as a munitions store. Nowy Sącz therefore no longer enjoys a rich historic heritage. Lately, the town has made its mark in the field of industry and commerce. It is the headquarters of a competitive computer business, one of the top-listed companies on the Warsaw stock exchange.

Apart from the **Rynek**, built in 1895 in the neo-Renaissance and neo-Baroque styles, it is worth visiting the Gothic House, also known as the **Canons' House** (Dom Kanoniczy) *(Tue, Wed, Thu 10am-3pm)*, built at the beginning of the 16C. Since the 1960s, it has housed collections of religious and ethnographic art as well as a display illustrating the history of the monuments destroyed over the centuries.

Nowy Sącz boasts a **Skansen** (Sądecki Park Etnograficzny), *at the southern end of town, along the road to Stary Sącz (Sat-Sun 9am-2.30pm, 6 PLN)*, symbolizing the region's rich and varied culture. With its 18C wooden Orthodox church, its manor house, its farms and evidence of gypsy camps, the open-air museum offers a pleasant walk which throws invaluable light on the coexistence of the different communities.

Stary Sącz ★
From Nowy Sącz drive south along road 87 towards Piwniczna-Zdrój. Stary Sącz is on the right side of the road, about 6km further on.

During the Middle Ages, the town stood as an important centre at the junction of trade routes between Hungary and Northern Europe. Princess Kinga commissioned a convent to be built for the Clarisse order and became its first abbess on the death of her husband, King Bolesław the Chaste. The chapels of this fortified edifice, still dedicated to its illustrious initiator, are decorated with Baroque works of art. The treasury of the **Trinity Church** houses many relics concerning the princess. The small city of Stary Sącz, like its more important neighbour, Nowy Sącz, was devastated by fire and wars. The heart of the city, destroyed in 1795, was only rebuilt after the Second World War. Today, the **Rynek** is a vast paved square, still surrounded by a few old houses such as no 6, the "Na Dołkach" House, home to the **Regional Museum**. Except for the Clarisse Convent, the architectural ensemble does not convey the town's former atmosphere and importance.

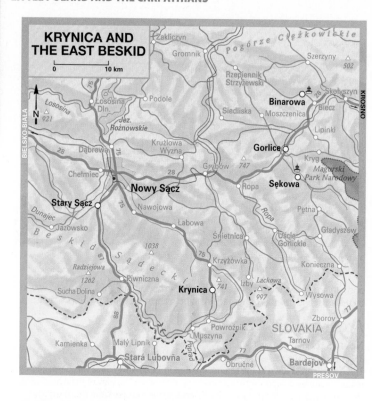

Around Gorlice

Wooden churches on UNESCO's World Heritage List★★
Sękowa

4km south-east of Gorlice, along road 977.

St Philip and St James's Church (kościół pw. św. św. Filipa i Jakuba) dates from 1520. The nave is entirely covered with shingles and the square tower is surmounted by an onion shaped spire. Although the building was greatly damaged during the First World War, the interior still retains Gothic fonts dating from 1522 and polychrome decorations dating from 1888.

Binarowa

From Gorlice, follow road 28 to Biecz then drive north along road 980 to Binarowa.

The **Church of St Michael the Archangel** was built around 1500, entirely from fir wood. The stencilled decorations on the ceiling and the Gothic sculptures date from the early 16C; as for the Baroque paintings, they are 17C works.

Around Krosno

Bóbrka

Oil Museum★ (Skansen Muzeum Przemysłu Naftowego)

Drive to Krosno, 105km east of Nowy Sącz along road 98. In Krosno, head for Dukla along roads 98 and 9. After 8km, turn right towards Bóbrka et Chorkówka. Follow signposts to "Skansen Muzeum Przemysłu Naftowego" for about 5km.

May-Sep: 9am-5pm, Oct-Apr: 9am-3pm. 6 PLN.

Lost in the middle of the Beskid, this open-air museum, covering an area of 20ha, offers an insight into a little-known aspect of 19C Polish economy: oil extraction, refining and transport. As early as the 15C, the chronicler Jan Długosz noted the presence of the precious liquid. A few attempts at exploiting and using the oil were made in the early 19C but it was only in the 1850s that the "father" of the oil industry, Ignacy Łukasiewicz, formed the first company.

The area around Krosno was not the only one involved in the exploitation of the black gold. Its presence was detected in the subsoil of a large strip of land stretching from Jasło to L'viv (Ukraine) via Sanok and the Bieszczady. Traces of this activity can still be seen along this itinerary and there are a few thematic displays in some museums.

However, Bóbrka is without a doubt the most informative and pertinent place of collective memory. The museum, located on a former working site, displays a lot of the original equipment as well as copies. The various aspects of the activity are dealt with: technology, industrial development, working conditions. A fascinating and instructive place.

Haczów wooden church

From Krosno, head for Iskzynia, then Haczów. The Church of the Blessed Virgin and of St Michael the Archangel (kościół pw. św Michała Archanioła) was erected in the 15C. The Gothic polychrome decoration dates from the late 15C. At the beginning of the 16C, the church was surrounded by a defensive wall. The roof, damaged in 1914, was restored in 1915. Today it is on UNESCO's World Heritage List.

Practical East Beskid

Postal code (Krynica) – 33-380
Postal code (Nowy Sącz) – 33-300

Useful addresses

Phone code – 018
Tourist office –
Krynica : *Ul Piłsudskiego 8* - 471 56 54 – www.krynica.pl - *10am-noon, 2-5pm. Located beneath the cinema.*
Nowy Sącz : *Ul Piotra Skargi 2* - 444 24 22 – www.cit.com.pl - cit@sarr.com.pl - *9am-5pm, Mon-Fri: 8am-6pm, Sat: 9am-2pm.*

Getting around

Railway station – *ul. Kolejowa.* Warsaw, Kraków, Gdynia, Budapest (Hungary) and Kosice (Slovakia) are linked to Nowy Sącz.

Bus station – *Situated on a square at the junction of Długosza and Wolności streets.* Buses leave regularly for the spas and villages of the Beskid in the Nowy Sącz area. Nowy Sącz et Krynica are linked by many bus and minibus services. The journey lasts around 30min. There are bus services to all the large towns in southern and central Poland: Warsaw, Kraków, Zakopane, Lublin, as well as Bardejov in Slovakia.

Where to stay

KRYNICA
Nikifor Hotel– *Ul Świdzińskiego 20 -* 477 87 00 - www.nikifor.pl - *24 rooms: 135 PLN.* The hotel is a real art gallery. Paintings, frescoes, sculptures are everywhere. The sauna and relaxation rooms appear to have been dug out of the rock. In addition, there is an upstairs restaurant serving inventive dishes and a traditional inn on the ground floor. All in all, a charming place!
Pensjonat Willa Witoldówka – *Ul Bulwary Dietla 10 -* 471 55 77 - http://www.witoldowka.com.pl - *40 rooms:*

120 PLN. Built in the heart of the spa, this large wooden building, characteristic of Krynica's architectural style, is one of the most famous "pensjonat". The slightly quaint atmosphere does not in the least spoil the pleasure of staying in a comfortable historic monument.
Pensjonat Małopolanka – *Ul Bulwary Dietla 13 -* 471 58 96 - www.malopolanka.com.pl - *20 rooms: 185 PLN.* Conveniently situated close to the promenade, this "pensjonat" is ideal for people looking first and foremost for relaxation. Yoga is the star activity offered to customers.

Eating out

KRYNICA
Zielona Górka – *Ul Nowotarskiego 5 -* 471 21 77 - *11am-10pm - 40 PLN.* This colourful inn is located at the beginning of the promenade (Deptak). Traditional cuisine and pizzas are both on the menu. Musicians sometimes liven up the evenings, when beer replaces sulphured water!

Shopping

Cepelia – *Rynek 21 - 33-300 Nowy Sącz -* 442 00 45 - www.cepelia.pl - cepelia@cepelia.com.pl - Far from the main tourist areas, this small handicraft gallery displays shimmering fabrics, wooden objects, painted eggs and tea sets.

Festive events

Jan Kiepura Festival. The famous Polish opera singer used to come to Krynica regularly. Every year, his admirers, many orchestras and singers all gather for two weeks in mid-August for a series of concerts in his honour.
Information: Centrum Kultury ul Piłsudskiego 19 - 33-380 - Krynica - 471 56 48 – kiepurafestival@o2.pl

Zakopane★★★

Nestling at the foot of the Tatras mountains, in the region of Podhale, Zakopane is an attractive town as much for it geographic position as for its architectural style. This green city, lying at an altitude of 838 metres and dominated by peaks culminating at almost 2 500 metres, proudly displays its mountain culture, making sure it remains authentic and thus expressing a determination to hold onto its roots which has never wavered since Zakopane was discovered by the Polish aristocracy around 1850.

▶ **Getting your bearings** – 100km south of Kraków along the E77 then road 95.

👁 **Not to be missed** – The many art galleries in town.

🕐 **Planning your visit** – Allow two days for visiting the museums and exploring on foot the long streets lined with wooden houses.

Background

An evolution respectful of tradition – For the past 150 years, Zakopane has shown its extraordinary capacity for adaptation and transformation. Until the 19C, the village was known only for its population of rebellious shepherds, who loved freedom passionately and were sometimes prone to commit robbery. It was then that Kraków's intelligentsia took control of the town's destiny. Doctors, scientists and artists were about to discover the beneficial mountain air and the area's tourist potential. Among them was Father Józef Stolarczyk who, as early as 1850, suggested to the members of his congregation that they should let rooms to visitors and then launched the idea of building guesthouses. Tytus Chałubiński, a doctor and a botanist, established the therapeutic qualities of the Tatras in the fight against tuberculosis. This scholar understood that very soon the sick would not be the only ones to come on holiday and that it was necessary to provide facilities and entertainment for the tourists. He initiated the creation of the Guides Company and invited musicians and dancers to come and provide evening entertainment in restaurants. According to legend, the "good doctor" laid the foundations of a true mountain resort. Last but not least was Stanisław Witkiewicz, the man who thought that the development of the resort could only be considered if the rules of traditional architecture were upheld. This poet, art critic and writer lived in Zakopane from 1890 to 1908. He is said to be the initiator of the "Zakopane style", a real school of architecture rooted in the traditions of the Podhale region. He argued that it would have been damaging for the region had its architectural style been modified according to Swiss or Tyrolean criteria, as had happened in other mountain regions in Poland.

> ### "Air as pure as crystal"
>
> This has been Zakopane's motto for many years. Before the 1990s, a disgusting cloud, due to the coal-fired heating of the houses, hovered over the town. This polluted fog became just a bad memory when the municipality decided to use the hot springs tapped at a depth of 2 000 metres to heat the town. Interest-free loans were granted to the inhabitants to encourage them to change their heating systems and this initiative was very successful.
> The municipality also undertook to maintain the open spaces and wooded areas within the limits of Zakopane, which represent 12% of the town's total area. This concerns in particular Równia Krupowa, the meadow where people go for a stroll and summer activities take place.

Most of the houses which are at least one hundred years old consist of two buildings: the house and the farm. The house is split into two separate parts by an entrance hall: the black room is on the left, the white room on the right. Originally, only the black room was occupied by the family because it was heated, the smoke accounting for the colour of the walls and of the furniture. The white room's main function was that of a reception room, it was here that festivities and ceremonies took place: weddings, funeral meals or religious feasts. Its decoration and furniture testified to the wealth and savoir vivre of its owners. An exposed beam (*sosreb*) is engraved with a star within a circle, the year the house was built and the name of the family. The frames of the front door and of the windows are also adorned with decorations (*zastrzaly*). Even if the interior has been remodelled, the outside appearance of modern houses is often in keeping with the criteria of the *"Zakopane style"*, which enables the town to retain its most enjoyable harmonious look.

The "Zakopane style" trail★★

Zakopane is best explored on foot. It is important to note that houses illustrating the "Zakopane style" are mostly privately owned. It is therefore essential to observe the rules of correct behaviour. There are several possible itineraries. One of them starts from the bus and railway station.

Chramcówki Street

Walk along this street and don't hesitate to turn into the narrow pedestrian streets on the left. The most characteristic traditional houses are often not in evidence. Note the **"Pyszna" Villa** at no 22a, which shows that recent constructions adhere to the rules of traditional architecture. Look also at the **Polonia House** at no 22. A contemporary church, surmounted by an original shingle roof, stands on the right side of the street.

Nowotarska Street

Next comes this street lined on either side by a fine group of houses level with no 30. When you reach the junction with Krupówki Street, continue towards Kościeliska Street.

Kościeliska Street

This very long street is Zakopane's architectural masterpiece. In addition to a wealth of houses, it offers the town's **oldest church**, dating from 1845, and its cemetery where a great many writers, artists and mountaineers, who form part of the resort's legend, are buried. The funeral monuments are often real works of art, sometimes adorned with **icons painted on glass** in true Podhale tradition.

Further on, at no 18, you will see the villa known as "**Koliba**". Built in 1893, from drawings by Stanisław Witkiewicz, it now houses the **Stanisław Witkiewicz Zakopane style Museum★★**. *Wed-Sat 9am-4.30pm, Sun 9am-3pm. Closed Mon and Tue. 6 PLN.* At the end of the 19C, Zygmunt Gnatowski, an ethnologist with a passion for the Tatras, wanted to have a summer residence built in Zakopane. Stanisław Witkiewicz succeeded in persuading him to let him have carte blanche so that he could put his architectural theories into practice. Therefore, when Villa "Koliba" was built in 1892, the "Zakopane style" was applied for the first time. Situated in a wooded area with a foaming stream running alongside, it is now a museum presenting Zygmunt Gnatowski's personal collections of furniture and handicraft. It is the ideal place for visitors to understand the building criteria of the houses. From the decorations to the method used for insulation, from the objects of daily life to the furniture, everything seems to have sprung straight out of a charming fairy tale. This is no doubt a means of masking the harshness of life in the Tatras at that time.

Koliba House, Stanisław Witkiewicz Zakopane style Museum

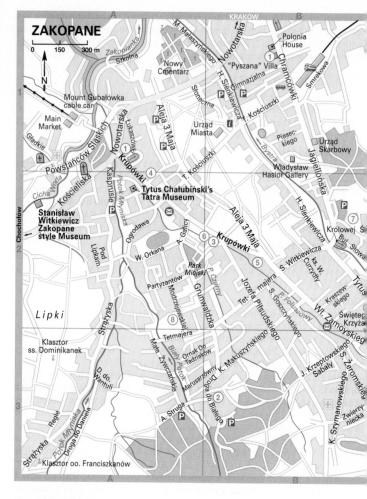

The Witkiewicz Houses

Further away, east of the town centre, there are three buildings designed by Stanisław Witkiewicz or his son: **Villa "Pod Jedlami"** at no 1 Koziniec Street; **Villa "Witkiewiczówka"**, built during the 1930s on Antałówka Road, and, further on, **the Jaszczurówka chapel** erected between 1904 and 1908 for the Uznański family. *To get there, follow signposts marked "Kaplica Jaszczurówka" on the way to the Łysa Polana border post between Poland and Slovakia.*

Krupówki Street★

This long pedestrian street runs through the town and is prolonged by the access path to the cable car leading to **Mount Gubałówka.** Although not the richest in terms of architectural heritage, this street is undoubtedly the most visited. Shops, restaurants, luxury hotels and street entertainment argue strongly in its favour.

No 10 is home to the **Tytus Chałubiński's Tatra Museum★ (Muzeum Tatrzańskie)** *(Tue-Sun 9am-4.30pm. 6 PLN).* Founded by Doctor Tytus Chałubiński and his faithful companion, mountain storyteller Jan Krzeptowski Sabała, this museum is housed in one of the rare "Zakopane-style" stone buildings. It shows how the shepherd village became a spa and sport resort. The ethnographic section is divided into two major parts: the first describes the layout of the houses, in particular the role of the black rooms and of the white rooms. The second presents the Podhale region's economic activity: hunting, sheep farming and farming. Many glass cases or galleries display costumes, tools, pottery and paintings on glass. The first floor is devoted to the geological aspect of the Tatras and of the Pieniny range, north-east of Zakopane. The museum also provides many informative panels and displays collections illustrating the varied flora and fauna found in an alpine-type mountain range. Look out, chamois and marmots are watching you!

HOTELS

Willa Pyszna .... ①
Belvedere .... ②
Fian .... ③
Kasprowy Wierch .... ⑤
Litwor .... ⑥
Pensjonat Antałówka . ⑦

Pensjonat Lipowy
Dwór .... ⑧
Pensjonat Renesens .. ⑨

RESTAURANTS

Gazdowo Kuźnia .. ①
Karcma Zapiecek .. ③
Restauracja Sabała ... ④

The Tatra Museum also runs the **Władysław Hasior Gallery** *(Ul Jagiellońska 18B. Wed-Sat 11am-6pm, Sun 9am-3pm. Closed Mon and Tue. 4.30 PLN)* devoted to the works of this artist (1928-2000) who lived in Zakopane for many years and achieved celebrity in the 1960s. Władysław Hasior is in a class of his own, borrowing from Dadaïsm, Surrealism and Pop-Art to create works brought to life by the wind or placing side by side objects of daily life.

A short distance from the museum, horse-drawn carriages and their owners dressed in Podhale costumes await tourists keen on a ride through the most picturesque streets. At the lower end of the street, beyond the junction with Kościeliska street, one enters Zakopane's **big market**. Woollen clothes, wooden objects and famous **oscypek cheese** made from ewe's milk are on sale at all the stalls, right up to the entrance of the cable-car station.

Nearby

Rambles around Zakopane★★★

These are described in the next chapter entitled "The Tatras".

In Zakopane itself *(south-east of the town)* you can visit the **Tatra Park Information Centre**, which houses a small museum devoted to the fauna and flora.

Chochołów★

Leave Zakopane along Kościeliska Street. The village of Chochołów lies some 15km on the way to Czarny Dunajec, along road 958. See the map of the Tatras p. 274-275.

The village was founded in the 16C but most of the present houses date from the 19C. The construction of these houses, lining the road over a distance of one kilometre, shows remarkable coherence and originality. The fir-tree logs stacked on top of each other are amazingly large. All this is far removed from the refined decorations of the "*Zakopane style*".

Standing opposite the stone church is the small **Chochołów Museum (***Wed-Sun 10am-2pm. 4 PLN),* housed in a building dating from 1798. In addition to the ethnographic information it provides, this tiny place tells us that the village is famous for its bravery in dealing with the various occupying forces. The Polish kings granted Chochołów and its inhabitants a particularly advantageous status as early as the 17C, to thank them for standing up to the Swedish invaders. Again in 1846, the brave villagers took up arms, two years before the rest of the country, in order to boot the Austrians out of their lands. In spite of their failure, Chochołów continued to operate in secret, sheltering patriots on the run; secret societies were formed for the sole purpose of liberating the Podhale region. Even though most of the activists were caught and executed by the Austrians before they had time to accomplish their mission, they are still considered as valiant fighters for freedom and independence.

Practical Zakopane

Postal code – 34-500
Phone code – 0-18

Useful addresses

Tourist office – Ul Kościuszki 17 - ✆ 201 22 11 - www.zakopane.pl - info@um. zakopane.pl - 10am-5pm.

Main post office – Ul Krupówki 20.

Police – ✆ 997.

Fire brigade – ✆ 998.

Mountain emergency – Ul Piłsudskiego 63a - ✆ 206 34 44.

Getting around

The bus and railway stations are adjacent and are situated some 100 metres from the Tourist office.

Railway station – Ul Chramcówki 23 - ✆ 201 45 04.

Bus station – Ul Kościuszki 25 - ✆ 201 46 03.

There are bus services to all the starting points of rambling tours through the Tatras and to the outlying districts of Zakopane.

Kraków is the destination with the most links with Zakopane. There are many bus and train services daily. The average journey time is 1hr 30min.

Airport – The nearest international airports are those of Kraków and Poprad in Slovakia.

Border posts

The two busiest border posts between Poland and Slovakia in the vicinity of Zakopane are Chochołów and Łysa Polana. They are both open to private cars and goods vehicles below 3.5t; in addition, the second allows freight through without tonnage limits. They are open 24hr a day.

Where to stay

Belvedere Hotel – Droga do Białego 3 - ✆ 202 12 00 - www.belvederehotel.pl - belvedere@trip.pl - 144 rooms: 300 PLN. This central luxury establishment is fitted up in 1920s style with a regional touch. Fitness, beauty centre and gourmet cuisine are the key words.

Litwor Hotel – Ul Krupówki 40 - ✆ 202 42 00 - www.litwor.pl - recepja@litwor.pl - 58 rooms : 200 PLN. Most of the rooms are very bright and offer a panoramic view of the Tatras. The friendy welcome and the decoration create a warm atmosphere. Swimming pool, solarium, sauna...

Kasprowy Wierch Hotel – Ul Krupówki 50B - ✆ 201 27 38 - kasprowy@mati.zakopane.pl - 30 rooms: 180 PLN. Very friendy hotel boasting a large peaceful courtyard away from the hustle and bustle of the street. Experience the pleasure of living in an old yet perfectly comfortable house.

Fian Hotel – Ul Chałubińskiego 38 - ✆ 201 50 71 - www.fian.pl - fian@fian.pl - 38 rooms: 195 PLN. Away from the town centre, this family hotel is modern and comfortable. It has struck the perfect compromise between quality services and reasonable prices.

Pensjonat Antałówka – Ul Wierchowa 2 - ✆ 201 32 71 - anatalowka@polskietatry.pl - 21 rooms: 200 PLN - 10 apart: 300 PLN. The facilities and decoration of this establishment are devoid of regional charm but are perfectly adequate for a prolonged stay. Tennis, sauna, jacuzzi and solarium are available.

Pensjonat Lipowy Dwór – Ul H. Modrzejewskiej 7 - ✆ 206 67 96 - www. sosnica.pl - sosnica@zakopane.pl - 15 rooms: 220 PLN. Situated 5min from the town centre, in a large wooden chalet-style house. Convivial welcome. Fine furniture and traditional fabrics create an elegant atmosphere.

Pensjonat Renesens – Ul Chałubińskiego 26 - ✆ 206 62 02 - www.renesans.pl - recepcja@renesans.pl - 23 rooms: 190 PLN. This fine residence with character offers all the comfort one could wish for. Mountain songs and dances provide entertainment on some evenings and guides or leisure activities can be recommended.

Willa Pyszna Rooms – Ul Chramcówki 22 - ✆ 206 85 42 - 3 rooms: 40 PLN - 1 apart 6-8 pers. : 300 PLN. Experience the pleasure of staying in a modern and comfortable house in authentic traditional style.

Eating out

Gazdowo Kuźnia – Ul Krupówki 1 - ✆ 201 72 01 - 40 PLN. The dining room looks like an antique shop or a skansen! Foodwise, don't expect any surprises, but look forward to savoury and very tasty traditional mountain dishes.

Restauracja Sabała – Ul Krupówki 11 - ✆ 201 50 92 - 10am-11pm - 40 PLN. The large chalet-style house, which also includes a luxury hotel, dominates the street. Restorative dishes can be enjoyed while watching the incessant movement of passers-by and horses.

Karcma Zapiecek – Ul Krupówki 43 - ✆ 201 56 99 - 11am-11pm - 40 PLN. For those who wish to experience the atmosphere of a "koliba". The palate and the ears can enjoy traditional folk flavours and sounds.

Pizzeria Kasprowy Wierch – At the top of the cable car which climbs to the summit of the Kasprowy Wierch (alt 1 988 mètres) - 30 PLN. The pizzas are quite edible, but the main interest lies in the photo gallery where all the great mountaineers and skiers are represented.

Taking a break

Sanacja Café – *Ul Krupówki 71 - ℘ 201 61 59 - noon-11pm.* For all those who have grown tired of listening to mountain folk music, this tiny café puts on jazz, latino-jazz or blues.

On the town

Paparazzi – *Ul Gen Galicy 8 – ℘ 206 32 51 - noon-10pm.* A place favoured by young people for its music and cyberspace.

Armstrong- Jazz Club – *Jagiellońska 18 - ℘ 201 29 04 -* From 7pm onwards one can have a drink here while listening to some jazz and sometimes attend a concert.

Art galleries

Many artists now have their own studios and galleries in Zakopane. Most of them are painters, sculptors, photographers or graphic designers. Exhibitions are temporary, styles and materials varied. Opening hours can also vary according to the seasons and the artists' work; it is therefore recommended to apply to the Tourist office before venturing on a visit. Here is a selection of galleries:

Miejska Galeria Sztuki – *Ul Krupówki 41 - ℘ 201 27 92.*

Galeria Politechniki Krakowskiej «Stara Polana» – *Ul Nowotarska 59 - ℘ 206 40 15.*

Galeria Sztuki im. W.i J. Kulczyckich – *Ul Koziniec 8 - ℘ 201 29 36.*

Galeria Podróży i Przygody « Globus » – *Ul Nowotarska 10.*

Shopping

ABC Shopping arcade (Elegancki pasaż handlowy) – *Ul Krupówki 29.* The shops are housed in a contemporary wooden structure. They include antique shops and art galleries as well as shops selling CDs, sports equipment, clothes and souvenirs.

Sport and leisure

Outdoor swimming pool and tennis

Stok Antałówki – *Ul Jaggiellońska 18 - ℘ 206 39 34.*

Indoor swimming pool

DW Sośnika – *Ul Modrzejewskiej 7 - ℘ 206 67 96.*

Indoor swimming pool and outdoor tennis

DW Biały Potok – *Droga do Białego 7 - ℘ 201 43 80.*

Ice-skating rink, with speed-skating loop – *Ul Br.Czecha.*

Festive events

May – Country Festival *(Majówka)*
This festival which takes place in early May and sometimes in late April consists of one week of festivities to celebrate the return of the fine weather. An opportunity for visitors to discover local cheeses (Oscypek), to go mountain biking or to dance to the sound of Carpathian instruments.

August – The Mountain Areas Folk Festival. During the last week in August, Polish and international companies meet in Zakopane to take part in impressive and colourful dancing parades. Zakopane then becomes the centre of mountain culture.

Typical wooden houses on the Chochołów road

R. Mattes / MICHELIN

The Tatras★★★

MAP OF POLAND C4 – WOJEWÓDZTWO OF LITTLE POLAND

Forming a natural border between Poland and Slovakia, the Tatras (Tatry) are the highest mountains in the western Carpathians. Some call them the "pocket-size mountains" for, although the area they cover is relatively small, they offer all the geological characteristics of an Alpine range. Zakopane and its region are the gateway to the Tatras, opening the way to numerous rambles and winter sports resorts.

▶ **Getting your bearings** – 100km from Kraków, the Tatra mountains tower over Zakopane and mark the border with Slovakia.

👁 **Not to be missed** – The ramble to Lake Morskie Oko

🕐 **Planning your visit** – Allow two days if you are an occasional rambler, much more if you are a mountain lover.

Background

The birth of a park – Before Zakopane developed economically and became a tourist destination, the mountains were occupied by shepherds, hunters, bears, chamois and marmots. In the 19C, hunting became widely practised as an aristocratic sport as well as an activity for subsistence and this upset the natural balance. The National Assembly in Lwów (today L'viv in Ukraine), which ran the affairs of Galicia, became aware of the danger and in 1869 it banned the shooting of marmots and deer. However, this realization did not prove sufficient and soon many scientists and lovers of the Tatra mountains got worried about the destructive trend. As years went by, because of the development of Zakopane's economy and tourist industry, the local fauna had to share their environment with the Sunday mountain dwellers and the chamois didn't stand a chance against trophy hunters. In 1873, scientists supported by the local authorities created the Tatra Association (Towarzystwo Tatrzańskie), intended to make the tourist welcome while safeguarding endangered animal and plant species. In 1885, the association launched an ambitious project to safeguard the forests surrounding Zakopane. The idea of creating a Park was slowly forming in the minds of the association's members,

> ### Geographical and Toponymic Facts
>
> The Carpathians, which extend from Ukraine to Poland via Romania and Hungary, are a mountain range of moderate altitude except for the Tatra mountains situated at their western extremity. Astride Poland and Slovakia, this range reaches altitudes of over 2 000m. The Rysy Peak, on the Polish side, culminates at 2 499m whereas, on the Slovak side, the Gierlach rises to 2 654m. The Polish Tatras are divided into three sections: to the east, **Tatry Bielskie**, a small area of 67sq km featuring many caves around Łysa Polana. Further south, the **High Tatras (Tatry Wysokie)** which extend over 335sq km and boast the highest summits (Gierlach, Rysy and Świnica…). And last the **Western Tatras (Tatry Zachodnie)**, covering some 400sq km and including the Kasprowy Wierch, the summit which attracts the most tourists.

but political and financial support was still lacking. At the beginning of the 20C, two sides confronted each other. Those who were opposed to the establishment of the leisure industry and those who wanted to cash in on it whatever the cost to the environment. The two World Wars stopped both sides in their tracks but, in 1947, the project was considered once more and, in 1954, the Council of Ministers announced the creation of the Tatra National Park (Tatrzański Park Narodowy - TPN). Today the Park's mission is to explore and protect the natural resources of 21 164ha of forests, valleys and rocky peaks. In addition to dealing with the purely environmental aspect, the TNP also gives its advice on farming, cultural and architectural problems. This mission is carried out in close cooperation with the Park's Slovak equivalent (TANAP) which covers an area about five times its size.

Rambling around Zakopane

What you need to know before setting off: *There is a charge for admission to the park and for parking. These relatively low charges (about 4 PLN) go towards financing part of the cost of the TPN.*

No matter which itinerary they choose, ramblers should bear in mind that mountains sometimes have surprises in store for them. It is essential to wear adequate shoes and to anticipate a change in the weather by taking warm, waterproof clothing.

Every year, over three million tourists ramble along the paths and tracks of the TPN. In order to preserve the park's natural resources and to ensure the safety of its visitors, it is necessary for everyone to respect elementary rules.

Elementary rules for ramblers

- ◗ Walk along marked paths
- ◗ Do not pick flowers or fruit
- ◗ Avoid making any noise
- ◗ Take your rubbish out with you
- ◗ Do not set up camp or light a fire
- ◗ Do not get near wild animals
- ◗ Do not leave food lying around

Mount Gubałówka★★

The ascent of Mount Gubałówka by cable car or on foot starts near the Zakopane handicraft market. Allow 50min on foot and 5min by cable car.

The Gubałówka culminates at an altitude of only 1 120m and its ascent is by no means a sporting achievement. It is nevertheless one of the favourite rambles of tourists and locals alike. In addition to the restaurants and shops located near the cable car terminal, the summit offers a fabulous panoramic view south towards Zakopane and the Tatra mountain range and north towards the Podhale region and the Beskid. Near the summit, several colourful farms and a small wooden church built in 1971 create an atmosphere straight out of an old postcard. The path leading from the Gubałówka to Butorowy Wierch in 40min is accessible to everyone without special equipment.

Ramble to Lake Morskie Oko (Eye of the Sea)★★

Starting from Zakopane, drive east along the road to Łysa Polana. Leave the border post on the left of the road and drive on to the parking area at the entrance to the Park.
Reckon on about 20km there and back including a tour of the lake. Difference in height: 450m. Minimum 6 hours' walk. There is no special difficulty as far as the lake. It is possible to call on a horse-drawn cart which stops less than 2km from the lake. 45 PLN there and back.

Several lakes throughout the world are nicknamed "eye of the sea" on account of the many legends linking mountain lakes and the sea.

Ramblers climb towards Lake Morskie Oko along a car-free surfaced road cut through a forest of fir trees, following the River Białka which marks the border between Poland and Slovakia. Some of the trees have been torn to shreds by the violent wind (the foehn) whirling round along the corridor formed by the valley. From the very beginning of the ascent, **Mount Gierlach (2 564m)**, the highest summit of the Slovak Tatras, comes into view. Soon after, one reaches several waterfalls. The **Mickiewicz Falls**, named after the poet. In winter the climb stops at this point because, beyond it, avalanches frequently occur. Farther up, after walking for 6km, one reaches Polana Włosienica, a wide clearing where carts deposit and pick up their customers. Part of the panorama known as Mięguszowieckie Szczyty unfolds in front of one's eyes. It encompasses the summits surrounding Lake Morskie Oko. After reaching the refuge

C. Hervé-Bazin / MICHELIN

Walking the the ridge of Kasprowy Wierch

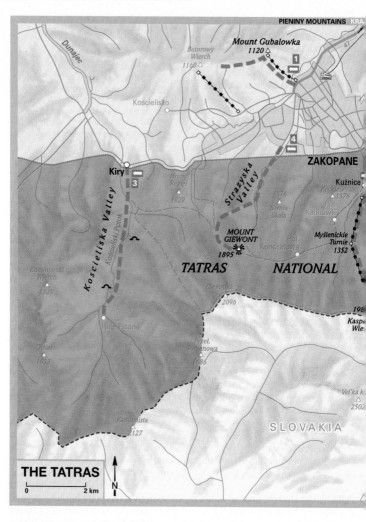

overlooking the lake, one gets an overall view of the whole range including the **Rysy (2 499m), the Czarny (2 410m) and the Wielki (2 438m)**. Lake Morskie Oko extending over 35ha at an altitude of 1 395m is 50m deep, which makes it the most important trout reserve in the Polish Tatras. An easy path with red markings runs right round it and offers magnificent views of the level of vegetation known as the "forested land". Fir trees and beeches gradually give way to spruce which, in turn disappear, until only scrub and dwarf pines remain. Then, above 1 800m, Alpine pastures entirely cover the ground until they are replaced by arid rocks culminating at over 2 200m.

Ramble through Kościeliska Valley★★ (Dolina Kóscieliska)

Leave Zakopane via Kościeliska Street and head for the village of Kiry 5km away. Buses link Zakopane and Kiry. Take the Zakopane – Ciche Górne line and get off at "Dolina Kóscieliska". Allow about 3hr on foot to cover the 6km and 180m difference in height. This ramble offers no special difficulty and is not colour-coded. The track is wide enough to allow horse-drawn carts to take ramblers to more distant junctions.

The path runs along the Kościeliski Potoka, a tumultuous stream separating a vast expanse of grazing land from the forest. Beyond a forestry worker's house, the path crosses a bridge over the Kościeliski Potok. *(To the left is the starting point of a longer itinerary which skirts the Slovak border, heading for the Czerwone Wierchy (4hr) and the Kasprowy Wierch (6hr). The path climbs above 2 000m and this ramble is only suitable for experienced hikers. Note that it is possible to take a cable car from the top of the Kasprowy Wierch to Zakopane-Kuźnice. A few hundred metres beyond the bridge, a path runs off to the right towards the Chochołów Valley (Dolina Chochołowska). Allow about 3hr to reach Polana Chochołowska, where the ramble ends.)*

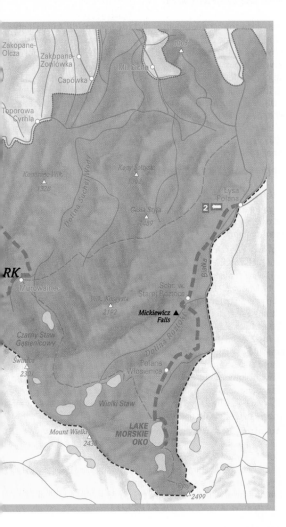

The path of the main itinerary leads to a wide valley offering a splendid panoramic view of the summits marking the Slovak border. A picturesque altar built long ago by miners looking for iron can be seen during the second part of the ramble. There are many **caves** along the path, some of them open to visitors. There is an admission charge and visitors must take a guided tour. It is advisable to take warm clothing and a torch. The difference in level is usually negligible and the tours are open to all visitors. The caves which are most popular with Polish visitors are **Jaskinia Mroźna and Jaskinia Zimna.** They are tunnels several hundred metres long, with chambers decorated with stalactites and stalagmites. The path continues towards Hala Pisana and its refuge where the ramble ends. Those who do not wish to retrace their steps can choose between several itineraries heading for Slovakia in the east or joining the Chochołów Valley to the west.

Ramble through the Strążyska Valley and ascent of Mount Giewont ★★★

The ramble starts in Zakopane. At the beginning of Kościeliska Street, turn left onto Kasprusi Street which becomes Strążyska Street. The latter ends at a parking area and the entrance to the Park. Allow a total of 5hr on foot. It takes 45min for the first part of the ramble which has a difference in height of 250m, then over 2hr to cover the 600m difference in altitude to the top of Mount Giewont.

During the first part of the itinerary, the stony path runs alongside a stream through a fairly dense forest, sometimes climbing steeply; however, the ramble remains accessible to families. The path leads to a steep pasture where a **shepherd's house has been turned into a tearoom** serving tea and herbal tea. The setting is delightful and the products served by the establishment really taste homemade. A little higher up, in the thick of the forest, one can hear waterfalls, a very pleasant and refreshing sound in summer. Many Polish ramblers make this convivial place the purpose of their outing. However, it is possible to go further along a more uneven and steeper path up to the top of the Giewont, one of the most famous summits of the Tatra mountains. During the ascent, one climbs from the fir forest level to the sub-Alpine scrub level and finally to the stony ground of Alpine pastures. One learns a lot about geology while walking. From the top of its 1 895m, the Giewont offers an overall view of the Zakopane Valley and of **the small Pieniny mountains**, 50km further away. The summit of the Giewont is surmounted by a 17m high metal cross , planted there in 1901 by Zakopane's parishioners.

From Zakopane-Kuźnice to the summit of Mount Kasprowy Wierch★★

Kuźnice is situated 3km south-west of Zakopane. Access by car is not allowed, therefore one must walk there or take no 59 bus. The Kasprowy Wierch rises to 1 959m. Its summit is accessible on foot or by cable car. The journey by cable car takes 20min; on foot, one should allow 5hr there and back.

Ascent of the Kasprowy Wierch by cable car – The Kasprowy Wierch cable car was the first of its kind built in Poland. It was inaugurated in 1936 after a long debate opposing members of the Union of Polish Skiers to those concerned with the safeguard of the environment. The total length is 4 000m with a difference in altitude of 936m. Each trip involves two cars carrying 36 persons each and travelling in opposite directions. The ascent is in two sections, separated by a halfway station Myślenickie Turnie, clinging to the rock face at an altitude of 1 028m. The first section reveals the Giewont and the Czerwone Wierchy. The 2 290m long second section, at an angle of 30 degrees, offers **splendid panoramic views** of the valleys and the Zakopane ski area at Sucha Dolina Kasprowa. The summit of the Kasprowy Wierch, often windswept and shrouded by clouds, is equipped with a restaurant, souvenirs shops and a meteorological station. It offers a spectacular panorama consisting of a **rocky barrier** rising to an average height of 2 200m (Świnica 2 301m ; Krywań 2 495m). Slovakia extends beyond this barrier featuring snow-covered peaks in all seasons.

The descent to Kuźnice – Two paths lead down from the Kasprowy Wierch to Kuźnice.

The first *(allow about 2hr 30min)* follows the cable-car route.

The second, more uneven, *(allow 3hr 30min)* has yellow markings as far as Hala Gąsienicowa, then yellow or blue ones down to Kuźnice.

Note that a footpath runs from Hala Gąsienicowa to Lake Morskie Oko. *Allow about 6hr on foot.*

Exploring the Pieniny

The Pieniny and the raft trip down the Dunajec Gorge★★★

Starting from Zakopane, drive to Nowy Targ then follow road 969 towards Krościenko. In Krośnica, turn right towards Sromowce Wyżne - Kąty. The pier is by the roadside, follow the signposts marked: Polskie Stowarzyszenie Flisaków Pienińskich.

Sromowce Wyżne - Kąty Pier: Apr-Aug 8.30am-5pm; Sep 8.30am-4pm; Oct 9am-3pm. Closed Sun, Easter and Corpus Christi. 39 PLN. About 3hr. www.flisacy.com.pl

The Pieniny National Park (Pieniński Park Narodowy) – The Park includes almost the entire Jurassic-chalk mountain range whose summits only rise to 982m (**Trzy Korony**) and 1 050m (**Wysoka**). Famous for their varied flora and luxuriant vegetation, the Pieniny are undeniably attractive. From the crests, one catches sight of the Tatras lining the horizon, at the extremity of a wide cultivated valley rather sparsely populated. The River Dunajec flows down from the Tatras through the Pieniny before joining the Wisła north-east of Kraków. The raft trip down the Dunajec Gorge is the region's main attraction.

Rafting down the Gorge – The trip is remarkably well organised and is absolutely safe thanks to the cooperation between the Pieniny Park and the Association of Boatmen. The latter use all their expertise in navigating the tumultuous waters of this natural frontier between Poland and Slovakia for the benefit of tourists. On the banks of the river in Sromowce Wyżne – Kąty, men in regional costumes help the would-be sailors into small flat-bottomed boats, rendered perfectly watertight by branches of fir trees pushed between the planks. Each raft, steered by two men, takes about ten passengers.

The trip starts at the foot of **Mount Macelowa** (802m). During the first few kilometres, the Dunajec is wide and calm. Very soon one catches sight of the high summits of the Tatras, then the boat sails past Slovak villages on the right bank and Polish ones on the left bank. It enters the Gorge some 6km after the starting point. The sheer cliffs are sometimes covered with vegetation, sometimes completely bare, which attracts rock-climbers. As the crow flies, the Gorge is 3km long, but **seven wide meanders** almost multiply this distance by three. The riverbed suddenly narrows as the raft reaches a place called **Bandit janosik's Jump (Zbójnicki Skok)**. According to legend, while he was fighting against the oppession of the wealthy monarch, a famous bandit called Janosik escaped his pursuers by jumping over the narrow river. At that point, the river is very deep and 10m wide! After a tumultuous stretch, it resumes its lazy course (Leniwe). According to another legend, the blessed who drink from the Slovak spring, which gushes forth in a spot known as "Stuletnie Źródło", "the hundred-year spring", will live a century. The Dunajec flows on to the landing stage at **Szczawnica**. There are many restaurants on the banks of this small spa resort. *The bus terminal, where buses are waiting to take tourists back to Sromowce Wyżne – Kąty, is situated below the bridge, on the right. The mini-buses only leave when they are full. You might therefore have to wait at certain times of the year.* The road followed on the return trip affords an exceptional view of the valley and of the Tatras.

Note that **Szczawnica** is the starting point of several cycle tracks 🚲 and footpaths 🐾 giving access to the Pieniny Park and then to the highest summit, the Wysoka (1 100m) or to the Trzy Korony (the Three Crowns).

Around Czorsztyn Reservoir; Czorsztyn and Niedzica Castles
The lake at Czorsztyn was created as a result of the construction of a hydraulic dam on the river Dunajec. A few wooden structures, including several chapels, which would have been flooded by the rise of the water, were moved to a small skansen in Kluszkowce, a few kilometres north-west of Czorsztyn. Owing to their position, two castles were spared by the construction work and the flooding of the valley.

From road 969, in the village of Krośnica, head south towards Czorsztyn and then Niedzica.

Czorsztyn Castle
May-Sep daily 9am-7pm, Oct-Apr Tue-Sun 9am-5pm.
The ruins of Czorsztyn Castle are worth a visit if only for the panoramic view of the lake, the Pieniny range and the Tatras. This small fortress, built in the 13C, at the time of Kazimierz the Great, for the Clarisse Sisters of Stary Sącz, was struck by lightning in 1790 and destroyed by fire. It was never rebuilt.

Niedzica Castle
May-Sep daily 9am-6pm, Oct-Apr Tue-Sun 10am-3pm. Closed 1 Jan, 1 Nov, 25-26 Dec. Easter hols.
Niedzica Castle stands on the opposite shore of the lake. As th e two castles face each other, they offer the same kind of spectacular view of the surrounding area. However, Niedzica Castle is historically more interesting than its neighbour. Built in the Gothic style in 1325, it was used for centuries to guard the frontier. It was successively captured by the Poles and the Hungarians, both wanting to control it. Today it is run by the Association of Art Historians which has turned the castle into an exhibition centre. Several rooms are devoted to local history and archaeology.

Dębno Church★★
Situated along road 969 between Nowy Targ and Krościenko. Mon-Fri 9am-noon, 2-4.30pm, Sat 9am-noon.
The first mention of the Church of St Michael the Archangel in Dębno goes back to 1335. Probably built on the initiative of one of the region's noble families, it only became the local parish church in 1400. The tower was added in 1601, the outside arcades and the porch later on during the 17C.

Rafting party, Dunajec Gorge

W. Buss / MICHELIN

The outside walls and the roof are covered with larch shingles. The church boasts an exceptional interior decorated with beautiful Gothic stencilled paintings and sculptures dating from the 15C and 16C. The gem is a remarkably well-preserved medieval polychrome. The oldest carving is a 14C crucifix. In 2003 the church was added to **UNESCO's World Heritage List**. Several wooden churches were built around Dębno. The most characteristic of 15C and 16C religious art are located in the villages of Grywałd and Harklowa, along road 969, and in Trybsz , south of Dębno.

Practical Tatras

Useful addresses

Regional Tourist Office (Redykołka) – Ul Kościeliska 1 - 34-500 Zakopane - ℘ (18) 201 32 53 - www.tatratour.pl - tatratours@ redykolka.prv.pl

The Tatra National Park - Tatrzański Park Narodowy – Ul Chałubińskiego 42a - 34-500 Zakopane - ℘ 202 32 00 - www. cyf-kr.edu.pl/tpn - kozica@tpn.zakopane.pl

The Pieniny National Park - Pieniński Park Narodowy – Ul Jagiellońska 107b - 34-450 Krościenko - ℘ 262 56 01 - www. pieninypn.pl - biuro@pieninypn.pl

Tourist office – Ul Drohojowskich 7 - 34-440 Czorsztyn - ℘(18) 265 03 66 - www. czorsztyn.pl - czorsztyn@czorsztyn.pl

Where to stay

Most hotels are located in Zakopane or in the town's close surroundings. See also "Practical Zakopane".

Farm Holidays Association - Galicyjskie Gospodarstwa Gościnne – Ul Meiselsa 1 - 31-063 Kraków - www.agroturystyka-ggg.pl - at.ggg@inetia.pl

CHMIEL Jadwiga and Stanisław – Ul Ks. J. Kosibowicza 41 - 33443 Sromowce Wyżne – ℘ 262 97 80 - stchmiel@poczta.onet.pl - www.chmiel.pieniny.net -4 rooms: 42 PLN. Fine rooms, a sauna and a solarium in a house classified as "ecological accommodation", a stone's throw from the raft trips down the River Dunajec, with a view of Slovakia.

WRÓBEL Zofia and Stanisław – 34 424 Szaflary - Bańska Niżna 154 - ℘ 275 42 62 - www.wrobel.infotatry.com - 4 rooms: 80 PLN ½ B – (Between Zakopane and Nowy Targ) - A mountain place where the owners lend their guests folk costumes for the purpose of souvenir photographs and where a wood fire burns in the fireplace.

PAŃSZCZYK Bożena and Józef – Dom wczasowy "Borowy" - 34 425 Biały Dunajec -

ul. Jana Pawła II 35 - ℘ 207 35 42 - www. borowy.zakopane.biz - 140 beds: 60 PLN ½ B. This is a mountain holiday centre, situated 12km from Zakopane on the way to Nowy Targ. Rambles, folk evenings, children's playground and many more facilities make this an ideal place for large families or groups of nature lovers.

Sport and leisure

Spelunking - Cave visits – Information available from the Tatra National Park.

Polish Association of Mountain Guides – www.pspw.pl

Mountain Kayaking and Rafting School – Ul Maszyńskiego 28 - 30-698 Kraków - ℘ (12) 654 73 45 - www.retendo. com.pl

Gliding School (hang-gliding and paragliding) – 34-500 Zakopane Nosal - ℘ 206 31 81

Central Parachuting School – Ul Lotników 1 - 34-400 Nowy Targ - ℘ (18) 266 23 23

Nowy Targ Flying Club – Flights offering bird's-eye-views of the Tatras and of the Podhale region - Ul Lotników 1 - 34-400 Nowy Targ - ℘ (18) 266 23 23 - www. aeroklub.nowy-targ.pl

River and lake fishing

Polish Fishing Association (Polski Związek Wędkarski - PZW) – Ul Ochronek 24 - 33-100 Tarnów - ℘ (14) 621 33 92. The association provides general information about fishing and the conditions required for practising this sport.

Foundation for the Regional Development of Czorsztyn Lake (Fundacja Rozwoju Regionalnego Jeziora Czorsztyńskiego) – Al Tysiąclecia 37 - 34-400 Nowy Targ - ℘ (18) 264 13 30. The foundation supervises fishing in the Czorsztyn lake.

The West Beskid ★★
Beskid Żywiecki
MAP OF POLAND C 4– WOJEWÓDZTWO OF SILESIA

Mount Babia Góra culminating at an altitude of 1 725 metres is the highest summit of the West Beskid mountains, known here as the Beskid Żywiecki. Listed by UNESCO as a World Biosphere Reserve, this region bordering Slovakia, proudly retains its folklore and traditions highly appreciated by the inhabitants of Kraków who come here on a Sunday outing or for a holiday in the country. Sucha Beskidzka and above all Zawoja are the starting points of many explorations off the beaten track.

▶ **Getting your bearings** – 80km north-west of Zakopane and 80km south-east of Kraków, on the Slovak border.

👁 **Not to be missed** – The view of Mount Babia Góra from the Józef Żak skansen in Zawoja.

🕐 **Planning your visit** – Allow one day to discover the natural environment around the Babia Góra and Zawoja, and half a day to visit Sucha Beskidzka.

Background

International recognition of its environment – The Babia Góra range is the second highest in Poland after the Tatra mountains. The vegetation on its lower slopes, up to 1 400m, includes beeches, spruce, fir trees and a few white maples. Higher up, scrub and pastures fight hard with the omnipresent rocks. Lynx, bears, wolves and capercaillies occupy the sparsely populated natural spaces, hardly affected by industry. Sheep farming by nomadic shepherds, the exploitation of pine forests and woodwork are the main economic activities, sustained by the controlled development of tourism. In 1976, UNESCO decided to classify the Babia Góra region as a living laboratory for the study of the biosphere, particularly water. As inhabitants of a World Reserve of Biosphere, local scientists and officials undertook to study and watch various parameters such as the impact of tourism on the environment, forest management, the quality of water and the survival of rare species, while encouraging economic and human growth. Control over these issues as a whole was made easier by the creation of the Babia Góra Park, whose head office is in Zawoja.

Around the Babia Góra Park

Zawoja
The Park's head office is in this village which stretches for several kilometres along road 957, at the foot of Mount Babia Góra. In winter, it becomes a family winter sports resort.

In Zawoja, the flock returning from pasture

A. Galy / MICHELIN

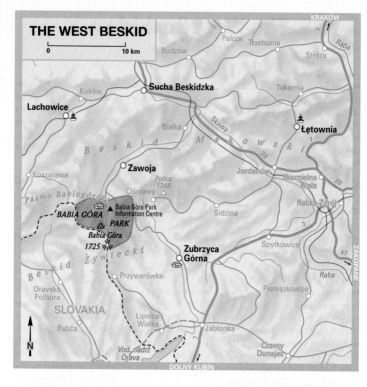

The wooden St-Clement's Church, situated in the village centre, on a mound overlooking the road, dates from 1759 but was rebuilt and restored on many occasions, the last time in 1888. The interior is decorated with murals. The wooden altar and the stone fonts show a Baroque influence.

Drive south from Zawoja's centre towards Zubrzyca Górna and turn right in Zawoja-Widły towards the Skansen and a place called Markowa.

The Babia Góra Park Information Centre – *May-Sep daily 9am-4.30pm, Oct-Apr Mon-Sat 9am-4.30pm. 3 PLN.* The exhibitions are devoted to the Park's natural area and to the region's folk traditions. The small Józef Żak Skansen is situated a short distance from the Centre, along the road.

Ramble to the top of the Babia Góra – *From Markowa, drive about 500 m to the refuge "PTTK Markowa Szczawiny".* From there, allow at least 2 hours to reach the summit of the Babia Góra; from the top, the view extends over the Beskid, Slovakia and, farther afield, the Tatra mountains. The yellow-marked track offers no difficulty, so long as you wear adequate shoes and clothing.

Zubrzyca Górna - Skansen
Located 20km south of Zawoja along road 957. May-Aug 8.30am-4.30pm; Sep-Apr 8.30am-2pm. 4 PLN.
The Skansen illustrates the settlement of different communities of shepherds and farmers from Moldavia or from the northern part of Little Poland. The path runs through woods and vast meadows dotted with farms, windmills or weaving work-shops. Note the fine collection of beehives. The group of buildings date from the late 18C and from the 19C. Most of the structures were moved from nearby locations.

Sucha Beskidzka - The Palace
Mon-Sat 8am-4pm. 2 PLN.
In 1614 Piotr Komorowski, a wealthy local scholar, had an extension added to a small fortified house built in 1554. The ensemble, turned into a Renaissance palace, became a cultural centre. A library containing some 55 000 works collected by the owner and later by his descendants, paintings and drawings furnished the wings of the palace until the 1930s. The collections are now scattered in Poland's major museums yet, spite of this, the palace continues to perform its cultural mission by organising regular temporary exhibitions devoted to painting and sculpture. A stroll through the beautiful park leads visitors to the dilapidated

orangerie in English neo-Gothic style: it once contained 1 200 lemon and orange trees which provided a decent income for the family of its initiator Anna Konstancja Wielopolska. Further on, the **Gardener's House** is a small ethnographic museum illustrating the handicraft activity and spiritual life of the inhabitants of the Babia Góra region in the 19C.

Sucha Beskidzka also boasts a fine example of religious architecture consisting of a monastery and several chapels dating from the 17C. Note, however, that this ensemble, grouped round the Church of the Annunciation, is a popular place of worship and not, strictly speaking, a tourist destination.

The **Roman Inn** (Karczma Rzym), built in the 17C, stands in the village centre. Although the building was restored in 1960, its traditional wooden architecture remains intact. The fact that the poet Adam Mickiewicz probably used it as the setting of one of his short stories, reinforces its status as a memorial.

Lachowice's wooden church

From Sucha Beskidzka, follow road 946 to Stachówska then turn left to Lachowice.
The church of the Apostles-Peter-and-Paul (Apostołów Piotra i Pawła) was built between 1789 and 1790 on the site of the former village cemetery. Its unusual roof, which nearly reaches down to the ground, forms a gallery supported by columns. The interior is in the classical Baroque style.

Łętownia's wooden church

Drive to Jordanów, 25km south of Sucha Beskidzka along road 28.
Erected between 1760 and 1765 on the site of two former 15C churches, the church of St-Simon-and-St-Jude (St Szymon and Juda Tadeusz) is one of the largest churches in the region lying at the foot of the Carpathians. Its interior decoration is in the Rococo-Baroque style. The high altar, the organ and the pulpit are very characteristic of that period.

Practical West Beskid

Postal code (Sucha Beskidzka) – 34-200
Postal code (Zawoja) – 34-223
Phone code – 033

Useful addresses

Tourist office – There are few information centres for foreigners. The Babia Góra Park Information centre in Zawoja can, however, fill this purpose. *www.bpn. babia-gora.pl - park@bpn.babia-gora.pl.* It is advisable to write in English. Website in Polish.

Tourist information services in Sucha Beskidzka and Zawoja can be contacted in English, through their websites (at present in Polish only). Sucha Beskidzka: *promocja@powiatsuski.pl - www.powiatsuski.pl* -Zawoja: *zawoja@ zawoja.pl - www.zawoja.pl*

Getting around

There are many bus services from Sucha Beskidzka and Zawoja to Kraków. Journey time: 1hr 30min.

Where to stay

Lajkonik Hotel – *34-200 Zawoja* – ℘ *874 51 00 – www.lajkonik.zawoja.pl - lajkonik@ zawoja.pl - 20 rooms: 195 PLN.* On leaving Zawoja in the direction of Jabłonka.

Backing onto a wooded hill, the hotel is housed in a large stone building of the 1930s. The decor is elegant and the establishment offers high-quality services. Sports activities and excursions are organised.

Pensjonat Jawor – *34-223 Zawoja Wilczna - ℘ 877 51 98 – www.pensjonat-jawor. com - recepcja@pensjonat-jawor.com - 16 rooms: 560 PLN per week.* This large new house, on the road leading to the Babia Góra Park Information Centre, offers all modern conveniences and a warm welcome so that you may enjoy your green...or white holidays depending on the season.

Eating out

Karczma «Przykiec» – *34-240 Jordanów - ℘ 277 35 61 - www.przykiec.iap.pl - 11am-10pm - 35 PLN.* - Along road 28, between Sucha Beskidzka and Jordanów. This is a real traditional gourmet inn. Try the onion soup served in a loaf of bread.

Festive events

A Folk Dance and Song Festival takes place in Zawoja in late September, when grazing animals return from their summer pastures.

Wrocław Town Hall

Pszczyna

POPULATION 26 830 – MAP OF POLAND C4 – WOJEWÓDZTWO OF SILESIA

Six consonants – five of them in a row at the beginning – in an eight-letter word, that might seem like an impossible challenge to a foreigner. In fact, this name – pronounced "pshchina" – belongs to a small unassuming provincial town known as "the pearl of Upper Silesia". A somewhat flattering yet true description of this city surrounded by lakes and forests, in striking contrast with the industrial landscapes of the coal mining region of Upper Silesia.

▶ **Getting your bearings** – 28km from Auschwitz, 88km from Kraków.

👁 **Not to be missed** – "The Telemann Evenings": a festival of Baroque music held inside the castle in September and October (inquire at the tourist office).

🕐 **Planning your visit** – Allow 2hr to visit the town and the castle, more if you wish to stroll through the park.

Background

Pszczyna, just like Silesia (Śląsk), had a troubled history. Annexed to Little Poland at the end of the 10C by the region's first king, Mieszko I, it became a Silesian city in 1178 when it fell under the authority of the Piast Princes. When the Princes of Bohemia took control, Pszczyna became, thanks to its fortress, the centre of a small independent state which, under the rule of the duchess Helena Korybutówna, successfully fought off Hussite attacks. In 1546, the free state was sold to Balthasar von Promnitz, the bishop of Wrocław. During the reign of his family and later of the Anhalt-Köthen, the ties between the Princes of Pless (the German name of the town) and the Polish kings on Wawel Hill were strengthened. In 1846, the estate passed into the hands of the counts Von Hochberg, who imposed the germanization and industrialization of Silesia. One of the two printing works set up in the early 20C undertook the publication of Upper Silesia's 1st newspaper in Polish and the first of the three Silesian uprisings took place in August 1919. In the 1921 referendum, 74% of local voters opted for unification with Poland, which became effective on 22 June 1922.

Things to see

The Rynek★

This attractive square, surrounded by a fine group of low 18C-19C houses, is dominated by the extremely wide neo-Baroque façade of the **evangelical church** adjacent to the **town hall** (Ratusz). Erected in the early 17C, the town hall was remodelled in the neo-Renaissance style in 1931. In the north-west corner of the square stands the 17C guardhouse with its elegant **Gate of the Chosen** (Brama Wybrańców), the only way into the castle.

Once a Piast dynasty holding, today a museum, the castle was carefully restored after 1945

Castle Museum (Muzeum Zamkowe)★

Ul. Brama Wybrańców 1. ☎ 210 30 37. www.zamek-pszczyna.pl . Nov-15 Dec and Feb-Mar Tue 11am-3pm, Wed 9am-4pm, Thu-Fri 9am-3pm, Sat 10am-3pm, Sun 10am-4pm; Apr-Jun and Sep-Oct Mon 11am-3pm, Tue 10am-3pm, Wed 9am-5pm, Thu-Fri 9am-4pm, Sat 10am-4pm, Sun 10am-5pm; Jul-Aug Mon 11am-3pm, Tue 10am-3pm, Wed-Fri 9am-5pm, Sat 10am-5pm, Sun 10am-6pm. Closed Jan, Easter Mon, Corpus Christi, 1 and 11 Nov, 14-31 Dec and Mondays Nov-Mar. Last admission 1hr before closing. 12 PLN.

This 15C Gothic castle was rebuilt between 1870 and 1876 in the neo-Classical style by French architect Alexandre Destailleur. Owned by the Piast dynasty until the end of the 14C, it was handed over to the Promnitz family then to the Anhalt-Köthen-Pless before becoming in 1846 the property of the counts von Hochberg who occupied it until it was nationalised in 1945. The members of this family, who originally came from the medieval castle of Książ in Lower Silesia, were allowed to keep the title of Princes von Pless. During the First World War, the German high command took over the castle and Emperor William made it his residence. One of the rare castles not to have been plundered during the Second World War – no doubt because of the German origins of its owners –, it was turned into a museum in 1946. The vast and sumptuous apartments were reconstructed to the last detail from old photographs. All the rooms were decorated in accordance with the principle of *horror vacui*, fear of empty spaces. For visitors, the absolute must is undoubtedly the prince's office. His "work" mainly consisted of hunting, judging by the impressive number of trophies on display.

Every September since 1979, the imposing Hall of Mirrors has been the setting of a **Festival of Baroque Music** (Sviatoslav Richter took part on several occasions) in honour of the composer Georg Philipp Telemann (1681-1767) who spent the summer months in the castle from 1704 to 1707.

The castle is also famous to a great extent for its 156ha English-style park (*Zabytkowy Park Pszczyński*), through which flows the River Pszczynka and which is crisscrossed by many footpaths and cycle tracks. The bison reserve (*rezerwat żubrów*) which contributed to the park's attraction is now closed.

Regional Ethnographic Museum (Zagroda wsi Pszczyńskiej)

In the eastern part of the castle's park. Apr-Oct Tue-Sat 10am-3pm, Sun 10am-6pm (8pm in summer). By appointment in winter ☎ 06 03131186. 5 PLN.

This unpretentious yet charming Skansen consists of a house and its outbuildings located in the heart of the forest. Just before arriving, you will see a restaurant called Stary Młyn, housed in an old traditional wooden mill, similar in style to the buildings of the open-air museum.

Practical Pszczyna

Postal code – 43-200
Phone code – 032

Useful addresses

Tourist office – *Brama Wybrańców 1. To the left of the gate giving access to the castle - ☎212 99 99 - www.pszczyna.pl - Dec-Apr: Mon-Fri 8am-4pm; May-Nov: Tue-Fri 8am-4pm, Sat-Sun and hols 10am-4pm.*

Getting around

Minibus, bus and train services (the most convenient are mentioned first) link Pszczyna and Kraków.Allow 2 to 3hr.

Where to stay

Rezydencja Retro – *Ul. Warowna 31 - ☎ 210 12 63 - www.retro.pl - hotel@retro.pl – 16 rooms: 150 PLN* 🅿: This true family guesthouse close to the Rynek is very appropriately named and you will be able to appreciate the old-world charm of the rooms.

Hôtel Michalika – *Ul. Dworcowa 11 - ☎210 13 55 - fax 210 13 88 - www.umichalika.pl - 16 rooms: 150 PLN* 🖃 🅿 Halfway between the station and the Rynek, this modern comfortable hotel has a restaurant on the premises and another one in town, bearing the same name.

Eating out

Restauracja Kmieć – *Ul. Piekarska 10 - ☎210 36 38 - noon-9pm - 50 PLN.* Located in the old town, this establishment features a surprising colour scheme and boasts good traditional Polish cooking. Terrace in the inner courtyard.

Restauracja Va Banque – *Ul. Bankowa 2 - ☎210 34 72 - 10am-10pm - 70PLN.* Reputed to be the best in town, this restaurant prides itself on having counted among its customers the former owner of the castle, the 6th prince von Pless and his family. Refined cuisine.

Opole

POPULATION 130 000 – MAP OF POLAND B3 – WOJEWÓDZTWO OF OPOLE

The capital of the region of the same name, Opole, on an island in the River Odra, is a pleasant, bright and spacious city boasting great architectural unity. It is famous throughout the country for the festival of Polish song held here since 1963. Not to be missed are the nearby chapels with Gothic frescoes and Brzeg Castle.

- ▶ **Getting your bearings** – 100km south-east of Wrocław and west of Częstochowa.
- 👁 **Not to be missed** – Opale's peaceful Rynek, the Gothic churches.
- 🕐 **Planning your visit** – Allow half a day to visit Opale, a few hours to see the churches scattered across the countryside and 2 hours for a tour of Brzeg Castle.

Background

Opole was founded in the 8C on a small island in the middle of the River Odra. Protected by its castle, of which all that remains is the 13C **Piast Tower** (Wieża Piastowska), it was, from the 13C to 1532, the headquarters of the ruling Silesian Piasts. The town then fell under the control of the Habsburgs and later of the Hohenzollerns. Over the centuries, the town centre gradually moved to its present location on the east bank of the Odra.

Things to see

The Rynek

The square is surrounded by Baroque and Renaissance houses, carefully restored after the war. In the centre stands the town hall, built in 1936 in the style of the Palazzio Vecchio in Florence. All the sights are near the Rynek.

Franciscan Church (Kościół Franciszkanów)

Ul. Zamkowa, south of the Rynek.
An atmosphere of deep meditation emanates from the nave and its ceilings decorated with an interlacing of foliage. The tiny **St Anne's Chapel** (Kaplica Św. Anny)★ containing the mausoleum of the Piasts, whose family tree is painted on the wall, has, since the 14C, been housing the recumbent figures of Bolko I, Bolko II, Bolko III and his wife Anna of Oświęcim. The Gothic ribbed vaulting is adorned with oak leaves, angels and brightly coloured coats of arms.

Opole's Silesian Museum (Muzeum Śląska Opolskiego)

Mały Rynek 7. Open Tue-Fri 9am-4pm, Sat 10am-3pm, Sun noon-5pm. 3 PLN.
This interesting museum, housed in a former Jesuit college, is devoted to regional history. In the basement, prehistory is illustrated by a loom and pieces of pottery. A Bronze-Age wooden boat (7sq m) and funeral urns are displayed on the ground floor.

Baroque façades

The upper floor is devoted to 19C religious painting and sculpture and also has an ethnographic section (traditional costumes, farming implements). The town's history is illustrated by archaeological finds, press cuttings and 19C documents. The top floor houses a small collection of 19C paintings.

North of the Rynek stand the twin towers of the **Cathedral of the Holy Cross** (Katedra Św. Krzyża).

Nearby

Opole's Village Museum (Muzeum Wsi Opolskiej)
Ul. Wrocławska 174. 5km from the town centre, on the way to Brzeg. Open 15 Apr-15 Oct Tue-Sun 10am-6pm; in winter Mon-Fri 9am-2pm. 6 PLN. This open-air museum is a real village comprising some forty traditional Silesian houses, illustrating rural life in Silesia in the 18C and 19C.

Brzeg★
45km north-west of Opole towards Wrocław. The town boasts an interesting 16C Renaissance town hall, designed by two Italian architects, Francesco Parra and André Walther. But the town's main attraction is the **Museum of Silesian Piasts★** (Muzeum Piastów Śląskich) *(Tue and Thu-Sun 10am-4pm, Wed 10am-6pm, 8 PLN, free on Sat, explanations in Polish)* located in Zamkowy square. It is housed in the castle, one of the finest examples of Renaissance architecture in Poland. The Piasts occupied it until their dynasty became extinct in 1675. The richly carved façade is crowned by the busts of members of this illustrious family and the three arcaded storeys of the inner courtyard are reminiscent of the Wawel in Kraków. The fine collections are displayed in the beautifully restored rooms, some of which have retained a monumental door frame or a fireplace. The basement, devoted to funerary art, contains copies of 13C and 14C recumbent figures and decorated lead sarcophagi. On the ground floor, the history of the town is illustrated by engravings and models of Brzeg in the Middle Ages and in the 18C. The second floor is more interesting. Devoted to Silesian art, it features delicate paintings and sculptures from the 15C to the 18C, including seven large statues, part of a crucifixion dating from 1420, formerly exhibited in St Elizabeth's Church in Wrocław.

The Gothic churches trail★★
The small churches in **Małujowice**, **Krzyżowice**, **Pogorzela**, **Strzelniki** and **Łosiów**, near Brzeg, are well worth a detour. Their frescoes, painted around the 14C, were systematically plastered over by the Protestants. This helped to preserve them from the ravages of time and today moving polychromes representing scenes of Christ's Life and Passion are being rediscovered. You're bound to fall in love with the Małujowice and Strzelniki churches with their walls entirely covered with frescoes. *Ask for the keys next door.*

Practical Opole

Postal code – 45 000
Phone code – 077

Useful addresses

Tourist office – *Ul. Krakowska 15 – ℘ 451 19 87 - Open Sep-Jun, Mon-Fri 10am-5pm, Sat 10am-1pm, Jul-Aug, Mon-Fri 10am-6pm, Sat 10am-1pm. Wide selection of brochures in English.*

Getting around

Railway station - *Ul. Krakowska 48 - ℘ 453 22 80 - www.pkp.com.pl*

Bus station - *Ul. 1-go Maja 4 - ℘ 454 51 64 - www.pks.opole.pl*

Where to stayr

Piast Hotel – *Ul.Piastowska - ℘ 454 97 10 - www.hotelpiast.com.pl - 25 rooms - 359 PLN, 240 PLN weekends, breakfast included.*

Ideally situated near the town centre, this luxury hotel overlooks the River Odra. Spacious rooms and quality service.

Eating out

Maska – *Rynek 4 - ℘ 453 92 67 - 25 PLN.* Excellent inventive Polish cuisine served on the terrace or in a charming vaulted room with walls artistically flaking to reveal frescoes.

Starka – *Ul. Ostrówek 19 - ℘ 453 12 14 - 50 PLN.* Perched above the Odra, this restaurant offers a wide choice of beers and cocktails and serves refined Polish dishes. A few specialities on request including lamb's trotters and Polish-style goose.

Festive events

Festival of Polish Song: Late June. An institution for over 40 years.

Wrocław★★★

POPULATION 630 000 –MAP OF POLAND B3 – WOJEWÓDZTWO OF LOWER SILESIA

The capital of Lower Silesia, which is also the largest town in south-west Poland, is a multi-faceted city. The hustle and bustle of the Rynek with its colourful façades contrasts with the peace and quiet pervading the streets of Ostrów Tumski, the cathedral district. With 110 bridges over the Odra and dozens of islands, the Polish Venice is a continually changing student town whose dynamism is reflected in its architectural innovations.

▶ **Getting your bearings** – 340km south-east of Warsaw, 270km north-west of Kraków.

👁 **Not to be missed** – Night strolls through Ostrów Tumski, the panoramic view of the town from the cathedral tower.

🕐 **Planning your visit** – Wrocław deserves two or three days of your time for you to appreciate its different facets to the full. Sights and museums are of real interest and the town is quite attractive by night.

👫 **With your children** – A visit to the zoo is a must.

Cathedral Bridge links Ostrów Tumski Island to Sand Island

Background

Wrocław was founded around the 9C on the island of Ostrów Tumski. In the year 1000, the Polish King Boleslas the Brave endowed the town with a cathedral and a bishop's palace. Wrocław then proudly resisted various raids and, in 1138, became the capital of Silesia, a region soon to grow prosperous. The expansion of the town led to its centre being moved to the south bank of the Odra. In 1335, Poland lost control over the region which fell under Bohemian rule. The Habsburgs took over in the 16C but were replaced in 1741 by the Prussians who definitively acquired the town in 1763, at the end of the Seven Years War against the Austrians. They named it Breslau and turned it into a supposedly impregnable fortress. In the 19C, the city became one of Silesia's major industrial centres. After the Second World War, the town was returned to Poland following the Potsdam agreement. The German population fled and a few thousand Poles were transferred from Lwów (now in Ukraine under the name of L'viv). They brought with them their lifestyle and part of their cultural heritage, including the statue of the writer Aleksander Fredro, the Racławice Panorama and the library collections of the Ossoliński Institute. The closeness of the German border in itself explains the flood of German tourists who often undertake a nostalgic journey to the place where they spent their childhood.

Exploring

THE RYNEK A-B2

This vast rectangle measuring 173 x 208 m is the heart of the medieval city laid out in 1241 in a grid pattern. East of the town hall stands a copy of the stocks used for torture from the 15C onwards. On the west side is the statue of comic author Aleksander Fredro, brought back from Lwów (or L'viv) after the war. The original Gothic houses surrounding the Rynek were later remodelled in the Renaissance, Baroque or Classical style. Most of them were restored after 1945. The massive grey building in the south-west corner was supposed to prefigure a new Rynek but, fortunately, the project never got off the ground. Note the **House of the Seven Electors** at no 8, the **House of the Golden Sun** at no 5, the **Griffin House** at no 2 and, in the north-west corner, the two houses known as **Hansel and Gretel** (Jaś i Małgosia). Standing in the middle of the square is the town hall next to a group of municipal buildings separated by a complex network of passageways; these buildings include the present town hall erected on the site of a cloth market. The glass fountain which has pride of place in the western part of the Rynek is one of the locals' favourite meeting places.

Town Hall (Ratusz)★★★ B2

This complex building, remodelled many times, is a real patchwork of styles, Late Gothic being predominant. The first wooden edifice, which stood here in the 13C, was replaced by a rectangular brick structure flanked by Renaissance corner turrets topped with conical roofs. It used to house the town's administrative offices and the basement was used as a beer cellar. The east façade boasts Flamboyant ornamentation and features an astronomical clock from 1580. The south façade is richly decorated with carvings depicting medieval scenes and characters. The main entrance is on the west side.

Interior – *Tue-Sat 11am-5pm, Sun 10am-6pm. 4 PLN.* The elaborately decorated interior comprises a succession of rooms where the city museum's collections are normally displayed but they are regularly replaced by temporary exhibitions. The most outstanding rooms are the small **Council Chamber** upstairs and the **Burghers' Hall** on the ground floor entered through a richly decorated wooden door with an intricately carved stone frame. Near the main door, a colour-coded map shows when the different parts of the edifice were built. The top of the tower features the oldest reproduction of the coat of arms adopted by the town in 1534.

Salt Square (Plac Solny) A2

Laid out at the same time as the Rynek and accessed from the latter's south-west corner, the square is surrounded by chiefly Baroque and Classical houses. Note the **"Negro Sign" House** (Pod Murzynem) at no 2/3 and, at no 16 on the south side, the old **Stock Exchange** (Starej Giełdy) dating from 1822. Today, the square is occupied 24 hours a day by flower stalls surrounding a fountain and a modern sculpture.

St Elizabeth's Church (Kościół Św. Elżbiety) A1

In the north-west corner of the Rynek.

The porch linking the Hansel and Gretel houses symbolically guards the entrance to the church. The layout of the paving stones recalls the path which once wound its way through gravestones up to the entrance of St Elizabeth's. This church, dating from the 14C and 15C, was for a long time the town's main sanctuary; it remained a Protestant place of worship until the end of the Second World War. The interior has retained fine Renaissance, Baroque and Mannerist epitaphs. From the 83m high **tower** (302 steps to the top), there is a splendid view of the town, sometimes extending as far as the mountains. *(summer: Mon-Fri 9am-7pm, Sat 11am-5pm, Sun 1-5pm; winter: Mon-Sat 10am-5pm, Sun 1-5pm, 5 PLN).* Before the spire surmounting it was destroyed by fire, the tower was 128m high.

ON THE WAY TO THE UNIVERSITY

Walk along Kiełbaśnicza Street towards the River Odra. Turn right onto the tiny Stare Jatki Street.

Old Butchers' Street (Stare Jatki) A1

A timeless atmosphere lingers along this narrow paved street which gives an idea of what Wrocław was like in the past. The former butchers' shops now house galleries belonging to artists and designers. At the end of the street, the sculpture of a pig and a goat pays tribute to the animals slaughtered here since the 12C.

Kotlarska Street leads to Więzienna Street, where a former prison has been turned into a pub. Continue towards the University.

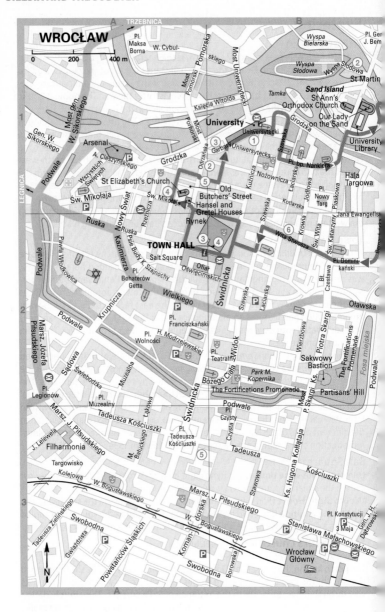

University (Uniwersytet)★★

Pl. Uniwersytecki 1. Mon-Fri 10am-3.30pm. 3 PLN.

The town's largest monumental ensemble of Baroque architecture was erected by the Jesuits in 1670 on the site of the Piasts' ducal castle. The Austro-Prussian war turned the building into a military hospital. From 1811 onwards, the Prussian authorities took over the running of the university founded in 1702 by Emperor Leopold I. This Baroque edifice was erected between 1728 and 1742. The square tower of the observatory dominating the ensemble houses a collection of old astronomical instruments; it is crowned by four allegorical statues representing medicine, philosophy, law and theology, subjects once taught here. Located on the ground floor of the University is the **Oratorium Marianum** where concerts still take place today. Upstairs, a heavy intricately carved wooden door leads into the **Leopoldine Hall** (Aula Leopoldina) *(Mon-Tue, Thu-Sun, 10am-3.30pm. 4.5 PLN)*, an impressive 18C Baroque hall decorated with cherubs and gilded ornaments; all round the room are portraits of the founding fathers of the university. Note the painted ceiling above ancient wooden benches facing the pulpit surmounted by a statue

of Leopold I in majesty. He seems to be watching over the receptions and symposia which are often organised here. In front of the building adjacent to the **Chuch of the Blessed Name of Jesus** (Kościół Najświętszego Imienia Jezus) stands the statue of a naked swashbuckler which has stood there since 1904 and been the butt of facetious students. They regularly replace his foil with the oddest accessories. Nearby, at no 8 Kuźnicza Street, is a small university museum devoted to anthropology *(open afternoons Tue-Sat)*.

Turn left past the Church of the Blessed Name of Jesus then right onto the embankment. Walk up the narrow Szewska Street which skirts the library and turn right again onto Bp.Nankiera Street. Walk across Piaskowski Bridge (Most Piaskowy), the town's oldest bridge, mentioned as early as the 12C. It spans the river in front of the Market Hall (Hala Targowa), reminiscent of markets during the communist era, and leads to Sand Island.

Sand Island (Wypa Pisłowa) B1

The street, shared by tramways and cars, is lined on the left by **St Ann's Orthodox Church** (Kościół Św. Anny) and on the right by the Baroque building of the University library, a former Augustinian convent. Next to it stands the Gothic **Church of Our Lady on the Sand** (Kościół NMP na Piasku). Inside, one of the chapels, dedicated to the deaf and the blind, houses a miscellaneous collection of movable figures.

At the extremity of the island, turn right onto the metallic bridge (Most Tumski) leading to the beginning of Cathedral Street (Ul. Katedralna). It is guarded by the statues of the patron saints of Silesia (St Hedwig) and of Wrocław (St John the Baptist).

OSTRÓW TUMSKI C1

This is the oldest part of Wrocław. The town was founded here in the 9C, on an island joined to the river bank in 1810 when an arm of the Odra was filled in. The streets, where one can still see lamplighters at work when night falls, have retained a peaceful, serene, almost insular atmosphere. The island, fortified against invasions, was the seat of the ducal authority; in the 11C, a bishopric was established and, after the 13C, when the new town developed on the south bank of the river, the island remained the seat of the church authorities.

Church of the Holy Cross and St Bartholomew (Kościół Św. Krzyża) C1

Built in the 13C and 14C, this Gothic edifice features a very unusual structure consisting of two churches, one on top of the other. The lower one is dedicated to St Bartholomew, the patron saint of the Piast dynasty.

Walking up Św. Marcina Street, one comes across the small **St Martin's Church** (Kościół Św. Marcina), the former castle chapel dating from the 13C, featuring a mixture of Romanesque and Gothic styles.

Return to Katedralna Street and continue until you reach the cathedral. The building is surrounded by the seat of the archbishopric and the former archbishop's palace.

Cathedral of St John the Baptist (Katedra Św. Jana Chrzciciela)★ C1

It stands on the site of the first Romanesque cathedral built around 1000, destroyed in 1037 by Bratislav, a Bohemian duke, rebuilt in the 12C and reduced to rubble once more by the Mongols in 1241. Work began almost immediately on the present brick-built cathedral, the first to be erected in Poland. The foundation stone was laid in 1244, but the building was only completed two centuries later, when the roof was covered with copper sheeting. In 1945, only 30% of the edifice remained standing. The present state of the medieval stone doorway, where one can see, close to the ground, the statue of a lion from the original 12C sanctuary, testifies to the scale of the damage. At the end of the nave, the high altar is surmounted by a triptych, painted in Lublin in 1522, depicting the Dormition of the Virgin Mary. In the east end of the cathedral, note the two chapels on either side of the Lady Chapel, St Elizabeth's Chapel decorated with Italian sculptures and the Corpus Christi Chapel. Note also, along the north wall, the oval-shaped Chapel of the Dead. Next to it, a door opens onto a narrow spiral staircase leading to the lift which takes visitors to the top of the North Tower (Mon-Sat except during religious holidays 10am-6pm, 4 PLN). This viewpoint, surmounted like its twin by a 45m spire in 1941, offers a panoramic view of the whole town.

Leave the cathedral and walk along the north side. Turn left under the arch on the corner of the small brick church dedicated to St Giles (Kościół Św. Idziego), undoubtedly Ostrów Tumski's oldest church. This leads to one of the entrances of the Botanical Gardens.

Botanical Gardens (Ogród Botaniczny)★ C1

Entrance via Kanonicza street and 23 Sienkiewicza Street. Mar-Oct 8am-6pm, hothouse open 10am-6pm. 5 PLN.

Part of the fortifications of the town, built alongside the arm of the Odra now filled in, used to stand on this site. Nature is cleverly given pride of place in an area which contains over 11 000 plant species spread around two vast expanses of water with ducks splashing about. This is the ideal place to escape the hustle and bustle of the town. Various buildings contain a hothouse, an aquarium, a palm grove, a collection of succulent plants, including many cacti, and an exhibition presenting the successive geological eras.

Return to the cathedral and continue eastwards to Katedralny Square.

Archdiocesan Museum (Muzeum Archidiecezjalne) C1

Pl. Katedralny 16. Tue-Sun 9am-3pm. 3 PLN. Captions and comments in English.

This museum, one of the town's oldest, is devoted to religious art: chalices, chasubles, paintings and sculptures including an awe-inspiring statue of the scourging of Christ; no real care seems to have been taken to make the displays attractive. However, the top-floor room is interesting for its collection of impressive archive cabinets dating from 1455, its equestrian statue of St George Slaying the Dragon, two 15C antiphonaries and a superb 13-14C manuscript, Henryków's Book (Księga Henrykowska), which contains the first text written in Polish.

Walk around Katedralny Square, take Św. Józefa Street and get back to the south bank of the Odra via Pokoju Bridge leading to the National Museum.

On the banks of the River Oder, the elegant façade of the University

Things to see

National Museum (Muzeum Narodowe)★ C1

Pl. Powstańców Warszawy 5. Wed, Fri, Sun 10am-4pm, Thu 9am-4pm, Sat 10am-6pm. 15 PLN, free on Sat.

The museum is housed in a late-19C neo-Renaissance building. Each of the three levels is laid out around a huge central staircase.

The first floor is devoted to Silesian art. The superb medieval collection includes polychrome wooden sculpture and a few paintings. Note in particular a very realistic 15C carved representation of the Flagellation and a Stations of the Cross with 11 life-size characters originally in St Mary Magdalene's Church in Wrocław. The rooms, devoted to the period stretching from the Renaissance to the 19C, contain mannerist and modernist painting and sculpture. The second floor presents Polish art from the 17C to the 19C. The interesting collection of contemporary art includes expressionist, surrealist and abstract works. A room dedicated to Magdalena Abakanowicz presents a sculpture entitled *Crowd*, which expresses the individual's anonymity in a crowd. One last room contains contemporary ceramic and glass works.

Panorama of the Battle of Racławice (Panorama Racławicka)★★ C2

Ul. Purkyniego 11. Summer 9am-5pm; winter 9am-4pm. Closed Mon. 20 PLN, the ticket also gives admission to the National Museum. 30 min. Audioguides in English on loan.

This vast panoramic painting measuring 120m x 15m is a real national monument. Its fame is such that it is essential to make a reservation if you wish to see it. The work gives a realistic rendering of the Battle of Racławice on 4 April 1794 which, following the Kościuskowska uprising, ended with the victory of the Polish people led by General Tadeusz Kościuszko over the Russian invaders.

Follow Jana Ewangelisty Purkyniego Street, then turn right onto Bernardyńska Street.

Museum of Architecture
(Muzeum Architektury) C2

Ul. Bernardyńska 5. Tue-Wed, Fri-Sat 10am-4pm, Thu noon-6pm, Sun 11am-5pm. 7 PLN.

The museum is housed in a former church and the adjoining cloister. Its moderately interesting collections consist of architectural elements from the 12C to the 20C, somewhat clumsily displayed in rooms which have, in fact, been carefully restored. However, the church contains some fine stained-glass windows and an unusual collection of ceramic stoves.

Return to the Rynek via J Słowackiego avenue prolonged by Wita Stwosza Street.

A Controversial Subject

The work was painted in Lwów (L'viv) at the end of the 19C by Jan Styka and Wojciech Kossak to celebrate the centenary of the Battle of Racławice. It was immediately popular and it nurtured the Poles' nationalist feelings in relation to the Russians. After the war, L'viv having become Ukrainian, the Soviet authorities sent the work to Wrocław. However, the subject was deemed too controversial by the communist authorities and the work was only finally exhibited in 1985, following the construction of a place fit to receive it.

Arsenal (Arsenał) A1

Ul. Cieszyńskiego 9

Situated north-west of the town centre, along the banks of the Odra, the former 15C arsenal, recently restored, houses the archaeological and military museums.

Archaeological Museum (Muzem Archeologiczne)

Wed-Sat 11am-5pm, Sun 10am-6pm. 7 PLN, Wed free.

Explanations in Polish only tend to spoil the interesting scenography and the fine displays: funeral urns, fibulae, bronze axes and swords, sigillated pottery, even the grave of a horseman buried with his horse. The second floor presents many neolithic items: tools made of cut and polished stone, reconstruction of a loom as well as artefacts dating from the early Bronze Age.

Military Museum (Muzeum Arsenał)

Wed-Sat 11am-5pm, Sun 10am-6pm. 7 PLN, Wed free.

The first floor, devoted to firearms, presents an impressive variety of handguns and rifles, and above all one of the most important collections of military helmets in Europe. A small room illustrates the history of bladed weapons from sharpened flints to medieval swords. The second floor houses a fine collection of Polish sabres from the 19C and 20C.

The Fortifications Promenade B2

Laid out at the beginning fo the 19C, this promenade runs through greenery along the line of fortifications which once enclosed the south bank of the Odra. The moat is still intact. The most interesting section lies to the south-east of the town centre, on both sides of P Skargi Street. **Partisans' Hill** (Wzgórze Partyzantów), the site of a former bastion, was laid out in 1868 and it is still possible to reach the neo-Renaissance panoramic platforms, unfortunately neglected.

The People's Hall (Hala Ludowa)

Ul. Wystawowa 1. Daily 8am-7pm. 3 PLN.

This vast circular building, in glass and reinforced concrete, is flanked by four apses and covered with a dome; 23m in height and 67m in diameter, it was designed by the modernist architect Max Berg and built in 1912-13 to commemorate the centenary of Napoleon's defeat at Leipzig. It is the venue for exhibitions, concerts and sporting events. In front of the building stands a 95m-high spire erected after the war by the communist authorities anxious to show their know-how and possibly outdo this masterpiece of German architecture.

Japanese Garden (Ogród Japoński)

Park Szczytnicki. Avr.-oct. 9h-19h. 2/1 PLN.

These gardens, located inside Park Szczytnicki, were laid out in 1913 and remodelled in 1997 with the help of Japanese specialists; they offer a gentle stroll in a setting of foaming waterfalls, of peaceful streams, elaborate floral and mineral displays enhanced by constructions in a typical Japanese style.

Zoo

Ul. Wróblewskiego 1. Daily Apr-Sep 9am-6pm. 10 PLN.

Founded in 1865, this is one of Europe's oldest zoos. In the 1970s, its inmates (nearly 5 000 of them!) became the stars of a television show, "A camera among animals", which delighted children for three decades, each show captivating some 9 million spectators. Today the zoo is home to kangaroos, giraffes, lions, elephants, antelopes, black panthers, tigers … there is also a reptile and amphibian house.

Jewish Cemetery

Ul. Ślężna 37/39. Open Apr-Sep Tue-Sat 11am-5pm, Sun 10am-6pm.

Situated in the southern part of town, the cemetery opened in 1856. With some 1 200 graves, it is one of Poland's best preserved Jewish cemeteries. Closed in 1942, it was only reopened in 1991, following extensive restoration work. Today, it is regarded as an open-air museum of Jewish funerary art.

Nearby

Trzebnica

22km north of Wrocław along the E261.

The town's history is linked to that of the first **Cistercian Convent** in Poland, established in the 13C by Duke Henry the Bearded at the request of his wife Hedwig.

The Ducal Hall in Lubiąż Abbey

In 1218, she managed to have Trzebnica Abbey accepted as the first monastery for women by the Cistercian Order and her daughter Gertrude became one of the first abbesses.

Of the vast monastic group of buildings, only St Hedwig's Basilica is open to visitors. Originally built in a mixture of Gothic and Romanesque styles, destroyed many times, it was entirely remodelled in the 18C in the purest Baroque style. The church has retained its Gothic structure. A tower now stands in front of the main entrance. On the left are the remains of a Romanesque doorway with a carved tympanum depicting King David playing on the psaltery for Queen Bathsheba and her ladies-in-waiting. Rediscovered behind an 18C wall, it is one of the three original doorways leading into the church. Inside, the profusion of Baroque decoration is at its most lavish in the chapel dedicated to the saint resting in the black-marble **tomb**★ watched over, it seems, by a 15C crucifix. On 16 October, the feast day of the saint, a crowd of pilgrims gathers in this peaceful hilly countryside.

Lubiąż★★

55km west of Wrocław. Open Jun-Sep 9am-6pm, Oct-Mar 10am-3pm. 8 PLN.
Situated in the middle of the countryside and rising above a clump of trees planted on the east bank of the Odra, the impressive abbey complex boasts a troubled history.

> ### Hedwig, Patron Saint of Silesia
>
> Born in 1178, Hedwig was the daughter of the Duke of Moravia. At age 12, her father sent her to the court in Wrocław. She was married at 18 to the Duke of Greater Poland, later to be known as Henry the Bearded (in keeping with the vow he made to her to refrain from shaving). She cared for the poor, the sick, victims of war, and those in prison. After the death of her son Henry the Pious at the Battle of Legnickie Pole, she retired to Trzebnica monastery where she died in 1243. After her death, her cult spread rapidly and pilgrims flocked to her grave in Trzebnica, not only from Silesia but also from Great Poland and Pomerania. She was canonized in 1267 and her feast-day established on 16 October.

Benedictine monks, who occupied the site as early as 1150, were soon replaced by Cistercian monks. After a period of decline, the monastery prospered once more during the 17C. Extensive building work, carried out between 1690 and 1720, gave the complex its present appearance; the predominantly Baroque church nevertheless retained a few Gothic features. The abbey was then one of Europe's largest monastic ensembles, 223m long and 118m wide, with over 300 rooms. In 1810, the abbey was abandoned and, for the next two centuries, it remained empty and stripped of its ornaments.

This imposing place, now being restored, conveys a somewhat ghostly impression. The breathtaking façade seems to crush visitors who can only see a few rooms containing an exhibition devoted to the history of the abbey, a railway museum, a sugar museum and a third one illustrating navigation along the River Odra.

The surprise waiting for you on the first floor is in itself worth the trip. At the end of a corridor, a monumental doorway supported by the giant statues of two Africans, opens onto the huge Baroque **Ducal Hall**. Beneath a vast ceiling decorated with frescoes, large windows on two levels let daylight flood in and play on the stucco decorations, the statues and the dazzling pink marbles.

Practical Wrocław

Postal code – 50 000 - 53 000
Phone code – 071

Useful addresses

Tourist office –Rynek 14 – ☎ 344 31 11 – www.wroclaw.pl - daily 9am-9pm. Run by a competent and dynamic polyglot team, this centre is a mine of information with a wide selection of books and brochures about the town and Lower Silesia. Bike hire (50 PLN/day), free Internet access, guided tours.

Police : ☎ 997

Main post office: Rynek 28. Open 24hr/day.

Pharmacy open 24hr/day – Apteka pod Lwami - Pl. 1-go Maja 7a, Apteka Katedralna - ul. H. Sienkiewicza 54/56.

Internet Café – W Sercu Miasta – Żelaźnicze 8 - daily 10am-midnight. In the centre of the rynek. 4 PLN/hr.

Where to go

Two small magazines in English offer a wealth of information. Wroław in your Pocket lists and comments on hôtels, restaurants and out-on-the-town places, whereas The Visitor (monthly) is more culturally oriented.

Getting around

Driving in the town centre crisscrossed by pedestrian streets is difficult. Opt for public transport. No fewer than 54 bus lines and 23 tramway lines insure a more than adequate service for a town this size. Allow 25 PLN for a 5-day travel card, 10 PLN for a day ticket.

Railway station – Ul. Piłsudskiego 105 - ☎ 367 58 82 - www.pkp.pl. The main station is situated 1km south of the town centre. There are trains to Warsaw, Kraków and Poznań several times a day.

Bus station– Ul. Sucha 1/11 – ☎ 361 01 77, informations 361 81 22 - www.pks.pl. Next door to the railway station.

Airport – Ul. Skarżyńskiego 36 – ☎ 358 11 00, 849 22 61 - www.airport.wroclaw.pl. Some 12km north-west of the town centre. Journey time: 20 min by bus no 406. Regular links with London; several flights daily to and from Warsaw.

Car hire – Autocash – ul. Powstańców Śląskich - ☎ 793 09 75. Budget (☎ 358 12 92), Avis (☎ 372 35 67), Hertz (☎ 358 12 94) and Europcar (☎ 358 12 91) at the airport.

Taxis– Several companies including Radio Serc (☎ 9629), Mini Radio Taxi (☎ 9626).

Where to stay

Savoy Hotel – Pl. Kościuszki 19 - ☎ 344 30 71 - 26 rooms - 110/130 PLN, ☕10 PLN. Close to the station, very cheap and recently restored in true functional style, the Savoy should not be judged on the first impression one gets from its somewhat austere façade. Advance booking advisable.

Tumski Hotel – Wyspa Słodowa 10 - ☎ 322 60 99 - www.hotel-tumski.com- 55 rooms - 290, 250 PLN weekends ☕. 40 PLN in the youth hostel section (6 rooms). Situated on a small island between the town centre and Ostrów Tumski, this well-kept hotel suits all budgets. Apart from their more basic decoration and fittings, the cheap rooms on the ground floor are comparable to the more expensive ones on the floors above.

Zaułek Hotel – Ul. Garbary 11 - ☎ 375 29 45 - www.hotel.uni.wroc.pl - 12 rooms - 290 PLN, 245 PLN weekends ☕. 🅿. The place has a quaint charm in spite of its favourable position in the university district, close to the hustle and bustle of the town centre; you won't find better value for money.

Dom Jana Pawła II – Ul. Św. Idziego 2 - ☎ 322 16 92 - www.pensjonat-jp2.pl - 60 rooms - 295 PLN, 257 PLN weekends ☕. 🅿. Located on Ostrów Tumski, between the cathedral and the botanical gardens, this brand new hotel boasts luxury facilities. The restaurant caters for communion and wedding receptions and gets crowded at teatime by people wanting to taste John Paul II's favourite cake. Internet connection in the rooms.

Patio Hotel – Ul. Kiełbaśnicza 24 - ☎ 375 04 00 - www.hotelpatio.pl - 49 rooms - 360 PLN, 267 PLN weekends 🅿. 50m from the rynek. The rooms are vast and very comfortable. Ask for one on the street side, as it will be much brighter and more pleasant than any of those overlooking the tiny alleyway lined with flashy modern buildings.

Eating out

Bazylia – Pl. Uniwersytecki - daily 8am-9pm - 20 PLN. This university restaurant, open to everybody, serves a carefully prepared cuisine. It is probably one of the most trendy establishments in town. It is situated on the ground floor of the new law faculty buildings, at the very hub of student life.

Kurna Chata – Ul. Odrzańska 7 - ☎ 341 06 68 - daily 10am-midnight, weekends noon-midnight - 20 PLN. Good traditional cooking at a reasonable price is served here, in a rustic decor. A young and not-so young eclectic clientele gathers round the few tables.

Bistrot Parisien –Ul. Nożownicza 7 - ☎ 343 76 98 - tlj. 10am-midnight, Sun noon-8pm - 20 PLN. A great many books from Balzac to Boris Vian and Malraux stacked up in the window create the atmosphere of the place. This French-speaking Francophile den serves copious French dishes (salads, crepes).

Paśnik – *Ul. Wita Stwosza 37 - ℘ 342 57 18 - daily 10am-midnight - 30 PLN*. This milkbar offering a classic menu is also the rendezvous of the town's chess players who take over the tables at any time of day. The atmosphere is unique and somewhat stylish.

Gospoda Wrocławska – *Ul. Sukiennice 7 - ℘ 342 74 56 - daily noon-midnight - 50 PLN*. Situated in one of the passageways of the rynek. The medieval-style decoration is slightly overdone but the menu offers all the classic dishes of Polish cuisine (roast pig and special soup made with blood...). In another room, fresh fish and seafood are served with just as much care.

Spiż – *Ul. Rynek Ratusz 9 - ℘ 344 72 25 - daily noon-midnight - 70 PLN*. Housed in the vaulted cellars of the town hall, this restaurant offers a cosy, refined atmosphere and an eclectic cuisine. Tasty specialities, such as soup made with beer; that very beer, brewed on the premises, flows freely late into the night in the large brewery room.

Taking a break

K2 – *Ul. Kiełbaśnicza 2 - daily 11am-11pm*. Perched up a narrow lane, at the top of a flight of steps, this tiny tearoom decorated with pastel colours offers a choice of pastries and teas in a friendly, cosy atmosphere.

Pod Kalamburem – *Ul. Kuźnicza 29 - 10am-11pm, Sun 3pm-midnight*. TheArt Nouveau decoration and the large mirrors account for the unique cachet of this slightly bohemian student bistro, close to the university.

Mleczarnia – *Ul. Włodkowica 5 - daily 10am-1am*. With its parquet flooring shiny with age, its old-fashioned photos covering the walls and its wooden tables, this large café, extending inwards from the street, recalls the 1930s. Let yourself be tempted byits quiet daytime atmosphere and enjoy a delicious homemade cake.

On the town

Piwnica Świdnicka – *Rynek Ratusz 1 - ℘ 369 95 00 - daily 10am-1am - 60 PLN*. This place is housed in a 15C cellar beneath the town hall. The kitsch medieval decor might put you off, but this is nevertheless a must. Plenty of beer and food served in a string of rooms where you will find side by side a snack, a high-class restaurant and an informal eating place with an exuberant atmosphere.

Klub Pracowania – *Ul. Włózienna 6 - daily 4pm-1am*. This former prison housed in a brick building is now more hospitable. The paved courtyard is used as a terrace in fine weather but to get to the bar you will have to enter the vaulted cellar crowded with locals and an assortment of miscellaneous objects.

Shopping

Stare Jatki – *Ul. Stare Jatki*. No fewer than 20 boutiques belonging to artists and designers have taken over the old houses lining the former Butchers' Street. Papers, arti st's materials, linen clothes, framing, glasswork, painting, pottery, sculpture and costume jewellery...an assortment of unique quality items.

Covered market – *Ul. Piaskowa 6 - daily 4pm-1am*. This market hall gives a highly authentic impression of what markets were like during the communist period. People come here mainly to buy foodstuffs.

Festive events

Festival of Singing Actors: Concerts and recitals as well as a singing competition. March.

Wrocław Jazz Festival: 3 days of jazz during this world-renowned festival. April.

Wrocław Non-Stop: During this festival, live shows take over the sights and streets of the town. Late June.

Vratislavia Cantans: Ancient music both sacred and classical invades the city during this international ten-day festival in September.

M. Ostrowska / MICHELIN

Sundial

Kłodzko Region★★

MAP OF POLAND B3 – WOJEWÓDZTWO OF LOWER SILESIA

This region, which tapers to a point jutting out into the Czech Republic, was coveted many times and fell into many hands over the centuries. It is an area of underground galleries and caves and of spectacular rock formations, where hydrotherapy is a major activity.

- ▶ **Getting your bearings** – Kłodzko lies 80km south of Wrocław along the E67.
- 👁 **Not to be missed** – Take time to explore the minor roads meandering through wooded hills dotted with isolated chapels and remote villages.
- 🕐 **Planning your visit** – Ideally, you need to devote three days to this region, to discover its monuments and its caves, to ramble through the countryside and stroll through the towns.
- 👪 **With your children** – The Erratic Boulders site.

Gothic Bridge with statues of saints

Kłodzko

Kłodzko is a thousand-year-old hillside city, once surrounded by ramparts, which, like other Silesian towns, successiveley belonged to the Poles, the Habsburgs and the Prussians before being returned to Poland in 1945.

Its steep, narrow, winding streets, often featuring flights of steps, greatly contribute to the charm of the city. The town hall, remodelled in the 19C, stands on the picturesque **Rynek** surrounded by elegant houses sometimes adorned with subtle decorations.

Gothic Bridge (Most Gotycki)

The pride of the town, built in 1390, looking to some extent like a miniature replica of St Charles's Bridge in Prague, spans the Młynówka canal; its parapets are adorned with six groups of statues representing various saints, erected in the 17C and 18C.

Church of the Assumption (Kościół Wniebowzięcia NMP)

The church stands in the centre of a pleasant square, one street away from the Rynek. Built in the 14C, it has retained its Gothic appearance on the outside decorated with sculptures and gargoyles. The interior, entirely remodelled from the 17C onwards, boasts a wealth of Baroque ornamentation. The 16C Gothic vaulting over the cental nave features stucco decorations from 1673. The Baroque altar dates from 1729.

Kłodzko Regional Museum (Muzeum Ziemi Kłodzkiej)

Ul. Łukasiewicza 4. Tue-Fri 10am-4pm, Sat-Sun 11am-5pm. 5 PLN.

The museum's main interest lies in its impressive collection of clocks. Cuckoo clocks, wooden mechanisms, enamel, porcelain or carved-wood clock-faces are displayed throughout the second level. The floor of a strange, dark room, paved with mirrors, reflects a profusion of clocks hanging from the ceiling. The museum also houses contemporary glassware dating from the 1950s and 1960s.

Underground Tourist Route (Prodziemna Trasa Turystyczna)

Access via no 3 Zawiszy Czarnego Street, under the Church of the Assumption and exit at the foot of the fortress. Apr-Oct 9am-5pm, Nov-Mar 10am-3pm. 4 PLN.

Discovered during the 1970s, after a series of cave-ins, this vast network of Medieval tunnels is a warren beneath the city, linking the cellars of some of the town's houses. Merchants once used them as storage space. Today the route consists of 600m of galleries (the rest having been filled in for safety reasons), which are nice and cool on hot summer days. The many cellars along the way often feature picturesque scenes and objects intended to create a gloomy and mysterious atmosphere.

Fortress

May-Oct 9am-6pm, Nov-Apr 9am-4pm. 4 PLN.

Castles and forts have always stood on the strategic hill overlooking Kłodzko, which   used to defend the buffer zone that this part of Silesia was in the past. The present fortress was built in the 18C by the Prussian authorities. Deep ditches and glacis were literally carved out of the terrain and high walls erected as reinforcements. The stronghold withstood 11 sieges without ever surrendering. An ingenious defence system, which prefigured mine fields, made it virtually impregnable. 45km of low, narrow and dark galleries run under the foundations and the idea was to blow up the sections located beneath enemy positions. Today the tour includes 600m of these galleries – some of them no higher than 50cm – which form a real labyrinth.

West of Kłodzko

There are more worthwhile sights in this area than in the rest of the region. Don't hesitate to stop somewhere for the night. If, on the other hand, you can only spare one day, make a point of seeing the Paper Industry Museum, the Chapel of Skulls and the Erratic Boulders site.

THE SPA TOWNS ROAD

Polanica Zdrój
15km west of Kłodzko.

This very pleasant spa resort, nestling inside a valley, offers shaded promenades along the River Bystrzyca.

Duszniki Zdrój
23km west of Kłodzko.

This is the second spa town on the way to the Czech Republic. The beneficial effects of the region's mineral springs have been known since the Middle Ages, but the resort only became flourishing and internationally renowned in the 19C. Chopin took the waters in 1826 and gave concerts for charity while he was there. Every year, a festival is held in his honour. This itinerary forms a loop starting from Kłodzko and extending westward as far as the Table Mountains.

Paper Industry Museum (Muzeum Papiernictwa)★★
May-Sep 9am-5pm; Oct-Apr 9am-3pm. Closed Mon and hols.

This fine museum is worth a detour for its superb presentation, its handsome building and the activities on offer. The paper mill, powered by a paddle wheel, itself driven by the river current, was built in 1605. It is an elegant piece of Baroque architecture, with its wooden scrolls and panelled façade. Recently restored, the mill is operational once more. It produces paper using traditional techniques pleasantly presented in the museum and illustrated by paper samples and a collection of watermarks. Visitors can pitch in if they wish.

Kudowa Zdrój
35km west of Kłodzko.

The region's main resort lies at an altitude of 400m, only a few kilometres from the border with the Czech Republic. People come to the neo-Baroque pump room, situated in the middle of the English-style park surrounded by dales, to take the waters from eight hot and cold mineral springs (inhalations, baths and drinks from the public fountain). It is also possible to visit a small but charming **Toy Museum** (Muzeum Zabawek, *ul. Zdrojowa 41*).

KŁODZKO REGION

0   10 km

Chapel of Skulls (Kaplica Czaszek)★★
In Czermna near Kudowa Zdrój. Ul. Kościuszki.

Situated in a parish close comprising a 17C church, cemetery and tower, this tiny unassuming chapel gives visitors no forewarning of the sight that awaits them when they enter. The interior is entirely lined with bones, some 3 000 skulls and shinbones representing the remains of victims of the Silesian and Seven Years Wars and of the epidemics which marked the second half of the 18C. This unusual presentation was set up by the local priest, Wacław Tomaszek, between 1776 and 1804. The guide ends the visit by lifting the trap door of the crypt where another 20 000 bones are deposited.

Open-air Museum of Sudeten Popular Culture in Pstrążna
(Muzeum Kultury Ludowej Pogórza Sudeckiego w Pstrążnej)
Mai-Oct. 10am-6pm. Closed Mon. 4 PLN.

This museum recreating a traditional valley village is located at the end of the road *(5km)* running past the Chapel of Skulls. The smithy, the bread oven, the potter's workshop all come to life during summer open-air festivals.

Table Mountains National Park (Park Narodowy Góry Stołowe)★★
30km west of Kołdzko. Access via the road linking Kudowa Zdrój and Radków.

Taking advantage of the horizontal geological structure of the area – a unique occurrence in Poland –, nature gave free course to her own fantasy by letting erosion carve the spectacular landscape into the most bizarre shapes. The National Park, created in 1993, is covered with a forest consisting mainly of conifers, which provides a habitat for protected flora and fauna. The most spectacular and also the most secluded site is the **Erratic Boulders Reserve (Błędne Skały)★★** *(alternate access from the road every 45min, 8am-7.15pm, 5 PLN. Admission to the Labyrinth 5 PLN).* This 21ha labyrinth, dug into the sedimentary rocks, is up to 6-8m high and no wider than 20 to 30cm in places. It meanders between boulders polished by streaming water, which sometimes look as if they're about to topple over.

From the village of Karłów, one can climb 665 steps hewn out of the rock *(1hr there and back)* to the **Szczeliniec Wielki★★** Reserve where the mountains reach their highest point (919m). From this viewpoint covering an area of 50ha, the view extends eastwards to the Kłodzko region and westwards beyond the Czech border. Further on, between Radków and Wambierzyce, the wooded valleys of the **Petrified Mushrooms** (Skalne Grzyby) Reserve are crisscrossed by footpaths.

Wambierzyce

20km north-west of Kłodzko.

Nestling at the foot of the Table Mountains, this Marian sanctuary, built in the Italian Baroque style, boasts an ochre façade preceded by a 56-step monumental staircase. The basilica contains a forty-centimetre high statue of Our Lady of Wambierzyce who is said to have special powers. Also of interest is the moving crib including no fewer than 800 characters carved out of lime-tree wood by a local locksmith who started in 1882 and took 28 years to complete his masterpiece. On the hill facing the sanctuary, a giant Way of the Cross including 29 Stations has been attracting penitents and pilgrims since the end of the 18C.

South-east of Kłodzko

Bear's Cave★★

In Kletno, 30km south-east of Kłodzko. From the parking area, allow 20min on foot through woodland. Open daily 9am-4.40pm except Dec-Jan, Mon and Thu Sep-Apr. Reservations essential ℘ (074) 814 12 50. The visit lasts 45min. Come prepared: the temperature does not rise above 6°C and the extreme humidity creates slippery and rainy conditions. Not recommended for young children.

The cave was discovered during the quarrying of a marble seam near the village of Kletno, in the Śnieżnik mountains. It is undoubtedly one of Poland's finest caves. Extending over a distance of 2km are vast chambers – the largest is 60m long and 45m high – , narrow passageways and forests of stalactites. The most delicate concretions suggest draperies while the most spectacular looks like an 8m high calcite cascade. Remains of animals, such as lions and foxes, were found in the cave, together with the impressive skeleton of a bear dating from the Ice Age. The highlight of the tour is the total darkness and silence experienced by visitors when the guide switches off the lights.

Paczków

33km east of Kłodzko.

Situated in the Opole region, in an area bordering the former principality of the bishops of Wrocław, Paczków is known as Poland's Carcassonne. The comparison, although exaggerated, is based on the well-preserved **ramparts** surrounding the town, which have been protecting it since the 14C. There are 19 semi-circular towers dotted around the 1.2km long, 9m high walls pierced by four doors flanked by towers.

The town follows a grid plan; in its centre is the small **Rynek** featuring a 16C **town hall** with a belfry reminiscent of northern Italy's Renaissance towers. From the **top of the belfry** *(access daily 10am-5pm, 3 PLN)*, there is a fine overall view of the almost perfect oval ring of ramparts. The so-called **Wrocław Tower** *(access Mon-Sat 7.30am-6pm, Sun 10am-5pm, 3 PLN, tickets on sale at the newspaper kiosk),* closing off the ring to the north-east, also offers a fine panoramic view extending to the mountains marking the border with the Czech Republic. South-east of the Rynek, the church of **St John the Evangelist** (Kościół Św. Jana Ewangelisty), a squat, almost cubic-shaped building

Kudowa Zdrój spa

crowned by defensive crenellations, is a typical example of a fortified church from the first half of the 14C. North of the ramparts, at no 6 Pocztowa Street, a fine **museum** housed in former gasworks (Muzeum Gazownictwa, *Mon-Fri 9am-4pm, free admission*) offers a fascinating presentation of the production and use of town gas.

Practical Kłodzko

Useful addresses

Kłodzko's Tourist office – *Pl. B. Chrobrego 1* – ℘ *(074) 865 89 70 - fax (074) 865 89 71 - www.ziemiakklodzka.pl and www.hrabstwo.pl – open Mon and Sat 9am-4pm, Tue-Fri 9am-6pm, Sun (May-Aug) 9am-1pm.* Well stocked with all kinds of guide books and maps (only a few are in English), this office centralizes all the information about the region.

Kudowa Zdrój Tourist office – *Ul. Zdrojowa 44* – ℘ *(074) 866 13 87 - www. kudowa.pl – May-Sep: Mon-Fri 9am-8pm, Sat 8am-6pm, Sun 9am-5pm. The rest of the year daily 9am-6pm.* This office can provide all the necessary information about the Table Montains as well as a few guide books and brochures (some in English) about the spa resorts.

Paczków Tourist office – *Ul. Słowackiego 4* – ℘ *(077) 431 67 91 - www.paczkow.pl - open Mon-Fri 8am-4pm.* Convivial welcome, useful information. Free Internet access.

Where to go

There are all kinds of maps of the Kłodzko region: road map, sightseeing map, rambling map. There is also a detailed map of the Table Mountains, showing all the footpaths and the estimated time needed to walk along each of them. Very useful to be able to ramble serenely through the National Park.

Getting around

By car: Parking is easy in the region's towns, except perhaps in the spa resorts during the high season. Many car parks in Kłodzko.

Railway station - Kłodzko has two train stations. Main station: Ul. Dworcowa, ℘ *(074) 867 34 72* and town station: Pl. Jedności, ℘ *(074) 867 34 72, www.pkp.pl.* Kudowa Zdrój station: Ul. Obrońców Pokoju, ℘ *(074) 866 17 85.*

Bus station - Pl. Jednosci - ℘ *(074) 867 37 32.* Buses link Kłodzko with various sights and towns throughout the region.

Where to stay

Kłodzko's accommodation facilities are inadequate. The nearby spa towns have luxury hotels often providing fitness equipment. Enjoy ecotourism: the region has a wealth of B & Bs where comfort and country scenery favourably compare with what luxury hotels have to offer.

KŁODZKO

Korona Hotel – *Ul. Noworudzka 1* - ℘ *(074) 867 37 37 - 18 rooms - 150 PLN with breakfast.* 🅿 As you arrive from the north. Cheap prices and basic comfort combine to offer good value for money.

MIĘDZYGÓRZE

Villa Millenium – *Ul. Wojska Polskiego 9* - ℘ *(071) 813 52 87 - www.millenium.ta.pl - 11 rooms - 65 PLN in winter, 100 PLN the rest of the year.* At the entrance to the village. all the rooms are similar: neat, bright, some with a balcony. Cosy atmosphere and courteous welcome.

Słoneczna Willa – *Ul. Śnieżna 27* – ℘ *(074) 813 52 70 - www.slonecznawilla.vir.pl - 22 rooms - 140 PLN with breakfast, half board 200 PLN.* Beyond the village, the road meanders on and finally reaches this house that looks like a hunting lodge. Plush family establishment. The mountains lie beyond.

KUDOWA ZDRÓJ

Tadeusz and Agnieszka Jesionowscy's Place – *Ul. Kościuszki 95* - ℘ *(074) 866 23 85 - 25 PLN per person.* As you leave town, in a wooded vale, 3km beyond the Chapel of Skulls. A few rooms available on two floors, the kitchen and living room are shared with the owners. Warm family welcome in this fine restored house dating from 1877.

POLANICA ZDRÓJ

Camping nr 169 – *Ul. Sportowa 7* - ℘ *(074) 868 12 10 - 30 PLN for two persons with a tent and a car.* North of the resort, near the road but far enough to offer peace and quiet. Nicely shaded with good grass-covered pitches.

Pod Rogaczem – *At "Studzienna", 15km north-west of Polanica Zdrój* - ℘ *(074) 868 17 97 - 30 PLN per pers, 22 PLN without bath.* This B & B, located on the slopes of a vale, offers informal yet comfortable accommodation. It's ideal for those wishing to ramble through the region on the edge of the Table Mountains National Park. Riding and fishing available, consistent end-of-ramble snack on request. Accommodation in dormitory or double rooms.

LĄDEK ZDRÓJ

Dom "Skowronki" – *3km before the village when arriving from Kłodzko along road 392; follow signposts from the main road* – ℘ *(074) 814 78 02 - 4 rooms with bath - 80 PLN/pers full board.* In a well-preserved 200-year-old house. Quality family welcome and service. The owner sometimes plays the accordeon after meals. You won't want to leave. If you prefer to be more autonomous, you can rent (for the same price) the small adjoining house with its traditional interior and ceramic stove, which accomodates 5 persons.

Cztery Kąty – *1.5km further along from the previous address -* ✆ *(074) 814 78 05 - 4 rooms with bath - 28 PLN/pers,* 🛏 *10 PLN.* 4 charming rooms, two of them with a balcony, in this restored house which has managed to retain its quaint charm. The place is peacefully located in the heart of a hamlet nestling in a vale. Communal kitchen and living room.

Little girl enjoying a treat

Eating out

KŁODZKO

W Ratuszu – *Pl. B. Chrobrego 3 -* ✆ *(074) 865 81 45 - 40 PLN.* Housed in the town hall building; large room with dark woodwork and chairs covered with blue velvet. Refined inventive cuisine: pork with walnuts and grape sauce, or Portuguese-style beef (skewered meat with cheese). It's delicious and tastefully served.

Pan Tadeusz – *Ul. Grottgera 7 -* ✆ *(074) 865 87 35 - 40 PLN.* Undoubtedly the best

restaurant in town. Cosy surroundings, excellent cuisine denoting Italian and Hungarian influences, very carefully served. Portions are huge and desserts are delicious.

POLANICA ZDRÓJ

This lively spa resort boasts many restaurants, particularly along Zdrojowa Street, shaded by chestnut trees.

Krokus – *Ul. Zdrojowa 3 -* ✆ *(074) 869 08 90 - 30 PLN.* Tiny, very pleasant restaurant with a relaxed atmosphere. Classic meat and fish dishes as well as pizzas are served in the dining room or at the tables set out in the pedestrian street.

Swojska Chata – *Ul. Sienkiewicza 24 -* ✆ *(074) 868 30 12 - 40 PLN.* 3km north of the resort. This restaurant, featuring a friendly rustic setting, serves restorative Polish food. Pork and potatoes are on the menu. Fine terrace and games for children.

Taking a break

Two pleasant pubs have tables outside on Kłodzko's Rynek. A few uninspiring bars line Kudowa Zdrój's high street. But Polanica Zdrój remains by far the most pleasant town for a break at an outdoor café selling drinks or ice-cream.

POLANICA ZDRÓJ

Zielony Domek – *Ul. Zdrojowa 8 -* ✆ *(074) 868 21 45.* Excellent ice-cream parlour in one of the spa resort's most pleasant pedestrian streets.

Festive events

International Music Festival (Międzynarodowy Festiwal Moniuszkowski) – *In Kudowa Zdrój.* The festival, dedicated to the founder of Polish opera, Stanisław Moniuszko, takes place in August.

Duszniki Zdrój Chopin Festival: in August.

Kłodzko Theatre Festival: in September.

Legnica

POPULATION 106 000 – MAP OF POLAND B3 – WOJEWÓDZTWO OF LOWER SILESIA

Legnica is the most western town on our Polish itinerary. Life in this former capital of the Silesian Piasts is peaceful and revolves around the Rynek and the ducal castle. The village of Legnickie Pole, a few kilometres away, still remembers the dreadful battle during which, in 1241, the Silesian army confronted the hordes of Tatar invaders.

- ▶ **Getting your bearings** – 62km west of Wrocław.
- 👁 **Not to be missed** – The castle and the old houses surrounding the Rynek.
- 🕐 **Planning your visit** – A short break is sufficient to discover the town.

Background

The Silesian Piasts' town – A village defended by a fort already stood on the site of Legnica which really got off the ground after the Battle of Legnickle Pole. The Silesian Piasts made it one of their capitals, surrounded it with ramparts (a few towers are still standing) and built one of Poland's first stone fortresses before moving on to Brzeg in the 18C. The 1745 partition ceded it to Prussia who renamed it Liegnitz. Badly damaged during the Second World War, it was returned to Poland in 1945.

Exploring

Start from the **Rynek** lined with a few elegant edifices as well as less pleasing ones built of grey concrete to heal the wounds inflicted by war. The imposing buildings standing in the centre of the square are dominated by the belfry of the **Town Hall,** a fine Baroque structure backing onto the theatre. Behind is a row of eight arcaded houses: these arcades, once occupied by herring-mongers, lead to a **16C house**, its façade decorated with sgraffiti depicting hunting scenes. South of the square rise the two brick towers of the **Cathedral of St Peter and St Paul** (Katedra Św. Piotra i Pawła). Massive and almost square, it houses the recumbent figures of Wacław 1, Duke of Legnica around 1400 and of his wife Anna of Cieszyn. The tympanum of the north doorway is carved with a representation of the Adoration of the Magi.

From the Rynek, Św Jana Street leads to a small **museum** *(Wed-Mon 11am-5pm, 5/2.5 PLN)*, which stages historical and contemporary exhibitions. Farther on, the Baroque west front of **St John's Church** (Kościół Św Jana) can be seen at the end of the street. Of the previous church built on this site, it only retained a chapel containing the mausoleum of the Silesian Piasts' dynasty which died out in 1675 *(Mon-Fri 9am-3pm)*.

Walk along Partyzantów Street to the **Piasts' castle**, an elongated edifice dominated by two Gothic red-brick towers looking like minarets. Built in the 13C, the castle is a strange mixture of architectural styles. Note the superb Renaissance doorway designed in 1532 by George of Amberg. Extended in the 16C, then partially rebuilt in a romantic style during the 19C, the castle is not open to the public. A pavilion standing in the inner courtyard shelters the **remains of the Romanesque chapel** with an unusual twelve-sided plan, built by Duke Henry the Bearded at the same time as the original 13C fortress.*(Apr-Oct Tue-Sat 11am-6pm. 5 PLN, free on Sat.).*

Nearby

Legnickie Pole
10km south-east of Legnica.
This is the place where, on 9 April 1241, the Silesian troops of Duke Henry the Pious were crushed by Tatar invaders. According to legend, the headless duke was identified from the sixth toe on his foot and a Gothic chapel was erected on the spot where he lay among his companions. Remodelled several times, the chapel today houses a small **museum** *(Wed-Sat 11am-5pm, 4.50/2.50 PLN, ticket valid also for the monastery)*. The battle is explained through an interactive map, reproductions of weapons, a copy of the recumbent figure of Henry the Pious and facsimiles of the Codex Lubiński which describes the arrival of the Mongols and the premonitory dream of St Hedwig, the Duke's mother; the church of the imposing **Benedictine monastery,** built nearby in the early 18C by the architect Kilian Ignatius Dientzenhofer, is dedicated to her. Note the outside sculptures carved by Wacław Laurentius Reiner and the interior frescoes recalling the fateful battle of 1241. The museum will open the church on request.

Świdnica and Jawor Churches★★

MAP OF POLAND B3 AND A3 – WOJEWÓDZTWO OF LOWER SILESIA

Nestling in the Silesian countryside, these half-timbered churches, now on UNESCO's World Heritage List, are both a technical feat and a symbol of religious resistance.

- **Getting your bearings** – Świdnica and Jawor, 30 km apart, are respectively situated 50km and 60km south-west of Wrocław.
- **Planning your visit** – Allow less than an hour to visit both churches.

Background

The Peace Churches (Kościół Pokoju)
The Treaty of Westphalia, which put an end to the Thirty Years War in 1648, granted religious freedom to the Protestants living in Catholic Silesia. But, no doubt to restrain religious practice, Protestant churches were submitted to certain conditions: they had to be built of wood, straw and clay, with no tower or sign revealing their religious function. Lastly, the edifice had to be built out of gun range from the town centre. Far from being discouraged, the Protestants performed a real act of faith by erecting the largest timber religious buildings in Europe, the austere appearance of their exterior contrasting with the splendour and exuberance of their Baroque interior. Three such churches were built but only those at Świdnica and Jawor, designed by the architect Albrecht von Saebisch, remain today.

Things to see

The churches are open Mar-Oct 10am-1pm, 2-5pm. 5/3/ PLN.

Świdnica Church★★
Ul. Pokoju 6 - Built in the shape of a cross from 1656 onwards, the church is flanked on both sides by porches and chapels which make it look to some extent like a Catholic church. It stands in the middle of an ancient cemetery and could hold 7 500 people, including 3 000 on the two-tiered galleries with balustrades decorated with epitaphs. Dedicated to the Holy Trinity, the church contains a high altar from 1752 and a Baroque pulpit.

Jawor Church★★
Park Pokoj. - Erected in 1654-55, it could welcome a 6000-strong congregation in the rectangular nave with its polychrome ceiling and in the four galleries surrounding it. The balconies are decorated with scenes of the Old and New Testaments and enhanced by the donators' coats of arms. The church, dedicated to the Holy Spirit, later acquired a bell tower which, according to regulations, does not rise above the roof.

A Baroque masterpiece, the interior of Jawor Church

Jelenia Góra ★

POPULATION 95 000– MAP OF POLAND B3 – WOJEWÓDZTWO OF LOWER SILESIA

This former border town occupies a strategic position in the hilly wooded region which precedes the Silesian summits and the Karkonosze National Park. It feels almost like a mountain town and those who like hydrotherapy will enjoy the peaceful atmosphere of the Cieplice Zdrój spa resort a few kilometres away.

- ▶ **Getting your bearings** – 125km south-west of Wrocław.
- 👁 **Not to be missed** – The view of the area from Szybowisko Hill.
- 🕐 **Planning your visit** – Spend one night in town. The surrounding area is rich in forests and sites suitable for rambling along itineraries suggested by the Tourist office.

Background

Deer Hill – Legend has it that in the 12C, during a hunting session, King Bolesław Bent-Mouth followed a wounded deer to the top of this hill. The place changed hands several times over the centuries, ruled in turn by the neighbouring Czechs, the Austrians and the Germans before being finally returned to Poland in 1945. It used to be an important manufacturing centre of cut-crystal.

Things to see

Start the visit from the supervised parking area next to the Tourist office.

Close by, a late-16C round tower, later raised by one polygonal storey, recalls the architectural style of northern Italy. It marks the western limit of the town's former fortifications flanked at this point by a gatehouse. From there, walk to the Rynek.

Rynek (Plac Ratuszowy)

Steep and rather small, the square is surrounded by Baroque and Rococo arcaded houses from the 17C and 18C, painted in an array of pleasant colours from ochre to blue. This is the heart of the old town and one of the best-preserved ryneks in Lower Silesia. Behind a Baroque fountain overlooked by an effigy of Neptune, stands the **Town Hall**, built in the 18C in a mixed Baroque and Classical style, on the site of a medieval edifice. It is prolonged by a group of buildings known as the **Seven Houses** (Siedem Domów). The town's main sights are located east of the Rynek, in the area around Konopnickiej Street and its continuation 1 Maja (1 May) Street.

St Erasmus and St Pancras's Church (Kościół Św. Św. Erazma i Pankracego)

Away from Konopnickiej Street, this austere Gothic church dates from the 14C. The interior was modified during the Baroque period as was the dome surmounting the bell tower.

1 Maja Street

it is possible to recognise the site of the former fortifications from the presence of the tiny **St Anne's Chapel** (Kaplica Św. Anny), which seems crushed by a tower that was originally part of these fortifications. Leaning against the chapel, the **Wojanowska Gate** (Brama Wojanowska) is all that remains of the medieval walls. It is surmounted by Rococo ornamentations including a cartouche bearing the coat-of-arms of Jelenia Góra, Silesia and Prussia.

Further down the street stands **St Peter and St Paul's** Orthodox Church (Kościół Św. Św. Piotra i Pawła), the former chapel of Our Lady. Built in the 18C on the site of a sanctuary destroyed during the Thirty Years War, it features two penance crosses on the north side.

Holy Cross Church (Kościół Świętego Krzyża)

Standing in the middle of a vast open space, the church, shaped like a Greek cross was built between 1709 and 1718 by a Swedish architect who took his inspiration from a church in Stockholm. A festival of organ music takes place every year. Tombstones, engraved with ornamental epitaphs, cover the outside walls; they were originally in the cemetery surrounding the church. Funerary chapels and family vaults can be seen along the west side of the enclosure.

Karkonosze Museum (Muzeum Karkonoskie)★

Ul. Matejki 28. Open Tue, Thu-Fri 9am-3.30pm, Wed, Sat-Sun 9am-4.30pm. 5 PLN.
The museum's impressive collection of glassware includes no fewer than 8 000 items. Other fine rooms are devoted to local painting, ethnography and archaeology.

Winter scene near Jelenia Góra

Nearby

Góra Szybowisko ★
5km north of Jelenia Góra.
This hill offers a superb view of the surrounding area.

Cieplice Zdrój
5km south-west of Jelenia Góra.
The water springing up at a temperature of 86°C is recommended for the treatment of rheumatism and eye complaints. Already famous in the 12C for its curative properties, the resort was ceded to the Knights of St John in 1281. Shaded by the Baroque church is a very pleasant, if tiny, pedestrian centre, popular with people taking the waters. More pleasant still are walks through the two large wooded parks, one of which boasts a small **Natural History Museum** housed in a Norwegian-style pavilion.

Perched on a rocky spur, 3km south-west of the resort, the stately **Chojnik Castle** (Zamek Chojnik) is still an impressive fortress; the stone pilori standing in the inner courtyard is a reminder of the kind of punishment inflicted upon criminals. From the top of the highest tower, there is a fine **view** of the surrounding area.

Practical Jelenia Góra

Postal code – 58 500
Phone code – 075

Useful addresses

Tourist office – *Grodzka 16* – ✆ *767 69 25* - *www.jeleniagora.pl* - *open Mon-Fri 9am-6pm, Sat 10am-2pm.*

Getting around

Railway station– *Ul. 1 Maja* - ✆ *94 36 and 75 29 327* - *www.pkp.pl.*

Bus station – *Ul. Obrońców Pokoju 16* - ✆ *642 21 01* - *www.pks.pl.*

Where to stay

Pałac Staniszów – *Staniszów, 3km south of Jelenia Góra* – ✆ *755 84 45* - *220/26 PLN.* Refined rooms and meals in an authentic manor set in an area of peaceful dales. Unforgettable.

Eating out

Kurna Chata – *Pl. Ratuszowy 23/24* - *15 PLN.* Cheap yet excellent Polish cuisine served under the arcades of the Rynek.

Piwnice Rajców – *In the town hall cellars* – ✆ *645 00 55* - *open noon-10pm. 35 PLN.* A creative cuisine concentrating on meat and fish dishes is served in superb vaulted cellars.

Quirino – *Pl. Piastowski 23 à Cieplice- open noon-midnight. 50 PLN.* Restaurant with a wine bar atmosphere in the very centre of Cieplice. Fine Polish cuisine.

Karkonosze National Park★★
Karkonoski Park Narodowy

MAP OF POLAND A3 – WOJEWÓDZTWO OF LOWER SILESIA

Acting as a natural border between Poland and the Czech Republic, the Karkonosze mountains rise abruptly beyond the hilly southern part of the Sudeten. Dense forests and high summits subjected to a harsh climate form the ideal environment for skiers in winter and for ramblers in summer.

▷ **Getting your bearings** – Karpacz: 125km south-west of Wrocław, 20km from Jelenia Góra.

◉ **Not to be missed** – The ascent of Mount Śnieżka.

◐ **Planning your visit** – 2hr are sufficient to catch the atmosphere of Karpacz but you need to spend at least a day rambling through the national park.

▲▲ **With your children** – Some footpaths are safe for children.

Background

The Giants' Mountains – The name "Giants' Mountains" (Karkonosze in Polish) was given to this range as early as the Middle Ages. The park, covering 5 575ha of crystalline rocks, extends along a 35km north-west/south-east axis. Forests of spruce, maples and limes cover two thirds of the area, giving way as the altitude increases to pines, replaced higher up still by scrub and peat bogs. The summit of Mount Śnieżka which, with an altitude of 1 603m, towers 200m above the rest of the range, consists of barren stony expanses. On the mountain slopes, post-glacial cirques, waterfalls, mountain lakes and streams welcome visitors who are likely to meet Corsican mouflons or boars during the course of their ramble. There are spectacular granite rock formations such as the **Pilgrims** (Pielgrzymy), three twenty-metre high outcroppings, and the **Sunflower** (Słonecznik), a rock visible from the lowest part of the Jelenia Góra Valley. Walloons who came from Belgium in the 14C were the first miners to take an interest in the wealth of minerals to be found in the valleys. Tourism started in the 19C as a result of the pilgrimage to the Baroque church of St Lawrence (Św. Wawrzyniec), patron saint of mountain guides, which stands at the top of Mount Śnieżka. Since then, tourism has considerably developed, particularly among ramblers and skiers.

Rambling through the National Park

Access – *From Karpacz and Szklarska Poręba. Admission 4 PLN, 3-day pass 8 PLN*
The park is the paradise of ramblers.

🚡 **Mount Śnieżka** – If you are short of time, take the chair lift *(daily 8.30am-5pm. 20 PLN, cheaper after 1pm)* linking Karpacz and Mount Kopa. Mount Śnieżka is then 1 hour's walk away.

In the National Park

M. Ostrowska / MICHELIN

Other rambling trails

They all start from the upper part of Karpacz, next to the service station, where Konstytucji 3 Maja avenue becomes Karkonoska avenue, except for the blue trail which starts from the Wang chapel. Allow 4 to 5hr for each of the trails. All are moderately difficult.

The red trail leads to the **Łomniczka cirque** (Kocioł Łomniczki) and to **Mount Śnieżka**. Perched at the top like a stranded flying saucer, the **Meteorological Observatory** (Wysokogórskie Obserwatorium Meteorologiczne) *(daily 10am-4pm)*, houses a mountain refuge and now competes with St Lawrence's Chapel. In fine weather, the view extends as far as Wrocław.

The blue, green and yellow trails lead to **Lake Wielki and Lake Mały** (Wielki Staw and Mały Staw) contained within impressive glacial cirques.

Things to see

Karpacz

Karpacz stretches along a road winding its way through the eastern part of the Karkonosze Mountains. Prospectors who, in the 14C, looked for gold and precious stones in the Łomniczka and Łomnica valleys, built the first village. Bohemia's Protestant community, fleeing from religious persecution, joined them around 1622. Being skilled botanists, they made use of the wealth of medicinal plants growing in the area. The first tourists arrived in the 19C, attracted by the Wang Chapel and by the fact that the village is the gateway to the mountains. Nowadays, snow cannons and seven lifts insure that visitors can reach and use some ten ski runs.

Situated in the upper part of Karpacz is the **Wang Chapel★★** *(open 15 Apr-Oct: Mon-Sat 9am-6pm, Sun 11.30am-5pm ; Nov-14 Apr: Mon-Sat 9am-5pm, Sun 11am-5pm. Service on Sun at 10am. 4.50 PLN)*. The 12C pine building assembled in northern Norway was bought by King Friedrich-Wilhelm IV of Prussia in 1841. Countess Frederika von Reden suggested he should present it to the Lutheran community in Karpacz. After a long voyage via Berlin, the reassembled or rather restored chapel was inaugurated on 28 July 1844. All that remains of the original edifice are the doorways and, inside, some capitals decorated with animals, floral motifs and interlacing. Note the elegant structure which combines the Viking and Romanesque styles, as well as the intricate timberwork put together with wooden pegs. A gallery, running right round the chancel and pierced with windows featuring a thousand glass discs, shelters the congregation from the cold weather outside.

The Museum of Sport and Tourism (Muzeum Sportu i Turystyki) *(Ul. M. Kopernika 2. Open Tue-Sun 9am-5pm. 4 PLN, free on Wed)*, housed inside a chalet, away from the main road, is devoted to the region's natural environment, to the development of tourism and of winter sports.

Higher up is the local **Toy Museum** (Miejskie Muzeum Zabawek).

Szklarska Poręba

25km west of Karpacz.

Szklarska Poręba, Karpacz's sister resort, is situated in the Kamienna Valley, at the eastern end of the Karkonosze. The town, which developed in the 14C around its glass workshops, boasts a vast ski area. Cross-country skiing is available a short distance away, at Jakuszyce, where the Piasts' Race (Bieg Piastów) takes place every year.

Practical Karkonoszce

Karpacz Tourist office – *Ul. Konstytucji 3 Maja 25* – ✆ *(075) 761 97 16 - www.karpacz. pl - open Mon-Sat. 9am-7pm, Sun 10am-4pm.* Numerous brochures about sports activities on offer in the resort as well as Ordnance Survey maps showing the various rambling trails.

Where to stay

Villa Rosa - *Ul. Okrzei 8 à Karpacz -* ✆ *(075) 761 95 50 - www.republika.pl/ willa_rosa - 5 rooms - 60 PLN, 50 PLN with shared bathroom.* This guesthouse occupies a magnificent 17C house on the fringe of a fir forest. Some of the rooms have a verandah or a balcony. Family atmosphere and large garden at the guests' disposal.

TOTUS TUUS

Toruń's Rynek

B. Brillion / MICHELIN

GREATER POLAND

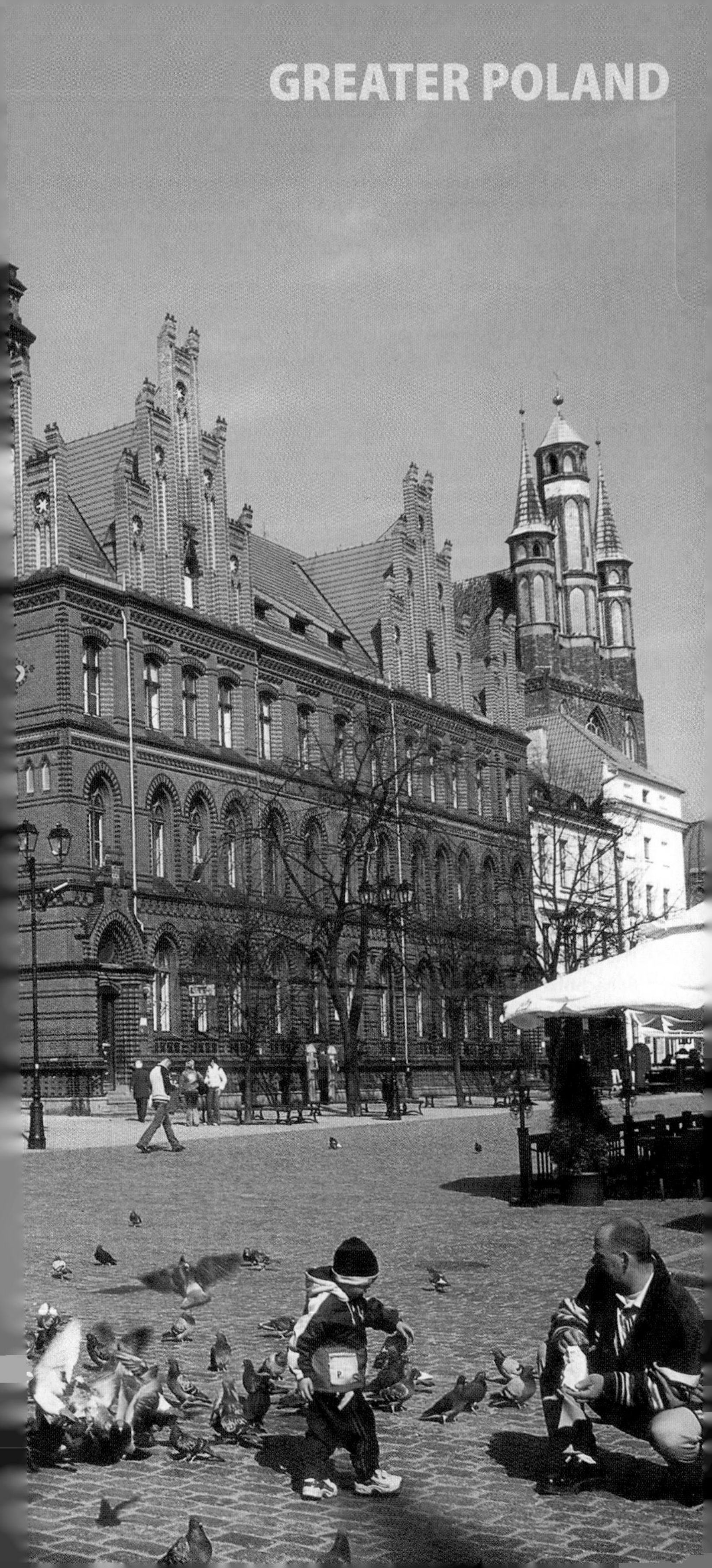

Kalisz

POPULATION 108 000– MAP OF POLAND B3 – WOJEWÓDZTWO OF GREATER POLAND

Situated at the confluence of the rivers Prosna and Bernardynka, Kalisz prides itself in being Poland's oldest city. Even though the ravages of time and war, particularly the First World War, somewhat altered its historic appearance, it still remains a pleasant town with a wealth of religious architecture.

▶ **Getting your bearings** – 140km north-east of Wrocław, 115km south-east of Poznań and 107km west of Łódź.

👁 **Not to be missed** – Walks through Gołuchów's parks.

🕓 **Planning your visit** – Allow one or two hours for strolling through the town.

Background

The pride of Kalisz (Calisia in Latin) is the mention of its name on Ptolemy's famous 2C map. During the Roman period, and even well before that, it was a trading settlement on the Amber Route. In the 9C, a fortress guarded this strategic confluence and the small city to which Bolesias the Pious granted a charter in 1257. In 1342, peace was signed between Poland and the Teutonic Knights. From 1583 onwards, the Jesuits contributed to the town's intellectual and artistic flourishing. But the 1792 fire and the Prussian occupation that lasted until 1806, signalled the city's decline which reached its lowest ebb in August 1914 when the Germans destroyed Kalisz. Returned to Poland in 1920, it was rebuilt with due respect to its medieval structure. But the Germans struck another blow in 1942 when they deported the entire Jewish population.

Things to see

Rynek

Bright and spacious, it is surrounded by fine houses, one of them arcaded and decorated with carved medallions. In the centre stands the town hall restored in 1920. From the top of the belfry *(Mon-Fri 9am-3pm)*, fine view of the bell towers rising above the roofs.

Franciscan Monastery (Zespół klasztorny OO Franciszkanów)

South-east of the Rynek, between Kazimierzowska, Sukiennicza and Rzeźnicza streets.
The church, founded in 1257 but later decorated in the Renaissance style, houses a reliquary of St Jolanta as well as an unusual boat-shaped pulpit. The monastery buildings date from the 17C.

Return to the Rynek, follow Zamkowa and Kanonicka streets to the cathedral.

St Nicholas's Cathedral (Katedra św. Mikołaja)

Erected in the 13C, It was often remodelled over the centuries. Beneath the Renaissance vaulting, the high altar is surmounted by a copy of the Descent from the Cross by

Laurent / Agence TOP

Gołuchów Castle

Rubens. Outside, one can see the remains of the town's medieval walls, which once included 15 towers and 2 gates but were destroyed by the Prussians in the 19C .

Continue along Zamkowa Street then turn right onto the narrow Chodyńkiego Street to reach Św. Józefa Square where St Joseph's Church and the Basilica stand.

Basilica of the Assumption (Bazylika Wniebowzięcia NMP)

This Baroque edifice has retained a 14C chancel, a fine Gothic polyptych and a painting depicting the Holy Family said to have miraculous powers. The Classical-style bell tower was erected in 1820.

Kalisz's Regional Museum (Muzeum Okręgowe Ziemi Kaliskiej)

Ul. Kościuszki 12 – Tue, Thu, Fri 11am-3pm, Wed 11am-5.30pm, Sat-Sun, 10.30am-2.30pm.

The ethnographic collection being something of a shambles, visitors can focus their interest on the history rooms, devoted to prehistory, the Roman occupation and the medieval town, and displaying photos of the town before its destruction in 1914.

Nearby

Gołuchów Castle

16km north-east of Kalisz. Castle (8 PLN) and museum (3.50 PLN) open Tue-Sun 10am-4pm.

Nestling among dales, ponds and forests, this Renaissance manor, built in 1560, may have been inspired by the Loire châteaux. Abandoned in the 17C, it was restored by Izabela Działyńska from 1872 onwards and turned into a museum. The stocky castle, flanked by polygonal towers with pepper-pot roofs, boasts numerous passageways leading to rooms with beautiful parquet floors and neo-Gothic panelled ceilings which enhance the works of art they contain. Note the Greek vases, medieval and classical paintings and sculptures as well as superb wall hangings.

Antonin's Palace

40km south of Kalisz.

When he was governor of the Grand Duchy of Poznań, Prince Antoni Radziwłł, had this elegant wooden hunting palace built in the shape of a cross between 1822 and 1824. The centre is occupied by a vast octagonal hall, surrounded by two-tiered galleries and featuring a huge central column carved with scenes of deer hunting in the surrounding woods. A friend of the arts, the prince invited many artists who were no doubt fascinated by the romantic appeal of this lakeside residence. Chopin stayed in the palace in 1827 and 1829. An annual piano festival takes place in his honour.Today the palace is a middle-of-the-range hotel and a fine game restaurant.

Practical Kalisz

Postal code – 62 800
Phone code – 062

Useful addresses

Tourist office – Ul. Garbarska 2 – ℰ 764 21 84 - www.kalisz.pl. Maps and guides, including a small accurate booklet devoted to the town (in English).
Police : Ul. Jasna 1-3 – ℰ 765 59 00 et 997
Pharmacies open 24h/day – Ul. Babina 4, ul. Kanonicka 6, ul. Serbinowska 19 (in turn).

Getting around

Railway station – Ul. Dworcowa 1 - ℰ 9436 - 2km south-east of the centre.
Bus station– Ul. Górnośląska 82-84 - ℰ 768 73 73 et 94 33 – www.pks.kalisz.pl. Near the above. Buses leave for Wrocław and Poznań.

Where to stay

Europa Hotel – Al. Wolności 5 - ℰ 767 20 32 - www.hotel-europa.pl - 41 rooms including 2 with air-cond - 100/190 PLN, 80/160 PLN weekends ☲ 🅿. Entirely refurbished, the hotel offers calm, well-equipped rooms near the town centre.
Calisia Hotel – Al. Ul. Nowy Swiat 1-3 - ℰ 767 91 00 - www.hotel-calisia.pl - 80 rooms - 220/260 PLN, 140 PLN weekends ☲ 🅿. Straightforward, comfortable modern hotel, 1km south of the old town.

Eating out

The restaurant of the Calisia hotel is by far the best in town.

Festive events

International Jazz Festival – 3 to 4 days in autumn.

Poznań★★

POPULATION 570 000– MAP OF POLAND B2 – WOJEWÓDZTWO OF GREATER POLAND

The capital of Greater Poland has many assets. This dynamic town, of manageable size, can be visited on foot and boasts a wealth of architectural and cultural heritage round one of the country's finest central market squares. The narrow streets are ideal for strolling as is the surrounding area offering excursions to wonderful castles and rambles through forests. Birthplace of the Polish State in the 10C, Poznań is now a lively youthful city, famous for its trade fairs, a tradition which has come down from the Middle Ages.

- ▶ **Getting your bearings** – 300km east of Warsaw, 147km south of Toruń and 170km north of Wrocław.
- 👁 **Not to be missed** – The narrow streets around the Rynek, the noon ceremony at the foot of the town hall.
- 🕐 **Planning your visit** – Allow a full day to visit the town and the main museums.
- 👪 **With your children** – Malta Park, its choice of activities and tourist train, the zoos and the botanical garden.

Background

Birthplace of the Polish State

In the 10C, Mieszko I made the small settlement nestling on an island in the River Warta one of the two capitals of his duchy. In 968 he established Poland's first bishopric in the town and soon had a cathedral built. Taking over where his father left off, Bolesław Chrobry (the Brave) became the first Polish king. Poznań developed and its position near the western borders of the kingdom made it an obvious target for its restless neighbours. Although the capital was eventually moved to Kraków, the city felt cramped on its island and, in 1253, the new town centre situated on the west bank of the river was granted privileges which stimulated the activity of the trade fairs. The town reached the peak of its power in the 16C, but its partial destruction by fire marked the beginning of a dark period. The decline brought about by the Swedish invasion in the 17C continued during the next century with the Prussian and Russian invasions, the Black Death and floods. The town finally fell under Prussian rule in 1793 and became Posen, the capital of the grand duchy of the same name. In December 1918, the rebellion of Greater Poland, launched in Poznań, led to the liberation of the region. This was short-lived since the province was annexed to Nazi Germany after 1939. Subsequently, over half the town was destroyed by bombings. During the communist era, it was here that the first uprising against the regime took place on 28 June 1956. The terrible repression that followed caused 76 deaths. Today, Poznań's activities revolve round its universities and the major trade fairs going back

Poznań Town Hall

W. Buss / MICHELIN

to the Middle Ages. The most emblematic of these, traditionally held on Midsummer's Day, still takes place on 24 June with antique dealers and collectors gathering on the Rynek. Other more international fairs comfort Poznań's position as Poland's major international trade centre.

Exploring

OLD MARKET SQUARE (STARY RYNEK)★★★ PLAN II

The perfectly square paved Rynek is the heart of the city, where everyone ends up, locals and visitors alike. It is surrounded by Gothic, Renaissance or Baroque houses, most of them destroyed in 1945 and splendidly restored after the war. Some of the façades painted with warm pastel colours are decorated with paintings, for instance nos 58, 66 and 73. Note the façade of nos 78-79 with its pediment surmounted by sculptures from the **Działyński Palace** (Pałac Działyńskich) built in the Baroque style in the 18C, over which a pelican hovers with its wings spread out. The square, where the sounds of an accordeon often waft through the air, is continuously teeming with people and, in fine weather, it is covered with wooden platforms and parasols.

The centre of the Rynek A1

In front of the town hall stand the **Baroque Proserpine Fountain** and a copy of the 1535 **pillory**, the original being kept in the town's history museum. A nearby row of arcades marks the former **traders' houses** (Domki Budnicze)★. A narrow street leads to the **Bamberka Fountain,** a reminder that part of the population originally came from the German town of Bamberg. Standing behind it, the elegant **Weigh House** offsets the austere appearance and lack of charm of the building erected on its left during the communist era. Finally, the small 17C **Guardhouse** (Odwach), features a west-facing Classical colonnade.

Town Hall (Ratusz)★★★ B1

Stary Rynek 1. Mon-Tue 10am-4pm, Wed noon-6pm, Fri 10am-6pm, Sun 10am-5pm. 5.50/3.50 PLN. Free on Fri.

Standing like a large cake in the middle of the Rynek and surmounted by a high belfry, this is one of Poland's most spectacular town halls. Destroyed by fire in 1536, it was restored in the Renaissance style by Italian architect Giovanni Battista Quadro. The façade featuring a three-storey arcade is topped with three pinnacles. At noon, all eyes converge on the middle one to watch the two goats of Poznań appear. Inside, the **Historical Museum of Poznań** (Muzeum Historii Miasta Poznania) is housed on the two floors and in the Gothic cellars. It illustrates the history of the town from the 10C to 1945: local archaeological discoveries, paintings, sculptures and an amazing exhibition of

> ### The Goats of Poznań
>
> Legend has it that in 1511 the cook in charge of the town hall's inauguration banquet unfortunately let the meat burn. Two goats were brought in but, unwilling to finish up on the grill, they escaped to the top of the building and confronted each other in front of the dumbfounded crowd. The governor took this as a good omen and ordered that mechanical effigies of the goats be coupled to the clock so that the event could be celebrated daily. Since then, the mechanical goats have been replying to the twelve strokes of midday by butting their horns twelve times.

photographs showing what the town looked like at the end of the war, thus enabling visitors to appreciate the extent of the restoration work undertaken. The highlight of the visit is the **Great Hall** (Wielka Sień). This Renaissance gem boasts a coffered ceiling from 1555, resting on two impressive columns and richly decorated with coats of arms, painted scenes and finely carved motifs.

Museum of Musical Instruments (Muzeum Instrumentów Muzycznych)★ B2

Stary Rynek 45. Tue-Sat 11am-5pm, Sun 11am-4pm. 5.50/3.50 PLN, free on Sat.

This interesting museum contains a unique collection of musical instruments. The ground floor presents unusual music boxes whose mechanisms, a cross between a barrel organ and a turntable, uses perforated discs, as well as harmoniums and wind instruments. The first floor contains string instruments and a large harpsi-chord decorated, like a Baroque altarpiece, with paintings and gilt motifs. One room, dedicated to Chopin, displays his death mask, a cast of his right hand and a piano he played around 1820. The upper floor, reminiscent of an ethnographic museum, is devoted to ancient and traditional instruments from Poland, Asia, Africa, Oceania and America.

POZNAŃ Plan II

0 — 100 — 200 m

HOTELS		RESTAURANTS	
Dom Polonii	①	Bażanciarnia	①
Brovaria	②	Cymes	②
Rezydencja Solei	③	Chimera	③
		Orfeusz	④

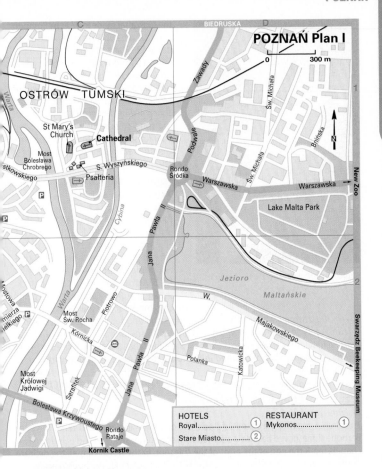

POZNAŃ Plan I

0   300 m

OSTRÓW TUMSKI

St Mary's Church
Cathedral
Most Bolesława Chrobrego
stkowskiego
S. Wyszyńskiego
Psałteria
Rondo Śródka
Warszawska
Warszawska
New Zoo
Lake Malta Park
Cybina
Pawła II
Jana
Jezioro
W.
Maltańskie
Mostowa
Most Sw. Rocha
Piotrowo
Kórnicka
Majakowskiego
Polanka
Katowicka
Most Królowej Jadwigi
Saraficka
Jana
Pawła II
Bolesława Krzywoustego
Rondo Rataje
Kórnik Castle
BIEDRUSKA
Sw. Michała
Brńska
Sw. Michała
Swarzędz Beekeeping Museum

HOTELS	RESTAURANT
Royal............................(1)	Mykonos....................(1)
Stare Miasto..............(2)	

Henryk Sienkiewicz Literature Museum
(Muzeum Literackie Im. H. Sienkiewicza)
Stary rynek 84. Mon-Fri 10am-5pm. 3/2 PLN.
Fans of the author of *Quo Vadis* will be rewarded, others will be glad of this opportunity to visit one of the imposing residences around the Rynek. Mementoes of the 1905 Noble Prize winner include editions of his work in 39 languages, original manuscripts as well as his death mask.

TOUR OF THE TOWN
The main sites being located close to the Rynek, the tour starts from the south-east corner of the square. Follow Wodna Street. Facing the arcades is the façade of the Górka Palace (Pałac Górka) which now houses the Archaeological Museum.

Archaeological Museum (Muzeum Archeologiczne)★ B2
Ul. Wodna 27. Tue-Fri 10am-4pm, Sat 10am-6pm, Sun 10am-3pm. 5/2 PLN, free on Sat.
A large room presents Greater Poland's Prehistory, from the Stone Age to the great migrations. Life-size reconstructions illustrate archaeological discoveries and recall the daily life of hunters, pickers and farmers. However, the most interesting part deals with funerary art in ancient Egypt. The somewhat modest collection includes the mummy of a boy, those of a cat and of a crocodile as well as funerary papyri and a "guide to the beyond".
Retrace your steps and turn left onto Świętosławska Street. The street dominated by the west front of the parish church forms an impressive picture, particularly when lit at night.

St Stanislas Parish Church★★ (Kościół Farny Św. Stanisława) B2
Ul. Klasztorna 11.
Erected for the Jesuits, this monumental Baroque church, boasting three naves supported by Corinthian columns, retains a certain stateliness in spite of its profuse ornamentation. Stuccoes, paintings, sculptures and a trompe-l'oeil dome frame

Church on Żydowska Street in the Old Town

the high altar made in 1727 by Pompeo Ferrari. Free concerts take place every day at 12.15pm from June to September and on Saturdays the rest of the year.

On leaving the church, turn right onto Gołębia Street. Through the railing of no 8, one can get a glimpse of the arcaded courtyard of the former Jesuit school (Dawna Szkoła Jezuicka), now housing a ballet school. Farther on stands the elegant belfry-doorway of the former Jesuit college.

Former Jesuit College
(Kolegium Pojezuickie) B2
Pl. Kolegiacki 17.
Today it houses the town's administrative offices. The refined outline of this elegant 18C building forms with the parish church a horseshoe-shaped ensemble. Napoleon stayed here in 1806. Across the street, on Kolegiacki Square, a bronze sculpture of two goats pays tribute to the town's mascots.

Follow Klasztorna Street lined with restaurants and antique shops. Beyond a bend, it leads to Żydowska Street which, together with the parallel Wroniecka Street, marked the limits of the Jewish district. At the end of the street stands the last of the three synagogues that once stood in the town; it has been a swimming pool ever since the Nazi occupation.

Return to the Rynek then follow Góra Przemysła Street to the Franciscan Church.

Franciscan Church (Kościoł Franciszkanów) A1
Ul. Franciszkańska 2.
The church, reached via a flight of steps, was built between 1674 and 1728. This late-Baroque three-naved basilica is adorned with sculptures, stuccoes and paintings. Two chapels mark the end of the arms of the transept. In the north chapel, the delicate rendering of a tiny painting of the Virgin with Child outshines the huge black-wood altarpiece with gilded decorations in which it is set.

Walk up the street then turn right towards the ruined ramparts pierced by a doorway leading to the esplanade in front of the Royal Castle.

Royal Castle (Zamek Królewski) A1
Góra Przemysła 1. Tue-Wed, Fri-Sat 10am-4pm, Sun 10am-3pm. 5/2 PLN, free on Sat.
Erected in the 13C, the hilltop castle towers above the town; it was once the residence of the governors of Greater Poland. Destroyed and remodelled many times, it now devotes one floor to a small **Museum of Decorative Arts** (Muzeum Sztuk Użytkowych) featuring a collection of works from medieval times to the present. It is particularly interesting for amateurs of ornaments, furniture, ceramics and glassware. A few swords and a well-preserved ceremonial costume are also on display. From the terrace, fine view of the town's roofs as far as the cathedral and of the town hall.

Ludgardy Street and Paderewskiego Street lead to the National Museum of Painting.

Gallery of the National Museum of Painting and Sculpture
(Muzeum Narodowe Galeria Malarstwa i Rzeźby)★★ A1
Al. Marcinkowskiego 9. Tue 10am-6pm, Wed 9am-5pm, Thu 10am-4pm, Fri-Sat 10am-5pm, Sun 10am-4pm. 10/6 PLN. Free on Sat.
The recently restored museum is housed in an austere early-20C building to which was added a modern extension featuring a refined architectural outline and providing vast exhibition areas for the contemporary, one could even say avant-garde, collections of painting and sculpture. The old building houses Romanesque and Gothic works together with a large collection of Italian painting from the 15C to the 18C, of 16C Flemish art and of Dutch works from the 18C. The museum also houses one of the most important collections of Spanish painting, including works by Jose Ribera and Francisco Zurbaran.

Return to the Rynek along Paderewskiego Street.

Things to see

OSTRÓW TUMSKI PLAN I

This island, now away from the town centre, was the birthplace not only of Poznań, but also of the Polish State and Church. The town's oldest monuments are gathered here, shrouded in a slightly austere ecclesiastical atmosphere.

Cathedral (Katedra)★ C1

Poland's first cathedral was built in 968 and dedicated to St Peter and St Paul. Destroyed and remodelled several times, it is now a three-naved basilica with traces of Romanesque architecture. The two towers surmounted by Baroque cupolas rise above the main doorway featuring doors decorated with scenes of the lives of St Paul and St Peter. Some fifteen chapels surround the nave, including the noteworthy **Golden Chapel**. Decorated in the Byzantine style in the 19C, it contains the sarcophagi and the statues of Mieszko I and of his son King Bolesław Chrobry (the Brave). The crypt, symbolically just as important, houses the foundations of the early-Romanesque edifice as well as remains of the fonts and of the original tombs of the two sovereigns.

St Mary's Church (Kościół Najświętszej Marii Panny) C1

This slender brick-built Gothic church, featuring a very steep roof, stands opposite the cathedral. Erected during the first half of the 15C, it is in the process of being restored and is not open to visitors. Excavations carried out beneath the church uncovered the foundations of a royal palace, the first seat of the Polish State.

Psałteria C1

Situated next to the church, this early-16C red-brick building used to be the residence of the cathedral's choristers.

WEST OF THE TOWN

The district lying at the end of Św. Marcin Street, near the station, livens up when one of the major trade fairs takes place in a vast centre (**Międzynarodowe Targi Poznańskie**) located on the other side of the railway track.

Imperial Castle
(Dawny Zamek Cesarski)
Ul. św. Marcin 80/82.

This imposing edifice, stone-built in neo-Romanesque style at the beginning of the 20C and greatly damaged during the Second World War, today houses a cultural centre and a theatre. The beautiful park laid out behind the building offers a different view of the arcaded façade with its somewhat Moorish feel.

Next to it stand the huge entertwined crosses of the **28 June 1956 Memorial** which pays tribute to the 76 protestors killed during confrontations with the police. The first Polish uprising against communist domination rallied nearly 120 000 people.

The Cathedral in Poznań

PARKS AND GARDENS PLAN I

Poznań boasts many open spaces. Whether they are just good places for a stroll or offer a choice of recreational activities, your children will love them.

Lake Malta Park D1
2km east of the town centre on the way to Warsaw.
This vast artificial lake surrounded by open spaces is the favourite recreation area of Poznań's inhabitants. Activities on offer include swimming, rock-climbing and even skiing on a 150m long artificial run. Regattas and other competitions are organised. A **tourist train** (*4.20/2.70 PLN, daily May-Sep and Sat-Sun*) runs through the park

from the western end (Zamenhofa Street) towards the **New Zoo** (Nowe Zoo) *(daily 9am-7pm, 9/7 PLN)* which shelters nearly 2 000 animals in woodland watered by a stream. A pavilion is devoted to nocturnal species.

Old Zoo D1
Ul. Zwierzyniecka 19, 1km west of the town centre. Daily 9am-7pm, 9/7 PLN.
Opened during the second half of the 19C, this venerable zoo covering 4.4ha is home to elephants, lions, dwarf hippopotami, giraffes and a few monkeys. An aquarium stands next to a reptile house and an aviary.

Botanical gardens A1
3km west of the town centre. Daily May-Oct 9am-6pm. Free admission.
Opened in 1925, these gardens belonging to the Adam Mickiewicz University and covering 22ha, contain nearly 8 000 species of plants from all over the world, representing all the known ecosystems: steppe, dunes...

Citadel Park (Cytadela) B1
Picnics, impromptu ball games on the vast lawns, students busy revising or couples relaxing in the shade of the trees, it is hard to imagine that the locals' favourite place for lazing around was once a powerful fortress. The terrain and a few remains are the only reminders of the citadel built by the Prussians, which the German and Soviet armies fought for in 1945. A cemetery recalls these events as does a **Military Museum** (Muzeum Uzbrojenia) *(Tue-Sat 9am-4pm, Sun 10am-4pm, 4/2 PLN, free on Fri)*. Important collection of weapons and open-air exhibition of tanks, planes and military vehicles.

Nearby
It is possible to make a round tour and include the following sites. Allow a whole day, leaving Poznań early in the morning. You won't need much time for the Rogalin site and even less for the Swarzędz site. Devote the afternoon to the National Park if you intend to go on a ramble.

Swarzędz Beekeeping Museum (Skansen i Muzeum Pszczelarstwa)
In Swarzędz, 10km east of Poznań, alongside the E30. 9am-3pm. Closed Mon and hols. 5 PLN.
Opened in 1963 by Professor Ryszard Kostecki, this small museum contains more than 200 exhibits including an important open-air collection of beehives. Usually impressive in size, these are carved in the shape of characters or animals, for instance a very life-like bear. The oldest beehive goes back to the 15C and most of them are still used to house bees.

Greater Poland National Park (Wielkopolski Park Narodowy)
15km south of Poznań along road 430.
The Poznań park is accessible by train or bus via Mosina and Puszczykowo on the east side and via Stęszew on the west side. The Mosina parking on the edge of the forest is close to the most interesting sites (lake Góreckie, most picturesque dales).
The park is crisscrossed by 85km of hiking trails forming five itineraries of 10 to 14km each. A detailed map is available at the Tourist office in Poznań:
Extending over an area of 7 584ha, this national park is the lungs of Poznań. The landscape, carved by glaciers, features 130m high hills, a dozen or so lakes including six where swimming is possible, marshy areas and dense woods planted with conifers and oak trees which shelter deer, boars and other protected species. As for birds, many of them only passing through, they splash about on the calm waters of the lakes or in the marshes.

If you wish to follow the footpaths:

Yellow footpath: round tour from Puszczykowo through the woods as far as Lake Jarosławieckie.

Red footpath: this is the most interesting one; it leaves the Mosina parking area and skirts Lake Kociołek and Lake Góreckie on its way to Puszczykowo. It is also possible to continue along the path to Rogalin, 15km further on.

Black footpath: It runs along Lake Łódzko Dymaczewskie in a south-north direction and goes through the only village in the park, Trzebaw.

Green footpath: it explores the north-western part of the park, between the villages of Szreniawa and Stęszew.

Blue footpath: it starts from the centre of Mosina and leads to Stęszew, through forests and along lakes ideal for fishing.

Rogalin Palace

If you are short of time, follow the blue footpath from the Mosina parking area then turn right onto the red footpath by Lake Góreckie. This is the domaine of wild geese that can be seen relaxing round a tiny island overlooked by the ruins of a castle. Continue until you join the yellow footpath (turn right again) which will take you back through a wooded dale to Puszczykowo Station or to Mosina if you carry on along the road.

Kórnik Castle

20km south-east of Poznań along road 11. 9am-4pm (arboretum closed Dec-Mar). 8 PLN (arboretum 3 PLN).

The medieval fortress built on this mound surrounded by a moat, near the River Warta, was remodelled several times until it became, in the 18C, a Baroque palace transformed in the 19C into a massive castle in English neo-Gothic style by Tytus Działyński who made it his residence and furnished it with the impressive collections we see today. The felt pads one puts on at the entrance make the visit both recreational and slippery *(be careful on the stairs)*. The ornaments, inlaid parquet flooring and period furniture dispayed on two floors are just as interesting as the collections of paintings and weapons the former owner liked so much. Note, on the first floor, the splendid Moorish room containing Hussars' armours. The castle overlooks the oldest and largest botanical garden in Poland: a 30ha park housing 3 000 plant species from Europe, Asia and America. It is at the height of its splendour during the spring flowering period, when magnificent magnolias are in bloom.

Rogalin Palace★

10km west of Kórnik. Open 10am-4pm, closed Mon.

The sumptuous neo-Classical residence of the Raczyński family was built on the banks of the River Warta by Kazimierz Raczyński, Greater Poland's governor at the end of the 18C. A vast lawn lined with chestnut trees leads to a horseshoe-shaped building; the right wing houses a reconstruction of the London study of the former Polish president in exile, Edward Raczyński; the left wing contains furniture (including an unusual cot gilded with gold leaf) and ornaments. The outbuildings house an exhibition of modern Polish painting and a garage contains 19C barouches, carts and sleighs. Behind the palace, a magnificent French-style garden leads to an English-style wooded park. 945 oak trees, among the oldest in Europe, grow in this magic place near the river; the three most famous are named after the legendary brothers, Lech, Czech and Rus who founded Poland, the Czech lands and Russia respectively.

Practical Poznań

Postal code – 60 900
Phone code – 061

Useful addresses

Tourist office – *Stary Rynek 59* – ☎ *852 61 56* - open Mon-Fri 9am-5pm, Sat 10am-2pm. Excellent advice, selection of brochures, maps and books about Poznań and its region. A lot of free literature. English-speaking staff.

Glob-Tour – *Ul. Dworcowa 1* – ☎ *866 06 67*. Tourist information centre at the station. Open 24hr/day.

Police : ☎ *997, 112 from a mobile phone.* Main station: al. K. Marcinkowskiego 31, ☎ *841 24 12.*

Post office : Main post office: *ul. Kościuszki 77*. In the old town: *ul. Wodna 17.*

Pharmacy open 24h/day – *Kalifarm, ul. Strzelecka 33/35,* ☎ *852 18 70. Galenica, ul. Srzelecka 2/6,* ☎ *852 99 22.*

Internet Café – *Klik – ul. Szkolna 15* - daily 10am-midnight. A few streets south of the Rynek.

Where to go

The three-monthly guide *Poznań In Your Pocket* is a mine of practical information about hotels, restaurants and out-on-the-town places as well as sights and museums.

PTTK office – *Stary Rynek 90* – ☎ *852 37 56* - www.bort.pl (in English). Access through the Londoner Pub. Guided tours of the town.

Poznańska Karta Miejska : A public transport pass with free admission to the main museums. Discounts in some restaurants and attractions. 30 PLN for one day, 25 PLN for two days and 40 PLN for three days.

Getting around

Parking – Driving in the vicinity of the Rynek is difficult because there are many one-way streets. Park your car in one of the numerous supervised car parks on the outskirts of town.

Train – *Ul. Dworcowa 1* - ☎ *866 12 12* - www.pkp.pl. The main railway station is situated 1km west of the Rynek. Links with Warsaw (3hr), Kraków and Wrocław several times a day.

Bus station – *Ul. Towarowa 17* - ☎ *833 15 11* - www.pks.pl.

Ławica Airport – *Ul. Bukowska 285* - ☎ *849 22 51, 849 22 61* - www.airport-poznan.com.pl. 7km west of the town centre.

Wasteels Travel Agency – *Ul. Dworcowa* - ☎ *865 26 26* – www.wasteels.com.pl. Train and bus tickets. English-speaking staff.

Where to stay

Most hotels are located around the Rynek and along Św. Marcin Avenue. Prices hit the roof when international fairs are on (50 to 150 % increases!).

Dom Polonii – *Stary Rynek 51* - ☎ *853 19 61 et 852 71 21* - 2 rooms - 230 PLN. Two rooms under the roof; they are vast, in need of a fresh coat of paint but cheap and ideally situated on the top floor of a building overlooking the Rynek.

Rezydencja Solei – *Ul. Szewska 2* - ☎ *855 73 50* - www.hotel-solei.pl - 11 rooms - 259 PLN, 219 PLN weekends, ☲. Tiny rooms in a hotel with a guesthouse feel, situated a few streets away from the Rynek. English spoken.

Stare Miasto Hotel – *Ul. Rybaki 36* - ☎ *663 62 42* - www.hotelstaremiasto.pl - 23 rooms. - 295 PLN, 220 PLN weekends, ☲. In spite of its name, this hotel lies some distance from the centre, 20min west of the Rynek. It is a fine establishment housed in a new building, with bright comfortable rooms.

Brovaria Hotel – *Stary Rynek 73/74* - ☎ *858 68 68* - fax 858 68 69 - www.brovaria.pl - 17 rooms - 290 PLN, ☲. Ideally situated on top of the Rynek, this luxury hotel has a lot of character and brews its own beers, including a delicious one with honey. The bar and the restaurant are sought after by a trendy crowd.

Royal Hotel – *Ul. Św. Marcin 71* - ☎ *858 23 00* - fax 853 78 84 - www.hotel-royal.com.pl - 16 rooms - 336/378 PLN, 252 PLN weekends, ☲ P. Close to the station and slightly away from the old town, this charming hotel is attractive on account of its setting in spite of the rather cool welcome.

Eating out

Cymes – *Ul. Woźna 2/3* - ☎ *851 66 38* - Tue-Sun noon-midnight, Mon 4pm-midnight - 30 PLN. Tiny restaurant serving Jewish specialities, simple, generous and nicely decorated. The food, served on wooden

Rynek

L. Gontier / MICHELIN

tables, includes herring, gefilte fisch and a delicious Hungarian steak cooked with lard.

Mykonos – *Pl. Wolności - ℘ 853 34 36 - daily 11am-midnight - 35 PLN*. Between the village-style setting and the refined cuisine (including all the classics from tarama to mussaka) the Greek illusion is perfect.

Chimera – *Ul. Dominikańska 7 - ℘ 852 03 17 - Mon-Sat 10am-midnight, Sun noon-midnight - 35 PLN*. A delightful restaurant-tearoom decorated with pastel colours. Behind the counter, some 100 tea caddies let off the most fascinating fragrances. Small menu offering carefully prepared dishes: roast camembert with sesame and salmon with green peppercorns.

Orfeusz – *Ul. Świętosławska 12 - ℘ 851 98 44 - noon-midnight - 70 PLN*. Good Polish cooking: bigos (sauerkraut and meat), venison and seafood, served in a refined decor with embroidered tablecloths; attentive staff.

Bażanciarnia – *Stary Rynek 94 - ℘ 855 33 58 - daily noon-midnight - 80 PLN*. This is an institution. A refined Polish cuisine is served in the dining room enhanced by fine woods and worthy of formal receptions: venison and game every day except on Thu, traditional seafood delivery day.

Taking a break

There is a wide choice in the vicinity of the Rynek. The cafés lining the east side of the square (**Arvezo** and **Pub Columbus**) are ideal for an ice-cream on summer afternoons.

Cacao Republika – *Ul. Zamkowa 7 - Mon-Sat 10am-midnight, Sun 11am-11pm*. The temple of hot chocolate a stone's throw from the Rynek. A few tables on the ground floor but, above all, sofas and thick cushions upstairs. Fifteen different kinds of chocolate and homemade cakes.

Cocorico – *Ul. Świętosławska 9 - Mon-Thu, Sun 10am-midnight, Fri-Sat 10-1am*. The atmosphere of the two dining rooms with a Parisian feel is charming enough, but who could resist the coolness of the small flower-decked courtyard where ice-cream and drinks are served?

On the town

Lizard King – *Stary Rynek 86 - www. lizardking.pl - daily noon-2am*. Night time brings out the highly charged atmosphere of the Lizard King. Rock and blues concerts on Fridays around 10pm. As for the decor... 'cellos instead of columns and bar shaped like a giant saxophone!

Behemot café – *Ul. Kramarska - Mon-Fri 10am-11pm, Sat 10am-midnight, Sun noon-midnight*. Bar with an intimate feel and an atmosphere as soft and mischievous as the feline mascot decorating the bar sign. Beer and cocktails galore.

Shopping

Antyki – *Ul. Wodna, under the arcades - Mon-Fri 10am-6pm, Sat 10am-2pm*. A real three-room loft containing the most unusual objects, from stamps to old 78s, gramophones and ancient typewriters.

Antykwariat – *Ul. Klasztorna 1 - Mon-Fri 11am-6pm, Sat 11am-2pm*. A small choice of objects carefully selected: ornaments, seals, a few rare books and documents, as well as small pieces of furniture.

R. Mattes / MICHELIN

An evening out in Poznań

Festive events

The calendar is mainly filled with the major trade fairs which take place throughout the year.

Malta International Theatre Festival: June.

Midsummer: craftsmen and bric-a-brac traders invade the streets. 24 June.

Jazz Festival: March.

Masks: International Theatre Festival. November.

Feast of Św. Marcin Street : Feast of St Martin Street. November.

Gniezno

POPULATION 70 200– MAP OF POLAND B2 – WOJEWÓDZTWO OF GREATER POLAND

The cradle of the Polish State is a small peaceful town built on a height overlooking a lake. Life flows on undisturbed in the shade of the towers of the cathedral which contains the relics of St Adalbert, patron saint of Poland.

▶ **Getting your bearings** – 50km north-west of Poznań.

👁 **Not to be missed** – The panorama of the town from the cathedral towers.

🕐 **Planning your visit** – Allow two hours for Cniezno and as much for Ostrów Lednicki.

👤👶 **With your children** – The ethnographic park and its activities.

Background

The Cradle of the Polish state

According to legend, it was here that Lech, the Poles' legendary ancestor, said good-bye to his brothers Rus and Czech and founded his tribe's first city. Duke Mieszko I introduced Christianism in 966 but chose to establish Poland's first bishopric in Poznań. His son Bolesław the Brave, Poland's first king, was crowned here and the tradition was perpetuated over the centuries. Around the year 1000, Emperor Otto III made a pilgrimage to the grave of St Adalbert, acknowledged the newly founded Polish nation and crowned Bolesław the Brave as its first king.

Things to see

Cathedral (Katedra)★

Erected at the end of the 14C, the cathedral was in fact the fourth sanctuary built on this site since the late 10C. The crypt contains part of the foundations of the pre-Romanesque edifice. This symbol of Polish Christianism houses the 17C silver tomb of the patron saint of Poland, Adalbert, who silently witnessed the coronation of Polish kings over the centuries. The Gothic interior features a Baroque nave surrounded by an ambulatory housing the tombstones of Archbishop Zbigniew Oleśnicki and Archbishop Ignacy Krasicki. On the south side, a wooden door hides two monumental **bronze doors ★★★** (11 PLN, free on Sun, access from outside), dating from 1175. Eighteen scenes illustrate the life of St Adalbert. This masterpiece of medieval art justifies in itself a visit to the cathedral. Fine panoramic view from the top of the towers (3 PLN).

> ### St Adalbert
>
> Born in Bohemia in 956, the son of a Czech prince, Adalbert studied in Magdeburg then became bishop of Prague. From Rome he went on missionary work throughout Italy, Germany and Hungary then visited the court of Bolesław the Brave in Gniezno. He was murdered by pagans in 997 while on an evangelizing mission on the shores of the Baltic, but his body was bought for its weight in gold by Bolesław who had him buried in Gniezno. Stolen in 1039 and partly recovered, the saint's body was buried a second time in Prague.

Archdiocesan Museum (Muzeum Archidiecezji)

Ul. Kolegiaty 2. May-Oct Mon-Sat 9am-5.30pm, Sun 9am-4pm; Nov-Apr Wed-Sat 9am-3pm. 3 PLN. 16C wooden sculptures can be seen next to a large Entombment from 1430 and three superb Romanesque chalices from Trzemeszno Abbey. One of them, made of gold and agate, dating from the 10C, is known as the St Adalbert chalice; another one from the 12C is carved in relief. Also displayed are liturgical objects, chasubles, episcopal seals. Fine collection of coffin portraits representing the deceased during their funeral. Upstairs, a miniature replica of St Adalbert's grave enables visitors to admire all the details. A long gallery displays a series of polychrome wooden statues and wooden panels painted with religious scenes.

Museum of the Origins of the Polish State
(Muzeum Początków Państwa Polskiego)

Ul. prof. Józefa Kostrzewskiego 1. Tue-Sun 10am-5pm. 5.50 PLN.

The museum is housed in a large cold-looking building. A few models of the town show its development since the Middle Ages. Upstairs, an austere exhibition recalls the history of Gniezno through documents, objects, seals and maps.

Also displayed is an amusing series of French engravings featuring allegorical representations of various trades. In the basement there is an audiovisual presentation (in English) about the origins of Polish society, Christianism and royalty. Videos, models, manuscripts and archaeological finds make the show even more interesting.

Nearby

Lake Lednica's Archaeological and Ethnographic Reserve
(Ostrów Lednicki)
15km west of Gniezno on the way to Poznań.
An island in the lake shelters the remains of the fortified residence where Mieszko I was probably christened in the 10C. On the shore, the **Museum of the First Piasts** (Muzeum Pierwszych Piastów) contains the finds discovered on the site of this palatial

Gniezno Cathedral (14C)

ensemble comprising a chapel and surrounded by a defensive earth embankment. On the south shore lies **Greater Poland's Ethnographic Park** (Wielkopolski Park Etnograficzny) *(Open Tue-Sun 15 Apr-Nov 9am-5pm, Feb-14 Apr 9am-3pm. 6 PLN.)*, a 20ha open-air museum featuring a reconstructed village brought to life by extras. Note in particular the beautiful wooden church and, slightly away from the rest, just beyond the cemetery and its tiny log-built chapel, a large landowner's house.

Practical Gniezo

Postal code – 62 200
Phone code – 061

Useful addresses

Tourist office – *Ul. Tumska 12* – ℘ *428 41 00* - *www.turystyka.gniezno.pl* – open Apr-Sep Mon-Fri 7.30am-6pm, Sat 9am-3pm, Sun 10am-2pm; Sep-Mar Mon-Fri 8am-4pm. Inside a small shopping arcade.

Getting around

Railway station – *Ul. Dworcowa 13* - ℘ *863 43 99* - *www.pkp.com.pl*
Bus station – *Ul. Dworcowa 15* - ℘ *426 38 93* - *www.pks.gniezno.pl*

Where to stay

Awo Hotel - *Ul. Warszawska 32* - t *426 11 97* - *www.hotel-awo.pl* - *27 rooms* -170 PLN ☕. Situated inside a courtyard opening on a quiet street, this small, recently restored hotel offers very cheap rooms.

Pietrak Hotel - *Ul. Chrobrego 3* - t *426 14 97* - *www.pietrak.pl* - *26 rooms* - 230 PLN ☕. 🅿. Luxury chain hotel located in the heart of the old town. The brand new establishment offers spacious, tastefully furnished rooms with high ceilings.

Eating out

Many restaurants, particularly along Chrobrego Street where you will find one after the other. The best choice is the restaurant of the Pietrak Hotel, which is good value for money and stays open late.

Festive events

The town's annual festivities, which include a lot of varied entertainment, take place in May.

Biskupin★★

Nestling at the extremity of a peninsula jutting out into a marshy lake between Toruń and Poznań, Biskupin offers a major archaeological insight into Poland's prehistory. The phrase "Polish Pompei" was even used to convey the remarkable state of preservation of the remains and the total immersion in the past experienced by visitors during the fascinating tour of this archaeological park.

▶ **Getting your bearings** – 80km south-west of Toruń and 85km north-east of Poznań.

🕐 **Planning your visit** – Two hours are sufficient to visit the site. Allow an afternoon to take in all the activities, particularly in September.

👪 **With your children** – The recreational introduction to archaeology during the September festivities.

Background

A chance discovery – In 1933, during one of his walks, a local teacher made one of the most fascinating archaeological discoveries in Poland. He found fragments of fossilised wood once carved by man imbedded in the peat covering the ground of Lake Biskupin's peninsula. Excavations led by Professor Józef Kostrzewski of Poznań University started the following year. They represented a real human adventure as well as a technological one which laid the foundations of modern Polish archaeology. Captive balloons were used to guide the search, pinpoint possible evidence and map out the site covering 2ha. The wooden remains were perfectly preserved in the marshy soil. Elements that were on the ground remained in place and, once the debris from the roofs and the walls had been cleared, it was possible to piece together the structure of the buildings. Rows of logs forming streets became visible as did the sites of houses and the oval line of 6m-high ramparts consisting of a coffer-wall surmounted by a watch path. A fortified gate guarded the entrance to the village and, when clearing the wooden way leading to it, archaeologists realised that a moat used to separate the fortress from the shore. 1936 marked the beginning of the reconstruction of the site, half of which had been explored by 1939. The war interrupted the excavation work which started again in 1946 and was completed in 1974. It was then decided to fill in the site to preserve it from destruction.

History spanning many centuries – The study of this and other similar sites provided a fairly accurate insight into the life of the populations that lived in the area over the centuries. 10 000 years ago, the fact that glaciers receded towards Northern Europe changed the topography of the region and forests grew round the lakes. This new environment became a real paradise for local tribes living from picking, hunting and fishing. The farming revolution which ensued resulted in the first Neolothic settlements. Then, at the beginning of the Iron Age, no doubt because of the occurrence of rivalries between the different communities, fortified camps like that of Biskupin were set up.

A haven in the middle of marshes – Built around 700 BC, the Biskupin site is linked to the Lusatian culture. It is thought that the lake's level rose in the 6C BC forcing the inhabitants to abandon the village which was soon repopulated. Around 1 000 people lived in it then, representing about 100 families occupying as many houses laid out in 13 parallel rows. Each house consisted of two to three rooms, the main one having a central stone hearth 2.5m in diameter. The lake offered a certain amount of protection reinforced by stakes set like chevaux de frise below the ramparts. It also provided a supply of fish and water fowl, as well as reeds used on the roofs of houses. The surrounding area was cleared for use as arable land and for breeding cattle, sheep, goats and pigs. Horses, as a painting on a vase shows, were used for game hunting in the surrounding forests. Situated at the junction of east-west and north-south trade routes, the community exchanged pottery, furs, textiles and metal objects. Amber pearls and Egyptian objects were found during the excavations. Biskupin's decline seems to have been sudden. Various hypotheses were put forward: intensive agriculture could have made the soil barren, the lake's level may have risen as a result of climatic changes in the 5C BC or Scythian raiders may have destroyed

Biskupin Archaeological Site

L. Gontier / MICHELIN

the settlement. Whatever it was, the fact that Lusatian cemeteries disappeared proves that the population abandoned the area. The site was intermittently occupied until the 12C when it is recorded as the property of Gniezno's diocese in a bull from Pope Innocent II.

Things to see

Biskupin Archaeological Site (Muzeum Archeologiczne w Biskupinie)★★
Access via the E261 to Żnin. From there, it is 15km south of Żnin by car or narrow-gauge tourist train to Biskupin (40min, ℘302 04 91, May to September).
Museum: ℘ 052 302 54 20 and 052 302 50 55 - www.biskupin.pl - daily 8am-6pm, 7/5 PLN. Boat trips on the lake Tue-Sun 9am-5pm.
From the vast parking area lined with stalls and snack bars, one reaches the entrance to the site on the other side of the tiny platform of the narrow-gauge tourist train linking Żnin and Biskupin. The archaeological park covers 28ha.
The Archaeological Museum stands next to a reconstructed 18C farm. Panels in Polish and English recall the discovery of the site and the different communities that inhabited the region from the Palaeolithic to the Middle Ages. Life in Biskupin at the time of the Lusatians is illustrated by objects found durind excavations. Floats made of bark, harpoons and hooks provide information about fishing techniques, pottery and weaving-loom weights illustrate various crafts. Urns suggest the Lusatians' funeral pratice of cremation. A large model of the fortress shows the site in its heyday, when the best use was made of the space within the enclosure.

Outside, a **wildlife park** shelters the different species that once lived in the area. Up on the hill, open-air **workshops** are set in a clearing. The place comes to life on the third weekend in September, during **Poland's Great Archeological Festival** which succeeded the experimental archaeology annual meetings. Visitors can watch the smelting process, see potters and basket makers at work. Reconstruction and dating techniques used by archaeologists are also explained.

Camped on its peninsula, the **fortress** is accessible via two gates, one of which is the historic fortified gateway linked by a wooden floating bridge and protected by chevaux de frise. Half the ramparts and two long buildings out of the 13 which made up the village were reconstructed; they now contain an exhibition of photographs illustrating the progress of the excavations as well as two houses with their furniture, weaving loom and stone hearth. In summer, extras recreate the lively atmosphere of the place so many centuries ago. A marshy area which was never excavated shows what the site was like before the excavation work started.

Boat trips on the lake allow visitors to view the site from different angles and to get a better insight into its environment.

During the year, Biskupin is often invaded by Polish students on educational school trips, who come here to learn about this aspect of their national history.

Toruń★★

POPULATION 200 000 – MAP OF POLAND B2 – WOJEWÓDZTWO OF KUYAVIA-POMERANIA

It is difficult not to succumb to Toruń's charm which entices you to stay a few days. Nestling inside its ramparts, on the north bank of the Wisła, the town conveys an impression of serenity in spite of the animation created by its important student population. It is proud of being Copernicus's birthplace and of its past as a Hanseatic port whose warehouses were always full. Pleasant hotels, a variety of restaurants, numerous cafés, theatre performances add to the list of Toruń's assets, not forgetting, of course, its wealth of architectural heritage which prompted UNESCO in 1997 to include the city on its World Heritage List.

▶ **Getting your bearings:** 200km north-west of Warsaw on the way to Gdańsk.

👁 **Not to be missed:** The views of the town from the tower of the cathedral of SS John and from the belfry of the town hall.

🕐 **Planning your visit:** Allow one whole day to visit the city and its main sights, museums and monuments. Staying overnight will enable you to discover the many facets of the town.

Background

A wealthy trading city

In 1233, Hermann von Salza, the grand master of the Order of the Teutonic Knights, granted Toruń a foundation charter. In order to protect its construction, a castle was erected on the river banks. The settlement grew rapidly. Commerce, stimulated in 1252 by tax exemptions, brought about the town's prosperity and markets were soon trading cloth, salt, spices, wood, fruit

The Town's Coat of Arms

Carried by an angel, it features a rampart with three towers and a gate. One door is ajar as a symbol that the town is open to outside influences which brought prosperity while the other is closed as a symbol of protection.

and fish. It became imperative to fortify the city and create a municipal council. In 1264, another charter established the eastern suburb as the New Town, where new inhabitants arriving from all over Europe settled. At the end of the 13C, Toruń, then called Thorn and known as the "Queen of the Wisła", joined the Hanseatic League. The town's expansion reached its climax in the 14C and 15C. Wooden buildings, considered unsafe, were replaced by brick ones. However, over the years, the city challenged the political and economic power of the Teutonic Knights and, in 1454, the population took over their fortress and chased them away. The open conflict ceased in 1466 when a second treaty was signed, returning to Poland territories stretching as far as Gdańsk. It is around that time that Copernicus was born. The town fell into decline in the 17C. The Swedish wars dealt a severe blow to the town, damaged several times by weapons and by fire. In 1793, following the partition of Poland, Toruń fell under Prussian rule. In the 19C, it became a fortress surrounded in 1878 by a 22km long perimeter of forts. 127 years later, the Treaty of Versailles returned it to Poland and it became the capital of the great Województwo (province) of Pomerania, getting through the Second World War practically unscathed.

Exploring the old town

Lying inside the ramparts is the old town prolonged eastwards by the new town. The former, to the west, centres round the Rynek Staromiejski, the latter, to the east, surrounds the Rynek Nowomiejski (note that the new town dates from the 13C!). In fact, the two districts are linked and we propose one itinerary for both.
Start the tour from the Rynek, in front of the tourist office.

THE RYNEK STAROMIEJSKI★★ B1-2

109m long and 104m wide, the Rynek Staromiejski is the historic centre of the city. The square is dominated by the Old Town Hall (Ratusz Staromiejski). On the west side stands the imposing neo-Gothic **post office** from 1881 next to the **Church of the Holy Spirit** (Kościół św. Ducha) erected in 1756. In front, a **fountain** featuring a young fiddler charming an assembly of frogs represents the local version of the Pied Piper legend.

The banks of the River Wisła near town

Old Town Hall (Ratusz Staromiejski)★★ B1

15 Apr-Jun: Tue-Sun 10am-7pm, Jul-Aug 10am-6pm, Sep-14 Apr 10am-4pm. 10 PLN.
Its massive red-brick outline dominates the centre of the Rynek. The original town hall built in the 13C was remodelled in 1393 in pure Gothic style, with two storeys surrounding an inner courtyard. In 1602-04, Dutch architect Anton van Obberghen added another storey, adorned it with stone sculptures and topped the angles with octagonal turrets in Dutch mannerist style. Burned down by the Swedes during the 1703 siege, the edifice was rebuilt between 1722 and 1738 and late-Baroque elements were added at the same time. Today, the former conference hall is a concert venue.

The Regional Museum (Muzeum Okręgowe) was housed inside in 1958. Note, on the first floor, an imposing 19C painting celebrating the signing of the Treaty of Toruń in 1466. Further on, the Royal Bedroom, decorated with portraits of Polish monarchs, opens onto other rooms devoted to 18C, 19C and 20C Polish painters. The museum also houses collections of Gothic stained glass, painting and sculpture as well as an exhibition of sacred art.

Do not miss the **panoramic view** of the town from the tower. *(Apr-Sep: Tue-Sun 10am-7pm, 10 PLN).*

Statue of Copernicus (Pomnik Kopernika) B2

Erected in 1853, this bronze statue by Friedrich Tieck from Berlin is the favourite meeting place of the local population. The Latin inscription on the base reads: "Nicolaus Copernicus from Toruń stopped the sun and the sky and got the earth moving". This, of course, refers to the fact that Copernicus was the first to prove that the earth revolved round the sun and not the contrary. Pointing a finger at the sky, the astronomer holds an armillary sphere in his left hand.

House of Artus (Dwór Artusa) B2

Built between 1889 and 1891, this large neo-Renaissance residence stands on the site of a building destroyed at the beginning of the 19C, where the Treaty of Toruń was signed in 1466, ending the conflict with the Teutonic Knights. Today, the edifice houses a cultural centre.

House Under the Star (Kamienica pod Gwiazdą)★★ B1-2

Tue-Sun 10am-4pm. 7 PLN.
This elegant house was, in the late 15C, the residence of Filippo Buonacorsi, the tutor of King Kazimierz Jagellon's sons. The Gothic building, restored at the end of the 17C, became the Italian-inspired Baroque edifice with a stucco-decorated façade that we see today. Its gable is topped with a golden star to which it owes its name. It houses a small but interesting museum of Far-Eastern art hosting collections of Chinese porcelain and painting, Japanese prints and ceramics, Indian sculptures as well as bronzes going back to the 17C BC. Displayed on the first floor is an Empire dining room denoting an Egyptian influence.

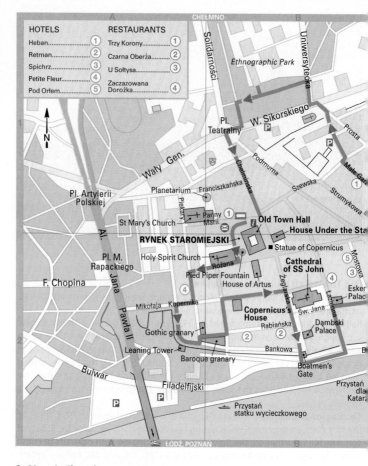

HOTELS		RESTAURANTS	
Heban	(1)	Trzy Korony	(1)
Retman	(2)	Czarna Oberża	(2)
Spichrz	(3)	U Sołtysa	(3)
Petite Fleur	(4)	Zaczazowana	(4)
Pod Orłem	(5)	Dorożka	

St Mary's Church (Kościół NMP) A1

Ul. Panny Marii.

This massive brick-built hall church was erected by the Franciscans between 1343 and 1370. According to the rule of the order, three pinnacles replaced the usual bell tower. Inside, the three naves soaring to a height of 27m contain large frescoes from the late 14C representing scenes from Christ's life. The star vaulting, decorated with floral motifs adds the final touch to this ensemble which seems to have been adorned like medieval manuscripts once were. Note the 15C stalls, the high altar from 1731 featuring the Visitation and the Baroque mausoleum of the Swedish princess Anna Vasa, sister of King Sigismund III.

TOUR OF THE TOWN

Starting from the Rynek, follow Różana Street, lined with arcades sheltering waffle sellers, then turn left onto Piekary Street. Pod Krzywą Wieżą Street skirts the ramparts and the Leaning Tower (Krzywa Wieża).

Leaning Tower (Krzywa Wieża) A2

This is one of the city's emblems, both unassuming and surprising. The 13C square tower was turned into a prison in the 18C before becoming a residence. It gave rise to a few legends and if its inclination (1.40m) is in reality due to subsidence, some think it is a punishment inflicted upon the town which was the birthplace of Copernicus, the astronomer who conceived heretical theories.

Rabiańska Street runs between two granaries, one Gothic and one Baroque, both due to be restored. Note the windows of the latter, on the right: their frames are shaped like wheat sacks. Turn left onto Ducha św. Street then right onto Kopernika.

Copernicus's House★ (Dom Kopernika) B2

Ul. Kopernika 15/17. 15 Apr-23 Jun: Tue-Sun 9am-6pm; 25 Jun-Aug: Tue-Sun 10am-7pm; Sep-14 Apr: Tue-Sun 10am-4pm. 10 PLN.

These two 15C Gothic houses featuring elegant gables were restored in the early 1960s. The museum is housed in both buildings but Copernicus was born in no 15 on 19 February 1473. An exhibition on five levels recalls the astronomer's life and works through documents and objects. It shows how his theories, very unorthodox in his day, fit in with the main currents of thought which completely changed our idea of the universe. One room contains a model of the town in the 15C. The building on the left displays the reconstructed interior of a Gothic house with its kitchen and money-changer's office. Other rooms show portraits of Copernicus and facsimiles of his works.

Cathedral of SS John
(Katedra śś. Janów)★ B2
Ul. Żeglarska 16
Work began on the sanctuary dedicated to St John the Baptist and St John the Evangelist shortly after the foundation of the town. A 52m high tower was added in 1433. It houses Poland's second-largest bell, the Tuba Dei (God's Trumpet), cast in 1500. The brick building with Gothic frescoes on the walls was remodelled until the end of the 15C and Copernicus was probably christened inside. Around 1530, it was taken over by the Protestants who whitewashed the walls to hide the frescoes and only one, depicting the Crucifixion, is visible today in the north part of the chancel. Returned to the Catholics in 1596, the church became the cathedral of Toruń's diocese in 1992. From the top of the tower, there is a striking view of the town and the river.

Walking down Żeglarska Street towards the river, note, at no 8 on your right, the Baroque stucco decoration of the façade of the **Dąmbski Palace** erected in 1693 for the bishop of Kujawy, now occupied by the Fine Arts Department of the Copernicus University. The Banks of the River Wisła are reached through the **Boatmen's Gate** (Brama Żeglarska), once the official gateway for visitors arriving by way of the river and later turned into a prison. Walking along the banks of the Wisła, one gets an unobstructed view of the city's ramparts. This is where the merchant ships used to be moored and where, today, you will find a floating restaurant and boats inviting you for a trip on the river. *Walk up Łazienna Street.*

Esken Palace (Pałac Eskenów) B2
Ul. Łazienna 16. Tue-Sun 10am-4pm. 7 PLN.
This former medieval house, today known as the "red granary" belonged to the Esken family in about 1460. The edifice was modified at the end of the 16C into a Renaissance palace featuring a doorway carved by Willem van den Blocke, a sculptor from Gdańsk. At the end of the 19C, it was turned into a granary then into a warehouse for the Prussian army before being finally restored at the end of the 20C. It now houses the History and Archaeology Department of the Regional Museum.

Nicolaus Copernicus

(Toruń 19 Feb 1473 – Frombork 24 May 1543). A native of the town, Copernicus was not born as it was once believed at no 30 Kopernika. A document discovered in the 19C gave rise to controversy tinged with nationalism. For, if the Poles now consider no 17 to be the astronomer's birthplace, the German authorities still support the original theory. The Polish version prevailed after 1945 and has since been confirmed by recently discovered documents dating from 1474.

Toruń's Rynek

Mementoes of the different stages of German occupation in the 19C are displayed on the first floor.

A collection of weapons and an exhibition about daily life in Toruń from prehistoric times to the Middle Ages take up the whole of the second floor. The third floor is devoted to the discovery of heliocentricism, from Copernicus to Newton.

Follow Ciasna Street and cross Mostowa Street at the end of which stands the Bridge Gate (Brama Mostowa), which used to be the starting point of ferries crossing the river. It owes its name to a bridge built around 1500 which was for a long time one of only two bridges to span the Wisła (the other was in Kraków), and disappeared in the 18C. Continue along the narrow Ciasna Street and walk across the ramparts to the castle of the Teutonic Knights.

Teutonic Knights' Castle (Zamek Krzyżacki) C2
Ul. Przedzamcze. Daily 10am-7pm. 1 PLN.
Erected around 1235 to become the seat of the Teutonic authority and to protect the town's builders from Prussian raids, it originally stood in the south-east corner of the fortifications. On 8 February 1454, it was taken and destroyed by the population rising against the order's domination.

Today its ruins are spread over an open space overlooking the castle, surrounded by the ramparts which separated the old town from the new town. They are grouped in a horseshoe shape around the base of a large octagonal tower and give a fair idea of what the austere brick structue of the imposing fortress looked like. The best-preserved part, the Gdanisko Tower, reached via a suspended gallery, was originally used as latrines. The cellars now host concerts and cultural events.

Pass through the fortified gate to reach Wielkie Garbary Street and walk towards the Rynek Nowomiejski along Ślusarska Street.

The New Town Square (Rynek Nowomiejski) C1
It marks the centre of the new town erected from 1264 onwards, when the old town became too small to absorb the influx of new inhabitants. In the south corner stands the **Blue Apron Tavern** (Gospoda Pod Modrym Fartuchem) opened in 1489. The middle of the square is occupied by the Evangelical church built in the 19C on the site of the former Gothic town hall. It was until 1945 the city's Lutheran church. The lofty St James's Church rises in the eastern corner of the Rynek.

St James's Church (Kościół Św. Jakuba) C1
Built from 1309 onwards to serve as the new town's parish church, it was only completed en 1424. Its basilica plan, unique in Toruń, comprises a 21m high central nave, twice as high as the two naves flanking it. The ensemble is dominated by an unusual tower with a double roof. The 14C pointed-arched doorway heralds the interior featuring a predominance of glazed green and yellow bricks. It opens onto late-14C polychrome frescoes on the walls and ceiling, which depict characters from the New Testament. Note, at the end of the south nave, a Gothic Crucifix known as "Christ and the Tree of Life" originally in a Dominican church, and, in the chancel, an 18C Baroque high altar with a representation of St James. The church changed

hands several times: from the Cistercians it passed to the Benedictines then was a Protestant church between 1557 and 1667 before being returned to the Benedictines who occupied it until their order was dissolved in 1834.

Walk to Małe Garbary Street via Król. Jadwigi Street and continue as far as Wały Gen. Sikorskiego Avenue.

Ethnographic Park B1

Ul. Wały gen. Sikorskiego 19. 15 Apr-Sep: Mon, Wed, Fri 9am-4pm, Tue, Thu Sat-Sun 9am-6pm, Oct-14 Apr: Tue-Sun 9am-4pm. 8 PLN.

A Prussian arsenal built in 1824 and a bastion from the 19C fortifications guard the entrance to this traditional village erected in the middle of town. Standing next to each other are various houses typical of Toruń's surrounding area, representing rural architecture from the Kujawy region in the south, Ziemia Chełmińska and Bory Tucholskie in the north and Ziemia Dobrzyńska in the east. There are farms, watermills and windmills, a bread oven, a smithy and beehives which, all together, contain some 50 000 pieces of furniture, tools, implements and objects of daily life. The complex is at its most lively in summer when dozens of costumed extras and craftsmen bring past trades back to life.

Cross the avenue towards the Theatre Square then return to the Rynek Staromiejski along the pedestrian Chełmińska Street.

Nearby

Golub Dobrzyń

37km north-west of Toruń along road 52.

The town was the result of the fusion in 1951 of Golub and the village of Dobrzyń on opposite banks of the River Drwęca. Golub, mentioned for the first time around 1258, was protected by a Gothic castle erected by the Teutonic Knights in 1309. The town was damaged repeatedly between 1414 and 1422 during conflicts opposing the Poles and the Teutonic Order and it became one of the Polish Crown's possessions following the Treaty of Toruń signed in 1466. The city prospered under King Sigismund III (1611-25) whose sister, Anna Vasa, settled in the castle. She softened the austere appearance of the brick building by adding Renaissance elements, raised the walls and built round turrets in the corners. She lived surrounded by erudites and apparently liked the castle so much that her ghost is said to haunt it on New Year's Eve in the hope of being invited to dance a polonaise. The city was damaged during the Swedish wars and the Seven Years War between 1756 and 1763. It passed through several hands before being finally returned to Poland in 1920.

The massive silhouette of **the castle** *(daily 7am-7pm. 10 PLN)* perched on a hill still seems to be protecting the River Drwęca. A gatehouse, flanked by a round tower and forming part of the wall, guards the entrance. In a building on the courtyard, a small museum displays objects of daily life in the past. A potter's wheel and a spinning wheel can be seen next to a dug-out wooden canoe; a traditional interior occupies a corner of the room. Upstairs, a room illustrates the three-day tournament which has taken place every July since 1976 on the esplanade in front of the castle. One of the most famous tournaments in Poland, it features jousts, knights' parades and crossbow competitions.

R. Mattes / MICHELIN

Chełmno Town Hall

Chełmno

45km north-west of Toruń.

The "city of the nine hills" is built on a promontory overlooking the Wisła. The town is mentioned in a chronicle dating from 1065 under the name of Culmen, but its expansion came later, with the arrival of the Teutonic Knights. In 1226, Prince Conrad of Masovia gave them control of the Chełmno region lying between the Wisła and the rivers Drwęca and Osa. The town was granted a foundation charter on 28 December 1233 and this marked the beginning of its expansion. After joining the Hanseatic League, it prospered rapidly. The signing of the second Treaty of Toruń in 1466 resulted in the eviction of the Teutonic Knights and the return of the town to Poland. However, it went into decline during the 18C. After the plague, the War of the Austrian Succession and the Seven Years War, Chełmno fell under Prussian domination. Returned to Poland in 1920, it was once more caught in the war in 1939.

Chełmno is today a peaceful city which has retained its original grid plan. The centre boasts a vast **Rynek**, bright and open, dominated by a fine **Town Hall★** housing a small museum. Built in Gothic style in 1298, the edifice now features an elegant Renaissance outline. Its south-west façade bears the standard metre, the unit of measure used by the town from medieval times.

Chełmno boasts six churches and monasteries. **The Parish Church of the Assumption** (Kościół Farny pw Wniebowzięcia NMP) is the most impressive. This brick-built Gothic edifice, one of the largest in Pomerania, houses the relics of St Valentine, the patron saint of lovers.

The town has retained its medieval ramparts, with a few towers here and there. From the **Grudziądzka Gate** (Brama Grudziądzka) closing off the north-west section of the walls, a wooded promenade leads down into the moat.

Practical Toruń

Postal code – 87100
Phone code – 056

Useful addresses

Tourist office – *Rynek Staromiejski 25 –* ✆ *621 09 31 - fax 621 09 30 - www.it.torun. pl – open Mon and Sat 9am-4pm, Tue-Fri 9am-6pm, Sun May-Aug 9am-1pm.* Well stocked with guides and maps, some in English. English-speaking staff.

Police : ✆ *637 (central)*, stations: *ul. PCK* ✆ *637 24 30 and ul. Grudziądzka* ✆ *637 23 80*

Post offices: *Rynek Staromiejski 15 and Rynek Nowomiejski 24.*

Pharmacy open 24h/day – *Ul. Św. Faustyny 14/4a.*

Internet Café – *Jeremi – Rynek Staromiejski 33.*

Where to go

Boat trips along the Wisła: *Statek Pasażerski Wanda – ticket office* ✆ *0501 07 83 05* – 40min cruises. Departures every hour 9am-7pm, except in winter.

Getting around

Parking – A parking space in the street only costs a few złotys to be paid to a mobile parking attendant. Allow 30 PLN for a night in a supervised car park.

Train– *Ul. Kujawska 1 -* ✆ *69436.* The main station is situated on the opposite river bank. Access by buses 22 and 27 from John Paul II Avenue. Warsaw-Toruń train journey 2hr 30min, Poznań-Toruń 2hr 30min.

Bus station – *Ul. Dąbrowskiego 8-24 -* ✆ *655 53 33 – www.pks.torun.com*

Car hire – *Firma Bonus* ✆ *648 07 47.*

Travel agency – *Kompas – Ul. Kopernika 5 -* ✆ *621 05 87 - Mon-Fri 10am-6pm, Sat 10am-1pm.*

Where to stay

Most hotels are situated in the old town, in the vicinity of the Rynek.

Pod Orłem – *Ul. Mostowa 17 -* ✆ *622 50 24 – www.hotel.torun.pl – 41 rooms - 140/180 PLN,* ⌷ *10 PLN.* A venerable institution, over a century old which gets rid of its quaint appearance a little more with each refurbishment. The rooms are clean but basic; pleasant family-style welcome from English-speaking staff.

Retman Hotel – *Ul. Rabiańska 15 - t 657 44 60 – www.hotelretman.pl – 30 rooms - 210 PLN, 170 PLN weekends,* ⌷. The rooms are plain but very comfortable in this high building situated between the Rynek and the Wisła. Very good value for money (quality-service-price). English spoken.

Petite Fleur – *Ul. Piekary 25 -* ✆ *663 44 00 et 663 44 02 - fax 663 54 54 - www. petitefleur.pl – 22 rooms - 250/290 PLN* ⌷☺. The hotel is as renowned as its restaurant serving good Franco-Polish cuisine at reasonable prices. Fine, tastefully decorated rooms; preference should be given to those in front, overlooking the street. Internet connection in each room, English spoken.

Spichrz Hotel – *Ul. Mostowa 1 -* ✆ *657 11 40 – fax 657 11 44 - www.spichrz.pl – 19 rooms - 250 PLN* ⌷, 🅿. Backing onto the Mostowa Gate, this hotel is housed in a former granary built in 1719 and restored in 2003. The rooms have large windows; their decor of wood and natural fibres adds a distinctive warm touch to their comfort. Copious varied breakfast. Internet connection in all rooms. English-speaking staff.

Heban Hotel – *ul. Małe Garbary 7 -* ✆ *652 15 55 - www.hotel-heban.com.pl – 40 rooms -300/350 PLN* ⌷. This high-class establishment is housed in a former

Renaissance residence refurbished in a modern style. The professional welcome and spotless rooms will satisfy the most demanding travellers. Wifi in all rooms, English-speaking staff.

Eating out

Oberża – *ul. Rabiańska 9 – daily 11am-midnight - 15 PLN*. Wooden decor and furniture give this self-service restaurant a rustic feel; good Polish cooking at unbeatable prices. The welcome is more than convivial and even though the menu is in Polish, you can see what's on offer.

Manekin – *Stary Rynek 16 - ☏ 621 05 04 – Mon-Fri noon-11pm, Sat-Sun 10am-midnight – 30 PLN*. This popular restaurant deserves its success. Crêpes are the stars of the menu which lists no fewer than 40 different kinds of savoury and sweet ones. When the weather is fine, tables are set up on the square outside and customers can enjoy their meal in the very heart of town. Menu in Polish.

Zaczarowana Dorżka – *ul. Łazienna 24 – ☏ 621 14 01 – Mon-Thu noon-11pm, Fri-Sat noon-1am, Sun noon-10pm – 50 PLN*. Creative cuisine (lamb marinated with tomatoes and celery, potato strudel) served in a refined decor featuring a lovely wooden ceiling and trompe-l'oeil frescoes illustrating the streets of a city. Velvet-covered chairs and subdued lighting create a cosy atmosphere. Menu in English.

U Sołtysa – *ul. Mostowa 17 - ☏ 652 26 56 – 10am-midnight – 60 PLN*. A must if you wish to taste traditional Polish cuisine. Tables made of rough wood and farming implements recreate a mountain-inn setting with costumed staff. On the menu: pierogi, bigos (sauerkraut and meat), soups and barszcz but also herrings, sausages and grilled meat. Restorative cuisine and relaxed atmosphere. Menu in English.

Taking a break

Dublin Pub – *ul. Mostowa 6/10 – ☏ 657 50 21 – daily noon-midnight*. A few steps lead down to the basement which houses this pub located in Mostowa Street. The atmosphere is undoubtedly Irish with draught Guinness, chips with vinegar and jovial customers, particularly on football-match evenings.

Róze Izen – *ul. Podmurna 18 - ☏ 621 05 21 – open Mon-Thu 11am-10pm, Fri-Sat 11am-11pm, Sun 11am-10pm*. A delightful unassuming place with an impressive menu offering a comprehensive choice of food and drink, in particular tea served in a very cosy 1930s-style room or in the courtyard set up like an open-air house with dressers, mirrors and paintings on the walls and stairs leading up to an imaginary first floor.

Pod Aniołem – *Beneath the town hall, entrance opposite Copernicus's statue - ☏ 658 54 82 – www.podaniolem.art.pl*. This meeting place, housed in the superb vaulted cellars of the town hall, is a must: people come in for a drink or a concert. The calendar of festive events is posted up at the entrance.

Kafeteria Artus – *Rynek Staromiejski 6 - ☏ 621 11 43 – daily 10am-midnight*. A very classy and slightly formal bar-tearoom located in the inner courtyard of the House of Artus. The glass-and-metal modern architecture blends well with the brick structure of the historic building. Café, beer and generous portions of ice-cream on offer.

Shopping

Pierniczek – *ul. Żeglarska 24 – daily 10am-8pm*. Gingerbread is the speciality here.

Emporium – *ul. Piekary 28 – t 657 61 08, www.emporium.torun.com.pl, open Mon-Fri 10am-6pm, Sat 10am-4pm, Jul-Aug Sun 10am-4pm*. Gingerbread and T-shirts on the theme of Copernicus and his theories.

Toruń's Gingerbread

(Piernik Toruński).

The recipe of this speciality, already mentioned in the 14C, remained a secret for a long time and was only revealed in 1725 in a medical publication. Honey and spices are the main ingredients. Made in different carefully sculpted shapes (characters, buildings), this gingerbread owes its taste and its crispness to a long maturing process in a cellar. It is a prize gift which was once traditionally included in dowries and offered to kings.

Festive events

Song of Songs Festival: International Ecumenical Festival of Christian Music. Early June.

Toruń's Feast : celebrated on 24 June, the feast-day of St John the Baptist, the patron saint of the town.

Toruń Muzyka i Architektura : concerts given in outstanding monuments. July and August.

Jazz Old NoWa Festival: 2 to 3 days in late February.

Klamra : 7-day theatre festival in March.

Toruński Festiwal Nauki i Sztuki: Art and science festival. Four days in late April. **Kontakt** : Theatre festival. First weekend in May.

Malbork Castle

Gdańsk★★★

POPULATION 461 653 – MAP OF POLAND B1 – WOJEW ÓDZ TWO OF POMERANIA

Some may never have heard of the "Pearl of the Baltic", yet for others its German name brings back a host of painful memories. The free city of Danzig, an old Hanseatic town, hit the world's headlines during the first few days of September 1939 when Hitler invaded the country. Its return to Poland was marked by a devastating fire which left it drained of all vitality under a heap of smouldering rubble. Although reduced to ashes, the town was rebuilt and some districts were meticulously reconstructed brick by brick, as if nothing had happened. That is saying a lot about the character of this proud city. The architectural style is reminiscent of Flanders, and the city is an inviting place for those who love to stroll at liesure. The birthplace of the "Solidarność" trade union, it is also famous as the capital of the amber trade. Gdańsk celebrated its millennium in 1997, an occasion to express its exuberance. Together with Gdynia and Sopot, its sister cities on the coast, it is part of the Trójmiasto (Tri-City) conurbation extending 35km along the coast and home to some 800 000 inhabitants. Each town has its own well-defined role: Gdańsk concentrates its efforts on historic and cultural tourism, Sopot takes care of seaside tourism, and Gdynia has the economic role, mainly centred on an active industrial sector (light industry).

- ▶ **Getting your bearings** – 348km north-west of Warsaw, around Gdańsk Bay (*Zatoka Gdańska*), on the shores of the Baltic Sea.
- 👁 **Not to be missed** – The Royal Way, Hans Memling's Last Judgement in the National Museum, the view from the tower of St Mary's Church, the boat trip to Westerplatte, organ concerts in Oliwa Cathedral, Sopot's pier.
- 🕑 **Planning your visit** – Allow a minimum of two days to explore Gdańsk's Old Town, half a day for a tour of Westerplatte, another half a day to wander through the Oliwa district and a whole day to make the most of Sopot and Gdynia.

Background

A troubled history – The missionary bishop Adalbert of Bohemia visited Gyddanyzc in 997, the year it was granted its town charter. After becoming the capital of the Dukes of Pomerania in the 12C, the city fell into the hands of the Teutonic Knights in 1308 and began its life as a trading town by joining the Hanseatic League in 1361. It remained under the domination of the Knights until 1454, when the Polish population rebelled and destroyed the fortress. A few years later, in 1466, the Polish Crown regained the whole coastal fringe and gradually granted many privileges and liberties to the city which, welcoming the Renaissance influence, became flourishing and prosperous and had its heyday in the 16C-17C. Twice besieged by the Swedes in the 17C and by the Russians in 1734, it fell under Prussian rule in 1793 following the second partition of Poland, was renamed Danzig and lost many of its privileges. Between 1807 and 1815, while the area was under French control, the western part of the coastal fringe, including Sopot, was given to the free city of Gdańsk while the eastern part remained in Polish hands; an enclave in Polish territory was thus created. Returned to Prussia in 1815 following the Congress of Vienna, on account of its mainly German-speaking population, the town went through virtually the same process at the end of the First World War when, in 1919, under the terms of the Treaty of Versailles, the territory of the free city of Danzig, under the authority of the League of Nations, was created between Poland and Germany. The accession to power of Hitler, who wanted to deprive Poland of an outlet to the sea and to annexe Danzig by linking it to Germany via a secure militarised strip, progressively undermined the foundations of the free city system. On 1 September 1939, the battleship *Schleswig-Hollstein* attacked the Polish garrison in Westerplatte and Hitler, intent on breaking through the Danzig corridor, invaded Poland, thus sparking off the great disaster. The heavy fighting, which led to the town's liberation by Russian troops in March 1945, left it in ruins. After the Allied victory, Gdańsk was returned to Poland which thus gained greater access to the coast.

A city in ruins – When it was time to assess the damage in April 1945, life seemed to have come to a halt. About 90% of the historic centre and 60% of the periphery were entirely destroyed. Some 6 000 buildings were completely wiped out, 1 300 partially. Three million cubic metres of rubble remained to be cleared. However, the

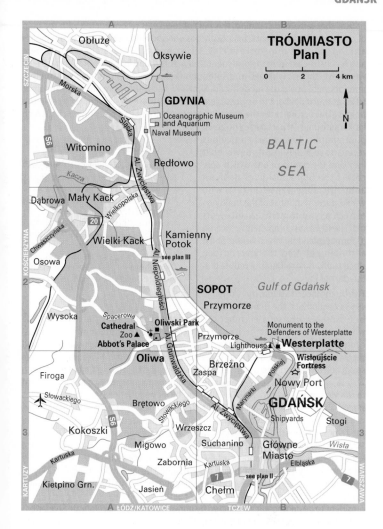

end of the war did not only result in an assessment of the architectural heritage, it also meant important and significant demographic changes. The census conducted on 16 June 1945, recorded 8 000 Poles and 124 000 Germans who were forced to leave for Germany in 1946. Its German population having been expelled and nearly all its original inhabitants having disappeared, the newly Polish city was able to start afresh and to plan its repopulation and reconstruction process. Operation "Wisła" launched in 1947-48 consisted in moving to Pomerania, Warmia and Masuria several thousand Polish families, originally from Galicia, who, when the new frontiers were established, found themselves in Soviet territory. New Polish immigrants from the region of Vilnius, looking for work and a roof, also came to bring the town back to life. Even though the change in the population was such that today there is little chance of finding long-established inhabitants, it is immediately obvious that the will to preserve the soul of the town, without making a clean sweep of its past and erasing its German character forever, weighed heavily on the decision taken in 1948 to rebuild Gdańsk exactly as it was before.

A remarkable reconstruction – Begun in 1949, it lasted almost 20 years, was only undertaken in earnest at the beginning of the 1960s, and, judging by Granary Island which is being redeveloped for the third time since 1947, it is not quite finished yet. While the town's peripheral districts were being crowned with concrete buildings, it was decided to give top priority to the reconstruction of the Main Town (Główne Miasto), otherwise known as the Right-hand Town as opposed to the Old Town (Stare Miasto), which was certainly not the oldest district but, in fact the most important, the most densely populated and the richest. From the shells of monuments and houses that remained standing, this part of town was reconstructed with the help of the available documents, mainly photos and souvenirs since most of the town's archives had gone up in smoke in 1945. Several houses, such as Steffens House, were also reconstructed from the ornamental elements found in the rubble. A few streets were nevertheless widened and, although façades were faithfully reconstructed, interiors were obviously modernised. Similarly, backyards were not rebuilt in order to let as much daylight in as possible and thus increase the level of comfort in the homes. This accounts for the empty space in the middle of housing blocks, which looks quite unusual particularly on aerial photographs. Today, this meticulous reconstruction has lost its newly built look and the patina of age which now covers the buildings gives them an authentic appearance. In fact, who would guess that most of the buildings one can see are no more than fifty years old. The town has completely recovered its former splendour which visitors find it all the more pleasant to admire on foot, since traffic is considerably reduced in this part of town.

Gdańsk's Who's Who

In addition to Lech Wałęsa, Gdańsk can take pride in having had several illustrious children, such as astronomer Jan Heweliusz (1611-1687), Gabriel Daniel Fahrenheit (1686-1736), the inventor of the mercury thermometer, philosopher Arthur Schopenhauer (1788-1860) and German-speaking writer and winner of the Nobel Prize for literature Günter Grass, born in 1927. The actor Klaus Kinski (1926-1991) was born in Sopot.

The birthplace of Solidarity – After the 1956 Poznań riots, the demonstrations by Gdańsk's workers in December 1970 and their brutal repression by the militia which resulted in 27 deaths, had already contributed in undermining the Poles' confidence in their communist leaders. Ten years later, social unrest continued and the whole workforce of the Lenin Shipyards went on strike on 14 August 1980. The strike quickly turned into a sit-in and the workers, led by a laid-off electrician, Lech Wałęsa, presented a list of 21 demands, including the construction of a monument to the victims of December 1970. Following bitter negotiations, an agreement was signed, allowing the foundation of the first legal independent trade union, *Solidarność*, which soon counted in its ranks over 10 million members; for 16 months they defied the regime and worried the Soviet Union. During the night of 12 to 13 December 1981, a state of war was proclaimed by the Military Committee of National Defence led by General Jaruzelski and a curfew was imposed. The state of war was officially lifted on 22 July 1983 but the union only regained its legitimacy in April 1989, just before the beginning of the events which changed the face of this part of Europe and contributed to making Lech Wałęsa, winner of the Nobel Peace Prize, the first Polish president to be democratically elected by universal suffrage. To celebrate Solidarity's 25th anniversary, Jean-Michel Jarre gave a huge concert within the compound of the shipyards on 26 August 2005.

The districts – Located at the extremity of the western arm of the Wisła, known as the dead Wisła (Wisła Martwa), Gdańsk's historic town used to lie between the

On the River Motława

River Motława and the Radunia Canal (Kanał Raduni). It formerly consisted of the **Old Town** (Stare Miasto) in the north, the **Main Town** (Główne Miasto), the **Old Suburb** (Stare Przedmieście), **Wheat Granary Island** (Wyspa Spichrzów)) and the **Lower Town** (Dolne Miasto) in the south. Following the war damage, the Main Town was the only one to be reconstructed exactly as it was before and the Old Town only recovered some of its buildings and a few churches. Gdańsk's plan is that of a medieval port town with some of its streets running parallel to the quay while others are perpendicular to it.

1 The Main Town (Główne Miasto)★★★ PLAN II

ROYAL WAY (Trakt Królewski) ★★★ B3

Running perpendicular to the River Motława between the Upland Gate and the Green Gate, it forms the town's main thoroughfare, on which was staged the ceremonial parade of the Polish kings who came on official visit to Gdańsk every year. The Royal Way begins with Długla Street, literally the Long Street, which in fact extends only over a distance of 200m from the Golden Gate to the Town Hall, and continues with Długi Targ, once the market square and old Gdańsk's main square near the harbour.

Upland Gate (Brama Wyższa) B3

The gate, which was the ceremonial entrance to the town and the starting point of the Royal Way, was erected in 1574-76 outside the existing walls, to reinforce the medieval fortifications. It was here that the king was given the keys to the city by the municipal authorities. The frieze decorating the west side features the coats of arms of Royal Prussia (with two unicorns), of Poland (with the arms of the "Ciołek") and of Gdańsk (with two lions). The coat of arms of the House of Hohenzollern was added to the east side in 1884. The following maxims in Latin are inscribed below the coat of arms: "Justice and Piety are the foundations of all kingdoms", "The citizens' most cherished possessions are peace, liberty and concord" and finally "There can be no wiser deed than what is done for the community".

Just behind the Upland Gate stands the Gothic **Foregate** at the start of Długa (Zespół przedbramia ulicy Długiej), a barbican comprising the **Prison Tower** (Wieża Więzienna) linked to the **Torture House** (Katownia) BY, on the town side. The buildings, at present closed for restoration, are scheduled to house a new amber museum.

Golden Gate (Złota Brama)★ B3

It was erected between 1612 and 1614 in Renaissance style by the architect Jan Strakowski from drawings by Abraham van den Blocke. Added in 1648 by Piotr Ringering, the eight ornamental sculptures surmounting the gate feature allegorical representations of civic virtues (west side: Peace, Justice, Glory and Concord; opposite side: Prudence, Piety, Liberty and Unity). On the town side, just above the porch, a maxim in Latin claims that "Concord helps small states to develop, discord makes large states disappear".

St George's Court (Bractwo Św Jerzego)★ B3

Adjoining the left side of the gate, this Gothic brick building is topped with an imposing 16C lantern surmounted by a replica of the statue of St George and the Dragon (the 1556 original is in the National Museum). Built between 1487 and 1494 by Hans Glotau for a military brotherhood, the court is now the headquarters of the Polish Architects' Society)

Turn left onto Coal Market Square (Targ Węglowy) to see the silver **Millennium Tree** erected by blacksmiths in 1997 to commemorate the town's millennium.

Długa Street★ B3

The slight curve of the Long Street (Długa) reveals the slender outline of the Town Hall tower standing at its eastern end. The street is lined with tall narrow mansions with splendid façades and elaborately decorated gables, dating from the 15C to the 20C and mostly rebuilt. Note in particular:
At **no 12**, the Rococo façade of the **Uphagens' House** (Dom Uphagena) now a **museum** devoted to 18C bourgeois interiors (✆ 326 07 10 - 15 Jun-15 Oct Mon 10am-3pm, Tue-Sat 10am-6pm, Sun 11am-6pm, 16 Oct-14 Jun Tue-Sat 10am-4pm, Sun 11am-4pm - 6 PLN - free on Sun in winter). Behind the façade featuring large windows, the lofty entrance hall – typical of merchants' houses – boasts a fine staircase leading to the upper floor. The fairly bare rooms are almost exact reproductions of the original setting, judging by old photographs.
At **no 28**, a Renaissance house built in 1560.

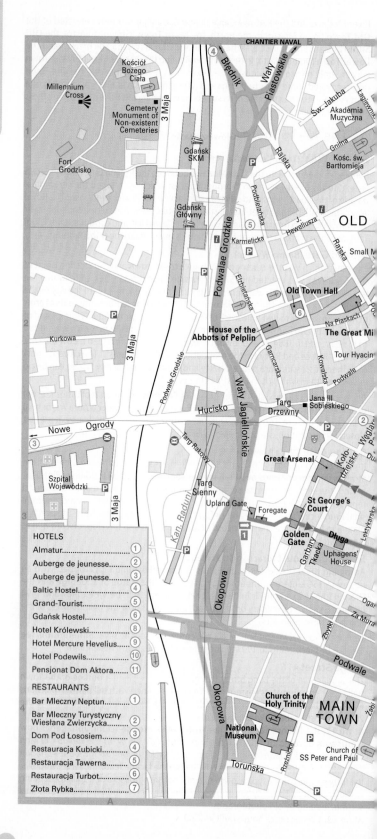

HOTELS

Almatur	①
Auberge de jeunesse	②
Auberge de jeunesse	③
Baltic Hostel	④
Grand-Tourist	⑤
Gdańsk Hostel	⑥
Hotel Królewski	⑧
Hotel Mercure Hevelius	⑨
Hotel Podewils	⑩
Pensjonat Dom Aktora	⑪

RESTAURANTS

Bar Mleczny Neptun	①
Bar Mleczny Turystyczny Wiesłana Zwierzycka	②
Dom Pod Łososiem	③
Restauracja Kubicki	④
Restauracja Tawerna	⑤
Restauracja Turbot	⑥
Złota Rybka	⑦

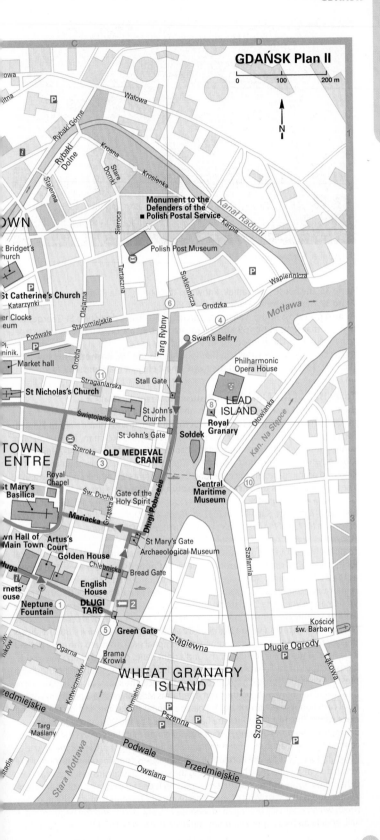

GDAŃSK Plan II

0   100   200 m

N

Wałowa

Rybaki Górne

Rybaki Dolne

Krosna

Stare Domki

Krosienka

Kanał Raduni

Karpia

Monument to the Defenders of the Polish Postal Service ■

Polish Post Museum

Wapiennicza

Grodzka

Sukiennicza

Motława

Tartaczna

Sieroca

Olejarna

Staromiejskie

Katarzynki

...OWN

...t Bridget's ...hurch

St Catherine's Church

...er Clocks ...eum

Podwale

...ninik.

Grobla

Market hall

Straganiarska

St Nicholas's Church

Targ Rybny

Swan's Belfry

⑥

④

Philharmonic Opera House

LEAD ISLAND

Ołowianka

Stall Gate

Świętojańska

St John's Church

St John's Gate

OLD MEDIEVAL CRANE

⑪

⑧

Royal Granary

Sołdek

Kan. Na Stępce

TOWN ...ENTRE

Szeroka

③

Royal Chapel

Św. Ducha

Gate of the Holy Spirit

Central Maritime Museum

⑩

...t Mary's Basilica

Mariacka

Grząska

Długi Pobrzeże

Szafarnia

...wn Hall of ...Main Town

Artus's Court

Golden House

Chlebnicka

St Mary's Gate

Archaeological Museum

...ługa

English House

Bread Gate

...rnets' ...ouse

Neptune Fountain ①

DŁUGI TARG

２

Kościół św. Barbary

⑤ Green Gate

Stągiewna

Długie Ogrody

Ogarna

Brama Krowia

Łąkowa

Konwiktorska

WHEAT GRANARY ISLAND

...edmiejskie

Targ Maślany

Chmielna

Pszenna

Szopy

...stadia

Stara Motława

Podwale

Przedmiejskie

Owsiana

Długa Street, Neptune fountain

At **no 35**, the house (Lwi Zamek) known as the Lions' Castle (1569).

At **no 37**, the fine stone façade carved in 1563.

At **no 47**, a recess in the wall houses an original mosaic depicting St George. The late-19C mansions at **nos 69 and 70** are among the rare buildings along the street to have survived the war and still be intact today.

At the east end of the street, on the right, stands the 16C **Kornets' House★** (now the PTTK Tourist office), one of the town's most elegant mansions; the Town Hall is on the left.

Town Hall of the Main Town (Ratusz Głównego Miasta)★★ C3

Built in 1379-81 by Henryk Ungeradin on the site of a previous edifice, mentioned in 1327, and damaged by the fire of October 1556, it was remodelled in Flemish Renaissance style. Its slender tower, designed by a Dutchman, Dirk Daniels, is surmounted by a tall spire topped with a golden statue of Sigismund II August who looks down on the town from a height of 82m; a tribute paid by the population to the king who promulgated an edict granting the same rights to Catholics and Protestants. The building houses the **Historical Museum of Gdańsk** (Muzeum Historii Miasta Gdańska)★★, *Ul. Długa 47 - ℘ 767 91 00 - 15 Jun-4 Sep Mon 10am-3pm, Tue-Sat 10am-6pm, Sun 11am-6pm, 5 Sep-14 Jun Tue-Sat. 10am-4pm, Sun 11am-4pm - 8 PLN. The ticket office is on the left of the fine access staircase, at the end of the passageway leading to the Palowa Restaurant, on the left.* Housed on the upper floors of the Town Hall, which was completely destroyed at the end of March 1945, the museum is worth a visit above all for its ceremonial rooms, in particular the large **Council Chamber★★★**, also known as the Red or Summer Room, decorated in Dutch mannerist style in 1589-91 with remarkable sculptures by Szymon Herle and seven murals by the Dutch artist Hans Vredeman de Vries. The 25 mythological and biblical paintings on the ceiling are the work of another Dutchman Izaac van den Blocke, including the oval centrepiece, the famous "**Glorification of the Unity of Gdańsk with Poland**"★★★ (1608). It shows the city resting on top of a monumental triumphal arch, rising to the west behind its Upland Gate and its fortifications. God's right hand, coming through the clouds, holds the spire of the Town Hall tower, surrounded by an eagle, symbolizing the divine presence embodied on earth by the municipal council. The source of the Wisła is linked by a divine rainbow with, on the right, the Tatras Mountains and a panorama of the royal castle on Wawel Hill in Kraków, Poland's capital at the time, and, on the left, the place where the river flows into the Baltic, guarded by the Wisłoujście fortress.

Below, the river flows by Long Market Square where members of the town's various communities, engaged in conversation, are gathered in front of the façade of Artus's Court (before its 1616 transformation). The treasures contained in this room were fortunately dismantled and hidden during the war, which explains why they survived. Other remarkable but reconstructed rooms include the small Council Chamber or Winter Room, the vast White Court Room entered through a fine stone doorway (1520) which originally belonged to a house in Long Street, and the large entrance hall, enhanced by a superb wooden spiral staircase from the 17C. The upper floor contains a fine display of ancient maps and interesting temporary exhibitions about the town's history. One of the last rooms is devoted to the chronology of the destructions suffered by the town during the last war from the first British bombing of July 1942 to the particularly devastating Soviet ones of 25 March 1945. Evocative photographs show the magnitude of the disaster. In summer, it is possible to climb to the top of the tower.

The Long Market (Długi Targ)★★★ C4

Lined with the town's most outstanding houses, each with its characteristic front steps, this square, formed by a widening of the Long Street, is the real heart of the town. The rich mansions were patiently rebuilt after the war.

In the top north-east corner stands the **Neptune Fountain** (Fontanna Neptuna)★★★, dating from 1633. An emblem of the town and a symbol of the proud city's wealth, this splendid fountain is surmounted by a bronze statue cast in 1615 by Peter Hussen. Neptune, the god of the sea and of navigation, represents the tight bond that exists between the town and the sea. Dismantled during the war, Neptune did not hold his trident again until 1954. Since then, the fountain has been the locals' favourite meeting point.

Behind the Neptune Fountain rises the sumptuous arcaded façade of **Artus's Court** (Dwór Artusa)★★★. Built between 1476 and 1481, this Gothic Court was the meeting place of six of the town's guilds. Its name suggest the Knights of the Round Table with whom the wealthy merchants identified for their democratic functioning. In 1616-17, the building was given a mannerist façade by Abraham van den Blocke. Its royal doorway is decorated with two medallions of members of the Vasa dynasty, Sigismund III and his son Ladisław IV. Level with the arcaded windows are statues of Scipio Africanus, Themistocles, Marius Camillus and Judas Maccabaeus, surmounted beneath the balustrade of the attic by personified allegories of Strength and Justice. Towering above the edifice is a well-chosen statue of the goddess of Fortune. The building is preceded by a vast unusual perron guarded by two stone lions holding the town's coat of arms whereas, on the left, the door leading to the basement is flanked by a cupola topped with a statue of Mercury, the protector of merchants, standing naked and pointing a finger to the sky. Behind the façade, the only part to have been spared, the entirely rebuilt edifice houses a museum reached on the left through the adjoining **Old Jury House** (Stary Dom Ławy), but also linked from the inside to the adjacent house on the right, the **New Jury House** (Nowy Dom Ławy)★. Sometimes called the **Aldermen's House** or **Gdańsk's Hall** (Sień Gdańska), this building boasts a mainly Gothic façade with a fine Renaissance porch and its gable, added in the 18C, has become the focus of attention on account of a local attraction: the "Maiden at the window" *(see box)*.

Visit of Artus's Court – ☏ 767 91 80 - 15 Jun-4 Sep: Mon 10am-3pm, Tue-Sat 10am-6pm, Sun 11am-6pm; 5 Sep-14 Jun Tue-Sat 10am-4pm, Sun 11am-4pm. 8 PLN.

> ### Now you see her, now you don't...
>
> The "Maiden at the window" (*Panienka z Okienka*) is a novel, written in 1891 by Deotyma, alias Jadwiga Łuszczewska, in which Hedwig, a 17C fair maiden from Gdańsk locked up by her uncle, watches the world from her window. She can now be seen at her window, recently located in the gable of the Aldermen's House. Coveted by photographers, the fair lady only appears at 1pm... for a few seconds... so make sure your camera is ready. On the other hand, that won't be of any use to you in the adjoining Golden House where, according to a persistent legend, the ghost of Judyta Bahr, the wife of burgomaster Jan Speymann who once lived in the house, haunts the corridors whispering reassuring words: "Always do what is just, fear no one".

At the entrance to the great hall (450sq m) with its fine starred web **vaulting**★★ supported by four slender granite columns, visitors are greeted by a suspended ship fitted with tiny guns that used to fire a salute on special occasions. In the right-hand corner stands the prize exhibit, a large **ceramic stove**★★★, looking like a five-tier obelisk. Built in 1545 by master potter Georg Stelzener, this "king of stoves", 10.64m high and 2.5m wide at the base, is covered over with 520 painted tiles (including 437 original ones) portraying the most prominent figures of the early-16C Catholic and Lutheran world, in particular Charles V, his brother Ferdinand I and their respective spouses, and also featuring allegorical representations of the cardinal virtues and the planets. The top of the stove bears the coats of arms of Gdańsk, royal Prussia and Poland. It was filled with coal through an opening located in the north wall. The upper part was dismantled and hidden in 1943 but the base was damaged by fire and restoration work was only completed in 1995. The *Last Judgement* (1603) by Anton Möller and *Orpheus Among the Animals* (1594) by Hans Vredeman de Vries were not so lucky and the paintings we see are replicas. Note, on the left, an expressive late-Gothic polychrome **low relief**★ by Hans Brandt depicting St George and the Dragon. Walk through the hall of the adjoining house (New Aldermen's House), which also belonged to Gdańsk's noble citizens and was entirely reconstructed. The upper floor houses temporary exhibitions.

Golden House (Złota Kamieniczka)★★★ C3

Shifting one's attention two gables to the right of Artus's Court (at no 41), one notices the wealth of ornamentation on the fine façade of this mansion. Built in 1609 by Abraham van den Blocke for the then mayor, it features a blend of the three architectural orders but is mostly noteworthy for its twelve friezes carved between 1609 and 1618 by Rostok-born Johann Voigt. These are separated, level with each cornice, by four busts, including those of Polish kings Ladisław Jagellon and Sigismund III Vasa, whereas, at the top, the balustrade is surmounted by statues of well-known figures from Antiquity, Cleopatra, Oedipus, Achilles and Antigone.

Green Gate (Zielona Brama)★ C3

Closing off the Long Market in front of the banks of the Motława, this gate features four arches. It was erected between 1568 and 1571 by Jan Kramer and Regnier, on the site of a 14C defensive gate known as Koga, to serve as the king's residence. Apart from Marie Louise de Gonzague just before she married Ladisław IV in 1646, no Polish monarch ever stayed in it and today, the former President of the Polish Republic, Lech Wałęsa has his office inside.

Beyond the arcades, the axis of the Długi Targ is prolonged by the **Green Bridge** (Most Zielony) spanning the Motława to reach **Granary Island** (Wyspa Spichrzów); the **Long Quay** (Długie Pobrzeże), extending to the left along the river, leads to the famous wooden crane.

② From the banks of the Motława to the old town

The Long Quay (Długie Pobrzeże)★★ C3

Before it was moved during the second half of the 19C to the "dead" Wisła and its side canals, the port of Gdańsk stretched along the Motława, at the foot of the town. All the perpendicular streets leading to the harbour opened onto the riverfront through fortified river gates that formed part of the medieval walls. In front of them, wooden landing-piers on stilts, set at right angles to the bank, served as moorings for the ships. The increase in maritime traffic rendered these numerous jetties impractical and, at the beginning of the 17C, one long wooden quay was built for the loading and unloading of goods. Today, the quay is a promenade lined with fine gabled houses reflecting in the still waters of the Motława and, at intervals, with gates opening onto perpendicular streets.

Beyond the Green Gate, the first and probably the oldest of these gates is the **Bread Gate** (Brama Chlebnicka), closing off the street of the same name. Built around 1450, it is surmounted by the town's oldest coat of arms: two crosses without a crown, which is the emblem of the Teutonic Knights. No 12 in Chlebnicka Street, known as the **Schlieff House**, was not reconstructed so right down to the last detail because it was damaged during the war but because the Emperor of Prussia, Friedrich Wilhelm III, decided in 1820 to have it entirely taken apart and reassembled in Potsdam, Germany, where it still is.

At no 16 stands the large gabled **English House** (Dom Angielski)★, also known as the House Under the Angels because of the angels decorating the façade. Built in 1569-70, it featured eight levels rising to a height of 30m and was the highest burgher's house in town. Owned by English merchants in the 17C, it later became a Masonic lodge and is now an annexe of the Fine Arts Academy.

No 26 along the quay is a tall unusual-looking house of which only the façades were saved in 1945. Topped with a turret used to keep watch over the ships before being turned into an astronomical observatory, the building features a fine five-storey oriel. Erected in 1598 by Anton van Obberghen for a wealthy merchant, it became in 1845 the House of the Naturalists' Society (attended by Humboldt); since 1962 it has been the home of the **Archaeological Museum** (Muzeum Archeologiczne) (*Tue and Thu-Fri 9am-4pm, Wed 10am-5pm, Sat-Sun 10am-4pm - Museum 5 PLN - Tower 2 PLN*

- Museum alone free on Sat). This museum is concerned with the region's population during the proto-Slav and Slav periods. One room presents the series of excavations undertaken by Poland in the Sudan, another is devoted to amber from the Baltic, which has been at the root of an important trans-European trade since Antiquity. The top of the tower offers a fine panoramic view of the town and the River Motława. Standing in front of the museum are two ancient statues from proto-Slav pagan tribes called "Baba".

Going right through the adjoining twin-turreted house, the Gothic **St Mary's Gate** (Brama Mariacka), surmounted by the town's coat of arms, leads to the famous street of the same name pervaded by a unique atmosphere. Before entering it, you can continue along the quay, passing the **Gate of the Holy Spirit** (Brama Św. Ducha), the **Gate of the Great Crane** (Brama Żuraw), **St John's Gate** (Brama Świętojańska) followed by the **Stall Gate** (Brama Straganiarska)**,** and arrive at the **Old Fishmarket Square** (Targ Rybny), in front of the **Swan's Belfry** (Baszta Łabędź) which marked the northern end of the medieval fortifications. Beyond, the space extending between Grodzka and Na Dylach Streets was occupied by **Gdańsk's Castrum** and the **Teutonic Knights' Castle** (Zamczysko), built in 1340 and destroyed by the inhabitants in 1454, which has given its name to the district.

Retrace your steps.

Old Medieval Crane (Stary Żuraw)★★★ C3

While strolling along the quay, you cannot miss the imposing and photogenic outline of this wooden crane once used for the loading and unloading of goods. The largest harbourside lifting gear in medieval Europe, it was also one of the gates for entering the town of which it is still the emblem. Mentioned in 1367, it was rebuilt in 1444 following a fire. The upper crane, added in the 17C, was designed to hoist loads of up to two tonnes to a height of 27m but also to fit long masts onto ships. The winch was activated by two wooden drums – 6m and 6.5m in diameter – put in motion by men who, like tireless hamsters, climbed the steps lining the inside of the drums. Severely damaged during the war, the crane, restored between 1955 and 1962, forms part of the Central Maritme Museum whose main buildings are located on Lead Island opposite.

Granary Island and Lead Island ★ D2-3

The splendid sailing ships of the Baltic are no longer moored in front of the island and the northern extremity of **Granary Island** (Wyspa Spichrzów) sometimes looks like a rubbish dump, yet the place offers a superb **panoramic view★★★** of the Long Quay with the outline of Old Gdańsk in the background.

On **Lead Island**, facing the wooden crane across the River Motława, are three adjacent granaries, Oliwa (Oliwski), Copper (Miedź) and the Virgin (Panna), now housing the **Central Maritime Museum** which includes the **Sołdek Museum Ship.** Further along stands the equally proud and characteristic structure of the **Royal Granary** (Spichrz Królewski)★ erected between 1606 and 1608 at the town's expense to store goods produced by the royal estates and recently turned into a fine modern hotel.

Behind it are the massive buildings of the new **Philharmonic Opera House** (Polska Filharmonia Bałtycka) on the site of a former thermoelectric power station.

The museum on Lead Island can be reached by taking the Motława River Shuttle(1 PLN) in front of the Old Crane or on foot (allow half an hour). Walk along Stągiewna Street, lined on the right with former granaries converted into offices, to the arm of the New Motława, preceded on the right by the Gothic Stągiewna Gate, which has retained former milk storing tanks formed by two adjoining towers. After crossing the bridge, turn left and walk alongside the marina before taking the first bridge to Lead Island (Wyspa Ołowianka).

What's to become of Granary Island?

This picturesque warehouse district facing the Main Town was built from the 13C onwards and, in the 14C, there were already 200 granaries on the island; their number kept on increasing and chronicles mention that the 1536 fire destroyed some 340 of them. A few years later, in 1576, a canal (known as the New Motława) was dug to avoid the spreading of fires, thus forming a peninsula which was again ravaged by fires and the 200 or so granaries which escaped were laid waste by the 1945 bombings. The island is still in ruins today but, since the 1990s, it has aroused a lot of interest and prompted endless projects. There are rumours about a theatre and a car park. What will be will be...

Mariacka Street★★ C3

This emblem of Old Gdańsk is one of the town's most charming and most picturesque streets. Practically razed to the ground during the war, it was meticulously reconstructed in the 1970s with its façades, its front steps, its railings and its shop signs exactly as they were. Today the street is lined with most of the souvenir shops, in particular those selling amber jewellery, an ancient tradition to which Gdańsk owes its reputation as the capital of the amber trade.

St Mary's Basilica (Bazylika Mariacka)★★ C3

Free admission, contribution to the upkeep and restoration of the church (2 PLN).

Known as "Gdańsk's Crown", this imposing basilica towering unchallenged above the town centre is the largest brick church ever built in Europe (105.5m x 66m). Covering an area of 4 900sq m, it can accommodate 20 000 people (that is to say the town's entire population around 1450). It was often full to capacity during the martial-law period when the inhabitants wanted to show their support for the members of the Solidarity trade union who took refuge inside.

Work began in 1343, but the church was built in stages and only completed in 1502. Initially used by the Catholics, it passed to the Protestants in 1572, after the death of King Sigismund II August, before becoming a Catholic place of worship once more in 1945.

It was severely damaged during the war, its upper structure was reduced to ashes, 40% of its vaulting collapsed and all its frescoes were destroyed, yet 80% of its artistic treasures were removed in time and saved. However, many of them are still not back in their original place; such is the case of the original of Hans Memling's triptych depicting *The Last Judgement*, which is now housed in Gdańsk's National Museum. The basilica's other gem is the magnificent **astronomical clock★★** made by Hans Düringer between 1464 and 1470. Located in the north transept, it is 14m high and comprises three sections; it

> ### Gdańsk's "Drawing Rooms"
>
> The *przedproża*, typical architectural features of Old Gdańsk, are those forecourts or perrons which stood in front of the smart mansions lining the street. While the terraces were turned into drawing rooms or summer dining rooms, the basements were used as shops, warehouses or workshops. Surrounded by balustrades and elaborately carved stone sculptures, these perrons were often ringed by gutters ending with splendid water outlets shaped like gargoyles. Unlike the fine perrons along Mariacka Street which were reconstructed, those lining Długa Street were demolished in the 19C to make way for the tramway ... now also vanished.

functioned until 1553 then was not put back in working order until 1993. The lowest part is the *calendarium* featuring two screens which show the hour and the date as well as the liturgical calendar. In the middle is the *planetarium* indicating the phases of the moon, the signs of the zodiac and the positions of the sun and of the moon in relation to the signs of the zodiac. The upper part is a kind of theatre with a selection of biblical characters and a device allowing them to appear in rotation and on two levels (the twelve Apostles, the four Evangelists, the three Wise Kings and Death holding a scythe) to strike the hours (noon is the most spectacular time). Right at the top, Adam and Eve standing on either side of the Tree of Knowledge, ring the bells. Also noteworthy are the octagonal **fonts** dating from 1553, the **high altar**, a late-Gothic polyptych by Master Michael of Augsburg dating from 1511-17, a lovely pietà (1410) by an anonymous master who also carved the beautiful **Madonna of Gdańsk**, situated in St Anne's Chapel (north side), as well as the fine Baroque **organ**, entirely rebuilt after the war. If you have enough stamina, climb the 408 steps to the top of the only tower and enjoy the beautiful **panoramic view★★** you get from the platform towering 82m above the town's roofs *(Mon-Sat 9am-5pm, Sun 1-5pm – 3PLN).*

Royal Chapel (Kaplica Królewska) C3

The chapel, adjoining the presbytery, on the north side of the basilica, was commissioned by King John III Sobieski after the municipality refused, in 1677, to give the cathedral back to the Catholics. Designed by the Dutch architect Tillmann van Gameren, it was built in the shape of a Greek cross between 1678 and 1683 and surmounted by a dome topped with a lantern; it is the town's only Baroque church and the only evidence of the Counter Reformation *(not open to the public).*

Great Arsenal
(Wielka Zbrojownia)★★ B3

This elegant edifice barring the view at the end of Piwna Street (Beer Street) is the town's finest example of the influence of Flemish Renaissance on local architecture. Built between 1600 and 1605, it was used until the 19C. Beneath the statue of Minerva, there used to be a well from which munitions were brought to the surface. The ground floor unexpectedly houses a small supermarket and a shopping arcade of moderate size, whereas the upper floors are occupied by the Fine Arts Academy. Walk through to **Coal Market Square** on the other side and turn round to admire the superb façade featuring four adjoining gables and flanked on the right by the 14C **Straw Tower**. Note the so-called Cossak's statue adorning the centre of the western façade.

Mariacka Street

R. Mattes / MICHELIN

From the Basilica to the Old Town

Return to the north side of the Basilica and follow the street successively named Globla (dyke) I to IV and turn right onto Świętojańska Street.

St John's Church (Kościół Św. Jana) C2

Its construction, begun in the second half of the 14C, was completed at the end of the 15C. Destroyed during the war, it has not been fully restored yet. The edifice is surrounded by a picturesque alleyway, also reconstructed, and carved stones from the ruined building are strewn all round, forming a lapidary museum.

St Nicholas's Church (Kościół Św. Mikołaja)★ C2

Believed to be the town's oldest church, St Nicholas was probably a wooden church in the 12C before being rebuilt in brick by the Dominicans who settled in 1227; its present appearance goes back to the period between 1340 and 1380. The church was miraculoulsy spared during the Second World War, suffering very little damage. Note the great organ from 1755 and the five-register altarpiece dating from 1643. The church always remained in Catholic hands and, in 1945, a religious community from Lwów (now L'viv in Ukraine) took charge of it.

Walk along Pańska Street to the octagonal **Hyacinthus's Tower** (Baszta Jacek) erected around 1400 on the site of the medieval fortifications which separated the Old Town from the Main Town. Known as the "Kitchen Window", it was used as a watchtower. Facing the tower is the fine 19C **Covered Market** (Hala Targowa), still in use.

The Old Town (Stare Miasto)★★

Cross the Podwale Staromiejskie to enter the Old Town where today, paradoxically, only a few reconstructed buildings stand out against a modern background.

Monument to the Defenders of the Polish Postal Service

This monument was erected in 1979 in front of the Post Office (**Poczta Polska**) attacked by the Nazis at the same time as Westerplatte on the morning of 1 September 1939. Some fifty Polish post-office employees defended it for 14 hours. Four of them succeeded in escaping when they surrendered, the 35 who survived were shot on 5 October and their bodies were thrown into a pit in Wrzeszcz, which was only discovered in 1991. This episode is recalled by Günter Grass in his novel *The Tin Drum* adapted for the screen by Volker Schlöndorff.

The reconstructed building houses a small museum which includes a room devoted to this tragic event; other rooms illustrate communication techniques (*Muzeum Poczty Polskiej - Tue-Fri 10am-4pm, Sat-Sun 10.30am-2pm - 3 PLN - free on Sun*).

St Catherine's Church (Kościół Św. Katarzyny)★ C2

This is one of Gdańsk's oldest parish churches; founded at the end of the 12C, it was built in stages during the 14C and 15C. At one end of the church, a few photographs show the extent of the destruction (collapsed vaulting) that it suffered. During the restoration work undertaken from 1953 to 1957, fragments of frescoes were brought to light. Several panels provide some information about the astronomer Johannes Hevelius (1611-87) whose grave was recently discovered in the church together with his epitaph. The high altar features a Crucifixion by Anton Möller (1610) and, occupying a prominent position under the organ loft on the left, is a huge painting by Bartolomeo Milwitz depicting "Jesus Christ Entering Jerusalem" (1590). A small door to the right of the porch gives access to the church tower and to the **Tower Clocks Museum** (Muzeum Zegarów Wieżowych) which contains a collection of clock mechanisms from the 15C to the 20C *(open in summer only Tue-Sun 10am-5pm – off season, groups can make an appointment ☏ 305 64 92).*

The magnificent **peal** (normally activated every Friday at 11am) had a troubled history. The original dating from 1738 was destroyed by fire in 1905; it was replaced in 1910 by another one which the Germans took down during the war and transferred to Lübeck. It only came back from there in 1989, as part of the German-Polish reconciliation. The fourth octave, which increased the number of bells from 37 to 49 was installed in 1999.

St Bridget's Church (Kościól Św. Brygidy) C2

Situated behind St Catherine's, St Bridget's Church was erected in 1396 to house the relics of the saint brought back from Rome and surmounted in the 17C by an unusual squat tower. Entirely destroyed during the war, it was rebuilt in the early 1970s and features contemporary furnishings including a monumental amber high altar. It became the sanctuary of the Solidarity trade union during the 1980s' strikes, after a group of striking workers sought refuge inside and were welcomed by Henryk Jankowski, the controversial parish priest.

The Great Mill (Wielki Młyn)★ B2

Having reached the Raduna Canal, you will notice on your left the outline of this imposing mill which, from the time it was founded in 1350 by the Teutonic Knights until its destruction by fire in 1945, never stopped grinding nearly 200 tonnes of grain per day, thanks to its 18 hydraulic wheels. Rebuilt in 1962, this impressive Gothic edifice now houses a shopping centre. Almost facing it is the 14C **Small Mill** (Mały Młyn) spanning one arm of the canal.

Close to the mill, the tip of the island is occupied by a 17C house once owned by the Millers' Guild (Dwór Młyński) and now turned into a café-restaurant with a pleasant terrace at the back.

Old Town Hall (Ratusz Staromiejski)★★ B2

It stands facing a small park and a monument to Hevelius; its elegant façade, characteristic of Flemish mannerist architecture, is surmounted by a slender turret. The edifice, built between 1587 and 1595 by Anton van Obberghen, retains the memory of the famous astronomer and brewer, Johannes Hevelius (1611-87). In 1945, it became the headquarters of the Soviet troops and today you will find, on either side of the entrance hall occupied by a pleasant café, a room devoted to art exhibitions and a bookshop which form **Gdańsk's Cultural Centre** (*daily 10am-6pm - free admission*). It is worth going upstairs to see the richly decorated municipal council's great chamber: 17C paintings by Adolf Boy and Herman Han, fine wooden spiral staircase, ceramic tiles from Delft and various 19C decorative elements from houses which were destroyed.

West of the Town Hall you will see the so-called **House of the Abbots of Pelplin** (Dom Opatów Pelplińskich) dating from 1612, one of the rare houses to come through the war unscathed; note the fine Renaissance **façade★**.

The Shipyard

If you continue to follow the itinerary, you will reach the limits of the Old Town and eventually come to Solidarity Square (Pl. Solidarności) marking the entrance to Gdańsk's Shipyard (Stocznia Gdańska), known as the Lenin Shipyard until 1980.

Monument to the Shipyard Workers Killed
(Pomnik Poległych Stoczniowców)★

Overlooking the square, it comprises a set of three 42m tall stainless-steel crosses weighing 133 tonnes, supporting crucified anchors, symbolizing hope. Their bases feature 12 low-relief sculptures illustrating scenes of the workers' daily life accompanied by several emphatic inscriptions such as "they gave their life so that you could live with dignity". It was inaugurated on 16 December 1980 to commemorate those who were killed or wounded ten years previously, during the workers' strikes

Monument and shipyard

of 16 and 17 December 1970. For the first time the authorities of a communist country recognised the victims of their own regime and allowed a commemorative monument to be erected in their honour. Behind it, against the wall, is a series of commemorative plaques laid by trade unions from all over the world as a tribute to the victims of communism. Note the plaque and its expressive sculpture dedicated to the memory of Father Jerzy Popiełuszko, assassinated in 1984. A passageway, situated on the right of the entrance to the shipyard, leads to the historic "Sala BHP" which houses the exhibition of the Solidarity Museum: "The Road to Freedom".

"The Road to Freedom" Exhibition (Wystawa "Drogi do Wolności")★★

Ul. Doki 1 - ℘ 769 29 20 - May-Sep Tue-Sun 10am-5pm, Oct-Apr 10am-4pm- 6 PLN (with leaflet). This multimedia exhibition situated at the entrance to the former Lenin Shipyard is intended to recount the history of the Solidarity (*Solidarność*) trade union which started the famous strike on 14 August 1980. A trail, starting from Solidarity Square, dotted with fragments of the Berlin Wall and of the Shipyard wall (which electrician Lech Wałęsa climbed over to get access to the establishment that had fired him for his trade union activities) leads, along the road to freedom, to the building now turned into a museum. One can see the famous **"Work Hygiene and Safety** room where, on 31 August 1980, negotiations took place and a historic agreement was signed. An audiovisual presentation with many dioramas and archive films recalls the chronology of events (with captions in English) and, in the exact place where it all happened, an amazingly realistic reconstruction enables visitors to imagine the background to the negotiations with tables strewn with files, radio sets (the shipyard radio gave a live transmission of the talks between the MKS and the government commission) and overflowing ashtrays lined up in front of the platform where the representatives of Solidarity stood.

Gdańsk's Heights

A nice way to end the itinerary is to climb from the back of the bus station up to the city's heights dominated by **Grodzisko Fort**, a group of military buildings connected with the siege of the town by the Russians in 1734 and later with the intrusion of Napoleon's troops led by Marshal Lefebvre in 1807. The **Millennium Cross** (Kryż Milenijny) has been standing since 2000 at the top of the hill (64m), near the Jerusalem Bastion, offering a fine **view**★ of the town and the shipyard and giving a good idea of the extent of the Tri-City and Gdańsk Bay. On the way down, you will catch a glimpse of the symbolic **Cemetery Monument of Non-Existent Cemeteries** (near the Church of the Blessed Sacrament), intended to commemorate Gdańsk's populations whose burying places have disappeared, wiped out by the passing of time or the furious assaults of history.

Museums

National Museum (Muzeum Narodowe)★★ B4

Ul. Toruńska 1 - ℘ 301 68 04 – Tue-Fri 9am-4pm, Sat-Sun 10am-4pm – 10 PLN – free on Sat – www.muzeum.narodowe.gda.pl

This fine museum is located in a former Franciscan convent in the **Old Suburb**; the cloister galleries and vaulted rooms on the ground floor house an interesting set of Gothic statues, religious gold and silverware, beautiful wrought-iron items, as well as the original statue of St George and the Dragon (1556) from the lantern of the Court of the Brotherhood of St George. One wing contains antique furniture including a kind of carved wardrobe, typical of Gdańsk and once famous throughout Europe. The upper floor is devoted to painting; the works are displayed against a brightly coloured background. Immediately on the left is the unmissable **Altarpiece of the Last Judgement★★★**, Hans Memling's (c 1433-94) most famous triptych, displayed in a glass case. The central panel depicts St Michael the Archangel among the Dead coming out of their graves, the right-hand panel shows the Chosen and the left-hand one the Damned. Walk round to see the magnificent portraits of the benefactors. Start with the department on the left, devoted to 16C-18C local painting (Malarstwo Gdańskie); the first and most interesting room precedes a long portrait gallery. Proceed to the department of Flemish and Dutch painting (Malarstwo Flamandzkie i Holenderskie) which has a few nice surprises in store for you and end the visit with the department of 19C-20C Polish painting (Malarstwo Polskie), where you will see, among others, works by Wyspiański, Malczewski and Pankiewicz.

Standing near the museum, the **Church of the Holy Trinity** (kościół Św. Trójcy)★ boasts beautiful vaulting and elaborate interior decoration. Completed in 1514, it features an unusual east end separated from the nave by a wall adorned with fine late-Gothic polyptychs. Commissioned by King Kazimierz Jagellon for the benefit of the Catholic Polish population, **St Anne's Chapel** (1480-84) houses a pulpit from 1721 and a Baroque organ from 1710.

Central Maritime Museum
(Centralne Muzeum Morskie)★★ D3
Ul. Ołowianka 9/13 - ℘ 301 86 11 - www. cmm.pl - Sep-18 Jun Tue-Sun 10am-4pm, 19 Jun-Aug 10am-6pm - 6 PLN (Granary) - 6 PLN (Sołdek Museum Ship) - 14 PLN (pass + ferry 2 PLN). The entrance is not easy to find; walk round the building to the right. Comprehensive informative booklets in English are available in each room. Tawerna Marina, a modest restaurant-cafeteria, enables visitors to have a snack on the premises. Allow at least two hours even for a selective visit.

This museum is in several sections. The main one is housed in the three former wheat granaries rebuilt on Lead Island. It also comprises a tour of the *Sołdek* moored to the quay in front of the granaries. On the town side, there is another building linked to the wooden crane.

III-Gotten Possessions Sometimes Bring Profit

The Altarpiece of the Last Judgement, the famous jewel by the master of Bruges, had a very troubled history. Commissioned by Angelo Tani (seen on the back with his wife Catherine), the Medici's banker in Bruges, to decorate a church in his native Florence, the work was intercepted while travelling through England owing to the blockade of English ports by Hanseatic towns. Brought to Gdańsk, the triptych was offered to St Mary's Church. The town staunchly refused to sell it to Emperor Rodolphus II or to give it to Tsar Peter the Great who asked for it as an "extra" contribution from the town. Napoleon, less scrupulous, asked Vivant Denon to take it back to Paris in 1807. Transferred from the Louvre to Berlin after Waterloo, it was sent back to Danzig in 1817 later to be seized by the Nazis. Recovered by the Russians it went to Leningrad before being returned to Poland in 1956 and placed... not in the church where it was originally but, under pressure from the communist authorities, in the National Museum.

The island's granaries – The collections, displayed on several floors, illustrate river and harbour traffic in Gdańsk as well as seafaring along the Baltic coast from the origins to the present through paintings, documents, engravings, scale models and objects. The long succession of rooms offers an exhaustive account of all the aspects of maritime life, from the naval battle against the Swedes, that took place in the Bay of Gdańsk on 28 November 1627 and is known as the Battle of Oliwa, to the great discoveries, Polish emigration or famous travellers, one area being devoted to the young sailor of Polish origin, Józef Korzeniowski, better known under his name as an English writer, Joseph Conrad.

Sołdek Museum Ship – The visit continues with a thorough, signposted tour of the first ship to come out of the town's shipyards in 1948, named after her first captain, Stanisław Sołdek. For the Poles, this ship embodies their regained self-esteem and remains a symbol of national independence.

The visit ends with the ferry crossing of the Motława to the annexe of the museum partly located inside the medieval crane.

Museum annexe and wooden crane – Inside the annexe, one room in particular is devoted to traditional boats from all over the world; as for the crane, it was partly turned into a dwelling in the 17C and now houses several reconstructed scenes with dummies, illustrating traditional trades and crafts connected with the sea and fishing. The crane's lifting gear is also on show.

Westerplatte★ PLAN I B3

7km north of the historic town. Accessible by shuttle boat from Gdańsk's Long Quay. The ticket office is located near the bridge, beyond the Green Gate, set back from the lowered quay. 50min one way to Westerplatte (26 PLN), 1hr 40min for the full tour (39 PLN). The landing-stage is situated between the monument and the fortress. From the central station, the journey by bus no 106 takes visitors through an area of plots of land cultivated by the workers.

Situated north-east of the town, mainly to the east of the Wisła estuary, the **shipyards** cover a considerable area. It is possible to visit them, but one already gets a good glimpse of them during the boat trip to Westerplatte, at the eastern extremity of the harbour canal. A town within the town, this fascinating area, where everything seems to be rusting away, gives the paradoxical impression of being both abandoned and full of activity. The uninterrupted succession of large sheds and warehouses, all extremely dilapidated, and the forest of huge cranes standing out against the sky like ghostly figures, create an awe-inspiring scene.

Monument to the Defenders of Westerplatte B2

Take the opportunity to breathe the invigorating Baltic air by going to this narrow peninsula where the Nazis began the first hostilities of a world conflict which set Europe ablaze for over five years. On 1 September 1939 at 4.47 in the morning, the battleship *Schleswig-Hollstein* opened fire on the Polish garrison guarding the military transport depot created on this site in 1924 by decision of the League of Nations. In spite of the obvious disproportion between the opposing forces and their respective military equipment, the 182 soldiers led by major Henryk Sucharski only surrendered on 7 September after putting up a fierce resistance (which commanded the Germans' admiration and earned their heroic leader military honours during the surrender ceremony as well as the privilege of keeping his sword in prison). On 21 September, Hitler himself inspected the place where over 300 of his soldiers had died against just 15 Poles. One of the shelled buildings remains as it was then for memory's sake and a tiny **museum**, housed inside the former Guardhouse no 1, to the left of the car park, recalls (in Polish) these terrible times *(1 May-14 Jun 9am-4pm, 15 Jun-Sep 9am-7pm – 3 PLN)*.

In order to commemorate this event symbolizing Polish resistance, a 25m high mono-lithic **monument**, representing the hilt of a sword planted in the ground, was erected in 1968 at the top of a 22.5m high artificial mound. Pope John Paul II celebrated mass there on 12 June 1987. Facing it on the opposite bank is the **lighthouse** (*latarnia morska*) of the **Nowy Port** (New Harbour) district. Built in 1893 and rising to a height of 90m, it has been reopened to the public *(May-Sep daily 10am-7pm)*.

Wisłoujście Fortress (Twierdza Wisłoujście)★★ B3

Designed to guard the entrance to the Wisła estuary (and at the same time to the whole of Poland!), which ships had to negotiate in order to reach the port of Gdańsk on the Motława, this fine fortress surrounded by water originally consisted of a Gothic lighthouse-tower (1482); in 1572, it was surrounded by a fort reinforced by bastions which was itself remodelled by Anton van Obberghen between 1584 and 1587. At that time, the sea was very close and now, although it looks fairly close from the Westerplatte landing-stage, it is a good twenty minutes' walk along the road *(bus no 106 stops near the junction where the path leading to it branches off)*. Abandoned for many years to the ravages of time, this ensemble is undergoing a thorough restoration which should last another few years. Note that the site looks good on film on account of the 17C barracks surrounding the tower.

Oliwa★★ PLAN I A3

Oliwa is accessible by tramway (no 6 and no 12; get off where the track runs round a roundabout) and by SKM regional train (get off at the Gdańsk Oliwa station and take the passageway on the left. As you come out of the station, take the 1st right then the

1st left. Cross a large avenue and walk to the right). There is no tourist office and what is supposed to be an information office, opposite the cathedral, is in fact a shop selling amber souvenirs.

This peaceful district next to Sopot, at the foot of the wooded Pachołek hill, 5km north-west of Gdańsk, is famous for its park, featuring a formal French garden in the south-west and an English-style park in the north, and adjoining a former Cistercian abbey which became a cathedral in 1925, when it was incorporated into the city of Gdańsk. Walk to the east entrance of the **Oliwski Park★** *(open 5am-6pm/8pm/11pm according to the season)* and follow a small tree-lined canal until you reach a pool (main gate) then bear right towards the Abbot's Palace and the cathedral.

Abbot's Palace (Pałac Opatów)★ A2

Ul. Cystersów 15a - ℘ 552 12 71 - Tue-Fri 9am-4pm - 9 PLN - free on Tue - last admission 45min before closing.

This fine Baroque edifice built in 1754-56 now houses the much ignored but restful **Department of Contemporary Art** (Oddział Sztuki Współczesnej)★, an annexe of Gdańsk's National Museum which offers a fine overview of 20C Polish art. Several fine rooms in succession, decorated in pure white, contain around 300 modern and contemporary paintings ranging from figurative works displayed in the first rooms to works of pure abstraction and cinetic art shown in the rooms situated in the eastern wing (remodelled Gothic). One room is entirely devoted to Henryk Starzewski (1894-1988), one of the leading figures of the Blok movement. Also worth seeing, at least out of curiosity, are two works by Tadeusz Kantor, when he was still painting.

Nearby, the former granary of the Abbey (Spichlerz Opacki) accommodates the **Ethnographic Museum** (Muzeum Etnograficzne), *Ul. Cystersów 19 - May-Sep Tue-Fri 9am-4pm, Sat-Sun 10am-5pm, Oct-Apr 9am-4pm - 5 PLN - free on Sat.* This other annexe of the National Museum houses an exhibition devoted to popular art of Low Powiśle and Kashubia.

Walk along the wall of the cloister to the cathedral entrance, next to the park.

Oliwa Cathedral (Katedra Oliwska)★★ A2

A troubled history and many modifications –Invited in 1186 by Sanbor I, Duke of Pomerania, Danish Cistercian monks settled here and founded their abbey in 1188. Erected in the 13C, over a previous brick-built sanctuary dating from 1200, the three-nave basilica was rebuilt in Gothic style after the 1350 fire. Next it was burned down by Prussian pagans then again, on four occasions, by the Teutonic Knights and finally in 1577 by Gdańsk's Protestant population, in retaliation for the support given by the abbots to King Stefan Batory who wanted to curb the town's independence. In the end, the king forced them to pay for its reconstruction which was completed in 1582. In 1626, the Swedes wrecked the church once more but in 1660 the **Treaty of Oliwa** was signed inside. It had its heyday in the 18C, under the authority of the last Polish abbot, Jacek Rybiński, acquiring a magnificent organ and the Abbot's Palace. Between the 16C and the 19C, many industrial ins-tallations grew around it (powder mills, fulling mills, paper mills, ironworks, sawmills). In 1831, the Cistercian abbey was definitively abolished by the king of Prussia. The church became a cathedral in 1925 and came through the Second World War relatively unscathed.

Interior – Bright and white with a long narrow nave and an extended chancel, the edifice is one of the three longest churches in Poland (107m). The undisputed jewel of the church is the magnificent dark-wood **organ★★★**, elaborately carved and framing a stained-glass window representing the Virgin and Child. Designed on the initiative of the Abbot Józef Rybiński, it was made by a Cistercian monk, Jan Wulf of Orneta, who, during 25 years from 1763 to 1788, worked on his project which was completed by organ master Friedrich R

Oliwa Cathedral

ONT Pologne

Dalitz in 1791-93. The sumptuous wood decoration was carved in a local workshop run by the monks Alanus and Joseph Gross. The church is often crowded, particularly on Sundays, when the renowned demonstrations of the amazing instrument take place *(weekdays at 11am and noon, Sundays at 3 and 4pm. It is advisable to arrive early as the doors are closed during the demonstration)*. The nuns ask visitors to stand up and invite them to say a paternoster before the beginning of the programme which includes a choice of varied music. The 101 registers of the instrument allow amazing sounds in both quality and power to come out of the 7 876 pipes.

The chancel boasts a **Baroque high altar★** (1688) featuring an impressive black-marble colonnade in striking contrast with the white-stucco vaulting which suggests a cloudy sky dotted with some 150 angels' heads. The delicately carved former **Renaissance high altar★** (1606) of the Holy Trinity was moved to the north transept. Note, on the opposite side, the unadorned black-marble **sarcophagus** of the Dukes of Pomerania (1615). Fine 17C **stalls★** and superb 18C **pulpit★**, decorated with scenes of the life of St Bernard, at the beginning of the chancel. The ambulatory contains

> ## The Treaty of Oliwa
>
> The name of Oliwa was recorded in History on account of the *Treaty of Oliwa* signed in 1660, between Poland, Prussia and Sweden. This treaty put an end to the frightful Swedish invasion known as *"the Deluge"*; in addition, John II Kazimierz of Poland lost Livonia and gave up his suzerainty over eastern Prussia.

the altar of the Four Evangelists and the altar of St Peter and St Paul, both adorned with 17C paintings by Hermann Han. Elegant 17C and 18C funeral stelae furnish the vaulted north aisle. Before leaving, take a look, on the south side, at the unusual funeral monument (1620) of the Kos family.

It is possible to prolong a tour of Oliwa by going northwards to the well-kept, flower-decked cemetery, always brightly lit with a thousand candles, or eastwards in the direction of the **Valley of Joy** (Dolina Radości), towards the former hydraulic forge and the **zoo**.

Sopot PLAN 1 A2

(Population 41 410)

Sopot, situated 12km north of Gdańsk's historic centre, is accessible by train from platforms 3-6 of the SKM regional network station. Trains every 10min, journey time 25min, 9th stop (Sopot) from Gdańsk Główny.

Wedged between the two large towns of Gdańsk and Gdynia on the one hand and between the sea and the wooded escarpment of the cliff on the other, Sopot boasts no special monument in spite of the fact that it is the country's poshest seaside resort. **The "Polish Deauville", created by a native of Alsace** – Given in the 13C to the monks of the Cistercian abbey of Oliwa, this former fishing village owed its real expansion to an Alsatian, Georges Haffner, a former surgeon in Napoleon's army, who settled there, had the first baths built in 1823 and the hydrotherapy establishment the following year. Despite its growing success, Sopot only obtained its urban charter in 1901 and, after the First World War, it was included within the limits of the free city of Gdańsk. It was soon the favourite destination of wealthy world travellers and had its heyday in the interwar period (thanks, in particular, to its casino founded in 1920) before becoming an ordinary Polish town once more in 1945. Today, it is a sought-after holiday destination, offering visitors a particularly pleasant atmosphere in striking contrast to the urban and densely historic feel of its imposing neighbour. As the day draws to an end, it becomes the paradise of night-time revellers and of all those who are looking for alternative restaurants and trendy bars. Although the equivalent of the Deauville film festival takes place next door in Gdynia, the nickname of "Polish Deauville" suits Sopot rather well.

Exploring Sopot

Walk down **Monte Cassino** Street, a pedestrian mall which owes its name to the battle and is called Monciak. It leads from the railway line to the beach. You can't miss the **façade of no 53** *(Rezydent)* looking as if it were facing a distorting mirror, even if the interior houses a score of uninspiring cafés. At the very end, beyond Zdrojowy Square, you will come to the wooden **pier★** *(molo)* which is the main attraction along the seafront *(Oct-Apri Mon-Fri 2.50 PLN; Sat-Sun and May-Sep Mon-Fri 3.70 PLN)*. Presented as Poland's longest pier, this 511m-long promenade will give you the impression of walking over the sea over a distance of at least 450m. The first 41m-long jetty built by Haffner was lengthened by 22m in 1842. Extended to 94m in 1882, it reached its present length in 1925, on the occasion of the 25th anniversary of the town's foundation.

The fine-sand **beach** stretches on both sides. Near the beginning of the pier, it is possible to climb inside a **viewpoint-lighthouse** *(2.50 PLN)* to get a bird's-eye view of the surrounding area.

To the north, one can see the massive outline of the **Grand Hotel** where Hitler stayed in September 1939 while his troops were rushing towards Warsaw.

Walk along the promenade which skirts the beach and extends southwards to Gdańsk's Brzeźno district; this will lead you to **Sopot Museum** *(Muzeum Sopotu. Ul. Poniatowskiego 8ńń- ✆ 551 22 66 - Tue-Fri 9am-4pm, Sat-Sun 11am-5pm - 5 PLN)*. Housed in a fine villa dating from 1903, the small museum is devoted to middle-class interiors and hosts temporary exhibitions. Series of fine photographs of prewar Sopot in the staircase. On the ground floor, there is a pleasant small café-restaurant.

If the beach is too hot, you can always walk in the opposite direction towards the forest, on the heights of the town, offering some fine rambles. Built in 1909 and modernised in the early 1960s, the **open-air opera** *(Opera Leśna / Ul. Moniuszki 12)* is an amphitheatre with some 5 000 seats nestling in the heart of the forest and protected by an impressive folding roof. In summer, it hosts a famous international song festival. A ski-lift takes visitors to the summit of the Bare Mountain (Łysa Góra), the highest point in the surrounding area.

HOTELS
Hotel Orbis Grand.. ①
Hotel Villa Sedan.... ②
Hotel Zhong Hua.... ③
Pensjonat Irena...... ④

RESTAURANTS
Bar Przystań............. ①
Klub Wieloryb......... ②

Gdynia A1
(Population 253 508)

Gdynia, situated 12km north of Gdańsk's historic centre, is accessible by train from platforms 3-6 of the SKM regional network station. Trains every 10min, journey time 40min, 14th stop (Gdynia Główna Osobowa) from Gdańsk Główny. There is a tourist office inside the station (at the end of the corridor on the left, Mon-Fri 10am-5pm, Sat 10am-3pm) and another one standing like a lookout at the end of the jetty on the right (May-Aug Mon-Fri 9am-6pm, Sat 10am-5pm, Sun 10am-4pm).

This is the youngest member of the three sister cities in the Trójmiasto, an ambitious town which goes on expanding and attracting many investments. It could, at first, appear less welcoming and convivial than its two older sisters; in fact, although it has fewer sights, it offers more entertainment thanks to its numerous cafés and restaurants and to its fine boutiques where Gdańsk's inhabitants like to shop. On Sundays, this harbour city attracts families who come for a stroll along the quays.

Access to the sea – Built on the site of a Kashubian fishing village founded in the 13C, this new town symbolizes the effort made by the Poles to regain their lost access to the sea. At the end of the First World War, when Sopot and Gdańsk again formed a free town, the new independent Republic of Poland needed a worthwhile harbour along the 72km-long strip of land allotted to the country. In 1921, the engineer, Tadeusz Wenda undertook the phenomenal construction of the harbour and, in August 1923, the first ship to enter the port was the *Kentucky* flying the French flag (the French had invested in the building of the harbour).

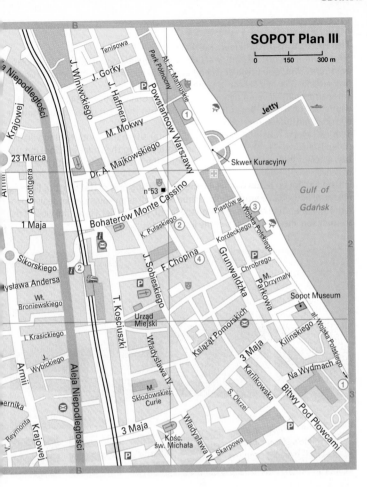

SOPOT Plan III

0   150   300 m

In 1934, it was already the largest and most modern port in the Baltic. Following the spectacular development of the city, its population, which consisted of 1 268 inhabitants in 1921, topped the 127 000 mark in 1939, when the Germans annexed the town and renamed it Gothafen. Severely damaged during the Second World War, the harbour was rebuilt and modernised and, today, Gdynia is Poland's main commercial port.

Exploring Gdynia

There are no beaches and Gdynia's main tourist attractions are located around Kościuszko Garden (Skwer Kościuszki) prolonged by a very wide pier. Two **museum ships** are moored along the north quay, the *Błyskawica* (Lightning), a destroyer built in 1937, and the three-masted frigate *Dar Pomorza* (Gift from Pomerania); they can be visited year-round. The latter, once used as a training ship, was replaced by the *Dar Młodzieży* (Gift of Youth) also moored nearby. Two commemorative monuments stand at the end of the jetty, a metal one known as the *Gra Masztów* (Play of Masts), and a stone one dedicated to the writer of Polish origin, Józef Teodor Konrad Nałęcz Korzeniowski, better known as Joseph Conrad.

On the south side near the end of the pier stands the **Oceanographic Museum and Aquarium** *(Muzeum Oceanograficzne i Akwarium Morskie - daily 9am-4.30pm - closed 1 Jan, Easter Sun, 1 Nov, 24-25 and 31 Dec - 12 PLN)*, not the most modern museum in the world, but interesting enough for those who love watching a selection of sealife swimming round a tank.

To the south-west of the pier, the **Stone Mountain** (Kamienna Góra), rising to a height of 52.40m, is the area's culminating point, from which one can see the full extent of the harbour and the coastal strip formed by the Hel Peninsula. Beneath is the **Naval Museum** (Muzeum Marynarki Wojennej) largely devoted to military armament.

Nearby

The Hel Peninsula (Mierzeja Helska)★

60km north of Gdańsk, 32km north of Gdynia. The small fishing port of Hel is accessible by train from Gdynia (fairly regular service), but also by boat from Gdańsk, Sopot or Gdynia between mid-May and the end of September.

This narrow pine-covered peninsula, closing off Gdańsk's Bay, is 34km long with a width varying from 200m at the base to 2.9km at the tip. It is particularly sought after by windsurfers.

Seaside resorts (Chałupy, Kuźnica and Jurata) alternating with fishing villages (Władysławowo, Jastarnia and Hel) are dotted along the shore overlooking the bay, whereas the north shore, turned towards the open sea, is lined with fine sandy beaches.

Situated at the tip of the peninsula, the small fishing port of **Hel** boasts a **Fishing Museum** housed in a former Gothic church as well as an aquarium for seals (Foka-rium) and offers fine rambles through the forest; you can get a beautiful view of the surrounding area from the top of the lighthouse.

Sopot beach and the Orbis Grand Hotel

Practical Gdańsk

Postal code – 80-000 to 80-900 (Gdańsk)
81-700 to 81-900 (Sopot)
81-300 to 81- 600 (Gdynia)

Phone code – (0)58

Useful addresses

IN GDAŃSK

www.trojmiasto.pl

Tourist Offices

Gdańska Informacja Turystyczna PTTK. *Ul. Długa 45* - ✆/fax *301 91 50* - *it@pttk-Gdańsk.pl* - *www.pttk-Gdańsk.pl* - *May-Aug Mon-Fri 9am-5pm, Sat-Sun 9am-3pm, Sep-Apr Mon-Fri 9am-5pm.* Opposite the Town Hall of the Main Town. The staff speaks English and some literature is available in English. Central reservation service for finding accommodation in private rooms: the office provides addresses and charges 5 PLN for booking. Sale of maps, books, guides, bus and ferry tickets.

Pomorska Regionalna Organizacja Turystyczna. Punkt IT. *Galeria Handlowa «Madison». Ul. Rajska 10* - ✆/fax *766 74 66* - *info@prot.gda.pl* - *www.pot.gov.pl* - *www.prot.pomorskie.info* - *Mon-Sat 9am-9pm, Sun 10am-9pm.* Turn right as you enter the "Madison" Gallery. Narrow office bearing the sign "Tourism Information" and including a bureau de change. Supposed to provide information about Pomerania, but the information available is incomplete.

Pomorze Gdańskie Tourist Association. *Ul. Heweliusza 27* - ✆ *301 43 55 fax 301 66 37* - *itGdańsk@op.pl* - *Mon-Fri 9am-4pm.* At the end of the street where Hotel Mercure Hevelius is situated. Has an annexe in a green kiosk located opposite the main station (take the subway and come up on the central island). *Ul. Podwale Grodzkie* - *Mon-Fri 8am-4pm, Sat-Sun 10am-2pm.*

Centrum Kultury Gdańsk. *Ul. Korzenna 33/35* - ✆ *301 10 51* - *www.nck.org.pl* - *daily 10am-6pm.* Here is your opportunity to visit the former Town Hall of the Old Town which stages free exhibitions and concerts. Pleasant café in the entrance hall. Bookshop.

Useful tips. The fortnightly brochure in English *Gdańsk inyourpocket* (5 PLN) is an excellent handbook to carry around, as is the *Tricity Guide*, published in English in 2004. The free monthly brochure *Poland What Where When* also provides a wealth of information about Gdańsk and Sopot.

Post Office – *Urząd Pocztowy. Ul Długa 22/26* - *Mon-Fri 8am-8pm, Sat 9am-3pm.* A fine 19C building. Telephone exchange on the right of the entrance. Annexe inside the building of the Postal Museum.

Guides Office – For information, contact the Tourist Office in Długa Street or the PTTK Regional Division - *Ul. Zakopiańska 40* - ✆/fax *301 48 18.*

Police – ✆ 997 ou 321 62 22 - Police station: *Ul. Piwna 32/35* - ✆ *301 09 42.*

Emergency – ✆ *999*

Municipal police – ✆ *986*

Fire brigade – ✆ *998*

Pharmacy open 24hr/day – *Apteka Plus* - *Dworzec Główny (central station)* - ✆ *346 25 40.*

Hospitals – *Szpital Wojewódzki* - *Ul. Nowe Ogrody 1/6* - ✆ *302 30 31.*

Medicover - *Ul. Beniowskiego 23* - ✆ *557 55 55.*

Internet – *Jazz'n'Java Internet Cafe. Ul. Tkacka 17/18* - ✆/fax *305 36 16* - *daily 10am-10pm - 10 min/1 PLN, 30 min/3 PLN, 1hr/5PLN.* Almost on the corner of Długa Street towards the Upland Gate.

Internet Café (Krewetka). Śródmieście - ✆ *320 92 30* - *Mon-Sat 9am-1am, Sun 9.30am-1am.* On the left-hand side of the ground floor of the Krewetka Cinema, opposite the station.

Banks – A *kantor* is open 24hr/day inside the central station.

IN SOPOT

Tourist Office (Informacja Turystyczna Sopot IT) – *Ul. Dworcowa 4* - ✆ *550 37 83 fax 555 12 27* - *it@sopot.pl* - *www.sopot.pl* - *Jun-Sep daily 9am-8pm, Oct-May daily 10am-6pm.* On the left as you leave the station, behind the Rezydent Hotel as you go up Monte Cassino Street. Deals with accommodation in private rooms. A second office, situated along the main road to Gdynia, is specially intended for motorists.

PTTK. Ul. Niepodległości 771 - ✆/fax *551 06 18* - *pttk@sopot.pl* - *Mon-Fri 9am-5pm, Sat 10am-3pm.*

Post Office – *Ul. Kościuszki 2 (Sopot)* - *www.poczta-polska.pl*

Pharmacy open 24hr/day – *Apteka «Pod Orłem»* - *Ul. Boh. Monte Cassino 37* - ✆ *551 10 18.*

IN GDYNIA

Tourist Office (Miejska Informacja Turystyczna IT Gdynia) – *Plac Konstytucji 1* ✆/fax *628 54 66 it@gdynia.pl* - *www.gdynia.pl/it* - *Mon-Fri 10am-5pm, Sat 10am-3pm* - In the hall of Gdynia Główna railway station. At the end of the left-hand corridor on the way out. Boutique with Internet access next door.

Baltic Tourist Information Centre (Bałtycki Punkt Informacji Turystycznej) – *Al. Zjednoczenia* - *t/fax 620 77 11* - *bpit@gdynia.pl* - *May-Aug Mon-Fri 10am-6pm, Sat 10am-5pm, Sun 10am-4pm.* A real lookout at the extremity of the long pier, on the right, beyond the aquarium.

Where to go

A combined ticket makes it possible, for 16 PLN (concessions 8 PLN), to visit the

Ratusz, the Dom Uphagena and the Dwór Artusa. Information from the ticket offices of these monuments.

Getting around

Airport – **Lech Wałęsa Gdańsk-Trójmiasto Airport** - *Ul. Słowakiego 200 - Rębiechowo* - ☎ *93 16 (24hr)* or *348 11 11* - *www.airport.Gdańsk.pl*. 10km west of the centre. Flights to and from Warsaw, London, Hamburg, Copenhagen, Frankfurt and Munich. B bus to central station or no 110 bus to Gdańsk Wrzeszcz Station.

Railway stations – **Gdańsk Główny Central Station** is a 10min walk from the town centre. Kolejowa PKP (*Ul. Podwale Grodzkie 1* - ☎ *94 36 / 301 11 12*). The SKM Regional Network Station (towards Sopot and Gdynia) is situated next door (accessible via the subway). Trains every 10min from platforms no 3-6.

Bus station – PKS (*Ul. 3 Maja 12* - ☎ *302 15 32*. Behind the railway station via the subway.

Car hire – **Avis** (☎ 348 12 89), **Budget** (☎ /fax 348 12 98 - www.budget.pl) and **Hertz** have a counter at the airport (*Ul. Słowackiego 200*).

Avis – *Ul. Podwale Grodzkie 9* - ☎ *300 60 05* - *www.avis.pl* - 8.30am-6pm, Sat 9am-5pm.

Hertz –*Ul. Brygidki 14b* - ☎ *301 40 45* - *fax 346 26 64* - www.hertz.com.pl - Mon-Fri 8am-5pm, Sat 10am-2pm.

Harbour station – The ferry landing stage is in Nowy Port (*Ul. Przemysłowa 1* - ☎ *343 00 78*), 7km north of the town centre. Access by train from Gdańsk Glowny Station , get off at Gdańsk-Brzeźno. The main shipping lines are:

Polferries. *Ul. Portowa 3 (Gdynia)* - ☎ *620 87 61* - www.polferries.pl

Stena Line. *Ul. Kwiatkowskiego 60 (Gdynia)* - ☎ *665 14 14* - www.stenaline.pl

Żegluga Gdańska. *Ul. Pończosników 2* - ☎ *301 63 35* - www.zegluga.pl

This ferry line has, since 1946, been providing a shuttle service to Westerplatte, Sopot, Gdynia and Hel. The ticket office is located near the bridge, beyond the Green Gate, set back from the lowered quay. 50min one way to Westerplatte, 1hr 40min for the full tour.

Where to stay

IN GDAŃSK

Private rooms

Grand-Tourist – *Ul. Podwale Grodzkie 8* - ☎ 301 17 27 fax 301 63 01 - kwatery@gt.com.pl - www.grand-tourist.pl - Mon-Fri 10am-6pm, Sat 10am-4pm (Jul-Aug daily 8am-8pm) - 💳. Situated in the basement of the City Forum, the shopping mall of the Holiday Inn Hotel. From the station, take the subway then turn right as you come out. Yellow sign and sliding door. This agency centralises private-room

accommodation offers in the town centre. It has a stock of some fifty rooms (100 PLN in the centre, 80 at the periphery) and around thirty apartments (1 room + kitchen + bathroom = 180 PLN). No breakfast. Cash payments to be made at the office which has the keys. English spoken.

Hotels

Almatur – *Ul. Długi Targ 11* - ☎ *301 24 03 fax 301 78 18* - www.almatur.gda.pl - *Mon-Fri 10am-5pm (Jun-Aug 6pm), Sat 10am-2pm*. This student travel agency deals with accommodation in university hostels during the months of June, July, August and September: about 10 sites in all, particularly near the University of Technology, situated between Gdańsk Politechnika and Gdańsk Wrzeszcz railway stations. For those who enjoy a Bohemian lifestyle, the agency also offers a few more centrally located rooms in the Fine Arts Academy Student Hostel, situated in the imposing English House, the largest mansion in Old Gdańsk.

Youth Hostel – *Ul. Wałowa 21* - ☎/fax *301 23 13* - biuro@mokf.com.pl - www.mokf.com.pl - *96 beds* - *70 PLN*. Located deep inside a small park, on the edge of the Old Town, not far from the shipyard's entrance, the most central of the three permanent youth hostels in town has rooms suitable for 1 to 10 persons. 17.50 PLN in a dormitory and 35 PLN per person in a double room.

Youth Hostel – *Grunwaldzka 244* - ☎ *341 41 08* - biuro@mokf.com.pl - *198 beds* - *102 PLN* - 💳. Inaugurated in 1997, the largest and most functional youth hostel in Poland, combined with a sports complex, is situated 6km north of the town centre, between the districts of Wrzeszcz and Oliwa. Easily accessible by train (Gdańsk Zaspa) or by trams no 6 and 12 tramways. Double rooms or rooms with four beds, plain but comfortable.

Baltic Hostel – *Ul. 3 Maja 25* - ☎ *721 96 57* - baltichostel@hotmail.com - www.baltichostel.com - 💳 - *6 rooms* - *90 PLN*. This annexe of the Gdańsk Hostel is located in the middle of a huge red-brick collective housing complex standing behind the central station (entrance on the bridge side). The rather dilapidated staircase contrasts with the brand new interior, pleasantly decorated with bright colours. This guesthouse, which is more suitable for young people, offers rooms with 3/4 to 6 beds (45 PLN per pers) and dormitories (35 PLN) with communal bathrooms.

Gdańsk Hostel – *Ul. Grodzka 21* - ☎ *301 56 27* - Gdańskhostel@hotmail.com - www.Gdańskhostel.com - 🅿 - 💳 - *6 rooms* - *120 PLN*. Well situated near the Old Fishmarket Square, this youth hostel offers a few rooms pleasantly decorated with vivid colours, most of them with a shared bath, as well as two mixed dormitories (40

PLN). The convivial manager is full of good advice. Bike and kayak rental. Laundry service, Internet access, free coffee and tea.

Pensjonat Dom Aktora – *Ul. Straganiarska 55/56 -* ☎ *301 61 93 - fax 301 59 01 - biuro@domaktora.pl - www. domaktora.pl - 12 rooms - 280 PLN -* ☐. An exclusively female staff, speaking German rather than English, runs this convivial guesthouse well situated north of the Old Town, in a small modern twin-gabled building. Fairly spacious rooms and fully equipped apartments for 2 to 4 persons costing between 350 and 500 PLN. Reception desk open 8am-10pm.

Hotel Królewski – *Ul. Ołowianka 1 -* ☎ *326 11 11 fax 326 11 10 - office@ hotelkrolewski - www.hotelkrolewski.pl - 30 rooms - 340 PLN -* ☐. Discreet establishment with a fine but austere façade featuring characteristic windows; one of the rare 17C royal granaries still standing on Lead Island; restored in 2003 to house this handsome four-storey hotel. For the same price, you can have a room – they all boast the same green-and-yellow colour scheme – overlooking the quayside. Fine suites at the top of the building. Dining room service from 7 to 9pm.

Hotel Mercure Hevelius – *Ul. Jana Heweliusza 22 -* ☎ *321 00 00 fax 321 00 20 - mer.hevelius@orbis.pl - www.mercure.pl -* ☐ *- 281 rooms - 470 PLN -* ☐. This unusual 17-storey building erected on the edge of the Old Town is the headquarters of many groups of tourists; entirely renovated in 2000 when it was taken over by the Accor chain, it features spacious rooms with all the usual comforts and exceptional views of the Old Town on one side and of the shipyards on the other.

Hotel Podewils – *Ul. Szafarnia 2 -* ☎ *300 95 60 fax 300 95 70 - Gdańsk@podewils-hotel.pl - www.podewils.pl - 10 rooms - 725 PLN* ☐. This small 5-star hotel, housed in one of the rare 18C buildings still standing, occupies a magnificent location opposite the famous crane, across the River Motława, and near the marina. A bell-boy stands in front of the Baroque door surmounted by a shield. Classic decor in the rooms. Discounts for last-minute bookings. Expensive but charming restaurant with peaceful terrace at the back.

IN SOPOT

Pensjonat Irena – *Ul. Chopina 36 -* ☎ *551 20 73 fax 551 34 90 - biuro@pensjonat-irena.gda.pl - www.pensjonat-irena.gda.pl - 16 rooms - 240 PLN -* ☐. Note the discreet charm of this guesthouse occupying a large seaside villa on four levels and offering good value for money. Rooms on two floors round a vast entrance hall. Small yet with high ceilings, they are all decorated with the same golden beige wallpaper. Very pleasant dining room for

lunch only *(50 PLN – daily 8am-5pm)* where time seems to have stopped in 1925, and splendid Karczma pub on the ground floor: an amazing restaurant serving traditional Polish cuisine *(daily 1pm-midnight)* from the reign of King Jan III Sobieski.

Villa Sedan Hotel – *Ul. Pułaskiego 18-20 -* ☎ *555 09 80 fax 551 06 17 - sedan@sedan. pl - www.sedan.pl -* ☐ *- 21 rooms - 295 PLN -* ☐. Housed in a fine turn-of-the-century villa, this peaceful hotel offers pleasant, comfortable rooms that won't disappoint you. Discounts at weekends except in July and August. Bright restaurant in restful setting *(70 PLN – daily 11am-11pm)*.

Orbis Grand Hotel – *Ul. Powstańców Warszawy 12/14 -* ☎ *551 00 41 fax 551 61 24 - sogrand@orbis.pl - www.orbis.pl - 113 rooms - 450 PLN -* ☐. This huge Art Nouveau building erected in 1924-27 looks quite impressive both on the street side, with its colossal double ramp for cars, and on the beach side. Vast corridors lead, on either side of the elegant central cupola, to bright, high-ceilinged rooms. Rooms with a view of the Baltic are more expensive *(550 to 650 PLN)*... a luxury that Hitler allowed himself in September 1939. Elegant dining room facing the sea.

Hotel Zhong Hua. *Al. Wojska Polskiego 1 -* ☎ *550 20 20 fax 551 72 75 - www. zhonghua.com.pl - 49 rooms - 440 PLN-* ☐. Situated by the beach in former baths transformed into pagodas, this hotel offers classic rooms as well as apartments with private terraces right on the beach. Bike rental (5 PLN/hr or 25 PLN/day). The north wing houses a restaurant – highly recommended and sought after by Polish people – boasting an oriental-style decor, which has the great advantage of facing the sea. The serving staff is Polish as is the kitchen staff apparently and the result is a selection of tasty and copious Chinese-style dishes *(1-11pm – 60 PLN)*.

Eating out

It seems that, even when it comes to gastronomy and entertainment, Gdańsk and Sopot have cleverly agreed on their respective roles. After trying out Gdańsk's classic restaurants, you could try Sopot's more trendy restaurants and attractive cafés. Note also that all Sopot's hotels mentioned above have restaurants worth trying.

IN GDAŃSK

Bar Mleczno-Turystyczny Wiesłana Zwierzycka – *Ul. Szeroka 8/10 - Mon-Fri 8am-6pm, Sat-Sun 9am-4pm -* ☒ *- 15 PLN.* The Poles flock to this providential establishment where it is possible to eat for a moderate price. Canary-yellow, budgie-green surroundings in this authentic "milk bar" – they were run as subsidised cafeterias under the former communist regime – give it the nostalgic feel of days past.

Bar Mleczny Neptun – *Ul. Długa 33/34 - Mon-Fri 7.30am-6pm, Sat-Sun 9am-5pm - ⊠ - 15 PLN*. Milk bar known to everyone and, what's more, superbly located on the most prestigious avenue in town. Perfect for a quick lunch: express menu of Polish family-style cooking. Dining room upstairs.

Złota Rybka – *Ul. Piwna 50/51 - ℘ 301 39 24 - Sun-Thu 11am-10pm, Fri-Sat 11am-midnight - 35 PLN*. Situated on the ground floor of the Klub Yesterday (which makes it possible for party animals to have a snack at the beginning of the evening), this small snack bar boasts a convivial atmosphere in pleasant surroundings; note in particular the mezzanine with its ceiling lined with sea shells. The walls are decorated with local stars' autographs accompanied by their comments about the "Gold Fish".

Restauracja Kubicki – *Ul. Wartka 5 - ℘ 301 00 50 - daily noon-10pm (midnight in summer) - ⊠ - 60 PLN*. This quayside restaurant, the oldest in town, boasts continuous activity since 1918. Hushed atmosphere in this large room where crimson and gold are the predominant colours and where time seems to have stopped; there are two smaller rooms on the side, decorated in a refreshing apple green. The background music is regrettably superfluous. Basic traditional cuisine fortunately less expensive than the refined decor might imply. Don't go there too late; off season at 9.30pm.

Turbot Restauracja – *Ul. Korzenna 33/35 - ℘ 307 51 48 - daily noon-last customers - 70 PLN*. Stairs on the right of the former Town Hall of the Old Town lead straight into the Turbot, a pleasant restaurant situated in a cellar. The easygoing, polyglot owner is the president of the Association of the Friends of Günter Grass, whom he unmistakably imitates. Naturally, flounder is featured on the menu in this restaurant, named for the eponymous novel in which men who make history are in fact under the control of women's art of cooking. Why not start a literary discussion while savouring one of the famous potatoes grown in the bay of the Wisła.

Dom Pod Łososiem – *Ul. Szeroka 52/54 - ℘ 301 56 48 - daily noon-midnight - 100 PLN*. The "Salmon" restaurant, which claims to have been opened in 1598, undoubtedly deserves to rank among the most elegant restaurants in town. Destroyed during the war, it only reopened in 1976. The speciality of the house is a mouth-watering roast duck with a crisp skin...Why not try the other local speciality: goldwasse, a sweet drink made from herbs and... 22-carat gold (Catherine II's favourite alcoholic drink). This traditional German drink from Poznań was made here, in the "Salmon"'s distillery actually founded in 1598.

Restauracja Tawerna – *Ul. Powroźnicza 19/20 - ℘ 301 41 14 - daily 11am-2am (last orders at 10.30pm - 120 PLN*. Quite close to the quay, near the Green Gate, this high-class restaurant specialises in fish dishes, in spite of the fact that the menu mentions "specialities from Poland and French Limousin"(reference to beef). Decor on a maritime theme enhanced by the long bar made of a splendid piece of wood with a dragon's head which you will find familiar (think of the gargoyles in Mariacki Street). Terrace in front and in the back used when the weather is fine.

IN SOPOT

Bar Przystań – *Al. Wojska Polskiego 11 - ℘ 550 02 41 - daily 11am-11pm - 25 PLN*. Located to the south of the seaside promenade, this beach restaurant is a real local institution. The long beached ship where one goes to place an order and eventually settle down, also offers a large terrace with a fine view of the sea and of the fishing boats. The menu (in English) of this "fast seafood" establishment naturally proposes fish specialities.

Klub Wieloryb – *Ul. Podjazd 2 - ℘ 551 57 22 - daily 1pm-1am*. An almost oppressive decor that Enki Bilal would certainly not disown, unless the greenish grey atmosphere is supposed to suggest the insides of a whale as the name implies. This very trendy restaurant, serving a French-inspired cuisine, may seem rather overdone, but it is at least surprising. Outside terrace.

IN GDYNIA

Bar Mleczny Słoneczny – *Ul. Władysława IV - Mon-Fri 6.30am-7pm - 15 PLN* – This milk bar occupies a vast room behind large white curtains with a floral motif. The rows of tables laid out close to one another, lead you to share your meal with strangers who come to spend as little as possible on dishes of invigorating Polish cooking.

Restauracja w Ogrodach – *Ul. Władysława IV 49- ℘ 781 5377 - Mon-Fri 11am-10pm, Sat-Sun 1-10pm - 40 PLN*. Feel free to appreciate or not the decor of this new place, a trifle too sophisticated, but you can on no account remain insensitive to the plain yet excellent cuisine prepared with care from fresh produce at very reasonable prices.

Taking a break

IN GDAŃSK

Cafe π Kawa – *Ul. Piwna 5/6 - ℘ 309 14 44 - daily 10am-10pm*. This small, charming café, which always draws the crowds, offers a cosy environment for a teatime break. The main decorative element is a collection of bags from elegant shops - forgotten by customers or artistic works, who knows? - hanging from the ceiling. This self-acclaimed brain-box café – "3.14116...Café" – has a branch in Gdynia. No smoking.

Cup of tea – *Ul. Szeroka 119/120 - ☎ 301 23 86 - daily 10am-10pm.* Near St Nicholas's Church; a tiny place to visit for a.cuppa.

IN SOPOT

Kawiarnia u Hrabiego. *Ul. Czyżewskiego 12 - ☎ 550 19 97 - daily 10am-10pm.* This very pleasant café cum tearoom cum art gallery occupies one of the oldest houses (200 years old) in Sopot. Forming part of the municipal heritage, this fine single-storey villa, now located right in the town centre, proposes a different exhibition every month and concerts every Thursday evening. Pleasant small summer garden. Coffee, tea (4.50 PLN).

Cafe Art déco – *Ul. Boh. Monte Cassino 9 A - ☎ 555 01 60 - daily 11am-10pm.* Situated at the very beginning of the unavoidable Monte Cassino Street, above the railway line, set back from the street, on the right. This tiny delightful café, boasting a literary atmosphere, is decorated with old photographs. Coffee made and served in Italian coffee pots (5.50 PLN) and tea ((5 PLN). Excellent fresh cheese and grape cake.

IN GDYNIA

Kawiarnia Cyganeria –*Ul. 3-go Maja 27/31 - ☎ 620 18 44 - 10am-midnight (1.30am on Sat).* With its transatlantic liner look, this fine spacious café owes its delicate feel to its unmistakable art deco style; its well-worn settees where one can lounge around beautiful wooden tables – nicely spaced out to protect private conversations – are perfect for dreaming of faraway destinations.

Czasostop Artystyczny – *Ul. Derdowskiego 11 - t 661 83 33 - Mon-Fri 11am-midnight,Sat-Sun noon-1am* – Arty highbrow café where books literally fall like rain from the ceiling.

On the town

IN GDAŃSK

Cafe Plastykon – *Ul. Długa 57 - ☎ 0606 490 590 - Sun-Wed 4pm-midnight, Thu-Sat 4pm-2am - closed in August.* Located in the same building as the Neptun, Cameron and Helicon cinemas and the Nahoru restaurant, the former Casablanca is no longer the venue for endless evenings and heated debates, but a vast room filled with miscellaneous furniture where the local youth drink beer with a straw.

Klub Yesterday – *Ul. Piwna 50/51 - ☎ 301 39 24 - Sun-Thu 6pm-2am, Fri-Sat 6pm-4am.* THE alternative bar in the town centre, buried deep down in vast cellars near St Mary's Church. Current dance music chosen by a DJ who takes his role very seriously, even when the audience is down to three people.

IN SOPOT

Galeria Kiński. *Ul. Kościuszki 10 - ☎ 802 56 38 - daily 11am-3am.* This café is entirely devoted to the actor Klaus Kiński, alias Nikolaus Gunther Nakszyński. It's no surprise really since he was born in this house (built in 1898) in 1926.

Błękitny Pudel – *Ul. Boh. M. Cassino 44 - ☎ 551 16 72 - daily 10am-1am.* Standing opposite the pretentious façade of the Centrum Rezydent, the unassuming but surprising Blue Poodle looks like a surrealist collage. Yet who would think on entering this dark paved courtyard (with false sewer grate) full of miscellaneous objects found in bric-a-bracs that it is only a decor set up barely ten years ago.

Spatif – *Ul. Boh. Monte Cassino 54 - ☎ 550 26 83 - daily 3pm-last customers.* Up a steep flight of stairs; you have to ring and prove you're acceptable if you wish to gain access to the vast room with its eccentric and bizarre decor or to the attractive bar with its huge mirror multiplying the number of bottles. Vodka between 6 and 8 PLN.

Shopping

Known as the "Gold of the Baltic", amber is a great speciality of the city of Gdańsk. Workshops making and selling **amber handicrafts** are concentrated in Mariacka Street, the Długi Targ and the Długie Pobrzeże (quay).

Ogród Sztuk – *Ul. Piwna 48/49 - ☎ 305 76 82 - Jun-Sep daily 9am-9pm, Oct-May daily 11am-8pm.* This bookshop facing the cathedral has a wide selection of books about Gdańsk and the surrounding region, some of them in English.

Festive events

Dominican Fair (since 1260), during the first two weeks in August.

Gdynia's Polish Feature-length Film Festival, in September.

St Catherine's Fair, at the end of November.

International Festival of Organ Music, in Oliwa's Cathedral from mid-June to the end of August (Tuesdays and Fridays).

Northern Peoples Folk Festival, mid-July.

"Baltic Sail": International yacht regatta during the 3rd week in July.

Street Theatre Festival, mid-July.

Festival of Peals, end of July and beginning of August.

Shakespeare Festival, beginning of August.

Sopot's International Song Festival (Open-air Opera), in August.

Słowiński National Park★★
Słowiński Park Narodowy
MAP OF POLAND B1 – WOJEW ÓDZ TWO OF POMERANIA

The amazing shifting dunes (ruchome wydmy) characterising this Polish Sahara are the main attraction of the National Park established along the coast, on the border of western Pomerania (Pomorze Zachodnie, pomorze meaning "coastal region") and of eastern Pomerania. The park gets its name from a small ancient tribe of Slav origin, the Slovincians, who settled permanently in the area south-west of Lake Łebsko, around the villages of Smołdzino and in particular Kluki, where there is a small skansen devoted to traditional village architecture. The seaside resort of Łeba is one of the main gateways to the park.

- ▶ **Getting your bearings** – Łeba, situated in the eastern part of the park, lies 110km from Gdańsk, 55km from Słupsk, 30km from Lębork.
- 👁 **Not to be missed** – A climb to the top of the shifting dunes, the fine beach at Łeba, a bike tour round Lake Łebsko returning to Łeba along the beach.
- 🕐 **Planning your visit** – Allow at least one whole day to enjoy the park, more if you wish to make the most of Łeba's seaside activities.

Background

Created in 1967, the Słowiński National Park was included in 1977 on Unesco's List of World Biosphere Reserves. It extends along the 33km of coastline separating Łeba in the east and Rowy in the west, and its landscape combines beaches, dunes, marshes, moors and peat bogs. A quarter of its 186sq km total area is covered with forest, another quarter consists of a string of four lakes (Jezioro Łebsko, Jezioro Gardno, Jezioro Sarbsko and Jezioro Dołgie Wielkie), which were once bays progressively cut off from the sea by the formation of a sand bar. With some 250 different bird species, both temporary and permanent inhabitants of the park, including the rare white-tailed eagle, the shores of Lake Łebsko – Pomerania's largest lake covering 70sq km – are a real paradise for ornithologists. The most spectacular part of the park is the narrow sand bank, covered with pines, which separates Lake Łebsko from the Baltic. This is where you will find the semi-circular shifting dunes, swept by the winds and constantly moving inland to the east. The dunes which form a sand mountain covering some 5sq km, the highest topping 42m, advance at a speed of several metres a year (up to 9m) and one can observe the relentless process of the sand burying the pine forest and creating a highly moving but very photogenic desolate landscape.

At the beginning of the Second World War, General Rommel's Afrika Korps took over the dunes as their training ground and the site was also used to establish launching pads for the V1 and V2 rockets aimed at England.

Dunes in Dunes Słowiński National Park

Discovering Łeba

(Population 3 892)

Framed by two lakes, the Baltic and a river of the same name, the peaceful little fishing port of Łeba (pronounce Weba) changes every summer into a seaside resort sought after by Polish holidaymakers. This Kashubian village founded in the 10C, lying west of the mouth of the River Łeba, was devastated by a terrible storm in 1558. The town was rebuilt on the opposite bank and the ruins of the former village disappeared under the sand. When the sand later invaded the cultivated land and the harbour, the town's economy went into decline, a process that was stopped by the construction of a dyke protecting the entrance to the new harbour at the end of the 19C and by the arrival of settlers of Jewish origin who contributed to its new-found dynamism. After the construction of the road to Lębork in 1869 and of the railway line in 1899, Łeba was no longer isolated and set about developing its tourist industry at the beginning of the 20C, as shown by the former Kurhaus Hotel (now called **Neptun Hotel**), an impressive building erected on the seafront in 1903. The expressionist painter, Max Pechstein, a member of the "Die Brücke" group, lived in Łeba between 1921 and 1945. Returned to Poland in 1945, the small town, which has no historic heritage whatsoever, is worth a visit for its fine **beach** which offers visitors a pleasant stay, even if the water temperature barely reaches 20°C in summer. It is above all the ideal gateway to the Słowiński National Park.

Exploring the National Park★★

The park's headquarters are located in Smołdzino (ul. Bohaterów Warszawy 1a, ☏ 811 72 04 fax 811 75 09), but information is available from the tourist office in Łeba (see Practical Słowiński National Park).

To enter the park, which can be explored on foot or by bike, there is a charge in high season of 4 PLN - 0.50 PLN per bike. Open May-Sep 7am-9pm, Oct-Apr 8am-4pm. Cars and buses are not allowed beyond the Rąbka parking area situated 2.5km from Łeba.

The Góra Łącka Dune★★

From the Rąbka parking area, allow 3hr 30min on foot there and back or 1hr by bike.

This 42m high dune, the highest of the shifting dunes, is easily accessible and, from the top, one can admire this strange, almost "sahara-like" landscape.

Bike Tour round Lake Łebsko

About 50km. Allow a whole day. Bike hire in Rąbka: 6 PLN /hr.

Start from the southern part of the lake. After cycling 21km, you will reach the village of Kluki, where the museum described below is situated; continue via Czołpino and return to Łeba by the "beach road", along the packed sand licked by the waves, on the very edge of the Baltic.

Kluki

Slovincian Skansen (Muzeum Wsi Słowińskiej w Klukach)★

An annexe of Słupsk's Museum of Central Pomerania. If you are not cycling, Kluki's Skansen is accessible by car from Słupsk (Swoupsk), 41km away. During the high season, a shuttle boat sails across the lake between Rąbka and Kluki.

76-214 Smołdzino - ☏/fax 846 30 20 - 15 May-15 Sep Mon 9am-4pm, Tue-Sun 10am-6pm; 16 Sep-14 May daily 9am-4pm - 7.50 PLN - www.muzeum.slupsk.pl.

Lying in a remote position south-west of Lake Łebsko, within the perimeter of the Słowiński National Park, the historic village of Kluki (Klucken in German) was turned into an ethnographic museum in 1963. This authentic village, comprising original houses (not ones that had been moved) was inhabited by Kashubians from western Pomerania called Słowińcy (Slovincians). Isolated by the massive germanisation forced on the region in the 19C, Slovincian traditions and culture survived longer in this micro-region, and yet after the war there were only a few people left who still had vague notions of a dialect now lost. Every year from 1 to 3 May, on the occasion of the "black-wedding feast", an important traditional festival, resembling a fête and intended to revive Slovincian traditions, attracts crowds of spectators. The 18C cemetery is situated on a mound, alongside the road, at the entrance to the village.

Smołdzino

Not on the bike itinerary. Allow 10km more there and back.

The National Park's headquarters are located here and Smołdzino also houses the Park Museum which presents local flora and fauna.

🐾 1km south-west of the village, a path leads (in 15min) to the summit of **Mount Rowokół**(114m). From the top of the observation tower, there is a superb view of the whole region.

Czołpino

From Czołpino (furthest spot accessible by car), you can climb (10min) up to the **lighthouse (Latarnia Morska)** standing at the top of the highest dune rising to an altitude of 55.10m above sea level *(Jun-Aug 10am-7pm - 3 PLN)*.

Kashubia (Kaszuby)★★

Kashubian Switzerland (Szwajcaria Kaszubska) boasting fine landscapes dotted with lakes, forests and morainic hills is a region of picturesque folk traditions lying west of Gdańsk. Its 200 000-strong community does not speak a Polish dialect but an original language which mixes some German with archaïc Slavic expressions. It was thanks to the Kashubians' deep attachment to Poland that, in 1918, the country obtained a 72km access to the sea.

Kartuzy

33km west of Gdańsk.

This small town, which is the region's unofficial capital, gets it name from the Carthusian monks who founded a monastery at the end of the 14C.

Of the Carthusian monastery on the shores of Lake Klasztorne, there remains a Gothic collegiate church with an unusual Baroque roof designed to remind the monks of the shape of a coffin and therefore of impending death. A surprising white angel of death, symbolically cutting down all new entrants into the church, and a *memento mori* placed at the top of the east end's buttresses add the finishing touch to this macabre setting.

Ethnographic Musuem – *Ul. Kościerska 1 - t 681 14 42 - www.muzeum-kaszubskie.gda. pl - May-Sep Tue-Fri 8am-4pm, Sat 8am-3pm, Sun and public hols 10am-2pm; Oct-Apr Tue-Fri 8am-4pm, Sat 8am-3pm.* The museum displays costumes, toys and objects illustrating the traditions of the Kashubian people.

Practical Słowiński National Park

Phone code – (0)59

Useful addresses

Tourist office – Informacja Turystyczna (Łeba) - *Ul. 11 Listopada 5a, 84-360 Łeba - ☎/fax (059) 866 25 65 - www.leba.pt - Jul-Sep Mon-Fri 8am-8pm, Sat 8am-6pm, Sun 10am-4pm; Oct-Jun Mon-Fri 8am-4pm.*

Internet – Internet access at the post office *(Mon-Fri 8am-6pm, Sat 9am-3pm).*

Getting around

Train and bus – Access from Gdynia station (4 trains/day) to Lębork then bus (1/ hr) to Łeba.

Bus – Buses link Gdynia and Łeba (94km) 2 to 4/day according to the season.

Bike – Bike hire on leaving Łeba towards the entrance to the park. Allow about 40 PLN for the day.

Where to stay

You'd have to do it on purpose not to find accommodation in Łeba for there are many private rooms on offer.

Arkun. *Ul. Wróblewskiego 11 - ☎/ fax 866 24 19 - arkun@ta.pl - www.arkun.ta.pl - 🅿 -* 22 rooms - 160 PLN - 🍽 35 PLN. This yellow-brick hotel near the canal was originally intended for the employees of the Handlowy Bank, recently bought by the American CitiBank. Let us hope that the reasonable prices applied up to now will be maintained.

Hotel Neptun – *Ul. Sosnowa 1 - ☎/fax 866 23 57 - hotel@neptun.2com.pl - www. neptunhotel.pl - 🅿 - 32 rooms - 635 PLN - 🍽.* Grand Hotel atmosphere (since 1903) in this fine building looking like a castle reigning supreme over the seafront. Compulsory half board in summer. Off season double room at 380 PLN.

Eating out

Tawerna Rybacka. *Ul. Wybrzeże - 40 PLN.* You wouldn't think of leaving Łeba without having eaten some fish! Why not do so along the canal, in the centre of a large courtyard, under an arbour of fake drooping seaweed.

Karczma Kaszubianka – *Ul. Kościuszki 28 - daily noon-midnight - 60 PLN.* Dark but not unpleasant room, if you can put up with the obtrusive background music. Fish & chips (*Smażalnie*) served outside.

Malbork Castle★★★

MAP OF POLAND B1– WOJEW ÓDZ TWO OF POMERANIA

Formerly known as Marienburg (the Fortress of Mary), Malbork Castle was the residence of the grand masters of the Order of the Teutonic Knights and later the capital of that order from 1308 to 1457. It is Europe's largest medieval castle, an impressive red-brick fortress covering an area of 21 hectares, standing on the east bank of the River Nogat. Even though the patina of age may seem somewhat artificial, this castle, admired as a model of its kind by the romantic 19C, has been on UNESCO's World Heritage List since 1997.

▶ **Finding your bearings** – 58km from Gdańsk, 30km from Elbląg, 315km from Warsaw.

👁 **Not to be missed** – The overall view from the pedestrian bridge spanning the Nogat.

🕐 **Planning your visit** – Minimum 3hr for a complete tour of the castle.

Background

The Teutonic Knights' domination – In 1309, Hermann von Salza, the 4th grand master of the order of the Teutonic Knights, made Marienburg (Malbork) the capital of the order. The castle subsequently expanded throughout the 14C. In 1457, during the "Thirteen Years" war (1454-1466) caused by the rebellion of the German middle class allied to the Polish nobility against the order, the Polish king, Kazimierz IV seized the castle and the war ended with the defeat of the Teutonic Knights. In 1525, when the Teutonic State was dissolved, Malbork became the regional administrative centre.

Destructions and reconstructions – Partially destroyed during the Swedish wars of 1655-60, the castle was turned into barracks by the Prussians after the first partition of Poland in 1772. A rebuilding programme, which was more romantic than medieval was undertaken during the first half of the 19C followed, from 1882 onwards, by a more serious historic reconstruction. It is this replica, more or less true to the original Teutonic castle and half destroyed in 1945, which the Poles set about rebuilding.

Tour of the castle

Ticket office on the esplanade, facing the castle entrance. ☎ *(055) 647 09 78 - www. zamek.malbork.pl - 15 Apr-15 Sep Tue-Sun 9am-8pm (exhibitions until 7pm, ticket office until 7.30pm); 16-30 Sep Tue-Sun 9am-5pm (courtyard until 7pm, ticket office until 6pm); Oct-14 Apr Tue-Sun 10am-5pm (exhibitions until 3pm, ticket office until 4pm) - 30 PLN. The courtyard is the only part of the castle accessible on Mondays.*

You will be amazed by the huge size of Malbork Castle as you get nearer to Malbork. The best way to appreciate it is to walk onto the footbridge leading to the opposite bank.

The Teutonic Knights

Founded in 1190, during the 3rd crusade to the Holy Land, the Order of the Teutonic Knights of the Hospital of St Mary of Jerusalem was a military and religious order. Established in Venice, the knights were called upon in 1226 to help the Polish Duke Konrad of Mazovia subdue the Prussians, a pagan tribe from the shores of the Baltic; having duly exterminated the Prussians and been rewarded with the gift of the stronghold of Chełmno, they eventually imposed their military strength and consolidated their power over the whole of Pomerania, then the Baltic coast and threatened the kingdom of Poland. At the same time as they moved eastwards, they settled in their path German colonies which contributed, through the expansion of trade, to accelerating the development of towns like Toruń, founded in 1233 by the order, or Gdańsk, conquered in 1308. One year later, the capital of the order was transferred from Venice to Marienburg (Malbork). The knights' domination of the region lasted 146 years. Faced with a growing conflict with the Polish Crown to whom they denied access to the sea, the order started declining in 1410, after being defeated by the Polish-Lithuanian alliance at the battle of Grunwald-Tannenberg and, following the Treaty of Toruń signed in 1466, it had to give back to Poland "Royal Prussia" or Gdańsk's Pomerania. Dissolved in 1525, the Teutonic State became a Protestant duchy of eastern Prussia, with the Polish king as its overlord.

The monumental fortress, surrounded by a double ring of ramparts, consists of three castles: in the north is the Low Castle or Esplanade covering half the total area, in the centre is the MIddle Castle with the Grand Masters' Palace and finally, in the south stands the High Castle.

The Low Castle (Zamek Niski) or Esplanade (Przedzamcze)

Dating mainly from the 14C, this freely accessible part comprises several annexees such as the arsenal, the armourer's or the bell foundry as well as Gothic defensive structures. The ticket office (kassa) is also here.

The Middle Castle (Zamek Średni)★★

Ticket in hand, walk over the bridge spanning the large moat and enter the vast courtyard of the Middle Castle. To the west, on the river's side, stands the

Detail on a fountain

Grand Masters' Palace (Pałac Wielkich Mistrzów)★★★, begun in the early 14C and completed between 1383 and 1393; note its fine façade, particularly at the 3rd floor level. Open to the public following a lengthy restoration, this part comprises three different buildings. The **palace** itself, erected before 1305, containing the grand masters' living quarters, the tower known as the **"Winter Refectory"**, built between 1330 and 1340, and the main building housing the **"Summer Refectory"**, built between 1330 and 1390. These two refectories, situated on the 3rd floor, feature splendid palm vaulting and traces of polychrome decorations. Adjoining the Grand Masters' Palace, along the whole length of the west wing, is the largest room in the castle (450sq m), the **Knights' Hall** (Sala Rycerska) or **Great Refectory** (Wielki Refektarz), boasting further palm vaulting, which is however closed to the public because its foundations are subsiding. The building situated in the east wing, on the other side of the courtyard, contains a remarkable **collection of amber** (Dzieje Bursztynu)★★

The High Castle (Zamek Wysoki)★★★

The tour continues with the High Castle, the third and oldest part of the castle but also the best preserved of the three, where the order's treasure was kept. To get to it, cross the second drawbridge over the "Dry Moat" situated on the right of a group of sculptures representing four grand masters of the order. Note the ceramic low relief depicting a Teutonic knight above the doorway. Beyond the entrance is a courtyard framed by Gothic galleries with, in its centre, a covered well surmounted by a pelican nourishing its offspring. The cloister feel of the place comes from the fact that the construction of this quadrangle began in 1280, before the transfer of the order's seat to Malbork, and that it was therefore intended to be a stronghold to house the soldier-monks.

After visiting the **kitchens** and **utility rooms** on the ground floor (note that there is no set direction to follow, so be inquisitive), go up to the first floor to look at the dignitaries' **bedrooms** and the **dormitories**, then to the second floor where you will find the **refectory★** and the **Room with the two fireplaces** followed by the **Convention Communal Room**. On the way down, the north wing of the cloister leads to the **Chapter House★★★** then to the famous **Golden Gate** (Złota Brama) ★★★ marking the entrance to the **Church of Our Lady★★★** (accessible and interesting because it has not been restored yet). This fine 13C carved doorway, covered with polychrome decorations, frames a rare oak door from the early 14C. From there, it is possible to reach the top of the **square tower** *(15 Apr-15 Sep - additional charge: 6 PLN)*, affording a **view★★★** which extends over the whole surrounding Żuławy.

A walk along the terraces surrounding the castle will lead you to the **Crypt of St Anne★**, a funeral chapel with fine portals at the north and south entrances; the chapel houses the funeral stelae of three grand masters of the order, dating from the 14C and 15C. The terrace above was the monks's cemetery. A spiral staircase (near the main door) gives access via the "Dry Moat" to the outer defences.

Nearby

Gniew★ (Population 6 929)

33km south of Malbork.

This charming little town, situated on high ground on the north bank of the Wisła, is one of the oldest cities in Pomerania. Founded in 1297, Gniew (*Gnief* which means anger in Polish) also has its own **Teutonic castle** built in 1282 and partly preserved 14C **ramparts** which account for it being sometimes called the "Polish Carcassonne". The outline of the castle hill (Wzgórze Zamkowe) offers from a distance an impressive view of this massive stronghold. Mostly destroyed by fire in 1921, it is gradually recovering its original appearance thanks to scrupulous restoration work. Today, the fortress, which is a real conservatory of medieval customs and traditions, houses the **medieval section of Gdańsk's Archaeological Museum** (*May-Oct Tue-Sun 9am-6pm - 8 PLN*) and is the setting of several festive events in summer. The town's annual festival (Gniewinki), from 24 to 29 June, recreates the atmosphere of the medieval city in its heyday. Fine restaurant in the vaulted cellars.

The small **medieval town** boasts a lovely gently sloping **Rynek** with a Gothic 14C Town Hall in its centre and, on the side, a Gothic parish church.

Pelplin Cathedral★★

14km north-west of Gniew.

In spite of Pelplin being known as the "Pomeranian Athens", the small town's only treasure is its Gothic cathedral, the former church of a Cistercian abbey founded in 1274 by the duke of Pomerania. The brick edifice, built between 1280 and 1320, features amazing dimensions and late-15C Gothic vaulting. The interior is sumptuously furnished: apart from its monumental Renaissance high altar from 1623 framing a painting by Herman Han (1625) and its 21 other altars, it boasts a Baroque organ and pulpit as well as remarkable Gothic stalls.

Practical Malbork

Postal code – 82-200
Phone code – 0(55)

Useful addresses

Tourist Information Centre – *Ul. Piastowska 15 - ℘ 273 49 90 - Tue-Fri 10.30am-6pm, Sat-Sun 10.30am-2pm.*This is more of a gallery than a real tourist office, but the town should soon acquire a "Malbork Welcome Center" worthy of the name in the former library , in Kościuszki Street.

Getting around

Railway station – Malbork station is a 15 minutes' walk from the castle. Several trains a day to Warsaw, Gdańsk and Olsztyn.

Where to stay

Youth Hostel (Schronisko Młodzieżowe) – *Ul. Żeromskiego 45 - ℘ 272 24 08 - fax 272 25 11 - 50 PLN.* 500m from the castle. Open year-round, this HI approved hostel, adjoining an accessible school gymnasium, has only two double bedrooms.

Hotel Stary Malbork – *Ul. 17 Marca 26 - 27 - ℘ 647 24 00 - fax 647 24 12 - www. hotelstarymalbork.com.pl - 30 rooms - 340 PLN -* 🍴. Decorated in various shades of pastel green, this art nouveau-style hotel offers convenient facilities in recently restored 19C twin houses.

Hotel Zamek – *Ul. Starościńska 14 - ℘/fax 272 84 00 - www.zlotehotele.pl/ zamek - 42 rooms -* 🅿 *- 379 PLN -* 🍴. A little of the dark austere atmosphere of the castle pervades this hotel housed inside the former Teutonic hospital, in the Low Castle. The dining room is also somewhat austere (*60 PLN*).

GNIEW
Youth-hostel type of accommodation inside the castle (*33 PLN*).

Hotel Restauracja Pałac Marysieńki – *Pl. Zamkowy 3, 83-140 Gniew - t 535 49 49 - fax 535 49 39 - www.hotelmarysienki.pl - 40 rooms - 175 PLN -* 🍴. Fine view of the peaceful Wisła from some of the back rooms of this 17C palace, once the residence of Queen MK Sobieska, built by Jan III Sobieski. The restaurant linked to the hotel is less picturesque (*50 PLN*).

Eating out

In the restaurants of the above hotels. Snacks available inside the castle.

Pizzeria D.M. Patrzałkowie – *Ul. Kościuszki 25 - ℘ 272 39 91 - daily 11am-9pm - 25 PLN.* At the very beginning of the street; bright room decorated with old photos of Marienburg in the past; thick soft pizzas to be enjoyed.

Festive events

Town Festival, 1st week in June.
Grand May Festival, 1st weekend in May.

NOTES

NOTES

NOTES

NOTES

NOTES

Kraków: towns, attractions and tourist areas.
Copernic, Nicolas: people and events, subjects addressed in the guide.
Sights in of main towns (musuems, synagogues, monuments, etc): look under the name of the town
Sights outside of main towns (castles, abbeys, caves, etc): look under the name of the sight.

INDEX

MAPS AND PLANS

Manufacture française des pneumatiques Michelin

Société en commandite par actions au capital de 304 000 000 EUR
Place des Carmes-Déchaux - 63000 Clermont-Ferrand (France)
R.C.S. Clermont-Fd B 855 200 507

© Michelin et Cie, Propriétaires-éditeurs.
Pre-Press: Nord Compo à Villeneuve-d'Ascq
Printing and binding: Aubin à Ligugé
Printed in France 05/ 2006/1.1